The Official
SCRABBLE®
Players
Dictionary

PUBLISHED BY POCKET BOOKS NEW YORK

Distributed in Canada by PaperJacks Ltd., a Licensee
of the trademarks of Simon & Schuster, a division of
Gulf+Western Corporation.

POCKET BOOKS, a Simon & Schuster division of
GULF & WESTERN CORPORATION
1230 Avenue of the Americas, New York, N.Y. 10020
In Canada distributed by PaperJacks Ltd.,
330 Steelcase Road, Markham, Ontario.

Copyright © 1978 by Selchow & Righter Company

Published by arrangement with G. & C. Merriam Company
Library of Congress Catalog Card Number: 78-3681

All rights reserved, including the right to reproduce
this book or portions thereof in any form whatsoever.
For information address G. & C. Merriam Company,
47 Federal Street, Springfield, Mass. 01101

ISBN: 0-671-43269-9

First Pocket Books printing October, 1979

10 9 8 7 6 5

POCKET and colophon are trademarks of Simon & Schuster.

Printed in Canada

REFACE ● This word book has been long awaited by lovers of the SCRABBLE® Brand crossword games, and Scrabble® Crossword Game Players, Inc., a subsidiary of Selchow & Righter Co., is very pleased to present it to them. All who have looked for a guide to settle challenges that arise in the course of play now have one of authority. This is the dictionary of first reference for all official SCRABBLE® Players crossword game tournaments.

It is important to remember that The Official Scrabble® Players Dictionary was edited solely with this limited purpose in mind. It is not intended to serve as a general dictionary of English; thus, such important features of general dictionaries as definitions of multiple senses, pronunciation respellings, etymologies, and usage labels are omitted.

The plan of the dictionary and the policies that governed its editing were developed under the direction of Scrabble® Crossword Game Players, Inc. The finished manuscript was prepared for the typesetter and the dictionary was seen into print by members of the Editorial Department of G. & C. Merriam Company under the supervision of James G. Lowe, Associate Editor.

The detailed organization and special features of the dictionary are explained in the Introduction which immediately follows. It should be read with care by all who use the dictionary. Now that this work is available, we are confident that it will afford satisfaction and enjoyment to SCRABBLE® crossword game players everywhere.

Scrabble® Crossword Game Players, Inc.

I₁

NTRODUCTION ● MAIN ENTRIES ● Main entries are listed in boldface type and are set flush with the left-hand margin of each column. Except for an occasional cross-reference (such as **GUNFOUGHT** past tense of gunfight), main entries contain from two to eight letters since words within this range are considered to be most useful to SCRABBLE® crossword game players. Only words that are permissible in SCRABBLE® crossword games are included in this dictionary. Thus, proper names, words requiring hyphens or apostrophes, words considered foreign, and abbreviations have been omitted. Because dictionaries have different standards for selecting entries, several current desk dictionaries were consulted in preparing the list of main entries of this book in order to insure a wider range of entries than any single dictionary of that kind offers. Words that exceed eight letters in length and are not inflected forms of words entered in this dictionary should be looked up in a desk dictionary such as Webster's New Collegiate Dictionary. No attempt was made to omit obsolete, archaic, slang, or nonstandard words since they are permitted by the rules of the game. All variant forms of a main entry are shown at their own alphabetical places and defined in terms of the principal form.

RUN-ON ENTRIES ● A main entry may be followed by one or more derivatives in boldface type with a different part-of-speech label. These are run-on entries. Run-on entries are not defined since their meanings are readily derivable from the meaning of the root word.

JOYOUS   *adj* joyful **JOYOUSLY** *adv*
KNOW   *v* KNEW, KNOWN, KNOWING,
               KNOWS to have a true
               understanding of **KNOWABLE**
               adj

No entry has been run on at another if it would fall alphabetically more than two places from the entry. When you do not find a word at its own place, it is always wise to check several entries above and below to see if it is run on.

CROSS-REFERENCES ● A cross-reference is a main entry that is an inflected form (such as the plural form of a noun, the past tense form of a verb, or the comparative form of an adjective) of another word. An inflected form is entered as a main entry only if it undergoes a spelling change in addition to or instead of suffixation *and* if it falls alphabetically three or more places away from the root word.

For example, in the entries reproduced below **GAGGED** is a main entry because it involves a spelling change (the final -*g* of *gag* is doubled) besides the addition of the -*ed* ending and because it falls alphabetically three or more places away from the entry **GAG**. On the other hand, *gags* is not a main entry because it involves no spelling change beyond the addition of the ending *-s*. Equally, while **GAGING** is a main entry, *gaged* is not, because, even though it involves a spelling change (the final *-e* of *gage* is dropped) beyond the addition of the *-ed* ending, it would not fall three or more places from **GAGE**.

GAG	*v* GAGGED, GAGGING, GAGS to stop up the mouth	
GAGA	*adj* crazy	
GAGE	*v* GAGED, GAGING, GAGES to pledge as security	
GAGER	*n* pl. -S gauger	
GAGGED	past tense of gag	
GAGGER	*n* pl. -S one that gags	
GAGGING	present participle of gag	
GAGGLE	*v* -GLED, -GLING, -GLES to cackle	
GAGING	present participle of gage	

This policy is intended to make the word desired as easy to find as possible without wasting space. Nevertheless, many inflected forms will appear only at the main entry.

Users of the book should always look at several entries above and below the expected place if they do not find the desired word as a main entry.

Cross-reference entries for present tense third person singular forms of verbs use the abbreviation "sing."

PARTS OF SPEECH   ●   An italic label indicating a part of speech follows each main entry except cross-references (such as **JOLLIED, JOLLIER, JOLLIES, JOLLIEST**), for which the label is given at the root word. The eight traditional parts of speech are indicated as follows:

n	noun	*pron*	pronoun
v	verb	*prep*	preposition
adj	adjective	*conj*	conjunction
adv	adverb	*interj*	interjection

The label *n/pl* is given to two kinds of nouns. One is the plural noun that has no singular form.

VIBES   *n/pl* a percussion instrument

The other is the plural noun of which the singular is not entered in this dictionary. Singular forms are omitted if they contain more than eight letters.

ROSTELLA   *n/pl* small, beaklike structures

Rostellum, the singular form, has nine letters and is not entered.

    When a word can be used as more than one part of speech, each part of speech is entered separately if the inflected forms are not spelled alike. For example, both the adjective *lazy* and the verb *lazy* are entered because the inflected forms vary.

LAZY   *adj* LAZIER, LAZIEST disinclined
           to work or exertion
LAZY   *v* LAZIED, LAZYING, LAZIES to
           move or lie lazily

On the other hand, the verb *suit* is entered while the noun *suit* is not because the inflected form *suits* at the verb is spelled the same as the plural form of the noun. In a dictionary for SCRABBLE® crossword game players, entry of the noun is therefore redundant. Homographs (words spelled alike) which may be used as the same of part of speech are treated in the same way. For example, *lepton* is entered as a noun twice because the plurals are spelled differently.

LEPTON   *n* pl. -TA a monetary unit of
           Greece
LEPTON   *n* pl. -S an atomic
           particle . . .

If both plurals were spelled alike, only one *lepton* would be entered in this dictionary. In this way the dictionary includes as many different spellings as possible yet avoids wasting space with repeated entry of words spelled in the same way. The SCRABBLE® crossword game player, after all, needs only one entry to justify his play.

INFLECTED FORMS   ●   Inflected forms include the past tense, past participle, present participle, and present tense third person singular of verbs, the plural of nouns, and the comparative and superlative of adjectives and adverbs. They are shown in capital letters immediately following the part-of-speech label. Irregular inflected forms are listed as main entries when they fall three or more alphabetical places away from the root word (see **Cross-References** above). All inflected forms are allowable as entries in SCRABBLE® crossword games.

    The principal parts of the majority of verbs are shown as -ED, -ING, -S (or -ES when applicable). This indicates that the past tense and past participle are formed simply by adding -*ed* to the entry word, that the present participle is formed simply by adding -*ing* to the entry word, and that the present third person singular is formed simply by adding -*s* (or -*es*) to the entry word.

TALK   *v* -ED, -ING, -S to communicate
           by speaking

When inflection of an entry word involves any spelling change in addition to the suffixal ending (such as the dropping of a final -e, the doubling of a final consonant, or the changing of a final -y to -i-) or when the inflection is irregular, the inflected forms given indicate such changes.

WASTE	v WASTED, WASTING, WASTES to use thoughtlessly
DIM	v DIMMED, DIMMING, DIMS to make dim
TRY	v TRIED, TRYING, TRIES to attempt
RISE	v ROSE, RISEN, RISING, RISES to move upward

For verbs of more than one syllable either the last syllable or the last two syllables are shown.

ABDICATE	v -CATED, -CATING, -CATES to give up formally
BEGIN	v -GAN, -GUN, -GINNING, -GINS to start

The plurals of nouns are preceded by the abbreviation "pl." Most plurals are shown as -S (or -ES when applicable) to indicate that the plural is formed simply by adding the given suffix to the entry word.

VINTNER	n pl. -S a wine merchant

When pluralizing a noun involves any spelling change in addition to the suffixal ending (such as the changing of a final -y to -i- or a final -f to -v-) or when the plural is irregular, the plural form shown indicates such change.

BEVY	n pl. BEVIES a group
LEAF	n pl. LEAVES a usually green, flattened organ of vascular plants
CHILD	n pl. CHILDREN a young person

In such cases involving polysyllabic nouns at least the last syllable is shown.

SUDATORY	n pl. -RIES a hot-air bath for inducing sweating

For the sake of clarity, two groups of nouns that are confusing to many, those ending in -o and those ending in -y, are always indicated in this dictionary by showing at least the last syllable, even though no spelling change is involved.

RONDO	n pl. -DOS a type of musical composition
SAWNEY	n pl. -NEYS a foolish person

Variant plurals are shown wherever they add another word permissible in SCRABBLE® crossword games.

GLOSSA   *n* pl. -SAE or -SAS the tongue

Plurals which have the same form as the singular are shown only when they are the only plural for that entry. This is done to show that for the entry in question it is not permissible to add -*s* (or -*es*) to the singular to create a plural.

HAIKU   *n* pl. HAIKU a Japanese poem
CALENDS   *n* pl. CALENDS the first day of
the Roman month

Otherwise, they are omitted and only the plural with the inflection is shown.

DEER   *n* pl. -S a ruminant mammal

The comparative and superlative forms of adjectives and adverbs are shown, when applicable, immediately following the part-of-speech label. Any spelling changes are indicated in the forms shown.

WEAK   *adj* WEAKER, WEAKEST lacking
strength
OFTEN   *adv* -ENER, -ENEST frequently
BALKY   *adj* BALKIER, BALKIEST
stubborn . .

Not all adjectives or adverbs can be inflected, and only those inflected forms shown are acceptable. None of the adjectives and adverbs listed as run-on entries in this dictionary have inflected forms.

DEFINITIONS ● In most cases, only one very brief definition is given for each main entry since definitions do not play a significant role in the SCRABBLE® crossword game. This definition serves only to orient the player in a general way to a single meaning of the word. It is not intended to have all the precision and detail of a definition in a good general dictionary.

When a word consisting of eight letters or less appears in a definition but is not an entry in this dictionary, it is glossed in parentheses. For example, at the entry for the verb *bomb*, the noun "bombs" is used in the definition and is glossed because the noun *bomb* is not a separate entry.

BOMB   *v* -ED, -ING, -S to attack with
bomba (explosive projectiles)

A main entry that is a variant form of another entry is defined in terms of the most common form, which is entered and defined at its own alphabetical place.

AMPOULE   *n* pl. -S ampule
AMPUL   *n* pl. -S ampule
AMPULE   *n* pl. -S a small glass vial

SCRABBLE® crossword game players in Canada will be pleased to learn that variant forms such as *honour, centre,* and *cheque,* which are often omitted from general dictionaries, have also been included in this book.

LISTS OF UNDEFINED WORDS   ●   Lists of undefined words
appear after the entries of the prefixes **RE-** and **UN-**. These words are not defined because they are self-explanatory: their meanings are simply the sum of a meaning of the prefix combined with a meaning of the root word. All of their inflected forms are given, however.

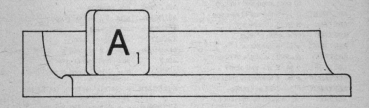

AA	*n* pl. -S rough, cindery lava	**ABATOR**	*n* pl. -S one that unlawfully seizes an inheritance
AAH	*v* -ED, -ING, -S to exclaim in amazement, joy, or surprise	**ABATTIS**	*n* pl. -TISES abatis
AAL	*n* pl. -S an East Indian shrub	**ABATTOIR**	*n* pl. -S a slaughterhouse
AALII	*n* pl. -S a tropical tree	**ABAXIAL**	*adj* situated away from the axis
AARDVARK	*n* pl. -S an African mammal	**ABAXILE**	*adj* abaxial
AARDWOLF	*n* pl. -WOLVES an African mammal	**ABBACY**	*n* pl. -CIES the office of an abbot
AASVOGEL	*n* pl. -S a vulture	**ABBATIAL**	*adj* pertaining to an abbot
ABA	*n* pl. -S a sleeveless garment worn by Arabs	**ABBE**	*n* pl. -S an abbot
ABACA	*n* pl. -S a Philippine plant	**ABBESS**	*n* pl. -ES the female superior of a convent of nuns
ABACK	*adv* toward the back	**ABBEY**	*n* pl. -BEYS a monastery or convent
ABACUS	*n* pl. -CI or -CUSES a calculating device	**ABBOT**	*n* pl. -S the superior of a monastery
ABAFT	*adv* toward the stern	**ABBOTCY**	*n* pl. -CIES abbacy
ABAKA	*n* pl. -S abaca	**ABDICATE**	*v* -CATED, -CATING, -CATES to give up formally
ABALONE	*n* pl. -S an edible shellfish	
ABAMP	*n* pl. -S abampere	**ABDOMEN**	*n* pl. -MENS or -MINA the body cavity containing the viscera
ABAMPERE	*n* pl. -S a unit of electric current	
ABANDON	*v* -ED, -ING, -S to leave or give up completely	**ABDUCE**	*v* -DUCED, -DUCING, -DUCES to abduct
ABASE	*v* ABASED, ABASING, ABASES to lower in rank, prestige, or esteem **ABASEDLY** *adv*	**ABDUCENS**	*n* pl. -CENTES a cranial nerve
		ABDUCENT	*adj* serving to abduct
		ABDUCING	present participle of abduce
ABASER	*n* pl. -S one that abases	**ABDUCT**	*v* -ED, -ING, -S to draw away from the original position
ABASH	*v* -ED, -ING, -ES to make ashamed or embarrassed	
ABASING	present participle of abase	**ABDUCTOR**	*n* pl. -ES or -S an abducent muscle
ABATE	*v* ABATED, ABATING, ABATES to reduce in degree or intensity **ABATABLE** *adj*	**ABEAM**	*adv* at right angles to the keel of a ship
		ABED	*adv* in bed
ABATER	*n* pl. -S one that abates	**ABELE**	*n* pl. -S a Eurasian tree
ABATIS	*n* pl. -TISES a barrier made of felled trees	**ABELMOSK**	*n* pl. -S a tropical herb

ABERRANT	*n* pl. -S a deviant
ABET	*v* ABETTED, ABETTING, ABETS to encourage and support
ABETMENT	*n* pl. -S the act of abetting
ABETTAL	*n* pl. -S abetment
ABETTED	past tense of abet
ABETTER	*n* pl. -S abettor
ABETTING	present participle of abet
ABETTOR	*n* pl. -S one that abets
ABEYANCE	*n* pl. -S temporary inactivity
ABEYANCY	*n* pl. -CIES abeyance
ABEYANT	*adj* marked by abeyance
ABFARAD	*n* pl. -S a unit of capacitance
ABHENRY	*n* pl. -RIES or -RYS a unit of inductance
ABHOR	*v* -HORRED, -HORRING, -HORS to loathe
ABHORRER	*n* pl. -S one that abhors
ABIDANCE	*n* pl. -S the act of abiding
ABIDE	*v* ABODE or ABIDED, ABIDING, ABIDES to accept without objection
ABIDER	*n* pl. -S one that abides
ABIGAIL	*n* pl. -S a lady's maid
ABILITY	*n* pl. -TIES the quality of being able to do something
ABIOSIS	*n* pl. -OSES absence of life ABIOTIC *adj*
ABJECT	*adj* sunk to a low condition ABJECTLY *adv*
ABJURE	*v* -JURED, -JURING, -JURES to renounce under oath
ABJURER	*n* pl. -S one that abjures
ABLATE	*v* -LATED, -LATING, -LATES to remove by cutting
ABLATION	*n* pl. -S surgical removal of a bodily part
ABLATIVE	*n* pl. -S a grammatical case
ABLAUT	*n* pl. -S a patterned change in root vowels of verb forms
ABLAZE	*adj* being on fire
ABLE	*adj* ABLER, ABLEST having sufficient power, skill, or resources
ABLE	*n* pl. -S a communications code word for the letter A
ABLEGATE	*n* pl. -S a papal envoy
ABLER	comparative of able
ABLEST	superlative of able
ABLINGS	*adv* ablins
ABLINS	*adv* perhaps
ABLOOM	*adj* blooming
ABLUENT	*n* pl. -S a cleansing agent
ABLUSH	*adj* blushing
ABLUTED	*adj* washed clean
ABLUTION	*n* pl. -S a washing
ABLY	*adv* in an able manner
ABMHO	*n* pl. -MHOS a unit of electrical conductance
ABNEGATE	*v* -GATED, -GATING, -GATES to deny to oneself
ABNORMAL	*n* pl. -S a mentally deficient person
ABO	*n* pl. ABOS an aborigine (an original inhabitant)
ABOARD	*adv* into, in, or on a ship, train, or airplane
ABODE	*v* ABODED, ABODING, ABODES to forebode
ABOHM	*n* pl. -S a unit of electrical resistance
ABOIDEAU	*n* pl. -DEAUS or -DEAUX a type of dike
ABOIL	*adj* boiling
ABOITEAU	*n* pl. -TEAUS or -TEAUX aboideau
ABOLISH	*v* -ED, -ING, -ES to do away with
ABOLLA	*n* pl. -LAE a cloak worn in ancient Rome
ABOMA	*n* pl. -S a South American snake
ABOMASAL	*adj* pertaining to the abomasum
ABOMASUM	*n* pl. -SA the fourth stomach of a ruminant
ABOMASUS	*n* pl. -MASI abomasum
ABOON	*adv* above
ABORAL	*adj* situated away from the mouth ABORALLY *adv*
ABORNING	*adv* while being born
ABORT	*v* -ED, -ING, -S to bring forth a fetus prematurely
ABORTER	*n* pl. -S one that aborts
ABORTION	*n* pl. -S induced expulsion of a nonviable fetus
ABORTIVE	*adj* failing to succeed
ABOUGHT	past tense of aby and abye
ABOULIA	*n* pl. -S abulia ABOULIC *adj*

ABOUND   v -ED, -ING, -S to have a large number or amount

ABOUT   adv approximately

ABOVE   n pl. -S something that is above (in a higher place)

ABRADANT   n pl. -S an abrasive

ABRADE   v ABRADED, ABRADING, ABRADES to wear away by friction

ABRADER   n pl. -S a tool for abrading

ABRASION   n pl. -S the act of abrading

ABRASIVE   n pl. -S an abrading substance

ABREACT   v -ED, -ING, -S to release repressed emotions by reliving the original traumatic experience

ABREAST   adv side by side

ABRI   n pl. -S a bomb shelter

ABRIDGE   v ABRIDGED, ABRIDGING, ABRIDGES to reduce the length of

ABRIDGER   n pl. -S one that abridges

ABROACH   adj astir

ABROAD   adv out of one's own country

ABROGATE   v -GATED, -GATING, -GATES to abolish by authoritative action

ABRUPT   adj -RUPTER, -RUPTEST rudely brief **ABRUPTLY** adv

ABSCESS   v -ED, -ING, -ES to form an abscess (a localized collection of pus surrounded by inflamed tissue)

ABSCISE   v -SCISED, -SCISING, -SCISES to cut off

ABSCISIN   n pl. -S a regulatory substance found in plants

ABSCISSA   n pl. -SAS or -SAE a particular geometric coordinate

ABSCOND   v -ED, -ING, -S to depart suddenly and secretly

ABSENCE   n pl. -S the state of being away

ABSENT   v -ED, -ING, -S to take or keep away

ABSENTEE   n pl. -S one that is not present

ABSENTER   n pl. -S one that absents himself

ABSENTLY   adv in an inattentive manner

ABSINTH   n pl. -S absinthe

ABSINTHE   n pl. -S a bitter liqueur

ABSOLUTE   adj -LUTER, -LUTEST free from restriction

ABSOLUTE   n pl. -S something that is absolute

ABSOLVE   v -SOLVED, -SOLVING, -SOLVES to free from the consequences of an action

ABSOLVER   n pl. -S one that absolves

ABSONANT   adj unreasonable

ABSORB   v -ED, -ING, -S to take up or in

ABSORBER   n pl. -S one that absorbs

ABSTAIN   v -ED, -ING, -S to refrain voluntarily

ABSTERGE   v -STERGED, -STERGING, -STERGES to cleanse by wiping

ABSTRACT   adj -STRACTER, -STRACTEST difficult to understand

ABSTRACT   v -ED, -ING, -S to take away

ABSTRICT   v -ED, -ING, -S to form by cutting off

ABSTRUSE   adj -STRUSER, -STRUSEST difficult to understand

ABSURD   adj -SURDER, -SURDEST ridiculously incongruous or unreasonable **ABSURDLY** adv

ABSURD   n pl. -S the condition in which man exists in an irrational and meaningless universe

ABUBBLE   adj bubbling

ABULIA   n pl. -S loss of will power **ABULIC** adj

ABUNDANT   adj present in great quantity

ABUSE   v ABUSED, ABUSING, ABUSES to use wrongly or improperly **ABUSABLE** adj

ABUSER   n pl. -S one that abuses

ABUSIVE   adj characterized by wrong or improper use

ABUT   v ABUTTED, ABUTTING, ABUTS to touch along a border

ABUTILON   n pl. -S a flowering plant

ABUTMENT   n pl. -S something that abuts

ABUTTAL   n pl. -S an abutment

ABUTTED   past tense of abut

ABUTTER   n pl. -S one that abuts

ABUTTING   present participle of abut

ABUZZ   adj buzzing

ABVOLT   n pl. -S a unit of electromotive force

ABWATT   n pl. -S a unit of power

ABY   v ABOUGHT, ABYING, ABYS to pay the penalty for

ABYE	*v* ABOUGHT, ABYING, ABYES to aby
ABYSM	*n pl.* -S an abyss
ABYSMAL	*adj* immeasurably deep
ABYSS	*n pl.* -ES a bottomless chasm ABYSSAL *adj*
ACACIA	*n pl.* -S a flowering tree or shrub
ACADEME	*n pl.* -S a place of instruction
ACADEMIA	*n pl.* -S scholastic life or environment
ACADEMIC	*n pl.* -S a college student or teacher
ACADEMY	*n pl.* -MIES a secondary school
ACAJOU	*n pl.* -S a tropical tree
ACALEPH	*n pl.* -LEPHAE or -LEPHS a jellyfish
ACALEPHE	*n pl.* -S acaleph
ACANTHUS	*n pl.* -THI or -THUSES a prickly herb
ACARI	*pl.* of acarus
ACARID	*n pl.* -S any of an order of arachnids
ACARIDAN	*n pl.* -S acarid
ACARINE	*n pl.* -S acarid
ACAROID	*adj* resembling an acarid
ACARPOUS	*adj* not producing fruit
ACARUS	*n pl.* -RI a mite
ACAUDAL	*adj* having no tail
ACAUDATE	*adj* acaudal
ACAULINE	*adj* having no stem
ACAULOSE	*adj* acauline
ACAULOUS	*adj* acauline
ACCEDE	*v* -CEDED, -CEDING, -CEDES to consent
ACCEDER	*n pl.* -S one that accedes
ACCENT	*v* -ED, -ING, -S to pronounce with prominence
ACCENTOR	*n pl.* -S a songbird
ACCEPT	*v* -ED, -ING, -S to receive willingly
ACCEPTEE	*n pl.* -S one that is accepted
ACCEPTER	*n pl.* -S one that accepts
ACCEPTOR	*n pl.* -S accepter
ACCESS	*v* -ED, -ING, -ES to get at
ACCIDENT	*n pl.* -S an unexpected or unintentional occurrence
ACCIDIE	*n pl.* -S acedia
ACCLAIM	*v* -ED, -ING, -S to shout approval of
ACCOLADE	*n pl.* -S an expression of praise
ACCORD	*v* -ED, -ING, -S to bring into agreement
ACCORDER	*n pl.* -S one that accords
ACCOST	*v* -ED, -ING, -S to approach and speak to first
ACCOUNT	*v* -ED, -ING, -S to give an explanation
ACCOUTER	*v* -ED, -ING, -S to equip
ACCOUTRE	*v* -TRED, -TRING, -TRES to accouter
ACCREDIT	*v* -ED, -ING, -S to give official authorization to
ACCRETE	*v* -CRETED, -CRETING, -CRETES to grow together
ACCRUAL	*n pl.* -S the act of accruing
ACCRUE	*v* -CRUED, -CRUING, -CRUES to come as an increase or addition
ACCURACY	*n pl.* -CIES the quality of being accurate
ACCURATE	*adj* free from error
ACCURSED	*adj* damnable
ACCURST	*adj* accursed
ACCUSAL	*n pl.* -S the act of accusing
ACCUSANT	*n pl.* -S an accuser
ACCUSE	*v* -CUSED, -CUSING, -CUSES to make an assertion against
ACCUSER	*n pl.* -S one that accuses
ACCUSTOM	*v* -ED, -ING, -S to make familiar
ACE	*v* ACED, ACING, ACES to score a point against in a single stroke
ACEDIA	*n pl.* -S apathy
ACELDAMA	*n pl.* -S a place of bloodshed
ACENTRIC	*adj* having no center
ACEQUIA	*n pl.* -S an irrigation ditch or canal
ACERATE	*adj* acerose
ACERATED	*adj* acerose
ACERB	*adj* ACERBER, ACERBEST sour
ACERBATE	*v* -BATED, -BATING, -BATES to make sour
ACERBIC	*adj* acerb
ACERBITY	*n pl.* -TIES sourness
ACEROLA	*n pl.* -S a West Indian shrub
ACEROSE	*adj* needle-shaped
ACEROUS	*adj* acerose

ACERVATE   *adj* growing in compact clusters

ACERVULI   *n/pl* spore-producing organs of certain fungi

ACESCENT   *n* pl. -S something that is slightly sour

ACETA   pl. of acetum

ACETAL   *n* pl. -S a flammable liquid

ACETAMID   *n* pl. -S an amide of acetic acid

ACETATE   *n* pl. -S a salt of acetic acid **ACETATED** *adj*

ACETIC   *adj* pertaining to vinegar

ACETIFY   *v* -FIED, -FYING, -FIES to convert into vinegar

ACETONE   *n* pl. -S a flammable liquid **ACETONIC** *adj*

ACETOSE   *adj* acetous

ACETOUS   *adj* tasting like vinegar

ACETOXYL   *n* pl. -S a univalent radical

ACETUM   *n* pl. -TA vinegar

ACETYL   *n* pl. -S a univalent radical **ACETYLIC** *adj*

ACHE   *v* ACHED, ACHING, ACHES to suffer a dull, continuous pain

ACHENE   *n* pl. -S a type of fruit **ACHENIAL** *adj*

ACHIER   comparative of achy

ACHIEST   superlative of achy

ACHIEVE   *v* ACHIEVED, ACHIEVING, ACHIEVES to carry out successfully

ACHIEVER   *n* pl. -S one that achieves

ACHINESS   *n* pl. -ES the state of being achy

ACHING   present participle of ache

ACHINGLY   *adv* in an aching manner

ACHIOTE   *n* pl. -S a yellowish red dye

ACHOO   *interj* ahchoo

ACHROMAT   *n* pl. -S a type of lens

ACHROMIC   *adj* having no color

ACHY   *adj* ACHIER, ACHIEST aching

ACICULA   *n* pl. -LAE or -LAS a needlelike part or process **ACICULAR** *adj*

ACID   *n* pl. -S a type of chemical compound

ACIDHEAD   *n* pl. -S one who uses LSD

ACIDIC   *adj* sour

ACIDIFY   *v* -FIED, -FYING, -FIES to convert into an acid

ACIDITY   *n* pl. -TIES sourness

ACIDLY   *adv* sourly

ACIDNESS   *n* pl. -ES acidity

ACIDOSIS   *n* pl. -DOSES an abnormal condition of the blood **ACIDOTIC** *adj*

ACIDY   *adj* sour

ACIERATE   *v* -ATED, -ATING, -ATES to turn into steel

ACIFORM   *adj* needle-shaped

ACING   present participle of ace

ACINUS   *n* pl. -NI a small, saclike division of a gland **ACINAR, ACINIC, ACINOSE, ACINOUS** *adj*

ACLINIC   *adj* having no inclination

ACME   *n* pl. -S the highest point **ACMATIC, ACMIC** *adj*

ACNE   *n* pl. -S a skin disease **ACNED** *adj*

ACNODE   *n* pl. -S an element of a mathematical set that is isolated from the other elements

ACOCK   *adj* cocked

ACOLD   *adj* cold

ACOLYTE   *n* pl. -S an assistant

ACONITE   *n* pl. -S a poisonous herb **ACONITIC** *adj*

ACONITUM   *n* pl. -S aconite

ACORN   *n* pl. -S the fruit of the oak tree

ACOUSTIC   *n* pl. -S a hearing aid

ACQUAINT   *v* -ED, -ING, -S to cause to know

ACQUEST   *n* pl. -S something acquired

ACQUIRE   *v* -QUIRED, -QUIRING, -QUIRES to come into possession of

ACQUIRER   *n* pl. -S one that acquires

ACQUIT   *v* -QUITTED, -QUITTING, -QUITS to free or clear from a charge of fault or crime

ACRASIN   *n* pl. -S a substance secreted by the cells of a slime mold

ACRE   *n* pl. -S a unit of area

ACREAGE   *n* pl. -S area in acres

ACRED   *adj* owning many acres

ACRID   *adj* -RIDER, -RIDEST sharp and harsh to the taste or smell

ACRIDINE   *n* pl. -S a chemical compound

ACRIDITY   *n* pl. -TIES the state of being acrid

ACRIDLY   *adv* in an acrid manner

ACRIMONY n pl. -NIES sharpness or bitterness of speech or temper

ACROBAT n pl. -S one skilled in feats of agility and balance

ACRODONT n pl. -S an animal having rootless teeth

ACROGEN n pl. -S a plant growing at the apex only

ACROLEIN n pl. -S a flammable liquid

ACROLITH n pl. -S a type of statue

ACROMION n pl. -MIA the outward end of the shoulder blade ACROMIAL adj

ACRONIC adj occurring at sunset

ACRONYM n pl. -S a word formed from the initials of a compound term or series of words

ACROSS prep from one side of to the other

ACROSTIC n pl. -S a poem in which certain letters taken in order form a word or phrase

ACROTISM n pl. -S weakness of the pulse ACROTIC adj

ACRYLATE n pl. -S an acrylic

ACRYLIC n pl. -S a type of resin

ACT v -ED, -ING, -S to do something

ACTA n/pl recorded proceedings

ACTABLE adj suitable for performance on the stage

ACTIN n pl. -S a protein in muscle tissue

ACTINAL adj having tentacles

ACTING n pl. -S the occupation of an actor

ACTINIA n pl. -IAE or -IAS a marine animal

ACTINIAN n pl. -S actinia

ACTINIC adj pertaining to actinism

ACTINIDE n pl. -S any of a series of radioactive elements

ACTINISM n pl. -S the property of radiant energy that effects chemical changes

ACTINIUM n pl. -S a radioactive element

ACTINOID n pl. -S an actinide

ACTINON n pl. -S an isotope of radon

ACTION n pl. -S the process of acting

ACTIVATE v -VATED, -VATING, -VATES to set in motion

ACTIVE n pl. -S a participating member of an organization

ACTIVELY adv with activity

ACTIVISM n pl. -S a doctrine that emphasizes direct and decisive action

ACTIVIST n pl. -S an advocate of activism

ACTIVITY n pl. -TIES brisk action or movement

ACTOR n pl. -S a theatrical performer ACTORISH adj

ACTRESS n pl. -ES a female actor

ACTUAL adj existing in fact ACTUALLY adv

ACTUARY n pl. -ARIES a statistician who computes insurance risks and premiums

ACTUATE v -ATED, -ATING, -ATES to set into action or motion

ACTUATOR n pl. -S one that actuates

ACUATE adj sharp

ACUITY n pl. -ITIES sharpness

ACULEATE adj having a sting

ACUMEN n pl. -S mental keenness

ACUTANCE n pl. -S a measure of photographic clarity

ACUTE adj ACUTER, ACUTEST marked by sharpness or severity ACUTELY adv

ACUTE n pl. -S a type of accent mark

ACYCLIC adj not cyclic

ACYL n pl. -S a univalent radical

ACYLATE v -ATED, -ATING, -ATES to introduce acyl into

AD n pl. -S an advertisement

ADAGE n pl. -S a traditional saying expressing a common observation ADAGIAL adj

ADAGIO n pl. -GIOS a musical composition or movement played in a slow tempo

ADAMANCE n pl. -S adamancy

ADAMANCY n pl. -CIES unyielding hardness

ADAMANT n pl. -S an extremely hard substance

ADAMSITE n pl. -S a lung-irritating gas

ADAPT v -ED, -ING, -S to make suitable

ADAPTER n pl. -S one that adapts

ADAPTION n pl. -S the act of adapting ADAPTIVE adj

ADAPTOR   *n* pl. -S adapter

ADAXIAL   *adj* situated on the same side as

ADD   *v* -ED, -ING, -S to combine or join so as to bring about an increase ADDABLE *adj*

ADDAX   *n* pl. -ES a large antelope

ADDEDLY   *adv* additionally

ADDEND   *n* pl. -S a number to be added to another

ADDENDUM   *n* pl. -DA something added or to be added

ADDER   *n* pl. -S a venomous snake

ADDIBLE   *adj* capable of being added

ADDICT   *v* -ED, -ING, -S to devote or surrender to something habitually or compulsively

ADDITION   *n* pl. -S something added

ADDITIVE   *n* pl. -S a substance added to another to impart desirable qualities

ADDLE   *v* -DLED, -DLING, -DLES to confuse

ADDRESS   *v* -DRESSED or -DREST, -DRESSING, -DRESSES to speak to

ADDUCE   *v* -DUCED, -DUCING, -DUCES to bring forward as evidence

ADDUCENT   *adj* serving to adduct

ADDUCER   *n* pl. -S one that adduces

ADDUCING   present participle of adduce

ADDUCT   *v* -ED, -ING, -S to draw toward the main axis

ADDUCTOR   *n* pl. -S an adducent muscle

ADEEM   *v* -ED, -ING, -S to take away

ADENINE   *n* pl. -S an alkaloid

ADENITIS   *n* pl. -TISES inflammation of a lymph node

ADENOID   *n* pl. -S an enlarged lymphoid growth behind the pharynx

ADENOMA   *n* pl. -MAS or -MATA a tumor of glandular origin

ADENYL   *n* pl. -S a univalent radical

ADEPT   *adj* ADEPTER, ADEPTEST highly skilled ADEPTLY *adv*

ADEPT   *n* pl. -S an adept person

ADEQUACY   *n* pl. -CIES the state of being adequate

ADEQUATE   *adj* sufficient for a specific requirement

ADHERE   *v* -HERED, -HERING, -HERES to become or remain attached or close to something

ADHEREND   *n* pl. -S the surface to which an adhesive adheres

ADHERENT   *n* pl. -S a supporter

ADHERER   *n* pl. -S one that adheres

ADHERING   present participle of adhere

ADHESION   *n* pl. -S the act of adhering

ADHESIVE   *n* pl. -S a substance that causes adhesion

ADHIBIT   *v* -ED, -ING, -S to take or let in

ADIEU   *n* pl. ADIEUS or ADIEUX a farewell

ADIOS   *interj* — used to express farewell

ADIPOSE   *n* pl. -S animal fat ADIPIC *adj*

ADIPOSIS   *n* pl. -POSES obesity

ADIPOUS   *adj* pertaining to adipose

ADIT   *n* pl. -S an entrance

ADJACENT   *adj* next to

ADJOIN   *v* -ED, -ING, -S to lie next to

ADJOINT   *n* pl. -S a type of mathematical matrix

ADJOURN   *v* -ED, -ING, -S to suspend until a later time

ADJUDGE   *v* -JUDGED, -JUDGING, -JUDGES to determine judicially

ADJUNCT   *n* pl. -S something attached in a subordinate position

ADJURE   *v* -JURED, -JURING, -JURES to command solemnly

ADJURER   *n* pl. -S one that adjures

ADJUROR   *n* pl. -S adjurer

ADJUST   *v* -ED, -ING, -S to bring to a more satisfactory state

ADJUSTER   *n* pl. -S one that adjusts

ADJUSTOR   *n* pl. -S adjuster

ADJUTANT   *n* pl. -S an assistant

ADJUVANT   *n* pl. -S an assistant

ADMAN   *n* pl. -MEN a man employed in the advertising business

ADMASS   *adj* pertaining to a society strongly influenced by advertising

ADMIRAL   *n* pl. -S a high-ranking naval officer

ADMIRE   *v* -MIRED, -MIRING, -MIRES to regard with wonder, pleasure, and approval

ADMIRER *n* pl. -S one that admires

ADMIT *v* -MITTED, -MITTING, -MITS to allow to enter

ADMITTER *n* pl. -S one that admits

ADMIX *n* -MIXED or -MIXT, -MIXING, -MIXES to mix

ADMONISH *n* -ED, -ING, -ES to reprove mildly or kindly

ADNATE *adj* joined to another part or organ

ADNATION *n* pl. -S the state of being adnate

ADNEXA *n/pl* conjoined anatomical parts **ADNEXAL** *adj*

ADNOUN *n* pl. -S an adjective when used as a noun

ADO *n* pl. ADOS bustling excitement

ADOBE *n* pl. -S an unburnt, sun-dried brick

ADOPT *v* -ED, -ING, -S to take into one's family by legal means

ADOPTEE *n* pl. -S one that is adopted

ADOPTER *n* pl. -S one that adopts

ADOPTION *n* pl. -S the act of adopting **ADOPTIVE** *adj*

ADORABLE *adj* worthy of being adored **ADORABLY** *adv*

ADORE *v* ADORED, ADORING, ADORES to love deeply

ADORER *n* pl. -S one that adores

ADORN *v* -ED, -ING, -S to add something to for the purpose of making more attractive

ADORNER *n* pl. -S one that adorns

ADOWN *adv* downward

ADOZE *adj* dozing

ADRENAL *n* pl. -S an endocrine gland

ADRIFT *adj* drifting

ADROIT *adj* ADROITER, ADROITEST skillful ADROITLY *adv*

ADSCRIPT *n* pl. -S a distinguishing symbol written after another character

ADSORB *v* -ED, -ING, -S to gather on a surface in a condensed layer

ADULARIA *n* pl. -S a mineral

ADULATE *v* -LATED, -LATING, -LATES to praise excessively

ADULATOR *n* pl. -S one that adulates

ADULT *n* pl. -S a fully developed individual

ADULTERY *n* pl. -TERIES voluntary sexual intercourse between a married person and someone other than his or her spouse

ADULTLY *adv* in a manner typical of an adult

ADUMBRAL *adj* shadowy

ADUNC *adj* bent inward

ADUNCATE *adj* adunc

ADUNCOUS *adj* adunc

ADUST *adj* scorched

ADVANCE *v* -VANCED, -VANCING, -VANCES to move or cause to move ahead

ADVANCER *n* pl. -S one that advances

ADVENT *n* pl. -S arrival

ADVERB *n* pl. -S a word used to modify the meaning of a verb, adjective, or other adverb

ADVERSE *adj* acting in opposition

ADVERT *v* -ED, -ING, -S to call attention

ADVICE *n* pl. -S recommendation regarding a decision or course of conduct

ADVISE *v* -VISED, -VISING, -VISES to give advice to

ADVISEE *n* pl. -S one that is advised

ADVISER *n* pl. -S one that advises

ADVISING present participle of advise

ADVISOR *n* pl. -S adviser

ADVISORY *n* pl. -RIES a report giving information

ADVOCACY *n* pl. -CIES the act of advocating

ADVOCATE *v* -CATED, -CATING, -CATES to speak in favor of

ADVOWSON *n* pl. -S the right of presenting a nominee to a vacant church office

ADYNAMIA *n* pl. -S lack of physical strength ADYNAMIC *adj*

ADYTUM *n* pl. -TA an inner sanctuary in an ancient temple

ADZ *n* pl.-ES a cutting tool

ADZE *n* pl. -S adz

AE *adj* one

AECIA pl. of aecium

AECIAL *adj* pertaining to an aecium

AECIDIUM *n* pl. -IA an aecium

AECIUM *n* pl. -IA a spore-producing organ of certain fungi

AEDES *n* pl. AEDES any of a genus of mosquitoes

AEDILE *n* pl. -S a magistrate of ancient Rome

AEDINE *adj* pertaining to an aedes

AEGIS *n* pl. -GISES protection

AENEOUS *adj* having a greenish gold color

AENEUS *adj* aeneous

AEOLIAN *adj* eolian

AEON *n* pl. -S eon

AEONIAN *adj* eonian

AEONIC *adj* eonian

AERATE *v* -ATED, -ATING, -ATES to supply with air

AERATION *n* pl. -S the act of aerating

AERATOR *n* pl. -S one that aerates

AERIAL *n* pl. -S a metallic apparatus for sending and receiving electromagnetic waves

AERIALLY *adv* in a manner pertaining to the air

AERIE *n* pl. -S a bird's nest built high on a mountain or cliff AERIED *adj*

AERIER comparative of aery

AERIES pl. of aery

AERIEST superlative of aery

AERIFORM *adj* having the form of air

AERIFY *v* -FIED, -FYING, -FIES to aerate

AERILY *adv* in an aery manner

AERO *adj* pertaining to aircraft

AEROBE *n* pl. -S an organism that requires oxygen to live AEROBIC *adj*

AEROBIUM *n* pl. -BIA aerobe

AERODUCT *n* pl. -S a type of jet engine

AERODYNE *n* pl. -S an aircraft that is heavier than air

AEROFOIL *n* pl. -S airfoil

AEROGEL *n* pl. -S a highly porous solid

AEROGRAM *n* pl. -S an airmail letter

AEROLITE *n* pl. -S a meteorite containing more stone than iron

AEROLITH *n* pl. -S aerolite

AEROLOGY *n* pl. -GIES the study of the atmosphere

AERONAUT *n* pl. -S one who operates an airship

AERONOMY *n* pl. -MIES the study of the upper atmosphere

AEROSOL *n* pl. -S a gaseous suspension of fine solid or liquid particles

AEROSTAT *n* pl. -S an aircraft that is lighter than air

AERUGO *n* pl. -GOS a green film that forms on copper

AERY *adj* AERIER, AERIEST airy

AERY *n* pl. AERIES aerie

AESTHETE *n* pl. -S esthete

AESTIVAL *adj* estival

AETHER *n* pl. -S the upper region of the atmosphere AETHERIC *adj*

AFAR *n* pl. -S a great distance

AFEARD *adj* afraid

AFEARED *adj* afeard

AFF *adv* off

AFFABLE *adj* easy to talk to AFFABLY *adv*

AFFAIR *n* pl. -S anything done or to be done

AFFAIRE *n* pl. -S a brief amorous relationship

AFFECT *v* -ED, -ING, -S to give a false appearance of

AFFECTER *n* pl. -S one that affects

AFFERENT *adj* conducting toward an organ or part

AFFIANCE *v* -ANCED, -ANCING, -ANCES to betroth

AFFIANT *n* pl. -S one who makes a written declaration under oath

AFFICHE *n* pl. -S a poster

AFFINE *n* pl. -S a relative by marriage

AFFINED *adj* closely related

AFFINELY *adv* in the manner of a type of mathematical mapping

AFFINITY *n* pl. -TIES a natural attraction or inclination

AFFIRM *v* -ED, -ING, -S to state positively

AFFIRMER *n* pl. -S one that affirms

AFFIX *v* -ED, -ING, -ES to attach

AFFIXAL *adj* pertaining to a prefix or suffix

AFFIXER *n* pl. -S one that affixes

AFFIXIAL *adj* affixal

AFFLATUS *n* pl. -ES a creative inspiration

AFFLICT *v* -ED, -ING, -S to distress with mental or physical pain

AFFLUENT *n* pl. -S a stream that flows into another

AFFLUX *n* pl. -ES a flowing toward a point

AFFORD *v* -ED, -ING, -S to have sufficient means for

AFFOREST *v* -ED, -ING, -S to convert into forest

AFFRAY *v* -ED, -ING, -S to frighten

AFFRAYER *n* pl. -S one that affrays

AFFRIGHT *v* -ED, -ING, -S to frighten

AFFRONT *v* -ED, -ING, -S to insult openly

AFFUSION *n* pl. -S an act of pouring a liquid on

AFGHAN *n* pl. -S a woolen blanket or shawl

AFGHANI *n* pl. -S a monetary unit of Afghanistan

AFIELD *adv* in the field

AFIRE *adj* being on fire

AFLAME *adj* flaming

AFLOAT *adj* floating

AFLUTTER *adj* nervously excited

AFOOT *adv* on foot

AFORE *adv* before

AFOUL *adj* entangled

AFRAID *adj* filled with apprehension

AFREET *n* pl. -S an evil spirit in Arabic mythology

AFRESH *adv* anew

AFRIT *n* pl. -S afreet

AFT *adv* toward the stern

AFTER *prep* behind in place or order

AFTERS *n/pl* dessert

AFTERTAX *adj* remaining after payment of taxes

AFTMOST *adj* nearest the stern

AFTOSA *n* pl. -S a disease of hoofed mammals

AGA *n* pl. -S a high-ranking Turkish military officer

AGAIN *adv* once more

AGAINST *prep* in opposition to

AGALLOCH *n* pl. -S the fragrant wood of a tropical tree

AGALWOOD *n* pl. -S agalloch

AGAMA *n* pl. -S a tropical lizard

AGAMETE *n* pl. -S an asexual reproductive cell

AGAMIC *adj* asexual

AGAMOUS *adj* agamic

AGAPE *n* pl. -PAE or -PAI the love of God for mankind **AGAPEIC** *adj*

AGAR *n* pl. -S a viscous substance obtained from certain seaweeds

AGARIC *n* pl. -S any of a family of fungi

AGATE *n* pl. -S a variety of quartz **AGATOID** *adj*

AGATIZE *v* -IZED, -IZING, -IZES to cause to resemble agate

AGAVE *n* pl. -S a tropical plant

AGAZE *adj* gazing

AGE *v* AGED, AGING or AGEING, AGES to grow old

AGEDLY *adv* oldly

AGEDNESS *n* pl. -ES oldness

AGEE *adv* to one side

AGEING *n* pl. -S aging

AGELESS *adj* never growing old

AGELONG *adj* lasting for a long time

AGENCY *n* pl. -CIES an organization that does business for others

AGENDA *n* pl. -S a list of things to be done

AGENDUM *n* pl. -S an item on an agenda

AGENE *n* pl. -S a chemical compound used in bleaching flour

AGENESIA *n* pl. -S agenesis

AGENESIS *n* pl. AGENESES absence or imperfect development of a bodily part **AGENETIC** *adj*

AGENIZE *v* -NIZED, -NIZING, -NIZES to treat with agene

AGENT *n* pl. -S one who is authorized to act for another **AGENTIAL** *adj*

AGENTRY *n* pl. -RIES the office or duties of an agent

AGER *n* pl. -S one that ages

AGERATUM *n* pl. -S a flowering plant

AGGER *n* pl. -S a mound of earth used as a fortification

AGGIE *n* pl. -S a type of playing marble

AGGRADE *v* -GRADED, -GRADING, -GRADES to fill with detrital material

MYOSOTE	*n* pl. -S myosotis
MYOSOTIS	*n* pl. -TISES a flowering plant
MYOTIC	*n* pl. -S miotic
MYOTOME	*n* pl. -S a portion of an embryonic somite
MYOTONIA	*n* pl. -S temporary muscular rigidity **MYOTONIC** *adj*
MYRIAD	*n* pl. -S a very large number
MYRIAPOD	*n* pl. -S a multi-legged arthropod
MYRICA	*n* pl. -S a medicinal tree bark
MYRIOPOD	*n* pl. -S myriapod
MYRMIDON	*n* pl. -S a loyal follower
MYRRH	*n* pl. -S an aromatic gum resin **MYRRHIC** *adj*
MYRTLE	*n* pl. -S an evergreen shrub
MYSELF	*pron* a form of the 1st person sing. pronoun
MYSOST	*n* pl. -S a mild cheese
MYSTAGOG	*n* pl. -S a teacher of religious mysteries
MYSTERY	*n* pl. -TERIES something that is not or cannot be known, understood, or explained
MYSTIC	*n* pl. -S one who professes to have had mystical experiences
MYSTICAL	*adj* spiritually significant or symbolic
MYSTICLY	*adv* in a mystical manner
MYSTIFY	*v* -FIED, -FYING, -FIES to perplex
MYSTIQUE	*n* pl. -S an aura of mystery or mystical power surrounding a particular person or thing
MYTH	*n* pl. -S a type of traditional story
MYTHIC	*adj* mythical
MYTHICAL	*adj* based on or described in a myth
MYTHOS	*n* pl. -THOI a myth
MYXEDEMA	*n* pl. -S a disease caused by decreased activity of the thyroid gland
MYXOCYTE	*n* pl. -S a large cell found in mucous tissue
MYXOID	*adj* containing mucus
MYXOMA	*n* pl. -MAS or -MATA a tumor composed of mucous tissue

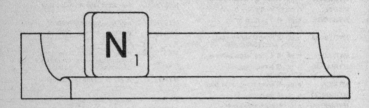

NA	*adv* no; not
NAB	*v* NABBED, NABBING, NABS to capture or arrest
NABIS	*n pl.* NABIS a group of French artists
NABOB	*n pl.* -S one who has become rich in India
NABOBERY	*n pl.* -ERIES the state of being a nabob
NABOBESS	*n pl.* -ES a female nabob
NABOBISM	*n pl.* -S great wealth and luxury
NACELLE	*n pl.* -S a shelter on an aircraft
NACRE	*n pl.* -S the pearly internal layer of certain shells NACRED, NACREOUS *adj*
NADIR	*n pl.* -S a point on the celestial sphere NADIRAL *adj*
NAE	*adv* no; not
NAETHING	*n pl.* -S nothing
NAEVUS	*n pl.* -VI nevus NAEVOID *adj*
NAG	*v* NAGGED, NAGGING, NAGS to find fault incessantly
NAGANA	*n pl.* -S a disease of horses in Africa
NAGGER	*n pl.* -S one that nags
NAGGING	present participle of nag
NAIAD	*n pl.* -S or -ES a water nymph
NAIF	*n pl.* -S a naive person
NAIL	*v* -ED, -ING, -S to fasten with a nail (a slender piece of metal)
NAILER	*n pl.* -S one that nails
NAILFOLD	*n pl.* -S a fold of skin around the fingernail
NAILHEAD	*n pl.* -S the top of a nail
NAILSET	*n pl.* -S a steel rod for driving a nail into something
NAINSOOK	*n pl.* -S a cotton fabric
NAIVE	*adj* NAIVER, NAIVEST lacking sophistication NAIVELY *adv*
NAIVE	*n pl.* -S a naive person
NAIVETE	*n pl.* -S the quality of being naive
NAIVETY	*n pl.* -TIES naivete
NAKED	*adj* -KEDER, -KEDEST being without clothing or covering NAKEDLY *adv*
NALED	*n pl.* -S an insecticide
NALOXONE	*n pl.* -S a chemical compound
NAME	*v* NAMED, NAMING, NAMES to give a title to NAMABLE, NAMEABLE *adj*
NAMELESS	*adj* lacking distinction or fame
NAMELY	*adv* that is to say
NAMER	*n pl.* -S one that names
NAMESAKE	*n pl.* -S one who is named after another
NAMING	present participle of name
NANA	*n pl.* -S a grandmother
NANCE	*n pl.* -S an effeminate male
NANDIN	*n pl.* -S an evergreen shrub
NANISM	*n pl.* -S abnormal smallness
NANKEEN	*n pl.* -S a cotton fabric
NANKIN	*n pl.* -S nankeen
NANNIE	*n pl.* -S nanny
NANNY	*n pl.* -NIES a children's nurse
NANOGRAM	*n pl.* -S a unit of mass and weight
NANOWATT	*n pl.* -S a unit of power

NAOS *n pl.* NAOI an ancient temple

NAP *v* NAPPED, NAPPING, NAPS to sleep briefly

NAPALM *v* -ED, -ING, -S to assault with a type of incendiary bomb

NAPE *n pl.* -S the back of the neck

NAPERY *n pl.* -PERIES table linen

NAPHTHA *n pl.* -S a volatile liquid

NAPHTHOL *n pl.* -S a chemical compound

NAPHTHYL *adj* containing a certain chemical group

NAPHTOL *n pl.* -S naphthol

NAPIFORM *adj* shaped like a turnip

NAPKIN *n pl.* -S a piece of material used to wipe the hands and mouth

NAPLESS *adj* threadbare

NAPOLEON *n pl.* -S a type of pastry

NAPPE *n pl.* -S a type of rock formation

NAPPED past tense of nap

NAPPER *n pl.* -S one that naps

NAPPIE *n pl.* -S a diaper

NAPPING present participle of nap

NAPPY *adj* -PIER, -PIEST kinky

NARC *n pl.* -S an undercover drug agent

NARCEIN *n pl.* -S narceine

NARCEINE *n pl.* -S an opium derivative

NARCISM *n pl.* -S excessive love of oneself

NARCISSI *n/pl* bulbous flowering plants

NARCIST *n pl.* -S one given to narcism

NARCO *n pl.* -COS narc

NARCOSE *adj* characterized by stupor

NARCOSIS *n pl.* -COSES a drug-induced stupor

NARCOTIC *n pl.* -S a drug that dulls the senses

NARD *n pl.* -S a fragrant ointment NARDINE *adj*

NARES *pl.* of naris

NARGHILE *n pl.* -S a hookah

NARGILE *n pl.* -S narghile

NARGILEH *n pl.* -S narghile

NARIS *n pl.* NARES a nostril NARIAL, NARIC, NARINE *adj*

NARK *v* -ED, -ING, -S to spy or inform

NARRATE *v* -RATED, -RATING, -RATES to tell a story

NARRATER *n pl.* -S narrator

NARRATOR *n pl.* -S one that narrates

NARROW *adj* -ROWER, -ROWEST of little width NARROWLY *adv*

NARROW *v* -ED, -ING, -S to make narrow

NARTHEX *n pl.* -ES a vestibule in a church

NARWAL *n pl.* -S narwhal

NARWHAL *n pl.* -S an arctic aquatic mammal

NARWHALE *n pl.* -S narwhal

NARY *adj* not one

NASAL *n pl.* -S a sound uttered through the nose

NASALISE *v* -ISED, -ISING, -ISES to nasalize

NASALITY *n pl.* -TIES the quality or an instance of being produced nasally

NASALIZE *v* -IZED, -IZING, -IZES to produce sounds nasally

NASALLY *adv* through the nose

NASCENCE *n pl.* -S nascency

NASCENCY *n pl.* -CIES birth; origin

NASCENT *adj* coming into existence

NASION *n pl.* -S a point in the skull NASIAL *adj*

NASTIC *adj* pertaining to an automatic response of plants

NASTY *adj* -TIER, -TIEST offensive to the senses NASTILY *adv*

NATAL *adj* pertaining to one's birth

NATALITY *n pl.* -TIES birth rate

NATANT *adj* floating or swimming NATANTLY *adv*

NATATION *n pl.* -S the act of swimming

NATATORY *adj* pertaining to swimming

NATES *n/pl* the buttocks

NATHLESS *adv* nevertheless

NATION *n pl.* -S a politically organized people who share a territory, customs, and history

NATIONAL *n pl.* -S a citizen of a nation

NATIVE *n pl.* -S an original inhabitant of an area

NATIVELY *adv* in an inborn manner

NATIVISM *n pl.* -S a policy of favoring the interests of native inhabitants

NATIVIST *n pl.* -S an advocate of nativism

NATIVITY *n pl.* -TIES the process of being born

NATRIUM *n pl.* -S sodium

NATRON *n pl.* -S a chemical compound

NATTER *v* -ED, -ING, -S to chatter

NATTY *adj* -TIER, -TIEST neatly dressed **NATTILY** *adv*

NATURAL *n pl.* -S a type of musical note

NATURE *n pl.* -S the essential qualities of a person or thing **NATURED** *adj*

NAUGHT *n pl.* -S a zero

NAUGHTY *adj* -TIER, -TIEST disobedient

NAUMACHY *n pl.* -CHIES a mock sea battle

NAUPLIUS *n pl.* -PLII a form of certain crustaceans **NAUPLIAL** *adj*

NAUSEA *n pl.* -S a stomach disturbance

NAUSEANT *n pl.* -S an agent that induces nausea

NAUSEATE *v* -ATED, -ATING, -ATES to affect with nausea

NAUSEOUS *adj* affected with nausea

NAUTCH *n pl.* -ES a dancing exhibition in India

NAUTICAL *adj* pertaining to ships

NAUTILUS *n pl.* -LUSES or -LI a spiral-shelled mollusk

NAVAID *n pl.* -S a navigational device

NAVAL *adj* pertaining to ships **NAVALLY** *adv*

NAVAR *n pl.* -S a system of air navigation

NAVE *n pl.* -S the main part of a church

NAVEL *n pl.* -S a depression in the abdomen

NAVETTE *n pl.* -S a gem cut in a pointed oval form

NAVICERT *n pl.* -S a document permitting a vessel passage through a naval blockade

NAVIES pl. of navy

NAVIGATE *v* -GATED, -GATING, -GATES to plan and control the course of

NAVVY *n pl.* -VIES a manual laborer

NAVY *n pl.* -VIES a nation's warships

NAWAB *n pl.* -S a nabob

NAY *n pl.* NAYS a negative vote

NAZI *n pl.* -S a type of fascist

NAZIFY *v* -FIED, -FYING, -FIES to cause to be like a nazi

NEAP *n pl.* -S a tide of lowest range

NEAR *adj* NEARER, NEAREST situated within a short distance

NEAR *v* -ED, -ING, -S to approach

NEARBY *adj* near

NEARLY *adv* -LIER, -LIEST with close approximation

NEARNESS *n pl.* -ES the state of being near

NEAT *adj* NEATER, NEATEST being in a state of cleanliness and order

NEAT *n pl.* -S a bovine

NEATEN *v* -ED, -ING, -S to make neat

NEATH *prep* beneath

NEATHERD *n pl.* -S a cowherd

NEATLY *adv* in a neat manner

NEATNESS *n pl.* -ES the state of being neat

NEB *n pl.* -S the beak of a bird

NEBBISH *n pl.* -ES a meek person

NEBULA *n pl.* -LAS or -LAE a cloud-like interstellar mass **NEBULAR** *adj*

NEBULE *adj* composed of successive short curves

NEBULISE *v* -LISED, -LISING, -LISES to nebulize

NEBULIZE *v* -LIZED, -LIZING, -LIZES to reduce to a fine spray

NEBULOSE *adj* nebulous

NEBULOUS *adj* unclear

NEBULY *adj* nebule

NECK *v* -ED, -ING, -S to kiss and caress in lovemaking

NECKBAND *n pl.* -S a band worn around the neck (the part of the body joining the head to the trunk)

NECKING *n pl.* -S a small molding near the top of a column

NECKLACE *n pl.* -S an ornament worn around the neck

NECKLESS *adj* having no neck

NECKLIKE *adj* resembling the neck

NECKLINE *n pl.* -S the line formed by the neck opening of a garment

NECKTIE *n pl.* -S a strip of fabric worn around the neck

NECKWEAR *n pl.* -S something that is worn around the neck

NECROPSY *v* -SIED, -SYING, -SIES to perform an autopsy on

NECROSE v -CROSED, -CROSING, -CROSES to affect with necrosis

NECROSIS n pl. -CROSES the death of living tissue **NECROTIC** adj

NECTAR n pl. -S a delicious drink

NECTARY n pl. -TARIES a plant gland

NEE adj born with the name of

NEED v -ED, -ING, -S to have an urgent or essential use for

NEEDER n pl. -S one that needs

NEEDFUL n pl. -S something that is needed

NEEDIER comparative of needy

NEEDIEST superlative of needy

NEEDILY adv in a needy manner

NEEDLE v -DLED, -DLING, -DLES to sew with a slender, pointed instrument

NEEDLER n pl. -S one that needles

NEEDLESS adj not necessary

NEEDLING n pl. -S the act of one who needles

NEEDY adj NEEDIER, NEEDIEST in a state of poverty

NEEM n pl. -S an East Indian tree

NEEP n pl. -S a turnip

NEGATE v -GATED, -GATING, -GATES to nullify

NEGATER n pl. -S one that negates

NEGATION n pl. -S the act of negating

NEGATIVE v -TIVED, -TIVING, -TIVES to veto

NEGATON n pl. -S negatron

NEGATOR n pl. -S negater

NEGATRON n pl. -S an electron

NEGLECT v -ED, -ING, -S to fail to pay attention to

NEGLIGE n pl. -S negligee

NEGLIGEE n pl. -S a woman's dressing gown

NEGRO n pl. -GROES a member of the black race of mankind

NEGROID n pl. -S a negro

NEGUS n pl. -ES an alcoholic beverage

NEIF n pl. -S nieve

NEIGH v -ED, -ING, -S to utter the cry of a horse

NEIGHBOR v -ED, -ING, -S to live close to

NEIST adj next

NEITHER adj not one or the other

NEKTON n pl. -S free-swimming marine animals **NEKTONIC** adj

NELSON n pl. -S a wrestling hold

NELUMBO n pl. -BOS an aquatic herb

NEMA n pl. -S a nematode

NEMATIC adj pertaining to a phase of a liquid crystal

NEMATODE n pl. -S a kind of worm

NEMESIS n pl. NEMESES an unbeatable opponent

NENE n pl. NENE a Hawaiian goose

NEOLITH n pl. -S an ancient stone implement

NEOLOGY n pl. -GIES a new word or phrase **NEOLOGIC** adj

NEOMORPH n pl. -S a type of biological structure

NEOMYCIN n pl. -S an antibiotic drug

NEON n pl. -S a gaseous element **NEONED** adj

NEONATE n pl. -S a newborn child **NEONATAL** adj

NEOPHYTE n pl. -S a novice

NEOPLASM n pl. -S a tumor

NEOPRENE n pl. -S a synthetic rubber

NEOTENY n pl. -NIES attainment of sexual maturity in the larval stage **NEOTENIC** adj

NEOTERIC n pl. -S a modern author

NEOTYPE n pl. -S a specimen of a species

NEPENTHE n pl. -S a drug that induces forgetfulness

NEPHEW n pl. -S a son of one's brother or sister

NEPHRIC adj renal

NEPHRISM n pl. -S ill health caused by a kidney disease

NEPHRITE n pl. -S a mineral

NEPHRON n pl. -S an excretory unit of a kidney

NEPOTISM n pl. -S favoritism shown to a relative **NEPOTIC** adj

NEPOTIST n pl. -S one who practices nepotism

NEREID n pl. -S a sea nymph

NEREIS n pl. -REIDES a marine worm

NERITIC adj pertaining to shallow water

NEROL	*n* pl. -S a fragrant alcohol
NEROLI	*n* pl. -S a fragrant oil
NERTS	*interj* — used to express defiance or disgust
NERTZ	*interj* nerts
NERVATE	*adj* having veins
NERVE	*v* NERVED, NERVING, NERVES to give courage to
NERVIER	comparative of nervy
NERVIEST	superlative of nervy
NERVILY	*adv* in a nervy manner
NERVINE	*n* pl. -S a soothing medicine
NERVING	*n* pl. -S a type of veterinary operation
NERVOUS	*adj* easily excited
NERVULE	*n* pl. -S nervure
NERVURE	*n* pl. -S a vascular ridge on a leaf
NERVY	*adj* NERVIER, NERVIEST impudent
NESCIENT	*n* pl. -S one who is ignorant
NESS	*n* pl. -ES a headland
NEST	*v* -ED, -ING, -S to build a nest (a structure for holding bird eggs)
NESTER	*n* pl. -S one that nests
NESTLE	*v* -TLED, -TLING, -TLES to lie snugly
NESTLER	*n* pl. -S one that nestles
NESTLIKE	*adj* resembling a nest
NESTLING	*n* pl. -S a young bird
NESTOR	*n* pl. -S a wise old man
NET	*v* NETTED, NETTING, NETS to catch in a net (a type of openwork fabric)
NETHER	*adj* situated below
NETLESS	*adj* having no net
NETLIKE	*adj* resembling a net
NETOP	*n* pl. -S friend; companion
NETSUKE	*n* pl. -S a button-like fixture on Japanese clothing
NETT	*v* -ED, -ING, -S to net
NETTABLE	*adj* capable of being netted
NETTED	past tense of net, nett
NETTER	*n* pl. -S one that nets
NETTIER	comparative of netty
NETTIEST	superlative of netty
NETTING	*n* pl. -S a net

NETTLE	*v* -TLED, -TLING, -TLES to make angry
NETTLER	*n* pl. -S one that nettles
NETTLY	*adj* -TLIER, -TLIEST prickly
NETTY	*adj* -TIER, -TIEST resembling a net
NETWORK	*v* -ED, -ING, -S to cover with or as if with crossing lines
NEUM	*n* pl. -S neume
NEUME	*n* pl. -S a sign used in musical notation **NEUMATIC**, **NEUMIC** *adj*
NEURAL	*adj* pertaining to the nervous system **NEURALLY** *adv*
NEURAXON	*n* pl. -S a part of a neuron
NEURITIC	*n* pl. -S one affected with neuritis
NEURITIS	*n* pl. -RITIDES or -RITISES inflammation of a nerve
NEUROID	*adj* resembling a nerve
NEUROMA	*n* pl. -MAS or -MATA a type of tumor
NEURON	*n* pl. -S the basic cellular unit of the nervous system **NEURONAL**, **NEURONIC** *adj*
NEURONE	*n* pl. -S neuron
NEUROSIS	*n* pl. -ROSES a type of emotional disturbance **NEUROSAL** *adj*
NEUROTIC	*n* pl. -S one affected with a neurosis
NEUSTON	*n* pl. -S an aggregate of small aquatic organisms
NEUTER	*v* -ED, -ING, -S to castrate
NEUTRAL	*n* pl. -S one that is impartial
NEUTRINO	*n* pl. -NOS an atomic particle
NEUTRON	*n* pl. -S an atomic particle
NEVE	*n* pl. -S a granular snow
NEVER	*adv* at no time
NEVUS	*n* pl. -VI a birthmark **NEVOID** *adj*
NEW	*adj* NEWER, NEWEST existing only a short time
NEW	*n* pl. -S something that is new
NEWBORN	*n* pl. -S a recently born infant
NEWCOMER	*n* pl. -S one that has recently arrived
NEWEL	*n* pl. -S a staircase support
NEWFOUND	*adj* newly found
NEWISH	*adj* somewhat new

NEWLY   adv recently

NEWLYWED   n pl. -S a person recently married

NEWMOWN   adj recently mown

NEWNESS   n pl. -ES the state of being new

NEWS   n/pl a report of recent events

NEWSBOY   n pl. -BOYS a boy who delivers or sells newspapers

NEWSCAST   n pl. -S a news broadcast

NEWSIER   comparative of newsy

NEWSIES   pl. of newsy

NEWSIEST   superlative of newsy

NEWSLESS   adj having no news

NEWSMAN   n pl. -MEN a news reporter

NEWSPEAK   n pl. -S a deliberately ambiguous language

NEWSREEL   n pl. -S a short movie presenting current events

NEWSROOM   n pl. -S a room where the news is gathered

NEWSY   adj NEWSIER, NEWSIEST full of news

NEWSY   n pl. NEWSIES a newsboy

NEWT   n pl. -S a small salamander

NEWTON   n pl. -S a unit of force

NEXT   adj coming immediately after; adjoining

NEXTDOOR   adj located in the next building or room

NEXUS   n pl. -ES a connection or link

NGWEE   n pl. NGWEE a Zambian unit of currency

NIACIN   n pl. -S a B vitamin

NIB   v NIBBED, NIBBING, NIBS to provide with a penpoint

NIBBLE   v -BLED, -BLING, -BLES to eat with small bites

NIBBLER   n pl. -S one that nibbles

NIBLICK   n pl. -S a golf club

NIBLIKE   adj resembling a penpoint

NICE   adj NICER, NICEST pleasing to the senses NICELY adv

NICENESS   n pl. -ES the quality of being nice

NICETY   n pl. -TIES a fine point or distinction

NICHE   v NICHED, NICHING, NICHES to place in a receding space or hollow

NICK   v -ED, -ING, -S to make a shallow cut in

NICKEL   v -ELED, -ELING, -ELS or -ELLED, -ELLING, -ELS to plate with nickel (a metallic element)

NICKELIC   adj pertaining to or containing nickel

NICKER   v -ED, -ING, -S to neigh

NICKLE   n pl. -S nickel

NICKNACK   n pl. -S a trinket

NICKNAME   v -NAMED, -NAMING, -NAMES to give an alternate name to

NICOL   n pl. -S a type of prism

NICOTIN   n pl. -S nicotine

NICOTINE   n pl. -S a poisonous alkaloid in tobacco

NICTATE   v -TATED, -TATING, -TATES to wink

NIDAL   adj pertaining to a nidus

NIDE   v NIDED, NIDING, NIDES to nest

NIDERING   n pl. -S a coward

NIDGET   n pl. -S an idiot

NIDI   a pl. of nidus

NIDIFY   v -FIED, -FYING, -FIES to nest

NIDING   present participle of nide

NIDUS   n pl. NIDI or NIDUSES a nest or breeding place

NIECE   n pl. -S a daughter of one's brother or sister

NIELLIST   n pl. -S one that niellos

NIELLO   n pl. -LI or -LOS a black metallic substance

NIELLO   v -ED, -ING, -S to decorate with niello

NIEVE   n pl. -S the fist or hand

NIFFER   v -ED, -ING, -S to barter

NIFTY   adj -TIER, -TIEST stylish; pleasing

NIFTY   n pl. -TIES something that is nifty

NIGGARD   v -ED, -ING, -S to act stingily

NIGGER   n pl. -S a black person — an offensive term

NIGGLE   v -GLED, -GLING, -GLES to worry over petty details

NIGGLER   n pl. -S one that niggles

NIGGLING   n pl. -S petty or meticulous work

NIGH   adj NIGHER, NIGHEST near

NIGH v -ED, -ING, -S to approach

NIGHNESS n pl. -ES the state of being nigh

NIGHT n pl. -S the period from sunset to sunrise

NIGHTCAP n pl. -S a cap worn to bed

NIGHTIE n pl. -S a nightgown

NIGHTIES pl. of nighty

NIGHTJAR n pl. -S a nocturnal bird

NIGHTLY adv every night; at night

NIGHTY n pl. NIGHTIES nightie

NIGRIFY v -FIED, -FYING, -FIES to make black

NIGROSIN n pl. -S a type of dye

NIHIL n pl. -S nothing

NIHILISM n pl. -S a doctrine that denies traditional values

NIHILIST n pl. -S an adherent of nihilism

NIHILITY n pl. -TIES the state of being nothing

NIL n pl. -S nothing

NILGAI n pl. -S a large antelope

NILGAU n pl. -S nilgai

NILGHAI n pl. -S nilgai

NILGHAU n pl. -S nilgai

NILL v -ED, -ING, -S to be unwilling

NIM v NIMMED, NIMMING, NIMS to steal

NIMBLE adj -BLER, -BLEST agile NIMBLY adv

NIMBUS n pl. -BI or -BUSES a luminous cloud NIMBUSED adj

NIMIETY n pl. -ETIES excess NIMIOUS adj

NIMMED past tense of nim

NIMMING present participle of nim

NIMROD n pl. -S a hunter

NINE n pl. -S a number

NINEBARK n pl. -S a flowering shrub

NINEFOLD adj nine times as great

NINEPIN n pl. -S a wooden pin used in a bowling game

NINETEEN n pl. -S a number

NINETY n pl. -TIES a number

NINNY n pl. -NIES a fool NINNYISH adj

NINON n pl. -S a sheer fabric

NINTH n pl. -S one of nine equal parts

NINTHLY adv in the ninth place

NIOBIUM n pl. -S a metallic element NIOBIC, NIOBOUS adj

NIP v NIPPED, NIPPING, NIPS to pinch

NIPA n pl. -S a palm tree

NIPPER n pl. -S one that nips

NIPPIER comparative of nippy

NIPPIEST superlative of nippy

NIPPILY adv in a nippy manner

NIPPING present participle of nip

NIPPLE n pl. -S a protuberance on the breast

NIPPY adj -PIER, -PIEST sharp or biting

NIRVANA n pl. -S a blessed state in Buddhism NIRVANIC adj

NISEI n pl. -S one born in America of immigrant Japanese parents

NISI adj not yet final

NISUS n pl. NISUS an effort

NIT n pl. -S the egg of a parasitic insect

NITCHIE n pl. -S an American Indian — an offensive term

NITER n pl. -S a chemical salt

NITID adj bright

NITON n pl. -S radon

NITPICK v -ED, -ING, -S to fuss over petty details

NITRATE v -TRATED, -TRATING, -TRATES to treat with nitric acid

NITRATOR n pl. -S one that nitrates

NITRE n pl. -S niter

NITRIC adj containing nitrogen

NITRID n pl. -S nitride

NITRIDE n pl. -S a compound of nitrogen

NITRIFY v -FIED, -FYING, -FIES to combine with nitrogen

NITRIL n pl. -S nitrile

NITRILE n pl. -S a chemical compound

NITRITE n pl. -S a salt of nitrous acid

NITRO n pl. -TROS a nitrated product

NITROGEN n pl. -S a gaseous element

NITROLIC adj pertaining to a class of acids

NITROSO adj containing nitrosyl

NITROSYL n pl. -S a univalent radical

NITROUS adj containing nitrogen

NITTY adj -TIER, -TIEST full of nits

NITWIT	*n* pl. -S a stupid person
NIVAL	*adj* pertaining to snow
NIVEOUS	*adj* resembling snow
NIX	*v* -ED, -ING, -ES to veto
NIXIE	*n* pl. -S a female water sprite
NIXY	*n* pl. NIXIES an undeliverable piece of mail
NIZAM	*n* pl. -S a former sovereign of India
NIZAMATE	*n* pl. -S the territory of a nizam
NO	*n* pl. NOS or NOES a negative reply
NOB	*n* pl. -S a wealthy person
NOBBIER	comparative of nobby
NOBBIEST	superlative of nobby
NOBBILY	*adv* in a nobby manner
NOBBLE	*v* -BLED, -BLING, -BLES to disable a racehorse
NOBBLER	*n* pl. -S one that nobbles
NOBBY	*adj* -BIER, -BIEST elegant
NOBELIUM	*n* pl. -S a radioactive element
NOBILITY	*n* pl. -TIES the social class composed of nobles
NOBLE	*adj* -BLER, -BLEST possessing qualities of excellence
NOBLE	*n* pl. -S a person of high birth, rank, or title
NOBLEMAN	*n* pl. -MEN a noble
NOBLER	comparative of noble
NOBLESSE	*n* pl. -S the nobility
NOBLEST	superlative of noble
NOBLY	*adv* in a noble manner
NOBODY	*n* pl. -BODIES an unimportant person
NOCENT	*adj* harmful
NOCK	*v* -ED, -ING, -S to notch a bow or arrow
NOCTUID	*n* pl. -S a night-flying moth NOCTUOID *adj*
NOCTULE	*n* pl. -S a large bat
NOCTURN	*n* pl. -S a religious service
NOCTURNE	*n* pl. -S a musical composition
NOCUOUS	*adj* harmful
NOD	*v* NODDED, NODDING, NODS to briefly lower the head forward
NODAL	*adj* of the nature of a node NODALLY *adv*
NODALITY	*n* pl. -TIES the state of being nodal
NODDED	past tense of nod
NODDER	*n* pl. -S one that nods
NODDIES	pl. of noddy
NODDING	present participle of nod
NODDLE	*v* -DLED, -DLING, -DLES to nod frequently
NODDY	*n* pl. -DIES a fool
NODE	*n* pl. -S a swollen enlargement
NODI	pl. of nodus
NODICAL	*adj* pertaining to an astronomical point
NODOSE	*adj* having nodes
NODOSITY	*n* pl. -TIES the state of being nodose
NODOUS	*adj* nodose
NODULE	*n* pl. -S a small node NODULAR, NODULOSE, NODULOUS *adj*
NODUS	*n* pl. -DI a difficulty
NOEL	*n* pl. -S a Christmas carol
NOESIS	*n* pl. -SISES the process of reason
NOETIC	*adj* pertaining to reason
NOG	*n* pl. -S a strong ale
NOGG	*n* pl. -S nog
NOGGIN	*n* pl. -S a small cup
NOGGING	*n* pl. -S a type of masonry
NOH	*n* pl. NOH the classical drama of Japan
NOHOW	*adv* in no manner
NOIL	*n* pl. -S a kind of short fiber NOILY *adj*
NOIR	*adj* black
NOISE	*v* NOISED, NOISING, NOISES to spread as a rumor or report
NOISOME	*adj* disgusting; harmful
NOISY	*adj* NOISIER, NOISIEST making loud sounds NOISILY *adv*
NOLO	*n* pl. -LOS a type of legal plea
NOM	*n* pl. -S a name
NOMA	*n* pl. -S a severe inflammation of the mouth
NOMAD	*n* pl. -S a wanderer NOMADIC *adj*
NOMADISM	*n* pl. -S the mode of life of a nomad
NOMARCH	*n* pl. -S the head of a nome

NOMARCHY *n pl.* -ARCHIES a nome

NOMBLES *n/pl* numbles

NOMBRIL *n pl.* -S a point on a heraldic shield

NOME *n pl.* -S a province of modern Greece

NOMEN *n pl.* -MINA the second name of an ancient Roman

NOMINAL *n pl.* -S a word functioning as a noun

NOMINATE *v* -NATED, -NATING, -NATES to name as a candidate

NOMINEE *n pl.* -S one that is nominated

NOMISM *n pl.* -S strict adherence to moral law **NOMISTIC** *adj*

NOMOGRAM *n pl.* -S a type of graph

NOMOLOGY *n pl.* -GIES the science of law

NOMOS *n pl.* NOMOI law

NONA *n pl.* -S a virus disease

NONACID *n pl.* -S a substance that is not an acid

NONADULT *n pl.* -S a person who is not an adult

NONAGE *n pl.* -S a period of immaturity

NONAGON *n pl.* -S a nine-sided polygon

NONBANK *adj* not involving a bank

NONBASIC *adj* not basic

NONBEING *n pl.* -S lack of being

NONBOOK *n pl.* -S a book of little literary merit

NONCASH *adj* other than cash

NONCE *n pl.* -S the present occasion

NONCOM *n pl.* -S a noncommissioned officer

NONDAIRY *adj* having no milk products

NONE *n pl.* -S one of seven canonical daily periods for prayer and devotion

NONEGO *n pl.* -GOS all that is not part of the ego

NONELECT *adj* not chosen

NONEMPTY *adj* not empty

NONENTRY *n pl.* -TRIES the fact of not entering

NONEQUAL *n pl.* -S one that is not equal

NONESUCH *n pl.* -ES a person or thing without an equal

NONEVENT *n pl.* -S an expected event that does not occur

NONFARM *adj* not pertaining to the farm

NONFAT *adj* having no fat solids

NONFATAL *adj* not fatal

NONFLUID *n pl.* -S a substance that is not a fluid

NONFOCAL *adj* not focal

NONFOOD *adj* pertaining to something other than food

NONGAME *adj* not hunted for food, sport, or fur

NONGREEN *adj* not green

NONGUILT *n pl.* -S the absence of guilt

NONHARDY *adj* not hardy

NONHERO *n pl.* -ROES an antihero

NONHUMAN *adj* not human

NONIDEAL *adj* not ideal

NONIONIC *adj* not ionic

NONJUROR *n pl.* -S one who refuses to take a required oath

NONLEGAL *adj* not legal

NONLIFE *n pl.* -LIVES the absence of life

NONLOCAL *n pl.* -S one that is not local

NONMAN *n pl.* -MEN a being that is not a man

NONMETAL *n pl.* -S an element that lacks metallic properties

NONMODAL *adj* not modal

NONMONEY *adj* not involving money

NONMORAL *adj* not pertaining to morals

NONNAVAL *adj* not naval

NONOBESE *adj* not obese

NONOWNER *n pl.* -S one who is not the owner

NONPAGAN *n pl.* -S one who is not a pagan

NONPAPAL *adj* not papal

NONPAR *adj* being a stock that has no face value

NONPARTY *adj* not affiliated with any political party

NONPLUS *v* -PLUSED, -PLUSING, -PLUSES or -PLUSSED, -PLUSSING, -PLUSSES to baffle

NONPOLAR *adj* not polar

NONPROS *v* -PROSSED, -PROSSING, -PROSSES to enter a judgment against a plaintiff who fails to prosecute

NONQUOTA *adj* not included in or subject to a quota

NONRATED adj not rated

NONRIGID adj not rigid

NONRIVAL n pl. -S an unimportant rival

NONROYAL adj not royal

NONRURAL adj not rural

NONSENSE n pl. -S behavior or language that is meaningless or absurd

NONSKED n pl. -S an airline without scheduled flying times

NONSKID adj designed to inhibit skidding

NONSKIER n pl. -S one that does not ski

NONSLIP adj designed to prevent slipping

NONSOLAR adj not solar

NONSOLID n pl. -S a substance that is not a solid

NONSTICK adj allowing of easy removal of cooked food particles

NONSTOP adj making no stops

NONSUCH n pl. -ES nonesuch

NONSUGAR n pl. -S a substance that is not a sugar

NONSUIT v -ED, -ING, -S to dismiss the lawsuit of

NONTAX n pl. -ES a tax of little consequence

NONTIDAL adj not tidal

NONTITLE adj pertaining to an athletic contest in which a title is not at stake

NONTOXIC adj not toxic

NONTRUMP adj not having a trump

NONTRUTH n pl. -S something that is not true

NONUNION n pl. -S failure of a broken bone to heal

NONUPLE n pl. -S a number nine times as great as another

NONURBAN adj not urban

NONUSE n pl. -S failure to use

NONUSER n pl. -S one that is not a user

NONUSING adj not using

NONVIRAL adj not viral

NONVOCAL adj not vocal

NONVOTER n pl. -S one that does not vote

NONWHITE n pl. -S a person who is not of the white race

NONWOODY adj not woody

NONWOVEN adj made without weaving

NONZERO adj having a value other than zero

NOO adv now

NOODLE v -DLED, -DLING, -DLES to play idly on a musical instrument

NOOK n pl. -S a corner, as in a room
NOOKLIKE adj

NOOKY n pl. NOOKIES sexual intercourse — usually considered vulgar

NOON n pl. -S midday

NOONDAY n pl. -DAYS noon

NOONING n pl. -S a meal eaten at noon

NOONTIDE n pl. -S noon

NOONTIME n pl. -S noon

NOOSE v NOOSED, NOOSING, NOOSES to secure with a type of loop

NOOSER n pl. -S one that nooses

NOPAL n pl. -S a cactus

NOPE adv no

NOR conj and not

NORIA n pl. -S a type of waterwheel

NORITE n pl. -S a granular rock
NORITIC adj

NORLAND n pl. -S a region in the north

NORM n pl. -S a standard regarded as typical for a specific group

NORMAL n pl. -S the usual or expected state or form

NORMALCY n pl. -CIES conformity with the norm

NORMALLY adv as a rule; usually

NORMED adj having a norm

NORMLESS adj having no norm

NORTH n pl. -S a point of the compass

NORTHER n pl. -S a wind or storm from the north

NORTHERN n pl. -S a person living in the north

NORTHING n pl. -S movement toward the north

NOSE v NOSED, NOSING, NOSES to sniff with the nose (the organ of smell)

NOSEBAG n pl. -S a feedbag

NOSEBAND n pl. -S a part of a horse's bridle

NOSED past tense of nose

NOSEGAY n pl. -GAYS a bouquet

NOSELESS	*adj* having no nose
NOSELIKE	*adj* resembling a nose
NOSEY	*adj* NOSIER, NOSIEST nosy
NOSH	*v* -ED, -ING, -ES to eat snacks between meals
NOSHER	*n* pl. -S one that noshes
NOSIER	comparative of nosy, nosey
NOSIEST	superlative of nosy, nosey
NOSILY	*adv* in a nosy manner
NOSINESS	*n* pl. -ES the quality of being nosy
NOSING	*n* pl. -S a projecting edge
NOSOLOGY	*n* pl. -GIES a classification of diseases
NOSTOC	*n* pl. -S a freshwater alga
NOSTRIL	*n* pl. -S an external opening of the nose
NOSTRUM	*n* pl. -S a medicine of one's own invention
NOSY	*adj* NOSIER, NOSIEST unduly curious
NOT	*adv* in no way
NOTA	pl. of notum
NOTABLE	*n* pl. -S a person of distinction
NOTABLY	*adv* in a distinguished manner
NOTAL	*adj* pertaining to a notum
NOTARIAL	*adj* pertaining to a notary
NOTARIZE	*v* -RIZED, -RIZING, -RIZES to certify through a notary
NOTARY	*n* pl. -RIES a public officer who certifies documents
NOTATE	*v* -TATED, -TATING, -TATES to put into notation
NOTATION	*n* pl. -S a system of symbols
NOTCH	*v* -ED, -ING, -ES to make an angular cut in
NOTCHER	*n* pl. -S one that notches
NOTE	*v* NOTED, NOTING, NOTES to write down
NOTEBOOK	*n* pl. -S a book in which to write
NOTECASE	*n* pl. -S a billfold
NOTED	past tense of note
NOTEDLY	*adv* in a famous manner
NOTELESS	*adj* undistinguished
NOTER	*n* pl. -S one that notes
NOTHING	*n* pl. -S the absence of all quantity or magnitude

NOTICE	*v* -TICED, -TICING, -TICES to become aware of
NOTIFIER	*n* pl. -S one that notifies
NOTIFY	*v* -FIED, -FYING, -FIES to inform
NOTING	present participle of note
NOTION	*n* pl. -S a general idea **NOTIONAL** *adj*
NOTORNIS	*n* pl. NOTORNIS a flightless bird
NOTTURNO	*n* pl. -NI a nocturne
NOTUM	*n* pl. -TA a part of the thorax of an insect
NOUGAT	*n* pl. -S a chewy candy
NOUGHT	*n* pl. -S naught
NOUMENON	*n* pl. -MENA an object of intellectual intuition **NOUMENAL** *adj*
NOUN	*n* pl. -S a word used to denote the name of something **NOUNAL, NOUNLESS** *adj* **NOUNALLY** *adv*
NOURISH	*v* -ED, -ING, -ES to sustain with food
NOUS	*n* pl. -ES mind, reason, or intellect
NOVA	*n* pl. -VAS or -VAE a type of star **NOVALIKE** *adj*
NOVATION	*n* pl. -S the substitution of a new legal obligation for an old one
NOVEL	*n* pl. -S a fictional prose narrative
NOVELISE	*v* -ISED, -ISING, -ISES to novelize
NOVELIST	*n* pl. -S a writer of novels
NOVELIZE	*v* -IZED, -IZING, -IZES to put into the form of a novel
NOVELLA	*n* pl. -LAS or -LE a short novel
NOVELLY	*adv* in a new or unusual manner
NOVELTY	*n* pl. -TIES something new or unusual
NOVENA	*n* pl. -NAS or -NAE a religious devotion lasting nine days
NOVERCAL	*adj* pertaining to a stepmother
NOVICE	*n* pl. -S a person new to any field or activity
NOW	*n* pl. -S the present time
NOWADAYS	*adv* in these times
NOWAY	*adv* in no way
NOWAYS	*adv* noway
NOWHERE	*n* pl. -S a nonexistent place

NOWISE   *adv* not at all

NOWT   *n* pl. -S naught

NOXIOUS   *adj* harmful to health

NOYADE   *n* pl. -S an execution by drowning

NOZZLE   *n* pl. -S a projecting spout

NTH   *adj* pertaining to an indefinitely large ordinal number

NU   *n* pl. -S a Greek letter

NUANCE   *n* pl. -S a slight variation **NUANCED** *adj*

NUB   *n* pl. -S a protuberance or knob

NUBBIER   comparative of nubby

NUBBIEST   superlative of nubby

NUBBIN   *n* pl. -S an undeveloped fruit

NUBBLE   *n* pl. -S a small nub

NUBBLY   *adj* -BLIER, -BLIEST having nubbles

NUBBY   *adj* -BIER, -BIEST having nubs

NUBIA   *n* pl. -S a woman's scarf

NUBILE   *adj* suitable for marriage

NUBILITY   *n* pl. -TIES the quality of being nubile

NUBILOSE   *adj* nubilous

NUBILOUS   *adj* cloudy

NUCELLUS   *n* pl. -LI the essential part of a plant ovule **NUCELLAR** *adj*

NUCHA   *n* pl. -CHAE the nape of the neck

NUCHAL   *n* pl. -S an anatomical part lying in the region of the nape

NUCLEAL   *adj* nuclear

NUCLEAR   *adj* pertaining to a nucleus

NUCLEASE   *n* pl. -S an enzyme

NUCLEATE   *v* -ATED, -ATING, -ATES to form into a nucleus

NUCLEI   a pl. of nucleus

NUCLEIN   *n* pl. -S a protein found in nuclei

NUCLEOLE   *n* pl. -S a part of a nucleus

NUCLEOLI   *n/pl* nucleoles

NUCLEON   *n* pl. -S an atomic particle

NUCLEUS   *n* pl. -CLEI or -CLEUSES an essential part of a cell

NUCLIDE   *n* pl. -S a species of atom **NUCLIDIC** *adj*

NUDE   *adj* NUDER, NUDEST being without clothing or covering **NUDELY** *adv*

NUDE   *n* pl. -S a nude figure

NUDENESS   *n* pl. -ES nudity

NUDER   comparative of nude

NUDEST   superlative of nude

NUDGE   *v* NUDGED, NUDGING, NUDGES to push gently

NUDGER   *n* pl. -S one that nudges

NUDICAUL   *adj* having leafless stems

NUDIE   *n* pl. -S a movie featuring nude performers

NUDISM   *n* pl. -S the practice of going nude

NUDIST   *n* pl. -S an advocate of nudism

NUDITY   *n* pl. -TIES the state of being nude

NUDNICK   *n* pl. -S nudnik

NUDNIK   *n* pl. -S an annoying person

NUGATORY   *adj* having no power

NUGGET   *n* pl. -S a mass of solid matter **NUGGETY** *adj*

NUISANCE   *n* pl. -S a source of annoyance

NUKE   *n* pl. -S a nuclear weapon or power plant

NULL   *v* -ED, -ING, -S to reduce to nothing

NULLAH   *n* pl. -S a ravine

NULLIFY   *v* -FIED, -FYING, -FIES to make useless or ineffective

NULLITY   *n* pl. -TIES something of no legal force

NUMB   *adj* NUMBER, NUMBEST lacking sensation

NUMB   *v* -ED, -ING, -S to make numb

NUMBER   *v* -ED, -ING, -S to count

NUMBERER   *n* pl. -S one that numbers

NUMBFISH   *n* pl. -ES a fish capable of emitting electric shocks

NUMBLES   *n/pl* animal entrails

NUMBLY   *adv* in a numb manner

NUMBNESS   *n* pl. -ES the state of being numb

NUMEN   *n* pl. -MINA a deity

NUMERAL   *n* pl. -S a symbol that expresses a number

NUMERARY   *adj* pertaining to numbers

NUMERATE   *v* -ATED, -ATING, -ATES to count

NUMERIC   *n* pl. -S a numeral

NUMEROUS *adj* many

NUMINA pl. of numen

NUMINOUS *n* pl. -ES the presence or revelation of the numen

NUMMARY *adj* pertaining to coins

NUMMULAR *adj* shaped like a coin

NUMSKULL *n* pl. -S a dunce

NUN *n* pl. -S a woman belonging to a religious order

NUNCIO *n* pl. -CIOS an ambassador from the pope

NUNCLE *n* pl. -S an uncle

NUNLIKE *adj* resembling a nun

NUNNERY *n* pl. -NERIES a religious house for nuns

NUNNISH *adj* of, pertaining to, or characteristic of a nun

NUPTIAL *n* pl. -S a wedding

NURL *n* -ED, -ING, -S to knurl

NURSE *v* NURSED, NURSING, NURSES to care for the sick or infirm

NURSER *n* pl. -S a baby's bottle

NURSERY *n* pl. -ERIES a room for young children

NURSING *n* pl. -S the profession of one who nurses

NURSLING *n* pl. -S an infant

NURTURE *v* -TURED, -TURING, -TURES to nourish

NURTURER *n* pl. -S one that nurtures

NUT *v* NUTTED, NUTTING, NUTS to gather nuts (hard-shelled dry fruits)

NUTANT *adj* drooping

NUTATE *v* -TATED, -TATING, -TATES to exhibit nutation

NUTATION *n* pl. -S an oscillatory movement of the axis of a rotating body

NUTBROWN *adj* of a dark brown

NUTGALL *n* pl. -S a galinut

NUTGRASS *n* pl. -ES a perennial herb

NUTHATCH *n* pl. -ES a small bird

NUTHOUSE *n* pl. -S an insane asylum

NUTLET *n* pl. -S a small nut

NUTLIKE *adj* resembling a nut

NUTMEAT *n* pl. -S the edible kernel of a nut

NUTMEG *n* pl. -S an aromatic seed used as a spice

NUTPICK *n* pl. -S a device for extracting the kernels from nuts

NUTRIA *n* pl. -S the coypu

NUTRIENT *n* pl. -S a nourishing substance

NUTSEDGE *n* pl. -S nutgrass

NUTSHELL *n* pl. -S the shell of a nut

NUTTED past tense of nut

NUTTER *n* pl. -S one that gathers nuts

NUTTING present participle of nut

NUTTY *adj* -TIER, -TIEST abounding in nuts NUTTILY *adv*

NUTWOOD *n* pl. -S a nut-bearing tree

NUZZLE *v* -ZLED, -ZLING, -ZLES to push with the nose

NYALA *n* pl. -S an antelope

NYLGHAI *n* pl. -S nilgai

NYLGHAU *n* pl. -S nilgai

NYLON *n* pl. -S a synthetic material

NYMPH *n* pl. -S a female spirit NYMPHAL, NYMPHEAN *adj*

NYMPHA *n* pl. -PHAE a fold of the vulva

NYMPHET *n* pl. -S a young nymph

NYMPHO *n* pl. -PHOS a woman obsessed by sexual desire

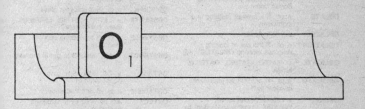

OAF   *n* pl. OAFS or OAVES a clumsy, stupid person **OAFISH** *adj* **OAFISHLY** *adv*

OAK   *n* pl. -S a hardwood tree or shrub **OAKEN, OAKLIKE** *adj*

OAKMOSS   *n* pl. -ES a lichen that grows on oak trees

OAKUM   *n* pl. -S loosely twisted hemp fiber

OAR   *v* -ED, -ING, -S to propel with oars (long, broad-bladed poles)

OARFISH   *n* pl. -ES a marine fish

OARLESS   *adj* having no oars

OARLIKE   *adj* resembling an oar

OARLOCK   *n* pl. -S a device for holding an oar in place

OARSMAN   *n* pl. -MEN a person who rows a boat

OASIS   *n* pl. OASES a green area in a desert region

OAST   *n* pl. -S a type of kiln

OAT   *n* pl. -S a cereal grass

OATCAKE   *n* pl. -S a cake made of oatmeal

OATEN   *adj* pertaining to oats

OATER   *n* pl. -S a cowboy movie

OATH   *n* pl. -S a formal declaration or promise to fulfill a pledge

OATLIKE   *adj* resembling oats

OATMEAL   *n* pl. -S meal made from oats

OAVES   a pl. of oaf

OBDURACY   *n* pl. -CIES the quality or an instance of being obdurate

OBDURATE   *adj* stubborn

OBE   *n* pl. -S obeah

OBEAH   *n* pl. -S a form of sorcery of African origin

OBEAHISM   *n* pl. -S the use of obeah

OBEDIENT   *adj* obeying or willing to obey

OBEISANT   *adj* showing reverence or respect

OBELI   pl. of obelus

OBELIA   *n* pl. -S a marine hydroid

OBELISE   *v* -LISED, -LISING, -LISES to obelize

OBELISK   *n* pl. -S a four-sided shaft of stone with a pyramidal top

OBELISM   *n* pl. -S the act of obelizing

OBELIZE   *v* -LIZED, -LIZING, -LIZES to mark with an obelus

OBELUS   *n* pl. -LI a symbol used in ancient manuscripts to indicate a doubtful passage

OBESE   *adj* very fat **OBESELY** *adv*

OBESITY   *n* pl. -TIES the state or condition of being obese

OBEY   *v* -ED, -ING, -S to follow the commands or guidance of **OBEYABLE** *adj*

OBEYER   *n* pl. -S one that obeys

OBI   *n* pl. -S obeah

OBIA   *n* pl. -S obeah

OBIISM   *n* pl. -S obeahism

OBIT   *n* pl. -S an obituary

OBITUARY   *n* pl. -ARIES a published notice of a death

OBJECT   *v* -ED, -ING, -S to argue in opposition

OBJECTOR   *n* pl. -S one that objects

OBLAST n pl. -LASTS or -LASTI an administrative division of the Soviet Union

OBLATE n pl. -S a layman residing in a monastery

OBLATELY adv elliptically

OBLATION n pl. -S the act of making a religious offering OBLATORY adj

OBLIGATE v -GATED, -GATING, -GATES to oblige

OBLIGATO n pl. -TI or -TOS an important musical part

OBLIGE v OBLIGED, OBLIGING, OBLIGES to put in one's debt by a favor or service

OBLIGEE n pl. -S one that is obliged

OBLIGER n pl. -S one that obliges

OBLIGING present participle of oblige

OBLIGOR n pl. -S one who places himself under a legal obligation

OBLIQUE v OBLIQUED, OBLIQUING, OBLIQUES to slant

OBLIVION n pl. -S the state of being forgotten; the act of forgetting

OBLONG n pl. -S something that is oblong (elongated)

OBLONGLY adv in an oblong manner

OBLOQUY n pl. -QUIES abusive language

OBOE n pl. -S a woodwind instrument

OBOIST n pl. -S one who plays the oboe

OBOL n pl. -S a coin of ancient Greece

OBOLE n pl. -S a coin of medieval France

OBOLUS n pl. -LI an obol

OBOVATE adj ovate with the narrow end at the base

OBOVOID adj ovoid with the narrow end at the base

OBSCENE adj -SCENER, -SCENEST indecent

OBSCURE adj -SCURER, -SCUREST dark or indistinct

OBSCURE v -SCURED, -SCURING, -SCURES to make obscure

OBSEQUY n pl. -QUIES a funeral rite

OBSERVE v -SERVED, -SERVING, -SERVES to look attentively

OBSERVER n pl. -S one that observes

OBSESS v -ED, -ING, -ES to dominate the thoughts of

OBSESSOR n pl. -S something that obsesses

OBSIDIAN n pl. -S a volcanic glass

OBSOLETE v -LETED, -LETING, -LETES to make out-of-date

OBSTACLE n pl. -S something that obstructs

OBSTRUCT v -ED, -ING, -S to get in the way of

OBTAIN v -ED, -ING, -S to gain possession of

OBTAINER n pl. -S one that obtains

OBTECT adj covered by a hardened secretion

OBTECTED adj obtect

OBTEST v -ED, -ING, -S to beseech

OBTRUDE v -TRUDED, -TRUDING, -TRUDES to thrust forward

OBTRUDER n pl. -S one that obtrudes

OBTUND v -ED, -ING, -S to deaden

OBTURATE v -RATED, -RATING, -RATES to close or stop up

OBTUSE adj -TUSER, -TUSEST dull OBTUSELY adv

OBVERSE n pl. -S the side of a coin bearing the main design

OBVERT v -ED, -ING, -S to turn so as to show a different surface

OBVIATE v -ATED, -ATING, -ATES to prevent or eliminate by effective measures OBVIABLE adj

OBVIATOR n pl. -S one that obviates

OBVIOUS adj easily perceived or understood

OBVOLUTE adj rolled or tuned in

OCA n pl. -S a South American herb

OCARINA n pl. -S a wind instrument

OCCASION v -ED, -ING, -S to cause

OCCIDENT n pl. -S the west

OCCIPUT n pl. -PITA or -PUTS the back part of the skull

OCCLUDE v -CLUDED, -CLUDING, -CLUDES to close or stop up

OCCLUSAL adj pertaining to the biting surface of a tooth

OCCULT v -ED, -ING, -S to conceal

OCCULTER n pl. -S one that occults

OCCULTLY adv secretly

OCCUPANT n pl. -S a resident

OCCUPIER n pl. -S one that occupies

OCCUPY   v -PIED, -PYING, -PIES to engage the attention or energies of

OCCUR   v -CURRED, -CURRING, -CURS to take place

OCEAN   n pl. -S the vast body of salt water that covers most of the earth's surface **OCEANIC** adj

OCELLAR   adj pertaining to an ocellus

OCELLATE   adj having ocelli

OCELLUS   n pl. -LI a minute simple eye

OCELOT   n pl. -S an American wildcat **OCELOID** adj

OCHER   v -ED, -ING, -S to color with ocher (a red or yellow iron ore used as a pigment)

OCHEROUS   adj containing or resembling ocher

OCHERY   adj ocherous

OCHONE   interj — used to express grief

OCHRE   v OCHRED, OCHRING, OCHRES to ocher

OCHREA   n pl. -REAE ocrea

OCHREOUS   adj ocherous

OCHRING   present participle of ochre

OCHROID   adj ocherous

OCHROUS   adj ocherous

OCHRY   adj ochery

OCOTILLO   n pl. -LOS a Mexican shrub

OCREA   n pl. -REAE a sheathing plant part

OCREATE   adj having ocreae

OCTAD   n pl. -S a group of eight **OCTADIC** adj

OCTAGON   n pl. -S an eight-sided polygon

OCTAL   adj pertaining to a number system with a base of eight

OCTANE   n pl. -S a liquid hydrocarbon

OCTANGLE   n pl. -S an octagon

OCTANT   n pl. -S an eighth of a circle **OCTANTAL** adj

OCTARCHY   n pl. -TARCHIES a government by eight persons

OCTAVE   n pl. -S a type of musical interval **OCTAVAL** adj

OCTAVO   n pl. -VOS a page size

OCTET   n pl. -S a group of eight

OCTETTE   n pl. -S octet

OCTONARY   n pl. -NARIES a stanza of eight lines

OCTOPI   a pl. of octopus

OCTOPOD   n pl. -S any of an order of eight-armed mollusks

OCTOPUS   n pl. -PUSES, -PI, or -PODES a nocturnal octopod

OCTOROON   n pl. -S a person of one-eighth black ancestry

OCTROI   n pl. -S a tax on certain articles brought into a city

OCTUPLE   v -PLED, -PLING, -PLES to multiply by eight

OCTUPLET   n pl. -S a group of eight related items

OCTUPLEX   adj being eight times as great

OCTUPLING   present participle of octuple

OCTUPLY   adv to eight times the degree

OCTYL   n pl. -S a univalent radical

OCULAR   n pl. -S an eyepiece

OCULARLY   adv by means of the eyes or sight

OCULIST   n pl. -S a physician who treats diseases of the eye

OD   n pl. -S a hypothetical force of natural power

ODALISK   n pl. -S a female slave in a harem

ODD   adj ODDER, ODDEST unusual

ODD   n pl. -S one that is odd

ODDBALL   n pl. -S an eccentric person

ODDISH   adj somewhat odd

ODDITY   n pl. -TIES one that is odd

ODDLY   adv in an odd manner

ODDMENT   n pl. -S a remnant

ODDNESS   n pl. -ES the state of being odd

ODE   n pl. -S a lyric poem

ODEON   n pl. -S odeum

ODEUM   n pl. ODEA a theater or concert hall

ODIC   adj pertaining to an ode

ODIOUS   adj deserving or causing hatred **ODIOUSLY** adv

ODIUM   n pl. -S hatred

ODOGRAPH   n pl. -S an odometer

ODOMETER   n pl. -S a device for measuring distance traveled

ODOMETRY   n pl. -TRIES the process of using an odometer

ODONATE   n pl. -S any of an order of predacious insects

ODONTOID n pl. -S a toothlike vertebral projection

ODOR n pl. -S the property of a substance that affects the sense of smell ODORED, ODORFUL adj

ODORANT n pl. -S an odorous substance

ODORIZE v -IZED, -IZING, -IZES to make odorous

ODORLESS adj having no odor

ODOROUS adj having an odor

ODOUR n pl. -S odor ODOURFUL adj

ODYL n pl. -S an od

ODYLE n pl. -S odyl

ODYSSEY n pl. -SEYS a long, wandering journey

OE n pl. -S a whirlwind off the Faeroe islands

OECOLOGY n pl. -GIES ecology

OEDEMA n pl. -MAS or -MATA edema

OEDIPAL adj pertaining to the libidinal feelings in a child toward the parent of the opposite sex

OEDIPEAN adj oedipal

OEILLADE n pl. -S an amorous look

OENOLOGY n pl. -GIES the study of wines

OENOMEL n pl. -S an ancient Greek beverage of wine and honey

OERSTED n pl. -S a unit of magnetic intensity

OESTRIN n pl. -S estrin

OESTRIOL n pl. -S estriol

OESTRONE n pl. -S estrone

OESTROUS adj estrous

OESTRUM n pl. -S estrum

OESTRUS n pl. -ES estrus

OEUVRE n pl. -S a work of art

OF prep coming from

OFAY n pl. OFAYS a white person — usually taken to be offensive

OFF v -ED, -ING, -S to go away

OFFAL n pl. -S waste material

OFFBEAT n pl. -S an unaccented beat in a musical measure

OFFCAST n pl. -S a castoff

OFFENCE n pl. -S offense

OFFEND v -ED, -ING, -S to commit an offense

OFFENDER n pl. -S one that offends

OFFENSE n pl. -S a violation of a moral or social code

OFFER v -ED, -ING, -S to present for acceptance or rejection

OFFERER n pl. -S one that offers

OFFERING n pl. -S a contribution

OFFEROR n pl. -S offerer

OFFHAND adv without preparation

OFFICE n pl. -S a position of authority

OFFICER v -ED, -ING, -S to furnish with officers (persons holding positions of authority)

OFFICIAL n pl. -S one that holds a position of authority

OFFING n pl. -S the near future

OFFISH adj aloof OFFISHLY adv

OFFLOAD v -ED, -ING, -S to unload

OFFPRINT v -ED, -ING, -S to reprint an excerpt

OFFSET v -SET, -SETTING, -SETS to compensate for

OFFSHOOT n pl. -S a lateral shoot from a main stem

OFFSHORE adv away from the shore

OFFSIDE adj being illegally in front of the ball in football

OFFSTAGE adj being on a part of the stage not visible to the audience

OFT adv OFTER, OFTEST often

OFTEN adv -ENER, -ENEST frequently

OFTTIMES adv often

OGAM n pl. -S ogham

OGDOAD n pl. -S a group of eight

OGEE n pl. -S an S-shaped molding

OGHAM n pl. -S an Old Irish alphabet OGHAMIC adj

OGHAMIST n pl. -S one who writes in ogham

OGIVE n pl. -S a pointed arch OGIVAL adj

OGLE v OGLED, OGLING, OGLES to stare at

OGLER n pl. -S one that ogles

OGRE n pl. -S a monster

OGREISH adj resembling an ogre

OGREISM n pl. -S the state of being ogreish

OGRESS n pl. -ES a female ogre

OGRISH adj ogreish OGRISHLY adv

OGRISM   *n* pl. -S ogreism

OH   *v* -ED, -ING, -S to exclaim in surprise, pain, or desire

OHIA   *n* pl. -S lehua

OHM   *n* pl. -S a unit of electrical resistance **OHMIC** *adj*

OHMAGE   *n* pl. -S electrical resistance expressed in ohms

OHMMETER   *n* pl. -S an instrument for measuring ohmage

OHO   *interj* — used to express surprise or exultation

OIDIUM   *n* pl. OIDIA a type of fungus

OIL   *v* -ED, -ING, -S to supply with oil (a greasy liquid used for lubrication, fuel, or illumination)

OILBIRD   *n* pl. -S a tropical bird

OILCAMP   *n* pl. -S a living area for workers at an oil well

OILCAN   *n* pl. -S a can for applying lubricating oil

OILCLOTH   *n* pl. -S a waterproof fabric

OILCUP   *n* pl. -S a closed cup for supplying lubricant

OILER   *n* pl. -S one that oils

OILHOLE   *n* pl. -S a hole through which lubricating oil is injected

OILIER   comparative of oily

OILIEST   superlative of oily

OILILY   *adv* in an oily manner

OILINESS   *n* pl. -ES the state of being oily

OILMAN   *n* pl. -MEN one who owns or operates oil wells

OILPAPER   *n* pl. -S a water-resistant paper

OILPROOF   *adj* impervious to oil

OILSEED   *n* pl. -S a seed from which oil is pressed out

OILSKIN   *n* pl. -S a waterproof fabric

OILSTONE   *n* pl. -S a stone for sharpening tools

OILTIGHT   *adj* being so tight as to prevent the passage of oil

OILWAY   *n* pl. -WAYS a channel for the passage of oil

OILY   *adj* OILIER, OILIEST covered or soaked with oil

OINK   *v* -ED, -ING, -S to utter the natural grunt of a hog

OINOLOGY   *n* pl. -GIES oenology

OINOMEL   *n* pl. -S oenomel

OINTMENT   *n* pl. -S a viscous preparation applied to the skin as a medicine or cosmetic

OITICICA   *n* pl. -S a South American tree

OKA   *n* pl. -S a Turkish unit of weight

OKAPI   *n* pl. -S an African ruminant mammal

OKAY   *v* -ED, -ING, -S to approve

OKE   *n* pl. -S oka

OKEH   *n* pl. -S approval

OKEYDOKE   *adj* perfectly all right

OKRA   *n* pl. -S a tall annual herb

OLD   *adj* OLDER, OLDEST or ELDER, ELDEST living or existing for a relatively long time

OLD   *n* pl. -S an individual of a specified age

OLDEN   *adj* pertaining to a bygone era

OLDIE   *n* pl. -S a popular song of an earlier day

OLDISH   *adj* somewhat old

OLDNESS   *n* pl. -ES the state of being old

OLDSTER   *n* pl. -S an old person

OLDSTYLE   *n* pl. -S a style of printing type

OLDWIFE   *n* pl. -WIVES a marine fish

OLE   *n* pl. -S a shout of approval

OLEA   pl. of oleum

OLEANDER   *n* pl. -S a flowering shrub

OLEASTER   *n* pl. -S a flowering shrub

OLEATE   *n* pl. -S a chemical salt

OLEFIN   *n* pl. -S an alkene **OLEFINIC** *adj*

OLEFINE   *n* pl. -S olefin

OLEIC   *adj* pertaining to oil

OLEIN   *n* pl. -S the liquid portion of a fat

OLEINE   *n* pl. -S olein

OLEO   *n* pl. OLEOS margarine

OLEUM   *n* pl. OLEA oil

OLEUM   *n* pl. -S a corrosive liquid

OLIBANUM   *n* pl. -S a fragrant resin

OLIGARCH   *n* pl. -S a ruler in a government by the few

OLIGOMER   *n* pl. -S a type of polymer

OLIO   *n* pl. OLIOS a miscellaneous collection

OLIVARY   *adj* shaped like an olive

OLIVE   *n* pl. -S the small oval fruit of a Mediterranean tree

OLIVINE	*n* pl. -S a mineral OLIVINIC *adj*
OLLA	*n* pl. -S a wide-mouthed pot or jar
OLOGIST	*n* pl. -S an expert in a particular ology
OLOGY	*n* pl. -GIES a branch of knowledge
OLYMPIAD	*n* pl. -S a celebration of the Olympic Games
OM	*n* pl. -S a mantra used in contemplation of ultimate reality
OMASUM	*n* pl. -SA the third stomach of a ruminant
OMBER	*n* pl. -S ombre
OMBRE	*n* pl. -S a card game
OMEGA	*n* pl. -S a Greek letter
OMELET	*n* pl. -S a dish of beaten eggs cooked and folded around a filling
OMELETTE	*n* pl. -S omelet
OMEN	*v* -ED, -ING, -S to be an omen (a prophetic sign) of
OMENTUM	*n* pl. -TA or -TUMS a fold in an abdominal membrane OMENTAL *adj*
OMER	*n* pl. -S a Hebrew unit of dry measure
OMICRON	*n* pl. -S a Greek letter
OMIKRON	*n* pl. -S omicron
OMINOUS	*adj* portending evil
OMISSION	*n* pl. -S something left undone
OMISSIVE	*adj* marked by omission
OMIT	*v* OMITTED, OMITTING, OMITS to leave out
OMNIARCH	*n* pl. -S an almighty ruler
OMNIBUS	*n* pl. -ES a bus
OMNIFIC	*adj* unlimited in creative power
OMNIFORM	*adj* of all forms
OMNIMODE	*adj* of all modes
OMNIVORA	*n/pl* omnivores
OMNIVORE	*n* pl. -S an animal that eats all kinds of food
OMOPHAGY	*n* pl. -GIES the eating of raw flesh
OMPHALOS	*n* pl. -LI a central point
ON	*n* pl. -S the side of the wicket where a batsman stands in cricket
ONAGER	*n* pl. -GERS or -GRI a wild ass of central Asia
ONANISM	*n* pl. -S coitus deliberately interrupted to prevent insemination
ONANIST	*n* pl. -S one who practices onanism
ONCE	*n* pl. -S one single time
ONCIDIUM	*n* pl. -S a tropical orchid
ONCOLOGY	*n* pl. -GIES the science of tumors
ONCOMING	*n* pl. -S an approach
ONDOGRAM	*n* pl. -S a graph of electric wave forms
ONE	*n* pl. -S a number
ONEFOLD	*adj* constituting a single, undivided whole
ONEIRIC	*adj* pertaining to dreams
ONENESS	*n* pl. -ES unity
ONEROUS	*adj* burdensome or oppressive
ONERY	*adj* -ERIER, -ERIEST ornery
ONESELF	*pron* a person's self
ONETIME	*adj* former
ONGOING	*adj* continuing without interruption
ONION	*n* pl. -S the edible bulb of a cultivated herb
ONIUM	*adj* characterized by a complex cation
ONLOOKER	*n* pl. -S a spectator
ONLY	*adv* with nothing or no one else
ONRUSH	*n* pl. -ES a forward rush or flow
ONSET	*n* pl. -S a beginning
ONSHORE	*adv* toward the shore
ONSIDE	*adj* not offside
ONSTAGE	*adj* being on a part of the stage visible to the audience
ONTIC	*adj* having real being or existence
ONTO	*prep* to a position upon
ONTOGENY	*n* pl. -NIES the development of an individual organism
ONTOLOGY	*n* pl. -GIES the branch of philosophy that deals with being
ONUS	*n* pl. -ES a burden or responsibility
ONWARD	*adv* toward a point ahead or in front
ONWARDS	*adv* onward
ONYX	*n* pl. -ES a variety of quartz
OOCYST	*n* pl. -S a zygote

OOCYTE *n pl.* -S an egg before maturation

OODLES *n pl.* OODLES a large amount

OODLINS *n pl.* OODLINS oodles

OOGAMETE *n pl.* -S a female gamete of certain protozoa

OOGAMOUS *adj* having structurally dissimilar gametes

OOGAMY *n pl.* -MIES the state of being oogamous

OOGENY *n pl.* -NIES the development of ova

OOGONIUM *n pl.* -NIA or -NIUMS a female sexual organ in certain algae and fungi OOGONIAL *adj*

OOH *v* -ED, -ING, -S to exclaim in amazement, joy, or surprise

OOLACHAN *n pl.* -S eulachon

OOLITE *n pl.* -S a variety of limestone OOLITIC *adj*

OOLITH *n pl.* -S oolite

OOLOGIST *n pl.* -S an expert in oology

OOLOGY *n pl.* -GIES the study of birds' eggs OOLOGIC *adj*

OOLONG *n pl.* -S a dark Chinese tea

OOMIAC *n pl.* -S umiak

OOMIACK *n pl.* -S umiak

OOMIAK *n pl.* -S umiak

OOMPH *n pl.* -S spirited vigor

OOPHYTE *n pl.* -S a stage of development in certain plants OOPHYTIC *adj*

OOPS *interj* — used to express mild apology, surprise, or dismay

OORALI *n pl.* -S curare

OORIE *adj* ourie

OOSPERM *n pl.* -S a fertilized egg

OOSPHERE *n pl.* -S an unfertilized egg within an oogonium

OOSPORE *n pl.* -S a fertilized egg within an oogonium OOSPORIC *adj*

OOT *n pl.* -S out

OOTHECA *n pl.* -CAE an egg case of certain insects OOTHECAL *adj*

OOTID *n pl.* -S one of the four sections into which a mature ovum divides

OOZE *v* OOZED, OOZING, OOZES to flow or leak out slowly

OOZINESS *n pl.* -ES the state of being oozy

OOZY *adj* OOZIER, OOZIEST containing or resembling soft mud or slime OOZILY *adv*

OP *n pl.* -S a style of abstract art

OPACIFY *v* -FIED, -FYING, -FIES to make opaque

OPACITY *n pl.* -TIES something that is opaque

OPAH *n pl.* -S a marine fish

OPAL *n pl.* -S a mineral

OPALESCE *v* -ESCED, -ESCING, -ESCES to emit an iridescent shimmer of colors

OPALINE *n pl.* -S an opaque white glass

OPAQUE *adj* OPAQUER, OPAQUEST impervious to light OPAQUELY *adv*

OPAQUE *v* OPAQUED, OPAQUING, OPAQUES to make opaque

OPE *v* OPED, OPING, OPES to open

OPEN *adj* OPENER, OPENEST affording unobstructed access, passage, or view

OPEN *v* -ED, -ING, -S to cause to become open OPENABLE *adj*

OPENER *n pl.* -S one that opens

OPENING *n pl.* -S a vacant or unobstructed space

OPENLY *adv* in an open manner

OPENNESS *n pl.* -ES the state of being open

OPENWORK *n pl.* -S ornamental or structural work containing numerous openings

OPERA *n pl.* -S a form of musical drama

OPERABLE *adj* usable OPERABLY *adv*

OPERAND *n pl.* -S a quantity on which a mathematical operation is performed

OPERANT *n pl.* -S one that operates

OPERATE *v* -ATED, -ATING, -ATES to perform a function

OPERATIC *n pl.* -S the technique of staging operas

OPERATOR *n pl.* -S a symbol that represents a mathematical function

OPERCELE *n pl.* -S opercule

OPERCULA *n/pl* opercules

OPERCULE *n pl.* -S an anatomical part that serves as a lid or cover

OPERETTA n pl. -S a light musical drama with spoken dialogue

OPERON n pl. -S a type of gene cluster

OPEROSE adj involving great labor

OPHIDIAN n pl. -S a snake

OPHITE n pl. -S an igneous rock **OPHITIC** adj

OPIATE v -ATED, -ATING, -ATES to treat with opium

OPINE v OPINED, OPINING, OPINES to hold or state as an opinion

OPING present participle of ope

OPINION n pl. -S a conclusion or judgment one holds to be true

OPIUM n pl. -S an addictive narcotic

OPIUMISM n pl. -S opium addiction

OPOSSUM n pl. -S an arboreal mammal

OPPIDAN n pl. -S a townsman

OPPILATE v -LATED, -LATING, -LATES to obstruct **OPPILANT** adj

OPPONENT n pl. -S one that opposes another

OPPOSE v -POSED, -POSING, -POSES to be in contention or conflict with

OPPOSER n pl. -S one that opposes

OPPOSITE n pl. -S one that is radically different from another in some related way

OPPRESS v -ED, -ING, -ES to burden by abuse of power or authority

OPPUGN v -ED, -ING, -S to assail with argument

OPPUGNER n pl. -S one that oppugns

OPSIN n pl. -S a type of protein

OPSONIC adj pertaining to opsonin

OPSONIFY v -FIED, -FYING, -FIES to opsonize

OPSONIN n pl. -S an antibody of blood serum

OPSONIZE v -NIZED, -NIZING, -NIZES to form opsonins in

OPT v -ED, -ING, -S to choose

OPTATIVE n pl. -S a mood of verbs that expresses a wish or desire

OPTIC n pl. -S an eye

OPTICAL adj pertaining to sight

OPTICIAN n pl. -S one who makes or deals in optical goods

OPTICIST n pl. -S one engaged in the study of light and vision

OPTIMA a pl. of optimum

OPTIMAL adj most desirable

OPTIME n pl. -S an honor student in mathematics at Cambridge University

OPTIMISE v -MISED, -MISING, -MISES to optimize

OPTIMISM n pl. -S a disposition to look on the favorable side of things

OPTIMIST n pl. -S one who exhibits optimism

OPTIMIZE v -MIZED, -MIZING, -MIZES to make as perfect, useful, or effective as possible

OPTIMUM n pl. -MA or -MUMS the most favorable condition for obtaining a given result

OPTION v -ED, -ING, -S to grant an option (a right to buy or sell something at a specified price within a specified time) on

OPTIONAL n pl. -S an elective course of study

OPTIONEE n pl. -S one who holds a legal option

OPULENCE n pl. -S wealth

OPULENCY n pl. -CIES opulence

OPULENT adj wealthy

OPUNTIA n pl. -S an American cactus

OPUS n pl. OPERA or OPUSES a literary or musical work

OPUSCULA n/pl opuscules

OPUSCULE n pl. -S a minor work

OQUASSA n pl. -S a small lake trout

OR n pl. -S the heraldic color gold

ORA pl. of os

ORACH n pl. -ES a cultivated plant

ORACHE n pl. -S orach

ORACLE n pl. -S a person through whom a deity is believed to speak **ORACULAR** adj

ORAL n pl. -S an examination requiring spoken answers

ORALITY n pl. -TIES the state of being produced orally

ORALLY adv through the mouth

ORANG n pl. -S a large ape

ORANGE n pl. -S a citrus fruit

ORANGERY n pl. -RIES a place where orange trees are cultivated

ORANGEY adj -ANGIER, -ANGIEST orangy

ORANGISH *adj* of a somewhat orange color

ORANGY *adj* -ANGIER, -ANGIEST resembling or suggestive of an orange

ORATE *v* ORATED, ORATING, ORATES to speak formally

ORATION *n pl.* -S a formal speech

ORATOR *n pl.* -S one that orates

ORATORIO *n pl.* -RIOS a type of musical composition

ORATORY *n pl.* -RIES the art of public speaking

ORATRESS *n pl.* -ES oratrix

ORATRIX *n pl.* -TRICES a female orator

ORB *v* -ED, -ING, -S to form into a circle or sphere

ORBIT *v* -ED, -ING, -S to move or revolve around

ORBITAL *n pl.* -S a subdivision of a nuclear shell

ORBITER *n pl.* -S one that orbits

ORC *n pl.* -S a marine mammal

ORCA *n pl.* -S orc

ORCEIN *n pl.* -S a reddish brown dye

ORCHARD *n pl.* -S an area for the cultivation of fruit trees

ORCHID *n pl.* -S a flowering plant

ORCHIL *n pl.* -S a purple dye

ORCHIS *n pl.* -CHISES an orchid

ORCHITIS *n pl.* -TISES inflammation of the testicle ORCHITIC *adj*

ORCIN *n pl.* -S orcinol

ORCINOL *n pl.* -S a chemical compound

ORDAIN *v* -ED, -ING, -S to invest with holy authority

ORDAINER *n pl.* -S one that ordains

ORDEAL *n pl.* -S a severely difficult or painful experience

ORDER *v* -ED, -ING, -S to give a command or instruction to

ORDERER *n pl.* -S one that orders

ORDERLY *n pl.* -LIES a male attendant

ORDINAL *n pl.* -S a number designating position in a series

ORDINAND *n pl.* -S a person about to be ordained

ORDINARY *adj* -NARIER, -NARIEST of a kind to be expected in the normal order of events

ORDINARY *n pl.* -NARIES something that is ordinary

ORDINATE *n pl.* -S a particular geometric coordinate

ORDINES a *pl.* of ordo

ORDNANCE *n pl.* -S artillery; a cannon

ORDO *n pl.* -DINES or -DOS a calendar of religious directions

ORDURE *n pl.* -S manure

ORE *n pl.* -S a mineral or rock containing a valuable metal

OREAD *n pl.* -S a mountain nymph in Greek mythology

ORECTIC *adj* pertaining to appetites or desires

ORECTIVE *adj* orectic

OREGANO *n pl.* -NOS an aromatic herb used as a seasoning

OREIDE *n pl.* -S oroide

ORFRAY *n pl.* -FRAYS orphrey

ORGAN *n pl.* -S a differentiated part of an organism performing a specific function

ORGANA a *pl.* of organon and organum

ORGANDIE *n pl.* -S organdy

ORGANDY *n pl.* -DIES a cotton fabric

ORGANIC *n pl.* -S a substance of animal or vegetable origin

ORGANISE *v* -NISED, -NISING, -NISES to organize

ORGANISM *n pl.* -S any form of animal or plant life

ORGANIST *n pl.* -S one who plays the organ (a keyboard musical instrument)

ORGANIZE *v* -NIZED, -NIZING, -NIZES to form into an orderly whole

ORGANON *n pl.* -GANA or -GANONS a system of rules for scientific investigation

ORGANUM *n pl.* -GANA or -GANUMS organon

ORGANZA *n pl.* -S a sheer fabric

ORGASM *n pl.* -S the climax of sexual excitement ORGASMIC, ORGASTIC *adj*

ORGEAT *n pl.* -S an almond-flavored syrup

ORGIAC *adj* of the nature of an orgy

ORGIC *adj* orgiac

ORGULOUS *adj* proud

ORGY n pl. -GIES a party marked by unrestrained sexual indulgence

ORIBATID n pl. -S any of a family of eyeless mites

ORIBI n pl. -S an African antelope

ORIEL n pl. -S a type of projecting window

ORIENT v -ED, -ING, -S to adjust in relation to something else

ORIENTAL n pl. -S an inhabitant of an eastern country

ORIFICE n pl. -S a mouth or mouthlike opening

ORIGAMI n pl. -S the Japanese art of paper folding

ORIGAN n pl. -S marjoram

ORIGANUM n pl. -S an aromatic herb

ORIGIN n pl. -S a coming into being

ORIGINAL n pl. -S the first form of something

ORINASAL n pl. -S a sound pronounced through both the mouth and nose

ORIOLE n pl. -S an American songbird

ORISON n pl. -S a prayer

ORLE n pl. -S a heraldic border

ORLOP n pl. -S the lowest deck of a ship

ORMER n pl. -S an abalone

ORMOLU n pl. -S an alloy used to imitate gold

ORNAMENT v -ED, -ING, -S to decorate

ORNATE adj elaborately or excessively ornamented ORNATELY adv

ORNERY adj -NERIER, -NERIEST stubborn and mean-spirited

ORNIS n pl. ORNITHES avifauna

ORNITHIC adj pertaining to birds

OROGENY n pl. -NIES the process of mountain formation OROGENIC adj

OROIDE n pl. -S an alloy used to imitate gold

OROLOGY n pl. -GIES the study of mountains

OROMETER n pl. -S a type of barometer

OROTUND adj full and clear in sound

ORPHAN v -ED, -ING, -S to deprive of both parents

ORPHIC adj mystical

ORPHICAL adj orphic

ORPHREY n pl. -PHREYS an ornamental band or border

ORPIMENT n pl. -S a yellow dye

ORPIN n pl. -S orpine

ORPINE n pl. -S a perennial herb

ORRA adj occasional

ORRERY n pl. -RERIES a mechanical model of the solar system

ORRICE n pl. -S orris

ORRIS n pl. -RISES a flowering plant

ORT n pl. -S a scrap of food

ORTHICON n pl. -S a type of television camera tube

ORTHO adj pertaining to reproduction in a photograph of the full range of colors in nature

ORTHODOX n pl. -ES one holding traditional beliefs

ORTHOEPY n pl. -EPIES the study of correct pronunciation

ORTHOTIC adj pertaining to the bracing of weak joints or muscles

ORTOLAN n pl. -S a European bird

ORYX n pl. -ES an African antelope

OS n pl. ORA an orifice

OS n pl. OSSA a bone

OS n pl. OSAR an esker

OSCINE n pl. -S any of a family of songbirds OSCININE adj

OSCITANT adj yawning

OSCULA pl. of osculum

OSCULANT adj adhering closely

OSCULAR adj pertaining to the mouth

OSCULATE v -LATED, -LATING, -LATES to kiss

OSCULE n pl. -S osculum

OSCULUM n pl. -LA an opening in a sponge

OSE n pl. -S an esker

OSIER n pl. -S a European tree

OSMATIC adj depending mainly on the sense of smell

OSMIUM n pl. -S a metallic element OSMIC, OSMIOUS adj

OSMOL n pl. -S a unit of osmotic pressure OSMOLAL adj

OSMOLAR adj osmotic

OSMOSE   v -MOSED, -MOSING, -MOSES to undergo osmosis

OSMOSIS   n pl. -MOSES a form of diffusion of a fluid through a membrane

OSMOTIC   adj pertaining to osmosis

OSMOUS   adj containing osmium

OSMUND   n pl. -S any of a genus of large ferns

OSMUNDA   n pl. -S osmund

OSNABURG   n pl. -S a cotton fabric

OSPREY   n pl. -PREYS an American hawk

OSSA   pl. of os

OSSEIN   n pl. -S a protein substance in bone

OSSEOUS   adj resembling bone

OSSIA   conj or else — used as a musical direction

OSSICLE   n pl. -S a small bone

OSSIFIC   adj pertaining to the formation of bone

OSSIFIER   n pl. -S one that ossifies

OSSIFY   v -FIED, -FYING, -FIES to convert into bone

OSSUARY   n pl. -ARIES a receptacle for the bones of the dead

OSTEAL   adj osseous

OSTEITIS   n pl. -ITIDES inflammation of bone OSTEITIC adj

OSTEOID   n pl. -S uncalcified bone matrix

OSTEOMA   n pl. -MAS or -MATA a tumor of bone tissue

OSTIA   pl. of ostium

OSTIARY   n pl. -ARIES a doorkeeper at a church

OSTINATO   n pl. -TOS a constantly recurring musical phrase

OSTIOLE   n pl. -S a small bodily opening OSTIOLAR adj

OSTIUM   n pl. OSTIA an opening in a bodily organ

OSTLER   n pl. -S hostler

OSTMARK   n pl. -S a monetary unit of East Germany

OSTOMY   n pl. -MIES a type of surgical operation

OSTOSIS   n pl. -TOSES or -TOSISES the formation of bone

OSTRACOD   n pl. -S a minute freshwater crustacean

OSTRICH   n pl. -ES a large, flightless bird

OTALGIA   n pl. -S pain in the ear OTALGIC adj

OTALGY   n pl. -GIES otalgia

OTHER   n pl. -S one that remains of two or more

OTIC   adj pertaining to the ear

OTIOSE   adj lazy OTIOSELY adv

OTIOSITY   n pl. -TIES the state of being otiose

OTITIS   n pl. OTITIDES inflammation of the ear OTITIC adj

OTOCYST   n pl. -S an organ of balance in many invertebrates

OTOLITH   n pl. -S a hard mass that forms in the inner ear

OTOLOGY   n pl. -GIES the science of the ear

OTOSCOPE   n pl. -S an instrument for examining the ear

OTOSCOPY   n pl. -PIES the use of an otoscope

OTTAR   n pl. -S attar

OTTAVA   n pl. -S an octave

OTTER   n pl. -S a carnivorous mammal

OTTO   n pl. -TOS attar

OTTOMAN   n pl. -S a type of sofa

OUABAIN   n pl. -S a cardiac stimulant

OUCH   n pl. -ES a setting for a precious stone

OUD   n pl. -S a stringed instrument of northern Africa

OUGHT   v -ED, -ING, -S to owe

OUISTITI   n pl. -S a South American monkey

OUNCE   n pl. -S a unit of weight

OUPH   n pl. -S ouphe

OUPHE   n pl. -S an elf

OUR   pron a possessive form of the pronoun we

OURANG   n pl. -S orang

OURARI   n pl. -S curare

OUREBI   n pl. -S oribi

OURIE   adj shivering with cold

OURS   pron a possessive form of the pronoun we

OURSELF   pron myself — used in formal or regal contexts

OUSEL   n pl. -S ouzel

OUST   v -ED, -ING, -S to expel or remove from a position or place

OUSTER   n pl. -S the act of ousting

OUT   v -ED, -ING, -S to be revealed

OUTACT   v -ED, -ING, -S to surpass in acting

OUTADD   v -ED, -ING, -S to surpass in adding

OUTAGE   n pl. -S a failure or interruption in use or functioning

OUTARGUE   v -GUED, -GUING, -GUES to get the better of by arguing

OUTASK   v -ED, -ING, -S to surpass in asking

OUTATE   past tense of outeat

OUTBACK   n pl. -S isolated rural country

OUTBAKE   v -BAKED, -BAKING, -BAKES to surpass in baking

OUTBARK   v -ED, -ING, -S to surpass in barking

OUTBAWL   v -ED, -ING, -S to surpass in bawling

OUTBEAM   v -ED, -ING, -S to surpass in beaming

OUTBEG   v -BEGGED, -BEGGING, -BEGS to surpass in begging

OUTBID   v -BID, -BIDDEN, -BIDDING, -BIDS to bid higher than

OUTBLAZE   v -BLAZED, -BLAZING, -BLAZES to surpass in brilliance of light

OUTBLEAT   v -ED, -ING, -S to surpass in bleating

OUTBLESS   v -ED, -ING, -ES to surpass in blessing

OUTBLOOM   v -ED, -ING, -S to surpass in blooming

OUTBLUFF   v -ED, -ING, -S to surpass in bluffing

OUTBLUSH   v -ED, -ING, -ES to surpass in blushing

OUTBOARD   n pl. -S a type of motor

OUTBOAST   v -ED, -ING, -S to surpass in boasting

OUTBOUND   adj outward bound

OUTBOX   v -ED, -ING, -ES to surpass in boxing

OUTBRAG   v -BRAGGED, -BRAGGING, -BRAGS to surpass in bragging

OUTBRAVE   v -BRAVED, -BRAVING, -BRAVES to surpass in courage

OUTBREAK   n pl. -S a sudden eruption

OUTBREED   v -BRED, -BREEDING, -BREEDS to interbreed relatively unrelated stocks

OUTBRIBE   v -BRIBED, -BRIBING, -BRIBES to surpass in bribing

OUTBUILD   v -BUILT, -BUILDING, -BUILDS to surpass in building

OUTBULLY   v -LIED, -LYING, -LIES to surpass in bullying

OUTBURN   v -BURNED or -BURNT, -BURNING, -BURNS to burn longer than

OUTBURST   n pl. -S a sudden and violent outpouring

OUTBY   adv outdoors

OUTBYE   adv outby

OUTCAPER   v -ED, -ING, -S to surpass in capering

OUTCAST   n pl. -S one that is cast out

OUTCASTE   n pl. -S a Hindu who has been expelled from his caste

OUTCATCH   v -CAUGHT, -CATCHING, -CATCHES to surpass in catching

OUTCAVIL   v -ILED, -ILING, -ILS or -ILLED, -ILLING, -ILS to surpass in caviling

OUTCHARM   v -ED, -ING, -S to surpass in charming

OUTCHEAT   v -ED, -ING, -S to surpass in cheating

OUTCHIDE   v -CHIDED or -CHID, -CHIDDEN, -CHIDING, -CHIDES to surpass in chiding

OUTCLASS   v -ED, -ING, -ES to surpass so decisively as to appear of a higher class

OUTCLIMB   v -CLIMBED or -CLOMB, -CLIMBING, -CLIMBS to surpass in climbing

OUTCOME   n pl. -S a result

OUTCOOK   v -ED, -ING, -S to surpass in cooking

OUTCRAWL   v -ED, -ING, -S to surpass in crawling

OUTCRIED   past tense of outcry

OUTCRIES   present 3d person sing. of outcry

OUTCROP   v -CROPPED, -CROPPING, -CROPS to protrude above the soil

OUTCROSS   v -ED, -ING, -ES to cross with a relatively unrelated individual

OUTCROW v -ED, -ING, -S to surpass in crowing

OUTCRY v -CRIED, -CRYING, -CRIES to cry louder than

OUTCURSE v -CURSED, -CURSING, -CURSES to surpass in cursing

OUTCURVE n pl. -S a type of pitch in baseball

OUTDANCE v -DANCED, -DANCING, -DANCES to surpass in dancing

OUTDARE v -DARED, -DARING, -DARES to surpass in daring

OUTDATE v -DATED, -DATING, -DATES to make out-of-date

OUTDO v -DID, -DONE, -DOING, -DOES to exceed in performance

OUTDODGE v -DODGED, -DODGING, -DODGES to surpass in dodging

OUTDOER n pl. -S one that outdoes

OUTDONE past participle of outdo

OUTDOOR adj pertaining to the open air

OUTDOORS adv in the open air

OUTDRANK past tense of outdrink

OUTDRAW v -DREW, -DRAWN, -DRAWING, -DRAWS to attract a larger audience than

OUTDREAM v -DREAMED or -DREAMT, -DREAMING, -DREAMS to surpass in dreaming

OUTDRESS v -ED, -ING, -ES to surpass in dressing

OUTDREW past tense of outdraw

OUTDRINK v -DRANK, -DRUNK, -DRINKS to surpass in drinking

OUTDRIVE v -DROVE, -DRIVEN, -DRIVING, -DRIVES to drive a golf ball farther than

OUTDROP v -DROPPED, -DROPPING, -DROPS to surpass in dropping

OUTDRUNK past participle of outdrink

OUTEAT v -ATE, -EATEN, -EATING, -EATS to surpass in eating

OUTECHO v -ED, -ING, -ES to surpass in echoing

OUTER n pl. -S a part of a target

OUTFABLE v -BLED, -BLING, -BLES to surpass in fabling

OUTFACE v -FACED, -FACING, -FACES to confront unflinchingly

OUTFALL n pl. -S the outlet of a body of water

OUTFAST v -ED, -ING, -S to surpass in fasting

OUTFAWN v -ED, -ING, -S to surpass in fawning

OUTFEAST v -ED, -ING, -S to surpass in feasting

OUTFEEL v -FELT, -FEELING, -FEELS to surpass in feeling

OUTFIELD n pl. -S a part of a baseball field

OUTFIGHT v -FOUGHT, -FIGHTING, -FIGHTS to defeat

OUTFIND v -FOUND, -FINDING, -FINDS to surpass in finding

OUTFIRE v -FIRED, -FIRING, -FIRES to surpass in firing

OUTFIT v -FITTED, -FITTING, -FITS to equip

OUTFLANK v -ED, -ING, -S to gain a tactical advantage over

OUTFLOW v -ED, -ING, -S to flow out

OUTFLY v -FLEW, -FLOWN, -FLYING, -FLIES to surpass in speed of flight

OUTFOOL v -ED, -ING, -S to surpass in fooling

OUTFOOT v -ED, -ING, -S to surpass in speed

OUTFOUGHT past tense of outfight

OUTFOUND past tense of outfind

OUTFOX v -ED, -ING, -ES to outwit

OUTFROWN v -ED, -ING, -S to frown more than

OUTGAIN v -ED, -ING, -S to gain more than

OUTGAS v -GASSED, -GASSING, -GASSES to remove gas from

OUTGIVE v -GAVE, -GIVEN, -GIVING, -GIVES to give more than

OUTGLARE v -GLARED, -GLARING, -GLARES to surpass in glaring

OUTGLOW v -ED, -ING, -S to surpass in glowing

OUTGNAW v -GNAWED, -GNAWN, -GNAWING, -GNAWS to surpass in gnawing

OUTGO v -WENT, -GONE, -GOING, -GOES to go beyond

OUTGOING n pl. -S a departure

OUTGREW past tense of outgrow

OUTGRIN v -GRINNED, -GRINNING, -GRINS to surpass in grinning

OUTGROUP n pl. -S a group of people outside one's own group

OUTGROW v -GREW, -GROWN, -GROWING, -GROWS to grow too large for

OUTGUESS v -ED, -ING, -ES to anticipate the actions of

OUTGUIDE v -GUIDED, -GUIDING, -GUIDES to surpass in guiding

OUTGUN v -GUNNED, -GUNNING, -GUNS to surpass in firepower

OUTGUSH n pl. -ES a gushing out

OUTHAUL n pl. -S a rope for extending a sail along a spar

OUTHEAR v -HEARD, -HEARING, -HEARS to surpass in hearing

OUTHIT v -HIT, -HITTING, -HITS to get more hits than

OUTHOUSE n pl. -S a toilet housed in a small structure

OUTHOWL v -ED, -ING, -S to surpass in howling

OUTHUMOR v -ED, -ING, -S to surpass in humoring

OUTING n pl. -S a short pleasure trip

OUTJINX v -ED, -ING, -ES to surpass in jinxing

OUTJUMP v -ED, -ING, -S to surpass in jumping

OUTJUT v -JUTTED, -JUTTING, -JUTS to stick out

OUTKEEP v -KEPT, -KEEPING, -KEEPS to surpass in keeping

OUTKICK v -ED, -ING, -S to surpass in kicking

OUTKISS v -ED, -ING, -ES to surpass in kissing

OUTLAID past tense of outlay

OUTLAIN past participle of outlie

OUTLAND n pl. -S a foreign land

OUTLAST v -ED, -ING, -S to last longer than

OUTLAUGH v -ED, -ING, -S to surpass in laughing

OUTLAW v -ED, -ING, -S to prohibit

OUTLAWRY n pl. -RIES habitual defiance of the law

OUTLAY n -LAID, -LAYING, -LAYS to pay out

OUTLEAP v -LEAPED or -LEAPT, -LEAPING, -LEAPS to surpass in leaping

OUTLEARN v -LEARNED or -LEARNT, -LEARNING, -LEARNS to surpass in learning

OUTLET n pl. -S a passage for escape or discharge

OUTLIE v -LAY, -LAIN, -LYING, -LIES to lie beyond

OUTLIER n pl. -S an outlying area or portion

OUTLINE v -LINED, -LINING, -LINES to indicate the main features or different parts of

OUTLIVE v -LIVED, -LIVING, -LIVES to live longer than

OUTLIVER n pl. -S one that outlives

OUTLOOK n pl. -S a point of view

OUTLOVE v -LOVED, -LOVING, -LOVES to surpass in loving

OUTLYING present participle of outlie

OUTMAN v -MANNED, -MANNING, -MANS to surpass in manpower

OUTMARCH v -ED, -ING, -ES to surpass in marching

OUTMATCH v -ED, -ING, -ES to outdo

OUTMODE v -MODED, -MODING, -MODES to outdate

OUTMOST adj farthest out

OUTMOVE v -MOVED, -MOVING, -MOVES to move faster or farther than

OUTPACE v -PACED, -PACING, -PACES to surpass in speed

OUTPAINT v -ED, -ING, -S to surpass in painting

OUTPASS v -ED, -ING, -ES to excel in passing a football

OUTPITY v -PITIED, -PITYING, -PITIES to surpass in pitying

OUTPLAN v -PLANNED, -PLANNING, -PLANS to surpass in planning

OUTPLAY v -ED, -ING, -S to excel or defeat in a game

OUTPLOD v -PLODDED, -PLODDING, -PLODS to surpass in plodding

OUTPOINT v -ED, -ING, -S to score more points than

OUTPOLL v -ED, -ING, -S to get more votes than

OUTPORT n pl. -S a port of export or departure

OUTPOST n pl. -S a body of troops stationed at a distance from the main body

OUTPOUR   v -ED, -ING, -S to pour out

OUTPRAY   v -ED, -ING, -S to surpass in praying

OUTPREEN   v -ED, -ING, -S to surpass in preening

OUTPRESS   v -ED, -ING, -ES to surpass in pressing

OUTPRICE   v -PRICED, -PRICING, -PRICES to surpass in pricing

OUTPULL   v -ED, -ING, -S to attract a larger audience or following than

OUTPUSH   v -ED, -ING, -ES to surpass in pushing

OUTPUT   v -PUTTED, -PUTTING, -PUTS to produce

OUTQUOTE   v -QUOTED, -QUOTING, -QUOTES to surpass in quoting

OUTRACE   v -RACED, -RACING, -RACES to run faster or farther than

OUTRAGE   v -RAGED, -RAGING, -RAGES to arouse anger or resentment in

OUTRAISE   v -RAISED, -RAISING, -RAISES to surpass in raising

OUTRAN   past tense of outrun

OUTRANCE   n pl. -S the last extremity

OUTRANG   past tense of outring

OUTRANGE   v -RANGED, -RANGING, -RANGES to surpass in range

OUTRANK   v -ED, -ING, -S to rank higher than

OUTRAVE   v -RAVED, -RAVING, -RAVES to surpass in raving

OUTRE   adj deviating from what is usual or proper

OUTREACH   v -ED, -ING, -ES to reach beyond

OUTREAD   v -READ, -READING, -READS to surpass in reading

OUTRIDE   v -RODE, -RIDDEN, -RIDING, -RIDES to ride faster or better than

OUTRIDER   n pl. -S a mounted attendant who rides before or beside a carriage

OUTRIGHT   adj being without limit or reservation

OUTRING   v -RANG, -RUNG, -RINGING, -RINGS to ring louder than

OUTRIVAL   v -VALED, -VALING, -VALS or -VALLED, -VALLING, -VALS to outdo in a competition or rivalry

OUTROAR   v -ED, -ING, -S to roar louder than

OUTROCK   v -ED, -ING, -S to surpass in rocking

OUTRODE   past tense of outride

OUTROLL   v -ED, -ING, -S to roll out

OUTROOT   v -ED, -ING, -S to pull up by the roots

OUTRUN   v -RAN, -RUNNING, -RUNS to run faster than

OUTRUNG   past participle of outring

OUTRUSH   n pl. -ES a rushing out

OUTSAIL   v -ED, -ING, -S to sail faster than

OUTSANG   past tense of outsing

OUTSAT   past tense of outsit

OUTSAVOR   v -ED, -ING, -S to surpass in a distinctive taste or smell

OUTSAW   past tense of outsee

OUTSCOLD   v -ED, -ING, -S to surpass in scolding

OUTSCORE   v -SCORED, -SCORING, -SCORES to score more points than

OUTSCORN   v -ED, -ING, -S to surpass in scorning

OUTSEE   v -SAW, -SEEN, -SEEING, -SEES to see beyond

OUTSELL   v -SOLD, -SELLING, -SELLS to sell more than

OUTSERT   n pl. -S a folded sheet placed around a folded section of printed matter

OUTSERVE   v -SERVED, -SERVING, -SERVES to surpass in serving

OUTSET   n pl. -S a beginning

OUTSHAME   v -SHAMED, -SHAMING, -SHAMES to surpass in shaming

OUTSHINE   v -SHONE or -SHINED, -SHINING, -SHINES to shine brighter than

OUTSHOOT   v -SHOT, -SHOOTING, -SHOOTS to shoot better than

OUTSHOUT   v -ED, -ING, -S to shout louder than

OUTSIDE   n pl. -S the outer side, surface, or part

OUTSIDER   n pl. -S one that does not belong to a particular group

OUTSIGHT   n pl. -S the power of perceiving external things

OUTSIN   v -SINNED, -SINNING, -SINS to surpass in sinning

OUTSING v -SANG, -SUNG, -SINGING, -SINGS to surpass in singing

OUTSIT v -SAT, -SITTING, -SITS to remain sitting or in session longer than

OUTSIZE n pl. -S an unusual size
OUTSIZED adj

OUTSKIRT n pl. -S an outlying area

OUTSLEEP v -SLEPT, -SLEEPING, -SLEEPS to sleep later than

OUTSMART v -ED, -ING, -S to outwit

OUTSOAR v -ED, -ING, -S to soar beyond

OUTSMILE v -SMILED, -SMILING, -SMILES to surpass in smiling

OUTSMOKE v -SMOKED, -SMOKING, -SMOKES to surpass in smoking

OUTSNORE v -SNORED, -SNORING, -SNORES to surpass in snoring

OUTSOLD past tense of outsell

OUTSOLE n pl. -S the outer sole of a boot or shoe

OUTSPAN v -SPANNED, -SPANNING, -SPANS to unharness a draft animal

OUTSPEAK v -SPOKE, -SPOKEN, -SPEAKING, -SPEAKS to outdo in speaking

OUTSPELL v -SPELLED or -SPELT, -SPELLING, -SPELLS to surpass in spelling

OUTSPEND v -SPENT, -SPENDING, -SPENDS to exceed the limits of in spending

OUTSPOKE past tense of outspeak

OUTSPOKEN past participle of outspeak

OUTSTAND v -STOOD, -STANDING, -STANDS to endure beyond

OUTSTARE v -STARED, -STARING, -STARES to outface

OUTSTART v -ED, -ING, -S to get ahead of at the start

OUTSTATE v -STATED, -STATING, -STATES to surpass in stating

OUTSTAY v -ED, -ING, -S to surpass in staying power

OUTSTEER v -ED, -ING, -S to surpass in steering

OUTSTOOD past tense of outstand

OUTSTRIP v -STRIPPED, -STRIPPING, -STRIPS to go faster or farther than

OUTSTUDY v -STUDIED, -STUDYING, -STUDIES to surpass in studying

OUTSTUNT v -ED, -ING, -S to surpass in stunting

OUTSULK v -ED, -ING, -S to surpass in sulking

OUTSUNG past participle of outsing

OUTSWEAR v -SWORE or -SWARE, -SWORN, -SWEARING, -SWEARS to surpass in swearing

OUTSWIM v -SWAM, -SWUM, -SWIMMING, -SWIMS to swim faster or farther than

OUTTAKE n pl. -S a passage outwards

OUTTALK v -ED, -ING, -S to surpass in talking

OUTTASK v -ED, -ING, -S to surpass in tasking

OUTTELL v -TOLD, -TELLING, -TELLS to say openly

OUTTHANK v -ED, -ING, -S to surpass in thanking

OUTTHINK v -THOUGHT, -THINKING, -THINKS to get the better of by thinking

OUTTHROB v -THROBBED, -THROBBING, -THROBS to surpass in throbbing

OUTTHROW v -THREW, -THROWN, -THROWING, -THROWS to throw farther or more accurately than

OUTTOLD past tense of outtell

OUTTOWER v -ED, -ING, -S to tower above

OUTTRADE v -TRADED, -TRADING, -TRADES to get the better of in a trade

OUTTRICK v -ED, -ING, -S to get the better of by trickery

OUTTROT v -TROTTED, -TROTTING, -TROTS to surpass in trotting

OUTTRUMP v -ED, -ING, -S to outplay

OUTTURN n pl. -S a quantity produced

OUTVALUE v -UED, -UING, -UES to be worth more than

OUTVAUNT v -ED, -ING, -S to surpass in vaunting

OUTVOICE v -VOICED, -VOICING, -VOICES to surpass in loudness of voice

OUTVOTE v -VOTED, -VOTING, -VOTES to defeat by a majority of votes

OUTWAIT v -ED, -ING, -S to exceed in patience

OUTWALK v -ED, -ING, -S to surpass in walking

OUTWAR *v* -WARRED, -WARRING, -WARS to surpass in warring

OUTWARD *adv* toward the outside

OUTWARDS *adv* outward

OUTWARRED past tense of outwar

OUTWAR-RING present participle of outwar

OUTWASH *n pl.* -ES detritus washed from a glacier

OUTWASTE *v* -WASTED, -WASTING, -WASTES to surpass in wasting

OUTWATCH *v* -ED, -ING, -ES to watch longer than

OUTWEAR *v* -WORE, -WORN, -WEARING, -WEARS to last longer than

OUTWEARY *v* -RIED, -RYING, -RIES to surpass in wearying

OUTWEEP *v* -WEPT, -WEEPING, -WEEPS to weep more than

OUTWEIGH *v* -ED, -ING, -S to weigh more than

OUTWENT past tense of outgo

OUTWEPT past tense of outweep

OUTWHIRL *v* -ED, -ING, -S to surpass in whirling

OUTWILE *v* -WILED, -WILING, -WILES to surpass in wiling

OUTWILL *v* -ED, -ING, -S to surpass in willpower

OUTWIND *v* -ED, -ING, -S to cause to be out of breath

OUTWISH *v* -ED, -ING, -ES to surpass in wishing

OUTWIT *v* -WITTED, -WITTING, -WITS to get the better of by superior cleverness

OUTWORE past tense of outwear

OUTWORK *v* -WORKED or -WROUGHT, -WORKING, -WORKS to work faster or better than

OUTWORN past participle of outwear

OUTWRITE *v* -WROTE or -WRIT, -WRITTEN, -WRITING, -WRITES to write better than

OUT-WROUGHT a past tense of outwork

OUTYELL *v* -ED, -ING, -S to yell louder than

OUTYELP *v* -ED, -ING, -S to surpass in yelping

OUTYIELD *v* -ED, -ING, -S to surpass in yield

OUZEL *n pl.* -S a European bird

OUZO *n pl.* -ZOS a Greek liqueur

OVA pl. of ovum

OVAL *n pl.* -S an oval (egg-shaped) figure or object

OVALITY *n pl.* -TIES ovalness

OVALLY *adv* in the shape of an oval

OVALNESS *n pl.* -ES the state of being oval

OVARIAL *adj* ovarian

OVARIAN *adj* pertaining to an ovary

OVARIES pl. of ovary

OVARIOLE *n pl.* -S one of the tubes of which the ovaries of most insects are composed

OVARITIS *n pl.* -RITIDES inflammation of an ovary

OVARY *n pl.* -RIES a female reproductive gland

OVATE *adj* egg-shaped **OVATELY** *adv*

OVATION *n pl.* -S an expression or demonstration of popular acclaim

OVEN *n pl.* -S an enclosed compartment in which substances are heated **OVENLIKE** *adj*

OVENBIRD *n pl.* -S an American songbird

OVENWARE *n pl.* -S heat-resistant dishes for baking and serving food

OVER *v* -ED, -ING, -S to leap above and to the other side of

OVERABLE *adj* excessively able

OVERACT *v* -ED, -ING, -S to act with exaggeration

OVERAGE *n pl.* -S an amount in excess

OVERALL *n pl.* -S a loose outer garment

OVERAPT *adj* excessively apt

OVERARCH *v* -ED, -ING, -ES to form an arch over

OVERARM *adj* done with the arm above the shoulder

OVERATE past tense of overeat

OVERAWE *v* -AWED, -AWING, -AWES to subdue by inspiring awe

OVERBAKE *v* -BAKED, -BAKING, -BAKES to bake too long

OVERBEAR *v* -BORE, -BORNE or -BORN, -BEARING, -BEARS to bring down by superior weight or force

OVERBET v -BETTED, -BETTING, -BETS to bet too much

OVERBID v -BID, -BIDDEN, -BIDDING, -BIDS to bid higher than

OVERBIG adj too big

OVERBITE n pl. -S a faulty closure of the teeth

OVERBLOW v -BLEW, -BLOWN, -BLOWING, -BLOWS to give excessive importance to

OVERBOLD adj excessively bold or forward

OVERBOOK v -ED, -ING, -S to issue reservations in excess of the space available

OVERBORE past tense of overbear

OVERBORN a past participle of overbear

OVERBORNE a past participle of overbear

OVER-BOUGHT past tense of overbuy

OVERBRED adj bred too finely or to excess

OVERBUSY adj too busy

OVERBUY v -BOUGHT, -BUYING, -BUYS to buy in quantities exceeding need or demand

OVERCALL v -ED, -ING, -S to overbid

OVERCAME past tense of overcome

OVERCAST v -CAST, -CASTING, -CASTS to become cloudy or dark

OVERCOAT n pl. -S a warm coat worn over indoor clothing

OVERCOLD adj too cold

OVERCOME v -CAME, -COMING, -COMES to get the better of

OVERCOOK v -ED, -ING, -S to cook too long

OVERCOOL v -ED, -ING, -S to make too cool

OVERCOY adj too coy

OVERCRAM v -CRAMMED, -CRAMMING, -CRAMS to stuff or cram to excess

OVERCROP v -CROPPED, -CROPPING, -CROPS to exhaust the fertility of by cultivating to excess

OVERDARE v -DARED, -DARING, -DARES to become too daring

OVERDEAR adj too dear; too costly

OVERDECK v -ED, -ING, -S to adorn extravagantly

OVERDO v -DID, -DONE, -DOING, -DOES to do to excess

OVERDOER n pl. -S one that overdoes

OVERDOSE v -DOSED, -DOSING, -DOSES to give an excessive dose to

OVERDRAW v -DREW, -DRAWN, -DRAWING, -DRAWS to draw checks on in excess of the balance

OVERDRY adj too dry

OVERDUE adj not paid when due

OVERDYE v -DYED, -DYEING, -DYES to dye with too much color

OVEREASY adj too easy

OVEREAT v -ATE, -EATEN, -EATING, -EATS to eat to excess

OVERFAR adj too great in distance, extent, or degree

OVERFAST adj too fast

OVERFAT adj too fat

OVERFEAR v -ED, -ING, -S to fear too much

OVERFEED v -FED, -FEEDING, -FEEDS to feed too much

OVERFILL v -ED, -ING, -S to fill to overflowing

OVERFISH v -ED, -ING, -ES to deplete the supply of fish in an area by fishing to excess

OVERFLOW v -FLOWED, -FLOWN, -FLOWING, -FLOWS to flow over the top of

OVERFLY v -FLEW, -FLOWN, -FLYING, -FLIES to fly over

OVERFOND adj too fond or affectionate

OVERFOUL adj too foul

OVERFREE adj too free

OVERFULL adj too full

OVERGILD v -GILDED or -GILT, -GILDING, -GILDS to gild over

OVERGIRD v -GIRDED or -GIRT, -GIRDING, -GIRDS to gird to excess

OVERGLAD adj too glad

OVERGOAD v -ED, -ING, -S to goad too much

OVERGROW v -GREW, -GROWN, -GROWING, -GROWS to grow over

OVERHAND v -ED, -ING, -S to sew with short, vertical stitches

OVERHANG v -HUNG, -HANGING, -HANGS to hang or project over

OVERHARD adj too hard

OVERHATE v -HATED, -HATING, -HATES to hate to excess

OVERHAUL v -ED, -ING, -S to examine carefully for needed repairs

OVERHEAD *n* pl. -S the general cost of running a business

OVERHEAP *v* -ED, -ING, -S to heap up or accumulate to excess

OVERHEAR *v* -HEARD, -HEARING, -HEARS to hear without the speaker's knowledge or intention

OVERHEAT *v* -ED, -ING, -S to heat to excess

OVERHIGH *adj* too high

OVERHOLD *v* -HELD, -HOLDING, -HOLDS to rate too highly

OVERHOLY *adj* too holy

OVERHOPE *v* -HOPED, -HOPING, -HOPES to hope exceedingly

OVERHOT *adj* too hot

OVERHUNG past tense of overhang

OVERHUNT *v* -ED, -ING, -S to deplete the supply of game in an area by hunting to excess

OVERIDLE *adj* too idle

OVERJOY *v* -ED, -ING, -S to fill with great joy

OVERJUST *adj* too just

OVERKEEN *adj* too keen

OVERKILL *v* -ED, -ING, -S to destroy with more nuclear force than required

OVERKIND *adj* too kind

OVERLADE *v* -LADED, -LADEN, -LADING, -LADES to load with too great a burden

OVERLAID past tense of overlay

OVERLAIN past participle of overlie

OVERLAND *n* pl. -S a train or stagecoach that travels over land

OVERLAP *v* -LAPPED, -LAPPING, -LAPS to extend over and cover a part of

OVERLATE *adj* too late

OVERLAX *adj* too lax

OVERLAY *v* -LAID, -LAYING, -LAYS to lay over

OVERLEAF *adv* on the other side of the page

OVERLEAP *v* -LEAPED or -LEAPT, -LEAPING, -LEAPS to leap over

OVERLET *v* -LET, -LETTING, -LETS to let to excess

OVERLEWD *adj* too lewd

OVERLIE *v* -LAY, -LAIN, -LYING, -LIES to lie over

OVERLIVE *v* -LIVED, -LIVING, -LIVES to outlive

OVERLOAD *v* -ED, -ING, -S to load to excess

OVERLONG *adj* too long

OVERLOOK *v* -ED, -ING, -S to fail to notice

OVERLORD *v* -ED, -ING, -S to rule tyrannically

OVERLOUD *adj* too loud

OVERLOVE *v* -LOVED, -LOVING, -LOVES to love to excess

OVERLY *adv* to an excessive degree

OVERLYING present participle of overlie

OVERMAN *n* pl. -MEN a foreman

OVERMAN *v* -MANNED, -MANNING, -MANS to provide with more men than are needed

OVERMANY *adj* too many

OVERMEEK *adj* excessively meek

OVERMELT *v* -ED, -ING, -S to melt too much

OVERMEN pl. of overman

OVERMILD *adj* too mild

OVERMIX *v* -ED, -ING, -ES to mix too much

OVERMUCH *n* pl. -ES an excess

OVERNEAR *adj* too near

OVERNEAT *adj* too neat

OVERNEW *adj* too new

OVERNICE *adj* excessively nice

OVERPASS *v* -PASSED or -PAST, -PASSING, -PASSES to pass over

OVERPAY *v* -PAID, -PAYING, -PAYS to pay too much

OVERPERT *adj* too pert

OVERPLAY *v* -ED, -ING, -S to exaggerate

OVERPLUS *n* pl. -ES a surplus

OVERPLY *v* -PLIED, -PLYING, -PLIES to ply to excess; overwork

OVERRAN past tense of overrun

OVERRANK *adj* too luxuriant in growth

OVERRASH *adj* too rash

OVERRATE *v* -RATED, -RATING, -RATES to rate too highly

OVERRICH *adj* too rich

OVERRIDE *v* -RODE, -RIDDEN, -RIDING, -RIDES to ride over

OVERRIFE *adj* too rife

OVERRIPE   *adj* too ripe

OVERRODE   past tense of override

OVERRUDE   *adj* excessively rude

OVERRUFF   *v* -ED, -ING, -S to trump with a higher trump card than has already been played

OVERRULE   *v* -RULED, -RULING, -RULES to disallow the arguments of

OVERRUN   *v* -RAN, -RUNNING, -RUNS to spread or swarm over

OVERSAD   *adj* excessively sad

OVERSALE   *n* pl. -S the act of overselling

OVERSALT   *v* -ED, -ING, -S to salt to excess

OVERSAVE   *v* -SAVED, -SAVING, -SAVES to save too much

OVERSAW   past tense of oversee

OVERSEA   *adv* overseas

OVERSEAS   *adv* beyond or across the sea

OVERSEE   *v* -SAW, -SEEN, -SEEING, -SEES to watch over and direct

OVERSEED   *v* -ED, -ING, -S to seed to excess

OVERSEER   *n* pl. -S one that oversees

OVERSELL   *v* -SOLD, -SELLING, -SELLS to sell more of than can be delivered

OVERSET   *v* -SET, -SETTING, -SETS to turn or tip over

OVERSEW   *v* -SEWED, -SEWN, -SEWING, -SEWS to overhand

OVERSHOE   *n* pl. -S a protective outer shoe

OVERSHOT   *n* pl. -S a type of fabric weave

OVERSICK   *adj* too sick

OVERSIDE   *n* pl. -S the other side of a phonograph record

OVERSIZE   *n* pl. -S an unusually large size

OVERSLIP   *v* -SLIPPED or -SLIPT, -SLIPPING, -SLIPS to leave out

OVERSLOW   *adj* too slow

OVERSOAK   *v* -ED, -ING, -S to soak too much

OVERSOFT   *adj* too soft

OVERSOLD   past tense of oversell

OVERSOON   *adv* too soon

OVERSOUL   *n* pl. -S a supreme reality or mind in transcendentalism

OVERSPIN   *n* pl. -S a forward spin imparted to a ball

OVERSTAY   *v* -ED, -ING, -S to stay beyond the limits or duration of

OVERSTEP   *v* -STEPPED, -STEPPING, -STEPS to go beyond

OVERSTIR   *v* -STIRRED, -STIRRING, -STIRS to stir too much

OVERSUP   *v* -SUPPED, -SUPPING, -SUPS to sup to excess

OVERSURE   *adj* too sure

OVERT   *adj* open to view OVERTLY *adv*

OVERTAKE   *v* -TOOK, -TAKEN, -TAKING, -TAKES to catch up with

OVERTAME   *adj* too tame

OVERTART   *adj* too tart

OVERTASK   *v* -ED, -ING, -S to task too severely

OVERTAX   *v* -ED, -ING, -ES to tax too heavily

OVERTHIN   *adj* too thin

OVERTIME   *v* -TIMED, -TIMING, -TIMES to exceed the desired timing for

OVERTIRE   *v* -TIRED, -TIRING, -TIRES to tire excessively

OVERTOIL   *v* -ED, -ING, -S to wear out or exhaust by excessive toil

OVERTONE   *n* pl. -S a higher partial tone

OVERTOOK   past tense of overtake

OVERTOP   *v* -TOPPED, -TOPPING, -TOPS to rise above the top of

OVERTRIM   *v* -TRIMMED, -TRIMMING, -TRIMS to trim too much

OVERTURE   *v* -TURED, -TURING, -TURES to propose

OVERTURN   *v* -ED, -ING, -S to turn over

OVERURGE   *v* -URGED, -URGING, -URGES to urge too much

OVERUSE   *v* -USED, -USING, -USES to use too much

OVERVIEW   *n* pl. -S a summary

OVERVOTE   *v* -VOTED, -VOTING, -VOTES to defeat by a majority of votes

OVERWARM   *v* -ED, -ING, -S to warm too much

OVERWARY   *adj* too wary

OVERWEAK   *adj* too weak

OVERWEAR   *v* -WORE, -WORN, -WEARING, -WEARS to wear out

OVERWEEN   *v* -ED, -ING, -S to be arrogant

OVERWET   *v* -WETTED, -WETTING, -WETS to wet too much

OVERWIDE   *adj* too wide

OVERWILY   *adj* too wily

OVERWIND v -WOUND, -WINDING, -WINDS to wind too much, as a watch

OVERWISE adj too wise

OVERWORD n pl. -S a word or phrase repeated at intervals in a song

OVERWORE past tense of overwear

OVERWORK v -WORKED or -WROUGHT, -WORKING, -WORKS to cause to work too hard

OVERWORN past participle of overwear

OVER-WOUND past tense of overwind

OVER-WROUGHT a past tense of overwork

OVERZEAL n pl. -S excess of zeal

OVIBOS n pl. OVIBOS a wild ox

OVICIDE n pl. -S an agent that kills eggs **OVICIDAL** adj

OVIDUCT n pl. -S a tube through which ova travel from an ovary **OVIDUCAL** adj

OVIFORM adj shaped like an egg

OVINE n pl. -S a sheep or a closely related animal

OVIPARA n/pl egg-laying animals

OVIPOSIT v -ED, -ING, -S to lay eggs

OVISAC n pl. -S a sac containing an ovum or ova

OVOID n pl. -S an egg-shaped body **OVOIDAL** adj

OVOLO n pl. -LI or -LOS a convex molding

OVONIC adj pertaining to a branch of electronics

OVULATE v -LATED, -LATING, -LATES to produce ova

OVULE n pl. -S a rudimentary seed **OVULAR, OVULARY** adj

OVUM n pl. OVA the female reproductive cell of animals

OW interj — used to express sudden pain

OWE v OWED, OWING, OWES to be under obligation to pay or repay

OWL n pl. -S a nocturnal bird

OWLET n pl. -S a young owl

OWLISH adj resembling an owl **OWLISHLY** adv

OWLLIKE adj owlish

OWN v -ED, -ING, -S to have as a belonging **OWNABLE** adj

OWNER n pl. -S one that owns

OWSE n pl. OWSEN ox

OX n pl. OXEN a hoofed mammal

OX n pl. -ES a clumsy person

OXALATE v -LATED, -LATING, -LATES to treat with an oxalate (a chemical salt)

OXALIS n pl. -ALISES a flowering plant **OXALIC** adj

OXAZINE n pl. -S a chemical compound

OXBLOOD n pl. -S a deep red color

OXBOW n pl. -S a U-shaped piece of wood in an ox yoke

OXCART n pl. -S an ox-drawn cart

OXEN pl. of ox

OXEYE n pl. -S a flowering plant

OXFORD n pl. -S a type of shoe

OXHEART n pl. -S a variety of sweet cherry

OXID n pl. -S oxide

OXIDABLE adj capable of being oxidized

OXIDANT n pl. -S an oxidizing agent

OXIDASE n pl. -S an oxidizing enzyme **OXIDASIC** adj

OXIDATE v -DATED, -DATING, -DATES to oxidize

OXIDE n pl. -S a binary compound of oxygen with another element or radical **OXIDIC** adj

OXIDISE v -DISED, -DISING, -DISES to oxidize

OXIDISER n pl. -S oxidizer

OXIDIZE v -DIZED, -DIZING, -DIZES to combine with oxygen

OXIDIZER n pl. -S an oxidant

OXIM n pl. -S oxime

OXIME n pl. -S a chemical compound

OXLIP n pl. -S a flowering plant

OXPECKER n pl. -S an African bird

OXTAIL n pl. -S the tail of an ox

OXTER n pl. -S the armpit

OXTONGUE n pl. -S a European herb

OXY adj containing oxygen

OXYACID n pl. -S an acid that contains oxygen

OXYGEN n pl. -S a gaseous element **OXYGENIC** adj

OXYMORON	*n* pl. -MORA a combination of contradictory or incongruous words
OXYPHIL	*n* pl. -S oxyphile
OXYPHILE	*n* pl. -S an organism that thrives in a relatively acid environment
OXYSALT	*n* pl. -S of an oxyacid
OXYSOME	*n* pl. -S a structural unit of cellular cristae
OXYTOCIC	*n* pl. -S a drug that hastens the process of childbirth
OXYTOCIN	*n* pl. -S a pituitary hormone
OXYTONE	*n* pl. -S a word having heavy stress on the last syllable
OY	*interj* — used to express dismay or pain
OYER	*n* pl. -S a type of legal writ
OYES	*n* pl. OYESSES oyez
OYEZ	*n* pl. OYESSES a cry used to introduce the opening of a court of law
OYSTER	*v* -ED, -ING, -S to gather oysters (edible mollusks)
OYSTERER	*n* pl. -S one that gathers or sells oysters
OZONE	*n* pl. -S a form of oxygen OZONIC *adj*
OZONIDE	*n* pl. -S a compound of ozone
OZONISE	*v* -ISED, -ISING, -ISES to ozonize
OZONIZE	*v* -IZED, -IZING, -IZES to convert into ozone
OZONIZER	*n* pl. -S a device for converting oxygen into ozone
OZONOUS	*adj* pertaining to ozone

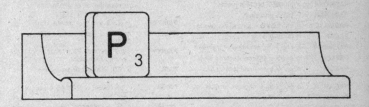

PA n pl. -S a father

PABULUM n pl. -S food PABULAR adj

PAC n pl. -S a shoe patterned after a moccasin

PACA n pl. -S a large rodent

PACE v PACED, PACING, PACES to walk with a regular step

PACER n pl. -S a horse whose gait is a pace

PACHA n pl. -S pasha

PACHADOM n pl. -S pashadom

PACHALIC n pl. -S pashalik

PACHISI n pl. -S a board game of India

PACHOULI n pl. -S an East Indian herb

PACHUCO n pl. -COS a flashy Mexican-American youth

PACIFIC adj peaceful

PACIFIED past tense of pacify

PACIFIER n pl. -S one that pacifies

PACIFIES present 3d person sing. of pacify

PACIFISM n pl. -S opposition to war or violence

PACIFIST n pl. -S an advocate of pacifism

PACIFY v -FIED, -FYING, -FIES to make peaceful

PACING present participle of pace

PACK v -ED, -ING, -S to put into a receptacle for transportation or storage PACKABLE adj

PACKAGE v -AGED, -AGING, -AGES to make into a package (a wrapped or boxed object)

PACKAGER n pl. -S one that packages

PACKER n pl. -S one that packs

PACKET v -ED, -ING, -S to make into a small package

PACKING n pl. -S material used to pack

PACKLY adv intimately

PACKMAN n pl. -MEN a peddler

PACKNESS n pl. -ES intimacy

PACKSACK n pl. -S a carrying bag to be worn on the back

PACKWAX n pl. -ES paxwax

PACT n pl. -S an agreement

PACTION n pl. -S a pact

PAD v PADDED, PADDING, PADS to line or stuff with soft material

PADAUK n pl. -S a tropical tree

PADDIES pl. of paddy

PADDING n pl. -S material with which to pad

PADDLE v -DLED, -DLING, -DLES to propel with a broad-bladed implement

PADDLER n pl. -S one that paddles

PADDLING n pl. -S the act of one who paddles

PADDOCK v -ED, -ING, -S to confine in an enclosure for horses

PADDY n pl. -DIES a rice field

PADISHAH n pl. -S a sovereign

PADLE n pl. -S a hoe

PADLOCK v -ED, -ING, -S to secure with a type of lock

PADNAG n pl. -S a horse that moves along at an easy pace

PADOUK n pl. -S padauk

PADRE *n* pl. PADRES or PADRI a Christian clergyman

PADRONE *n* pl. -NES or -NI a master

PADSHAH *n* pl. -S padishah

PADUASOY *n* pl. -SOYS a strong silk fabric

PAEAN *n* pl. -S a song of joy

PAEANISM *n* pl. -S the chanting of a paean

PAELLA *n* pl. -S a saffron-flavored stew

PAEON *n* pl. -S a metrical foot of four syllables

PAGAN *n* pl. -S an irreligious person

PAGANDOM *n* pl. -S the realm of pagans

PAGANISE *v* -ISED, -ISING, -ISES to paganize

PAGANISH *adj* resembling a pagan

PAGANISM *n* pl. -S an irreligious attitude

PAGANIST *n* pl. -S a pagan

PAGANIZE *v* -IZED, -IZING, -IZES to make irreligious

PAGE *v* PAGED, PAGING, PAGES to summon by calling out the name of

PAGEANT *n* pl. -S an elaborate public spectacle

PAGEBOY *n* pl. -BOYS a woman's hairstyle

PAGED past tense of page

PAGINAL *adj* pertaining to the pages of a book

PAGINATE *v* -NATED, -NATING, -NATES to number the pages of

PAGING present participle of page

PAGOD *n* pl. -S pagoda

PAGODA *n* pl. -S a Far Eastern temple

PAGURIAN *n* pl. -S a hermit crab

PAGURID *n* pl. -S pagurian

PAH *interj* — used as an exclamation of disgust

PAHLAVI *n* pl. -S a coin of Iran

PAID a past tense of pay

PAIK *v* -ED, -ING, -S to beat or strike

PAIL *n* pl. -S a watertight cylindrical container

PAILFUL *n* pl. PAILFULS or PAILSFUL as much as a pail will hold

PAIN *v* -ED, -ING, -S to cause pain (suffering or distress)

PAINCH *n* pl. -ES paunch

PAINFUL *adj* -FULLER, -FULLEST causing pain

PAINLESS *adj* not causing pain

PAINT *v* -ED, -ING, -S to make a representation of with paints (coloring substances)

PAINTER *n* pl. -S one that paints

PAINTING *n* pl. -S a picture made with paints

PAINTY *adj* PAINTIER, PAINTIEST covered with paint

PAIR *v* -ED, -ING, -S to arrange in sets of two

PAISA *n* pl. PAISE or PAISAS a coin of Pakistan

PAISAN *n* pl. -S paisano

PAISANO *n* pl. -NOS a fellow countryman

PAISE a pl. of paisa

PAISLEY *n* pl. -LEYS a patterned wool fabric

PAJAMA *n* pl. -S a garment for sleeping or lounging

PAL *v* PALLED, PALLING, PALS to associate as friends

PALABRA *n* pl. -S a word

PALACE *n* pl. -S a royal residence PALACED *adj*

PALADIN *n* pl. -S a knightly champion

PALAIS *n* pl. PALAIS a palace

PALATAL *n* pl. -S a bone of the palate

PALATE *n* pl. -S the roof of the mouth

PALATIAL *adj* resembling a palace

PALATINE *n* pl. -S a high officer of an empire

PALAVER *v* -ED, -ING, -S to chatter

PALAZZO *n* pl. -ZI an impressive building

PALE *adj* PALER, PALEST lacking intensity of color

PALE *v* PALED, PALING, PALES to make or become pale

PALEA *n* pl. -LEAE a small bract PALEAL *adj*

PALEFACE *n* pl. -S a white person

PALELY *adv* in a pale manner

PALENESS *n* pl. -ES the quality of being pale

PALER comparative of pale

PALEST superlative of pale

PALESTRA *n* pl. -TRAS or -TRAE a school for athletics in ancient Greece

PALET *n* pl. -S a palea

PALETOT *n* pl. -S a loose overcoat

PALETTE *n* pl. -S a board on which an artist mixes colors

PALEWAYS *adv* palewise

PALEWISE *adv* vertically

PALFREY *n* pl. -FREYS a riding horse

PALIER comparative of paly

PALIEST superlative of paly

PALIKAR *n* pl. -S a Greek soldier

PALING *n* pl. -S a picket fence

PALINODE *n* pl. -S a formal retraction

PALISADE *v* -SADED, -SADING, -SADES to fortify with a heavy fence

PALISH *adj* somewhat pale

PALL *v* -ED, -ING, -S to become insipid

PALLADIA *n/pl* safeguards

PALLADIC *adj* pertaining to the metallic element palladium

PALLED past tense of pal

PALLET *n* pl. -S a bed or mattress of straw

PALLETTE *n* pl. -S a piece of armor protecting the armpit

PALLIA a pl. of pallium

PALLIAL *adj* pertaining to a part of the brain

PALLIATE *v* -ATED, -ATING, -ATES to conceal the seriousness of

PALLID *adj* pale PALLIDLY *adv*

PALLIER comparative of pally

PALLIEST superlative of pally

PALLING present participle of pal

PALLIUM *n* pl. -LIA or -LIUMS a cloak worn in ancient Rome

PALLOR *n* pl. -S paleness

PALLY *adj* -LIER, -LIEST marked by close friendship

PALM *v* -ED, -ING, -S to touch with the palm (inner surface) of the hand

PALMAR *adj* pertaining to the palm

PALMARY *adj* worthy of praise

PALMATE *adj* resembling an open hand

PALMATED *adj* palmate

PALMER *n* pl. -S a religious pilgrim

PALMETTE *n* pl. -S a type of ornament

PALMETTO *n* pl. -TOS or -TOES a tropical tree

PALMIER comparative of palmy

PALMIEST superlative of palmy

PALMIST *n* pl. -S a fortune-teller

PALMITIN *n* pl. -S a chemical compound

PALMLIKE *adj* resembling a palm tree

PALMY *adj* PALMIER, PALMIEST marked by prosperity

PALMYRA *n* pl. -S a tropical tree

PALOMINO *n* pl. -NOS a slender-legged horse

PALOOKA *n* pl. -S an inferior boxer

PALP *n* pl. -S a palpus

PALPABLE *adj* capable of being felt PALPABLY *adv*

PALPAL *adj* pertaining to a palpus

PALPATE *v* -PATED, -PATING, -PATES to examine by touch

PALPATOR *n* pl. -S one that palpates

PALPEBRA *n* pl. -BRAE an eyelid

PALPUS *n* pl. -PI a sensory organ of an arthropod

PALSY *v* -SIED, -SYING, -SIES to paralyze

PALTER *v* -ED, -ING, -S to talk or act insincerely

PALTERER *n* pl. -S one that palters

PALTRY *adj* -TRIER, -TRIEST petty PALTRILY *adv*

PALUDAL *adj* pertaining to a marsh

PALUDISM *n* pl. -S malaria

PALY *adj* PALIER, PALIEST somewhat pale

PAM *n* pl. -S the jack of clubs in certain card games

PAMPA *n* pl. -S a grassland of South America

PAMPEAN *n* pl. -S a native of the pampas

PAMPER *v* -ED, -ING, -S to treat with extreme or excessive indulgence

PAMPERER *n* pl. -S one that pampers

PAMPERO *n* pl. -ROS a cold, dry wind

PAMPHLET *n* pl. -S a printed work with a paper cover

PAN *v* PANNED, PANNING, PANS to criticize harshly

PANACEA *n* pl. -S a remedy for all diseases or ills PANACEAN *adj*

PANACHE *n* pl. -S an ornamental tuft of feathers

PANADA _n_ pl. -S a thick sauce

PANAMA _n_ pl. -S a lightweight hat

PANATELA _n_ pl. -S a long, slender cigar

PANCAKE _v_ -CAKED, -CAKING, -CAKES to land an airplane in a certain manner

PANCHAX _n_ pl. -ES a tropical fish

PANCREAS _n_ pl. -ES a large gland

PANDA _n_ pl. -S a carnivorous mammal

PANDANUS _n_ pl. -NI or -NUSES a tropical plant

PANDECT _n_ pl. -S a complete body of laws

PANDEMIC _n_ pl. -S a widespread disease

PANDER _v_ -ED, -ING, -S to provide gratification for others' desires

PANDERER _n_ pl. -S one that panders

PANDIED past tense of pandy

PANDIES present 3d person sing. of pandy

PANDIT _n_ pl. -S a wise or learned man in India

PANDOOR _n_ pl. -S pandour

PANDORA _n_ pl. -S bandore

PANDORE _n_ pl. -S bandore

PANDOUR _n_ pl. -S a marauding soldier

PANDOWDY _n_ pl. -DIES an apple dessert

PANDURA _n_ pl. -S bandore

PANDY _v_ -DIED, -DYING, -DIES to punish by striking the hand

PANE _n_ pl. -S a sheet of glass for a window PANED _adj_

PANEL _v_ -ELED, -ELING, -ELS or -ELLED, -ELLING, -ELS to decorate with thin sheets of material

PANELING _n_ pl. -S material with which to panel

PANELIST _n_ pl. -S a member of a discussion or advisory group

PANELLED past tense of panel

PANELLING a present participle of panel

PANETELA _n_ pl. -S panatela

PANFISH _n_ pl. -ES any small fish that can be fried whole

PANFUL _n_ pl. -S as much as a pan will hold

PANG _v_ -ED, -ING, -S to cause to have spasm of pain

PANGA _n_ pl. -S a large knife

PANGEN _n_ pl. -S a hypothetical heredity-controlling particle of proto-plasm

PANGOLIN _n_ pl. -S a toothless mammal

PANHUMAN _adj_ pertaining to all humanity

PANIC _v_ -ICKED, -ICKING, -ICS to be overwhelmed by fear

PANICKY _adj_ -ICKIER, -ICKIEST tending to panic

PANICLE _n_ pl. -S a loosely branched flower cluster PANICLED _adj_

PANICUM _n_ pl. -S a grass

PANIER _n_ pl. -S pannier

PANMIXIA _n_ pl. -S random mating within a breeding population

PANNE _n_ pl. -S a lustrous velvet

PANNED past tense of pan

PANNIER _n_ pl. -S a large basket

PANNIKIN _n_ pl. -S a small saucepan

PANNING present participle of pan

PANOCHA _n_ pl. -S a coarse Mexican sugar

PANOCHE _n_ pl. -S panocha

PANOPLY _n_ pl. -PLIES a suit of armor

PANOPTIC _adj_ including everything visible in one view

PANORAMA _n_ pl. -S a complete view

PANPIPE _n_ pl. -S a musical instrument

PANSOPHY _n_ pl. -PHIES universal knowledge

PANSY _n_ pl. -SIES a flowering plant

PANT _v_ -ED, -ING, -S to breathe quickly and with difficulty

PANTHEON _n_ pl. -S a temple dedicated to all the gods

PANTHER _n_ pl. -S a leopard

PANTIE _n_ pl. -S a woman's or child's undergarment

PANTIES pl. of panty

PANTILE _n_ pl. -S a roofing tile PANTILED _adj_

PANTOFLE _n_ pl. -S a slipper

PANTOUM _n_ pl. -S a verse form

PANTRY _n_ pl. -TRIES a closet or room for storing kitchen utensils

PANTSUIT _n_ pl. -S a type of woman's suit

PANTY _n_ pl. PANTIES pantie

PANZER _n_ pl. -S an armored combat vehicle

PAP _n_ pl. -S a soft food for infants

PAPA   n pl. -S a father

PAPACY   n pl. -CIES the office of the pope

PAPAIN   n pl. -S an enzyme

PAPAL   adj pertaining to the pope PAPALLY adv

PAPAW   n pl. -S a fleshy fruit

PAPAYA   n pl. -S a melon-like fruit PAPAYAN adj

PAPER   v -ED, -ING, -S to cover or wrap with paper (a thin sheet material made of cellulose pulp)

PAPERBOY   n pl. -BOYS a newsboy

PAPERER   n pl. -S one that papers

PAPERY   adj resembling paper

PAPHIAN   n pl. -S a prostitute

PAPILLA   n pl. -LAE a nipple-like projection PAPILLAR adj

PAPILLON   n pl. -S a small dog

PAPIST   n pl. -S a Roman Catholic — usually used disparagingly PAPISTIC adj

PAPISTRY   n pl. -TRIES the Roman Catholic religion — usually used disparagingly

PAPOOSE   n pl. -S an American Indian baby

PAPPI   a pl. of peppus

PAPPIER   comparative of pappy

PAPPIES   pl. of pappy

PAPPIEST   superlative of pappy

PAPPOOSE   n pl. -S papoose

PAPPUS   n pl. -PI a tuft of bristles on the achene of certain plants PAPPOSE, PAPPOUS adj

PAPPY   adj -PIER, -PIEST resembling pap

PAPPY   n pl. -PIES a father

PAPRICA   n pl. -S paprika

PAPRIKA   n pl. -S a seasoning made from red peppers

PAPULA   n pl. -LAE papule

PAPULE   n pl. -S a pimple PAPULAN, PAPULAR, PAPULOSE adj

PAPYRUS   n pl. -RUSES or -RI a tall aquatic plant PAPYRAL, PAPYRIAN, PAPYRINE adj

PAR   v PARRED, PARRING, PARS to shoot in a standard number of strokes in golf

PARA   n pl. -S a monetary unit of Yugoslavia

PARABLE   n pl. -S a simple story conveying a moral or religious lesson

PARABOLA   n pl. -S a conic section

PARACHOR   n pl. -S a mathematical constant that relates molecular volume to surface tension

PARADE   v -RADED, -RADING, -RADES to march in a public procession

PARADER   n pl. -S one that parades

PARADIGM   n pl. -S a pattern or example

PARADING   present participle of parade

PARADISE   n pl. -S a place of extreme beauty or delight

PARADOS   n pl. -ES a protective embankment

PARADOX   n pl. -ES a statement seemingly contradictory or absurd yet perhaps true

PARADROP   v -DROPPED, -DROPPING, -DROPS to deliver by parachute

PARAFFIN   v -ED, -ING, -S to coat with a waxy substance

PARAFORM   n pl. -S a substance used as an antiseptic

PARAGOGE   n pl. -S the addition of a sound or sounds at the end of a word

PARAGON   v -ED, -ING, -S to compare with

PARAKEET   n pl. -S a small parrot

PARALLAX   n pl. -ES an apparent optical displacement of an object

PARALLEL   v -LELED, -LELING, -LELS or -LELLED, -LELLING, -LELS to be similar or analogous to

PARALYSE   v -LYSED, -LYSING, -LYSES to paralyze

PARALYZE   v -LYZED, -LYZING, -LYZES to render incapable of movement

PARAMENT   n pl. -MENTS or -MENTA an ornamental vestment

PARAMO   n pl. -MOS a plateau region of South America

PARAMOUR   n pl. -S an illicit lover

PARANG   n pl. -S a heavy knife

PARANOEA   n pl. -S paranoia

PARANOIA   n pl. -S a mental disorder

PARANOID   n pl. -S one affected with paranoia

PARAPET   n pl. -S a protective wall

PARAPH   *n pl.* -S a flourish at the end of a signature

PARAQUAT   *n pl.* -S a weed killer

PARAQUET   *n pl.* -S parakeet

PARASANG   *n pl.* -S a Persian unit of distance

PARASHAH   *n pl.* -SHOTH or -SHIOTH a passage in Jewish scripture

PARASITE   *n pl.* -S an organism that lives and feeds on or in another organism

PARASOL   *n pl.* -S a small, light umbrella

PARAVANE   *n pl.* -S an underwater device used to cut cables

PARBOIL   *v* -ED, -ING, -S to cook partially by boiling for a short time

PARCEL   *v* -CELED, -CELING, -CELS or -CELLED, -CELLING, -CELS to divide into parts or shares

PARCENER   *n pl.* -S a joint heir

PARCH   *v* -ED, -ING, -ES to make very dry

PARD   *n pl.* -S a leopard

PARDAH   *n pl.* -S purdah

PARDEE   *interj* pardi

PARDI   *interj* — used as a mild oath

PARDIE   *interj* pardi

PARDINE   *adj* pertaining to a leopard

PARDNER   *n pl.* -S chum; friend

PARDON   *v* -ED, -ING, -S to release from liability for an offense

PARDONER   *n pl.* -S one that pardons

PARDY   *interj* pardi

PARE   *v* PARED, PARING, PARES to cut off the outer covering of

PARECISM   *n pl.* -S the state of having the male and female sexual organs beside or near each other

PAREIRA   *n pl.* -S a medicinal plant root

PARENT   *v* -ED, -ING, -S to exercise the functions of a parent (a father or mother)

PARENTAL   *adj* pertaining to a parent

PARER   *n pl.* -S one that pares

PARESIS   *n pl.* -RESES partial loss of the ability to move

PARETIC   *n pl.* -S one affected with paresis

PAREU   *n pl.* -S a Polynesian garment

PAREVE   *adj* parve

PARFAIT   *n pl.* -S a frozen dessert

PARFLESH   *n pl.* -ES a rawhide smoked in lye to remove the hair and dried

PARFOCAL   *adj* having lenses with the corresponding focal points in the same plane

PARGE   *v* PARGED, PARGING, PARGES to parget

PARGET   *v* -GETED, -GETING, -GETS or -GETTED, -GETTING, -GETS to cover with plaster

PARGO   *n pl.* -GOS a food fish

PARHELIA   *n/pl* bright circular spots appearing on a solar halo

PARHELIC   *adj* pertaining to parhelia

PARIAH   *n pl.* -S a social outcast

PARIAN   *n pl.* -S a hard, white porcelain

PARIES   *n pl.* PARIETES the wall of an organ

PARIETAL   *n pl.* -S a bone of the skull

PARING   *n pl.* -S something pared off

PARIS   *n pl.* -ISES a European herb

PARISH   *n pl.* -ES an ecclesiastical district

PARITY   *n pl.* -TIES equality

PARK   *v* -ED, -ING, -S to leave a vehicle in a location for a time

PARKA   *n pl.* -S a hooded garment

PARKER   *n pl.* -S one that parks

PARKING   *n pl.* -S an area in which vehicles may be left

PARKLAND   *n pl.* -S a grassland region with isolated or grouped trees

PARKLIKE   *adj* resembling an outdoor recreational area

PARKWAY   *n pl.* -WAYS a wide highway

PARLANCE   *n pl.* -S a manner of speaking

PARLANDO   *adj* sung in a manner suggestive of speech

PARLANTE   *adj* parlando

PARLAY   *v* -ED, -ING, -S to bet an original wager and its winnings on a subsequent event

PARLE   *v* PARLED, PARLING, PARLES to parley

PARLEY   *v* -LEYED, -LEYING, -LEYS to discuss terms with an enemy

PARLEYER   *n pl.* -S one that parleys

PARLING   present participle of parle

PARLOR n pl. -S a room for the entertainment of visitors

PARLOUR n pl. -S parlor

PARLOUS adj dangerous

PARODIC adj comically imitative

PARODIED past tense of parody

PARODIES present 3d person sing. of parody

PARODIST n pl. -S one who parodies

PARODOS n pl. -DOI an ode sung in ancient Greek drama

PARODY v -DIED, -DYING, -DIES to imitate a serious literary work for comic effect

PAROL n pl. -S an utterance

PAROLE v -ROLED, -ROLING, -ROLES to release from prison before completion of the imposed sentence

PAROLEE n pl. -S one who is paroled

PARONYM n pl. -S a word having the same root as another

PAROQUET n pl. -S parakeet

PAROTIC adj situated near the ear

PAROTID n pl. -S a salivary gland

PAROTOID n pl. -S a gland of certain toads and frogs

PAROUS adj having produced offspring

PAROXYSM n pl. -S a sudden fit or attack

PARQUET v -ED, -ING, -S to furnish with a floor of inlaid design

PARR n pl. -S a young salmon

PARRAL n pl. -S parrel

PARRED past tense of par

PARREL n pl. -S a sliding loop of rope or chain used on a ship

PARRIDGE n pl. -S porridge

PARRIED past tense of parry

PARRIES present 3d person sing. of parry

PARRING present participle of par

PARRITCH n pl. -ES porridge

PARROKET n pl. -S parakeet

PARROT v -ED, -ING, -S to repeat or imitate without thought or understanding

PARROTER n pl. -S one that parrots

PARROTY adj resembling a parrot (a hook-billed tropical bird)

PARRY v -RIED, -RYING, -RIES to ward off a blow

PARSE v PARSED, PARSING, PARSES to describe and analyze grammatically **PARSABLE** adj

PARSEC n pl. -S a unit of astronomical distance

PARSER n pl. -S one that parses

PARSING present participle of parse

PARSLEY n pl. -LEYS a cultivated herb

PARSNIP n pl. -S a European herb

PARSON n pl. -S a clergyman **PARSONIC** adj

PART v -ED, -ING, -S to divide or break into separate pieces

PARTAKE v -TOOK, -TAKEN, -TAKING, -TAKES to participate

PARTAKER n pl. -S one that partakes

PARTAN n pl. -S an edible crab

PARTERRE n pl. -S a section of a theater

PARTIAL n pl. -S a simple component of a complex tone

PARTIBLE adj divisible

PARTICLE n pl. -S a very small piece or part

PARTIED past tense of party

PARTIES present 3d person sing. of party

PARTING n pl. -S a division or separation

PARTISAN n pl. -S a firm supporter of a person, party, or cause

PARTITA n pl. -S a set of related instrumental pieces

PARTITE adj divided into parts

PARTIZAN n pl. -S partisan

PARTLET n pl. -S a woman's garment

PARTLY adv in some measure or degree

PARTNER v -ED, -ING, -S to associate with in some activity of common interest

PARTON n pl. -S a hypothetical atomic particle

PARTOOK past tense of partake

PARTWAY adv to some extent

PARTY v -TIED, -TYING, -TIES to attend a social gathering

PARURA n pl. -S parure

PARURE n pl. -S a set of matched jewelry

PARVE adj made without milk or meat

PARVENU *n* pl. -S one who has suddenly risen above his class

PARVENUE *adj* characteristic of a parvenu

PARVIS *n* pl. -VISES an enclosed area in front of a church

PARVISE *n* pl. -S parvis

PARVOLIN *n* pl. -S an oily liquid obtained from fish

PAS *n* pl. PAS a dance step

PASCHAL *n* pl. -S a candle used in certain religious ceremonies

PASE *n* pl. -S a movement of a matador's cape

PASEO *n* pl. -SEOS a leisurely stroll

PASH *v* -ED, -ING, -ES to strike violently

PASHA *n* pl. -S a former Turkish high official

PASHADOM *n* pl. -S the rank of a pasha

PASHALIC *n* pl. -S pashalik

PASHALIK *n* pl. -S the territory of a pasha

PASQUIL *n* pl. -S a satire or lampoon

PASS *v* -ED, -ING, -ES to go by

PASSABLE *adj* fairly good or acceptable PASSABLY *adv*

PASSADE *n* pl. -S a turn of a horse backward or forward on the same ground

PASSADO *n* pl. -DOS or -DOES a forward thrust in fencing

PASSAGE *v* -SAGED, -SAGING, -SAGES to make a voyage

PASSANT *adj* walking with the farther forepaw raised — used of a heraldic animal

PASSBAND *n* pl. -S a frequency band that permits transmission with maximum efficiency

PASSBOOK *n* pl. -S a bankbook

PASSE *adj* outmoded

PASSEE *adj* passe

PASSEL *n* pl. -S a large quantity or number

PASSER *n* pl. -S one that passes

PASSERBY *n* pl. PASSERSBY one who passes by

PASSIBLE *adj* capable of feeling or suffering

PASSIM *adv* here and there

PASSING *n* pl. -S a death

PASSION *n* pl. -S an intense emotion

PASSIVE *n* pl. -S a verb form

PASSKEY *n* pl. -KEYS a key that opens several different locks

PASSLESS *adj* incapable of being traveled over or through

PASSOVER *n* pl. -S the lamb eaten at the feast of a Jewish holiday

PASSPORT *n* pl. -S a document allowing travel from one country to another

PASSUS *n* pl. -ES a section of a story or poem

PASSWORD *n* pl. -S a secret word that must be spoken to gain admission

PAST *n* pl. -S time gone by

PASTA *n* pl. -S a food made of dough

PASTE *v* PASTED, PASTING, PASTES to fasten with a sticky mixture

PASTEL *n* pl. -S a soft, delicate hue

PASTER *n* pl. -S one that pastes

PASTERN *n* pl. -S a part of a horse's foot

PASTICCI *n/pl* pastiches

PASTICHE *n* pl. -S an artistic work made of fragments from various sources

PASTIER comparative of pasty

PASTIES pl. of pasty

PASTIEST superlative of pasty

PASTIL *n* pl. -S pastille

PASTILLE *n* pl. -S a lozenge

PASTIME *n* pl. -S a recreational activity

PASTINA *n* pl. -S a type of macaroni

PASTING present participle of paste

PASTNESS *n* pl. -ES the state of being past or gone by

PASTOR *v* -ED, -ING, -S to serve as the spiritual overseer of

PASTORAL *n* pl. -S a literary or artistic work that depicts country life

PASTRAMI *n* pl. -S a highly seasoned smoked beef

PASTROMI *n* pl. -S pastrami

PASTRY *n* pl. -TRIES a sweet baked food

PASTURAL *adj* pertaining to a pasture

PASTURE *v* -TURED, -TURING, -TURES to put in a pasture (a grazing area)

PASTURER *n* pl. -S one that pastures livestock

PASTY   *adj* PASTIER, PASTIEST pale and unhealthy in appearance

PASTY   *n* pl. PASTIES a meat pie

PAT   *v* PATTED, PATTING, PATS to touch lightly

PATACA   *n* pl. -S a monetary unit of Macao

PATAGIUM   *n* pl. -GIA a wing membrane of a bat

PATAMAR   *n* pl. -S a sailing vessel

PATCH   *v* -ED, -ING, -ES to mend or cover a hole or weak spot in

PATCHER   *n* pl. -S one that patches

PATCHY   *adj* PATCHIER, PATCHIEST uneven in quality PATCHILY *adv*

PATE   *n* pl. -S the top of the head PATED *adj*

PATELLA   *n* pl. -LAE or -LAS the flat movable bone at the front of the knee PATELLAR *adj*

PATEN   *n* pl. -S a plate

PATENCY   *n* pl. -CIES the state of being obvious

PATENT   *v* -ED, -ING, -S to obtain a patent (a government grant protecting the rights of an inventor) on

PATENTEE   *n* pl. -S one that holds a patent

PATENTLY   *adv* obviously

PATENTOR   *n* pl. -S one that grants a patent

PATER   *n* pl. -S a father

PATERNAL   *adj* pertaining to a father

PATH   *n* pl. -S a trodden way or track

PATHETIC   *adj* arousing pity

PATHLESS   *adj* having no path

PATHOGEN   *n* pl. -S any disease-producing organism

PATHOS   *n* pl. -ES a quality that arouses feelings of pity or compassion

PATHWAY   *n* pl. -WAYS a path

PATIENCE   *n* pl. -S the quality of being patient

PATIENT   *adj* -TIENTER, -TIENTEST able to endure disagreeable circumstances without complaint

PATIENT   *n* pl. -S one who is under medical treatment

PATIN   *n* pl. -S paten

PATINA   *n* pl. -NAE or -NAS a green film that forms on bronze

PATINE   *v* -TINED, -TINING, -TINES to cover with a patina

PATIO   *n* pl. -TIOS an outdoor paved area adjoining a house

PATLY   *adv* suitably

PATNESS   *n* pl. -ES suitability

PATOIS   *n* pl. PATOIS a dialect

PATRIOT   *n* pl. -S one who loves his country

PATROL   *v* -TROLLED, -TROLLING, -TROLS to pass through an area for the purposes of observation or security

PATRON   *n* pl. -S a regular customer PATRONAL, PATRONLY *adj*

PATROON   *n* pl. -S a landowner granted manorial rights under old Dutch law

PATSY   *n* pl. -SIES a person who is easily fooled

PATTAMAR   *n* pl. -S patamar

PATTED   past tense of pat

PATTEE   *adj* paty

PATTEN   *n* pl. -S a shoe having a thick wooden sole

PATTER   *v* -ED, -ING, -S to talk glibly or rapidly

PATTERER   *n* pl. -S one that patters

PATTERN   *v* -ED, -ING, -S to make according to a prescribed design

PATTIE   *n* pl. -S patty

PATTING   present participle of pat

PATTY   *n* pl. -TIES a small, flat cake of chopped food

PATTYPAN   *n* pl. -S a pan in which patties are baked

PATULENT   *adj* patulous

PATULOUS   *adj* spreading; open

PATY   *adj* formee

PAUCITY   *n* pl. -TIES smallness of number or quantity

PAUGHTY   *adj* arrogant

PAULDRON   *n* pl. -S a piece of armor for the shoulder

PAULIN   *n* pl. -S a sheet of waterproof material

PAUNCH   *n* pl. -ES the belly or abdomen PAUNCHED *adj*

PAUNCHY   *adj* PAUNCHIER, PAUNCHIEST having a protruding belly

PAUPER	*v* -ED, -ING, -S to reduce to poverty
PAUSAL	*adj* pertaining to a break or rest in speaking or writing
PAUSE	*v* PAUSED, PAUSING, PAUSES to stop temporarily
PAUSER	*n* pl. -S one that pauses
PAVAN	*n* pl. -S a slow, stately dance
PAVANE	*n* pl. -S pavan
PAVE	*v* PAVED, PAVING, PAVES to cover with material that forms a firm, level surface
PAVEMENT	*n* pl. -S a paved surface
PAVER	*n* pl. -S one that paves
PAVID	*adj* timid
PAVILION	*v* -ED, -ING, -S to cover with a large tent
PAVIN	*n* pl. -S pavan
PAVING	*n* pl. -S pavement
PAVIOR	*n* pl. -S a paver
PAVIOUR	*n* pl. -S a paver
PAVIS	*n* pl. -ISES a large medieval shield
PAVISE	*n* pl. -S pavis
PAVISER	*n* pl. -S a soldier carrying a pavis
PAVONINE	*adj* resembling a peacock
PAW	*v* -ED, -ING, -S to strike or scrape with a beating motion
PAWER	*n* pl. -S one that paws
PAWKY	*adj* PAWKIER, PAWKIEST sly PAWKILY *adv*
PAWL	*n* pl. -S a hinged mechanical part
PAWN	*v* -ED, -ING, -S to give as security for something borrowed PAWNABLE *adj*
PAWNAGE	*n* pl. -S an act of pawning
PAWNEE	*n* pl. -S one to whom something is pawned
PAWNER	*n* pl. -S one that pawns something
PAWNOR	*n* pl. -S pawner
PAWNSHOP	*n* pl. -S a place where things are pawned
PAWPAW	*n* pl. -S papaw
PAX	*n* pl. -ES a ceremonial embrace given to signify Christian love and unity
PAXWAX	*n* pl. -ES the nuchal ligament of a quadruped
PAY	*v* PAID or PAYED, PAYING, PAYS to give money or something of value in exchange for goods or services
PAYABLE	*adj* profitable PAYABLY *adv*
PAYCHECK	*n* pl. -S a check in payment of wages or salary
PAYDAY	*n* pl. -DAYS the day on which wages are paid
PAYEE	*n* pl. -S one to whom money is paid
PAYER	*n* pl. -S one that pays
PAYLOAD	*n* pl. -S the part of a cargo producing income
PAYMENT	*n* pl. -S something that is paid
PAYNIM	*n* pl. -S a pagan
PAYOFF	*n* pl. -S the act of distributing gains
PAYOLA	*n* pl. -S a secret payment for favors
PAYOR	*n* pl. -S payer
PAYROLL	*n* pl. -S a list of employees entitled to payment
PE	*n* pl. -S a Hebrew letter
PEA	*n* pl. -S the edible seed of an annual herb
PEACE	*v* PEACED, PEACING, PEACES to be or become silent
PEACEFUL	*adj* -FULLER, -FULLEST undisturbed; calm
PEACH	*v* -ED, -ING, -ES to inform against someone
PEACHER	*n* pl. -S one that peaches
PEACHY	*adj* PEACHIER, PEACHIEST dandy
PEACING	present participle of peace
PEACOAT	*n* pl. -S a heavy woolen jacket
PEACOCK	*v* -ED, -ING, -S to strut vainly
PEACOCKY	*adj* -COCKIER, -COCKIEST vain
PEAFOWL	*n* pl. -S a large pheasant
PEAG	*n* pl. -S wampum
PEAGE	*n* pl. -S peag
PEAHEN	*n* pl. -S a female peafowl
PEAK	*v* -ED, -ING, -S to reach a maximum
PEAKIER	comparative of peaky
PEAKIEST	superlative of peaky
PEAKISH	*adj* somewhat sickly

PEAKLESS *adj* having no peak (a pointed top)

PEAKLIKE *adj* resembling a peak

PEAKY *adj* PEAKIER, PEAKIEST sickly

PEAL *v* -ED, -ING, -S to ring out

PEALIKE *adj* resembling a pea

PEAN *n pl.* -S paean

PEANUT *n pl.* -S the nutlike seed or pod of an annual vine

PEAR *n pl.* -S a fleshy fruit

PEARL *v* -ED, -ING, -S to adorn with pearls (smooth, rounded masses formed in certain mollusks)

PEARLASH *n pl.* -ES an alkaline compound

PEARLER *n pl.* -S one that dives for pearls

PEARLITE *n pl.* -S a cast-iron alloy

PEARLY *adj* PEARLIER, PEARLIEST resembling a pearl

PEARMAIN *n pl.* -S a variety of apple

PEART *adj* PEARTER, PEARTEST lively **PEARTLY** *adv*

PEASANT *n pl.* -S a person of inferior social rank

PEASCOD *n pl.* -S peasecod

PEASE *n pl.* PEASEN or PEASES a pea

PEASECOD *n pl.* -S a pea pod

PEAT *n pl.* -S a substance composed of partially decayed vegetable matter

PEATY *adj* PEATIER, PEATIEST resembling or containing peat

PEAVEY *n pl.* -VEYS a lever used to move logs

PEAVY *n pl.* -VIES peavey

PEBBLE *v* -BLED, -BLING, -BLES to cover with pebbles (small, rounded stones)

PEBBLY *adj* -BLIER, -BLIEST resembling pebbles

PECAN *n pl.* -S a nut-bearing tree

PECCABLE *adj* liable to sin

PECCANCY *n pl.* -CIES the state of being peccant

PECCANT *adj* sinful

PECCARY *n pl.* -RIES a hoofed mammal

PECCAVI *n pl.* -S a confession of sin

PECH *v* -ED, -ING, -S to pant

PECHAN *n pl.* -S the stomach

PECK *v* -ED, -ING, -S to strike with the beak or something pointed

PECKER *n pl.* -S one that pecks

PECKY *adj* PECKIER, PECKIEST marked by decay caused by fungi

PECTASE *n pl.* -S an enzyme

PECTATE *n pl.* -S a chemical salt

PECTEN *n pl.* -TENS or -TINES a comblike anatomical part

PECTIN *n pl.* -S a carbohydrate derivative **PECTIC** *adj*

PECTIZE *v* -TIZED, -TIZING, -TIZES to change into a jelly

PECTORAL *n pl.* -S something worn on the breast

PECULATE *v* -LATED, -LATING, -LATES to embezzle

PECULIAR *n pl.* -S something belonging exclusively to a person

PECULIUM *n pl.* -LIA private property

PED *n pl.* -S a natural soil aggregate

PEDAGOG *n pl.* -S a teacher

PEDAGOGY *n pl.* -GIES the work of a teacher

PEDAL *v* -ALED, -ALING, -ALS or -ALLED, -ALLING, -ALS to operate by means of foot levers

PEDALFER *n pl.* -S a type of soil

PEDALIER *n pl.* -S the pedal keyboard of an organ

PEDALLED past tense of pedal

PEDALLING present participle of pedal

PEDANT *n pl.* -S one who flaunts his knowledge **PEDANTIC** *adj*

PEDANTRY *n pl.* -RIES ostentatious display of knowledge

PEDATE *adj* resembling a foot **PEDATELY** *adv*

PEDDLE *v* -DLED, -DLING, -DLES to travel about selling wares

PEDDLER *n pl.* -S one that peddles

PEDDLERY *n pl.* -RIES the trade of a peddler

PEDDLING present tense of peddle

PEDERAST *n pl.* -S a man who engages in sexual activities with boys

PEDES *pl.* of pes

PEDESTAL *v* -TALED, -TALING, -TALS or -TALLED, -TALLING, -TALS to provide with an architectural support or base

PEDICAB *n* pl. -S a passenger vehicle that is pedaled

PEDICEL *n* pl. -S a slender basal part of an organism

PEDICLE *n* pl. -S pedicel PEDICLED *adj*

PEDICURE *v* -CURED, -CURING, -CURES to administer a cosmetic treatment to the feet and toenails

PEDIFORM *adj* shaped like a foot

PEDIGREE *n* pl. -S a line of ancestors

PEDIMENT *n* pl. -S a triangular architectural part

PEDIPALP *n* pl. -S an appendage of an arachnid

PEDLAR *n* pl. -S peddler

PEDLARY *n* pl. -LARIES peddlery

PEDLER *n* pl. -S peddler

PEDOCAL *n* pl. -S a type of soil

PEDOLOGY *n* pl. -GIES the scientific study of the behavior and development of children

PEDRO *n* pl. -DROS a card game

PEDUNCLE *n* pl. -S a flower stalk

PEE *v* PEED, PEEING, PEES to urinate — sometimes considered vulgar

PEEBEEN *n* pl. -S an evergreen tree

PEEK *v* -ED, -ING, -S to look furtively or quickly

PEEKABOO *n* pl. -BOOS a children's game

PEEL *v* -ED, -ING, -S to strip off an outer covering of PEELABLE *adj*

PEELER *n* pl. -S one that peels

PEELING *n* pl. -S a piece or strip that has been peeled off

PEEN *v* -ED, -ING, -S to beat with the non-flat end of a hammerhead

PEEP *v* -ED, -ING, -S to utter a short, shrill cry

PEEPER *n* pl. -S one that peeps

PEEPHOLE *n* pl. -S a small opening through which one may look

PEEPSHOW *n* pl. -S an exhibition viewed through a small opening

PEEPUL *n* pl. -S pipal

PEER *v* -ED, -ING, -S to look narrowly or searchingly

PEERAGE *n* pl. -S the rank of a nobleman

PEERESS *n* pl. -ES a noblewoman

PEERIE *n* pl. -S peery

PEERLESS *adj* having no equal

PEERY *n* pl. PEERIES a child's toy

PEESWEEP *n* pl. -S a lapwing

PEETWEET *n* pl. -S a wading bird

PEEVE *v* PEEVED, PEEVING, PEEVES to annoy

PEEVISH *adj* irritable

PEEWEE *n* pl. -S an unusually small person or thing

PEEWIT *n* pl. -S pewit

PEG *v* PEGGED, PEGGING, PEGS to fasten with a peg (a wooden pin)

PEGBOARD *n* pl. -S a board with holes for pegs

PEGBOX *n* pl. -ES a part of a stringed instrument

PEGGED past tense of peg

PEGGING present participle of peg

PEGLESS *adj* lacking a peg

PEGLIKE *adj* resembling a peg

PEIGNOIR *n* pl. -S a woman's gown

PEIN *v* -ED, -ING, -S to peen

PEISE *v* PEISED, PEISING, PEISES to weigh

PEKAN *n* pl. -S a carnivorous mammal

PEKE *n* pl. -S a small, long-haired dog

PEKIN *n* pl. -S a silk fabric

PEKOE *n* pl. -S a black tea

PELAGE *n* pl. -S the coat or covering of a mammal PELAGIAL *adj*

PELAGIC *adj* oceanic

PELE *n* pl. -S a medieval fortified tower

PELERINE *n* pl. -S a woman's cape

PELF *n* pl. -S money or wealth

PELICAN *n* pl. -S a large, web-footed bird

PELISSE *n* pl. -S a long outer garment

PELITE *n* pl. -S a rock composed of fine fragments PELITIC *adj*

PELLAGRA *n* pl. -S a niacin-deficiency disease

PELLET *v* -ED, -ING, -S to strike with pellets (small rounded masses)

PELLETAL *adj* resembling a pellet

PELLICLE *n* pl. -S a thin skin or film

PELLMELL *n* pl. -S a jumbled mass

PELLUCID *adj* transparent

PELON *adj* hairless

PELORIA *n* pl. -S abnormal regularity of a flower form **PELORIAN**, **PELORIC** *adj*

PELORUS *n* pl. -ES a navigational instrument

PELOTA *n* pl. -S a court game of Spanish origin

PELT *v* -ED, -ING, -S to strike repeatedly with blows or missiles

PELTAST *n* pl. -S a soldier of ancient Greece

PELTATE *adj* shaped like a shield

PELTER *n* pl. -S one that pelts

PELTRY *n* pl. -RIES an animal skin

PELVIC *n* pl. -S a bone of the pelvis

PELVIS *n* pl. -VES or -VISES a part of the skeleton

PEMBINA *n* pl. -S a variety of cranberry

PEMICAN *n* pl. -S pemmican

PEMMICAN *n* pl. -S a food prepared by North American Indians

PEMOLINE *n* pl. -S a drug used experimentally to improve memory

PEMPHIX *n* pl. -ES a skin disease

PEN *v* PENNED, PENNING, PENS to write with a pen (an instrument for writing with fluid ink)

PENAL *adj* pertaining to punishment

PENALISE *v* -ISED, -ISING, -ISES to penalize

PENALITY *n* pl. -TIES liability to punishment

PENALIZE *v* -IZED, -IZING, -IZES to subject to a penalty

PENALLY *adv* in a penal manner

PENALTY *n* pl. -TIES a punishment imposed for violation of a law, rule, or agreement

PENANCE *v* -ANCED, -ANCING, -ANCES to impose a type of punishment upon

PENANG *n* pl. -S a cotton fabric

PENATES *n/pl* the Roman gods of the household

PENCE a pl. of penny

PENCEL *n* pl. -S a small flag

PENCHANT *n* pl. -S a strong liking for something

PENCIL *v* -CILED, -CILING, -CILS or -CILLED, -CILLING, -CILS to produce by using a pencil (a writing and drawing implement)

PENCILER *n* pl. -S one that pencils

PEND *v* -ED, -ING, -S to remain undecided or unsettled

PENDANT *n* pl. -S a hanging ornament

PENDENCY *n* pl. -CIES a pending state

PENDENT *n* pl. -S pendant

PENDULUM *n* pl. -S a type of free swinging body **PENDULAR** *adj*

PENES a pl. of penis

PENGO *n* pl. -GOS a former monetary unit of Hungary

PENGUIN *n* pl. -S a flightless, aquatic bird

PENICIL *n* pl. -S a small tuft of hairs

PENIS *n* pl. -NES or -NISES the male organ of copulation **PENIAL**, **PENILE** *adj*

PENITENT *n* pl. -S a person who repents his sins

PENKNIFE *n* pl. -KNIVES a small pocketknife

PENLIGHT *n* pl. -S a small flashlight

PENLITE *n* pl. -S penlight

PENMAN *n* pl. -MEN an author

PENNA *n* pl. -NAE any of the feathers that determine a bird's shape

PENNAME *n* pl. -S a name used by an author instead of his real name

PENNANT *n* pl. -S a long, narrow flag

PENNATE *adj* having wings or feathers

PENNATED *adj* pennate

PENNED past tense of pen

PENNER *n* pl. -S one that pens

PENNI *n* pl. -NIA or -NIS a Finnish coin

PENNIES a pl. of penny

PENNINE *n* pl. -S a mineral

PENNING present participle of pen

PENNON *n* pl. -S a pennant **PENNONED** *adj*

PENNY *n* pl. PENNIES or PENCE a coin of the United Kingdom

PENOCHE *n* pl. -S penuche

PENOLOGY *n* pl. -GIES the science of the punishment of crime

PENONCEL *n* pl. -S a small pennon

PENPOINT *n* pl. -S the point of a pen

PENSEE n pl. -S a thought

PENSIL n pl. -S pencel

PENSILE adj hanging loosely

PENSION v -ED, -ING, -S to grant a retirement allowance to

PENSIONE n pl. -S a boarding house

PENSIVE adj engaged in deep thought

PENSTER n pl. -S a writer

PENSTOCK n pl. - S a conduit for conveying water to a waterwheel

PENT adj confined

PENTACLE n pl. -S a five-pointed star

PENTAD n pl. -S a group of five

PENTAGON n pl. -S a five-sided polygon

PENTANE n pl. -S a volatile liquid

PENTARCH n pl. -S one of five joint rulers

PENTOMIC adj made up of five battle groups

PENTOSAN n pl. -S a complex carbohydrate

PENTOSE n pl. -S a sugar having five carbon atoms per molecule

PENTYL n pl. -S amyl

PENUCHE n pl. -S a fudge-like candy

PENUCHI n pl. -S penuche

PENUCHLE n pl. -S pinochle

PENUCKLE n pl. -S pinochle

PENULT n pl. -S the next to last syllable in a word

PENUMBRA n pl. -BRAE or -BRAS a partial shadow

PENURY n pl. -RIES extreme poverty

PEON n pl. -S or -ES an unskilled laborer

PEONAGE n pl. -S the condition of being a peon

PEONISM n pl. -S peonage

PEONY n pl. -NIES a flowering plant

PEOPLE v -PLED, -PLING, -PLES to furnish with inhabitants

PEOPLER n pl. -S one that peoples

PEP v PEPPED, PEPPING, PEPS to fill with energy

PEPERONI n pl. -S a highly seasoned sausage

PEPLOS n pl. -ES a garment worn by women in ancient Greece

PEPLUM n pl. -LUMS or -LA a short section attached to the waistline of a garment PEPLUMED adj

PEPLUS n pl. -ES peplos

PEPO n pl. -POS a fruit having a fleshy interior and a hard rind

PEPONIDA n pl. -S pepo

PEPONIUM n pl. -S pepo

PEPPED past tense of pep

PEPPER v -ED, -ING, -S to season with pepper (a pungent condiment)

PEPPERER n pl. -S one that peppers

PEPPERY adj resembling pepper

PEPPING present participle of pep

PEPPY adj -PIER, -PIEST full of energy PEPPILY adv

PEPSIN n pl. -S a digestive enzyme of the stomach

PEPSINE n pl. -S pepsin

PEPTIC n pl. -S a substance that promotes digestion

PEPTID n pl. -S peptide

PEPTIDE n pl. -S a combination of amino acids PEPTIDIC adj

PEPTIZE v -TIZED, -TIZING, -TIZES to increase the colloidal dispersion of

PEPTIZER n pl. -S one that peptizes

PEPTONE n pl. -S a protein compound PEPTONIC adj

PER prep for each

PERACID n pl. -S a type of acid

PERCALE n pl. -S a cotton fabric

PERCEIVE v -CEIVED, -CEIVING, -CEIVES to become aware of through the senses

PERCENT n pl. -S one part in a hundred

PERCEPT n pl. -S something that is perceived

PERCH v -ED, -ING, -ES to sit or rest on an elevated place

PERCHER n pl. -S one that perches

PERCOID n pl. -S a spiny-finned fish

PERCUSS v -ED, -ING, -ES to strike with force

PERDIE interj pardi

PERDU n pl. -S a soldier sent on a dangerous mission

PERDUE n pl. -S perdu

PERDY interj pardi

PERE n pl. -S a father

PEREGRIN n pl. -S a swift falcon much used in falconry

PERFECT adj -FECTER, -FECTEST lacking fault or defect; of an extreme kind

PERFECT v -ED, -ING, -S to make perfect

PERFECTA n pl. -S a system of betting

PERFECTO n pl. -TOS a medium-sized cigar

PERFIDY n pl. -DIES deliberate breach of faith or trust

PERFORCE adj of necessity

PERFORM v -ED, -ING, -S to begin and carry through to completion

PERFUME v -FUMED, -FUMING, -FUMES to fill with a fragrant odor

PERFUMER n pl. -S one that perfumes

PERFUSE v -FUSED, -FUSING, -FUSES to spread over or through something

PERGOLA n pl. -S a shaded shelter or passageway

PERHAPS n pl. -ES something open to doubt or conjecture

PERI n pl. -S a supernatural being of Persian mythology

PERIANTH n pl. -S an outer covering of a flower

PERIAPT n pl. -S an amulet

PERIBLEM n pl. -S a region of plant tissue

PERICARP n pl. -S the wall of a ripened plant ovary or fruit

PERICOPE n pl. -PES or -PAE a selection from a book

PERIDERM n pl. -S an outer layer of plant tissue

PERIDIUM n pl. -IA the covering of the spore-bearing organ in many fungi PERIDIAL adj

PERIDOT n pl. -S a mineral

PERIGEE n pl. -S the point in the orbit of a celestial body which is nearest to the earth PERIGEAL, PERIGEAN adj

PERIGON n pl. -S an angle equal to 360 degrees

PERIGYNY n pl. -NIES the state of being situated on a cuplike organ surrounding the pistil

PERIL v -ILED, -ILING, -ILS or -ILLED, -ILLING, -ILS to imperil

PERILLA n pl. -S an Asian herb

PERILOUS adj dangerous

PERILUNE n pl. -S the point in the orbit of a celestial body which is nearest to the moon

PERINEUM n pl. -NEA a region of the body at the lower end of the trunk PERINEAL adj

PERIOD n pl. -S a portion of time

PERIODIC adj recurring at regular intervals

PERIODID n pl. -S an iodide

PERIOTIC adj surrounding the ear

PERIPETY n pl. -TIES a sudden change in a course of events

PERIPTER n pl. -S a structure with a row of columns around all sides

PERIQUE n pl. -S a dark tobacco

PERISARC n pl. -S a protective covering of certain hydrozoans

PERISH v -ED, -ING, -ES to die

PERIWIG n pl. -S a wig

PERJURE v -JURED, -JURING, -JURES to make a perjurer of

PERJURER n pl. -S one guilty of perjury

PERJURY n pl. -RIES the willful giving of false testimony under oath in a judicial proceeding

PERK v -ED, -ING, -S to carry oneself jauntily

PERKISH adj somewhat perky

PERKY adj PERKIER, PERKIEST jaunty PERKILY adv

PERLITE n pl. -S a volcanic glass PERLITIC adj

PERM n pl. -S a long-lasting hair setting

PERMEASE n pl. -S a catalyzing agent

PERMEATE v -ATED, -ATING, -ATES to spread through

PERMIT v -MITTED, -MITTING, -MITS to allow

PERMUTE v -MUTED, -MUTING, -MUTES to change the order of

PERONEAL adj pertaining to the fibula

PERORAL adj occurring through the mouth

PERORATE v -RATED, -RATING, -RATES to make a lengthy speech

PEROXID n pl. -S peroxide

PEROXIDE v -IDED, -IDING, -IDES to treat with peroxide (a bleaching agent)

PERPEND v -ED, -ING, -S to ponder

PERPENT n pl. -S a large building stone

PERPLEX   v -ED, -ING, -ES to make mentally uncertain

PERRON   n pl. -S an outdoor stairway

PERRY   n pl. -RIES a beverage of pear juice often fermented

PERSALT   n pl. -S a chemical salt

PERSE   n pl. -S a blue color

PERSIST   v -ED, -ING, -S to continue resolutely in some activity

PERSON   n pl. -S a human being

PERSONA   n pl. -NAE a character in a literary work

PERSONA   n pl. -S the public role that a person assumes

PERSONAL   n pl. -S a brief, private notice in a newspaper

PERSPIRE   v -SPIRED, -SPIRING, -SPIRES to give off moisture through the pores of the skin **PERSPIRY** adj

PERSUADE   v -SUADED, -SUADING, -SUADES to cause to do something by means of argument, reasoning, or entreaty

PERT   adj PERTER, PERTEST impudent **PERTLY** adv

PERTAIN   v -ED, -ING, -S to have reference or relation

PERTNESS   n pl. -ES the quality of being pert

PERTURB   v -ED, -ING, -S to disturb greatly

PERUKE   n pl. -S a wig

PERUSAL   n pl. -S the act of perusing

PERUSE   v -RUSED, -RUSING, -RUSES to read

PERUSER   n pl. -S one that peruses

PERVADE   v -VADED, -VADING, -VADES to spread through every part of

PERVADER   n pl. -S one that pervades

PERVERSE   adj willfully deviating from desired or expected conduct

PERVERT   v -ED, -ING, -S to turn away from the right course of action

PERVIOUS   adj capable of being penetrated

PES   n pl. PEDES a foot or footlike part

PESADE   n pl. -S the position of a horse when rearing

PESETA   n pl. -S a monetary unit of Spain

PESEWA   n pl. -S a monetary unit of Ghana

PESKY   adj -KIER, -KIEST annoying **PESKILY** adv

PESO   n pl. -SOS a monetary unit of various Spanish-speaking countries

PESSARY   n pl. -RIES a contraceptive device worn in the vagina

PEST   n pl. -S an annoying person or thing

PESTER   v -ED, -ING, -S to bother

PESTERER   n pl. -S one that pesters

PESTHOLE   n pl. -S a place liable to epidemic disease

PESTLE   v -TLED, -TLING, -TLES to crush with a club-shaped hand tool

PET   v PETTED, PETTING, PETS to caress with the hand

PETAL   n pl. -S a leaflike part of a corolla **PETALED, PETALLED** adj

PETALINE   adj resembling a petal

PETALODY   n pl. -DIES the metamorphosis of various floral organs into petals

PETALOID   adj resembling a petal

PETALOUS   adj having petals

PETARD   n pl. -S an explosive device

PETASOS   n pl. -ES petasus

PETASUS   n pl. -ES a broad-brimmed hat worn in ancient Greece

PETCOCK   n pl. -S a small valve or faucet

PETECHIA   n pl. -CHIAE a small hemorrhagic spot on a body surface

PETER   v -ED, -ING, -S to diminish gradually

PETIOLAR   adj pertaining to a petiole

PETIOLE   n pl. -S the stalk of a leaf **PETIOLED** adj

PETIT   adj small; minor

PETITE   n pl. -S a clothing size for short women

PETITION   v -ED, -ING, -S to make a formal request

PETREL   n pl. -S a small seabird

PETRIFY   v -FIED, -FYING, -FIES to convert into stone or a stony substance

PETROL   n pl. -S gasoline

PETROLIC   adj derived from petroleum

PETRONEL   n pl. -S a portable firearm

PETROSAL	*adj* petrous	**PHALLIST**	*n* pl. -S one who practices phallism
PETROUS	*adj* resembling stone in hardness	**PHALLUS**	*n* pl. -LI or -LUSES the penis
PETTED	past tense of pet	**PHANTASIED** past tense of phantasy	
PETTEDLY	*adv* peevishly	**PHANTASIES** present 3d person sing. of phantasy	
PETTER	*n* pl. -S one that pets		
PETTI	pl. of petto	**PHANTASM**	*n* pl. -S a creation of the imagination
PETTIER	comparative of petty	**PHANTAST**	*n* pl. -S fantast
PETTIEST	superlative of petty	**PHANTASY**	*v* -SIED, -SYING, -SIES to fantasy
PETTIFOG	*v* -FOGGED, -FOGGING, -FOGS to quibble		
PETTILY	*adv* in a petty manner	**PHANTOM**	*n* pl. -S something existing in appearance only
PETTING	present participle of pet	**PHARAOH**	*n* pl. -S a ruler of ancient Egypt
PETTISH	*adj* peevish	**PHARISEE**	*n* pl. -S a hypocritically self-righteous person
PETTLE	*v* -TLED, -TLING, -TLES to caress		
PETTO	*n* pl. -TI the breast	**PHARMACY**	*n* pl. -CIES a drugstore
PETTY	*adj* -TIER, -TIEST insignificant	**PHAROS**	*n* pl. -ES a lighthouse or beacon to guide seamen
PETULANT	*adj* peevish	**PHARYNX**	*n* pl. -YNGES or -YNXES a section of the digestive tract
PETUNIA	*n* pl. -S a tropical herb		
PETUNTSE	*n* pl. -S a mineral	**PHASE**	*v* PHASED, PHASING, PHASES to plan or carry out by phases (distinct stages of development) PHASEAL, PHASIC *adj*
PETUNTZE	*n* pl. -S petuntse		
PEW	*n* pl. -S a bench for seating people in church		
PEWEE	*n* pl. -S a small bird	**PHASEOUT**	*n* pl. -S a gradual stopping of operations
PEWIT	*n* pl. -S the lapwing	**PHASIS**	*n* pl. PHASES a phase
PEWTER	*n* pl. -S a tin alloy	**PHASMID**	*n* pl. -S a tropical insect
PEWTERER	*n* pl. -S one that makes articles of pewter	**PHAT**	*adj* susceptible of easy and rapid typesetting
PEYOTE	*n* pl. -S a cactus	**PHATIC**	*adj* sharing feelings rather than ideas
PEYOTL	*n* pl. -S peyote		
PEYTRAL	*n* pl. -S a piece of armor for the breast of a horse	**PHEASANT**	*n* pl. -S a large, long-tailed bird
PEYTREL	*n* pl. -S peytral	**PHELLEM**	*n* pl. -S a layer of plant cells
PFENNIG	*n* pl. -NIGS or -NIGE a bronze coin of Germany	**PHELONIA**	*n/pl* liturgical vestments
		PHENAZIN	*n* pl. -S a chemical compound
PHAETON	*n* pl. -S a light carriage	**PHENETIC**	*adj* pertaining to a type of classificatory system
PHAGE	*n* pl. -S an organism that destroys bacteria		
		PHENETOL	*n* pl. -S a volatile liquid
PHALANGE	*n* pl. -S any bone of a finger or toe	**PHENIX**	*n* pl. -ES phoenix
		PHENOL	*n* pl. -S a caustic compound
PHALANX	*n* pl. -ES a formation of infantry in ancient Greece	**PHENOLIC**	*n* pl. -S a synthetic resin
		PHENOM	*n* pl. -S a person of extraordinary ability or promise
PHALLI	a pl. of phallus		
PHALLIC	*adj* pertaining to a phallus	**PHENYL**	*n* pl. -S a univalent chemical radical PHENYLIC *adj*
PHALLISM	*n* pl. -S worship of the phallus as symbolic of nature's creative power		
		PHEW	*interj* — used to express relief, fatigue, or disgust
		PHI	*n* pl. -S a Greek letter

PHIAL   n pl. -S a vial

PHILABEG   n pl. -S filibeg

PHILIBEG   n pl. -S filibeg

PHILOMEL   n pl. -S a songbird

PHILTER   v -ED, -ING, -S to put under the spell of a love potion

PHILTRE   v -TRED, -TRING, -TRES to philter

PHIMOSIS   n pl. -MOSES the abnormal constriction of the opening of the prepuce PHIMOTIC adj

PHIZ   n pl. -ES a face or facial expression

PHLEGM   n pl. -S a thick mucus secreted in the air passages

PHLEGMY   adj PHLEGMIER, PHLEGMIEST resembling phlegm

PHLOEM   n pl. -S a complex plant tissue

PHLOX   n pl. -ES a flowering plant

PHOBIA   n pl. -S an obsessive or irrational fear PHOBIC adj

PHOCINE   adj pertaining to seals

PHOEBE   n pl. -S a small bird

PHOENIX   n pl. -ES a mythical bird

PHON   n pl. -S a unit of loudness

PHONAL   adj pertaining to speech sounds

PHONATE   v -NATED, -NATING, -NATES to produce speech sounds

PHONE   v PHONED, PHONING, PHONES to telephone

PHONEME   n pl. -S a unit of speech PHONEMIC adj

PHONETIC   adj pertaining to speech sounds

PHONEY   adj -NIER, -NIEST phony

PHONEY   n pl. -NEYS a phony

PHONIC   adj pertaining to the nature of sound

PHONICS   n/pl the science of sound

PHONIER   comparative of phoney and phony

PHONIES   pl. of phony

PHONIEST   superlative of phoney and phony

PHONILY   adv in a phony manner

PHONING   present participle of phone

PHONO   n pl. -NOS a record player

PHONON   n pl. -S a quantum of vibrational energy

PHONY   adj -NIER, -NIEST not genuine or real

PHONY   n pl. -NIES one that is phony

PHOOEY   interj — used as an exclamation of disgust or contempt

PHORATE   n pl. -S an insecticide

PHOSGENE   n pl. -S a poisonous gas

PHOSPHID   n pl. -S a chemical compound

PHOSPHIN   n pl. -S a poisonous gas

PHOSPHOR   n pl. -S a substance that will emit light when exposed to radiation

PHOT   n pl. -S a unit of illumination

PHOTIC   adj pertaining to light

PHOTICS   n/pl the science of light

PHOTO   v -ED, -ING, -S to photograph

PHOTOG   n pl. -S one who takes photographs

PHOTOMAP   v -MAPPED, -MAPPING, -MAPS to map by means of aerial photography

PHOTON   n pl. -S a quantum of radiant energy PHOTONIC adj

PHOTOPIA   n pl. -S vision in bright light PHOTOPIC adj

PHOTOSET   v -SET, -SETTING, -SETS to prepare for printing by photographic means

PHPHT   interj pht

PHRASAL   adj pertaining to a group of two or more associated words

PHRASE   v PHRASED, PHRASING, PHRASES to express in words

PHRASING   n pl. -S manner or style of verbal expression

PHRATRY   n pl. -TRIES a tribal unit among primitive peoples PHRATRAL, PHRATRIC adj

PHREATIC   adj pertaining to underground waters

PHRENIC   adj pertaining to the mind

PHRENSY   v -SIED, -SYING, -SIES to frenzy

PHT   interj — used as an expression of mild anger or annoyance

PHTHALIC   adj pertaining to a certain acid

PHTHALIN   n pl. -S a chemical compound

PHTHISIC   n pl. -S phthisis

PHTHISIS   n pl. PHTHISES a disease of the lungs

PHYLA   pl. of phylon and phylum

PHYLAE pl. of phyle

PHYLAR *adj* pertaining to a phylum

PHYLAXIS *n* pl. -AXISES an inhibiting of infection by the body

PHYLE *n* pl. -LAE a political subdivision in ancient Greece **PHYLIC** *adj*

PHYLESIS *n* pl. -LESES or -LESISES the course of evolutionary development **PHYLETIC** *adj*

PHYLLARY *n* pl. -RIES a bract of certain plants

PHYLLITE *n* pl. -S a foliated rock

PHYLLODE *n* pl. -S a flattened petiole that serves as a leaf

PHYLLOID *n* pl. -S a leaflike plant part

PHYLLOME *n* pl. -S a leaf of a plant

PHYLON *n* pl. -LA a genetically related group

PHYLUM *n* pl. -LA a taxonomic division

PHYSES pl. of physis

PHYSIC *v* -ICKED, -ICKING, -ICS to treat with medicine

PHYSICAL *n* pl. -S a medical examination of the body

PHYSIQUE *n* pl. -S the form or structure of the body

PHYSIS *n* pl. PHYSES the principle of growth or change in nature

PHYTANE *n* pl. -S a chemical compound

PHYTIN *n* pl. -S a chemical salt

PHYTOID *adj* resembling a plant

PHYTON *n* pl. -S a structural unit of a plant **PHYTONIC** *adj*

PI *n* pl. -S a Greek letter

PI *v* PIED, PIEING or PIING, PIES to jumble or disorder

PIA *n* pl. -S a membrane of the brain

PIACULAR *adj* atoning

PIAFFE *v* PIAFFED, PIAFFING, PIAFFES to perform a piaffer

PIAFFER *n* pl. -S a movement in horsemanship

PIAL *adj* pertaining to a pia

PIAN *n* pl. -S a tropical disease **PIANIC** *adj*

PIANISM *n* pl. -S performance on the piano

PIANIST *n* pl. -S one who plays the piano

PIANO *n* pl. -NOS a musical instrument

PIASABA *n* pl. -S piassava

PIASAVA *n* pl. -S piassava

PIASSABA *n* pl. -S piassava

PIASSAVA *n* pl. -S a coarse, stiff fiber

PIASTER *n* pl. -S a monetary unit of several Arab countries

PIASTRE *n* pl. -S piaster

PIAZZA *n* pl. -ZAS or -ZE a public square in an Italian town

PIBROCH *n* pl. -S a musical piece played on the bagpipe

PIC *n* pl. -S a photograph

PICA *n* pl. -S a craving for unnatural food

PICACHO *n* pl. -CHOS an isolated peak of a hill

PICADOR *n* pl. -ES or -S a horseman in a bullfight

PICAL *adj* resembling a pica

PICARA *n* pl. -S a female picaro

PICARO *n* pl. -ROS a vagabond

PICAROON *v* -ED, -ING, -S to act as a pirate

PICAYUNE *n* pl. -S a former Spanish-American coin

PICCOLO *n* pl. -LOS a small flute

PICE *n* pl. PICE a former coin of India and Pakistan

PICEOUS *adj* glossy-black in color

PICK *v* -ED, -ING, -S to select

PICKADIL *n* pl. -S a type of collar

PICKAX *v* -ED, -ING, -ES to use a pickax (a tool for breaking hard surfaces)

PICKAXE *v* -AXED, -AXING, -AXES to pickax

PICKEER *v* -ED, -ING, -S to skirmish in advance of an army

PICKER *n* pl. -S one that picks

PICKEREL *n* pl. -S a freshwater fish

PICKET *v* -ED, -ING, -ES to stand outside of some location, as a business, to publicize one's grievances against it

PICKETER *n* pl. -S one who pickets

PICKIER comparative of picky

PICKIEST superlative of picky

PICKING *n* pl. -S the act of one that picks

PICKLE v -LED, -LING, -LES to preserve or flavor in a solution of brine or vinegar

PICKLOCK n pl. -S a tool for opening locks

PICKOFF n pl. -S a play in baseball

PICKUP n pl. -S a small truck

PICKWICK n pl. -S a device for raising wicks in oil lamps

PICKY adj PICKIER, PICKIEST fussy

PICLORAM n pl. -S an herbicide

PICNIC v -NICKED, -NICKING, -NICS to go on a picnic (an outdoor excursion with food)

PICNICKY adj pertaining to a picnic

PICOGRAM n pl. -S one trillionth of a gram

PICOLIN n pl. -S picoline

PICOLINE n pl. -S a chemical compound

PICOT v -ED, -ING, -S to edge with ornamental loops

PICOTEE n pl. -S a variety of carnation

PICQUET n pl. -S piquet

PICRATE n pl. -S a chemical salt
PICRATED adj

PICRIC adj having a very bitter taste

PICRITE n pl. -S an igneous rock

PICTURE v -TURED, -TURING, -TURES to make a visual representation of

PICUL n pl. -S an Asian unit of weight

PIDDLE v -DLED, -DLING, -DLES to waste time

PIDDLER n pl. -S one that piddles

PIDDOCK n pl. -S a bivalve mollusk

PIDGIN n pl. -S a mixed language

PIE v PIED, PIEING, PIES to pi

PIEBALD n pl. -S a spotted animal

PIECE v PIECED, PIECING, PIECES to join into a whole

PIECER n pl. -S one that pieces

PIECING n pl. -S material to be sewn together

PIECRUST n pl. -S the crust of a pie

PIED past tense of pie

PIEDFORT n pl. -S piefort

PIEDMONT n pl. -S an area lying at the foot of a mountain

PIEFORT n pl. -S an unusually thick coin

PIEING a present participle of pi

PIEPLANT n pl. -S a rhubarb

PIER n pl. -S a structure extending from land out over water

PIERCE v PIERCED, PIERCING, PIERCES to cut or pass into or through

PIERCER n pl. -S one that pierces

PIERROT n pl. -S a clown

PIETA n pl. -S a representation of the Virgin Mary mourning over the body of Christ

PIETIES pl. of piety

PIETISM n pl. -S piety

PIETIST n pl. -S a pious person

PIETY n pl. -TIES the quality or state of being pious

PIFFLE v -FLED, -FLING, -FLES to babble

PIG v PIGGED, PIGGING, PIGS to bear pigs (cloven-hoofed mammals)

PIGBOAT n pl. -S a submarine

PIGEON n pl. -S a short-legged bird

PIGFISH n pl. -ES a marine fish

PIGGED past tense of pig

PIGGERY n pl. -GERIES a pigpen

PIGGIE n pl. -S piggy

PIGGIES pl. of piggy

PIGGIN n pl. -S a small wooden pail

PIGGING present participle of pig

PIGGISH adj greedy or dirty

PIGGY n pl. -GIES a small pig

PIGLET n pl. -S a small pig

PIGMENT v -ED, -ING, -S to add a coloring matter to

PIGMY n pl. -MIES pygmy

PIGNUS n pl. -NORA property held as security for a debt

PIGNUT n pl. -S a hickory nut

PIGPEN n pl. -S a place where pigs are kept

PIGSKIN n pl. -S the skin of a pig

PIGSNEY n pl. -NEYS a darling

PIGSTICK v -ED, -ING, -S to hunt for wild boar

PIGSTY n pl. -STIES a pigpen

PIGTAIL n pl. -S a tight braid of hair

PIGWEED n pl. -S a weedy plant

PIKA n pl. -S a small mammal

PIKAKE n pl. -S an East Indian vine

PIKE   v PIKED, PIKING, PIKES to pierce with a pike (a long spear)

PIKEMAN   n pl. -MEN a soldier armed with a pike

PIKER   n pl. -S a stingy person

PIKING   present participle of pike

PILAF   n pl. -S a dish made of seasoned rice and often meat

PILAFF   n pl. -S pilaf

PILAR   adj pertaining to hair

PILASTER   n pl. -S a rectangular column

PILAU   n pl. -S pilaf

PILAW   n pl. -S pilaf

PILCHARD   n pl. -S a small marine fish

PILE   v PILED, PILING, PILES to lay one upon the other

PILEA   pl. of pileum

PILEATE   adj having a pileus

PILEATED   adj pileate

PILED   past tense of pile

PILEI   pl. of pileus

PILEOUS   adj pilose

PILEUM   n pl. -LEA the top of a bird's head

PILEUP   n pl. -S a collision involving several motor vehicles

PILEUS   n pl. -LEI the umbrella-shaped portion of a mushroom

PILEWORT   n pl. -S a medicinal plant

PILFER   v -ED, -ING, -S to steal

PILFERER   n pl. -S one that pilfers

PILGRIM   n pl. -S a traveler or wanderer

PILI   n pl. -S a Philippine tree

PILIFORM   adj resembling a hair

PILING   n pl. -S a structure of building supports

PILL   v -ED, -ING, -S to dose with pills (small, rounded masses of medicine)

PILLAGE   v -LAGED, -LAGING, -LAGES to plunder

PILLAGER   n pl. -S one that pillages

PILLAR   v -ED, -ING, -S to provide with vertical building supports

PILLBOX   n pl. -ES a small box for pills

PILLION   n pl. -S a pad or cushion for an extra rider on a horse or motorcycle

PILLORY   v -RIED, -RYING, -RIES to expose to public ridicule or abuse

PILLOW   v -ED, -ING, -S to rest on a pillow (a cushion for the head)

PILLOWY   adj resembling a pillow

PILOSE   adj covered with hair

PILOSITY   n pl. -TIES the state of being pilose

PILOT   v -ED, -ING, -S to control the course of

PILOTAGE   n pl. -S the act of piloting

PILOTING   n pl. -S a branch of navigation

PILOUS   adj pilose

PILSENER   n pl. -S pilsner

PILSNER   n pl. -S a light beer

PILULE   n pl. -S a small pill PILULAR adj

PILUS   n pl. -LI a hair or hairlike structure

PILY   adj divided into a number of wedge-shaped heraldic designs

PIMA   n pl. -S a strong, high-grade cotton

PIMENTO   n pl. -TOS pimiento

PIMIENTO   n pl. -TOS a sweet pepper

PIMP   v -ED, -ING, -S to solicit clients for a prostitute

PIMPLE   n pl. -S an inflamed swelling of the skin PIMPLED adj

PIMPLY   adj -PLIER, -PLIEST covered with pimples

PIN   v PINNED, PINNING, PINS to fasten with a pin (a slender, pointed piece of metal)

PINA   n pl. -S a pineapple

PINAFORE   n pl. -S a child's apron

PINANG   n pl. -S a palm tree

PINASTER   n pl. -S a pine tree

PINATA   n pl. -S a pottery jar used in a Mexican game

PINBALL   n pl. -S an electric game

PINBONE   n pl. -S the hipbone

PINCER   n pl. -S one of the two pivoted parts of a grasping tool

PINCH   v -ED, -ING, -ES to squeeze between two edges or surfaces

PINCHBUG   n pl. -S a large beetle

PINCHECK   n pl. -S a fabric design

PINCHER   n pl. -S one that pinches

PINDER	*n* pl. -S an official who formerly impounded stray animals
PINDLING	*adj* puny or sickly
PINE	*v* PINED, PINING, PINES to yearn intensely
PINEAL	*adj* shaped like a pinecone
PINECONE	*n* pl. -S a cone-shaped fruit of a pine tree
PINED	past tense of pine
PINELIKE	*adj* resembling a pine (an evergreen tree)
PINENE	*n* pl. -S the main constituent of turpentine
PINERY	*n* pl. -ERIES an area where pineapples are grown
PINESAP	*n* pl. -S a fragrant herb
PINETUM	*n* pl. -TA a plantation of pine trees
PINEWOOD	*n* pl. -S the wood of a pine tree
PINEY	*adj* PINIER, PINIEST piny
PINFISH	*n* pl. -ES a small marine fish
PINFOLD	*v* -ED, -ING, -S to confine in an enclosure for stray animals
PING	*v* -ED, -ING, -S to produce a brief, high-pitched sound
PINGER	*n* pl. -S a device for producing pulses of sound
PINGO	*n* pl. -GOS a hill forced up by the effects of frost
PINGRASS	*n* pl. -ES a European weed
PINGUID	*adj* greasy
PINHEAD	*n* pl. -S the head of a pin
PINHOLE	*n* pl. -S a small hole made by a pin
PINIER	comparative of piney and piny
PINIEST	superlative of piney and piny
PINING	present participle of pine
PINION	*v* -ED, -ING, -S to remove or bind the wing feathers of to prevent flight
PINITE	*n* pl. -S a mineral
PINK	*adj* PINKER, PINKEST of a pale reddish hue
PINK	*v* -ED, -ING, -S to stab with a pointed weapon
PINKEYE	*n* pl. -S an inflammation of the eye
PINKIE	*n* pl. -S the little finger
PINKIES	pl. of pinky
PINKING	*n* pl. -S a method of cutting or decorating
PINKISH	*adj* somewhat pink
PINKLY	*adv* with a pink hue
PINKNESS	*n* pl. -ES the state of being pink
PINKO	*n* pl. PINKOS or PINKOES a person who holds somewhat radical political views
PINKROOT	*n* pl. -S a medicinal plant root
PINKY	*n* pl. PINKIES pinkie
PINNA	*n* pl. -NAE or -NAS a feather, wing, or winglike part
PINNACE	*n* pl. -S a small sailing ship
PINNACLE	*v* -CLED, -CLING, -CLES to place on a summit
PINNAE	a pl. of pinna
PINNAL	*adj* pertaining to a pinna
PINNATE	*adj* resembling a feather
PINNATED	*adj* pinnate
PINNED	past tense of pin
PINNER	*n* pl. -S one that pins
PINNING	present participle of pin
PINNIPED	*n* pl. -S a mammal with limbs modified into flippers
PINNULA	*n* pl. -LAE pinnule **PINNULAR** *adj*
PINNULE	*n* pl. -S a pinnate part or organ
PINOCHLE	*n* pl. -S a card game
PINOCLE	*n* pl. -S pinochle
PINOLE	*n* pl. -S a finely ground flour
PINON	*n* pl. -S or -ES a pine tree
PINPOINT	*v* -ED, -ING, -S to locate precisely
PINPRICK	*v* -ED, -ING, -S to puncture with a pin
PINSCHER	*n* pl. -S a large, short-haired dog
PINT	*n* pl. -S a liquid and dry measure of capacity
PINTA	*n* pl. -S a skin disease
PINTADA	*n* pl. -S pintado
PINTADO	*n* pl. -DOS or -DOES a large food fish
PINTAIL	*n* pl. -S a river duck
PINTANO	*n* pl. -NOS a tropical fish
PINTLE	*n* pl. -S a pin on which something turns
PINTO	*n* pl. -TOS or -TOES a spotted horse

PINTSIZE *adj* small

PINUP *n pl.* -S a picture that may be pinned up on a wall

PINWALE *n pl.* -S a type of fabric

PINWEED *n pl.* -S a perennial herb

PINWHEEL *n pl.* -S a child's toy resembling a windmill

PINWORK *n pl.* -S a type of embroidery

PINWORM *n pl.* -S a parasitic worm

PINY *adj* PINIER, PINIEST suggestive of or covered with pine trees

PINYON *n pl.* -S pinon

PIOLET *n pl.* -S an ice ax

PION *n pl.* -S an atomic particle PIONIC *adj*

PIONEER *v* -ED, -ING, -S to take part in the beginnings of

PIOSITY *n pl.* -TIES an excessive show of piety

PIOUS *adj* marked by religious reverence PIOUSLY *adv*

PIP *v* PIPPED, PIPPING, PIPS to break through the shell of an egg

PIPAGE *n pl.* -S a system of pipes

PIPAL *n pl.* -S a fig tree of India

PIPE *v* PIPED, PIPING, PIPES to convey by means of a pipe (a hollow cylinder)

PIPEAGE *n pl.* -S pipage

PIPEFISH *n pl.* -ES a slender fish

PIPEFUL *n pl.* -S a quantity sufficient to fill a tobacco pipe

PIPELESS *adj* having no pipe

PIPELIKE *adj* resembling a pipe

PIPELINE *v* -LINED, -LINING, -LINES to convey by a line of pipe

PIPER *n pl.* -S one that plays on a tubular musical instrument

PIPERINE *n pl.* -S a chemical compound

PIPESTEM *n pl.* -S the stem of a tobacco pipe

PIPET *v* -PETTED, -PETTING, -PETS to pipette

PIPETTE *v* -PETTED, -PETTING, -PETTES to measure liquid with a calibrated tube

PIPIER comparative of pipy

PIPIEST superlative of pipy

PIPING *n pl.* -S a system of pipes

PIPINGLY *adv* shrilly

PIPIT *n pl.* -S a songbird

PIPKIN *n pl.* -S a small pot

PIPPED past tense of pip

PIPPIN *n pl.* -S any of several varieties of apple

PIPPING present participle of pip

PIPY *adj* PIPIER, PIPIEST shrill

PIQUANCY *n pl.* -CIES the quality of being piquant

PIQUANT *adj* having an agreeably sharp taste

PIQUE *v* PIQUED, PIQUING, PIQUES to arouse anger or resentment in

PIQUET *n pl.* -S a card game

PIRACY *n pl.* -CIES robbery on the high seas

PIRAGUA *n pl.* -S a dugout canoe

PIRANA *n pl.* -S piranha

PIRANHA *n pl.* -S a voracious fish

PIRARUCU *n pl.* -S a large food fish

PIRATE *v* -RATED, -RATING, -RATES to commit piracy

PIRATIC *adj* pertaining to piracy

PIRAYA *n pl.* -S piranha

PIRN *n pl.* -S a spinning-wheel bobbin

PIROG *n pl.* -ROGEN, -ROGHI or -ROGI a large Russian pastry

PIROGUE *n pl.* -S piragua

PIROQUE *n pl.* -S piragua

PIROZHOK *n pl.* -ROZHKI, -ROSHKI or -ROJKI a small Russian pastry

PISCARY *n pl.* -RIES a place for fishing

PISCATOR *n pl.* -S a fisherman

PISCINA *n pl.* -NAE or -NAS a basin used in certain church ceremonies PISCINAL *adj*

PISCINE *adj* pertaining to fish

PISH *v* -ED, -ING, -ES to express contempt

PISIFORM *n pl.* -S a small bone of the wrist

PISMIRE *n pl.* -S an ant

PISOLITE *n pl.* -S a limestone

PISS *v* -ED, -ING, -ES to urinate — sometimes considered vulgar

PISSANT *n pl.* -S an ant

PISSOIR *n pl.* -S a public urinal

PISTACHE   n pl. -S a shade of green

PISTIL   n pl. -S the seed-bearing organ of flowering plants

PISTOL   v -TOLED, -TOLING, -TOLS or -TOLLED, -TOLLING, -TOLS to shoot with a small firearm

PISTOLE   n pl. -S a former European gold coin

PISTON   n pl. -S a part of an engine

PIT   v PITTED, PITTING, PITS to mark with cavities or depressions

PITA   n pl. -S a strong fiber

PITAPAT   v -PATTED, -PATTING, -PATS to make a repeated tapping sound

PITCH   v -ED, -ING, -ES to throw

PITCHER   n pl. -S a container for holding and pouring liquids

PITCHIER   comparative of pitchy

PITCHIEST   superlative of pitchy

PITCHILY   adv in a very dark manner

PITCHMAN   n pl. -MEN a salesman of small wares

PITCHOUT   n pl. -S a type of pitch in baseball

PITCHY   adj PITCHIER, PITCHIEST tarry

PITEOUS   adj pitiful

PITFALL   n pl. -S a hidden danger or difficulty

PITH   v -ED, -ING, -S to sever the spinal cord of

PITHEAD   n pl. -S a mine entrance

PITHLESS   adj lacking force

PITHY   adj PITHIER, PITHIEST concise PITHILY adv

PITIABLE   adj pitiful PITIABLY adv

PITIED   past tense of pity

PITIER   n pl. -S one that pities

PITIES   present 3d person sing. of pity

PITIFUL   adj -FULLER, -FULLEST arousing pity

PITILESS   adj having no pity

PITMAN   n pl. -MEN a mine worker

PITMAN   n pl. -S a connecting rod

PITON   n pl. -S a metal spike used in mountain climbing

PITSAW   n pl. -S a large saw for cutting logs

PITTANCE   n pl. -S a small allowance of money

PITTED   past tense of pit

PITTING   n pl. -S an arrangement of cavities or depressions

PITY   v PITIED, PITYING, PITIES to feel pity (sorrow aroused by another's misfortune)

PIU   adv more — used as a musical direction

PIVOT   v -ED, -ING, -S to turn on a shaft or rod

PIVOTAL   adj critically important

PIX   n pl. -ES pyx

PIXIE   n pl. -S pixy PIXIEISH adj

PIXINESS   n pl. -ES the state of being playfully mischievous

PIXY   n pl. PIXIES a playfully mischievous fairy or elf PIXYISH adj

PIZAZZ   n pl. -ES the quality of being exciting or attractive

PIZZA   n pl. -S an Italian open pie

PIZZERIA   n pl. -S a place where pizzas are made and sold

PIZZLE   n pl. -S the penis of an animal

PLACABLE   adj capable of being placated PLACABLY adv

PLACARD   v -ED, -ING, -S to publicize by means of posters

PLACATE   v -CATED, -CATING, -CATES to soothe or mollify

PLACATER   n pl. -S one that placates

PLACE   v PLACED, PLACING, PLACES to set in a particular position

PLACEBO   n pl. -BOS or -BOES a substance containing no medication that is given for its psychological effect

PLACEMAN   n pl. -MEN a political appointee to a public office

PLACENTA   n pl. -TAS or -TAE a vascular organ in most mammals

PLACER   n pl. -S one that places

PLACET   n pl. -S a vote of assent

PLACID   adj calm or peaceful PLACIDLY adv

PLACING   present participle of place

PLACK   n pl. -S a former coin of Scotland

PLACKET   n pl. -S a slit in a garment

PLACOID   n pl. -S a fish having platelike scales

PLAFOND   *n* pl. -S an elaborately decorated ceiling

PLAGAL   *adj* designating a medieval musical mode

PLAGE   *n* pl. -S a bright region on the sun

PLAGIARY   *n* pl. -RIES the act of passing off another's work as one's own

PLAGUE   *v* PLAGUED, PLAGUING, PLAGUES to harass or torment

PLAGUER   *n* pl. -S one that plagues

PLAGUEY   *adj* plaguy

PLAGUING   present participle of plague

PLAGUY   *adj* troublesome PLAGUILY *adv*

PLAICE   *n* pl. -S a European flatfish

PLAID   *n* pl. -S a woolen scarf of a checkered pattern PLAIDED *adj*

PLAIN   *adj* PLAINER, PLAINEST evident PLAINLY *adv*

PLAIN   *v* -ED, -ING, -S to complain

PLAINT   *n* pl. -S a complaint

PLAISTER   *v* -ED, -ING, -S to plaster

PLAIT   *v* -ED, -ING, -S to braid

PLAITER   *n* pl. -S one that plaits

PLAITING   *n* pl. -S something that is plaited

PLAN   *v* PLANNED, PLANNING, PLANS to formulate a plan (a method for achieving an end)

PLANAR   *adj* flat

PLANARIA   *n* pl. -S an aquatic flatworm

PLANATE   *adj* having a flat surface

PLANCH   *n* pl. -ES a plank

PLANCHE   *n* pl. -S a planch

PLANCHET   *n* pl. -S a flat piece of metal for stamping into a coin

PLANE   *v* PLANED, PLANING, PLANES to make smooth or even

PLANER   *n* pl. -S one that planes

PLANET   *n* pl. -S a celestial body

PLANFORM   *n* pl. -S the contour of an object as viewed from above

PLANGENT   *adj* resounding loudly

PLANING   present participle of plane

PLANISH   *v* -ED, -ING, -ES to toughen and smooth by hammering lightly

PLANK   *v* -ED, -ING, -S to cover with planks (long, flat pieces of lumber)

PLANKING   *n* pl. -S covering made of planks

PLANKTER   *n* pl. -S any organism that is an element of plankton

PLANKTON   *n* pl. -S the minute animal and plant life of a body of water

PLANLESS   *adj* having no plan

PLANNED   past tense of plan

PLANNER   *n* pl. -S one that plans

PLANNING   *n* pl. -S the establishment of goals or policies

PLANOSOL   *n* pl. -S a type of soil

PLANT   *v* -ED, -ING, -S to place in the ground for growing

PLANTAIN   *n* pl. -S a short-stemmed herb

PLANTAR   *adj* pertaining to the sole of the foot

PLANTER   *n* pl. -S one that plants

PLANTING   *n* pl. -S an area where plants are grown

PLANULA   *n* pl. -LAE the free-swimming larva of certain organisms PLANULAR *adj*

PLAQUE   *n* pl. -S an ornamental plate or disk

PLASH   *v* -ED, -ING, -ES to weave together

PLASHER   *n* pl. -S one that plashes

PLASHY   *adj* PLASHIER, PLASHIEST marshy

PLASM   *n* pl. -S plasma

PLASMA   *n* pl. -S the liquid part of blood PLASMIC *adj*

PLASMID   *n* pl. -S a hereditary structure of a cell

PLASMIN   *n* pl. -S an enzyme

PLASMOID   *n* pl. -S a type of high energy particle

PLASMON   *n* pl. -S a determinant of inheritance believed to exist in cells

PLASTER   *v* -ED, -ING, -S to cover with plaster (a mixture of lime, sand, and water)

PLASTERY   *adj* resembling plaster

PLASTIC   *n* pl. -S any of a group of synthetic or natural moldable materials

PLASTID   *n* pl. -S a structure in plant cells

PLASTRON   *n* pl. -S a part of the shell of a turtle PLASTRAL *adj*

PLASTRUM   *n* pl. -S plastron

PLAT   *v* PLATTED, PLATTING, PLATS to plait

PLATAN   *n* pl. -S a large tree

PLATANE   *n* pl. -S platan

PLATE   *v* PLATED, PLATING, PLATES to coat with a thin layer of metal

PLATEAU   *n* pl. -TEAUS or -TEAUX a level stretch of elevated land

PLATEAU   *v* -ED, -ING, -S to reach a period or condition of stability

PLATED   past tense of plate

PLATEFUL   *n* pl. PLATEFULS or PLATESFUL the quantity that fills a plate (a shallow dish)

PLATELET   *n* pl. -S a small, flattened body

PLATEN   *n* pl. -S the roller of a typewriter

PLATER   *n* pl. -S one that plates

PLATESFUL   a pl. of plateful

PLATFORM   *n* pl. -S a raised floor or flat surface

PLATIER   comparative of platy

PLATIES   a pl. of platy

PLATIEST   superlative of platy

PLATINA   *n* pl. -S platinum

PLATING   *n* pl. -S a thin layer of metal

PLATINIC   *adj* pertaining to platinum

PLATINUM   *n* pl. -S a metallic element

PLATONIC   *adj* purely spiritual and free from sensual desire

PLATOON   *v* -ED, -ING, -S to alternate with another player at the same position

PLATTED   past tense of plat

PLATTER   *n* pl. -S a large, shallow dish

PLATTING   present participle of plat

PLATY   *adj* PLATIER, PLATIEST split into thin, flat pieces

PLATY   *n* pl. PLATYS or PLATIES a small tropical fish

PLATYPUS   *n* pl. -PUSES or -PI an aquatic mammal

PLAUDIT   *n* pl. -S an expression of praise

PLAUSIVE   *adj* expressing praise

PLAY   *v* -ED, -ING, -S to engage in amusement or sport PLAYABLE *adj*

PLAYA   *n* pl. -S the bottom of a desert basin

PLAYACT   *v* -ED, -ING, -S to take part in a theatrical performance

PLAYBACK   *n* pl. -S the act of replaying a newly made recording

PLAYBILL   *n* pl. -S a program for a theatrical performance

PLAYBOOK   *n* pl. -S a book containing one or more literary works for the stage

PLAYBOY   *n* pl. -BOYS a man devoted to pleasurable activities

PLAYDAY   *n* pl. -DAYS a holiday

PLAYDOWN   *n* pl. -S a playoff

PLAYER   *n* pl. -S one that plays

PLAYFUL   *adj* frolicsome

PLAYGIRL   *n* pl. -S a female playboy

PLAYGOER   *n* pl. -S one who attends the theater

PLAYLAND   *n* pl. -S a recreational area

PLAYLESS   *adj* lacking playfulness

PLAYLET   *n* pl. -S a short theatrical performance

PLAYLIKE   *adj* resembling a theatrical performance

PLAYMATE   *n* pl. -S a companion in play

PLAYOFF   *n* pl. -S a series of games played to determine a championship

PLAYPEN   *n* pl. -S an enclosure in which a young child may play

PLAYROOM   *n* pl. -S a recreation room

PLAYSUIT   *n* pl. -S a sports outfit for women and children

PLAYTIME   *n* pl. -S a time for play or amusement

PLAYWEAR   *n* pl. -S clothing worn for leisure activities

PLAZA   *n* pl. -S a public square

PLEA   *n* pl. -S an entreaty

PLEACH   *v* -ED, -ING, -ES to weave together

PLEAD   *v* PLEADED or PLED, PLEADING, PLEADS to ask for earnestly

PLEADER   *n* pl. -S one that pleads

PLEADING   *n* pl. -S an allegation in a legal action

PLEASANT   *adj* -ANTER, -ANTEST pleasing

PLEASE   *v* PLEASED, PLEASING, PLEASES to give enjoyment or satisfaction to

PLEASER   *n* pl. -S one that pleases

PLEASURE   *v* -SURED, -SURING, -SURES to please

PLEAT   *v* -ED, -ING, -S to fold in an even manner

PLEATER   *n* pl. -S one that pleats

PLEB   *n* pl. -S a commoner

PLEBE   *n* pl. -S a freshman at a military or naval academy

PLEBEIAN   *n* pl. -S a commoner

PLECTRON   *n* pl. -TRONS or -TRA plectrum

PLECTRUM   *n* pl. -TRUMS or -TRA an implement used to pluck the strings of a stringed instrument

PLED   a past tense of plead

PLEDGE   *v* PLEDGED, PLEDGING, PLEDGES to give as security for something borrowed

PLEDGEE   *n* pl. -S one to whom something is pledged

PLEDGEOR   *n* pl. -S pledger

PLEDGER   *n* pl. -S one that pledges something

PLEDGET   *n* pl. -S a pad of absorbent cotton

PLEDGING   present participle of pledge

PLEDGOR   *n* pl. -S pledger

PLEIAD   *n* pl. -S or -ES a group of seven illustrious persons

PLENA   a pl. of plenum

PLENARY   *adj* complete in every respect

PLENISH   *v* -ED, -ING, -ES to fill up

PLENISM   *n* pl. -S the doctrine that space is fully occupied by matter

PLENIST   *n* pl. -S an advocate of plenism

PLENTY   *n* pl. -TIES a sufficient or abundant amount

PLENUM   *n* pl. -NUMS or -NA space considered as fully occupied by matter

PLEONASM   *n* pl. -S the use of needless words

PLEOPOD   *n* pl. -S an appendage of crustaceans

PLESSOR   *n* pl. -S plexor

PLETHORA   *n* pl. -S an excess

PLEURA   *n* pl. -RAE or -RAS a membrane that envelops the lungs **PLEURAL** *adj*

PLEURISY   *n* pl. -SIES inflammation of the pleura

PLEURON   *n* pl. -RA a part of a thoracic segment of an insect

PLEUSTON   *n* pl. -S aquatic vegetation

PLEXOR   *n* pl. -S a small, hammer-like medical instrument

PLEXUS   *n* pl. -ES an interlacing of parts

PLIABLE   *adj* easily bent **PLIABLY** *adv*

PLIANCY   *n* pl. -CIES the quality of being pliant

PLIANT   *adj* easily bent **PLIANTLY** *adv*

PLICA   *n* pl. -CAE a fold of skin **PLICAL** *adj*

PLICATE   *adj* pleated

PLICATED   *adj* plicate

PLIE   *n* pl. -S a movement in ballet

PLIED   past tense of ply

PLIER   *n* pl. -S one that plies

PLIES   present 3d person sing. of ply

PLIGHT   *v* -ED, -ING, -S to promise or bind by a solemn pledge

PLIGHTER   *n* pl. -S one that plights

PLIMSOL   *n* pl. -S plimsoll

PLIMSOLE   *n* pl. -S plimsoll

PLIMSOLL   *n* pl. -S a rubber-soled cloth shoe

PLINK   *v* -ED, -ING, -S to shoot at random targets

PLINKER   *n* pl. -S one that plinks

PLINTH   *n* pl. -S a stone or slab upon which a column or pedestal rests

PLISKIE   *n* pl. -S a practical joke

PLISKY   *n* pl. -KIES pliskie

PLISSE   *n* pl. -S a puckered texture of cloth

PLOD   *v* PLODDED, PLODDING, PLODS to walk heavily

PLODDER   *n* pl. -S one that plods

PLOIDY   *n* pl. -DIES the extent of repetition of the basic number of chromosomes

PLONK   *v* -ED, -ING, -S to plunk

PLOP   *v* PLOPPED, PLOPPING, PLOPS to drop or fall heavily

PLOSION   *n* pl. -S a release of breath after the articulation of certain consonants

PLOSIVE   *n* pl. -S a sound produced by plosion

PLOT   v PLOTTED, PLOTTING, PLOTS to plan secretly

PLOTLESS   adj planless

PLOTTAGE   n pl. -S an area of land

PLOTTED   past tense of plot

PLOTTER   n pl. -S one that plots

PLOTTIER   comparative of plotty

PLOTTIES   pl. of plotty

PLOTTING   present participle of plot

PLOTTY   adj -TIER, -TIEST full of intrigue, as a novel

PLOTTY   n pl. -TIES a hot, spiced beverage

PLOUGH   v -ED, -ING, -S to plow

PLOUGHER   n pl. -S one that ploughs

PLOVER   n pl. -S a shore bird

PLOW   v -ED, -ING, -S to turn up land with a plow (a farm implement) PLOWABLE adj

PLOWBACK   n pl. -S a reinvestment of profits in a business

PLOWBOY   n pl. -BOYS a boy who leads a plow team

PLOWER   n pl. -S one that plows

PLOWHEAD   n pl. -S the clevis of a plow

PLOWLAND   n pl. -S land suitable for cultivation

PLOWMAN   n pl. -MEN a man who plows

PLOY   v -ED, -ING, -S to move from a line into column

PLUCK   v -ED, -ING, -S to pull out or off

PLUCKER   n pl. -S one that plucks

PLUCKY   adj PLUCKIER, PLUCKIEST brave and spirited PLUCKILY adv

PLUG   v PLUGGED, PLUGGING, PLUGS to seal or close with a plug (a piece of material used to fill a hole)

PLUGGER   n pl. -S one that plugs

PLUGLESS   adj having no plug

PLUGUGLY   n pl. -LIES a hoodlum

PLUM   n pl. -S a fleshy fruit

PLUMAGE   n pl. -S the feathers of a bird PLUMAGED adj

PLUMATE   adj resembling a feather

PLUMB   v -ED, -ING, -S to determine the depth of

PLUMBAGO   n pl. -GOS graphite

PLUMBER   n pl. -S one who installs and repairs plumbing

PLUMBERY   n pl. -ERIES the work of a plumber

PLUMBIC   adj containing lead

PLUMBING   n pl. -S the pipe system of a building

PLUMBISM   n pl. -S lead poisoning

PLUMBOUS   adj containing lead

PLUMBUM   n pl. -S lead

PLUME   v PLUMED, PLUMING, PLUMES to cover with feathers

PLUMELET   n pl. -S a small feather

PLUMIER   comparative of plumy

PLUMIEST   superlative of plumy

PLUMING   present participle of plume

PLUMIPED   n pl. -S a bird having feathered feet

PLUMLIKE   adj resembling a plum

PLUMMET   v -ED, -ING, -S to drop straight down

PLUMMY   adj -MIER, -MIEST full of plums

PLUMOSE   adj having feathers

PLUMP   adj PLUMPER, PLUMPEST well-rounded and full in form

PLUMP   v -ED, -ING, -S to make plump

PLUMPEN   v -ED, -ING, -S to plump

PLUMPER   n pl. -S a heavy fall

PLUMPISH   adj somewhat plump

PLUMPLY   adv in a plump way

PLUMULE   n pl. -S the primary bud of a plant embryo PLUMULAR adj

PLUMY   adj PLUMIER, PLUMIEST covered with feathers

PLUNDER   v -ED, -ING, -S to rob of goods by force

PLUNGE   v PLUNGED, PLUNGING, PLUNGES to throw or thrust suddenly or forcibly into something

PLUNGER   n pl. -S one that plunges

PLUNK   v -ED, -ING, -S to fall or drop heavily

PLUNKER   n pl. -S one that plunks

PLURAL   n pl. -S a word that expresses more than one

PLURALLY   adv in a manner or form that expresses more than one

PLUS   n pl. PLUSES or PLUSSES an additional quantity

PLUSH	*adj* PLUSHER, PLUSHEST luxurious **PLUSHLY** *adv*
PLUSH	*n* pl. -ES a fabric with a long pile
PLUSHY	*adj* PLUSHIER, PLUSHIEST luxurious **PLUSHILY** *adv*
PLUSSAGE	*n* pl. -S an amount over and above another
PLUSSES	a pl. of plus
PLUTON	*n* pl. -S a formation of igneous rock **PLUTONIC** *adj*
PLUVIAL	*n* pl. -S a prolonged period of wet climate
PLUVIOSE	*adj* pluvious
PLUVIOUS	*adj* pertaining to rain
PLY	*v* PLIED, PLYING, PLIES to supply with or offer repeatedly **PLYINGLY** *adv*
PLYER	*n* pl. -S plier
PLYWOOD	*n* pl. -S a building material
PNEUMA	*n* pl. -S the soul or spirit
POACEOUS	*adj* pertaining to plants of the grass family
POACH	*v* -ED, -ING, -ES to trespass for the purpose of taking game or fish
POACHER	*n* pl. -S one that poaches
POACHY	*adj* POACHIER, POACHIEST swampy
POCHARD	*n* pl. -S a sea duck
POCK	*v* -ED, -ING, -S to mark with pocks (pustules caused by an eruptive disease)
POCKET	*v* -ED, -ING, -S to place in a pouch sewed into a garment
POCKETER	*n* pl. -S one that pockets
POCKMARK	*v* -ED, -ING, -S to mark with scars caused by an eruptive disease
POCKY	*adj* POCKIER, POCKIEST covered with pocks **POCKILY** *adv*
POCO	*adv* a little — used as a musical direction
POCOSIN	*n* pl. -S an upland swamp
POD	*v* PODDED, PODDING, PODS to produce seed vessels
PODAGRA	*n* pl. -S gout in the foot **PODAGRAL, PODAGRIC** *adj*
PODESTA	*n* pl. -S an Italian magistrate
PODGY	*adj* PODGIER, PODGIEST pudgy **PODGILY** *adv*
PODIA	a pl. of podium
PODIATRY	*n* pl. -TRIES the study and treatment of the human foot
PODITE	*n* pl. -S a limb segment of an arthropod **PODITIC** *adj*
PODIUM	*n* pl. -DIUMS or -DIA a small platform
PODOMERE	*n* pl. -S a podite
PODSOL	*n* pl. -S podzol **PODSOLIC** *adj*
PODZOL	*n* pl. -S an infertile soil **PODZOLIC** *adj*
POECHORE	*n* pl. -S a semiarid region
POEM	*n* pl. -S a composition in verse
POESY	*n* pl. -ESIES poetry
POET	*n* pl. -S one who writes poems
POETESS	*n* pl. -ES a female poet
POETIC	*adj* pertaining to poetry
POETICAL	*adj* poetic
POETICS	*n/pl* poetic theory or practice
POETISE	*v* -ISED, -ISING, -ISES to poetize
POETISER	*n* pl. -S poetizer
POETIZE	*v* -IZED, -IZING, -IZES to write poetry
POETIZER	*n* pl. -S one that poetizes
POETLESS	*adj* lacking a poet
POETLIKE	*adj* resembling a poet
POETRY	*n* pl. -RIES literary work in metrical form
POGEY	*n* pl. -GEYS any form of government relief
POGIES	pl. of pogy
POGONIA	*n* pl. -S a small orchid
POGONIP	*n* pl. -S a dense fog of suspended ice particles
POGROM	*v* -ED, -ING, -S to massacre systematically
POGY	*n* pl. -GIES a marine fish
POH	*interj* — used to express disgust
POI	*n* pl. -S a Hawaiian food
POIGNANT	*adj* emotionally distressing
POILU	*n* pl. -S a French soldier
POIND	*v* -ED, -ING, -S to seize and sell the property of to satisfy a debt
POINT	*v* -ED, -ING, -S to indicate direction with the finger
POINTE	*n* pl. -S a ballet position
POINTER	*n* pl. -S one that points

POINTMAN *n* pl. -MEN a certain player in hockey

POINTY *adj* POINTIER, POINTIEST coming to a sharp, tapering end

POISE *v* POISED, POISING, POISES to hold in a state of equilibrium

POISER *n* pl. -S one that poises

POISON *v* -ED, -ING, -S to administer a harmful substance to

POISONER *n* pl. -S one that poisons

POITREL *n* pl. -S peytral

POKE *v* POKED, POKING, POKES to push or prod

POKER *n* pl. -S one that pokes

POKEROOT *n* pl. -S pokeweed

POKEWEED *n* pl. -S a perennial herb

POKEY *n* pl. -KEYS poky

POKIER comparative of poky

POKIES pl. of poky

POKIEST superlative of poky

POKILY *adv* in a poky manner

POKINESS *n* pl. -ES the state of being poky

POKING present participle of poke

POKY *n* pl. POKIES a jail

POKY *adj* POKIER, POKIEST slow

POL *n* pl. -S a politician

POLAR *n* pl. -S a straight line related to a point

POLARISE *v* -ISED, -ISING, -ISES to polarize

POLARITY *n* pl. -TIES the possession of two opposite qualities

POLARIZE *v* -IZED, -IZING, -IZES to give polarity to

POLARON *n* pl. -S a type of electron

POLDER *n* pl. -S a tract of low land reclaimed from a body of water

POLE *v* POLED, POLING, POLES to propel with a pole (a long, thin piece of wood or metal)

POLEAX *v* -ED, -ING, -ES to strike with an axlike weapon

POLEAXE *v* -AXED, -AXING, -AXES to poleax

POLECAT *n* pl. -S a carnivorous mammal

POLED past tense of pole

POLEIS pl. of polis

POLELESS *adj* having no pole

POLEMIC *n* pl. -S a controversial argument

POLEMIST *n* pl. -S one who engages in polemics

POLEMIZE *v* -MIZED, -MIZING, -MIZES to engage in polemics

POLENTA *n* pl. -S a thick mush of cornmeal

POLER *n* pl. -S one that poles

POLESTAR *n* pl. -S a guiding principle

POLEWARD *adv* in the direction of either extremity of the earth's axis

POLEYN *n* pl. -S a protective piece of leather for the knee

POLICE *v* -LICED, -LICING, -LICES to make clean or orderly

POLICY *n* pl. -CIES an action or a procedure considered with reference to prudence or expediency

POLING present participle of pole

POLIO *n* pl. -LIOS an infectious virus disease

POLIS *n* pl. -LEIS an ancient Greek city-state

POLISH *v* -ED, -ING, -ES to make smooth and lustrous by rubbing

POLISHER *n* pl. -S one that polishes

POLITE *adj* -LITER, -LITEST showing consideration for others **POLITELY** *adv*

POLITIC *adj* shrewd

POLITICK *v* -ED, -ING, -S to engage in politics

POLITICO *n* pl. -COS or -COES one who politicks

POLITICS *n/pl* the art or science of government

POLITY *n* pl. -TIES a form or system of government

POLKA *v* -ED, -ING, -S to perform a lively dance

POLL *v* -ED, -ING, -S to question for the purpose of surveying public opinion

POLLACK *n* pl. -S a marine food fish

POLLARD *v* -ED, -ING, -S to cut the top branches of a tree back to the trunk

POLLEE *n* pl. -S one who is polled

POLLEN   v -ED, -ING, -S to convey pollen (the fertilizing element in a seed plant) to

POLLER   n pl. -S one that polls

POLLEX   n pl. -LICES the innermost digit of the forelimb **POLLICAL** adj

POLLINIA   n/pl masses of pollen grains

POLLINIC   adj pertaining to pollen

POLLIST   n pl. -S a poller

POLLIWOG   n pl. -S a tadpole

POLLOCK   n pl. -S a pollack

POLLSTER   n pl. -S a poller

POLLUTE   v -LUTED, -LUTING, -LUTES to make unclean or impure

POLLUTER   n pl. -S one that pollutes

POLLYWOG   n pl. -S polliwog

POLO   n pl. -LOS a game played on horseback

POLOIST   n pl. -S a polo player

POLONIUM   n pl. -S a radioactive element

POLTROON   n pl. -S a base coward

POLY   n pl. POLYS a type of white blood cell

POLYBRID   n pl. -S a type of hybrid plant

POLYCOT   n pl. -S a type of plant

POLYENE   n pl. -S a chemical compound **POLYENIC** adj

POLYGALA   n pl. -S a flowering plant

POLYGAMY   n pl. -MIES the condition of having more than one spouse at the same time

POLYGENE   n pl. -ES a type of gene

POLYGLOT   n pl. -S one that speaks or writes several languages

POLYGON   n pl. -S a closed plane figure bounded by straight lines

POLYGONY   n pl. -NIES an herb

POLYGYNY   n pl. -NIES the condition of having more than one wife at the same time

POLYMATH   n pl. -S a person of great and varied learning

POLYMER   n pl. -S a complex chemical compound

POLYNYA   n pl. -S an area of open water surrounded by sea ice

POLYP   n pl. -S an invertebrate

POLYPARY   n pl. -ARIES the common supporting structure of a polyp colony

POLYPI   a pl. of polypus

POLYPIDE   n pl. -S a polyp

POLYPNEA   n pl. -S rapid breathing

POLYPOD   n pl. -S a many-footed organism

POLYPODY   n pl. -DIES a fern

POLYPOID   adj resembling a polyp

POLYPORE   n pl. -S a type of fungus

POLYPOUS   adj pertaining to a polyp

POLYPUS   n pl. -PI or -PUSES a growth protruding from the mucous lining of an organ

POLYSEMY   n pl. -MIES diversity of meanings

POLYSOME   n pl. -S a cluster of protein particles

POLYTENE   adj having chromosomes of a certain type

POLYTENY   n pl. -NIES the state of being polytene

POLYTYPE   n pl. -S a crystal structure

POLYURIA   n pl. -S excessive urination **POLYURIC** adj

POLYZOAN   n pl. -S a bryozoan

POLYZOIC   adj composed of many zooids

POMACE   n pl. -S the pulpy residue of crushed fruits

POMADE   v -MADED, -MADING, -MADES to apply a perfumed hair dressing to

POMANDER   n pl. -S a mixture of aromatic substances

POMATUM   n pl. -S a perfumed hair dressing

POME   n pl. -S a fleshy fruit with a core

POMELO   n pl. -LOS a grapefruit

POMMEE   adj having arms with knoblike ends — used of a heraldic cross

POMMEL   v -MELED, -MELING, -MELS or -MELLED, -MELLING, -MELS to strike with the fists

POMOLOGY   n pl. -GIES the study of fruits

POMP   n pl. -S stately or splendid display

POMPANO   n pl. -NOS a marine food fish

POMPOM   n pl. -S an antiaircraft cannon

POMPON   n pl. -S an ornamental tuft or ball

POMPOUS   adj marked by exaggerated self-importance

PONCE n pl. -S a man who solicits clients for a prostitute

PONCHO n pl. -CHOS a type of cloak

POND n pl. -S a body of water smaller than a lake

PONDER v -ED, -ING, -S to consider something deeply and thoroughly

PONDERER n pl. -S one that ponders

PONDWEED n pl. -S an aquatic plant

PONE n pl. -S a corn bread

PONENT adj affirmative

PONGEE n pl. -S a type of silk

PONGID n pl. -S an anthropoid ape

PONIARD v -ED, -ING, -S to stab with a dagger

PONIED past tense of pony

PONIES present 3d person sing. of pony

PONS n pl. PONTES a band of nerve fibers in the brain

PONTIFEX n pl. -FICES an ancient Roman priest

PONTIFF n pl. -S a pope or bishop

PONTIFIC adj pertaining to a pope or bishop

PONTIFICES pl. of pontifex

PONTIL n pl. -S a punty

PONTINE adj pertaining to bridges

PONTON n pl. -S pontoon

PONTOON n pl. -S a flat-bottomed boat

PONY v -NIED, -NYING, -NIES to prepare lessons with the aid of a literal translation

PONYTAIL n pl. -S a hairstyle

POOCH n pl. -ES a dog

POOD n pl. -S a Russian unit of weight

POODLE n pl. -S a heavy-coated dog

POOH v -ED, -ING, -S to express contempt for

POOL v -ED, -ING, -S to combine in a common fund

POOLHALL n pl. -S a poolroom

POOLROOM n pl. -S an establishment for the playing of billiards

POON n pl. -S an East Indian tree

POOP v -ED, -ING, -S to tire out

POOR adj POORER, POOREST lacking the means of support

POORI n pl. -S a light, flat wheat cake

POORISH adj somewhat poor

POORLY adv in a poor manner

POORNESS n pl. -ES the state of being poor

POORTITH n pl. -S poverty

POP v POPPED, POPPING, POPS to make a sharp, explosive sound

POPCORN n pl. -S a variety of corn

POPE n pl. -S the head of the Roman Catholic Church POPELESS, POPELIKE adj

POPEDOM n pl. -S the office of a pope

POPERY n pl. -ERIES Roman Catholicism — usually used disparagingly

POPEYED adj having bulging eyes

POPGUN n pl. -S a toy gun

POPINJAY n pl. -JAYS a vain person

POPISH adj pertaining to the Roman Catholic Church — usually used disparagingly POPISHLY adv

POPLAR n pl. -S a fast-growing tree

POPLIN n pl. -S a durable fabric

POPLITIC adj pertaining to the part of the leg behind the knee

POPOVER n pl. -S a very light egg muffin

POPPA n pl. -S papa

POPPED past tense of pop

POPPER n pl. -S one that pops

POPPET n pl. -S a mechanical valve

POPPIED adj covered with poppies

POPPIES pl. of poppy

POPPING present participle of pop

POPPLE v -PLED, -PLING, -PLES to move in a bubbling or rippling manner

POPPY n pl. -PIES a flowering plant

POPULACE n pl. -S the common people

POPULAR adj liked by many people

POPULATE v -LATED, -LATING, -LATES to inhabit

POPULISM n pl. -S populists' doctrines

POPULIST n pl. -S a member of a party which represents the common people

POPULOUS adj containing many inhabitants

PORCH   *n* pl. -ES a covered structure at the entrance to a building

PORCINE   *adj* pertaining to swine

PORE   *v* PORED, PORING, PORES to gaze intently

PORGY   *n* pl. -GIES a marine food fish

PORISM   *n* pl. -S a type of mathematical proposition

PORK   *n* pl. -S the flesh of swine used as food

PORKER   *n* pl. -S a pig

PORKIER   comparative of porky

PORKIES   pl. of porky

PORKIEST   superlative of porky

PORKPIE   *n* pl. -S a man's hat

PORKWOOD   *n* pl. -S a tropical tree

PORKY   *adj* PORKIER, PORKIEST resembling pork

PORKY   *n* pl. -KIES a porcupine

PORN   *n* pl. -S pornography

PORNO   *n* pl. -NOS pornography

POROSE   *adj* porous

POROSITY   *n* pl. -TIES the state of being porous

POROUS   *adj* having minute openings POROUSLY *adv*

PORPHYRY   *n* pl. -RIES an igneous rock

PORPOISE   *n* pl. -S an aquatic mammal

PORRECT   *adj* extended forward

PORRIDGE   *n* pl. -S a soft food

PORT   *v* -ED, -ING, -S to shift to the left side

PORTABLE   *n* pl. -S something that can be carried

PORTABLY   *adv* so as to be capable of being carried

PORTAGE   *v* -TAGED, -TAGING, -TAGES to transport from one navigable waterway to another

PORTAL   *n* pl. -S a door, gate, or entrance PORTALED *adj*

PORTANCE   *n* pl. -S demeanor

PORTEND   *v* -ED, -ING, -S to serve as an omen of

PORTENT   *n* pl. -S an omen

PORTER   *n* pl. -S a person employed to carry luggage

PORTHOLE   *n* pl. -S a small window in a ship's side

PORTICO   *n* pl. -COS or -COES a type of porch

PORTIERE   *n* pl. -S a curtain for a doorway

PORTION   *v* -ED, -ING, -S to divide into shares for distribution

PORTLESS   *adj* having no place for ships to load or unload

PORTLY   *adj* -LIER, -LIEST rather heavy or fat

PORTRAIT   *n* pl. -S a likeness of a person

PORTRAY   *v* -ED, -ING, -S to represent pictorially

PORTRESS   *n* pl. -ES a female doorkeeper

POSADA   *n* pl. -S an inn

POSE   *v* POSED, POSING, POSES to assume a fixed position

POSER   *n* pl. -S one that poses

POSEUR   *n* pl. -S an affected or insincere person

POSH   *adj* POSHER, POSHEST stylish or elegant

POSIES   pl. of posy

POSING   present participle of pose

POSINGLY   *adv* in a posing manner

POSIT   *v* -ED, -ING, -S to place

POSITION   *v* -ED, -ING, -S to put in a particular location

POSITIVE   *adj* -TIVER, -TIVEST certain

POSITIVE   *n* pl. -S a quantity greater than zero

POSITRON   *n* pl. -S an atomic particle

POSOLOGY   *n* pl. -GIES a branch of medicine that deals with drug dosages

POSSE   *n* pl. -S a body of men summoned to aid a peace officer

POSSESS   *v* -ED, -ING, -ES to have as property

POSSET   *n* pl. -S a hot, spiced drink

POSSIBLE   *adj* -BLER, -BLEST capable of happening or proving true POSSIBLY *adv*

POSSUM   *n* pl. -S opossum

POST   *v* -ED, -ING, -S to affix in a public place

POSTAGE   *n* pl. -S the charge for mailing an item

POSTAL   *n* pl. -S a postcard

POSTALLY   *adv* in a manner pertaining to the mails

POSTANAL *adj* situated behind the anus

POSTBAG *n* pl. -S a mailbag

POSTBOX *n* pl. -ES a mailbox

POSTBOY *n* pl. -BOYS a boy who carries mail

POSTCARD *n* pl. -S a card for use in the mail

POSTCAVA *n* pl. -VAE a vein in higher vertebrates

POSTDATE *v* -DATED, -DATING, -DATES to give a date later than the actual date to

POSTEEN *n* pl. -S an Afghan outer garment

POSTER *n* pl. -S a printed or written notice for posting

POSTERN *n* pl. -S a rear door or gate

POSTFACE *n* pl. -S a brief note placed at the end of a publication

POSTFIX *v* -ED, -ING, -ES to affix at the end of something

POSTFORM *v* -ED, -ING, -S to shape subsequently

POSTHOLE *n* pl. -S a hole dug to secure a fence post

POSTICHE *n* pl. -S an imitation

POSTIN *n* pl. -S posteen

POSTING *n* pl. -S the act of transferring to a ledger

POSTIQUE *n* pl. -S postiche

POSTLUDE *n* pl. -S a closing musical piece

POSTMAN *n* pl. -MEN a mailman

POSTMARK *v* -ED, -ING, -S to stamp mail with an official mark

POSTORAL *adj* situated behind the mouth

POSTPAID *adv* with the postage prepaid

POSTPONE *v* -PONED, -PONING, -PONES to put off to a future time

POSTURAL *adj* pertaining to the position of the body

POSTURE *v* -TURED, -TURING, -TURES to assume a particular position

POSTURER *n* pl. -S one that postures

POSTWAR *adj* occurring or existing after a war

POSY *n* pl. -SIES a flower or bouquet

POT *v* POTTED, POTTING, POTS to put in a pot (a round, fairly deep container)

POTABLE *n* pl. -S a liquid suitable for drinking

POTAGE *n* pl. -S a thick soup

POTAMIC *adj* pertaining to rivers

POTASH *n* pl. -ES an alkaline compound

POTASSIC *adj* pertaining to potassium (a metallic element)

POTATION *n* pl. -S the act of drinking

POTATO *n* pl. -TOES the edible tuber of a cultivated plant

POTATORY *adj* pertaining to drinking

POTBELLY *n* pl. -LIES a protruding abdominal region

POTBOIL *v* -ED, -ING, -S to produce a literary or artistic work of poor quality

POTBOY *n* pl. -BOYS a boy who serves customers in a tavern

POTEEN *n* pl. -S Irish whiskey that is distilled unlawfully

POTENCE *n* pl. -S potency

POTENCY *n* pl. -CIES the quality of being potent

POTENT *adj* powerful **POTENTLY** *adv*

POTFUL *n* pl. -S as much as a pot can hold

POTHEAD *n* pl. -S one who smokes marijuana

POTHEEN *n* pl. -S poteen

POTHER *v* -ED, -ING, -S to trouble

POTHERB *n* pl. -S any herb used as a food or seasoning

POTHOLE *n* pl. -S a deep hole in a road **POTHOLED** *adj*

POTHOOK *n* pl. -S a hook for lifting or hanging pots

POTHOUSE *n* pl. -S a tavern

POTICHE *n* pl. -S a type of vase

POTION *n* pl. -S a magical or medicinal drink

POTLACH *n* pl. -ES a ceremonial feast

POTLACHE *n* pl. -S potlach

POTLATCH *v* -ED, -ING, -ES to hold a ceremonial feast for

POTLIKE *adj* resembling a pot

POTLUCK *n* pl. -S food which is incidentally available

POTMAN *n* pl. -MEN a man who serves customers in a tavern

POTPIE *n* pl. -S a deep-dish pie containing meat and vegetables

POTSHARD *n* pl. -S potsherd

POTSHERD   *n* pl. -S a fragment of broken pottery

POTSHOT   *v* -SHOT, -SHOTTING, -SHOTS to shoot randomly at

POTSIE   *n* pl. -S potsy

POTSTONE   *n* pl. -S a variety of steatite

POTSY   *n* pl. -SIES a children's game

POTTAGE   *n* pl. -S a thick soup

POTTED   past tense of pot

POTTEEN   *n* pl. -S poteen

POTTER   *v* -ED, -ING, -S to putter

POTTERER   *n* pl. -S one that potters

POTTERY   *n* pl. -TERIES ware molded from clay and hardened by heat

POTTIER   comparative of potty

POTTIES   pl. of potty

POTTIEST   superlative of potty

POTTING   present participle of pot

POTTLE   *n* pl. -S a drinking vessel

POTTO   *n* pl. -TOS a lemur of tropical Africa

POTTY   *adj* -TIER, -TIEST of little importance

POTTY   *n* pl. -TIES a small toilet seat

POUCH   *v* -ED, -ING, -ES to put in a pouch (a small, flexible receptacle)

POUCHY   *adj* POUCHIER, POUCHIEST resembling a pouch

POUF   *n* pl. -S a loose roll of hair POUFED *adj*

POUFF   *n* pl. -S pouf POUFFED *adj*

POUFFE   *n* pl. -S pouf

POULARD   *n* pl. -S a spayed hen

POULARDE   *n* pl. -S poulard

POULT   *n* pl. -S a young domestic fowl

POULTICE   *v* -TICED, -TICING, -TICES to apply a healing substance to

POULTRY   *n* pl. -TRIES domestic fowls kept for eggs or meat

POUNCE   *v* POUNCED, POUNCING, POUNCES to make a sudden assault or approach

POUNCER   *n* pl. -S one that pounces

POUND   *v* -ED, -ING, -S to strike heavily and repeatedly

POUNDAGE   *n* pl. -S the act of impounding

POUNDAL   *n* pl. -S a unit of force

POUNDER   *n* pl. -S one that pounds

POUR   *v* -ED, -ING, -S to cause to flow POURABLE *adj*

POURER   *n* pl. -S one that pours

POUSSIE   *n* pl. -S pussy

POUT   *v* -ED, -ING, -S to protrude the lips in ill humor

POUTER   *n* pl. -S one that pouts

POUTFUL   *adj* pouty

POUTY   *adj* POUTIER, POUTIEST tending to pout

POVERTY   *n* pl. -TIES the state of being poor

POW   *n* pl. -S an explosive sound

POWDER   *v* -ED, -ING, -S to reduce to powder (matter in a finely divided state)

POWDERER   *n* pl. -S one that powders

POWDERY   *adj* resembling powder

POWER   *v* -ED, -ING, -S to provide with means of propulsion

POWERFUL   *adj* possessing great force

POWTER   *n* pl. -S a domestic pigeon

POWWOW   *v* -ED, -ING, -S to hold a conference

POX   *v* -ED, -ING, -ES to infect with syphilis

POXVIRUS   *n* pl. -ES a type of virus

POYOU   *n* pl. -S an armadillo of Argentina

POZZOLAN   *n* pl. -S a finely divided material used to make cement

PRAAM   *n* pl. -S a pram

PRACTIC   *adj* practical

PRACTICE   *v* -TICED, -TICING, -TICES to perform often so as to acquire skill

PRACTISE   *v* -TISED, -TISING, -TISES to practice

PRAECIPE   *n* pl. -S a legal writ

PRAEDIAL   *adj* pertaining to land

PRAEFECT   *n* pl. -S prefect

PRAELECT   *v* -ED, -ING, -S to prelect

PRAETOR   *n* pl. -S an ancient Roman magistrate

PRAHU   *n* pl. -S prau

PRAIRIE   *n* pl. -S a tract of grassland

PRAISE   *v* PRAISED, PRAISING, PRAISES to express approval or admiration of

PRAISER   *n* pl. -S one that praises

PRALINE   n pl. -S a confection made of nuts cooked in sugar

PRAM   n pl. -S a flat-bottomed boat

PRANCE   v PRANCED, PRANCING, PRANCES to spring forward on the hind legs

PRANCER   n pl. -S one that prances

PRANDIAL   adj pertaining to a meal

PRANG   v -ED, -ING, -S to cause to crash

PRANK   v -ED, -ING, -S to adorn gaudily

PRANKISH   adj mischievous

PRAO   n pl. PRAOS prau

PRASE   n pl. -S a mineral

PRAT   n pl. -S the buttocks

PRATE   v PRATED, PRATING, PRATES to chatter

PRATER   n pl. -S one that prates

PRATFALL   n pl. -S a fall on the buttocks

PRATING   present participle of prate

PRATIQUE   n pl. -S clearance given a ship by the health authority of a port

PRATTLE   v -TLED, -TLING, -TLES to babble

PRATTLER   n pl. -S one that prattles

PRAU   n pl. -S a swift Malaysian sailing vessel

PRAWN   v -ED, -ING, -S to fish for prawns (edible shellfishes)

PRAWNER   n pl. -S one that prawns

PRAXIS   n pl. PRAXISES or PRAXES practical use of a branch of learning

PRAY   v -ED, -ING, -S to address prayers to

PRAYER   n pl. -S a devout petition to a deity

PREACH   v -ED, -ING, -ES to advocate or recommend urgently

PREACHER   n pl. -S one that preaches

PREACHY   adj PREACHIER, PREACHIEST tending to preach

PREACT   v -ED, -ING, -S to act beforehand

PREADAPT   v -ED, -ING, -S to adapt beforehand

PREADMIT   v -MITTED, -MITTING, -MITS to admit beforehand

PREADOPT   v -ED, -ING, -S to adopt beforehand

PREADULT   adj preceding adulthood

PREAGED   adj previously aged

PREALLOT   v -LOTTED, -LOTTING, -LOTS to allot beforehand

PREAMBLE   n pl. -S an introductory statement

PREAMP   n pl. -S an amplifier

PREANAL   adj situated in front of the anus

PREARM   v -ED, -ING, -S to arm beforehand

PREAVER   v -VERRED, -VERRING, -VERS to aver or assert beforehand

PREAXIAL   adj situated in front of an axis

PREBASAL   adj situated in front of a base

PREBEND   n pl. -S a clergyman's stipend

PREBILL   v -ED, -ING, -S to bill beforehand

PREBIND   v -BOUND, -BINDING, -BINDS to bind in durable materials for library use

PREBLESS   v -ED, -ING, -ES to bless beforehand

PREBOIL   v -ED, -ING, -S to boil beforehand

PREBOUND   past tense of prebind

PRECAST   v -CAST, -CASTING, -CASTS to cast and finish before placing into position

PRECAVA   n pl. -VAE a vein in higher vertebrates PRECAVAL adj

PRECEDE   v -CEDED, -CEDING, -CEDES to go before

PRECENT   v -ED, -ING, -S to lead a church choir in singing

PRECEPT   n pl. -S a rule of conduct

PRECESS   v -ED, -ING, -ES to rotate with a complex motion

PRECHECK   v -ED, -ING, -S to check beforehand

PRECHILL   v -ED, -ING, -S to chill beforehand

PRECIEUX   adj excessively refined

PRECINCT   n pl. -S a subdivision of a city or town

PRECIOUS   n pl. -ES a darling

PRECIPE   n pl. -S praecipe

PRECIS   v -ED, -ING, -ES to make a concise summary of

PRECISE   adj -CISER, -CISEST sharply and clearly defined or stated

PRENAME

435

PRECITED *adj* previously cited

PRECLEAN *v* -ED, -ING, -S to clean beforehand

PRECLUDE *v* -CLUDED, -CLUDING, -CLUDES to make impossible by previous action

PRECOOK *v* -ED, -ING, -S to cook beforehand

PRECOOL *v* -ED, -ING, -S to cool beforehand

PRECURE *v* -CURED, -CURING, -CURES to cure beforehand

PREDATE *v* -DATED, -DATING, -DATES to date before the actual or a specified time

PREDATOR *n* pl. -S one that plunders

PREDAWN *n* pl. -S the time just before dawn

PREDIAL *adj* praedial

PREDICT *v* -ED, -ING, -S to tell of or about in advance

PREDUSK *n* pl. -S the time just before dusk

PREE *v* PREED, PREEING, PREES to test by tasting

PREELECT *v* -ED, -ING, -S to elect or choose beforehand

PREEMIE *n* pl. -S an infant born prematurely

PREEMPT *v* -ED, -ING, -S to acquire by prior right

PREEN *v* -ED, -ING, -S to smooth or clean with the beak or tongue

PREENACT *v* -ED, -ING, -S to enact beforehand

PREENER *n* pl. -S one that preens

PREEXIST *v* -ED, -ING, -S to exist before

PREFAB *v* -FABBED, -FABBING, FABS to construct beforehand

PREFACE *v* -ACED, -ACING, -ACES to provide with an introductory statement

PREFACER *n* pl. -S one that prefaces

PREFECT *n* pl. -S an ancient Roman official

PREFER *v* -FERRED, -FERRING, -FERS to hold in higher regard or esteem

PREFIX *v* -ED, -ING, -ES to add as a prefix (a form affixed to the beginning of a root word)

PREFIXAL *adj* pertaining to or being a prefix

PREFOCUS *v* -CUSED, -CUSING, -CUSES or -CUSSED, -CUSSING, -CUSSES to focus beforehand

PREFORM *v* -ED, -ING, -S to form beforehand

PREFRANK *v* -ED, -ING, -S to frank beforehand

PREGAME *adj* preceding a game

PREGNANT *adj* carrying a developing fetus in the uterus

PREHEAT *v* -ED, -ING, -S to heat beforehand

PREHUMAN *n* pl. -S a prototype of man

PREJUDGE *v* -JUDGED, -JUDGING, -JUDGES to judge beforehand

PRELACY *n* pl. -CIES the office of a prelate

PRELATE *n* pl. -S a high-ranking clergyman PRELATIC *adj*

PRELECT *v* -ED, -ING, -S to lecture

PRELEGAL *adj* occurring before the commencement of studies in law

PRELIM *n* pl. -S a minor match preceding the main event

PRELIMIT *v* -ED, -ING, -S to limit beforehand

PRELUDE *v* -LUDED, -LUDING, -LUDES to play a musical introduction

PRELUDER *n* pl. -S one that preludes

PREMAN *n* pl. -MEN a hypothetical ancestor of man

PREMED *n* pl. -S a student preparing for the study of medicine

PREMEDIC *n* pl. -S a premed

PREMEN pl. of preman

PREMIE *n* pl. -S preemie

PREMIER *n* pl. -S a prime minister

PREMIERE *v* -MIERED, -MIERING, -MIERES to present publicly for the first time

PREMISE *v* -MISED, -MISING, -MISES to state in advance

PREMISS *n* pl. -ES a proposition in logic

PREMIUM *n* pl. -S an additional payment

PREMIX *v* -ED, -ING, -ES to mix before use

PREMOLAR *n* pl. -S a tooth

PREMORSE *adj* ending abruptly, as if bitten off

PREMUNE *adj* resistant to a disease

PRENAME *n* pl. -S a forename

PRENATAL *adj* prior to birth

PRENOMEN *n pl.* -MENS or -MINA the first name of an ancient Roman

PRENTICE *v* -TICED, -TICING, -TICES to place with an employer for instruction in a trade

PREP *v* PREPPED, PREPPING, PREPS to attend a preparatory school

PREPACK *v* -ED, -ING, -S to package before retail distribution

PREPAID past tense of prepay

PREPARE *v* -PARED, -PARING, -PARES to put in proper condition or readiness

PREPARER *n pl.* -S one that prepares

PREPAY *v* -PAID, -PAYING, -PAYS to pay in advance

PREPENSE *adj* planned in advance

PREPLACE *v* -PLACED, -PLACING, -PLACES to place beforehand

PREPLAN *v* -PLANNED, -PLANNING, -PLANS to plan in advance

PREPLANT *adj* occurring before planting

PREPPED past tense of prep

PREPPIE *n pl.* -S one who preps

PREPPING present participle of prep

PREPRINT *v* -ED, -ING, -S to print in advance

PREPUCE *n pl.* -S a fold of skin covering the penis

PREPUNCH *v* -ED, -ING, -ES to punch in advance

PRERENAL *adj* situated in front of the kidney

PRESA *n pl.* -SE a musical symbol

PRESAGE *v* -SAGED, -SAGING, -SAGES to foretell

PRESAGER *n pl.* -S one that presages

PRESCIND *v* -ED, -ING, -S to consider separately

PRESCORE *v* -SCORED, -SCORING, -SCORES to record the sound of before filming

PRESE pl. of presa

PRESELL *v* -SOLD, -SELLING, -SELLS to promote a product not yet being sold to the public

PRESENCE *n pl.* -S close proximity

PRESENT *v* -ED, -ING, -S to bring into the presence of someone

PRESERVE *v* -SERVED, -SERVING, -SERVES to keep free from harm or danger

PRESET *v* -SET, -SETTING, -SETS to set beforehand

PRESHAPE *v* -SHAPED, -SHAPING, -SHAPES to shape beforehand

PRESHOW *v* -SHOWED, -SHOWN, -SHOWING, -SHOWS to show beforehand

PRESIDE *v* -SIDED, -SIDING, -SIDES to occupy the position of authority

PRESIDER *n pl.* -S one that presides

PRESIDIA *n/pl* Soviet executive committees

PRESIDIO *n pl.* -DIOS a Spanish fort

PRESIFT *v* -ED, -ING, -S to sift beforehand

PRESOAK *v* -ED, -ING, -S to soak beforehand

PRESOLD past tense of presell

PRESS *v* -ED, -ING, -ES to act upon with steady force

PRESSER *n pl.* -S one that presses

PRESSMAN *n pl.* -MEN a printing press operator

PRESSOR *adj* causing an increase in blood pressure

PRESSRUN *n pl.* -S a continuous operation of a printing press

PRESSURE *v* -SURED, -SURING, -SURES to apply force to

PREST *n pl.* -S a loan

PRESTAMP *v* -ED, -ING, -S to stamp beforehand

PRESTER *n pl.* -S a priest

PRESTIGE *n pl.* -S distinction or reputation in the eyes of people

PRESTO *n pl.* -TOS a musical passage played in rapid tempo

PRESUME *v* -SUMED, -SUMING, -SUMES to take for granted

PRESUMER *n pl.* -S one that presumes

PRETASTE *v* -TASTED, -TASTING, -TASTES to taste beforehand

PRETAX *adj* existing before provision for taxes

PRETEEN *n pl.* -S a child under the age of thirteen

PRETENCE *n pl.* -S pretense

PRETEND *v* -ED, -ING, -S to assume or display a false appearance of

PRETENSE n pl. -S the act of pretending

PRETERIT n pl. -S a past tense in grammar

PRETEST v -ED, -ING, -S to give a preliminary test to

PRETEXT v -ED, -ING, -S to allege as an excuse

PRETOR n pl. -S praetor

PRETREAT v -ED, -ING, -S to treat beforehand

PRETTIED past tense of pretty

PRETTIER comparative of pretty

PRETTIES present 3d person sing. of pretty

PRETTIEST superlative of pretty

PRETTIFY v -FIED, -FYING, -FIES to make pretty

PRETTY v -TIED, -TYING, -TIES to make pretty

PRETTY adj -TIER, -TIEST pleasing to the eye PRETTILY adv

PRETZEL n pl. -S a glazed, salted cracker

PREUNION n pl. -S a union beforehand

PREUNITE v -UNITED, -UNITING, -UNITES to unite beforehand

PREVAIL v -ED, -ING, -S to triumph

PREVENT v -ED, -ING, -S to keep from happening

PREVIEW v -ED, -ING, -S to view or exhibit in advance

PREVIOUS adj coming or occurring before in time or order

PREVISE v -VISED, -VISING, -VISES to foresee

PREVISOR n pl. -S one that previses

PREVUE v -VUED, -VUING, -VUES to preview

PREWAR adj occurring or existing before a war

PREWARM v -ED, -ING, -S to warm beforehand

PREWARN v -ED, -ING, -S to warn in advance

PREWASH v -ED, -ING, -ES to wash beforehand

PREWRAP v -WRAPPED, -WRAPPING, -WRAPS to wrap beforehand

PREX n pl. -ES prexy

PREXY n pl. PREXIES a president

PREY v -ED, -ING, -S to seize and devour animals for food

PREYER n pl. -S one that preys

PRIAPEAN adj priapic

PRIAPI a pl. of priapus

PRIAPIC adj phallic

PRIAPISM n pl. -S a persistent erection of the penis

PRIAPUS n pl. -PUSES or -PI a representation of the phallus

PRICE v PRICED, PRICING, PRICES to set a value on

PRICER n pl. -S one that prices

PRICEY adj PRICIER, PRICIEST expensive

PRICIER comparative of pricey and pricy

PRICIEST superlative of pricey and pricy

PRICING present participle of price

PRICK v -ED, -ING, -S to puncture slightly

PRICKER n pl. -S one that pricks

PRICKET n pl. -S a spike for holding a candle upright

PRICKIER comparative of pricky

PRICKIEST superlative of pricky

PRICKLE v -LED, -LING, -LES to prick

PRICKLY adj -LIER, -LIEST having many sharp points

PRICKY adj PRICKIER, PRICKIEST prickly

PRICY adj PRICIER, PRICIEST pricey

PRIDE v PRIDED, PRIDING, PRIDES to feel pride (a feeling of self-esteem)

PRIDEFUL adj full of pride

PRIED past tense of pry

PRIEDIEU n pl. -DIEUS or -DIEUX a piece of furniture for kneeling on during prayer

PRIER n pl. -S one that pries

PRIES present 3d person sing. of pry

PRIEST v -ED, -ING, -S to ordain as a priest (one authorized to perform religious rites)

PRIESTLY adj -LIER, -LIEST characteristic of or befitting a priest

PRIG v PRIGGED, PRIGGING, PRIGS to steal

PRIGGERY n pl. -GERIES priggism

PRIGGISH adj marked by priggism

PRIGGISM n pl. -S prim adherence to convention

PRILL	v -ED, -ING, -S to convert into pellets
PRIM	adj PRIMMER, PRIMMEST formally precise or proper
PRIM	v PRIMMED, PRIMMING, PRIMS to give a prim expression to
PRIMA	n pl. -S primo
PRIMACY	n pl. -CIES the state of being first
PRIMAGE	n pl. -S an amount paid as an addition to freight charges
PRIMAL	adj being at the beginning or foundation
PRIMARY	n pl. -RIES a preliminary election
PRIMATE	n pl. -S any of an advanced order of mammals PRIMATAL adj
PRIME	v PRIMED, PRIMING, PRIMES to make ready
PRIMELY	adv excellently
PRIMER	n pl. -S a book that covers the basics of a subject
PRIMERO	n pl. -ROS a card game
PRIMEVAL	adj pertaining to the earliest ages
PRIMI	a pl. of primo
PRIMINE	n pl. -S the outer covering of an ovule
PRIMING	n pl. -S the act of one that primes
PRIMLY	adv in a prim manner
PRIMMED	past tense of prim
PRIMMER	comparative of prim
PRIMMEST	superlative of prim
PRIMMING	present participle of prim
PRIMNESS	n pl. -ES the state of being prim
PRIMO	n pl. -MOS or -MI the main part in a musical piece
PRIMP	v -ED, -ING, -S to dress or adorn carefully
PRIMROSE	n pl. -S a perennial herb
PRIMSIE	adj prim
PRIMULA	n pl. -S primrose
PRIMUS	n pl. -ES the head bishop of Scotland
PRINCE	n pl. -S a non-reigning male member of a royal family
PRINCELY	adj -LIER, -LIEST of or befitting a prince
PRINCESS	n pl. -ES a non-reigning female member of a royal family
PRINCIPE	n pl. -PI a prince
PRINCOCK	n pl. -S a coxcomb
PRINCOX	n pl. -ES princock
PRINK	v -ED, -ING, -S to dress or adorn in a showy manner
PRINKER	n pl. -S one that prinks
PRINT	v -ED, -ING, -S to produce by pressed type on a surface
PRINTER	n pl. -S one that prints
PRINTERY	n pl. -ERIES a place where printing is done
PRINTING	n pl. -S a reproduction from a printing surface
PRINTOUT	n pl. -S the printed output of a computer
PRIOR	n pl. -S an officer in a monastery
PRIORATE	n pl. -S the office of a prior
PRIORESS	n pl. -ES a nun corresponding in rank to a prior
PRIORIES	pl. of priory
PRIORITY	n pl. -TIES precedence established by importance
PRIORLY	adv previously
PRIORY	n pl. -RIES a religious house
PRISE	v PRISED, PRISING, PRISES to raise or force with a lever
PRISERE	n pl. -S a succession of vegetational stages
PRISM	n pl. -S a solid which disperses light into a spectrum
PRISMOID	n pl. -S a geometric solid
PRISON	v -ED, -ING, -S to imprison
PRISONER	n pl. -S one that is imprisoned
PRISS	n pl. -ES a prissy
PRISSY	adj -SIER, -SIEST excessively or affectedly proper PRISSILY adv
PRISSY	n pl. -SIES one who is prissy
PRISTANE	n pl. -S a chemical compound
PRISTINE	adj pertaining to the earliest time or state
PRITHEE	interj — used to express a wish or request
PRIVACY	n pl. -CIES the state of being private
PRIVATE	adj -VATER, -VATEST secluded from the sight, presence, or intrusion of others

PRIVATE   *n* pl. -S a soldier of lower rank

PRIVET   *n* pl. -S an ornamental shrub

PRIVIER   comparative of privy

PRIVIES   pl. of privy

PRIVITY   *n* pl. -TIES private knowledge

PRIVY   *adj* PRIVIER, PRIVIEST private **PRIVILY** *adv*

PRIVY   *n* pl. PRIVIES an outhouse

PRIZE   *v* PRIZED, PRIZING, PRIZES to value highly

PRIZER   *n* pl. -S one who vies for a reward

PRO   *n* pl. PROS an argument or vote in favor of something

PROA   *n* pl. -S prau

PROBABLE   *adj* likely to occur or prove true **PROBABLY** *adv*

PROBAND   *n* pl. -S one whose reactions or responses are studied

PROBANG   *n* pl. -S a surgical rod

PROBATE   *v* -BATED, -BATING, -BATES to establish the validity of

PROBE   *v* PROBED, PROBING, PROBES to investigate or examine thoroughly

PROBER   *n* pl. -S one that probes

PROBIT   *n* pl. -S a unit of statistical probability

PROBITY   *n* pl. -TIES complete and confirmed integrity

PROBLEM   *n* pl. -S a perplexing question or situation

PROCAINE   *n* pl. -S a compound used as a local anesthetic

PROCARP   *n* pl. -S a female sexual organ in certain algae

PROCEED   *v* -ED, -ING, -S to go forward or onward

PROCESS   *v* -ED, -ING, -ES to treat or prepare by a special method

PROCHAIN   *adj* prochein

PROCHEIN   *adj* nearest in time, relation, or degree

PROCLAIM   *v* -ED, -ING, -S to make known publicly or officially

PROCTOR   *v* -ED, -ING, -S to supervise

PROCURAL   *n* pl. -S the act of procuring

PROCURE   *v* -CURED, -CURING, -CURES to obtain by effort

PROCURER   *n* pl. -S one that procures

PROD   *v* PRODDED, PRODDING, PRODS to jab with something pointed

PRODDER   *n* pl. -S one that prods

PRODIGAL   *n* pl. -S one who spends lavishly and foolishly

PRODIGY   *n* pl. -GIES a child having exceptional talent or ability

PRODROME   *n* pl. -DROMES or -DROMATA a sign of impending disease

PRODUCE   *v* -DUCED, -DUCING, -DUCES to bring into existence

PRODUCER   *n* pl. -S one that produces

PRODUCT   *n* pl. -S something produced by labor or effort

PROEM   *n* pl. -S an introductory statement **PROEMIAL** *adj*

PROETTE   *n* pl. -S a female professional athlete

PROF   *n* pl. -S a professor

PROFANE   *v* -FANED, -FANING, -FANES to treat with irreverence or abuse

PROFANER   *n* pl. -S one that profanes

PROFESS   *v* -ED, -ING, -ES to affirm openly

PROFFER   *v* -ED, -ING, -S to present for acceptance

PROFILE   *v* -FILED, -FILING, -FILES to draw an outline of

PROFILER   *n* pl. -S one that profiles

PROFIT   *v* -ED, -ING, -S to gain an advantage or benefit

PROFITER   *n* pl. -S one that profits

PROFOUND   *adj* -FOUNDER, -FOUNDEST intellectually deep and penetrating

PROFOUND   *n* pl. -S something that is very deep

PROFUSE   *adj* pouring forth generously

PROG   *v* PROGGED, PROGGING, PROGS to prowl about for food or plunder

PROGENY   *n* pl. -NIES a descendant or offspring

PROGGER   *n* pl. -S one that progs

PROGGING   present participle of prog

PROGNOSE   *v* -NOSED, -NOSING, -NOSES to forecast the probable course of a disease

PROGRADE   *adj* pertaining to the orbital motion of a body

PROGRAM   v -GRAMED, -GRAMING, -GRAMMED, -GRAMMING, -GRAMS to arrange in a plan of proceedings

PROGRESS   v -ED, -ING, -ES to move forward or onward

PROHIBIT   v -ED, -ING, -S to forbid by authority

PROJECT   v -ED, -ING, -S to extend outward

PROJET   n pl. -S a plan or outline

PROLABOR   adj favoring organized labor

PROLAMIN   n pl. -S a simple protein

PROLAN   n pl. -S a sex hormone

PROLAPSE   v -LAPSED, -LAPSING, -LAPSES to fall or slip out of place

PROLATE   adj extended lengthwise

PROLE   n pl. -S a member of the working class

PROLEG   n pl. -S an abdominal leg of certain insect larvae

PROLIFIC   adj producing abundantly

PROLINE   n pl. -S an amino acid

PROLIX   adj tediously long and wordy PROLIXLY adv

PROLOG   v -ED, -ING, -S to prologue

PROLOGUE   v -LOGUED, -LOGUING, -LOGUES to preface

PROLONG   v -ED, -ING, -S to lengthen in duration

PROLONGE   n pl. -S a rope used for pulling a gun carriage

PROM   n pl. -S a formal dance

PROMISE   v -ISED, -ISING, -ISES to make a declaration of assurance

PROMISEE   n pl. -S one who is promised something

PROMISER   n pl. -S promisor

PROMISING   present participle of promise

PROMISOR   n pl. -S one that promises

PROMOTE   v -MOTED, -MOTING, -MOTES to contribute to the progress of

PROMOTER   n pl. -S one that promotes

PROMPT   adj PROMPTER, PROMPTEST quick to act or respond

PROMPT   v -ED, -ING, -S to induce to action

PROMPTER   n pl. -S one that prompts

PROMPTLY   adv in a prompt manner

PROMULGE   v -MULGED, -MULGING, -MULGES to proclaim

PRONATE   v -NATED, -NATING, -NATES to turn the palm downward or backward

PRONATOR   n pl. -S or -ES a forearm or forelimb muscle

PRONE   adj lying with the front or face downward PRONELY adv

PRONG   v -ED, -ING, -S to pierce with a pointed projection

PRONOTUM   n pl. -NOTA a hard outer plate of an insect

PRONOUN   n pl. -S a word that may be used in place of a noun

PRONTO   adv quickly

PROOF   v -ED, -ING, -S to examine for errors

PROOFER   n pl. -S one that proofs

PROP   v PROPPED, PROPPING, PROPS to keep from falling

PROPANE   n pl. -S a flammable gas

PROPEL   v -PELLED, -PELLING, -PELS to cause to move forward or onward

PROPEND   v -ED, -ING, -S to have a tendency toward

PROPENE   n pl. -S a flammable gas

PROPENOL   n pl. -S a flammable liquid

PROPENSE   adj tending toward

PROPENYL   adj pertaining to a certain chemical group

PROPER   adj -ERER, -EREST suitable PROPERLY adv

PROPER   n pl. -S a portion of the Mass

PROPERTY   n pl. -TIES something owned

PROPHAGE   n pl. -S a form of virus

PROPHASE   n pl. -S the first stage in mitosis

PROPHECY   n pl. -CIES a prediction

PROPHESY   v -SIED, -SYING, -SIES to predict

PROPHET   n pl. -S one who predicts

PROPINE   v -PINED, -PINING, -PINES to offer as a gift

PROPJET   n pl. -S a type of airplane

PROPMAN   n pl. -MEN a man in charge of stage properties

PROPOLIS   n pl. -LISES a resinous substance used as a cement by bees

PROPONE v -PONED, -PONING, -PONES to propose

PROPOSAL n pl. -S something that is proposed

PROPOSE v -POSED, -POSING, -POSES to put forward for consideration or acceptance

PROPOSER n pl. -S one that proposes

PROPOUND v -ED, -ING, -S to propose

PROPPED past tense of prop

PROPPING present participle of prop

PROPYL n pl. -S a univalent radical PROPYLIC adj

PROPYLON n pl. -LA an entrance to a temple

PRORATE v -RATED, -RATING, -RATES to divide proportionately

PROROGUE v -ROGUED, -ROGUING, -ROGUES to discontinue a session of

PROSAIC adj pertaining to prose

PROSAISM n pl. -S a prosaic style

PROSAIST n pl. -S a writer of prose

PROSE v PROSED, PROSING, PROSES to write prose (writing without metrical structure)

PROSECT v -ED, -ING, -S to dissect

PROSER n pl. -S a prosaist

PROSIER comparative of prosy

PROSIEST superlative of prosy

PROSILY adv in a prosy manner

PROSING present participle of prose

PROSIT interj — used as a drinking toast

PROSO n pl. -SOS millet

PROSODY n pl. -DIES the study of poetical forms PROSODIC adj

PROSOMA n pl. -S the front region of the body of an invertebrate PROSOMAL adj

PROSPECT v -ED, -ING, -S to explore for mineral deposits

PROSPER v -ED, -ING, -S to be successful or fortunate

PROST interj prosit

PROSTATE n pl. -S a gland in male mammals

PROSTYLE n pl. -S a building having a row of columns across the front only

PROSY adj PROSIER, PROSIEST prosaic

PROTAMIN n pl. -S a simple protein

PROTASIS n pl. -ASES the introductory part of a classical drama PROTATIC adj

PROTEA n pl. -S an evergreen shrub

PROTEAN adj readily taking on different shapes or forms

PROTEASE n pl. -S an enzyme

PROTECT v -ED, -ING, -S to keep from harm, attack, or injury

PROTEGE n pl. -S one whose career is promoted by an influential person

PROTEGEE n pl. -S a female protege

PROTEI pl. of proteus

PROTEID n pl. -S protein

PROTEIDE n pl. -S proteid

PROTEIN n pl. -S a nitrogenous organic compound

PROTEND v -ED, -ING, -S to extend

PROTEOSE n pl. -S a water-soluble protein

PROTEST v -ED, -ING, -S to express strong objection

PROTEUS n pl. -TEI any of a genus of aerobic bacteria

PROTIST n pl. -S any of a group of unicellular organisms

PROTIUM n pl. -S an isotope of hydrogen

PROTOCOL v -COLED, -COLING, -COLS or -COLLED, -COLLING, -COLS to form a preliminary draft of an official document

PROTON n pl. -S an atomic particle PROTONIC adj

PROTOPOD n pl. -S a part of a crustacean appendage

PROTOXID n pl. -S an oxide

PROTOZOA n/pl unicellular microscopic organisms

PROTRACT v -ED, -ING, -S to prolong

PROTRUDE v -TRUDED, -TRUDING, -TRUDES to extend beyond the main portion

PROTYL n pl. -S protyle

PROTYLE n pl. -S a hypothetical substance from which all the elements are supposedly derived

PROUD adj PROUDER, PROUDEST having or displaying pride PROUDLY adv

PROUDFUL adj prideful

PROUNION adj favoring labor unions

PROVE v PROVED, PROVEN, PROVING, PROVES to establish the truth or validity of **PROVABLE** adj **PROVABLY** adv

PROVENLY adv without doubt

PROVER n pl. -S one that proves

PROVERB v -ED, -ING, -S to make a byword of

PROVIDE v -VIDED, -VIDING, -VIDES to supply

PROVIDER n pl. -S one that provides

PROVINCE n pl. -S an administrative division of a country

PROVING present participle of prove

PROVIRUS n pl. -ES a form of virus **PROVIRAL** adj

PROVISO n pl. -SOS or -SOES a clause in a document introducing a condition or restriction

PROVOKE v -VOKED, -VOKING, -VOKES to incite to anger or resentment

PROVOKER n pl. -S one that provokes

PROVOST n pl. -S a high-ranking university official

PROW n pl. -S the forward part of a ship

PROW adj PROWER, PROWEST brave

PROWAR adj favoring war

PROWESS n pl. -ES exceptional ability

PROWL v -ED, -ING, -S to move about stealthily

PROWLER n pl. -S one that prowls

PROXEMIC adj pertaining to a branch of environmental study

PROXIES pl. of proxy

PROXIMAL adj located near the point of origin

PROXIMO adj of or occurring in the following month

PROXY n pl. PROXIES a person authorized to act for another

PRUDE n pl. -S a prudish person

PRUDENCE n pl. -S the quality of being prudent

PRUDENT adj having, showing, or exercising good judgment

PRUDERY n pl. -ERIES excessive regard for propriety, modesty, or morality

PRUDISH adj marked by prudery

PRUINOSE adj having a powdery covering

PRUNE v PRUNED, PRUNING, PRUNES to cut off branches or parts from **PRUNABLE** adj

PRUNELLA n pl. -S a strong woolen fabric

PRUNELLE n pl. -S a plum-flavored liqueur

PRUNELLO n pl. -LOS prunella

PRUNER n pl. -S one that prunes

PRUNING present participle of prune

PRURIENT adj having lustful thoughts or desires

PRURIGO n pl. -GOS a skin disease

PRURITUS n pl. -ES intense itching **PRURITIC** adj

PRUSSIC adj pertaining to a type of acid

PRUTA n pl. PRUTOT prutah

PRUTAH n pl. PRUTOTH a monetary unit of Israel

PRY v PRIED, PRYING, PRIES to inquire impertinently into private matters **PRYINGLY** adv

PRYER n pl. -S prier

PRYTHEE interj prithee

PSALM v -ED, -ING, -S to praise in psalms (sacred songs)

PSALMIC adj of or pertaining to a psalm

PSALMIST n pl. -S a writer of psalms

PSALMODY n pl. -DIES the use of psalms in worship

PSALTER n pl. -S a book of psalms

PSALTERY n pl. -TERIES an ancient stringed musical instrument

PSALTRY n pl. -TRIES psaltery

PSAMMITE n pl. -S a fine-grained rock

PSCHENT n pl. -S a crown worn by ancient Egyptian kings

PSEPHITE n pl. -S a rock composed of small pebbles

PSEUDO adj false or counterfeit

PSHAW v -ED, -ING, -S to utter an expression of disapproval

PSI n pl. -S a Greek letter

PSILOSIS n pl. -LOSES a tropical disease **PSILOTIC** adj

PSOAS n pl. PSOAI or PSOAE a muscle of the loin

PSOCID n pl. -S a minute winged insect

PSORALEA n pl. -S a plant of the bean family

PSST *interj* — used to attract someone's attention

PSYCH *v* -ED, -ING, -S to put into the proper frame of mind

PSYCHE *n pl.* -S the mental structure of a person

PSYCHIC *n pl.* -S one sensitive to extrasensory phenomena

PSYCHO *n pl.* -CHOS a mentally unstable person

PSYLLA *n pl.* -S any of various plant lice

PSYLLID *n pl.* -S psylla

PTERIN *n pl.* -S a chemical compound

PTEROPOD *n pl.* -S a type of mollusk

PTERYLA *n pl.* -LAE a feathered area on the skin of a bird

PTISAN *n pl.* -S a tea of herbs or barley

PTOMAIN *n pl.* -S ptomaine

PTOMAINE *n pl.* -S a compound produced by the decomposition of protein

PTOSIS *n pl.* PTOSES a drooping of the upper eyelid **PTOTIC** *adj*

PTYALIN *n pl.* -S a salivary enzyme

PTYALISM *n pl.* -S an excessive flow of saliva

PUB *n pl.* -S a tavern

PUBERTY *n pl.* -TIES a period of sexual maturation **PUBERAL, PUBERTAL** *adj*

PUBES *n pl.* PUBES the lower part of the abdomen

PUBIC *adj* pertaining to the pubes or pubis

PUBIS *n pl.* PUBES the forward portion of either of the hipbones

PUBLIC *n pl.* -S the community or the people as a whole

PUBLICAN *n pl.* -S one who owns or manages a pub

PUBLICLY *adv* by the public

PUBLISH *v* -ED, -ING, -ES to print and issue to the public

PUCCOON *n pl.* -S an herb that yields a red dye

PUCE *n pl.* -S a dark red color

PUCK *n pl.* -S a rubber disk used in ice hockey

PUCKA *adj* pukka

PUCKER *v* -ED, -ING, -S to gather into small wrinkles or folds

PUCKERER *n pl.* -S one that puckers

PUCKERY *adj* -ERIER, -ERIEST having a tendency to pucker

PUCKISH *adj* impish

PUD *n pl.* -S pudding

PUDDING *n pl.* -S a thick, soft dessert

PUDDLE *v* -DLED, -DLING, -DLES to strew with puddles (small pools of water)

PUDDLER *n pl.* -S one who subjects iron to puddling

PUDDLING *n pl.* -S the process of converting pig iron to wrought iron

PUDDLY *adj* -DLIER, -DLIEST full of puddles

PUDENCY *n pl.* -CIES modesty

PUDENDUM *n pl.* -DA the external genital organs of a woman **PUDENDAL** *adj*

PUDGY *adj* PUDGIER, PUDGIEST short and fat **PUDGILY** *adv*

PUDIC *adj* pertaining to the pudendum

PUEBLO *n pl.* -LOS a communal dwelling of certain Indian tribes

PUERILE *adj* childish

PUFF *v* -ED, -ING, -S to blow in short gusts

PUFFBALL *n pl.* -S any of various globular fungi

PUFFER *n pl.* -S one that puffs

PUFFERY *n pl.* -ERIES excessive public praise

PUFFIN *n pl.* -S a sea bird

PUFFY *adj* -FIER, -FIEST swollen **PUFFILY** *adv*

PUG *v* PUGGED, PUGGING, PUGS to fill in with clay or mortar

PUGAREE *n pl.* -S pugree

PUGGAREE *n pl.* -S pugree

PUGGED past tense of pug

PUGGIER comparative of puggy

PUGGIEST superlative of puggy

PUGGING present participle of pug

PUGGISH *adj* somewhat stubby

PUGGREE *n pl.* -S pugree

PUGGRY *n pl.* -GRIES pugree

PUGGY *adj* -GIER, -GIEST puggish

PUGH *interj* — used to express disgust

PUGILISM n pl. -S the art or practice of fighting with the fists

PUGILIST n pl. -S one who fights with his fists

PUGMARK n pl. -S a footprint

PUGREE n pl. -S a cloth band wrapped around a hat

PUISNE n pl. -S one of lesser rank

PUISSANT adj powerful

PUKE v PUKED, PUKING, PUKES to vomit

PUKKA adj genuine

PUL n pl. PULS or PULI a coin of Afghanistan

PULE v PULED, PULING, PULES to whine

PULER n pl. -S one that pules

PULI n pl. -LIK or -LIS a long-haired sheepdog

PULICENE adj pertaining to fleas

PULICIDE n pl. -S an agent used for destroying fleas

PULIK a pl. of puli

PULING n pl. -S a plaintive cry

PULINGLY adv in a whining manner

PULL v -ED, -ING, -S to exert force in order to cause motion toward the force

PULLBACK n pl. -S a restraint or drawback

PULLER n pl. -S one that pulls

PULLET n pl. -S a young hen

PULLEY n pl. -LEYS a device used for lifting weight

PULLMAN n pl. -S a railroad sleeping car

PULLOUT n pl. -S a withdrawal

PULLOVER n pl. -S a garment that is put on by being drawn over the head

PULMONIC adj pertaining to the lungs

PULMOTOR n pl. -S a respiratory device

PULP v -ED, -ING, -S to reduce to pulp (a soft, moist mass of matter)

PULPAL adj pertaining to pulp PULPALLY adv

PULPER n pl. -S one that pulps

PULPIER comparative of pulpy

PULPIEST superlative of pulpy

PULPILY adv in a pulpy manner

PULPIT n pl. -S a platform in a church PULPITAL adj

PULPLESS adj having no pulp

PULPOUS adj pulpy

PULPWOOD n pl. -S soft wood used in making paper

PULPY adj PULPIER, PULPIEST resembling pulp

PULQUE n pl. -S a fermented Mexican beverage

PULSANT adj pulsating

PULSAR n pl. -S a celestial source of radio waves

PULSATE v -SATED, -SATING, -SATES to expand and contract rhythmically

PULSATOR n pl. -S something that pulsates

PULSE v PULSED, PULSING, PULSES to pulsate

PULSEJET n pl. -S a type of engine

PULSER n pl. -S a device that causes pulsations

PULSING present participle of pulse

PULSION n pl. -S propulsion

PULSOJET n pl. -S pulsejet

PULVILLI n/pl pads between the claws of an insect's foot

PULVINUS n pl. -NI a swelling at the base of a leaf PULVINAR adj

PUMA n pl. -S a cougar

PUMELO n pl. -LOS pomelo

PUMICE v -ICED, -ICING, -ICES to polish with a porous volcanic rock

PUMICER n pl. -S one that pumices

PUMICITE n pl. -S a porous volcanic rock

PUMMEL v -MELED, -MELING, -MELS or -MELLED, -MELLING, -MELS to pommel

PUMP v -ED, -ING, -S to cause to flow by means of a pump (a device for moving fluids)

PUMPER n pl. -S one that pumps

PUMPKIN n pl. -S a large, edible fruit

PUMPLESS adj lacking a pump

PUMPLIKE adj resembling a pump

PUN v PUNNED, PUNNING, PUNS to make a pun (a play on words)

PUNA n pl. -S a cold, arid plateau

PUNCH v -ED, -ING, -ES to perforate with a type of tool

PUNCHEON n pl. -S a vertical supporting timber

PUNCHER   *n pl.* -S one that punches

PUNCHY   *adj* PUNCHIER, PUNCHIEST dazed

PUNCTATE   *adj* covered with dots

PUNCTUAL   *adj* being on time

PUNCTURE   *v* -TURED, -TURING, -TURES to pierce with a pointed object

PUNDIT   *n pl.* -S a Hindu scholar PUNDITIC *adj*

PUNDITRY   *n pl.* -RIES the learning of pundits

PUNG   *n pl.* -S a box-shaped sleigh

PUNGENCY   *n pl.* -CIES the state of being pungent

PUNGENT   *adj* sharply affecting the organs of taste or smell

PUNIER   comparative of puny

PUNIEST   superlative of puny

PUNILY   *adv* in a puny manner

PUNINESS   *n pl.* -ES the state of being puny

PUNISH   *v* -ED, -ING, -ES to impose a penalty on in requital for wrongdoing

PUNISHER   *n pl.* -S one that punishes

PUNITION   *n pl.* -S the act of punishing; punishment

PUNITIVE   *adj* inflicting punishment

PUNITORY   *adj* punitive

PUNK   *n pl.* -S dry, decayed wood used as tinder

PUNK   *adj* PUNKER, PUNKEST of inferior quality

PUNKA   *n pl.* -S a ceiling fan used in India

PUNKAH   *n pl.* -S punka

PUNKEY   *n pl.* -KEYS punkie

PUNKIE   *n pl.* -S a biting gnat

PUNKIN   *n pl.* -S pumpkin

PUNKY   *adj* PUNKIER, PUNKIEST resembling punk

PUNNED   past tense of pun

PUNNER   *n pl.* -S a punster

PUNNING   present participle of pun

PUNNY   *adj* -NIER, -NIEST being or involving a pun

PUNSTER   *n pl.* -S one who is given to punning

PUNT   *v* -ED, -ING, -S to propel through water with a pole

PUNTER   *n pl.* -S one that punts

PUNTO   *n pl.* -TOS a hit or thrust in fencing

PUNTY   *n pl.* -TIES an iron rod used in glassmaking

PUNY   *adj* PUNIER, PUNIEST of inferior size, strength, or significance

PUP   *v* PUPPED, PUPPING, PUPS to give birth to puppies

PUPA   *n pl.* -PAS or -PAE an intermediate stage of a metamorphic insect PUPAL *adj*

PUPARIUM   *n pl.* -IA a pupal shell PUPARIAL *adj*

PUPATE   *v* -PATED, -PATING, -PATES to pass through the pupal stage

PUPATION   *n pl.* -S the act of pupating

PUPFISH   *n pl.* -ES a small, freshwater fish

PUPIL   *n pl.* -S a student under the close supervision of a teacher

PUPILAGE   *n pl.* -S the state of being a pupil

PUPILAR   *adj* pertaining to a part of the eye

PUPILARY   *adj* pupilar

PUPPED   past tense of pup

PUPPET   *n pl.* -S a small figure, as of a person or animal, manipulated by the hand

PUPPETRY   *n pl.* -RIES the art of making or manipulating puppets

PUPPING   present participle of pup

PUPPY   *n pl.* -PIES a young dog PUPPYISH *adj*

PUPPYDOM   *n pl.* -S the world of puppies

PUR   *v* PURRED, PURRING, PURS to purr

PURANA   *n pl.* -S a Hindu scripture PURANIC *adj*

PURBLIND   *adj* partially blind

PURCHASE   *v* -CHASED, -CHASING, -CHASES to acquire by the payment of money

PURDA   *n pl.* -S purdah

PURDAH   *n pl.* -S a curtain used in India to seclude women

PURE   *adj* PURER, PUREST free from anything different, inferior, or contaminating

PUREBRED   *n pl.* -S an animal of unmixed stock

PUREE	v -REED, -REEING, -REES to reduce to a thick pulp by cooking and sieving
PURELY	adv in a pure manner
PURENESS	n pl. -ES the quality of being pure
PURER	comparative of pure
PUREST	superlative of pure
PURFLE	v -FLED, -FLING, -FLES to decorate the border of
PURFLING	n pl. -S an ornamental border
PURGE	v PURGED, PURGING, PURGES to purify
PURGER	n pl. -S one that purges
PURGING	n pl. -S the act of purifying
PURI	n pl. -S poori
PURIFIER	n pl. -S one that purifies
PURIFY	v -FIED, -FYING, -FIES to free from impurities
PURIN	n pl. -S purine
PURINE	n pl. -S a chemical compound
PURISM	n pl. -S strict adherence to traditional correctness
PURIST	n pl. -S one who practices purism PURISTIC adj
PURITAN	n pl. -S a rigorously moral or religious person
PURITY	n pl. -TIES the quality of being pure
PURL	v -ED, -ING, -S to knit with a particular stitch
PURLIEU	n pl. -S an outlying or neighboring area
PURLIN	n pl. -S a horizontal supporting timber
PURLINE	n pl. -S purlin
PURLOIN	v -ED, -ING, -S to steal
PURPLE	adj -PLER, -PLEST of a color intermediate between red and blue
PURPLE	v -PLED, -PLING, -PLES to make purple
PURPLISH	adj somewhat purple
PURPLY	adj purplish
PURPORT	v -ED, -ING, -S to profess or claim
PURPOSE	v -POSED, -POSING, -POSES to resolve to perform or accomplish
PURPURA	n pl. -S a disease characterized by purple spots on the skin
PURPURE	n pl. -S the heraldic color purple
PURPURIC	adj pertaining to purpura
PURPURIN	n pl. -S a reddish dye
PURR	v -ED, -ING, -S to utter a low, vibrant sound
PURRED	past tense of pur and purr
PURRING	present participle of pur and purr
PURSE	v PURSED, PURSING, PURSES to pucker
PURSER	n pl. -S an officer in charge of a ship's accounts
PURSIER	comparative of pursy
PURSIEST	superlative of pursy
PURSILY	adv in a pursy manner
PURSING	present participle of purse
PURSLANE	n pl. -S a common garden herb
PURSUANT	adv in accordance
PURSUE	v -SUED, -SUING, -SUES to follow in order to overtake or capture
PURSUER	n pl. -S one that pursues
PURSUIT	n pl. -S the act of pursuing
PURSY	adj PURSIER, PURSIEST short of breath
PURULENT	adj secreting pus
PURVEY	v -ED, -ING, -S to supply
PURVEYOR	n pl. -S one that purveys
PURVIEW	n pl. -S the extent of operation, authority, or concern
PUS	n pl. -ES a viscous fluid formed in infected tissue
PUSH	v -ED, -ING, -ES to exert force in order to cause motion away from the force
PUSHBALL	n pl. -S a type of ball game
PUSHCART	n pl. -S a light cart pushed by hand
PUSHDOWN	n pl. -S a store of computer data
PUSHER	n pl. -S one that pushes
PUSHFUL	adj pushy
PUSHIER	comparative of pushy
PUSHIEST	superlative of pushy
PUSHILY	adv in a pushy manner
PUSHOVER	n pl. -S an easily defeated person or team
PUSHPIN	n pl. -S a large-headed pin

PUSHUP n pl. -S a type of exercise

PUSHY adj PUSHIER, PUSHIEST offensively aggressive

PUSLEY n pl. -LEYS pussley

PUSLIKE adj resembling pus

PUSS n pl. -ES a cat

PUSSIER comparative of pussy

PUSSIES pl. of pussy

PUSSIEST superlative of pussy

PUSSLEY n pl. -LEYS purslane

PUSSLIKE adj catlike

PUSSLY n pl. -LIES pussley

PUSSY n pl. PUSSIES a cat

PUSSY adj -SIER, -SIEST full of pus

PUSSYCAT n pl. -S a cat

PUSTULE n pl. -S a small elevation of the skin containing pus **PUSTULAR, PUSTULED** adj

PUT v PUT, PUTTING, PUTS to place in a particular position

PUTAMEN n pl. -MINA the hard covering of the kernel of certain fruits

PUTATIVE adj generally regarded as such

PUTLOG n pl. -S a horizontal supporting timber

PUTOFF n pl. -S an excuse

PUTON n pl. -S a hoax or deception

PUTOUT n pl. -S an act of causing an out in baseball

PUTREFY v -FIED, -FYING, -FIES to make or become putrid

PUTRID adj being in a decomposed, foul-smelling state **PUTRIDLY** adv

PUTSCH n pl. -ES a suddenly executed attempt to overthrow a government

PUTT v -ED, -ING, -S to hit with a light stroke in golf

PUTTEE n pl. -S a strip of cloth wound around the leg

PUTTER v -ED, -ING, -S to occupy oneself in a leisurely or ineffective manner

PUTTERER n pl. -S one that putters

PUTTIED past tense of putty

PUTTIER n pl. -S one that putties

PUTTING present participle of put

PUTTY v -TIED, -TYING, -TIES to fill with a type of cement

PUZZLE v -ZLED, -ZLING, -ZLES to cause uncertainty and indecision in

PUZZLER n pl. -S something that puzzles

PYA n pl. -S a copper coin of Burma

PYAEMIA n pl. -S pyemia **PYAEMIC** adj

PYCNIDIA n/pl spore-bearing organs of certain fungi

PYE n pl. -S a book of ecclesiastical rules in the pre-Reformation English church

PYELITIS n pl. -TISES inflammation of the pelvis or the kidney **PYELITIC** adj

PYEMIA n pl. -S the presence of pus in the blood **PYEMIC** adj

PYGIDIUM n pl. -IA the posterior region of certain invertebrates **PYGIDIAL** adj

PYGMY n pl. -MIES a small person **PYGMAEAN, PYGMEAN, PYGMOID, PYGMYISH** adj

PYGMYISM n pl. -S a stunted or dwarfish condition

PYIC adj pertaining to pus

PYIN n pl. -S a protein compound contained in pus

PYJAMAS n pl. PYJAMAS pajamas

PYKNIC n pl. -S a person having a broad, stocky build

PYLON n pl. -S a tall structure marking an entrance or approach

PYLORUS n pl. -RI or -RUSES the opening between the stomach and the duodenum **PYLORIC** adj

PYODERMA n pl. -S a pus-causing skin disease

PYOGENIC adj producing pus

PYOID adj puslike

PYORRHEA n pl. -S a discharge of pus

PYOSIS n pl. -OSES the formation of pus

PYRALID n pl. -S a long-legged moth

PYRAMID v -ED, -ING, -S to raise or increase by adding amounts gradually

PYRAN n pl. -S a chemical compound **PYRANOID** adj

PYRANOSE n pl. -S a simple sugar

PYRE n pl. -S a pile of combustible material

PYRENE n pl. -S a putamen

PYRENOID *n* pl. -S a protein body of certain lower organisms

PYRETIC *adj* pertaining to fever

PYREXIA *n* pl. -S fever PYREXIAL, PYREXIC *adj*

PYRIC *adj* pertaining to burning

PYRIDINE *n* pl. -S a flammable liquid PYRIDIC *adj*

PYRIFORM *adj* pear-shaped

PYRITE *n* pl. -S a metallic sulfide PYRITIC, PYRITOUS *adj*

PYROGEN *n* pl. -S a substance that produces fever

PYROLA *n* pl. -S a perennial herb

PYROLOGY *n* pl. -GIES the scientific examination of materials by heat

PYROLYZE *v* -LYZED, -LYZING, -LYZES to affect compounds by the application of heat

PYRONE *n* pl. -S a chemical compound

PYRONINE *n* pl. -S a dye

PYROPE *n* pl. -S a variety of garnet

PYROSIS *n* pl. -SISES heartburn

PYROSTAT *n* pl. -S a thermostat

PYROXENE *n* pl. -S any of a group of minerals common in igneous rocks

PYRRHIC *n* pl. -S a type of metrical foot

PYRROL *n* pl. -S pyrrole

PYRROLE *n* pl. -S a chemical compound PYRROLIC *adj*

PYRUVATE *n* pl. -S a chemical salt

PYTHON *n* pl. -S a large snake PYTHONIC *adj*

PYURIA *n* pl. -S the presence of pus in the urine

PYX *n* pl. -ES a container in which the eucharistic bread is kept

PYXIDES pl. of pyxis

PYXIDIUM *n* pl. -IA a type of seed vessel

PYXIE *n* pl. -S an evergreen shrub

PYXIS *n* pl. PYXIDES a pyxidium

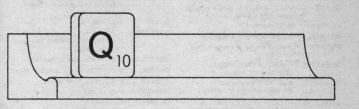

QAID	*n pl.* -S caid
QINDAR	*n pl.* -S qintar
QINTAR	*n pl.* -S a monetary unit of Albania
QIVIUT	*n pl.* -S the wool of a musk-ox
QOPH	*n pl.* -S koph
QUA	*adv* in the capacity of
QUACK	*v* -ED, -ING, -S to utter the characteristic cry of a duck
QUACKERY	*n pl.* -ERIES fraudulent practice
QUACKISH	*adj* fraudulent
QUACKISM	*n pl.* -S quackery
QUAD	*v* QUADDED, QUADDING, QUADS to space out by means of quadrats
QUADRANS	*n pl.* -RANTES an ancient Roman coin
QUADRANT	*n pl.* -S a quarter section of a circle
QUADRAT	*n pl.* -S a piece of type metal used for filling spaces
QUADRATE	*v* -RATED, -RATING, -RATES to correspond or agree
QUADRIC	*n pl.* -S a type of geometric surface
QUADRIGA	*n pl.* -GAE a chariot drawn by four horses
QUADROON	*n pl.* -S a person of one-quarter black ancestry
QUAERE	*n pl.* -S a question
QUAESTOR	*n pl.* -S an ancient Roman magistrate
QUAFF	*v* -ED, -ING, -S to drink deeply
QUAFFER	*n pl.* -S one that quaffs
QUAG	*n pl.* -S a quagmire
QUAGGA	*n pl.* -S an extinct zebralike mammal
QUAGGY	*adj* -GIER, -GIEST marshy
QUAGMIRE	*n pl.* -S an area of marshy ground
QUAGMIRY	*adj* -MIRIER, -MIRIEST marshy
QUAHAUG	*n pl.* -S quahog
QUAHOG	*n pl.* -S an edible clam
QUAI	*n pl.* -S quay
QUAICH	*n pl.* -ES or -S a small drinking vessel
QUAIGH	*n pl.* -S quaich
QUAIL	*v* -ED, -ING, -S to cower
QUAINT	*adj* QUAINTER, QUAINTEST pleasingly old-fashioned or unfamiliar **QUAINTLY** *adv*
QUAKE	*v* QUAKED, QUAKING, QUAKES to shake or vibrate
QUAKER	*n pl.* -S one that quakes
QUAKY	*adj* QUAKIER, QUAKIEST tending to quake **QUAKILY** *adv*
QUALE	*n pl.* -LIA a property considered apart from things having the property
QUALIFY	*v* -FIED, -FYING, -FIES to make suitable or capable
QUALITY	*n pl.* -TIES a characteristic or attribute
QUALM	*n pl.* -S a feeling of doubt or misgiving
QUALMISH	*adj* having qualms
QUALMY	*adj* QUALMIER, QUALMIEST qualmish
QUAMASH	*n pl.* -ES camass
QUANDANG	*n pl.* -S quandong

QUANDARY *n* pl. -RIES a dilemma

QUANDONG *n* pl. -S an Australian tree

QUANT *v* -ED, -ING, -S to propel through water with a pole

QUANTA pl. of quantum

QUANTAL *adj* pertaining to a quantum

QUANTIC *n* pl. -S a type of mathematical function

QUANTIFY *v* -FIED, -FYING, -FIES to determine the quantity of

QUANTITY *n* pl. -TIES a specified or indefinite amount or number

QUANTIZE *v* -TIZED, -TIZING, -TIZES to limit the possible values of to a discrete set

QUANTONG *n* pl. -S quandong

QUANTUM *n* pl. -TA a fundamental unit of energy

QUARE *adj* queer

QUARK *n* pl. -S a hypothetical atomic particle

QUARREL *v* -RELED, -RELING, -RELS or -RELLED, -RELLING, -RELS to engage in an angry dispute

QUARRIER *n* pl. -S one that quarries

QUARRY *v* -RIED, -RYING, -RIES to dig stone from an excavation

QUART *n* pl. -S a liquid measure of capacity

QUARTAN *n* pl. -S a recurrent malarial fever

QUARTE *n* pl. -S a fencing thrust

QUARTER *v* -ED, -ING, -S to divide into four equal parts

QUARTERN *n* pl. -S one-fourth of something

QUARTET *n* pl. -S a group of four

QUARTIC *n* pl. -S a type of mathematical function

QUARTILE *n* pl. -S a portion of a frequency distribution

QUARTO *n* pl. -TOS the size of a piece of paper cut four from a sheet

QUARTZ *n* pl. -ES a mineral

QUASAR *n* pl. -S a distant celestial object emitting strong radio waves

QUASH *v* -ED, -ING, -ES to suppress completely

QUASI *adj* similar but not exactly the same

QUASS *n* pl. -ES kvass

QUASSIA *n* pl. -S a tropical tree

QUASSIN *n* pl. -S a medicinal compound obtained from the wood of a quassia

QUATE *adj* quiet

QUATORZE *n* pl. -S a set of four cards of the same denomination scoring fourteen points

QUATRAIN *n* pl. -S a stanza of four lines

QUATRE *n* pl. -S the four at cards or dice

QUAVER *v* -ED, -ING, -S to quiver

QUAVERER *n* pl. -S one that quavers

QUAVERY *adj* quivery

QUAY *n* pl. QUAYS a wharf **QUAYLIKE** *adj*

QUAYAGE *n* pl. -S a charge for the use of a quay

QUAYSIDE *n* pl. -S the area adjacent to a quay

QUEAN *n* pl. -S a harlot

QUEASY *adj* -SIER, -SIEST easily nauseated **QUEASILY** *adv*

QUEAZY *adj* -ZIER, -ZIEST queasy

QUEEN *v* -ED, -ING, -S to make a queen (a female monarch) of

QUEENLY *adj* -LIER, -LIEST of or befitting a queen

QUEER *adj* QUEERER, QUEEREST deviating from the expected or normal

QUEER *v* -ED, -ING, -S to spoil the effect or success of

QUEERISH *adj* somewhat queer

QUEERLY *adv* in a queer manner

QUELL *v* -ED, -ING, -S to suppress

QUELLER *n* pl. -S one that quells

QUENCH *v* -ED, -ING, -ES to put out or extinguish

QUENCHER *n* pl. -S one that quenches

QUENELLE *n* pl. -S a type of dumpling

QUERCINE *adj* pertaining to oaks

QUERIDA *n* pl. -S a female sweetheart

QUERIED past tense of query

QUERIER *n* pl. -S a querist

QUERIES present 3d person sing. of query

QUERIST *n* pl. -S one who queries

QUERN *n* pl. -S a hand-turned grain mill

QUERY *v* -RIED, -RYING, -RIES to question

QUEST	v -ED, -ING, -S to make a search
QUESTER	n pl. -S one that quests
QUESTION	v -ED, -ING, -S to put a question (an inquiry) to
QUESTOR	n pl. -S quaestor
QUETZAL	n pl. -S or -ES a tropical bird
QUEUE	v QUEUED, QUEUING or QUEUEING, QUEUES to line up
QUEUER	n pl. -S one that queues
QUEY	n pl. QUEYS a young cow
QUEZAL	n pl. -S or -ES quetzal
QUIBBLE	v -BLED, -BLING, -BLES to argue over trivialities
QUIBBLER	n pl. -S one that quibbles
QUICHE	n pl. -S a custard-filled pastry
QUICK	adj QUICKER, QUICKEST acting or capable of acting with speed
QUICK	n pl. -S a sensitive area of flesh
QUICKEN	v -ED, -ING, -S to speed up
QUICKIE	n pl. -S something done quickly
QUICKLY	adv in a quick manner
QUICKSET	n pl. -S a plant suitable for hedges
QUID	n pl. -S a portion of something to be chewed
QUIDDITY	n pl. -TIES the true nature of a thing
QUIDNUNC	n pl. -S a nosy person
QUIET	adj -ETER, -ETEST making little or no noise
QUIET	v -ED, -ING, -S to cause to be quiet
QUIETEN	v -ED, -ING, -S to quiet
QUIETER	n pl. -S one that quiets
QUIETISM	n pl. -S a form of religious mysticism
QUIETIST	n pl. -S an advocate of quietism
QUIETLY	adv in a quiet manner
QUIETUDE	n pl. -S a state of tranquillity
QUIETUS	n pl. -ES a final settlement
QUIFF	n pl. -S a forelock
QUILL	v -ED, -ING, -S to press small ridges in
QUILLAI	n pl. -S an evergreen tree
QUILLET	n pl. -S a trivial distinction
QUILT	v -ED, -ING, -S to stitch together with padding in between
QUILTER	n pl. -S one that quilts
QUILTING	n pl. -S material that is used for making quilts
QUINARY	n pl. -RIES a group of five
QUINATE	adj arranged in groups of five
QUINCE	n pl. -S an apple-like fruit
QUINCUNX	n pl. -ES an arrangement of five objects
QUINELLA	n pl. -S a type of bet in horse racing
QUINIC	adj pertaining to quinine
QUINIELA	n pl. -S quinella
QUININ	n pl. -S quinine
QUININA	n pl. -S quinine
QUININE	n pl. -S a medicinal alkaloid
QUINNAT	n pl. -S a food fish
QUINOA	n pl. -S a weedy plant
QUINOID	n pl. -S a chemical compound
QUINOL	n pl. -S a chemical compound
QUINOLIN	n pl. -S a chemical compound
QUINONE	n pl. -S a chemical compound
QUINSY	n pl. -SIES an inflammation of the tonsils
QUINT	n pl. -S a group of five
QUINTAIN	n pl. -S an object used as a target in a medieval sport
QUINTAL	n pl. -S a unit of weight
QUINTAN	n pl. -S a recurrent fever
QUINTAR	n pl. -S qintar
QUINTET	n pl. -S a group of five
QUINTIC	n pl. -S a type of mathematical function
QUINTILE	n pl. -S a portion of a frequency distribution
QUINTIN	n pl. -S a fine linen
QUIP	v QUIPPED, QUIPPING, QUIPS to make witty remarks
QUIPPISH	adj witty
QUIPPU	n pl. -S quipu
QUIPSTER	n pl. -S one that quips
QUIPU	n pl. -S an ancient calculating device
QUIRE	v QUIRED, QUIRING, QUIRES to arrange sheets of paper in sets of twenty-four
QUIRK	v -ED, -ING, -S to twist
QUIRKY	adj QUIRKIER, QUIRKIEST tricky QUIRKILY adv

QUIRT *v* -ED, -ING, -S to strike with a riding whip

QUISLING *n* pl. -S a traitor who aids the invaders of his country

QUIT *v* QUITTED, QUITTING, QUITS to end one's engagement in or occupation with

QUITCH *n* pl. -ES a perennial grass

QUITE *adv* to the fullest extent

QUITRENT *n* pl. -S a fixed rent due from a socage tenant

QUITTED past tense of quit

QUITTER *n* pl. -S one that quits

QUITTING present participle of quit

QUITTOR *n* pl. -S an inflammation of an animal's hoof

QUIVER *v* -ED, -ING, -S to shake with a slight but rapid motion

QUIVERER *n* pl. -S one that quivers

QUIVERY *adj* marked by quivering

QUIXOTE *n* pl. -S a quixotic person

QUIXOTIC *adj* extremely idealistic

QUIXOTRY *n* pl. -TRIES quixotic action or thought

QUIZ *v* QUIZZED, QUIZZING, QUIZZES to test the knowledge of by asking questions

QUIZZER *n* pl. -S one that quizzes

QUOD *n* pl. -S a prison

QUOIN *v* -ED, -ING, -S to secure with a type of wedge

QUOIT *v* -ED, -ING, -S to play a throwing game similar to ringtoss

QUOMODO *n* pl. -DOS a means or manner

QUONDAM *adj* that once was

QUORUM *n* pl. -S a particularly chosen group

QUOTA *n* pl. -S a proportional part or share

QUOTE *v* QUOTED, QUOTING, QUOTES to repeat the words of **QUOTABLE** *adj* **QUOTABLY** *adv*

QUOTER *n* pl. -S one that quotes

QUOTH *v* said — QUOTH is the only accepted form of this verb; it cannot be conjugated

QUOTHA *interj* — used to express surprise or sarcasm

QUOTIENT *n* pl. -S the number resulting from the division of one number by another

QUOTING present participle of quote

QURSH *n* pl. -ES a monetary unit of Saudi Arabia

QURUSH *n* pl. -ES qursh

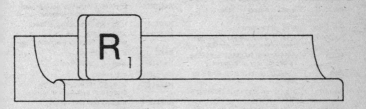

RABATO *n pl.* -TOS a wide, lace-edged collar

RABBET *v* -ED, -ING, -S to cut a groove in

RABBI *n pl.* -S or -ES a Jewish spiritual leader

RABBIN *n pl.* -S rabbi

RABBINIC *adj* pertaining to rabbis

RABBIT *v* -ED, -ING, -S to hunt rabbits (rodent-like mammals)

RABBITER *n pl.* -S one that rabbits

RABBITRY *n pl.* -RIES a place where rabbits are kept

RABBLE *v* -BLED, -BLING, -BLES to mob

RABBLER *n pl.* -S an iron bar used in puddling

RABBONI *n pl.* -S master; teacher — used as a Jewish title of respect

RABIC *adj* pertaining to rabies

RABID *adj* affected with rabies RABIDLY *adv*

RABIDITY *n pl.* -TIES the state of being rabid

RABIES *n pl.* RABIES an infectious virus disease RABIETIC *adj*

RACCOON *n pl.* -S a carnivorous mammal

RACE *v* RACED, RACING, RACES to compete in a contest of speed

RACEMATE *n pl.* -S a chemical salt

RACEME *n pl.* -S a mode of arrangement of flowers along an axis RACEMED *adj*

RACEMIC *adj* constituting a chemical compound that is optically inactive

RACEMISM *n pl.* -S the state of being racemic

RACEMIZE *v* -MIZED, -MIZING, -MIZES to convert into a racemic compound

RACEMOID *adj* pertaining to a raceme

RACEMOSE *adj* having the form of a raceme

RACEMOUS *adj* racemose

RACER *n pl.* -S one that races

RACEWAY *n pl.* -WAYS a channel for conducting water

RACHET *n pl.* -S ratchet

RACHIS *n pl.* -CHISES or -CHIDES the spinal column RACHIAL *adj*

RACHITIS *n pl.* -TIDES rickets RACHITIC *adj*

RACIAL *adj* pertaining to an ethnic group RACIALLY *adv*

RACIER comparative of racy

RACIEST superlative of racy

RACILY *adv* in a racy manner

RACINESS *n pl.* -ES the quality of being racy

RACING *n pl.* -S the sport of engaging in contests of speed

RACISM *n pl.* -S a doctrine of racial superiority

RACIST *n pl.* -S an advocate of racism

RACK *v* -ED, -ING, -S to place in a type of framework

RACKER *n pl.* -S one that racks

RACKET *v* -ED, -ING, -S to make a loud noise

RACKETY *adj* -ETIER, -ETIEST noisy

RACKLE *adj* impetuous; rash

RACKWORK *n* pl. -S a type of mechanism

RACLETTE *n* pl. -S a cheese dish

RACON *n* pl. -S a type of radar transmitter

RACOON *n* pl. -S raccoon

RACQUET *n* pl. -S a lightweight implement used in various ball games

RACY *adj* RACIER, RACIEST bordering on impropriety or indecency

RAD *v* RADDED, RADDING, RADS to fear

RADAR *n* pl. -S an electronic locating device

RADDLE *v* -DLED, -DLING, -DLES to weave together

RADIABLE *adj* capable of radiating

RADIAL *n* pl. -S a part diverging from a center

RADIALE *n* pl. -LIA a bone of the carpus

RADIALLY *adv* in a diverging manner

RADIAN *n* pl. -S a unit of angular measure

RADIANCE *n* pl. -S brightness

RADIANCY *n* pl. -CIES radiance

RADIANT *n* pl. -S a point from which rays are emitted

RADIATE *v* -ATED, -ATING, -ATES to emit rays

RADIATOR *n* pl. -S a heating device

RADICAL *n* pl. -S a group of atoms that acts as a unit in chemical compounds

RADICAND *n* pl. -S a quantity in mathematics

RADICATE *v* -CATED, -CATING, -CATES to cause to take root

RADICEL *n* pl. -S a rootlet

RADICES a pl. of radix

RADICLE *n* pl. -S a part of a plant embryo

RADII a pl. of radius

RADIO *v* -ED, -ING, -S to transmit by radio (an apparatus for wireless communication)

RADIOMAN *n* pl. -MEN a radio operator or technician

RADISH *n* pl. -ES a pungent, edible root

RADIUM *n* pl. -S a radioactive element

RADIUS *n* pl. -DII or -DIUSES a straight line from the center of a circle to the circumference

RADIX *n* pl. -DICES or -DIXES the root of a plant

RADOME *n* pl. -S a domelike device used to shelter a radar antenna

RADON *n* pl. -S a radioactive element

RADULA *n* pl. -LAE or -LAS a tonguelike organ of mollusks RADULAR *adj*

RAFF *n* pl. -S riffraff

RAFFIA *n* pl. -S a palm tree

RAFFISH *adj* tawdry

RAFFLE *v* -FLED, -FLING, -FLES to dispose of by a form of lottery

RAFFLER *n* pl. -S one that raffles

RAFT *v* -ED, -ING, -S to transport on a raft (a type of buoyant structure)

RAFTER *n* pl. -S a supporting beam

RAFTSMAN *n* pl. -MEN one who manages a raft

RAG *v* RAGGED, RAGGING, RAGS to scold

RAGA *n* pl. -S a Hindu musical form

RAGBAG *n* pl. -S a bag for storing scraps of cloth

RAGE *v* RAGED, RAGING, RAGES to act or speak with violent anger

RAGEE *n* pl. -S ragi

RAGGED *adj* -GEDER, -GEDEST tattered RAGGEDLY *adv*

RAGGEDY *adj* somewhat ragged

RAGGING present participle of rag

RAGGLE *n* pl. -S a groove cut in masonry

RAGGY *n* pl. -GIES ragi

RAGI *n* pl. -S an East Indian cereal grass

RAGING present participle of rage

RAGINGLY *adv* in a furious manner

RAGLAN *n* pl. -S a type of overcoat

RAGMAN *n* pl. -MEN one who gathers and sells scraps of cloth

RAGOUT *v* -ED, -ING, -S to make into a highly seasoned stew

RAGTAG *n* pl. -S riffraff

RAGTIME *n* pl. -S a style of American dance music

RAGWEED *n* pl. -S a weedy herb

RAGWORT *n* pl. -S a flowering plant

RAH *interj* — used to cheer on a team or player

RAIA   *n pl.* -S rayah

RAID   *v* -ED, -ING, -S to make a sudden assault on

RAIDER   *n pl.* -S one that raids

RAIL   *v* -ED, -ING, -S to scold in abusive or insolent language

RAILBIRD   *n pl.* -S a racing enthusiast

RAILER   *n pl.* -S one that rails

RAILHEAD   *n pl.* -S the end of a railroad line

RAILING   *n pl.* -S a fence-like barrier

RAILLERY   *n pl.* -LERIES good-natured teasing

RAILROAD   *v* -ED, -ING, -S to transport by railroad (a type of road on which locomotives are run)

RAILWAY   *n pl.* -WAYS a railroad

RAIMENT   *n pl.* -S clothing

RAIN   *v* -ED, -ING, -S to fall like rain (drops of water condensed from atmospheric vapor)

RAINBAND   *n pl.* -S a dark band in the solar spectrum

RAINBIRD   *n pl.* -S a type of bird

RAINBOW   *n pl.* -S an arc of spectral colors formed in the sky

RAINCOAT   *n pl.* -S a waterproof coat

RAINDROP   *n pl.* -S a drop of rain

RAINFALL   *n pl.* -S a fall of rain

RAINIER   comparative of rainy

RAINIEST   superlative of rainy

RAINILY   *adv* in a rainy manner

RAINLESS   *adj* having no rain

RAINOUT   *n pl.* -S atomic fallout occurring in precipitation

RAINWASH   *n pl.* -ES the washing away of material by rain

RAINWEAR   *n pl.* -S waterproof clothing

RAINY   *adj* RAINIER, RAINIEST marked by rain

RAISE   *v* RAISED, RAISING, RAISES to move to a higher position RAISABLE *adj*

RAISER   *n pl.* -S one that raises

RAISIN   *n pl.* -S a dried grape RAISINY *adj*

RAISING   *n pl.* -S an elevation

RAISONNE   *adj* arranged systematically

RAJ   *n pl.* -ES dominion; sovereignty

RAJA   *n pl.* -S rajah

RAJAH   *n pl.* -S a king or prince in India

RAKE   *v* RAKED, RAKING, RAKES to gather with a toothed implement

RAKEE   *n pl.* -S raki

RAKEHELL   *n pl.* -S a man lacking in moral restraint

RAKEOFF   *n pl.* -S a share of profits

RAKER   *n pl.* -S one that rakes

RAKI   *n pl.* -S a Turkish liqueur

RAKING   present participle of rake

RAKISH   *adj* dapper RAKISHLY *adv*

RALE   *n pl.* -S an abnormal respiratory sound

RALLIED   past tense of rally

RALLIER   *n pl.* -S one that rallies

RALLINE   *adj* pertaining to a family of marsh birds

RALLY   *v* -LIED, -LYING, -LIES to call together for a common purpose

RALLYE   *n pl.* -S a type of automobile race

RALLYING   *n pl.* -S the sport of driving in rallyes

RALLYIST   *n pl.* -S a participant in a rallye

RAM   *v* RAMMED, RAMMING, RAMS to strike with great force

RAMATE   *adj* having branches

RAMBLE   *v* -BLED, -BLING, -BLES to wander

RAMBLER   *n pl.* -S one that rambles

RAMBUTAN   *n pl.* -S the edible fruit of a Malayan tree

RAMEE   *n pl.* -S ramie

RAMEKIN   *n pl.* -S a cheese dish

RAMENTUM   *n pl.* -TA a scale formed on the surface of leaves

RAMEQUIN   *n pl.* -S ramekin

RAMET   *n pl.* -S an independent member of a clone

RAMI   *pl.* of ramus

RAMIE   *n pl.* -S an Asian shrub

RAMIFORM   *adj* shaped like a branch

RAMIFY   *v* -FIED, -FYING, -FIES to divide into branches

RAMILIE   *n pl.* -S ramillie

RAMILLIE   *n pl.* -S a type of wig

RAMJET   *n pl.* -S a type of engine

RAMMED past tense of ram

RAMMER n pl. -S one that rams

RAMMIER comparative of rammy

RAMMIEST superlative of rammy

RAMMING present participle of ram

RAMMISH adj resembling a ram (a male sheep)

RAMMY adj -MIER, -MIEST rammish

RAMOSE adj having many branches RAMOSELY adv

RAMOSITY n pl. -TIES the state of being ramose

RAMOUS adj ramose

RAMP v -ED, -ING, -S to rise or stand on the hind legs

RAMPAGE v -PAGED, -PAGING, -PAGES to move about wildly or violently

RAMPAGER n pl. -S one that rampages

RAMPANCY n pl. -CIES the state of being rampant

RAMPANT adj unrestrained

RAMPART v -ED, -ING, -S to furnish with a fortifying embankment

RAMPIKE n pl. -S a standing dead tree

RAMPION n pl. -S a European plant

RAMPOLE n pl. -S rampike

RAMROD n pl. -S a rod used in loading a firearm

RAMSHORN n pl. -S a snail used as an aquarium scavenger

RAMSON n pl. -S a broad-leaved garlic

RAMTIL n pl. -S a tropical plant

RAMULOSE adj having many small branches

RAMULOUS adj ramulose

RAMUS n pl. -MI a branch-like part of a structure

RAN past tense of run and rin

RANCE n pl. -S a variety of marble

RANCH v -ED, -ING, -ES to work on a ranch (an establishment for raising livestock)

RANCHER n pl. -S one that owns or works on a ranch

RANCHERO n pl. -ROS a rancher

RANCHMAN n pl. -MEN a rancher

RANCHO n pl. -CHOS a ranch

RANCID adj having an unpleasant odor or taste

RANCOR n pl. -S bitter and vindictive enmity RANCORED adj

RANCOUR n pl. -S rancor

RAND n pl. -S a strip of leather at the heel of a shoe

RANDAN n pl. -S a boat rowed by three persons

RANDIES pl. of randy

RANDOM n pl. -S a haphazard course

RANDOMLY adv in a haphazard manner

RANDY n pl. RANDIES a rude person

RANEE n pl. -S rani

RANG past tense of ring

RANGE v RANGED, RANGING, RANGES to place in a particular order

RANGER n pl. -S an officer supervising the care of a forest

RANGY adj RANGIER, RANGIEST tall and slender

RANI n pl. -S the wife of a rajah

RANID n pl. -S any of a large family of frogs

RANK v -ED, -ING, -S to determine the relative position of

RANK adj RANKER, RANKEST strong and disagreeable in odor or taste

RANKER n pl. -S an enlisted soldier

RANKISH adj somewhat rank

RANKLE v -KLED, -KLING, -KLES to cause irritation or resentment in

RANKLY adv in a rank manner

RANKNESS n pl. -ES the state of being rank

RANPIKE n pl. -S rampike

RANSACK v -ED, -ING, -S to search thoroughly

RANSOM v -ED, -ING, -S to obtain the release of by paying a demanded price

RANSOMER n pl. -S one that ransoms

RANT v -ED, -ING, -S to speak in a loud or vehement manner

RANTER n pl. -S one that rants

RANULA n pl. -S a cyst formed under the tongue

RAP v RAPPED, RAPPING, RAPS to strike sharply

RAPACITY n pl. -TIES the quality of being ravenous

RAPE   v RAPED, RAPING, RAPES to force to submit to sexual intercourse

RAPER   n pl. -S a rapist

RAPESEED   n pl. -S the seed of a European herb

RAPHE   n pl. RAPHAE or RAPHES a seamlike ridge between two halves of an organ or part

RAPHIA   n pl. -S raffia

RAPHIDE   n pl. -S a needle-shaped crystal occurring in plant cells

RAPHIS   n pl. -PHIDES raphide

RAPID   adj -IDER, -IDEST moving or acting with great speed RAPIDLY adv

RAPID   n pl. -S a fast-moving part of a river

RAPIDITY   n pl. -TIES the state of being rapid

RAPIER   n pl. -S a long, slender sword RAPIERED adj

RAPINE   n pl. -S the taking of property by force

RAPING   present participle of rape

RAPIST   n pl. -S one who rapes

RAPPAREE   n pl. -S a plunderer

RAPPED   past tense of rap

RAPPEE   n pl. -S a strong snuff

RAPPEL   v -PELLED, -PELLING, -PELS to descend from a steep height by means of a rope

RAPPEN   n pl. RAPPEN a Swiss coin

RAPPER   n pl. -S one that raps

RAPPING   present participle of rap

RAPPINI   n/pl immature turnip plants

RAPPORT   n pl. -S a harmonious relationship

RAPT   adj deeply engrossed RAPTLY adv

RAPTNESS   n pl. -ES the state of being rapt

RAPTOR   n pl. -S a bird of prey

RAPTURE   v -TURED, -TURING, -TURES to fill with great joy

RARE   adj RARER, RAREST occurring infrequently

RAREBIT   n pl. -S a cheese dish

RAREFIER   n pl. -S one that rarefies

RAREFY   v -EFIED, -EFYING, -EFIES to make less dense

RARELY   adv not often

RARENESS   n pl. -ES the quality of being rare

RARER   comparative of rare

RARERIPE   n pl. -S a fruit that ripens early

RAREST   superlative of rare

RARIFY   v -FIED, -FYING, -FIES to rarefy

RARING   adj full of enthusiasm

RARITY   n pl. -TIES rareness

RAS   n pl. -ES an Ethiopian prince

RASBORA   n pl. -S a tropical fish

RASCAL   n pl. -S an unscrupulous or dishonest person

RASCALLY   adj characteristic of a rascal

RASE   v RASED, RASING, RASES to raze

RASER   n pl. -S one that rases

RASH   adj RASHER, RASHEST acting without due caution or forethought

RASH   n pl. -ES a skin eruption RASHLIKE adj

RASHER   n pl. -S a thin slice of meat

RASHLY   adv in a rash manner

RASHNESS   n pl. -ES the state of being rash

RASING   present participle of rase

RASORIAL   adj habitually scratching the ground for food

RASP   v -ED, -ING, -S to rub with something rough

RASPER   n pl. -S one that rasps

RASPISH   adj irritable

RASPY   adj RASPIER, RASPIEST rough

RASSLE   v -SLED, -SLING, -SLES to wrestle

RASTER   n pl. -S the area reproducing images on the picture tube of a television set

RASURE   n pl. -S erasure

RAT   v RATTED, RATTING, RATS to hunt rats (long-tailed rodents)

RATABLE   adj capable of being rated RATABLY adv

RATAFEE   n pl. -S ratafia

RATAFIA   n pl. -S an almond-flavored liqueur

RATAL   n pl. -S an amount on which rates are assessed

RATAN   n pl. -S rattan

RATANY *n pl.* -NIES rhatany

RATAPLAN *v* -PLANNED, -PLANNING, -PLANS to make a rapidly repeating sound

RATATAT *n pl.* -S a quick, sharp rapping sound

RATCH *n pl.* -ES a ratchet

RATCHET *n pl.* -S a mechanism which allows motion in one direction only

RATE *v* RATED, RATING, RATES to estimate the value of

RATEABLE *adj* ratable **RATEABLY** *adv*

RATEL *n pl.* -S a carnivorous mammal

RATER *n pl.* -S one that rates

RATFINK *n pl.* -S a contemptible person

RATFISH *n pl.* -ES a marine fish

RATH *adj* rathe

RATHE *adj* appearing or ripening early

RATHER *adv* preferably

RATHOLE *n pl.* -S a hole made by a rat

RATICIDE *n pl.* -S a substance for killing rats

RATIFIER *n pl.* -S one that ratifies

RATIFY *v* -FIED, -FYING, -FIES to approve and sanction formally

RATINE *n pl.* -S a heavy fabric

RATING *n pl.* -S relative estimate or evaluation

RATIO *n pl.* -TIOS a proportional relationship

RATION *v* -ED, -ING, -S to distribute in fixed portions

RATIONAL *n pl.* -S a number that can be expressed as a quotient of integers

RATITE *n pl.* -S a flightless bird

RATLIKE *adj* resembling a rat

RATLIN *n pl.* -S ratline

RATLINE *n pl.* -S one of the ropes forming the steps of a rope ladder on a ship

RATO *n pl.* -TOS a rocket-assisted airplane takeoff

RATOON *v* -ED, -ING, -S to sprout from a root planted the previous year

RATOONER *n pl.* -S a plant that ratoons

RATSBANE *n pl.* -S rat poison

RATTAIL *n pl.* -S a marine fish

RATTAN *n pl.* -S a palm tree

RATTED past tense of rat

RATTEEN *n pl.* -S a coarse woolen fabric

RATTEN *v* -ED, -ING, -S to harass

RATTENER *n pl.* -S one that rattens

RATTER *n pl.* -S an animal used for catching rats

RATTIER comparative of ratty

RATTIEST superlative of ratty

RATTING present participle of rat

RATTISH *adj* ratlike

RATTLE *v* -TLED, -TLING, -TLES to make a quick succession of short, sharp sounds

RATTLER *n pl.* -S one that rattles

RATTLING *n pl.* -S ratline

RATTLY *adj* tending to rattle

RATTON *n pl.* -S a rat

RATTOON *v* -ED, -ING, -S to ratoon

RATTRAP *n pl.* -S a trap for catching rats

RATTY *adj* -TIER, -TIEST infested with rats

RAUCITY *n pl.* -TIES the state of being raucous

RAUCOUS *adj* loud and unruly

RAUNCHY *adj* -CHIER, -CHIEST slovenly

RAVAGE *v* -AGED, -AGING, -AGES to destroy

RAVAGER *n pl.* -S one that ravages

RAVE *v* RAVED, RAVING, RAVES to speak irrationally or incoherently

RAVEL *v* -ELED, -ELING, -ELS or -ELLED, -ELLING, -ELS to separate the threads of

RAVELER *n pl.* -S one that ravels

RAVELIN *n pl.* -S a type of fortification

RAVELING *n pl.* -S a loose thread

RAVELLED a past tense of ravel

RAVELLER *n pl.* -S raveler

RAVELLING *n pl.* -S raveling

RAVELLY *adj* tangled

RAVEN *v* -ED, -ING, -S to eat in a ravenous manner

RAVENER *n pl.* -S one that ravens

RAVENING *n pl.* -S rapacity

RAVENOUS *adj* extremely hungry

RAVER *n pl.* -S one that raves

RAVIGOTE *n pl.* -S a spiced vinegar sauce

RAVIN	v -ED, -ING, -S to raven	**REACCEPT**	v -ED, -ING, -S
RAVINE	n pl. -S a narrow, steep-sided valley	**REACCUSE**	v -CUSED, -CUSING, -CUSES
		READAPT	v -ED, -ING, -S
RAVING	n pl. -S irrational, incoherent speech	**READD**	v -ED, -ING, -S
		READDICT	v -ED, -ING, -S
RAVINGLY	adv in a delirious manner	**READJUST**	v -ED, -ING, -S
RAVIOLI	n pl. -S an Italian dish	**READMIT**	v -MITTED, -MITTING, -MITS
RAVISH	v -ED, -ING, -ES to seize and carry off by force	**READOPT**	v -ED, -ING, -S
		READORN	v -ED, -ING, -S
RAVISHER	n pl. -S one that ravishes	**REAFFIRM**	v -ED, -ING, -S
RAW	adj RAWER, RAWEST uncooked	**REAFFIX**	v -ED, -ING, -ES
RAW	n pl. -S a sore or irritated spot	**REALIGN**	v -ED, -ING, -S
RAWBONED	adj having little flesh	**REALLOT**	v -LOTTED, -LOTTING, -LOTS
RAWHIDE	v -HIDED, -HIDING, -HIDES to beat with a type of whip	**REALTER**	v -ED, -ING, -S
		REANNEX	v -ED, -ING, -ES
RAWISH	adj somewhat raw	**REANOINT**	v -ED, -ING, -S
RAWLY	adv in a raw manner	**REAPPEAR**	v -ED, -ING, -S
RAWNESS	n pl. -ES the state of being raw	**REAPPLY**	v -PLIED, -PLYING, -PLIES
RAX	v -ED, -ING, -ES to stretch out	**REARGUE**	v -GUED, -GUING, -GUES
RAY	v -ED, -ING, -S to emit rays (narrow beams of light)	**REARM**	v -ED, -ING, -S
		REAROUSE	v -AROUSED, -AROUSING, -AROUSES
RAYA	n pl. -S rayah		
RAYAH	n pl. -S a non-Muslim inhabitant of Turkey	**REARREST**	v -ED, -ING, -S
		REASCEND	v -ED, -ING, -S
RAYGRASS	n pl. -ES ryegrass	**REASSAIL**	v -ED, -ING, -S
RAYLESS	adj having no rays	**REASSERT**	v -ED, -ING, -S
RAYON	n pl. -S a synthetic fiber	**REASSESS**	v -ED, -ING, -ES
RAZE	v RAZED, RAZING, RAZES to tear down or demolish	**REASSIGN**	v -ED, -ING, -S
		REASSORT	v -ED, -ING, -S
RAZEE	v -ZEED, -ZEEING, -ZEES to make lower by removing the upper deck, as a ship	**REASSUME**	v -SUMED, -SUMING, -SUMES
		REASSURE	v -SURED, -SURING, -SURES
		REATTACH	v -ED, -ING, -ES
RAZER	n pl. -S one that razes	**REATTACK**	v -ED, -ING, -S
RAZING	present participle of raze	**REATTAIN**	v -ED, -ING, -S
RAZOR	v -ED, -ING, -S to shave or cut with a sharp-edged instrument	**REAVOW**	v -ED, -ING, -S
		REAWAKE	v -AWAKED or -AWOKE, -AWOKEN, -AWAKING, -AWAKES
RAZZ	v -ED, -ING, -ES to deride	**REAWAKEN**	v -ED, -ING, -S
RE	n pl. -S the second tone of the diatonic musical scale	**REBAIT**	v -ED, -ING, -S
		REBID	v -BID, -BIDDEN, -BIDDING, -BIDS
		REBILL	v -ED, -ING, -S
		REBIND	v -BOUND, -BINDING, -BINDS
		REBLOOM	v -ED, -ING, -S
		REBOARD	v -ED, -ING, -S
		REBOIL	v -ED, -ING, -S
		REBOUND	past tense of rebind
		REBUILD	v -BUILT or -BUILDED, -BUILDING, -BUILDS

R₁ E₁

Following is a list of self-explanatory verbs containing the prefix RE- (again):

REABSORB	v -ED, -ING, -S	**REBURY**	v -BURIED, -BURYING, -BURIES
		REBUTTON	v -ED, -ING, -S
REACCEDE	v -CEDED, -CEDING, -CEDES	**RECANE**	v -CANED, -CANING, -CANES
REACCENT	v -ED, -ING, -S	**RECARRY**	v -RIED, -RYING, -RIES
		RECAST	v -CAST, -CASTING, -CASTS

RECHANGE	v -CHANGED, -CHANGING, -CHANGES	**REEJECT**	v -ED, -ING, -S
RECHARGE	v -CHARGED, -CHARGING, -CHARGES	**REELECT**	v -ED, -ING, -S
		REEMBARK	v -ED, -ING, -S
RECHART	v -ED, -ING, -S	**REEMBODY**	v -BODIED, -BODYING, -BODIES
RECHECK	v -ED, -ING, -S	**REEMERGE**	v -EMERGED, -EMERGING, -EMERGES
RECHOOSE	v -CHOSE, -CHOSEN, -CHOOSING, -CHOOSES	**REEMIT**	v -EMITTED, -EMITTING, -EMITS
RECIRCLE	v -CLED, -CLING, -CLES	**REEMPLOY**	v -ED, -ING, -S
RECLAD	a past tense of reclothe	**REENACT**	v -ED, -ING, -S
RECLASP	v -ED, -ING, -S	**REENDOW**	v -ED, -ING, -S
RECLEAN	v -ED, -ING, -S	**REENGAGE**	v -GAGED, -GAGING, -GAGES
RECLOTHE	v -CLOTHED or -CLAD, -CLOTHING, -CLOTHES	**REENJOY**	v -ED, -ING, -S
		REENLIST	v -ED, -ING, -S
RECOAL	v -ED, -ING, -S	**REENTER**	v -ED, -ING, -S
RECOCK	v -ED, -ING, -S	**REEQUIP**	v -EQUIPPED, -EQUIPPING, -EQUIPS
RECODIFY	v -FIED, -FYING, -FIES	**REERECT**	v -ED, -ING, -S
RECOIN	v -ED, -ING, -S	**REEVOKE**	v -EVOKED, -EVOKING, -EVOKES
RECOLOR	v -ED, -ING, -S	**REEXPEL**	v -PELLED, -PELLING, -PELS
RECOMB	v -ED, -ING, -S	**REEXPORT**	v -ED, -ING, -S
RECOMMIT	v -MITTED, -MITTING, -MITS	**REFALL**	v -FELL, -FALLEN, -FALLING, -FALLS
RECOOK	v -ED, -ING, -S		
RECOPY	v -COPIED, -COPYING, -COPIES	**REFASTEN**	v -ED, -ING, -S
RECOUPLE	v -PLED, -PLING, -PLES	**REFEED**	v -FED, -FEEDING, -FEEDS
RECRATE	v -CRATED, -CRATING, -CRATES	**REFELL**	past tense of refall
RECROSS	v -ED, -ING, -ES	**REFIGHT**	v -FOUGHT, -FIGHTING, -FIGHTS
RECROWN	v -ED, -ING, -S	**REFIGURE**	v -URED, -URING, -URES
RECUT	v -CUT, -CUTTING, -CUTS	**REFILE**	v -FILED, -FILING, -FILES
REDATE	v -DATED, -DATING, -DATES	**REFILL**	v -ED, -ING, -S
REDEFEAT	v -ED, -ING, -S	**REFILM**	v -ED, -ING, -S
REDEFINE	v -FINED, -FINING, -FINES	**REFILTER**	v -ED, -ING, -S
REDEFY	v -FIED, -FYING, -FIES	**REFIND**	v -FOUND, -FINDING, -FINDS
REDEMAND	v -ED, -ING, -S	**REFIRE**	v -FIRED, -FIRING, -FIRES
REDENY	v -NIED, -NYING, -NIES	**REFIX**	v -ED, -ING, -ES
REDEPLOY	v -ED, -ING, -S	**REFLEW**	past tense of refly
REDESIGN	v -ED, -ING, -S	**REFLIES**	present 3d person sing. of refly
REDID	past tense of redo	**REFLOAT**	v -ED, -ING, -S
REDIGEST	v -ED, -ING, -S	**REFLOOD**	v -ED, -ING, -S
REDIP	v -DIPPED or -DIPT, -DIPPING, -DIPS	**REFLOW**	v -ED, -ING, -S
REDIVIDE	v -VIDED, -VIDING, -VIDES	**REFLOWER**	v -ED, -ING, -S
REDO	v -DID, -DONE, -DOING, -DOES	**REFLY**	v -FLEW, -FLOWN, -FLYING, -FLIES
REDOCK	v -ED, -ING, -S	**REFOCUS**	v -CUSED, -CUSING, -CUSES or -CUSSED, -CUSSING, -CUSSES
REDRAW	v -DREW, -DRAWN, -DRAWING, -DRAWS		
		REFOLD	v -ED, -ING, -S
REDRIED	past tense of redry	**REFORGE**	v -FORGED, -FORGING, -FORGES
REDRIES	present 3d person sing. of redry	**REFORMAT**	v -MATTED, -MATTING, -MATS
REDRILL	v -ED, -ING, -S	**REFOUGHT**	past tense of refight
REDRIVE	v -DROVE, -DRIVEN, -DRIVING, -DRIVES	**REFOUND**	v -ED, -ING, -S
		REFRAME	v -FRAMED, -FRAMING, -FRAMES
REDRY	v -DRIED, -DRYING, -DRIES	**REFREEZE**	v -FROZE, -FROZEN, -FREEZING, -FREEZES
REDYE	v -DYED, -DYEING, -DYES		
REEARN	v -ED, -ING, -S	**REFRONT**	v -ED, -ING, -S
REECHO	v -ED, -ING, -ES	**REFRY**	v -FRIED, -FRYING, -FRIES
REEDIT	v -ED, -ING, -S	**REFUEL**	v -ELED, -ELING, -ELS or -ELLED, -ELLING, -ELS

REGAIN   v -ED, -ING, -S

REGATHER   v -ED, -ING, -S

REGAUGE   v -GAUGED, -GAUGING, -GAUGES

REGAVE   past tense of regive

REGEAR   v -ED, -ING, -S

REGILD   v -GILDED or -GILT, -GILDING, -GILDS

REGIVE   v -GAVE, -GIVEN, -GIVING, -GIVES

REGLAZE   v -GLAZED, -GLAZING, -GLAZES

REGLOSS   v -ED, -ING, -ES

REGLOW   v -ED, -ING, -S

REGLUE   v -GLUED, -GLUING, -GLUES

REGRADE   v -GRADED, -GRADING, -GRADES

REGRAFT   v -ED, -ING, -S

REGRANT   v -ED, -ING, -S

REGREW   past tense of regrow

REGRIND   v -GROUND, -GRINDING, -GRINDS

REGROOVE   v -GROOVED, -GROOVING, -GROOVES

REGROUP   v -ED, -ING, -S

REGROW   v -GREW, -GROWN, -GROWING, -GROWS

REHAMMER   v -ED, -ING, -S

REHANDLE   v -DLED, -DLING, -DLES

REHANG   v -HUNG or -HANGED, -HANGING, -HANGS

REHARDEN   v -ED, -ING, -S

REHASH   v -ED, -ING, -ES

REHEAR   v -HEARD, -HEARING, -HEARS

REHEAT   v -ED, -ING, -S

REHEEL   v -ED, -ING, -S

REHEM   v -HEMMED, -HEMMING, -HEMS

REHINGE   v -HINGED, -HINGING, -HINGES

REHIRE   v -HIRED, -HIRING, -HIRES

REHUNG   a past tense of rehang

REIGNITE   v -NITED, -NITING, -NITES

REIMAGE   v -AGED, -AGING, -AGES

REIMPORT   v -ED, -ING, -S

REIMPOSE   v -POSED, -POSING, -POSES

REINCITE   v -CITED, -CITING, -CITES

REINCUR   v -CURRED, -CURRING, -CURS

REINDEX   v -ED, -ING, -ES

REINDUCE   v -DUCED, -DUCING, -DUCES

REINDUCT   v -ED, -ING, -S

REINFECT   v -ED, -ING, -S

REINFORM   v -ED, -ING, -S

REINFUSE   v -FUSED, -FUSING, -FUSES

REINJURE   v -JURED, -JURING, -JURES

REINSERT   v -ED, -ING, -S

REINSURE   v -SURED, -SURING, -SURES

REINTER   v -TERRED, -TERRING, -TERS

REINVENT   v -ED, -ING, -S

REINVEST   v -ED, -ING, -S

REINVITE   v -VITED, -VITING, -VITES

REINVOKE   v -VOKED, -VOKING, -VOKES

REISSUE   v -SUED, -SUING, -SUES

REJOIN   v -ED, -ING, -S

REJUDGE   v -JUDGED, -JUDGING, -JUDGES

REKEY   v -ED, -ING, -S

REKINDLE   v -DLED, -DLING, -DLES

REKNIT   v -KNITTED, -KNITTING, -KNITS

RELABEL   v -BELED, -BELING, -BELS or -BELLED, -BELLING, -BELS

RELACE   v -LACED, -LACING, -LACES

RELAUNCH   v -ED, -ING, -ES

RELAY   v -LAID, -LAYING, -LAYS

RELEARN   v -LEARNED or -LEARNT, -LEARNING, -LEARNS

RELEND   v -LENT, -LENDING, -LENDS

RELET   v -LET, -LETTING, -LETS

RELETTER   v -ED, -ING, -S

RELIGHT   v -LIGHTED or -LIT, -LIGHTING, -LIGHTS

RELINE   v -LINED, -LINING, -LINES

RELIST   v -ED, -ING, -S

RELIT   a past tense of relight

RELOAD   v -ED, -ING, -S

RELOAN   v -ED, -ING, -S

REMAIL   v -ED, -ING, -S

REMAKE   v -MADE, -MAKING, -MAKES

REMAP   v -MAPPED, -MAPPING, -MAPS

REMARRY   v -RIED, -RYING, -RIES

REMATCH   v -ED, -ING, -ES

REMEET   v -MET, -MEETING, -MEETS

REMELT   v -ED, -ING, -S

REMEND   v -ED, -ING, -S

REMERGE   v -MERGED, -MERGING, -MERGES

REMET   past tense of remeet

REMIX   v -MIXED or -MIXT, -MIXING, -MIXES

REMODIFY   v -FIED, -FYING, -FIES

REMOLD   v -ED, -ING, -S

REMOUNT   v -ED, -ING, -S

RENAME   v -NAMED, -NAMING, -NAMES

RENOTIFY   v -FIED, -FYING, -FIES

RENUMBER   v -ED, -ING, -S

REOBJECT   v -ED, -ING, -S

REOBTAIN   v -ED, -ING, -S

REOCCUPY   v -PIED, -PYING, -PIES

REOCCUR   v -CURRED, -CURRING, -CURS

REOIL   v -ED, -ING, -S

REOPEN   v -ED, -ING, -S

REOPPOSE   v -POSED, -POSING, -POSES

REORDAIN   v -ED, -ING, -S

REORDER   v -ED, -ING, -S

REORIENT   v -ED, -ING, -S

REPACIFY   v -FIED, -FYING, -FIES

REPACK   v -ED, -ING, -S

REPAINT   v -ED, -ING, -S

REPAPER	v -ED, -ING, -S	RESHOOT	v -SHOT, -SHOOTING, -SHOOTS
REPASS	v -ED, -ING, -ES	RESHOW	v -SHOWED, -SHOWN, -SHOWING, -SHOWS
REPAVE	v -PAVED, -PAVING, -PAVES		
REPEOPLE	v -PLED, -PLING, -PLES	RESIFT	v -ED, -ING, -S
REPERK	v -ED, -ING, -S	RESILVER	v -ED, -ING, -S
REPHRASE	v -PHRASED, -PHRASING, -PHRASES	RESIZE	v -SIZED, -SIZING, -SIZES
		RESMELT	v -ED, -ING, -S
REPIN	v -PINNED, -PINNING, -PINS	RESMOOTH	v -ED, -ING, -S
REPLAN	v -PLANNED, -PLANNING, -PLANS	RESOLD	past tense of resell
REPLANT	v -ED, -ING, -S	RESOLDER	v -ED, -ING, -S
REPLATE	v -PLATED, -PLATING, -PLATES	RESOLE	v -SOLED, -SOLING, -SOLES
REPLAY	v -ED, -ING, -S	RESOUGHT	past tense of reseek
REPLEDGE	v -PLEDGED, -PLEDGING, -PLEDGES	RESOW	v -SOWED, -SOWN, -SOWING, -SOWS
REPLUNGE	v -PLUNGED, -PLUNGING, -PLUNGES		
		RESPELL	v -SPELLED or -SPELT, -SPELLING, -SPELLS
REPOLISH	v -ED, -ING, -ES		
REPOUR	v -ED, -ING, -S	RESPREAD	v -SPREAD, -SPREADING, -SPREADS
REPOWER	v -ED, -ING, -S		
REPRICE	v -PRICED, -PRICING, -PRICES	RESPRING	v -SPRANG or -SPRUNG, -SPRINGING, -SPRINGS
REPRINT	v -ED, -ING, -S		
REPROBE	v -PROBED, -PROBING, -PROBES	RESTACK	v -ED, -ING, -S
REPURIFY	v -FIED, -FYING, -FIES	RESTAFF	v -ED, -ING, -S
REPURSUE	v -SUED, -SUING, -SUES	RESTAGE	v -STAGED, -STAGING, -STAGES
REREAD	v -READ, -READING, -READS	RESTAMP	v -ED, -ING, -S
RERECORD	v -ED, -ING, -S	RESTART	v -ED, -ING, -S
RERISE	v -ROSE, -RISEN, -RISING, -RISES	RESTATE	v -STATED, -STATING, -STATES
REROLL	v -ED, -ING, -S	RESTOCK	v -ED, -ING, -S
REROUTE	v -ROUTED, -ROUTING, -ROUTES	RESTRIKE	v -STRUCK, -STRICKEN, -STRIKING, -STRIKES
RESADDLE	v -DLED, -DLING, -DLES		
RESAID	past tense of resay	RESTRING	v -STRUNG, -STRINGING, -STRINGS
RESAIL	v -ED, -ING, -S	RESTRIVE	v -STROVE, -STRIVEN, -STRIVING, -STRIVES
RESALUTE	v -LUTED, -LUTING, -LUTES		
RESAMPLE	v -PLED, -PLING, -PLES	RESTRUCK	past tense of restrike
RESAW	v -SAWED, -SAWN, -SAWING, -SAWS	RESTRUNG	past tense of restring
		RESTUDY	v -STUDIED, -STUDYING, -STUDIES
RESAY	v -SAID, -SAYING, -SAYS	RESTUFF	v -ED, -ING, -S
RESCORE	v -SCORED, -SCORING, -SCORES	RESTYLE	v -STYLED, -STYLING, -STYLES
RESCREEN	v -ED, -ING, -S	RESUBMIT	v -MITTED, -MITTING, -MITS
RESEAL	v -ED, -ING, -S	RESUMMON	v -ED, -ING, -S
RESEAT	v -ED, -ING, -S	RESUPPLY	v -PLIED, -PLYING, -PLIES
RESEE	v -SAW, -SEEN, -SEEING, -SEES	RESURVEY	v -ED, -ING, -S
RESEED	v -ED, -ING, -S	RETAILOR	v -ED, -ING, -S
RESEEK	v -SOUGHT, -SEEKING, -SEEKS	RETASTE	v -TASTED, -TASTING, -TASTES
RESEEN	past participle of resee	RETEACH	v -TAUGHT, -TEACHING, -TEACHES
RESEIZE	v -SEIZED, -SEIZING, -SEIZES	RETELL	v -TOLD, -TELLING, -TELLS
RESELL	v -SOLD, -SELLING, -SELLS	RETEST	v -ED, -ING, -S
RESEND	v -SENT, -SENDING, -SENDS	RETHINK	v -THOUGHT, -THINKING, -THINKS
RESET	v -SET, -SETTING, -SETS	RETHREAD	v -ED, -ING, -S
RESETTLE	v -TLED, -TLING, -TLES	RETIE	v -TIED, -TYING, -TIES
RESEW	v -SEWED, -SEWN, -SEWING, -SEWS	RETIME	v -TIMED, -TIMING, -TIMES
		RETINT	v -ED, -ING, -S
		RETITLE	v -TLED, -TLING, -TLES
RESHAPE	v -SHAPED, -SHAPING, -SHAPES	RETOLD	past tense of retell
RESHIP	v -SHIPPED, -SHIPPING, -SHIPS	RETRACK	v -ED, -ING, -S
RESHOE	v -SHOD, -SHOEING, -SHOES	RETRAIN	v -ED, -ING, -S

RETRIM	v -TRIMMED, -TRIMMING, -TRIMS	**REACTANT**	n pl. -S one that reacts
RETRY	v -TRIED, -TRYING, -TRIES	**REACTION**	n pl. -S the act of reacting
RETUNE	v -TUNED, -TUNING, -TUNES	**REACTIVE**	adj tending to react
RETWIST	v -ED, -ING, -S	**REACTOR**	n pl. -S one that reacts
RETYING	present participle of retie	**READ**	v READ, READING, READS to
RETYPE	v -TYPED, -TYPING, -TYPES		look at so as to take in the
REUNIFY	v -FIED, -FYING, -FIES		meaning of, as something
REUNITE	v -UNITED, -UNITING, -UNITES		written or printed READABLE
REUSE	v -USED, -USING, -USES		adj READABLY adv
REUTTER	v -ED, -ING, -S	**READER**	n pl. -S one that reads
REVALUE	v -UED, -UING, -UES	**READIED**	past tense of ready
REVERIFY	v -FIED, -FYING, -FIES	**READIER**	comparative of ready
REVEST	v -ED, -ING, -S	**READIES**	present 3d person sing. of
REVIEW	v -ED, -ING, -S		ready
REVISIT	v -ED, -ING, -S	**READIEST**	superlative of ready
REVOICE	v -VOICED, -VOICING, -VOICES	**READILY**	adv in a ready manner
REWAKE	v -WAKED or -WOKE, -WOKEN, -WAKING, -WAKES	**READING**	n pl. -S material that is read
REWAKEN	v -ED, -ING, -S	**READOUT**	n pl. -S a presentation of
REWAN	a past tense of rewin		computer data
REWARM	v -ED, -ING, -S	**READY**	adj READIER, READIEST
REWASH	v -ED, -ING, -ES		prepared
REWAX	v -ED, -ING, -ES	**READY**	v READIED, READYING,
REWEAVE	v -WOVE or -WEAVED, -WOVEN, -WEAVING, -WEAVES		READIES to make ready
REWEIGH	v -ED, -ING, -S	**REAGENT**	n pl. -S a substance used in a
REWELD	v -ED, -ING, -S		chemical reaction to ascertain
REWIDEN	v -ED, -ING, -S		the nature or composition of
REWIN	v -WON or -WAN, -WINNING, -WINS		another
REWIND	v -WOUND or -WINDED, -WINDING, -WINDS	**REAGIN**	n pl. -S a type of antibody
REWIRE	v -WIRED, -WIRING, -WIRES		REAGINIC adj
REWOKE	a past tense of rewake	**REAL**	adj REALER, REALEST having
REWOKEN	past participle of rewake		actual existence
REWON	a past tense of rewin	**REAL**	n pl. -S or -ES a former
REWORK	v -WORKED or -WROUGHT, -WORKING, -WORKS		monetary unit of Spain
REWOUND	a past tense of rewind	**REAL**	n pl. REIS a former monetary
REWOVE	a past tense of reweave		unit of Portugal and Brazil
REWOVEN	past participle of reweave	**REALGAR**	n pl. -S a mineral
REWRAP	v -WRAPPED, or -WRAPT, -WRAPPING, -WRAPS	**REALIA**	n/pl objects used by a teacher
REWRITE	v -WROTE, -WRITTEN, -WRITING, -WRITES		to illustrate everyday living
REWROUGHT	a past tense of rework	**REALISE**	v -ISED, -ISING, -ISES to realize
REZONE	v -ZONED, -ZONING, -ZONES	**REALISER**	n pl. -S one that realises
		REALISM	n pl. -S concern with fact or
			reality
		REALIST	n pl. -S one who is concerned
			with fact or reality
		REALITY	n pl. -TIES something that is
			real
REACH	v -ED, -ING, -ES to stretch out or put forth	**REALIZE**	v -IZED, -IZING, -IZES to
			understand completely
REACHER	n pl. -S one that reaches	**REALIZER**	n pl. -S one that realizes
REACT	v -ED, -ING, -S to respond to a stimulus	**REALLY**	adv actually
		REALM	n pl. -S a kingdom

REALNESS *n pl.* -ES the state of being real

REALTY *n pl.* -TIES property in buildings and land

REAM *v* -ED, -ING, -S to enlarge with a reamer

REAMER *n pl.* -S a tool used to enlarge holes

REAP *v* -ED, -ING, -S to cut for harvest REAPABLE *adj*

REAPER *n pl.* -S one that reaps

REAPHOOK *n pl.* -S an implement used in reaping

REAR *v* -ED, -ING, -S to lift upright

REARER *n pl.* -S one that rears

REARMICE *n/pl* reremice

REARMOST *adj* coming or situated last

REARWARD *n pl.* -S the rearmost division of an army

REASCENT *n pl.* -S a new or second ascent

REASON *v* -ED, -ING, -S to derive inferences or conclusions from known or presumed facts

REASONER *n pl.* -S one that reasons

REATA *n pl.* -S riata

REAVE *v* REAVED or REFT, REAVING, REAVES to plunder

REAVER *n pl.* -S one that reaves

REB *n pl.* -S a Confederate soldier

REBATE *v* -BATED, -BATING, -BATES to deduct or return from a payment or bill

REBATER *n pl.* -S one that rebates

REBATO *n pl.* -TOS rabato

REBBE *n pl.* -S a rabbi

REBEC *n pl.* -S an ancient stringed instrument

REBECK *n pl.* -S rebec

REBEL *v* -BELLED, -BELLING, -BELS to oppose the established government of one's land

REBELDOM *n pl.* -S an area controlled by rebels

REBIRTH *n pl.* -S a new or second birth

REBOANT *adj* resounding loudly

REBOP *n pl.* -S a type of music

REBORN *adj* born again

REBOUND *v* -ED, -ING, -S to spring back

REBOZO *n pl.* -ZOS a long scarf

REBRANCH *v* -ED, -ING, -ES to form secondary branches

REBUFF *v* -ED, -ING, -S to reject or refuse curtly

REBUKE *v* -BUKED, -BUKING, -BUKES to criticize sharply

REBUKER *n pl.* -S one that rebukes

REBURIAL *n pl.* -S a second burial

REBUS *n pl.* -ES a type of puzzle

REBUT *v* -BUTTED, -BUTTING, -BUTS to refute

REBUTTAL *n pl.* -S argument or proof that rebuts

REBUTTER *n pl.* -S one that rebuts

REBUTTING present participle of rebut

REC *n pl.* -S recreation

RECALL *v* -ED, -ING, -S to call back

RECALLER *n pl.* -S one that recalls

RECANT *v* -ED, -ING, -S to make a formal retraction or disavowal of

RECANTER *n pl.* -S one that recants

RECAP *v* -CAPPED, -CAPPING, -CAPS to review by a brief summary

RECEDE *v* -CEDED, -CEDING, -CEDES to move back or away

RECEIPT *v* -ED, -ING, -S to mark as having been paid

RECEIVE *v* -CEIVED, -CEIVING, -CEIVES to come into possession of

RECEIVER *n pl.* -S one that receives

RECENCY *n pl.* -CIES the state of being recent

RECENT *adj* -CENTER, -CENTEST of or pertaining to a time not long past RECENTLY *adv*

RECEPT *n pl.* -S a type of mental image

RECEPTOR *n pl.* -S a nerve ending specialized to receive stimuli

RECESS *v* -ED, -ING, -ES to place in a receding space or hollow

RECHEAT *n pl.* -S a hunting call

RECIPE *n pl.* -S a set of instructions for making something

RECISION *n pl.* -S a cancellation

RECITAL *n pl.* -S a detailed account

RECITE *v* -CITED, -CITING, -CITES to declaim or say from memory

RECITER *n pl.* -S one that recites

RECK *v* -ED, -ING, -S to be concerned about

RECKLESS   *adj* foolishly heedless of danger

RECKON   *v* -ED, -ING, -S to count or compute

RECKONER   *n pl.* -S one that reckons

RECLAIM   *v* -ED, -ING, -S to make suitable for cultivation or habitation

RECLAME   *n pl.* -S publicity

RECLINE   *v* -CLINED, -CLINING, -CLINES to lean or lie back

RECLINER   *n pl.* -S one that reclines

RECLUSE   *n pl.* -S one who lives in solitude and seclusion

RECOIL   *v* -ED, -ING, -S to draw back in fear or disgust

RECOILER   *n pl.* -S one that recoils

RECON   *n pl.* -S a preliminary survey

RECONVEY   *v* -ED, -ING, -S to convey back to a previous position

RECORD   *v* -ED, -ING, -S to set down for preservation

RECORDER   *n pl.* -S one that records

RECOUNT   *v* -ED, -ING, -S to relate in detail

RECOUP   *v* -ED, -ING, -S to get back the equivalent of

RECOUPE   *adj* divided twice

RECOURSE   *n pl.* -S a turning or applying to someone or something for aid

RECOVER   *v* -ED, -ING, -S to obtain again after losing

RECOVERY   *n pl.* -ERIES an economic upturn

RECREANT   *n pl.* -S a coward

RECREATE   *v* -ATED, -ATING, -ATES to refresh mentally or physically

RECRUIT   *v* -ED, -ING, -S to engage for military service

RECTA   *a pl.* of rectum

RECTAL   *adj* pertaining to the rectum **RECTALLY** *adv*

RECTI   *pl.* of rectus

RECTIFY   *v* -FIED, -FYING, -FIES to correct

RECTO   *n pl.* -TOS a right-hand page of a book

RECTOR   *n pl.* -S a clergyman in charge of a parish

RECTORY   *n pl.* -RIES a rector's dwelling

RECTRIX   *n pl.* -TRICES a feather of a bird's tail

RECTUM   *n pl.* -TUMS or -TA the terminal portion of the large intestine

RECTUS   *n pl.* -TI a straight muscle

RECUR   *v* -CURRED, -CURRING, -CURS to happen again

RECURVE   *v* -CURVED, -CURVING, -CURVES to curve backward or downward

RECUSANT   *n pl.* -S one who refuses to accept established authority

RECUSE   *v* -CUSED, -CUSING, -CUSES to disqualify or challenge as judge in a particular case

RECYCLE   *v* -CLED, -CLING, -CLES to process in order to extract useful materials

RED   *adj* REDDER, REDDEST of the color of blood

RED   *v* REDDED, REDDING, REDS to redd

REDACT   *v* -ED, -ING, -S to prepare for publication

REDACTOR   *n pl.* -S one that redacts

REDAN   *n pl.* -S a type of fortification

REDARGUE   *v* -GUED, -GUING, -GUES to disprove

REDBAIT   *v* -ED, -ING, -S to denounce as Communist

REDBAY   *n pl.* -BAYS a small tree

REDBIRD   *n pl.* -S a bird with red plummage

REDBONE   *n pl.* -S a hunting dog

REDBRICK   *adj* pertaining to modern British universities

REDBUD   *n pl.* -S a small tree

REDBUG   *n pl.* -S a chigger

REDCAP   *n pl.* -S a porter

REDCOAT   *n pl.* -S a British soldier during the American Revolution

REDD   *v* -ED, -ING, -S to put in order

REDDED   past tense of red and redd

REDDEN   *v* -ED, -ING, -S to make or become red

REDDER   *n pl.* -S one that redds

REDDEST   superlative of red

REDDING   present participle of red and redd

REDDISH   *adj* somewhat red

REDDLE   *v* -DLED, -DLING, -DLES to ruddle

REDE   *v* REDED, REDING, REDES to advise

REDEAR   *n pl.* -S a common sunfish

REDEEM v -ED, -ING, -S to buy back

REDEEMER n pl. -S one that redeems

REDEYE n pl. -S a railroad danger signal

REDFIN n pl. -S a freshwater fish

REDFISH n pl. -ES an edible rockfish

REDHEAD n pl. -S a person with red hair

REDHORSE n pl. -S a freshwater fish

REDIA n pl. -DIAE or -DIAS the larva of certain flatworms **REDIAL** adj

REDING present participle of rede

REDIRECT v -ED, -ING, -S to change the course or direction of

REDLEG n pl. -S a bird with red legs

REDLY adv with red color

REDNECK n pl. -S a white, rural laborer of the southern United States

REDNESS n pl. -ES the state of being red

REDO n pl. -DOS something that is done again

REDOLENT adj fragrant

REDOUBLE v -BLED, -BLING, -BLES to double

REDOUBT n pl. -S an enclosed fortification

REDOUND v -ED, -ING, -S to have an effect or consequence

REDOUT n pl. -S a condition in which blood is driven to the head

REDOWA n pl. -S a lively dance

REDOX n pl. -ES a type of chemical reaction

REDPOLL n pl. -S a small finch

REDRAFT v -ED, -ING, -S to make a revised copy of

REDRAWER n pl. -S one that redraws

REDRESS v -ED, -ING, -ES to set right

REDROOT n pl. -S a perennial herb

REDSHANK n pl. -S a shore bird

REDSHIRT v -ED, -ING, -S to keep a college athlete out of varsity play in order to extend his eligibility

REDSKIN n pl. -S a North American Indian

REDSTART n pl. -S a small songbird

REDTOP n pl. -S a type of grass

REDUCE v -DUCED, -DUCING, -DUCES to diminish

REDUCER n pl. -S one that reduces

REDUVIID n pl. -S a bloodsucking insect

REDWARE n pl. -S an edible seaweed

REDWING n pl. -S a European thrush

REDWOOD n pl. -S a very tall evergreen tree

REE n pl. -S the female Eurasian sandpiper

REED v -ED, -ING, -S to fasten with reeds (the stalks of tall grasses)

REEDBIRD n pl. -S the bobolink

REEDBUCK n pl. -S an African antelope

REEDIER comparative of reedy

REEDIEST superlative of reedy

REEDIFY v -FIED, -FYING, -FIES to rebuild

REEDING n pl. -S a convex molding

REEDLING n pl. -S a marsh bird

REEDY adj REEDIER, REEDIEST abounding in reeds

REEF v -ED, -ING, -S to reduce the area of a sail

REEFER n pl. -S one that reefs

REEFY adj REEFIER, REEFIEST abounding in ridges of rock

REEK v -ED, -ING, -S to give off a strong, unpleasant odor

REEKER n pl. -S one that reeks

REEKY adj REEKIER, REEKIEST reeking

REEL v -ED, -ING, -S to wind on a type of rotary device **REELABLE** adj

REELER n pl. -S one that reels

REENTRY n pl. -TRIES a new or second entry

REEST v -ED, -ING, -S to balk

REEVE v REEVED or ROVE, ROVEN, REEVING, REEVES to fasten by passing through or around something

REF v REFFED, REFFING, REFS to referee

REFACE v -FACED, -FACING, -FACES to repair the outer surface of

REFECT v -ED, -ING, -S to refresh with food and drink

REFEL v -FELLED, -FELLING, -FELS to reject

REFER v -FERRED, -FERRING, -FERS to direct to a source for help or information

REFEREE   v -EED, -EEING, -EES to supervise the play in certain sports

REFERENT   n pl. -S something referred to

REFERRAL   n pl. -S one that is referred

REFERRED   past tense of refer

REFERRER   n pl. -S one that refers

REFERRING   present participle of refer

REFFED   past tense of ref

REFFING   present participle of ref

REFINE   v -FINED, -FINING, -FINES to free from impurities

REFINER   n pl. -S one that refines

REFINERY   n pl. -ERIES a place where crude material is refined

REFINING   present participle of refine

REFINISH   v -ED, -ING, -ES to give a new surface to

REFIT   v -FITTED, -FITTING, -FITS to prepare and equip for additional use

REFLATE   v -FLATED, -FLATING, -FLATES to inflate again

REFLECT   v -ED, -ING, -S to turn or throw back from a surface

REFLET   n pl. -S special brilliance of surface

REFLEX   v -ED, -ING, -ES to bend back

REFLEXLY   adv in a reflexed manner

REFLUENT   adj flowing back

REFLUX   v -ED, -ING, -ES to cause to flow back

REFOREST   v -ED, -ING, -S to replant with trees

REFORM   v -ED, -ING, -S to change to a better state

REFORMER   n pl. -S one that reforms

REFRACT   v -ED, -ING, -S to deflect in a particular manner, as a ray of light

REFRAIN   v -ED, -ING, -S to keep oneself back

REFRESH   v -ED, -ING, -ES to restore the well-being and vigor of

REFT   a past tense of reave

REFUGE   v -UGED, -UGING, -UGES to give or take shelter

REFUGEE   n pl. -S one who flees for safety

REFUGIUM   n pl. -GIA a stable area during a period of continental climactic change

REFUND   v -ED, -ING, -S to give back

REFUNDER   n pl. -S one that refunds

REFUSAL   n pl. -S the act of refusing

REFUSE   v -FUSED, -FUSING, -FUSES to express oneself as unwilling to accept, do, or comply with

REFUSER   n pl. -S one that refuses

REFUTAL   n pl. -S the act of refuting

REFUTE   v -FUTED, -FUTING, -FUTES to prove to be false or erroneous

REFUTER   n pl. -S one that refutes

REGAINER   n pl. -S one that regains

REGAL   adj of or befitting a king

REGALE   v -GALED, -GALING, -GALES to delight

REGALIA   n/pl the rights and privileges of a king

REGALITY   n pl. -TIES regal authority

REGALLY   adv in a regal manner

REGARD   v -ED, -ING, -S to look upon with a particular feeling

REGATTA   n pl. -S a boat race

REGELATE   v -LATED, -LATING, -LATES to refreeze ice by reducing the pressure

REGENCY   n pl. -CIES the office of a regent

REGENT   n pl. -S one who rules in the place of a sovereign **REGENTAL** adj

REGES   pl. of rex

REGICIDE   n pl. -S the killing of a king

REGIME   n pl. -S a system of government

REGIMEN   n pl. -S a systematic plan

REGIMENT   v -ED, -ING, -S to form into military units

REGINA   n pl. -NAE or -NAS queen **REGINAL** adj

REGION   n pl. -S an administrative area or division

REGIONAL   n pl. -S something that serves as a region

REGISTER   v -ED, -ING, -S to record officially

REGISTRY   n pl. -TRIES the act of registering

REGIUS   adj holding a professorship founded by the sovereign

REGLET   n pl. -S a flat, narrow molding

REGMA   n pl. -MATA a type of fruit

REGNA pl. of regnum

REGNAL *adj* pertaining to a king or his reign

REGNANCY *n* pl. -CIES the state of being regnant

REGNANT *adj* reigning

REGNUM *n* pl. -NA dominion

REGOLITH *n* pl. -S a layer of loose rock

REGORGE *v* -GORGED, -GORGING, -GORGES to vomit

REGOSOL *n* pl. -S a type of soil

REGRATE *v* -GRATED, -GRATING, -GRATES to buy up in order to sell for a higher price in the same area

REGREET *v* -ED, -ING, -S to greet in return

REGRESS *v* -ED, -ING, -ES to go back

REGRET *v* -GRETTED, -GRETTING, -GRETS to look back upon with sorrow or remorse

REGROWTH *n* pl. -S a new or second growth

REGULAR *n* pl. -S an habitual customer

REGULATE *v* -LATED, -LATING, -LATES to control according to rule

REGULUS *n* pl. -LI or -LUSES a mass that forms beneath the slag in a furnace REGULINE *adj*

REHEARSE *v* -HEARSED, -HEARSING, -HEARSES to practice in preparation for a public appearance

REHEATER *n* pl. -S one that reheats

REHOUSE *v* -HOUSED, -HOUSING, -HOUSES to establish in a new housing unit

REI *n* pl. -S an erroneous English form for a former Portuguese coin

REIF *n* pl. -S robbery

REIFIER *n* pl. -S one that reifies

REIFY *v* -IFIED, -IFYING, -IFIES to regard as real or concrete

REIGN *v* -ED, -ING, -S to exercise sovereign power

REIN *v* -ED, -ING, -S to restrain

REINDEER *n* pl. -S a large deer

REINLESS *adj* unrestrained

REINSMAN *n* pl. -MEN a skilled rider of horses

REIS pl. of real

REISSUER *n* pl. -S one that reissues

REITBOK *n* pl. -S the reedbuck

REIVE *v* REIVED, REIVING, REIVES to plunder

REIVER *n* pl. -S one that reives

REJECT *v* -ED, -ING, -S to refuse to accept, consider, or make use of

REJECTEE *n* pl. -S one that is rejected

REJECTER *n* pl. -S one that rejects

REJECTOR *n* pl. -S rejecter

REJIGGER *v* -ED, -ING, -S to alter

REJOICE *v* -JOICED, -JOICING, -JOICES to feel joyful

REJOICER *n* pl. -S one that rejoices

RELAPSE *v* -LAPSED, -LAPSING, -LAPSES to fall or slip back into a former state

RELAPSER *n* pl. -S one that relapses

RELATE *v* -LATED, -LATING, -LATES to give an account of

RELATER *n* pl. -S one that relates

RELATION *n* pl. -S a significant association between two or more things

RELATIVE *n* pl. -S one who is connected with another by blood or marriage

RELATOR *n* pl. -S relater

RELAX *v* -ED, -ING, -ES to make less tense or rigid

RELAXANT *n* pl. -S a drug that relieves muscular tension

RELAXER *n* pl. -S one that relaxes

RELAXIN *n* pl. -S a female hormone

RELAY *v* -ED, -ING, -S to send along by using fresh sets to replace tired ones

RELEASE *v* -LEASED, -LEASING, -LEASES to set free

RELEASER *n* pl. -S one that releases

RELEGATE *v* -GATED, -GATING, -GATES to assign

RELENT *v* -ED, -ING, -S to become less severe

RELEVANT *adj* pertaining to the matter at hand

RELIABLE *adj* suitable to be relied on RELIABLY *adv*

RELIANCE *n* pl. -S confident or trustful dependence

RELIANT *adj* showing reliance

RELIC	n pl. -S a surviving memorial of something past
RELICT	n pl. -S an organism surviving in a changed environment
RELIED	past tense of rely
RELIEF	n pl. -S aid in the form of money or necessities
RELIER	n pl. -S one that relies
RELIES	present 3d person sing. of rely
RELIEVE	v -LIEVED, -LIEVING, -LIEVES to lessen or free from pain or discomfort
RELIEVER	n pl. -S one that relieves
RELIEVO	n pl. -VOS the projection of figures or forms from a flat background
RELIGION	n pl. -S the worship of a god or the supernatural
RELIQUE	n pl. -S relic
RELISH	v -ED, -ING, -ES to enjoy
RELIVE	v -LIVED, -LIVING, -LIVES to experience again
RELOADER	n pl. -S one that reloads
RELOCATE	v -CATED, -CATING, -CATES to establish in a new place
RELUCENT	adj reflecting light
RELUCT	v -ED, -ING, -S to show opposition
RELUME	v -LUMED, -LUMING, -LUMES to light again
RELUMINE	v -MINED, -MINING, -MINES to relume
RELY	v -LIED, -LYING, -LIES to place trust or confidence
REM	n pl. -S a quantity of ionizing radiation
REMAIN	v -ED, -ING, -S to continue in the same state
REMAN	v -MANNED, -MANNING, -MANS to furnish with a fresh supply of men
REMAND	v -ED, -ING, -S to send back
REMANENT	adj remaining
REMANNED	past tense of reman
REMANNING	present participle of reman
REMARK	v -ED, -ING, -S to say or write briefly or casually
REMARKER	n pl. -S one that remarks
REMARQUE	n pl. -S a mark made in the margin of an engraved plate
REMEDIAL	adj intended to correct something
REMEDY	v -DIED, -DYING, -DIES to relieve or cure
REMEMBER	v -ED, -ING, -S to bring to mind again
REMEX	n pl. REMIGES a flight feather of a bird's wing REMIGIAL adj
REMIND	v -ED, -ING, -S to cause to remember
REMINDER	n pl. -S one that reminds
REMINT	v -ED, -ING, -S to melt down and make into new coin
REMISE	v -MISED, -MISING, -MISES to give up a claim to
REMISS	adj careless REMISSLY adv
REMIT	v -MITTED, -MITTING, -MITS to send money in payment
REMITTAL	n pl. -S the act of remitting
REMITTER	n pl. -S one that remits
REMITTING	present participle of remit
REMITTOR	n pl. -S remitter
REMNANT	n pl. -S something remaining
REMODEL	v -ELED, -ELING, -ELS or -ELLED, -ELLING, -ELS to make over
REMOLADE	n pl. -S a piquant sauce
REMORA	n pl. -S a type of marine fish REMORID adj
REMORSE	n pl. -S deep anguish caused by a sense of guilt
REMOTE	adj -MOTER, -MOTEST situated far away REMOTELY adv
REMOTION	n pl. -S the act of removing
REMOVAL	n pl. -S the act of removing
REMOVE	v -MOVED, -MOVING, -MOVES to take or move away
REMOVER	n pl. -S one that removes
REMUDA	n pl. -S a herd of horses
RENAL	adj pertaining to the kidneys
RENATURE	v -TURED, -TURING, -TURES to restore natural qualities
REND	v RENT or RENDED, RENDING, RENDS to tear apart forcibly
RENDER	v -ED, -ING, -S to cause to be or become
RENDERER	n pl. -S one that renders
RENDIBLE	adj capable of being rent
RENDZINA	n pl. -S a type of soil

RENEGADE v -GADED, -GADING, -GADES to become a traitor

RENEGADO n pl. -DOS or -DOES a traitor

RENEGE v -NEGED, -NEGING, -NEGES to fail to carry out a promise or commitment

RENEGER n pl. -S one that reneges

RENEW v -ED, -ING, -S to make new or as if new again

RENEWAL n pl. -S the act of renewing

RENEWER n pl. -S one that renews

RENIFORM adj kidney-shaped

RENIG v -NIGGED, -NIGGING, -NIGS to renege

RENIN n pl. -S an enzyme

RENITENT adj resisting physical pressure

RENNASE n pl. -S rennin

RENNET n pl. -S a lining membrane in the stomach of certain young animals

RENNIN n pl. -S an enzyme

RENOGRAM n pl. -S a photographic depiction of the course of renal excretion

RENOUNCE v -NOUNCED, -NOUNCING, -NOUNCES to disown

RENOVATE v -VATED, -VATING, -VATES to make like new

RENOWN v -ED, -ING, -S to make famous

RENT v -ED, -ING, -S to obtain temporary use of in return for compensation **RENTABLE** adj

RENTAL n pl. -S an amount paid or collected as rent

RENTE n pl. -S annual income under French law

RENTER n pl. -S one that rents

RENTIER n pl. -S one that receives a fixed income

RENVOI n pl. -S the expulsion by a government of an alien

REOFFER v -ED, -ING, -S to offer for public sale

REOVIRUS n pl. -ES a type of virus

REP n pl. -S a cross-ribbed fabric

REPAID past tense of repay

REPAIR v -ED, -ING, -S to restore to good condition

REPAIRER n pl. -S one that repairs

REPAND adj having a wavy margin **REPANDLY** adv

REPARTEE n pl. -S a quick, witty reply

REPAST v -ED, -ING, -S to eat or feast

REPAY v -PAID, -PAYING, -PAYS to pay back

REPEAL v -ED, -ING, -S to revoke

REPEALER n pl. -S one that repeals

REPEAT v -ED, -ING, -S to say or do again

REPEATER n pl. -S one that repeats

REPEL v -PELLED, -PELLING, -PELS to drive back

REPELLER n pl. -S one that repels

REPENT v -ED, -ING, -S to feel remorse or self-reproach for a past action

REPENTER n pl. -S one that repents

REPETEND n pl. -S a phrase or sound that is repeated

REPINE v -PINED, -PINING, -PINES to express discontent

REPINER n pl. -S one that repines

REPLACE v -PLACED, -PLACING, -PLACES to take the place of

REPLACER n pl. -S one that replaces

REPLETE adj abundantly supplied

REPLEVIN v -ED, -ING, -S to replevy

REPLEVY v -PLEVIED, -PLEVYING, -PLEVIES to regain possession of by legal action

REPLICA n pl. -S a close copy or reproduction

REPLIER n pl. -S one that replies

REPLY v -PLIED, -PLYING, -PLIES to answer

REPORT v -ED, -ING, -S to give an account of

REPORTER n pl. -S one that reports

REPOSAL n pl. -S the act of reposing

REPOSE v -POSED, -POSING, -POSES to lie at rest

REPOSER n pl. -S one that reposes

REPOSIT v -ED, -ING, -S to put away

REPOUSSE n pl. -S a raised design hammered in metal

REPP n pl. -S rep

REPPED adj resembling rep

REPRESS v -ED, -ING, -ES to keep under control

REPRIEVE v -PRIEVED, -PRIEVING, -PRIEVES to postpone the punishment of

REPRISAL n pl. -S an act of retaliation

REPRISE v -PRISED, -PRISING, -PRISES to take back by force

REPRO n pl. -PROS a trial sheet of printed material suitable for photographic reproduction

REPROACH v -ED, -ING, -ES to find fault with

REPROOF n pl. -S criticism for a fault

REPROVAL n pl. -S reproof

REPROVE v -PROVED, -PROVING, -PROVES to rebuke

REPROVER n pl. -S one that reproves

REPTANT adj creeping or crawling

REPTILE n pl. -S any of a class of cold-blooded, air-breathing verte-brates

REPUBLIC n pl. -S a constitutional form of government

REPUGN v -ED, -ING, -S to oppose

REPULSE v -PULSED, -PULSING, -PULSES to drive back

REPULSER n pl. -S one that repulses

REPUTE v -PUTED, -PUTING, -PUTES to consider to be as specified

REQUEST v -ED, -ING, -S to express a desire for

REQUIEM n pl. -S a musical composition for the dead

REQUIN n pl. -S a voracious shark

REQUIRE v -QUIRED, -QUIRING, -QUIRES to have need of

REQUIRER n pl. -S one that requires

REQUITAL n pl. -S something given in return, compensation, or retaliation

REQUITE v -QUITED, -QUITING, -QUITES to make equivalent return for

REQUITER n pl. -S one that requites

RERAN past tense of rerun

REREDOS n pl. -ES an ornamental screen behind an altar

REREMICE n/pl bats (flying mammals)

REREWARD n pl. -S rearward

REROLLER n pl. -S one that rerolls

RERUN v -RAN, -RUNNING, -RUNS to present a repetition of a recorded performance

RES n pl. RES a particular thing or matter

RESALE n pl. -S the act of selling again

RESCALE v -SCALED, -SCALING, -SCALES to plan on a new scale

RESCIND v -ED, -ING, -S to annul

RESCRIPT n pl. -S something rewritten

RESCUE v -CUED, -CUING, -CUES to free from danger

RESCUER n pl. -S one that rescues

RESEARCH v -ED, -ING, -ES to investigate thoroughly

RESEAU n pl. -SEAUS or -SEAUX a filter screen for making color films

RESECT v -ED, -ING, -S to excise part of an organ or structure surgically

RESEDA n pl. -S a flowering plant

RESELLER n pl. -S one that resells

RESEMBLE v -BLED, -BLING, -BLES to be similar to

RESENT v -ED, -ING, -S to feel or express annoyance or ill will at

RESERVE v -SERVED, -SERVING, -SERVES to keep back for future use

RESERVER n pl. -S one that reserves

RESETTER n pl. -S one that resets

RESH n pl. -ES a Hebrew letter

RESHAPER n pl. -S one that reshapes something

RESID n pl. -S a type of fuel oil

RESIDE v -SIDED, -SIDING, -SIDES to dwell permanently or continu-ously

RESIDENT n pl. -S one who resides

RESIDER n pl. -S a resident

RESIDUA a pl. of residuum

RESIDUAL n pl. -S something left over

RESIDUE n pl. -S something remaining after the removal of a part

RESIDUUM n pl. -SIDUA or -SIDUUMS residue

RESIGN v -ED, -ING, -S to give up one's office or position

RESIGNER n pl. -S one that resigns

RESILE v -SILED, -SILING, -SILES to spring back

RESIN v -ED, -ING, -S to treat with resin (a viscous substance obtained from certain plants)

RESINATE   v -ATED, -ATING, -ATES to resin

RESINIFY   v -FIED, -FYING, -FIES to convert into resin

RESINOID   n pl. -S a resinous substance

RESINOUS   adj resembling resin

RESINY   adj resinous

RESIST   v -ED, -ING, -S to strive against

RESISTER   n pl. -S one that resists

RESISTOR   n pl. -S a device in an electric circuit

RESOJET   n pl. -S a pulsejet

RESOLUTE   adj -LUTER, -LUTEST characterized by firmness or determination

RESOLUTE   n pl. -S one who is resolute

RESOLVE   v -SOLVED, -SOLVING, -SOLVES to make a firm decision about

RESOLVER   n pl. -S one that resolves

RESONANT   n pl. -S a resounding sound

RESONATE   v -NATED, -NATING, -NATES to resound

RESORB   v -ED, -ING, -S to absorb again

RESORCIN   n pl. -S a chemical compound

RESORT   v -ED, -ING, -S to go frequently or habitually

RESORTER   n pl. -S one that resorts

RESOUND   v -ED, -ING, -S to make a loud, long, or echoing sound

RESOURCE   n pl. -S an available supply

RESPECT   v -ED, -ING, -S to have a high regard for

RESPIRE   v -SPIRED, -SPIRING, -SPIRES to breathe

RESPITE   v -SPITED, -SPITING, -SPITES to relieve temporarily

RESPOND   v -ED, -ING, -S to say or act in return

RESPONSA   n/pl written rabbinic decisions

RESPONSE   n pl. -S a reply or reaction

REST   v -ED, -ING, -S to refresh oneself by ceasing work or activity

RESTER   n pl. -S one that rests

RESTFUL   adj -FULLER, -FULLEST tranquil

RESTIVE   adj difficult to control

RESTLESS   adj unable or disinclined to remain at rest

RESTORAL   n pl. -S the act of restoring

RESTORE   v -STORED, -STORING, -STORES to bring back to a former or original condition

RESTORER   n pl. -S one that restores

RESTRAIN   v -ED, -ING, -S to hold back from action

RESTRICT   v -ED, -ING, -S to keep within certain boundaries

RESULT   v -ED, -ING, -S to occur as a consequence

RESUME   v -SUMED, -SUMING, -SUMES to take up again after interruption

RESUMER   n pl. -S one that resumes

RESUPINE   adj lying on the back

RESURGE   v -SURGED, -SURGING, -SURGES to rise again

RET   v RETTED, RETTING, RETS to soak in order to loosen the fiber from the woody tissue

RETABLE   n pl. -S a raised shelf above an altar

RETAIL   v -ED, -ING, -S to sell in small quantities

RETAILER   n pl. -S one that retails

RETAIN   v -ED, -ING, -S to keep possession of

RETAINER   n pl. -S one that retains

RETAKE   v -TOOK, -TAKEN, -TAKING, -TAKES to take back

RETAKER   n pl. -S one that retakes

RETARD   v -ED, -ING, -S to slow the progress of

RETARDER   n pl. -S one that retards

RETCH   v -ED, -ING, -ES to make an effort to vomit

RETE   n pl. -TIA an anatomical mesh or network

RETEM   n pl. -S a desert shrub

RETENE   n pl. -S a chemical compound

RETIA   pl. of rete

RETIAL   adj pertaining to a rete

RETIARII   n/pl ancient Roman gladiators

RETIARY   adj resembling a net

RETICENT   adj tending to be silent

RETICLE   n pl. -S a network of lines in the eyepiece of an optical instrument

RETICULA   n/pl netlike structures

RETICULE   n pl. -S a woman's handbag

RETIFORM *adj* arranged like a net

RETINA *n* pl. -NAS or -NAE a membrane of the eye

RETINAL *n* pl. -S retinene

RETINENE *n* pl. -S a pigment in the retina

RETINITE *n* pl. -S a fossil resin

RETINOL *n* pl. -S a liquid hydrocarbon

RETINUE *n* pl. -S a group of attendants RETINUED *adj*

RETINULA *n* pl. -LAE or -LAS a neural receptor of an arthropod's eye

RETIRANT *n* pl. -S a retiree

RETIRE *v* -TIRED, -TIRING, -TIRES to go away or withdraw

RETIREE *n* pl. -S one who has retired from his vocation

RETIRER *n* pl. -S one that retires

RETIRING *adj* shy

RETOOK past tense of retake

RETOOL *v* -ED, -ING, -S to reequip with tools

RETORT *v* -ED, -ING, -S to answer back

RETORTER *n* pl. -S one that retorts

RETOUCH *v* -ED, -ING, -ES to add new details or touches to

RETRACE *v* -TRACED, -TRACING, -TRACES to go back over

RETRACT *v* -ED, -ING, -S to take back

RETRAIN *v* -ED, -ING, -S to train again

RETRAL *adj* situated toward the back RETRALLY *adv*

RETREAD *v* -ED, -ING, -S to furnish with a new tread

RETREAT *v* -ED, -ING, -S to go back or backward

RETRENCH *v* -ED, -ING, -ES to curtail

RETRIAL *n* pl. -S a second trial

RETRIEVE *v* -TRIEVED, -TRIEVING, -TRIEVES to get back

RETROACT *v* -ED, -ING, -S to act in return

RETROFIT *v* -FITTED, -FITTING, -FITS to furnish with new parts not originally available

RETRORSE *adj* bent backward

RETSINA *n* pl. -S a Greek wine

RETTED past tense of ret

RETTING present participle of ret

RETURN *v* -ED, -ING, -S to come or go back

RETURNEE *n* pl. -S one that has returned

RETURNER *n* pl. -S one that returns

RETUSE *adj* having a rounded apex with a shallow notch — used of leaves

REUNION *n* pl. -S a reuniting of persons after separation

REUNITER *n* pl. -S one that reunites

REUSABLE *adj* capable of being used again

REV *v* REVVED, REVVING, REVS to increase the speed of

REVAMP *v* -ED, -ING, -S to make over

REVAMPER *n* pl. -S one that revamps

REVANCHE *n* pl. -S a political policy designed to regain lost territory

REVEAL *v* -ED, -ING, -S to make known

REVEALER *n* pl. -S one that reveals

REVEHENT *adj* carrying back

REVEILLE *n* pl. -S a morning bugle call

REVEL *v* -ELED, -ELING, -ELS or -ELLED, -ELLING, -ELS to engage in revelry

REVELER *n* pl. -S one that revels

REVELLER *n* pl. -S reveler

REVELRY *n* pl. -RIES noisy merrymaking

REVENANT *n* pl. -S one that returns

REVENGE *v* -VENGED, -VENGING, -VENGES to inflict injury in return for

REVENGER *n* pl. -S one that revenges

REVENUE *n* pl. -S the income of a government REVENUAL, REVENUED *adj*

REVENUER *n* pl. -S a revenue officer

REVERB *n* pl. -S an echo effect in recorded music

REVERE *v* -VERED, -VERING, -VERES to regard with great respect

REVEREND *n* pl. -S a clergyman

REVERENT *adj* deeply respectful

REVERER *n* pl. -S one that reveres

REVERIE *n* pl. -S a daydream

REVERIES pl. of revery

REVERING present participle of revere

REVERS *n* pl. REVERS a part of a garment turned back to show the inside

REVERSAL *n* pl. -S the act of reversing

REVERSE *v* -VERSED, -VERSING, -VERSES to turn or move in the opposite direction

REVERSER *n* pl. -S one that reverses

REVERSO *n* pl. -VERSOS verso

REVERT *v* -ED, -ING, -S to return to a former state

REVERTER *n* pl. -S one that reverts

REVERY *n* pl. -ERIES reverie

REVET *v* -VETTED, -VETTING, -VETS to face with masonry

REVIEWAL *n* pl. -S the act of reviewing

REVIEWER *n* pl. -S one that reviews

REVILE *v* -VILED, -VILING, -VILES to denounce with abusive language

REVILER *n* pl. -S one that reviles

REVISAL *n* pl. -S a revision

REVISE *v* -VISED, -VISING, -VISES to make a new or improved version of

REVISER *n* pl. -S one that revises

REVISION *n* pl. -S a revised version

REVISOR *n* pl. -S a reviser

REVISORY *adj* pertaining to revision

REVIVAL *n* pl. -S renewed attention to or interest in something

REVIVE *v* -VIVED, -VIVING, -VIVES to bring back to life or consciousness

REVIVER *n* pl. -S one that revives

REVIVIFY *v* -FIED, -FYING, -FIES to give new life to

REVIVING present participle of revive

REVOKE *v* -VOKED, -VOKING, -VOKES to annul by taking back

REVOKER *n* pl. -S one that revokes

REVOLT *v* -ED, -ING, -S to rise up against authority

REVOLTER *n* pl. -S one that revolts

REVOLUTE *adj* rolled backward or downward

REVOLVE *v* -VOLVED, -VOLVING, -VOLVES to turn about an axis

REVOLVER *n* pl. -S a type of handgun

REVUE *n* pl. -S a type of musical show

REVUIST *n* pl. -S a writer of revues

REVULSED *adj* affected with revulsion

REVVED past tense of rev

REVVING present participle of rev

REWARD *v* -ED, -ING, -S to give recompense to for worthy behavior

REWARDER *n* pl. -S one that rewards

REWINDER *n* pl. -S one that rewinds

REWORD *v* -ED, -ING, -S to state again in other words

REWRITER *n* pl. -S one that rewrites

REX *n* pl. REGES king

REX *n* pl. -ES an animal with a single wavy layer of hair

REYNARD *n* pl. -S a fox

RHABDOM *n* pl. -S a rodlike structure in the retinula

RHABDOME *n* pl. -S rhabdom

RHACHIS *n* pl. -CHISES or -CHIDES rachie

RHAMNOSE *n* pl. -S a sugar found in plants

RHAMNUS *n* pl. -ES a thorny tree or shrub

RHAPHE *n* pl. -PHAE or -PHES raphe

RHAPSODE *n* pl. -S a reciter of epic poetry in ancient Greece

RHAPSODY *n* pl. -DIES an exalted expression of feeling

RHATANY *n* pl. -NIES a South American shrub

RHEA *n* pl. -S a flightless bird

RHEBOK *n* pl. -S a large antelope

RHEMATIC *adj* pertaining to a verb

RHENIUM *n* pl. -S a metallic element

RHEOBASE *n* pl. -S the smallest amount of electricity required to stimulate a nerve

RHEOLOGY *n* pl. -GIES the study of matter in the fluid state

RHEOPHIL *adj* living in flowing water

RHEOSTAT *n* pl. -S a resistor used to control electric current

RHESUS *n* pl. -ES as Asian monkey

RHETOR *n* pl. -S a teacher of rhetoric

RHETORIC *n* pl. -S the study of effective speech and writing

RHEUM *n* pl. -S a watery discharge from the eyes or nose RHEUMIC *adj*

RHEUMY *adj* RHEUMIER, RHEUMIEST marked by rheum

RHINAL *adj* pertaining to the nose

RHINITIS *n* pl. RHINITIDES inflammation of the mucous membranes of the nose

RHINO *n* pl. -NOS a rhinoceros

RHIZOBIA	*n/pl* rod-shaped bacteria
RHIZOID	*n* pl. -S a rootlike structure
RHIZOMA	*n* pl. -MATA rhizome
RHIZOME	*n* pl. -S a rootlike, underground stem **RHIZOMIC** *adj*
RHIZOPOD	*n* pl. -S any of a class of protozoans
RHIZOPUS	*n* pl. -PI or -PUSES any of a genus of mold fungi
RHO	*n* pl. RHOS a Greek letter
RHODAMIN	*n* pl. -S a red dye
RHODIUM	*n* pl. -S a metallic element **RHODIC** *adj*
RHODORA	*n* pl. -S a flowering shrub
RHOMB	*n* pl. -S a rhombus
RHOMBI	a pl. of rhombus
RHOMBIC	*adj* having the shape of a rhombus
RHOMBOID	*n* pl. -S a type of geometric figure
RHOMBUS	*n* pl. -BUSES or -BI a type of geometric figure
RHONCHUS	*n* pl. -CHI a rattling respiratory sound **RHONCHAL** *adj*
RHUBARB	*n* pl. -S a perennial herb
RHUMB	*n* pl. -S a point of the mariner's compass
RHUMBA	*v* -ED, -ING, -S to rumba
RHUS	*n* pl. -ES any of a genus of shrubs and trees
RHYME	*v* RHYMED, RHYMING, RHYMES to compose verse with corresponding terminal sounds
RHYMER	*n* pl. -S one that rhymes
RHYOLITE	*n* pl. -S a volcanic rock
RHYTA	pl. of rhyton
RHYTHM	*n* pl. -S movement or procedure with uniform recurrence of strong and weak elements
RHYTHMIC	*n* pl. -S the science of rhythm
RHYTON	*n* pl. -TA an ancient Greek drinking horn
RIAL	*n* pl. -S a monetary unit of Iran
RIALTO	*n* pl. -TOS a marketplace
RIANT	*adj* cheerful **RIANTLY** *adv*
RIATA	*n* pl. -S a lasso
RIB	*v* RIBBED, RIBBING, RIBS to poke fun at
RIBALD	*n* pl. -S one who uses crude language

RIBALDLY	*adv* crudely
RIBALDRY	*n* pl. -RIES crude language
RIBAND	*n* pl. -S a ribbon
RIBBAND	*n* pl. -S a long, narrow strip used in shipbuilding
RIBBED	past tense of rib
RIBBER	*n* pl. -S one that ribs
RIBBIER	comparative of ribby
RIBBIEST	superlative of ribby
RIBBING	*n* pl. -S the act of one that ribs
RIBBON	*v* -ED, -ING, -S to decorate with ribbons (narrow strips of fine fabric)
RIBBONY	*adj* resembling ribbon
RIBBY	*adj* -BIER, -BIEST marked by prominent ribs (curved bony rods in the body)
RIBES	*n* pl. RIBES a flowering shrub
RIBGRASS	*n* pl. -ES a weedy plant
RIBLESS	*adj* having no ribs
RIBLET	*n* pl. -S the rib end in a breast of lamb or veal
RIBLIKE	*adj* resembling a rib
RIBOSE	*n* pl. -S a pentose sugar
RIBOSOME	*n* pl. -S a particle composed of protein and ribonucleic acid
RIBWORT	*n* pl. -S ribgrass
RICE	*v* RICED, RICING, RICES to press through a ricer
RICEBIRD	*n* pl. -S the bobolink
RICER	*n* pl. -S a kitchen utensil consisting of a container perforated with small holes
RICERCAR	*n* pl. -S an instrumental composition
RICH	*adj* RICHER, RICHEST having wealth
RICHEN	*v* -ED, -ING, -S to make rich
RICHES	*n/pl* wealth
RICHLY	*adv* in a rich manner
RICHNESS	*n* pl. -ES the state of being rich
RICHWEED	*n* pl. -S a flowering plant
RICIN	*n* pl. -S a poisonous protein
RICING	present participle of rice
RICINUS	*n* pl. -ES a large-leaved plant
RICK	*v* -ED, -ING, -S to pile hay in stacks

RICKETS n/pl a disease resulting from vitamin D deficiency

RICKETY adj -ETIER, -ETIEST likely to fall or collapse

RICKEY n pl. -EYS an alcoholic beverage containing lime juice, sugar, and soda water

RICKRACK n pl. -S a flat braid used as a trimming

RICKSHA n pl. -S rickshaw

RICKSHAW n pl. -S a small, two-wheeled passenger vehicle

RICOCHET v -CHETED, -CHETING, -CHETS or -CHETTED, -CHETTING, -CHETS to rebound from a surface

RICOTTA n pl. -S an Italian cheese

RICRAC n pl. -S rickrack

RICTUS n pl. -ES the expanse of the open mouth RICTAL adj

RID v RID or RIDDED, RIDDING, RIDS to free from something objectionable

RIDABLE adj capable of being ridden

RIDDANCE n pl. -S deliverance

RIDDED past tense of rid

RIDDEN past participle of ride

RIDDER n pl. -S one that rids

RIDDING present participle of rid

RIDDLE v -DLED, -DLING, -DLES to pierce with many holes

RIDDLER n pl. -S one that riddles

RIDE v RODE, RIDDEN, RIDING, RIDES to sit on, control, and be conveyed by an animal or machine

RIDEABLE adj ridable

RIDENT adj laughing

RIDER n pl. -S one that rides

RIDGE v RIDGED, RIDGING, RIDGES to form into ridges (long, narrow elevations)

RIDGEL n pl. -S a ridgling

RIDGIER comparative of ridgy

RIDGIEST superlative of ridgy

RIDGIL n pl. -S a ridgling

RIDGING present participle of ridge

RIDGLING n pl. -S a male animal with undescended testicles

RIDGY adj RIDGIER, RIDGIEST having ridges

RIDICULE v -CULED, -CULING, -CULES to make fun of

RIDING n pl. -S the act of one that rides

RIDLEY n pl. -LEYS a sea turtle

RIDOTTO n pl. -TOS a public musical entertainment in 18th century England

RIEL n pl. -S a monetary unit of Cambodia

RIEVER n pl. -S reaver

RIFE adj RIFER, RIFEST abundant RIFELY adv

RIFENESS n pl. -ES the state of being rife

RIFF v -ED, -ING, -S to riffle

RIFFLE v -FLED, -FLING, -FLES to flip through hastily

RIFFLER n pl. -S a filing and scraping tool

RIFFRAFF n pl. -S the disreputable element of society

RIFLE v -FLED, -FLING, -FLES to search through and rob

RIFLEMAN n pl. -MEN a soldier armed with a rifle (a type of firearm)

RIFLER n pl. -S one that rifles

RIFLERY n pl. -RIE6 the practice of shooting at targets with a rifle

RIFLING n pl. -S the system of grooves in a gun barrel

RIFT v -ED, -ING, -S to form rifts (clefts)

RIFTLESS adj having no rift

RIG v RIGGED, RIGGING, RIGS to put in proper condition for use

RIGADOON n pl. -S a lively dance

RIGATONI n pl. -S a tubular pasta

RIGAUDON n pl. -S rigadoon

RIGGED past tense of rig

RIGGER n pl. -S one that rigs

RIGGING n pl. -S the system of lines, chains, and tackle used aboard a ship

RIGHT adj RIGHTER, RIGHTEST being in accordance with what is good, proper, or just

RIGHT v -ED, -ING, -S to put in proper order or condition

RIGHTER n pl. -S one that rights

RIGHTFUL adj just or proper

RIGHTIES pl. of righty

RIGHTISM n pl. -S a conservative political philosophy

RIGHTIST n pl. -S an advocate of rightism

RIGHTLY adv in a right manner

RIGHTO interj — used to express cheerful consent

RIGHTY n pl. RIGHTIES a right-handed person

RIGID adj not flexible

RIGIDIFY v -FIED, -FYING, -FIES to make rigid

RIGIDITY n pl. -TIES the state of being rigid

RIGIDLY adv in a rigid manner

RIGOR n pl. -S strictness or severity

RIGORISM n pl. -S strictness or severity in conduct or attitude

RIGORIST n pl. -S one that professes rigorism

RIGOROUS adj characterized by rigor

RIGOUR n pl. -S rigor

RIKISHA n pl. -S rickshaw

RIKSHAW n pl. -S rickshaw

RILE v RILED, RILING, RILES to anger

RILEY adj angry

RILIEVO n pl. -VI relievo

RILING present participle of rile

RILL v -ED, -ING, -S to flow like a rill (a small brook)

RILLE n pl. -S a valley on the moon's surface

RILLET n pl. -S a small rill

RIM v RIMMED, RIMMING, RIMS to provide with a rim (an outer edge)

RIME v RIMED, RIMING, RIMES to rhyme

RIMER n pl. -S one that rimes

RIMESTER n pl. -S a rimer

RIMFIRE adj designed for the use of certain cartridges

RIMIER comparative of rimy

RIMIEST superlative of rimy

RIMING present participle of rime

RIMLAND n pl. -S an outlying area

RIMLESS adj having no rim

RIMMED past tense of rim

RIMMER n pl. -S a reamer

RIMMING present participle of rim

RIMOSE adj marked by cracks RIMOSELY adv

RIMOSITY n pl. -TIES the state of being rimose

RIMOUS adj rimose

RIMPLE v -PLED, -PLING, -PLES to wrinkle

RIMROCK n pl. -S a type of rock formation

RIMY adj RIMIER, RIMIEST frosty

RIN v RAN, RINNING, RINS to run or melt

RIND n pl. -S a thick and firm outer covering RINDED adj

RING v -ED, -ING, -S to form a ring (a circular band) around

RING v RANG, RUNG, RINGING, RINGS to give forth a clear, resonant sound

RINGBARK v -ED, -ING, -S to make an encircling cut through the bark of

RINGBOLT n pl. -S a type of eyebolt

RINGBONE n pl. -S a bony growth on a horse's foot

RINGDOVE n pl. -S a European pigeon

RINGENT adj having open liplike parts

RINGER n pl. -S one that rings

RINGHALS n pl. -ES a venomous snake

RINGLET adj a small ring

RINGLIKE adj resembling a ring

RINGNECK n pl. -S a bird having a ring of color around the neck

RINGSIDE n pl. -S the area just outside a boxing or wrestling ring (a square enclosure)

RINGTAIL n pl. -S an animal having a tail with ringlike markings

RINGTAW n pl. -S a game of marbles

RINGTOSS n pl. -ES a game in which the object is to toss a ring onto an upright stick

RINGWORM n pl. -S a skin disease

RINK n pl. -S a surface of ice for skating

RINNING present participle of rin

RINSE v RINSED, RINSING, RINSES to cleanse with clear water RINSABLE, RINSIBLE adj

RINSER n pl. -S one that rinses

RINSING   n pl. -S the act of one that rinses

RIOT   v -ED, -ING, -S to take part in a violent public disturbance

RIOTER   n pl. -S one that riots

RIOTOUS   adj characterized by rioting

RIP   v RIPPED, RIPPING, RIPS to tear or cut apart roughly

RIPARIAN   adj pertaining to the bank of a river

RIPCORD   n pl. -S a cord pulled to release a parachute

RIPE   adj RIPER, RIPEST fully developed RIPELY adv

RIPE   v RIPED, RIPING, RIPES to cleanse

RIPEN   v -ED, -ING, -S to become ripe

RIPENER   n pl. -S one that ripens

RIPENESS   n pl. -ES the state of being ripe

RIPER   comparative of ripe

RIPEST   superlative of ripe

RIPIENO   n pl. -NI or -NOS tutti

RIPING   present participle of ripe

RIPOST   v -ED, -ING, -S to riposte

RIPOSTE   v -POSTED, -POSTING, -POSTES to make a return thrust in fencing

RIPPABLE   adj capable of being ripped

RIPPED   past tense of rip

RIPPER   n pl. -S one that rips

RIPPING   adj excellent

RIPPLE   v -PLED, -PLING, -PLES to form ripples (small waves)

RIPPLER   n pl. -S a toothed tool for cleaning flax fiber

RIPPLET   n pl. -S a small ripple

RIPPLING   present participle of ripple

RIPPLY   adj -PLIER, -PLIEST marked by ripples

RIPRAP   v -RAPPED, -RAPPING, -RAPS to strengthen with a foundation of broken stones

RIPSAW   n pl. -S a type of saw

RIPTIDE   n pl. -S a tide that opposes other tides

RISE   v ROSE, RISEN, RISING, RISES to move upward

RISER   n pl. -S one that rises

RISHI   n pl. -S a Hindu sage

RISIBLE   adj inclined to laugh RISIBLY adv

RISIBLES   n/pl a sense of the ridiculous

RISING   n pl. -S the act of one that rises

RISK   v -ED, -ING, -S to expose to a chance of injury or loss

RISKER   n pl. -S one that risks

RISKY   adj RISKIER, RISKIEST dangerous RISKILY adv

RISOTTO   n pl. -TOS a rice dish

RISQUE   adj bordering on impropriety or indecency

RISSOLE   n pl. -S a small roll filled with meat or fish

RISUS   n pl. -ES a grin or laugh

RITARD   n pl. -S a musical passage with a gradual slackening in tempo

RITE   n pl. -S a ceremonial act or procedure

RITTER   n pl. -S a knight

RITUAL   n pl. -S a system of rites

RITUALLY   adv ceremonially

RITZ   n pl. -ES pretentious display

RITZY   adj RITZIER, RITZIEST elegant RITZILY adv

RIVAGE   n pl. -S a coast, shore, or bank

RIVAL   v -VALED, -VALING, -VALS or -VALLED, -VALLING, -VALS to strive to equal or surpass

RIVALRY   n pl. -RIES competition

RIVE   v RIVED, RIVEN, RIVING, RIVES to tear apart

RIVER   n pl. -S a large, natural stream of water

RIVERBED   n pl. -S the area covered or once covered by a river

RIVERINE   adj pertaining to a river

RIVET   v -ETED, -ETING, -ETS or -ETTED, -ETTING, -ETS to fasten with a type of metal bolt

RIVETER   n pl. -S one that rivets

RIVIERA   n pl. -S a coastal resort area

RIVIERE   n pl. -S a necklace of precious stones

RIVING   present participle of rive

RIVULET   n pl. -S a small stream

RIYAL   n pl. -S a monetary unit of Saudi Arabia

ROACH   v -ED, -ING, -ES to cause to arch

ROAD   *n* pl. -S an open way for public passage

ROADBED   *n* pl. -S the foundation for a railroad track

ROADLESS   *adj* having no roads

ROADSIDE   *n* pl. -S the area along the side of a road

ROADSTER   *n* pl. -S a light, open automobile

ROADWAY   *n* pl. -WAYS a road

ROADWORK   *n* pl. -S outdoor running as a form of physical conditioning

ROAM   *v* -ED, -ING, -S to move about without purpose or plan

ROAMER   *n* pl. -S one that roams

ROAN   *n* pl. -S an animal having a coat sprinkled with white or gray

ROAR   *v* -ED, -ING, -S to utter a loud, deep sound

ROARER   *n* pl. -S one that roars

ROARING   *n* pl. -S a loud, deep sound

ROAST   *v* -ED, -ING, -S to cook with dry heat

ROASTER   *n* pl. -S one that roasts

ROB   *v* ROBBED, ROBBING, ROBS to take property from illegally

ROBALO   *n* pl. -LOS a marine food fish

ROBAND   *n* pl. -S a piece of yarn used to fasten a sail

ROBBED   past tense of rob

ROBBER   *n* pl. -S one that robs

ROBBERY   *n* pl. -BERIES the act of one who robs

ROBBIN   *n* pl. -S a roband

ROBBING   present participle of rob

ROBE   *v* ROBED, ROBING, ROBES to cover with a robe (a long, loose outer garment)

ROBIN   *n* pl. -S a songbird

ROBLE   *n* pl. -S an oak tree

ROBORANT   *n* pl. -S an invigorating drug

ROBOT   *n* pl. -S a humanlike machine that performs various functions

ROBOTICS   *n/pl* a field of interest concerned with robots

ROBOTISM   *n* pl. -S the state of being a robot

ROBOTIZE   *v* -IZED, -IZING, -IZES to make automatic

ROBOTRY   *n* pl. -RIES the science of robots

ROBUST   *adj* -BUSTER, -BUSTEST strong and healthy **ROBUSTLY** *adv*

ROC   *n* pl. -S a lengendary bird of prey

ROCHET   *n* pl. -S a linen vestment

ROCK   *v* -ED, -ING, -S to move back and forth

ROCKABY   *n* pl. -BIES a song used to lull a child to sleep

ROCKABYE   *n* pl. -S rockaby

ROCKAWAY   *n* pl. -WAYS a light carriage

ROCKER   *n* pl. -S a rocking chair

ROCKERY   *n* pl. -ERIES a rock garden

ROCKET   *v* -ED, -ING, -S to convey by means of a rocket (a device propelled by the reaction of escaping gases)

ROCKETER   *n* pl. -S one that designs or launches rockets

ROCKETRY   *n* pl. -RIES the science of rockets

ROCKFALL   *n* pl. -S a mass of fallen rocks

ROCKFISH   *n* pl. -ES a fish living around rocks

ROCKIER   comparative of rocky

ROCKIEST   superlative of rocky

ROCKLESS   *adj* having no rocks

ROCKLIKE   *adj* resembling a rock (a large mass of stone)

ROCKLING   *n* pl. -S a marine fish

ROCKOON   *n* pl. -S a small rocket

ROCKROSE   *n* pl. -S a flowering plant

ROCKWEED   *n* pl. -S a brown seaweed

ROCKWORK   *n* pl. -S a natural mass of rocks

ROCKY   *adj* ROCKIER, ROCKIEST unsteady

ROCOCO   *n* pl. -COS a style of architecture and decoration

ROD   *v* RODDED, RODDING, RODS to provide with a rod (a straight, slender piece of wood, metal, or other material)

RODE   past tense of ride

RODENT   *n* pl. -S a gnawing mammal

RODEO   *n* pl. -DEOS a public exhibition of cowboy skills

RODLESS   *adj* having no rod

RODLIKE   *adj* resembling a rod

RODMAN   *n* pl. -MEN a surveyor's assistant

RODSMAN *n* pl. -MEN rodman

ROE *n* pl. -S the mass of eggs within a female fish

ROEBUCK *n* pl. -S the male of a small Eurasian deer

ROENTGEN *n* pl. -S a unit of radiation dosage

ROGATION *n* pl. -S the proposal of a law in ancient Rome

ROGATORY *adj* requesting information

ROGER *n* pl. -S the pirate flag bearing the skull and crossbones

ROGUE *v* ROGUED, ROGUEING or ROGUING, ROGUES to defraud

ROGUERY *n* pl. -ERIES roguish conduct

ROGUISH *adj* dishonest

ROIL *v* -ED, -ING, -S to make muddy

ROILY *adj* ROILIER, ROILIEST muddy

ROISTER *v* -ED, -ING, -S to revel

ROLAMITE *n* pl. -S a nearly frictionless mechanical device

ROLE *n* pl. -S a part played by an actor

ROLL *v* -ED, -ING, -S to move along by repeatedly turning over

ROLLAWAY *adj* mounted on rollers for easy movement

ROLLBACK *n* pl. -S a return to a lower level of prices or wages

ROLLER *n* pl. -S a cylindrical device that rolls or rotates

ROLLICK *v* -ED, -ING, -S to frolic

ROLLICKY *adj* given to rollicking

ROLLING *n* pl. -S the act of one that rolls

ROLLMOP *n* pl. -S a fillet of herring

ROLLOUT *n* pl. -S a type of play in football

ROLLOVER *n* pl. -S a motor vehicle accident in which the vehicle overturns

ROLLTOP *adj* having a flexible, sliding cover

ROLLWAY *n* pl. -WAYS an incline for rolling logs

ROMAINE *n* pl. -S a variety of lettuce

ROMAN *n* pl. -S a metrical narrative of medieval France

ROMANCE *v* -MANCED, -MANCING, -MANCES to woo

ROMANCER *n* pl. -S one that romances

ROMANIZE *v* -IZED, -IZING, -IZES to write in the Roman alphabet

ROMANO *n* pl. -NOS an Italian cheese

ROMANTIC *n* pl. -S a fanciful person

ROMAUNT *n* pl. -S a long, medieval narrative

ROMP *v* -ED, -ING, -S to play boisterously

ROMPER *n* pl. -S one that romps

ROMPISH *adj* inclined to romp

RONDEAU *n* pl. -DEAUX a short poem of fixed form

RONDEL *n* pl. -S a rondeau of 14 lines

RONDELET *n* pl. -S a rondeau of 5 or 7 lines

RONDELLE *n* pl. -S a rondel

RONDO *n* pl. -DOS a type of musical composition

RONDURE *n* pl. -S a circle or sphere

RONION *n* pl. -S a mangy animal or person

RONNEL *n* pl. -S an insecticide

RONTGEN *n* pl. -S roentgen

RONYON *n* pl. -S ronion

ROOD *n* pl. -S a crucifix

ROOF *v* -ED, -ING, -S to provide with a roof (the external upper covering of a building)

ROOFER *n* pl. -S one that builds or repairs roofs

ROOFING *n* pl. -S material for a roof

ROOFLESS *adj* having no roof

ROOFLIKE *adj* resembling a roof

ROOFLINE *n* pl. -S the profile of a roof

ROOFTOP *n* pl. -S a roof

ROOFTREE *n* pl. -S a horizontal timber in a roof

ROOK *v* -ED, -ING, -S to swindle

ROOKERY *n* pl. -ERIES a colony of rooks (European crows)

ROOKIE *n* pl. -S a novice

ROOKY *adj* ROOKIER, ROOKIEST abounding in rooks

ROOM *v* -ED, -ING, -S to occupy a room (a walled space within a building)

ROOMER *n* pl. -S a lodger

ROOMETTE *n* pl. -S a small room

ROOMFUL *n* pl. -S as much as a room will hold

ROOMMATE *n* pl. -S one with whom a room is shared

ROOMY *adj* ROOMIER, ROOMIEST spacious ROOMILY *adv*

ROORBACK *n* pl. -S a false story used for political advantage

ROOSE *v* ROOSED, ROOSING, ROOSES to praise

ROOSER *n* pl. -S one that rooses

ROOST *v* -ED, -ING, -S to settle down for rest or sleep

ROOSTER *n* pl. -S a male chicken

ROOT *v* -ED, -ING, -S to put forth a root (an underground portion of a plant)

ROOTAGE *n* pl. -S a system of roots

ROOTER *n* pl. -S one that gives encouragement or support

ROOTHOLD *n* pl. -S the embedding of a plant to soil through the growing of roots

ROOTIER comparative of rooty

ROOTIEST superlative of rooty

ROOTLESS *adj* having no roots

ROOTLET *n* pl. -S a small root

ROOTLIKE *adj* resembling a root

ROOTY *adj* ROOTIER, ROOTIEST full of roots

ROPE *v* ROPED, ROPING, ROPES to bind with a rope (a thick line of twisted fibers) ROPABLE *adj*

ROPER *n* pl. -S one that ropes

ROPERY *n* pl. -ERIES a place where ropes are made

ROPEWALK *n* pl. -S a long path where ropes are made

ROPEWAY *n* pl. -WAYS an aerial cable used to transport freight

ROPIER comparative of ropy

ROPIEST superlative of ropy

ROPILY *adv* in a ropy manner

ROPINESS *n* pl. -ES the quality of being ropy

ROPING present participle of rope

ROPY *adj* ROPIER, ROPIEST resembling a rope or ropes

ROQUE *n* pl. -S a form of croquet

ROQUET *v* -ED, -ING, -S to cause one's own ball to hit another in croquet

RORQUAL *n* pl. -S a large whale

ROSARIA a pl. of rosarium

ROSARIAN *n* pl. -S a cultivator of roses

ROSARIUM *n* pl. -IA or -IUMS a rose garden

ROSARY *n* pl. -RIES a series of prayers in the Roman Catholic Church

ROSCOE *n* pl. -S a pistol

ROSE *v* ROSED, ROSING, ROSES to make the color of a rose (a reddish flower)

ROSEATE *adj* rose-colored

ROSEBAY *n* pl. -BAYS an evergreen shrub

ROSEBUD *n* pl. -S the bud of a rose

ROSEBUSH *n* pl. -ES a shrub that bears roses

ROSED past tense of rose

ROSEFISH *n* pl. -ES a marine food fish

ROSELIKE *adj* resembling a rose

ROSELLE *n* pl. -S a tropical plant

ROSEMARY *n* pl. -MARIES an evergreen shrub

ROSEOLA *n* pl. -S a rose-colored skin rash ROSEOLAR *adj*

ROSEROOT *n* pl. -S a perennial herb

ROSERY *n* pl. -ERIES a place where roses are grown

ROSET *n* pl. -S resin

ROSETTE *n* pl. -S an ornament resembling a rose

ROSEWOOD *n* pl. -S a tropical tree

ROSIER comparative of rosy

ROSIEST superlative of rosy

ROSILY *adv* in a rosy manner

ROSIN *v* -ED, -ING, -S to treat with rosin (a brittle resin)

ROSINESS *n* pl. -ES the state of being rosy

ROSING present participle of rose

ROSINOUS *adj* resembling rosin

ROSINY *adj* rosinous

ROSOLIO *n* pl. -LIOS a liqueur made from raisins and brandy

ROSTELLA *n/pl* small, beaklike structures

ROSTER *n* pl. -S a list of names

ROSTRA a pl. of rostrum

ROSTRAL *adj* pertaining to a rostrum

ROSTRATE *adj* having a rostrum

ROSTRUM *n* pl. -TRA or -TRUMS a beaklike process or part

ROSULATE *adj* arranged in the form of a rosette

ROSY *adj* ROSIER, ROSIEST rose-colored

ROT *v* ROTTED, ROTTING, ROTS to decompose

ROTA *n pl.* -S a roster

ROTARY *n pl.* -RIES a rotating part or device

ROTATE *v* -TATED, -TATING, -TATES to turn about an axis

ROTATION *n pl.* -S the act or an instance of rotating **ROTATIVE** *adj*

ROTATOR *n pl.* -S one that rotates

ROTATOR *n pl.* -ES a muscle serving to rotate a part of the body

ROTATORY *adj* pertaining to rotation

ROTCH *n pl.* -ES rotche

ROTCHE *n pl.* -S a seabird

ROTE *n pl.* -S mechanical routine

ROTENONE *n pl.* -S an insecticide

ROTGUT *n pl.* -S inferior liquor

ROTIFER *n pl.* -S a microscopic aquatic organism

ROTIFORM *adj* shaped like a wheel

ROTL *n pl.* ROTLS or ARTAL a unit of weight in Muslim countries

ROTO *n pl.* -TOS a type of printing process

ROTOR *n pl.* -S a rotating part of a machine

ROTOTILL *v* -ED, -ING, -S to till soil with a type of farming implement

ROTTED past tense of rot

ROTTEN *adj* -TENER, -TENEST being in a state of decay **ROTTENLY** *adv*

ROTTER *n pl.* -S a scoundrel

ROTTING present participle of rot

ROTUND *adj* marked by roundness **ROTUNDLY** *adv*

ROTUNDA *n pl.* -S a round building

ROTURIER *n pl.* -S a commoner

ROUBLE *n pl.* -S ruble

ROUCHE *n pl.* -S ruche

ROUE *n pl.* -S a lecherous man

ROUEN *n pl.* -S any of a breed of domestic ducks

ROUGE *v* ROUGED, ROUGING, ROUGES to color with a red cosmetic

ROUGH *adj* ROUGHER, ROUGHEST having an uneven surface

ROUGH *v* -ED, -ING, -S to make rough

ROUGHAGE *n pl.* -S coarse, bulky food

ROUGHDRY *v* -DRIED, -DRYING, -DRIES to dry without ironing, as washed clothes

ROUGHEN *v* -ED, -ING, -S to make rough

ROUGHER *n pl.* -S one that roughs

ROUGHHEW *v* -HEWED, -HEWN, -HEWING, -HEWS to shape roughly

ROUGHISH *adj* somewhat rough

ROUGHLEG *n pl.* -S a large hawk

ROUGHLY *adv* in a rough manner

ROUGING present participle of rouge

ROULADE *n pl.* -S a musical embellishment

ROULEAU *n pl.* -LEAUX or -LEAUS a roll of coins wrapped in paper

ROULETTE *v* -LETTED, -LETTING, -LETTES to make tiny slits in

ROUND *adj* ROUNDER, ROUNDEST shaped like a sphere

ROUND *v* -ED, -ING, -S to make round

ROUNDEL *n pl.* -S a round figure or object

ROUNDER *n pl.* -S a tool for rounding

ROUNDISH *adj* somewhat round

ROUNDLET *n pl.* -S a small circle

ROUNDLY *adv* in a round manner

ROUNDUP *n pl.* -S the driving together of cattle scattered over a range

ROUP *v* -ED, -ING, -S to auction

ROUPET *adj* roupy

ROUPY *adj* ROUPIER, ROUPIEST hoarse **ROUPILY** *adv*

ROUSE *v* ROUSED, ROUSING, ROUSES to bring out of a state of sleep or inactivity

ROUSER *n pl.* -S one that rouses

ROUSSEAU *n pl.* -S fried pemmican

ROUST *v* -ED, -ING, -S to arouse and drive out

ROUSTER *n pl.* -S a wharf laborer and deckhand

ROUT *v* -ED, -ING, -S to defeat overwhelmingly

ROUTE *v* ROUTED, ROUTING, ROUTES to send on a particular course

ROUTEMAN *n pl.* -MEN one who conducts business on a customary course

ROUTER   *n* pl. -S a scooping tool

ROUTEWAY   *n* pl. -WAYS an established course of travel

ROUTH   *n* pl. -S an abundance

ROUTINE   *n* pl. -S a regular course of procedure

ROUTING   present participle of route

ROUX   *n* pl. ROUX a mixture of butter and flour

ROVE   *v* ROVED, ROVING, ROVES to roam

ROVEN   a past participle of reeve

ROVER   *n* pl. -S one that roves

ROVING   *n* pl. -S a roll of textile fibers

ROVINGLY   *adv* in a roving manner

ROW   *v* -ED, -ING, -S to propel by means of oars **ROWABLE** *adj*

ROWAN   *n* pl. -S a Eurasian tree

ROWBOAT   *n* pl. -S a small boat designed to be rowed

ROWDY   *adj* -DIER, -DIEST disorderly in behavior **ROWDILY** *adv*

ROWDY   *n* pl. -DIES a rowdy person

ROWDYISH   *adj* tending to be rowdy

ROWDYISM   *n* pl. -S disorderly behavior

ROWEL   *v* -ELED, -ELING, -ELS or -ELLED, -ELLING, -ELS to prick with a spiked wheel in order to urge forward

ROWEN   *n* pl. -S a second growth of grass

ROWER   *n* pl. -S one that rows

ROWING   *n* pl. -S the sport of racing in light, long, and narrow rowboats

ROWLOCK   *n* pl. -S an oarlock

ROWTH   *n* pl. -S a routh

ROYAL   *n* pl. -S a size of printing paper

ROYALISM   *n* pl. -S support of a monarch or monarchy

ROYALIST   *n* pl. -S a supporter of a monarch or monarchy

ROYALLY   *adv* in a kingly manner

ROYALTY   *n* pl. -TIES the status or power of a monarch

ROYSTER   *v* -ED, -ING, -S to roister.

ROZZER   *n* pl. -S a policeman

RUB   *v* RUBBED, RUBBING, RUBS to move along the surface of a body with pressure

RUBABOO   *n* pl. -BOOS a type of soup

RUBACE   *n* pl. -S rubasse

RUBAIYAT   *n* pl. RUBAIYAT four-lined stanzas in Persian poetry

RUBASSE   *n* pl. -S a variety of quartz

RUBATO   *n* pl. -TOS a fluctuation of speed within a musical phrase

RUBBABOO   *n* pl. -BOOS rubaboo

RUBBED   past tense of rub

RUBBER   *n* pl. -S an elastic substance **RUBBERY** *adj*

RUBBING   *n* pl. -S an image produced by rubbing

RUBBISH   *n* pl. -ES worthless, unwanted matter **RUBBISHY** *adj*

RUBBLE   *v* -BLED, -BLING, -BLES to reduce to rubble (broken pieces)

RUBBLY   *adj* -BLIER, -BLIEST abounding in rubble

RUBDOWN   *n* pl. -S a brisk rubbing of the body

RUBE   *n* pl. -S a rustic

RUBELLA   *n* pl. -S a virus disease

RUBEOLA   *n* pl. -S a virus disease **RUBEOLAR** *adj*

RUBICUND   *adj* ruddy

RUBIDIUM   *n* pl. -S a metallic element **RUBIDIC** *adj*

RUBIED   past tense of ruby

RUBIER   comparative of ruby

RUBIES   present 3d person sing. of ruby

RUBIEST   superlative of ruby

RUBIGO   *n* pl. -GOS red iron oxide

RUBIOUS   *adj* ruby-colored

RUBLE   *n* pl. -S a monetary unit of the Soviet Union

RUBRIC   *n* pl. -S a part of a manuscript or book that appears in red **RUBRICAL** *adj*

RUBUS   *n* pl. RUBUS a plant of the rose family

RUBY   *v* -BIED, -BYING, -BIES to tint with the color of a ruby (a deep-red precious stone)

RUBY   *adj* -BIER, -BIEST of a deep-red color

RUBYLIKE   *adj* resembling a ruby

RUCHE   *n* pl. -S a pleated strip of fine fabric

RUCHING   *n* pl. -S a ruche

RUCK   v -ED, -ING, -S to wrinkle or crease

RUCKSACK   n pl. -S a knapsack

RUCKUS   n pl. -ES a noisy disturbance

RUCTION   n pl. -S a ruckus

RUCTIOUS   adj quarrelsome

RUDD   n pl. -S a freshwater fish

RUDDER   n pl. -S a vertical blade used to direct the course of a vessel

RUDDIER   comparative of ruddy

RUDDIEST   superlative of ruddy

RUDDILY   adv in a ruddy manner

RUDDLE   v -DLED, -DLING, -DLES to color with a red dye

RUDDOCK   n pl. -S a European bird

RUDDY   adj -DIER, -DIEST having a healthy, reddish color

RUDE   adj RUDER, RUDEST discourteous or impolite RUDELY adv

RUDENESS   n pl. -ES the quality of being rude

RUDERAL   n pl. -S a plant growing in poor land

RUDESBY   n pl. -BIES a rude person

RUDEST   superlative of rude

RUDIMENT   n pl. -S a basic principle or element

RUE   v RUED, RUING, RUES to feel sorrow or remorse for

RUEFUL   adj feeling sorrow or remorse RUEFULLY adv

RUER   n pl. -S one that rues

RUFF   v -ED, -ING, -S to trump

RUFFE   n pl. -S a freshwater fish

RUFFIAN   n pl. -S a tough, lawless person

RUFFLE   v -FLED, -FLING, -FLES to destroy the smoothness of

RUFFLER   n pl. -S one that ruffles

RUFFLIKE   adj resembling a ruff (a pleated collar)

RUFFLING   present participle of ruffle

RUFFLY   adj not smooth

RUFOUS   adj reddish

RUG   v RUGGED, RUGGING, RUGS to tear roughly

RUGA   n pl. -GAE an anatomical fold or wrinkle RUGAL, RUGATE adj

RUGBY   n pl. -BIES a form of football

RUGGED   adj -GEDER, -GEDEST having an uneven surface RUGGEDLY adv

RUGGER   n pl. -S rugby

RUGGING   present participle of rug

RUGLIKE   adj resembling a rug (a thick fabric used as a floor covering)

RUGOSE   adj full of wrinkles RUGOSELY adv

RUGOSITY   n pl. -TIES the state of being rugose

RUGOUS   adj rugose

RUGULOSE   adj having small wrinkles

RUIN   v -ED, -ING, -S to destroy RUINABLE adj

RUINATE   v -ATED, -ATING, -ATES to ruin

RUINER   n pl. -S one that ruins

RUING   present participle of rue

RUINOUS   adj destructive

RULE   v RULED, RULING, RULES to exercise control over RULABLE adj

RULELESS   adj not restrained or regulated by law

RULER   n pl. -S one that rules

RULING   n pl. -S an authoritative decision

RUM   n pl. -S an alcoholic liquor

RUM   adj RUMMER, RUMMEST odd

RUMBA   v -ED, -ING, -S to perform a ballroom dance

RUMBLE   v -BLED, -BLING, -BLES to make a deep, thunderous sound

RUMBLER   n pl. -S one that rumbles

RUMBLING   n pl. -S a deep, thunderous sound

RUMBLY   adj tending to rumble

RUMEN   n pl. -MINA or -MENS a part of the stomach of a ruminant RUMINAL adj

RUMINANT   n pl. -S a hoofed, even-toed mammal

RUMINATE   v -NATED, -NATING, -NATES to chew again

RUMMAGE   v -MAGED, -MAGING, -MAGES to search thoroughly through

RUMMAGER   n pl. -S one that rummages

RUMMER   n pl. -S a large drinking glass

RUMMEST   superlative of rum

RUMMY   n pl. -MIES a card game

RUMMY *adj* -MIER, -MIEST odd

RUMOR *v* -ED, -ING, -S to spread by hearsay

RUMOUR *v* -ED, -ING, -S to rumor

RUMP *n pl.* -S the lower and back part of the trunk **RUMPLESS** *adj*

RUMPLE *v* -PLED, -PLING, -PLES to wrinkle

RUMPLY *adj* -PLIER, -PLIEST rumpled

RUMPUS *n pl.* -ES a noisy disturbance

RUN *v* RAN, RUNNING, RUNS to move by rapid steps

RUNABOUT *n pl.* -S a small, open auto

RUNAGATE *n pl.* -S a deserter

RUNAWAY *n pl.* -AWAYS one that runs away

RUNBACK *n pl.* -S a type of run in football

RUNDLE *n pl.* -S a rung

RUNDLET *n pl.* -S a small barrel

RUNDOWN *n pl.* -S a summary

RUNE *n pl.* -S a letter of an ancient alphabet **RUNELIKE** *adj*

RUNG *n pl.* -S a crosspiece forming a step of a ladder **RUNGLESS** *adj*

RUNIC *adj* pertaining to a rune

RUNKLE *v* -KLED, -KLING, -KLES to wrinkle

RUNLESS *adj* scoring no runs in baseball

RUNLET *n pl.* -S a small stream

RUNNEL *n pl.* -S a small stream

RUNNER *n pl.* -S one that runs

RUNNING *n pl.* -S a race

RUNNY *adj* -NIER, -NIEST tending to drip

RUNOFF *n pl.* -S rainfall that is not absorbed by the soil

RUNOUT *n pl.* -S the end of a film strip

RUNOVER *n pl.* -S matter for publication that exceeds the allotted space

RUNROUND *n pl.* -S evasive action

RUNT *n pl.* -S a small person or animal **RUNTISH** *adj*

RUNTY *adj* RUNTIER, RUNTIEST small

RUNWAY *n pl.* -WAYS a landing and takeoff strip for aircraft

RUPEE *n pl.* -S a monetary unit of India

RUPIAH *n pl.* -S a monetary unit of Indonesia

RUPTURE *v* -TURED, -TURING, -TURES to burst

RURAL *adj* pertaining to the country

RURALISE *v* -ISED, -ISING, -ISES to ruralize

RURALISM *n pl.* -S the state of being rural

RURALIST *n pl.* -S one who lives in the country

RURALITE *n pl.* -S a ruralist

RURALITY *n pl.* -TIES the state of being rural

RURALIZE *v* -IZED, -IZING, -IZES to make rural

RURALLY *adv* in a rural manner

RURBAN *adj* partially rural and urban

RUSE *n pl.* -S a deception

RUSH *v* -ED, -ING, -ES to move swiftly

RUSHEE *n pl.* -S a college student seeking admission to a fraternity or sorority

RUSHER *n pl.* -S one that rushes

RUSHIER comparative of rushy

RUSHIEST superlative of rushy

RUSHING *n pl.* -S yardage gained in football by running plays

RUSHLIKE *adj* resembling a rush (a grasslike marsh plant)

RUSHY *adj* RUSHIER, RUSHIEST abounding in rushes

RUSINE *adj* pertaining to a genus of deer

RUSK *n pl.* -S a sweetened biscuit

RUSSET *n pl.* -S a reddish or yellowish brown color **RUSSETY** *adj*

RUSSIFY *v* -FIED, -FYING, -FIES to make Russian

RUST *v* -ED, -ING, -S to form rust (a reddish coating that forms on iron) **RUSTABLE** *adj*

RUSTIC *n pl.* -S one who lives in the country **RUSTICAL** *adj*

RUSTICLY *adv* in a rural manner

RUSTIER comparative of rusty

RUSTIEST superlative of rusty

RUSTILY *adv* in a rusty manner

RUSTLE *v* -TLED, -TLING, -TLES to make a succession of slight, soft sounds

RUSTLER *n pl.* -S one that rustles

RUSTLESS *adj* free from rust

RUSTLING present participle of rustle

RUSTY	*adj* RUSTIER, RUSTIEST covered with rust
RUT	*v* RUTTED, RUTTING, RUTS to make ruts (grooves) in
RUTABAGA	*n pl.* -S a plant having a thick, edible root
RUTH	*n pl.* -S compassion
RUTHENIC	*adj* pertaining to a rare, metallic element
RUTHFUL	*adj* full of compassion
RUTHLESS	*adj* having no compassion
RUTILANT	*adj* having a reddish glow
RUTILE	*n pl.* -S a mineral
RUTTED	past tense of rut
RUTTIER	comparative of rutty

RUTTIEST	superlative of rutty
RUTTILY	*adv* in a rutty manner
RUTTING	present participle of rut
RUTTISH	*adj* lustful
RUTTY	*adj* -TIER, -TIEST marked by ruts
RYA	*n pl.* -S a Scandinavian handwoven rug
RYE	*n pl.* -S a cereal grass
RYEGRASS	*n pl.* -ES a European grass
RYKE	*v* RYKED, RYKING, RYKES to reach
RYND	*n pl.* -S an iron support
RYOT	*n pl.* -S a tenant farmer in India

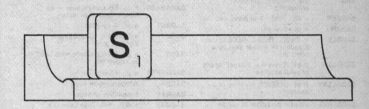

SAB   v SABBED, SABBING, SABS to sob

SABATON   n pl. -S a piece of armor for the foot

SABBAT   n pl. -S an assembly of demons and witches

SABBATH   n pl. -S sabbat

SABBATIC   adj bringing a period of rest

SABBED   past tense of sab

SABBING   present participle of sab

SABE   v SABED, SABEING, SABES to savvy

SABER   v -ED, -ING, -S to strike with a saber (a type of sword)

SABIN   n pl. -S a unit of sound absorption

SABINE   n pl. -S savin

SABIR   n pl. -S a French-based pidgin language

SABLE   n pl. -S a carnivorous mammal

SABOT   n pl. -S a wooden shoe

SABOTAGE   v -TAGED, -TAGING, -TAGES to destroy maliciously

SABOTEUR   n pl. -S one who sabotages

SABRA   n pl. -S a native Israeli

SABRE   v -BRED, -BRING, -BRES to saber

SABULOSE   adj sabulous

SABULOUS   adj sandy

SAC   n pl. -S a pouchlike structure in an animal or plant

SACATON   n pl. -S a perennial grass

SACBUT   n pl. -S sackbut

SACCADE   n pl. -S a rapid, jerky movement of the eye SACCADIC adj

SACCATE   adj having a sac

SACCULAR   adj resembling a sac

SACCULE   n pl. -S a small sac

SACCULUS   n pl. -LI saccule

SACHEM   n pl. -S a North American Indian chief SACHEMIC adj

SACHET   n pl. -S a small bag containing perfumed powder SACHETED adj

SACK   v -ED, -ING, -S to put into a sack (a large bag)

SACKBUT   n pl. -S a medieval trombone

SACKER   n pl. -S one that sacks

SACKFUL   n pl. SACKFULS or SACKSFUL as much as a sack will hold

SACKING   n pl. -S material for making sacks

SACKLIKE   adj resembling a sack

SACKSFUL   a pl. of sackful

SACLIKE   adj resembling a sac

SACQUE   n pl. -S a loose-fitting dress

SACRA   pl. of sacrum

SACRAL   n pl. -S a vertebra or nerve situated near the sacrum

SACRARIA   n/pl ancient Roman shrines

SACRED   adj dedicated to or set apart for the worship of a deity SACREDLY adv

SACRIST   n pl. -S a person in charge of a sacristy

SACRISTY   n pl. -TIES a room in which sacred vessels and vestments are kept

SACRUM *n pl.* -CRA a bone of the pelvis

SAD *adj* SADDER, SADDEST unhappy

SADDEN *v* -ED, -ING, -S to make sad

SADDHU *n pl.* -S sadhu

SADDLE *v* -DLED, -DLING, -DLES to put a saddle (a leather seat for a rider) on

SADDLER *n pl.* -S one that makes, repairs, or sells saddles

SADDLERY *n pl.* -DLERIES the shop of a saddler

SADDLING present participle of saddle

SADE *n pl.* -S a Hebrew letter

SADHE *n pl.* -S sade

SADHU *n pl.* -S a Hindu holy man

SADI *n pl.* -S sade

SADIRON *n pl.* -S a heavy flatiron

SADISM *n pl.* -S a tendency to take delight in inflicting pain

SADIST *n pl.* -S one marked by sadism SADISTIC *adj*

SADLY *adv* in a sad manner

SADNESS *n pl.* -ES the state of being sad

SAE *adv* so

SAFARI *v* -ED, -ING, -S to go on a hunting expedition

SAFE *adj* SAFER, SAFEST free from danger SAFELY *adv*

SAFE *n pl.* -S a metal receptacle for storing valuables

SAFENESS *n pl.* -ES the quality of being safe

SAFER comparative of safe

SAFEST superlative of safe

SAFETY *v* -TIED, -TYING, -TIES to protect against failure, breakage, or accident

SAFFRON *n pl.* -S a flowering plant

SAFRANIN *n pl.* -S a red dye

SAFROL *n pl.* -S safrole

SAFROLE *n pl.* -S a poisonous liquid

SAG *v* SAGGED, SAGGING, SAGS to bend or sink downward from weight or pressure

SAGA *n pl.* -S a medieval Scandinavian narrative

SAGACITY *n pl.* -TIES wisdom

SAGAMAN *n pl.* -MEN a writer of sagas

SAGAMORE *n pl.* -S an Algonquian Indian chief

SAGANASH *n pl.* -ES a white man — an Algonquian Indian term

SAGBUT *n pl.* -S sackbut

SAGE *adj* SAGER, SAGEST wise SAGELY *adv*

SAGE *n pl.* -S an aromatic herb used as seasoning

SAGENESS *n pl.* -ES wisdom

SAGER comparative of sage

SAGEST superlative of sage

SAGGAR *v* -ED, -ING, -S to bake in a saggar (a protective clay casing)

SAGGARD *n pl.* -S a saggar

SAGGED past tense of sag

SAGGER *v* -ED, -ING, -S to saggar

SAGGING present participle of sag

SAGIER comparative of sagy

SAGIEST superlative of sagy

SAGITTAL *adj* resembling an arrow or arrowhead

SAGO *n pl.* -GOS a tropical tree

SAGUARO *n pl.* -ROS a tall cactus

SAGUM *n pl.* -GA a cloak worn by ancient Roman soldiers

SAGY *adj* SAGIER, SAGIEST flavored with sage

SAHIB *n pl.* -S sir; master — used as a term of respect in colonial India

SAHIWAL *n pl.* -S any of a breed of humped dairy cattle

SAHUARO *n pl.* -ROS saguaro

SAICE *n pl.* -S syce

SAID *n pl.* -S sayyid

SAIGA *n pl.* -S a small antelope

SAIL *v* -ED, -ING, -S to move across the surface of water by the action of wind SAILABLE *adj*

SAILBOAT *n pl.* -S a boat that sails

SAILER *n pl.* -S a vessel that sails

SAILFISH *n pl.* -ES a large marine fish

SAILING *n pl.* -S the act of one that sails

SAILOR *n pl.* -S a member of a ship's crew SAILORLY *adj*

SAIN *v* -ED, -ING, -S to make the sign of the cross on

SAINFOIN *n pl.* -S a perennial herb

SAINT   *v* -ED, -ING, -S to declare to be a saint (a person of exceptional holiness)

SAINTDOM   *n* pl. -S the condition of being a saint

SAINTLY   *adj* -LIER, -LIEST of or befitting a saint

SAITH   a present 3d person sing. of say

SAITHE   *n* pl. SAITHE a marine food fish

SAIYID   *n* pl. -S sayyid

SAJOU   *n* pl. -S a capuchin

SAKE   *n* pl. -S benefit, interest, or advantage

SAKER   *n* pl. -S a Eurasian falcon

SAKI   *n* pl. -S a Japanese liquor

SAL   *n* pl. -S salt

SALAAM   *v* -ED, -ING, -S to greet with a low bow

SALABLE   *adj* capable of being or fit to be sold **SALABLY** *adv*

SALACITY   *n* pl. -TIES lewdness

SALAD   *n* pl. -S a dish of green, raw vegetables

SALADANG   *n* pl. -S a wild ox

SALAMI   *n* pl. -S a seasoned sausage

SALARIAT   *n* pl. -S the class of salaried persons

SALARY   *v* -RIED, -RYING, -RIES to pay a periodic, fixed compensation to

SALE   *n* pl. -S the act or an instance of selling

SALEABLE   *adj* salable **SALEABLY** *adv*

SALEP   *n* pl. -S a starchy meal ground from the roots of certain orchids

SALEROOM   *n* pl. -S a room in which goods are displayed for sale

SALESMAN   *n* pl. -MEN a man who sells merchandise

SALIC   *adj* pertaining to a group of igneous rocks

SALICIN   *n* pl. -S a chemical compound

SALICINE   *n* pl. -S salicin

SALIENCE   *n* pl. -S a projecting feature or detail

SALIENCY   *n* pl. -CIES salience

SALIENT   *n* pl. -S the part of a fortification projecting closest to the enemy

SALIFY   *v* -FIED, -FYING, -FIES to combine with a salt

SALINA   *n* pl. -S a pond, marsh, or lake containing salt water

SALINE   *n* pl. -S a salt solution

SALINITY   *n* pl. -TIES a concentration of salt

SALINIZE   *v* -NIZED, -NIZING, -NIZES to treat with salt

SALIVA   *n* pl. -S a fluid secreted by the glands of the mouth **SALIVARY** *adj*

SALIVATE   *v* -VATED, -VATING, -VATES to secrete saliva

SALL   *v* shall — SALL is the only form of this verb; it cannot be conjugated

SALLET   *n* pl. -S a light medieval helmet

SALLIED   past tense of sally

SALLIER   *n* pl. -S one that sallies

SALLIES   present 3d person sing. of sally

SALLOW   *adj* -LOWER, -LOWEST of a sickly yellowish color **SALLOWLY** *adv*

SALLOW   *v* -ED, -ING, -S to make sallow

SALLOWY   *adj* abounding in willow trees

SALLY   *v* -LIED, -LYING, -LIES to rush out suddenly

SALMI   *n* pl. -S a dish of roasted game birds

SALMON   *n* pl. -S a food fish

SALMONID   *n* pl. -S a fish of the salmon family

SALOL   *n* pl. -S a chemical compound

SALON   *n* pl. -S a large room in which guests are received

SALOON   *n* pl. -S a tavern

SALOOP   *n* pl. -S a hot drink made from an infusion of aromatic herbs

SALP   *n* pl. -S salpa

SALPA   *n* pl. -PAE or -PAS a free-swimming tunicate

SALPIAN   *n* pl. -S salpa

SALPID   *n* pl. -S salpa

SALPINX   *n* pl. -PINGES an anatomical tube

SALSIFY   *n* pl. -FIES a European herb

SALSILLA   *n* pl. -S a tropical plant

SALT   *v* -ED, -ING, -S to treat with salt (a crystalline compound used as a seasoning and preservative)

SALT   *adj* SALTER, SALTEST salty

SALTANT *adj* jumping or dancing

SALTBOX *n pl.* -ES a type of house

SALTBUSH *n pl.* -ES a salt-tolerant plant

SALTER *n pl.* -S one that salts

SALTERN *n pl.* -S a place where salt is produced

SALTIE *n pl.* -S a deep-sea vessel sailing the Great Lakes

SALTIER *n pl.* -S saltire

SALTIEST superlative of salty

SALTILY *adv* in a salty manner

SALTINE *n pl.* -S a salted cracker

SALTIRE *n pl.* -S a heraldic design

SALTISH *adj* somewhat salty

SALTLESS *adj* having no salt

SALTLIKE *adj* resembling salt

SALTNESS *n pl.* -ES the state of being salty

SALTPAN *n pl.* -S a large pan for making salt by evaporation

SALTWORK *n pl.* -S a saltern

SALTWORT *n pl.* -S a seaside herb

SALTY *adj* SALTIER, SALTIEST tasting of or containing salt

SALUKI *n pl.* -S a tall, slender dog

SALUTARY *adj* producing a beneficial effect

SALUTE *v* -LUTED, -LUTING, -LUTES to greet with a sign of welcome or respect

SALUTER *n pl.* -S one that salutes

SALVABLE *adj* capable of being saved SALVABLY *adv*

SALVAGE *v* -VAGED, -VAGING, -VAGES to save from loss or destruction

SALVAGEE *n pl.* -S one in whose favor salvage has been effected

SALVAGER *n pl.* -S one that salvages

SALVAGING present participle of salvage

SALVE *v* SALVED, SALVING, SALVES to soothe

SALVER *n pl.* -S a tray or serving platter

SALVIA *n pl.* -S a flowering plant

SALVIFIC *adj* having the power to save

SALVING present participle of salve

SALVO *v* -ED, -ING, -S or -ES to discharge firearms simultaneously

SALVOR *n pl.* -S a salvager

SAMARA *n pl.* -S a dry, one-seeded fruit

SAMARIUM *n pl.* -S a metallic element

SAMBA *v* -ED, -ING, -S to perform a Brazilian dance

SAMBAR *n pl.* -S a large Asian deer

SAMBHAR *n pl.* -S sambar

SAMBHUR *n pl.* -S sambar

SAMBO *n pl.* -BOS a Latin American of mixed black and Indian ancestry

SAMBUCA *n pl.* -S an ancient stringed instrument

SAMBUKE *n pl.* -S sambuca

SAMBUR *n pl.* -S sambar

SAME *adj* resembling in every relevant respect

SAMECH *n pl.* -S samek

SAMEK *n pl.* -S a Hebrew letter

SAMEKH *n pl.* -S samek

SAMENESS *n pl.* -ES lack of change or variety

SAMIEL *n pl.* -S the simoom

SAMISEN *n pl.* -S a Japanese stringed instrument

SAMITE *n pl.* -S a silk fabric

SAMLET *n pl.* -S a young salmon

SAMOVAR *n pl.* -S a metal urn for heating water

SAMP *n pl.* -S coarsely ground corn

SAMPAN *n pl.* -S a flat-bottomed Chinese skiff

SAMPHIRE *n pl.* -S a European herb

SAMPLE *v* -PLED, -PLING, -PLES to test a representative portion of a whole

SAMPLER *n pl.* -S one that samples

SAMPLING *n pl.* -S a small part selected for analysis

SAMSARA *n pl.* -S the cycle of birth, death, and rebirth in Buddhism

SAMSHU *n pl.* -S a Chinese liquor

SAMURAI *n pl.* -S a Japanese warrior

SANATIVE *adj* having the power to cure or heal

SANCTA a pl. of sanctum

SANCTIFY *v* -FIED, -FYING, -FIES to make holy

SANCTION *v* -ED, -ING, -S to authorize

SANCTITY *n pl.* -TIES holiness

SANCTUM *n* pl. -TUMS or -TA a sacred place

SAND *v* -ED, -ING, -S to cover with sand (a loose, granular rock material)

SANDAL *v* -DALED, -DALING, -DALS or -DALLED, -DALLING, -DALS to provide with sandals (light, open shoes)

SANDARAC *n* pl. -S an aromatic resin

SANDBAG *v* -BAGGED, -BAGGING, -BAGS to surround with bags of sand

SANDBANK *n* pl. -S a large mass of sand

SANDBAR *n* pl. -S a ridge of sand formed in a river or sea

SANDBOX *n* pl. -ES a box containing sand for children to play in

SANDBUR *n* pl. -S an annual herb

SANDBURR *n* pl. -S sandbur

SANDER *n* pl. -S one that sands

SANDFISH *n* pl. -ES a marine fish

SANDFLY *n* pl. -FLIES a biting fly

SANDHI *n* pl. -S a process of phonetic modification

SANDHOG *n* pl. -S a worker who digs or works in sand

SANDIER comparative of sandy

SANDIEST superlative of sandy

SANDLIKE *adj* resembling sand

SANDLING *n* pl. -S a marine fish

SANDLOT *n* pl. -S a vacant lot

SANDMAN *n* pl. -MEN a mythical person who makes children sleepy by sprinkling sand in their eyes

SANDPEEP *n* pl. -S a wading bird

SANDPILE *n* pl. -S a pile of sand

SANDPIT *n* pl. -S a pit dug in sandy soil

SANDSOAP *n* pl. -S a type of soap

SANDWICH *v* -ED, -ING, -ES to place between two layers or objects

SANDWORM *n* pl. -S a sand-dwelling worm

SANDWORT *n* pl. -S a flowering plant

SANDY *adj* SANDIER, SANDIEST containing or covered with sand

SANE *adj* SANER, SANEST mentally sound SANELY *adv*

SANE *v* SANED, SANING, SANES to sain

SANENESS *n* pl. -ES sanity

SANER comparative of sane

SANEST superlative of sane

SANG past tense of sing

SANGA *n* pl. -S sangar

SANGAR *n* pl. -S a temporary fortification for two or three men

SANGAREE *n* pl. -S an alcoholic beverage

SANGER *n* pl. -S sangar

SANGH *n* pl. -S an association promoting unity between the different groups in Hinduism

SANGRIA *n* pl. -S an alcoholic beverage

SANGUINE *n* pl. -S a red color

SANICLE *n* pl. -S a medicinal herb

SANIES *n* pl. SANIES a fluid discharged from wounds SANIOUS *adj*

SANING present participle of sane

SANITARY *n* pl. -TARIES a public urinal

SANITATE *v* -TATED, -TATING, -TATES to sanitize

SANITIES pl. of sanity

SANITISE *v* -TISED, -TISING, -TISES to sanitize

SANITIZE *v* -TIZED, -TIZING, -TIZES to guard against infection or disease by cleaning or sterilizing

SANITY *n* pl. -TIES the state of being sane

SANJAK *n* pl. -S an administrative district of Turkey

SANK past tense of sink

SANNOP *n* pl. -S sannup

SANNUP *n* pl. -S a married male American Indian

SANNYASI *n* pl. -S a Hindu monk

SANS *prep* without

SANSAR *n* pl. -S sarsar

SANSEI *n* pl. -S a grandchild of Japanese immigrants to the United States

SANSERIF *n* pl. -S a typeface without serifs

SANTALIC *adj* pertaining to sandalwood

SANTIMS *n* pl. -TIMI a former coin of Latvia

SANTIR *n* pl. -S a Persian dulcimer

SANTOL *n* pl. -S a tropical tree

SANTONIN *n* pl. -S a chemical compound

SANTOUR *n* pl. -S santir

SAP	v SAPPED, SAPPING, SAPS to deplete or weaken gradually	**SARCASM**	n pl. -S a sharply mocking or contemptuous remark
SAPAJOU	n pl. -S a capuchin	**SARCENET**	n pl. -S a silk fabric
SAPHEAD	n pl. -S a foolish, stupid, or gullible person	**SARCOID**	n pl. -S a disease of horses
SAPHENA	n pl. -NAE a vein of the leg	**SARCOMA**	n pl. -MAS or -MATA a type of tumor
SAPID	adj pleasant to the taste	**SARCOUS**	adj composed of flesh or muscle
SAPIDITY	n pl. -TIES the state of being sapid	**SARD**	n pl. -S a variety of quartz
SAPIENCE	n pl. -S wisdom	**SARDAR**	n pl. -S sirdar
SAPIENCY	n pl. -CIES sapience	**SARDINE**	n pl. -S a small food fish
SAPIENS	adj pertaining to recent man	**SARDIUS**	n pl. -ES sard
SAPIENT	adj wise	**SARDONIC**	adj mocking
SAPLESS	adj lacking vitality	**SARDONYX**	n pl. -ES a variety of quartz
SAPLING	n pl. -S a young tree	**SAREE**	n pl. -S sari
SAPONIFY	v -FIED, -FYING, -FIES to convert into soap	**SARGASSO**	n pl. -GASSOS a brownish seaweed
SAPONIN	n pl. -S a soapy substance obtained from plants	**SARGE**	n pl. -S sergeant
SAPONINE	n pl. -S saponin	**SARI**	n pl. -S an outer garment worn by Hindu women
SAPONITE	n pl. -S a mineral found in veins and cavities of rocks	**SARIN**	n pl. -S a toxic gas
SAPOR	n pl. -S flavor **SAPOROUS** adj	**SARK**	n pl. -S a shirt
SAPOTA	n pl. -S an evergreen tree	**SARMENT**	n pl. -S a type of plant stem
SAPOUR	n pl. -S sapor	**SARMENTA**	n/pl sarments
SAPPED	past tense of sap	**SAROD**	n pl. -S a lute of northern India
SAPPER	n pl. -S a military engineer	**SARODE**	n pl. -S sarod
SAPPHIC	n pl. -S a type of verse form	**SARODIST**	n pl. -S one who plays the sarod
SAPPHIRE	n pl. -S a blue gem	**SARONG**	n pl. -S an outer garment worn in the Pacific islands
SAPPHISM	n pl. -S lesbianism		
SAPPHIST	n pl. -S a lesbian	**SARSAR**	n pl. -S a cold, whistling wind
SAPPING	present participle of sap	**SARSEN**	n pl. -S a large sandstone block
SAPPY	adj -PIER, -PIEST silly **SAPPILY** adv	**SARSENET**	n pl. -S sarcenet
		SARTOR	n pl. -S a tailor
SAPREMIA	n pl. -S a form of blood poisoning **SAPREMIC** adj	**SARTORII**	n/pl flat, narrow thigh muscles
SAPROBE	n pl. -S an organism that derives its nourishment from decaying organic matter **SAPROBIC** adj	**SASH**	v -ED, -ING, -ES to furnish with a frame in which glass is set
		SASHAY	v -ED, -ING, -S to flounce
SAPROPEL	n pl. -S mud consisting chiefly of decaying organic matter	**SASHIMI**	n pl. -S a Japanese dish of sliced raw fish
SAPSAGO	n pl. -GOS a hard green cheese	**SASIN**	n pl. -S an antelope of India
SAPWOOD	n pl. -S the newly formed outer wood of a tree	**SASS**	v -ED, -ING, -ES to talk impudently to
SARABAND	n pl. -S a stately Spanish dance	**SASSABY**	n pl. -BIES an African antelope
		SASSIER	comparative of sassy
SARAPE	n pl. -S serape	**SASSIEST**	superlative of sassy
		SASSILY	adv in a sassy manner

SASSWOOD n pl. -S an African tree

SASSY n pl. -SIES sasswood

SASSY adj SASSIER, SASSIEST impudent

SASTRUGA n pl. -GI a ridge of snow formed by the wind in polar regions

SAT past tense of sit

SATANG n pl. -S a monetary unit of Thailand

SATANIC adj extremely evil

SATANISM n pl. -S worship of the powers of evil

SATANIST n pl. -S one who practices satanism

SATARA n pl. -S a woolen fabric

SATCHEL n pl. -S a small carrying bag

SATE v SATED, SATING, SATES to satiate

SATEEN n pl. -S a cotton fabric

SATEM adj pertaining to a group of Indo-European languages

SATI n pl. -S suttee

SATIABLE adj capable of being satiated SATIABLY adv

SATIATE v -ATED, -ATING, -ATES to satisfy to or beyond capacity

SATIETY n pl. -ETIES the state of being satiated

SATIN n pl. -S a smooth fabric

SATINET n pl. -S a thin satin

SATING present participle of sate

SATINPOD n pl. -S a flowering plant

SATINY adj resembling satin

SATIRE n pl. -S the use of derisive wit to attack folly or wickedness SATIRIC adj

SATIRISE v -RISED, -RISING, -RISES to satirize

SATIRIST n pl. -S one who satirizes

SATIRIZE v -RIZED, -RIZING, -RIZES to subject to satire

SATISFY v -FIED, -FYING, -FIES to provide fully with what is desired, expected, or needed

SATORI n pl. -S the illumination of spirit sought by Zen Buddhists

SATRAP n pl. -S a governor of a province in ancient Persia

SATRAPY n pl. -PIES the territory of a satrap

SATURANT n pl. -S a substance used to saturate

SATURATE v -RATED, -RATING, -RATES to fill completely with something that permeates

SATYR n pl. -S a woodland deity of Greek mythology SATYRIC adj

SATYRID n pl. -S a brownish butterfly

SAU n pl. SAU xu

SAUCE v SAUCED, SAUCING, SAUCES to season with sauce (a flavorful liquid dressing)

SAUCEBOX n pl. -ES a saucy person

SAUCEPAN n pl. -S a cooking utensil

SAUCER n pl. -S a small, shallow dish

SAUCH n pl. -S saugh

SAUCING present participle of sauce

SAUCY adj SAUCIER, SAUCIEST impudent SAUCILY adv

SAUGER n pl. -S a freshwater fish

SAUGH n pl. -S a willow tree SAUGHY adj

SAUL n pl. -S soul

SAULT n pl. -S a waterfall

SAUNA n pl. -S a Finnish steam bath

SAUNTER v -ED, -ING, -S to walk in a leisurely manner

SAUREL n pl. -S a marine fish

SAURIAN n pl. -S any of a suborder of reptiles

SAUROPOD n pl. -S any of a suborder of large dinosaurs

SAURY n pl. -RIES a marine fish

SAUSAGE n pl. -S finely chopped and seasoned meat stuffed into a casing

SAUTE v -TEED or -TED, -TEING, -TES to fry in a small amount of fat

SAUTERNE n pl. -S a sweet white wine

SAUTOIR n pl. -S a saltire

SAUTOIRE n pl. -S sautoir

SAVABLE adj capable of being saved

SAVAGE adj -AGER, -AGEST fierce SAVAGELY adv

SAVAGE v -AGED, -AGING, -AGES to attack or treat brutally

SAVAGERY n pl. -RIES the quality of being savage

SAVAGEST superlative of savage

SAVAGING present participle of savage

SAVAGISM n pl. -S savagery

SAVANNA n pl. -S a flat, treeless grassland

SAVANNAH n pl. -S savanna

SAVANT n pl. -S a man of profound learning

SAVATE n pl. -S a pugilistic sport

SAVE v SAVED, SAVING, SAVES to rescue from danger, injury, or loss SAVEABLE adj

SAVELOY n pl. -LOYS a highly seasoned sausage

SAVER n pl. -S one that saves

SAVIN n pl. -S an evergreen shrub

SAVINE n pl. -S savin

SAVING n pl. -S the act or an instance of saving

SAVINGLY adv in a thrifty manner

SAVIOR n pl. -S one that saves

SAVIOUR n pl. -S savior

SAVOR v -ED, -ING, -S to taste or smell with pleasure

SAVORER n pl. -S one that savors

SAVORIER comparative of savory

SAVORIES pl. of savory

SAVOROUS adj savory

SAVORY adj -VORIER, -VORIEST pleasant to the taste or smell SAVORILY adv

SAVORY n pl. -VORIES a savory dish served before or after a meal

SAVOUR v -ED, -ING, -S to savor

SAVOURER n pl. -S savorer

SAVOURY adj -VOURIER, -VOURIEST savory

SAVOURY n pl. -VOURIES a savory

SAVOY n pl. -VOYS a variety of cabbage

SAVVY v -VIED, -VYING, -VIES to understand

SAW v SAWED, SAWN, SAWING, SAWS to cut or divide with a saw (a type of cutting tool)

SAWBILL n pl. -S a tropical bird

SAWBONES n pl. -BONESES a surgeon

SAWBUCK n pl. -S a sawhorse

SAWDUST n pl. -S small particles of wood produced in sawing

SAWER n pl. -S one that saws

SAWFISH n pl. -ES a marine fish

SAWFLY n pl. -FLIES a winged insect

SAWHORSE n pl. -S a rack used to support a piece of wood being sawed

SAWLIKE adj resembling a saw

SAWLOG n pl. -S a log large enough to saw into boards

SAWMILL n pl. -S a place where logs are sawed

SAWN a past participle of saw

SAWNEY n pl. -NEYS a foolish person

SAWTOOTH n pl. -TEETH a cutting edge on a saw

SAWYER n pl. -S one that saws wood for a living

SAX n pl. -ES a saxophone

SAXATILE adj living or growing among rocks

SAXHORN n pl. -S a brass wind instrument

SAXONY n pl. -NIES a woolen fabric

SAXTUBA n pl. -S a bass saxhorn

SAY v SAID, SAYING, present sing. 2d person SAY, SAYEST, or SAYST, 3d person SAYS or SAITH to utter SAYABLE adj

SAYER n pl. -S one that says

SAYID n pl. -S sayyid

SAYING n pl. -S a maxim

SAYONARA n pl. -S goodby

SAYST a present 2d person sing. of say

SAYYID n pl. -S lord; sir — used as a title of respect for a Muslim dignitary

SCAB v SCABBED, SCABBING, SCABS to become covered with a scab (a crust that forms over a healing wound)

SCABBARD v -ED, -ING, -S to put into a sheath, as a sword

SCABBLE v -BLED, -BLING, -BLES to shape roughly

SCABBY adj -BIER, -BIEST covered with scabs SCABBILY adv

SCABIES n pl. SCABIES a skin disease

SCABIOSA n pl. -S scabious

SCABIOUS n pl. -ES a flowering plant

SCABLIKE adj resembling a scab

SCABROUS adj roughened with small projections

SCAD n pl. -S a marine fish

SCAFFOLD v -ED, -ING, -S to provide with a scaffold (a temporary platform for workmen)

SCAG n pl. -S heroin

SCALABLE adj capable of being scaled **SCALABLY** adv

SCALADE n pl. -S an act of scaling the walls of a fortification

SCALADO n pl. -DOS scalade

SCALAGE n pl. -S a percentage deduction to compensate for shrinkage

SCALAR n pl. -S a mathematical quantity possessing only magnitude

SCALARE n pl. -S a tropical fish

SCALAWAG n pl. -S a rascal

SCALD v -ED, -ING, -S to burn with hot liquid or steam

SCALDIC adj skaldic

SCALE v SCALED, SCALING, SCALES to climb up or over

SCALENE adj designating a triangle having no two sides equal

SCALENUS n pl. -NI a muscle of the neck

SCALEPAN n pl. -S a pan on a weighing scale

SCALER n pl. -S one that scales

SCALIER comparative of scaly

SCALIEST superlative of scaly

SCALING present participle of scale

SCALL n pl. -S a scaly eruption of the skin

SCALLION n pl. -S an onion-like plant

SCALLOP v -ED, -ING, -S to bake in a sauce topped with bread crumbs

SCALP v -ED, -ING, -S to remove an upper part from

SCALPEL n pl. -S a small surgical knife

SCALPER n pl. -S one that scalps

SCALY adj SCALIER, SCALIEST peeling off in flakes

SCAMMONY n pl. -NIES a climbing plant

SCAM n pl. -S a swindle

SCAMP v -ED, -ING, -S to perform in a hasty or careless manner

SCAMPER v -ED, -ING, -S to run playfully about

SCAMPI n pl. SCAMPI large shrimp used in Italian cooking

SCAMPISH adj rascally

SCAN v SCANNED, SCANNING, SCANS to examine closely

SCANDAL v -DALED, -DALING, -DALS or -DALLED, -DALLING, -DALS to defame

SCANDENT adj climbing, as a plant

SCANDIA n pl. -S an oxide of scandium

SCANDIUM n pl. -S a metallic element **SCANDIC** adj

SCANNED past tense of scan

SCANNER n pl. -S one that scans

SCANNING n pl. -S close examination

SCANSION n pl. -S the analysis of verse into metrical feet and rhythm patterns

SCANT adj SCANTER, SCANTEST meager

SCANT v -ED, -ING, -S to provide with a meager portion

SCANTIER comparative of scanty

SCANTIES n/pl brief panties for women

SCANTLY adv in a scant manner

SCANTY adj SCANTIER, SCANTIEST meager SCANTILY adv

SCAPE v SCAPED, SCAPING, SCAPES to escape

SCAPHOID n pl. -S a bone of the wrist

SCAPOSE adj bearing a leafless stalk

SCAPULA n pl. -LAE or -LAS a bone of the shoulder

SCAPULAR n pl. -S a sleeveless outer garment worn by monks

SCAR v SCARRED, SCARRING, SCARS to form a scar (a mark left by the healing of injured tissue)

SCARAB n pl. -S a large, black beetle

SCARCE adj SCARCER, SCARCEST infrequently seen or found

SCARCELY adv by a narrow margin

SCARCITY n pl. -TIES the quality of being scarce

SCARE v SCARED, SCARING, SCARES to frighten

SCARER n pl. -S one that scares

SCAREY adj SCARIER, SCARIEST scary

SCARF n pl. SCARFS or SCARVES a piece of cloth worn for warmth or protection

SCARF v -ED, -ING, -S to scarf

SCARFPIN *n* pl. -S a tiepin

SCARIER comparative of scarey and scary

SCARIEST superlative of scarey and scary

SCARIFY *v* -FIED, -FYING, -FIES to make superficial cuts in

SCARING present participle of scare

SCARIOSE *adj* scarious

SCARIOUS *adj* thin, dry, and membranous

SCARLESS *adj* having no scars

SCARLET *n* pl. -S a red color

SCARP *v* -ED, -ING, -S to cut or make into a steep slope

SCARPER *v* -ED, -ING, -S to flee

SCARPH *v* -ED, -ING, -S to unite by means of a type of joint

SCARRED past tense of scar

SCARRING present participle of scar

SCARRY *adj* -RIER, -RIEST marked with scars

SCART *v* -ED, -ING, -S to scratch

SCARVES a pl. of scarf

SCARY *adj* SCARIER, SCARIEST frightening

SCAT *v* SCATTED, SCATTING, SCATS to leave hastily

SCATBACK *n* pl. -S a type of player in football

SCATHE *v* SCATHED, SCATHING, SCATHES to criticize severely

SCATT *n* pl. -S a tax

SCATTED past tense of scat

SCATTER *v* -ED, -ING, -S to go or send in various directions

SCATTING present participle of scat

SCATTY *adj* -TIER, -TIEST crazy

SCAUP *n* pl. -S a sea duck

SCAUPER *n* pl. -S an engraving tool

SCAUR *n* pl. -S a protruding, isolated rock

SCAVENGE *v* -ENGED, -ENGING, -ENGES to search through rubbish for usable items

SCENA *n* pl. -S an elaborate composition for a single voice

SCENARIO *n* pl. -IOS a summary of the plot of a dramatic work

SCEND *v* -ED, -ING, -S to rise upward, as a ship on a wave

SCENE *n* pl. -S the place where some action or event occurs

SCENERY *n* pl. -ERIES a picturesque landscape or view

SCENIC *adj* pertaining to scenery

SCENICAL *adj* scenic

SCENT *v* -ED, -ING, -S to fill with an odor

SCEPTER *v* -ED, -ING, -S to invest with royal authority

SCEPTIC *n* pl. -S skeptic

SCEPTRAL *adj* pertaining to royal authority

SCEPTRE *v* -TRED, -TRING, -TRES to scepter

SCHAPPE *n* pl. -S a silk fabric

SCHAV *n* pl. -S a chilled soup

SCHEDULE *v* -ULED, -ULING, -ULES to assign to a certain date or time

SCHEMA *n* pl. -MATA a generalized diagram or plan

SCHEME *v* SCHEMED, SCHEMING, SCHEMES to plan or plot

SCHEMER *n* pl. -S one that schemes

SCHERZO *n* pl. -ZOS or -ZI a lively musical movement

SCHILLER *n* pl. -S a brownish luster occurring on certain minerals

SCHISM *n* pl. -S a division into opposing parties

SCHIST *n* pl. -S a rock that readily splits into parallel layers

SCHIZO *n* pl. SCHIZOS a schizoid

SCHIZOID *n* pl. -S a person affected with a type of psychotic disorder

SCHIZONT *n* pl. -S an organism that reproduces by a form of asexual reproduction

SCHLEP *v* SCHLEPPED, SCHLEPPING, SCHLEPS to lug or drag

SCHLEPP *v* -ED, -ING, -S to schlep

SCHLOCK *n* pl. -S inferior merchandise

SCHMALTZ *n* pl. -ES excessive sentimentality

SCHMALZ *n* pl. -ES schmaltz

SCHMALZY *adj* SCHMALZIER, SCHMALZIEST characterized by schmaltz

SCHMEER *v* -ED, -ING, -S to bribe

SCHMELZE *n* pl. -S a type of decorative glass

SCHMO *n* pl. SCHMOES a stupid person

SCHMOE *n* pl. -S schmo

SCHMOOS *v* -ED, -ING, -ES to schmooze

SCHMOOSE *v* SCHMOOSED, SCHMOOSING, SCHMOOSES to schmooze

SCHMOOZE *v* SCHMOOZED, SCHMOOZING, SCHMOOZES to gossip

SCHMUCK *n* pl. -S a foolish or clumsy person

SCHNAPPS *n* pl. SCHNAPPS a strong liquor

SCHNAPS *n* pl. SCHNAPS schnapps

SCHNECKE *n* pl. -KEN a sweet roll

SCHNOOK *n* pl. -S an easily deceived person

SCHOLAR *n* pl. -S a learned person

SCHOLIUM *n* pl. -LIA or -LIUMS an explanatory marginal note

SCHOOL *v* -ED, -ING, -S to educate in an institution of learning

SCHOONER *n* pl. -S a sailing vessel

SCHORL *n* pl. -S a mineral

SCHRIK *n* pl. -S sudden fright

SCHTICK *n* pl. -S shtick

SCHUIT *n* pl. -S a Dutch sailing vessel

SCHUL *n* pl. SCHULN shul

SCHUSS *v* -ED, -ING, -ES to make a fast, straight run in skiing

SCHWA *n* pl. -S a type of vowel sound

SCIAENID *n* pl. -S a carnivorous fish

SCIATIC *n* pl. -S a nerve, vein, or artery situated near the hip

SCIATICA *n* pl. -S a painful disorder of the hip and adjoining areas

SCIENCE *n* pl. -S a department of systematized knowledge

SCILICET *adv* namely

SCILLA *n* pl. -S a flowering plant

SCIMETAR *n* pl. -S scimitar

SCIMITAR *n* pl. -S a curved Oriental sword

SCIMITER *n* pl. -S scimitar

SCINCOID *n* pl. -S one of a family of smooth, short-limbed lizards

SCIOLISM *n* pl. -S superficial knowledge

SCIOLIST *n* pl. -S one whose knowledge is superficial

SCION *n* pl. -S a child or descendant

SCIROCCO *n* pl. -COS sirocco

SCIRRHUS *n* pl. -RHI or -RHUSES a hard tumor

SCISSILE *adj* capable of being cut or split easily

SCISSION *n* pl. -S the act of cutting or splitting

SCISSOR *v* -ED, -ING, -S to cut with a two-bladed cutting implement

SCISSURE *n* pl. -S a lengthwise cut

SCIURINE *n* pl. -S a rodent of the squirrel family

SCIUROID *adj* resembling a squirrel

SCLAFF *v* -ED, -ING, -S to strike the ground with the club before hitting the ball in golf

SCLAFFER *n* pl. -S one that sclaffs

SCLERA *n* pl. -RAS or -RAE the white, fibrous outer coat of the eyeball SCLERAL *adj*

SCLEREID *n* pl. -S a type of plant cell

SCLERITE *n* pl. -S one of the hard plates forming the outer covering of an arthropod

SCLEROID *adj* sclerous

SCLEROMA *n* pl. -MATA a hardened patch of cellular tissue

SCLEROSE *v* -ROSED, -ROSING, -ROSES to become hard, as tissue

SCLEROUS *adj* hardened

SCOFF *v* -ED, -ING, -S to express rude doubt or derision

SCOFFER *n* pl. -S one that scoffs

SCOFFLAW *n* pl. -S an habitual law violator

SCOLD *v* -ED, -ING, -S to rebuke harshly

SCOLDER *n* pl. -S one that scolds

SCOLDING *n* pl. -S a harsh reproof

SCOLEX *n* pl. -LECES or -LICES the knoblike head of a tapeworm

SCOLIOMA *n* pl. -S abnormal curvature of the spine

SCOLLOP *v* -ED, -ING, -S to scallop

SCONCE *v* SCONCED, SCONCING, SCONCES to fine

SCONE *n* pl. -S a flat, round cake

SCOOP *v* -ED, -ING, -S to take up with a scoop (a spoonlike utensil)

SCOOPER *n* pl. -S one that scoops

SCOOPFUL *n* pl. SCOOPFULS or SCOOPSFUL as much as a scoop will hold

SCOOT *v* -ED, -ING, -S to go quickly

SCOOTER *n* pl. -S a two-wheeled vehicle

SCOP   n pl. -S an Old English poet

SCOPE   n pl. -S extent

SCOPULA   n pl. -LAE or -LAS a dense tuft of hairs

SCORCH   v -ED, -ING, -ES to burn slightly so as to alter the color or taste

SCORCHER   n pl. -S one that scorches

SCORE   v SCORED, SCORING, SCORES to make a point in a game or contest

SCOREPAD   n pl. -S a pad on which scored points are recorded

SCORER   n pl. -S one that scores

SCORIA   n pl. -RIAE the refuse of a smelted metal or ore

SCORIFY   v -FIED, -FYING, -FIES to reduce to scoria

SCORING   present participle of score

SCORN   v -ED, -ING, -S to treat or regard with contempt

SCORNER   n pl. -S one that scorns

SCORNFUL   adj feeling or expressing contempt

SCORPION   n pl. -S a stinging arachnid

SCOT   n pl. -S a tax

SCOTCH   v -ED, -ING, -ES to put a definite end to

SCOTER   n pl. -S a sea duck

SCOTIA   n pl. -S a concave molding

SCOTOMA   n pl. -MAS or -MATA a blind spot in the field of vision

SCOTOPIA   n pl. -S vision in dim light SCOTOPIC adj

SCOTTIE   n pl. -S a short-legged terrier

SCOUR   v -ED, -ING, -S to cleanse or polish by hard rubbing

SCOURER   n pl. -S one that scours

SCOURGE   v SCOURGED, SCOURGING, SCOURGES to punish severely

SCOURGER   n pl. -S one that scourges

SCOURING   n pl. -S material removed by scouring

SCOUSE   n pl. -S a type of meat stew

SCOUT   v -ED, -ING, -S to observe for the purpose of obtaining information

SCOUTER   n pl. -S one that scouts

SCOUTH   n pl. -S plenty

SCOUTHER   v -ED, -ING, -S to scorch

SCOUTING   n pl. -S the act of one that scouts

SCOW   v -ED, -ING, -S to transport by scow (a flat-bottomed boat)

SCOWDER   v -ED, -ING, -S to scouther

SCOWL   v -ED, -ING, -S to frown angrily

SCOWLER   n pl. -S one that scowls

SCRABBLE   v -BLED, -BLING, -BLES to claw or grope about frantically

SCRABBLY   adj raspy

SCRAG   v SCRAGGED, SCRAGGING, SCRAGS to wring the neck of

SCRAGGLY   adj -GLIER, -GLIEST uneven

SCRAGGY   adj -GIER, -GIEST scrawny

SCRAICH   v -ED, -ING, -S to utter a shrill cry

SCRAIGH   v -ED, -ING, -S to scraich

SCRAM   v SCRAMMED, SCRAMMING, SCRAMS to leave quickly

SCRAMBLE   v -BLED, -BLING, -BLES to move or climb hurriedly

SCRANNEL   n pl. -S a thin person

SCRAP   v SCRAPPED, SCRAPPING, SCRAPS to discard

SCRAPE   v SCRAPED, SCRAPING, SCRAPES to rub so as to remove an outer layer

SCRAPER   n pl. -S one that scrapes

SCRAPIE   n pl. -S a disease of sheep

SCRAPING   n pl. -S something scraped off

SCRAPPED   past tense of scrap

SCRAPPER   n pl. -S a fighter

SCRAPPIER   comparative of scrappy

SCRAPPIEST   superlative of scrappy

SCRAPPING   present participle of scrap

SCRAPPLE   n pl. -S a seasoned mixture of ground meat and cornmeal

SCRAPPY   adj -PIER, -PIEST marked by fighting spirit

SCRATCH   v -ED, -ING, -ES to make a thin, shallow cut or mark on

SCRATCHY   adj SCRATCHIER, SCRATCHIEST uneven in quality

SCRAWL   v -ED, -ING, -S to write hastily or illegibly

SCRAWLER   n pl. -S one that scrawls

SCRAWLY   adj SCRAWLIER, SCRAWLIEST written hastily or illegibly

SCRAWNY   adj -NIER, -NIEST extremely thin

SCREAK v -ED, -ING, -S to screech

SCREAKY adj screechy

SCREAM v -ED, -ING, -S to utter a prolonged, piercing cry

SCREAMER n pl. -S one that screams

SCREE n pl. -S a mass of rocks at the foot of a slope

SCREECH v -ED, -ING, -S to utter a harsh, shrill cry

SCREECHY adj SCREECHIER, SCREECHIEST screeching

SCREED v -ED, -ING, -S to shred

SCREEN v -ED, -ING, -S to provide with a screen (a device designed to divide, conceal, or protect)

SCREENER n pl. -S one that screens

SCREW v -ED, -ING, -S to attach with a screw (a type of metal fastener)

SCREWER n pl. -S one that screws

SCREWY adj SCREWIER, SCREWIEST crazy

SCRIBAL adj pertaining to a public clerk or secretary

SCRIBBLE v -BLED, -BLING, -BLES to write hastily or carelessly

SCRIBE v SCRIBED, SCRIBING, SCRIBES to mark with a scriber

SCRIBER n pl. -S a pointed instrument used for marking off material to be cut

SCRIEVE v SCRIEVED, SCRIEVING, SCRIEVES to move along swiftly and smoothly

SCRIM n pl. -S a cotton fabric

SCRIMP v -ED, -ING, -S to be very or overly thrifty

SCRIMPIT adj meager

SCRIMPY adj SCRIMPIER, SCRIMPIEST meager

SCRIP n pl. -S a small piece of paper

SCRIPT v -ED, -ING, -S to prepare a written text for, as a play or motion picture

SCRIVE v SCRIVED, SCRIVING, SCRIVES to engrave

SCROD n pl. -S a young cod

SCROFULA n pl. -S a disease of the lymph glands

SCROGGY adj -GIER, -GIEST of stunted growth

SCROLL n pl. -S a roll of parchment or paper with writing on it

SCROOGE n pl. -S a miserly person

SCROOP v -ED, -ING, -S to make a harsh, grating sound

SCROTUM n pl. -TA or -TUMS the pouch of skin that contains the testes SCROTAL adj

SCROUGE v SCROUGED, SCROUGING, SCROUGES to crowd

SCROUNGE v SCROUNGED, SCROUNGING, SCROUNGES to gather by foraging

SCROUNGY adj SCROUNGIER, SCROUNGIEST dirty

SCRUB v SCRUBBED, SCRUBBING, SCRUBS to rub hard in order to clean

SCRUBBER n pl. -S one that scrubs

SCRUBBY adj -BIER, -BIEST inferior in size or quality

SCRUFF n pl. -S the back of the neck

SCRUFFY adj -FIER, -FIEST shabby

SCRUM n pl. -S a formation around the ball in rugby

SCRUNCH v -ED, -ING, -ES to crush

SCRUPLE v -PLED, -PLING, -PLES to hesitate because of ethical considerations

SCRUTINY n pl. -NIES a close examination

SCUBA n pl. -S an underwater breathing device

SCUD v SCUDDED, SCUDDING, SCUDS to run or move swiftly

SCUDO n pl. -DI a former Italian coin

SCUFF v -ED, -ING, -S to walk without lifting the feet

SCUFFLE v -FLED, -FLING, -FLES to struggle in a rough, confused manner

SCUFFLER n pl. -S one that scuffles

SCULK v -ED, -ING, -S to skulk

SCULKER n pl. -S skulker

SCULL v -ED, -ING, -S to propel with a type of oar

SCULLER n pl. -S one that sculls

SCULLERY n pl. -LERIES a room in which kitchen utensils are cleaned and stored

SCULLION n pl. -S a kitchen servant who does menial work

SCULP v -ED, -ING, -S to sculpt

SCULPIN n pl. -S a freshwater fish

SCULPT *v* -ED, -ING, -S to form an image or representation of from solid material

SCULPTOR *n* pl. -S one that sculpts

SCUM *v* SCUMMED, SCUMMING, SCUMS to remove the scum (impure or extraneous matter) from

SCUMBLE *v* -BLED, -BLING, -BLES to soften the outlines or colors of by rubbing lightly

SCUMLIKE *adj* resembling scum

SCUMMED past tense of scum

SCUMMER *n* pl. -S one that scums

SCUMMING present participle of scum

SCUMMY *adj* -MIER, -MIEST covered with scum

SCUNNER *v* -ED, -ING, -S to feel loathing or disgust

SCUP *n* pl. -S a marine food fish

SCUPPAUG *n* pl. -S scup

SCUPPER *v* -ED, -ING, -S to ambush

SCURF *n* pl. -S scaly or shredded dry skin

SCURFY *adj* SCURFIER, SCURFIEST covered with scurf

SCURRIED past tense of scurry

SCURRIES present 3d person sing. of scurry

SCURRIL *adj* scurrile

SCURRILE *adj* expressed in coarse and abusive language

SCURRY *v* -RIED, -RYING, -RIES to move hurriedly

SCURVY *adj* -VIER, -VIEST base or contemptible SCURVILY *adv*

SCURVY *n* pl. -VIES a disease resulting from vitamin C deficiency

SCUT *n* pl. -S a short tail, as of a rabbit

SCUTA pl. of scutum

SCUTAGE *n* pl. -S a tax exacted by a feudal lord in lieu of military service

SCUTATE *adj* shaped like a shield

SCUTCH *v* -ED, -ING, -ES to separate the woody fiber from by beating

SCUTCHER *n* pl. -S one that scutches

SCUTE *n* pl. -S a horny plate or scale

SCUTELLA *n/pl* small, scutate organs or parts

SCUTTER *v* -ED, -ING, -S to scurry

SCUTTLE *v* -TLED, -TLING, -TLES to scurry

SCUTUM *n* pl. -TA scute

SCYPHATE *adj* shaped like a cup

SCYTHE *v* SCYTHED, SCYTHING, SCYTHES to cut with a scythe (a single-bladed cutting implement)

SEA *n* pl. -S the ocean

SEABAG *n* pl. -S a bag used by a sailor

SEABEACH *n* pl. -ES a beach lying along the sea

SEABED *n* pl. -S a seafloor

SEABIRD *n* pl. -S a bird frequenting the ocean or seacoast

SEABOARD *n* pl. -S the seacoast

SEABOOT *n* pl. -S a waterproof boot

SEABORNE *adj* carried on or over the sea

SEACOAST *n* pl. -S land bordering on the sea

SEACOCK *n* pl. -S a valve in a ship's hull

SEACRAFT *n* pl. -S skill in sea navigation

SEADOG *n* pl. -S a fogbow

SEADROME *n* pl. -S an airport in the sea

SEAFARER *n* pl. -S a sailor

SEAFLOOR *n* pl. -S the bottom of a sea

SEAFOOD *n* pl. -S edible fish or shellfish from the sea

SEAFOWL *n* pl. -S a seabird

SEAFRONT *n* pl. -S an area along the edge of the sea

SEAGIRT *adj* surrounded by the sea

SEAGOING *adj* designed for use on the sea

SEAL *v* -ED, -ING, -S to close or make secure against access, leakage, or passage SEALABLE *adj*

SEALANT *n* pl. -S a sealing agent

SEALER *n* pl. -S one that seals

SEALERY *n* pl. -ERIES the occupation of hunting seals

SEALLIKE *adj* resembling a seal (an aquatic mammal)

SEALSKIN *n* pl. -S the skin of a seal

SEAM *v* -ED, -ING, -S to join with a seam (a line formed by sewing two pieces of fabric together)

SEAMAN *n* pl. -MEN a sailor SEAMANLY *adj*

SEAMARK n pl. -S a landmark serving as a navigational guide to mariners

SEAMER n pl. -S one that seams

SEAMIER comparative of seamy

SEAMIEST superlative of seamy

SEAMLESS adj having no seam

SEAMLIKE adj resembling a seam

SEAMOUNT n pl. -S an undersea mountain

SEAMSTER n pl. -S a person whose occupation is sewing

SEAMY adj SEAMIER, SEAMIEST unpleasant

SEANCE n pl. -S a meeting of persons seeking spiritualistic messages

SEAPIECE n pl. -S a seascape

SEAPLANE n pl. -S an airplane designed to take off from or land on the water

SEAPORT n pl. -S a harbor or town accessible to seagoing ships

SEAQUAKE n pl. -S an undersea earthquake

SEAR adj SEARER, SEAREST sere

SEAR v -ED, -ING, -S to burn the surface of

SEARCH v -ED, -ING, -ES to look through or over carefully in order to find something

SEARCHER n pl. -S one that searches

SEARER comparative of sear

SEAREST superlative of sear

SEASCAPE n pl. -S a picture of the sea

SEASCOUT n pl. -S a boy scout trained in water activities

SEASHELL n pl. -S the shell of a marine mollusk

SEASHORE n pl. -S land bordering on the sea

SEASICK adj affected with nausea caused by the motion of a vessel at sea

SEASIDE n pl. -S the seashore

SEASON v -ED, -ING, -S to heighten or improve the flavor of by adding savory ingredients

SEASONAL adj occurring at a certain time of the year

SEASONER n pl. -S one that seasons

SEAT v -ED, -ING, -S to place on a seat (something on which one sits)

SEATER n pl. -S one that seats

SEATING n pl. -S material for covering seats

SEATLESS adj having no seat

SEATMATE n pl. -S one with whom one shares a seat

SEATRAIN n pl. -S a ship equipped to carry railroad cars

SEATWORK n pl. -S work done at one's seat

SEAWALL n pl. -S a wall to protect a shoreline from erosion

SEAWAN n pl. -S wampum

SEAWANT n pl. -S seawan

SEAWARD n pl. -S the direction toward the open sea

SEAWARE n pl. -S seaweed used as fertilizer

SEAWATER n pl. -S water from the sea

SEAWAY n pl. -WAYS the headway made by a ship

SEAWEED n pl. -S a plant growing in the sea

SEBACIC adj derived from a certain acid

SEBASIC adj sebacic

SEBUM n pl. -S a fatty matter secreted by certain glands of the skin

SEC n pl. -S secant

SECANT n pl. -S a trigonometric function of an angle

SECANTLY adv in an intersecting manner

SECATEUR n pl. -S a pruning tool

SECCO n pl. -COS the art of painting on dry plaster

SECEDE v -CEDED, -CEDING, -CEDES to withdraw formally from an alliance or association

SECEDER n pl. -S one that secedes

SECERN v -ED, -ING, -S to discern as separate

SECLUDE v -CLUDED, -CLUDING, -CLUDES to remove or set apart from others

SECOND v -ED, -ING, -S to give support or encouragement to

SECONDE n pl. -S a position in fencing

SECONDER n pl. -S one that seconds

SECONDLY adv in the next place after the first

SECONDO n pl. -DI the lower part in a piano duet

SECPAR	*n* pl. -S a parsec	**SEDERUNT**	*n* pl. -S a prolonged sitting
SECRECY	*n* pl. -CIES the condition of being secret	**SEDGE**	*n* pl. -S a marsh plant
SECRET	*adj* -CRETER, -CRETEST kept from knowledge or view	**SEDGY**	*adj* SEDGIER, SEDGIEST abounding in sedge
SECRET	*n* pl. -S something kept from the knowledge of others	**SEDILE**	*n* pl. -LIA one of the seats in a church for the use of the officiating clergy
SECRETE	*v* -CRETED, -CRETING, -CRETES to generate and separate out from cells or bodily fluids	**SEDILIUM**	*n* pl. -LIA sedile
SECRETIN	*n* pl. -S a hormone	**SEDIMENT**	*v* -ED, -ING, -S to settle to the bottom of a liquid
SECRETLY	*adv* in a secret manner	**SEDITION**	*n* pl. -S incitement of rebellion against a government
SECRETOR	*n* pl. -S one that secretes		
SECT	*n* pl. -S a group of people united by common beliefs or interests	**SEDUCE**	*v* -DUCED, -DUCING, -DUCES to lead astray SEDUCIVE *adj*
SECTARY	*n* pl. -RIES a member of a sect	**SEDUCER**	*n* pl. -S one that seduces
SECTILE	*adj* capable of being cut smoothly	**SEDULITY**	*n* pl. -TIES the state of being sedulous
SECTION	*v* -ED, -ING, -S to divide into sections (distinct parts)	**SEDULOUS**	*adj* diligent
SECTOR	*v* -ED, -ING, -S to divide into sectors (sections)	**SEDUM**	*n* pl. -S a flowering plant
		SEE	*v* SAW, SEEN, SEEING, SEES to perceive with the eyes SEEABLE *adj*
SECTORAL	*adj* of or pertaining to a sector		
SECULAR	*n* pl. -S a layman	**SEECATCH**	*n* pl. -CATCHIE an adult male fur seal
SECUND	*adj* having the parts or organs arranged on one side only SECUNDLY *adv*	**SEED**	*v* -ED, -ING, -S to plant seeds (propagative plant structures) in
SECUNDUM	*adv* according to	**SEEDBED**	*n* pl. -S land prepared for seeding
SECURE	*adj* -CURER, -CUREST free from danger SECURELY *adv*	**SEEDCAKE**	*n* pl. -S a sweet cake containing aromatic seeds
SECURE	*v* -CURED, -CURING, -CURES to make firm or tight	**SEEDCASE**	*n* pl. -S a pericarp
SECURER	*n* pl. -S one that secures	**SEEDER**	*n* pl. -S one that seeds
SECUREST	superlative of secure	**SEEDIER**	comparative of seedy
SECURING	present participle of secure	**SEEDIEST**	superlative of seedy
SECURITY	*n* pl. -TIES the state of being secure	**SEEDILY**	*adv* in a seedy manner
		SEEDLESS	*adj* having no seeds
SEDAN	*n* pl. -S a type of automobile	**SEEDLIKE**	*adj* resembling a seed
SEDARIM	a pl. of seder	**SEEDLING**	*n* pl. -S a young plant
SEDATE	*adj* -DATER, -DATEST calm SEDATELY *adv*	**SEEDMAN**	*n* pl. -MEN seedsman
		SEEDPOD	*n* pl. -S a type of seed vessel
SEDATE	*v* -DATED, -DATING, -DATES to administer a sedative to	**SEEDSMAN**	*n* pl. -MEN a dealer in seeds
SEDATION	*n* pl. -S the reduction of stress or excitement by the use of sedatives	**SEEDTIME**	*n* pl. -S the season for sowing seeds
SEDATIVE	*n* pl. -S a drug that induces a calm state	**SEEDY**	*adj* SEEDIER, SEEDIEST containing seeds; inferior in condition or quality
		SEEING	*n* pl. -S the act of one that sees
SEDER	*n* pl. -DARIM or -DERS a Jewish ceremonial dinner	**SEEK**	*v* SOUGHT, SEEKING, SEEKS to go in search of
		SEEKER	*n* pl. -S one that seeks

SEEL   v -ED, -ING, -S to stitch closed the eyes of, as a falcon during training

SEELY   adj frail

SEEM   v -ED, -ING, -S to give the impression of being

SEEMER   n pl. -S one that seems

SEEMING   n pl. -S outward appearance

SEEMLY   adj -LIER, -LIEST of pleasing appearance

SEEN   past participle of see

SEEP   v -ED, -ING, -S to pass slowly through small openings

SEEPAGE   n pl. -S the quantity of fluid that has seeped

SEEPY   adj SEEPIER, SEEPIEST soaked or oozing with water

SEER   n pl. -S a prophet

SEERESS   n pl. -ES a female seer

SEESAW   v -ED, -ING, -S to move up and down or back and forth

SEETHE   v SEETHED, SEETHING, SEETHES to surge or foam as if boiling

SEGETAL   adj growing in fields of grain

SEGGAR   n pl. -S a saggar

SEGMENT   v -ED, -ING, -S to divide into sections

SEGNO   n pl. -GNI or -GNOS a musical sign

SEGO   n pl. -GOS a perennial herb

SEGUE   v -GUED, -GUEING, -GUES to proceed without pause from one musical theme to another

SEI   n pl. -S a rorqual

SEICENTO   n pl. -TOS the seventeenth century

SEICHE   n pl. -S an oscillation of the surface of a lake or landlocked sea

SEIDEL   n pl. -S a large beer glass

SEIGNEUR   n pl. -S seignior

SEIGNIOR   n pl. -S a feudal lord

SEIGNORY   n pl. -GNORIES the power of a seignior

SEINE   v SEINED, SEINING, SEINES to catch fish with a large, vertically hanging net

SEINER   n pl. -S one that seines

SEISE   v SEISED, SEISING, SEISES to seize **SEISABLE** adj

SEISER   n pl. -S seizer

SEISIN   n pl. -S seizin

SEISING   n pl. -S seizing

SEISM   n pl. -S an earthquake **SEISMAL, SEISMIC** adj

SEISMISM   n pl. -S the natural activity involved in earthquakes

SEISOR   n pl. -S seizor

SEISURE   n pl. -S seizure

SEIZE   v SEIZED, SEIZING, SEIZES to take hold of suddenly and forcibly **SEIZABLE** adj

SEIZER   n pl. -S one that seizes

SEIZIN   n pl. -S legal possession of land

SEIZING   n pl. -S the act of one that seizes

SEIZOR   n pl. -S one that takes seizin

SEIZURE   n pl. -S the act of seizing

SEJANT   adj represented in a sitting postion — used of a heraldic animal

SEJEANT   adj sejant

SEL   n pl. -S self

SELADANG   n pl. -S saladang

SELAH   n pl. -S a word of unknown meaning often marking the end of a verse in the Psalms

SELAMLIK   n pl. -S the portion of a Turkish house reserved for men

SELCOUTH   adj unusual

SELDOM   adj infrequent **SELDOMLY** adv

SELECT   v -ED, -ING, -S to choose

SELECTEE   n pl. -S one that is selected

SELECTLY   adv by selection

SELECTOR   n pl. -S one that selects

SELENATE   n pl. -S a chemical salt

SELENIC   adj pertaining to selenium

SELENIDE   n pl. -S a compound of selenium

SELENITE   n pl. -S a variety of gypsum

SELENIUM   n pl. -S a nonmetallic element **SELENOUS** adj

SELF   n pl. SELVES the total, essential, or particular being of one person

SELF   v -ED, -ING, -S to inbreed

SELFDOM   n pl. -S selfhood

SELFHEAL   n pl. -S a perennial herb

SELFHOOD *n* pl. -S the state of being an individual person

SELFISH *adj* concerned chiefly or only with oneself

SELFLESS *adj* unselfish

SELFNESS *n* pl. -ES selfhood

SELFSAME *adj* identical

SELFWARD *adv* toward oneself

SELL *v* SOLD, SELLING, SELLS to give up to another for money or other valuable consideration SELLABLE *adj*

SELLE *n* pl. -S a saddle

SELLER *n* pl. -S one that sells

SELLOUT *n* pl. -S a performance for which all seats have been sold

SELSYN *n* pl. -S a type of remote-control device

SELTZER *n* pl. -S carbonated mineral water

SELVAGE *n* pl. -S the edge of a woven fabric finished to prevent raveling SELVAGED *adj*

SELVEDGE *n* pl. -S selvage

SELVES pl. of self

SEMANTIC *adj* pertaining to meaning

SEMATIC *adj* serving as a warning

SEME *n* pl. -S a type of ornamental pattern

SEMEME *n* pl. -S the meaning of a morpheme

SEMEN *n* pl. -MINA or -MENS a fluid produced in the male reproductive organs

SEMESTER *n* pl. -S a period constituting half of an academic year

SEMI *n* pl. -S a freight trailer

SEMIARID *adj* characterized by light rainfall

SEMIBALD *adj* partly bald

SEMICOMA *n* pl. -S a coma from which a person can be aroused

SEMIDEAF *adj* partly deaf

SEMIDOME *n* pl. -S a half dome

SEMIDRY *adj* moderately dry

SEMIFIT *adj* conforming somewhat to the lines of the body

SEMIGALA *adj* somewhat gala

SEMIHARD *adj* moderately hard

SEMIHIGH *adj* moderately high

SEMIHOBO *n* pl. -BOS or -BOES a person having some of the characteristics of a hobo

SEMILOG *adj* having one scale logarithmic and the other arithmetic

SEMIMAT *adj* having a slight luster

SEMIMATT *adj* semimat

SEMIMUTE *adj* having partially lost the faculty of speech

SEMINA a pl. of semen

SEMINAL *adj* pertaining to semen

SEMINAR *n* pl. -S an advanced study group at a college or university

SEMINARY *n* pl. -NARIES a school for the training of priests, ministers, or rabbis

SEMINUDE *adj* partly nude

SEMIOSIS *n* pl. -OSES a process in which something functions as a sign to an organism

SEMIOTIC *n* pl. -S a general theory of signs and symbolism

SEMIPRO *n* pl. -PROS one who is engaged in some field or sport for pay on a part-time basis

SEMIRAW *adj* somewhat raw

SEMIS *n* pl. -MISES a coin of ancient Rome

SEMISOFT *adj* moderately soft

SEMITIST *n* pl. -S one who favors Jewish interests

SEMITONE *n* pl. -S a type of musical tone

SEMIWILD *adj* somewhat wild

SEMOLINA *n* pl. -S a granular product of wheat used for pasta

SEMPLE *adj* of humble birth

SEMPLICE *adj* simple — used as a musical direction

SEMPRE *adv* in the same manner throughout — used as a musical direction

SEN *n* pl. SEN a monetary unit of Japan

SENARIUS *n* pl. -NARII a Greek or Latin verse consisting of six metrical feet

SENARY *adj* pertaining to the number six

SENATE *n* pl. -S an assembly having high deliberative and legislative functions

SENATOR *n* pl. -S a member of a senate

SEND v SENT, SENDING, SENDS to cause to go **SENDABLE** adj

SENDAL n pl. -S a silk fabric

SENDER n pl. -S one that sends

SENDOFF n pl. -S a farewell celebration

SENECA n pl. -S senega

SENECIO n pl. -CIOS a flowering plant

SENEGA n pl. -S a medicinal plant root

SENGI n pl. SENGI a monetary unit of Zaire

SENHOR n pl. -S or -ES a Portuguese or Brazilian gentleman

SENHORA n pl. -S a married Portuguese or Brazilian woman

SENILE n pl. -S one who exhibits senility

SENILELY adv in a senile manner

SENILITY n pl. -TIES mental and physical infirmity due to old age

SENIOR n pl. -S a person who is older than another

SENITI n pl. SENITI a monetary unit of Tonga

SENNA n pl. -S a medicinal plant

SENNET n pl. -S a call sounded on a trumpet signaling the entrance or exit of actors

SENNIGHT n pl. -S a week

SENNIT n pl. -S braided straw used in making hats

SENOPIA n pl. -S an improvement of near vision

SENOR n pl. -S or -ES a Spanish gentleman

SENORA n pl. -S a married Spanish woman

SENORITA n pl. -S an unmarried Spanish girl or woman

SENSA pl. of sensum

SENSATE v -SATED, -SATING, -SATES to sense

SENSE v SENSED, SENSING, SENSES to perceive by the senses (any of certain agencies through which an individual receives impressions of the external world)

SENSEFUL adj sensible

SENSIBLE adj -BLER, -BLEST having or showing good judgment **SENSIBLY** adv

SENSIBLE n pl. -S something that can be sensed

SENSILLA n/pl simple sense organs

SENSING present participle of sense

SENSOR n pl. -S a device that receives and responds to a stimulus

SENSORIA n/pl the parts of the brain concerned with the reception and interpretation of sensory stimuli

SENSORY adj pertaining to the senses or sensation

SENSUAL adj pertaining to the physical senses

SENSUM n pl. -SA an object of perception or sensation

SENSUOUS adj pertaining to or derived from the senses

SENT past tense of send

SENTENCE v -TENCED, -TENCING, -TENCES to declare judicially the extent of punishment to be imposed

SENTI n pl. SENTI a monetary unit of Tanzania

SENTIENT n pl. -S a person or thing capable of sensation

SENTINEL v -NELED, -NELING, -NELS or -NELLED, -NELLING, -NELS to stand guard

SENTRY n pl. -TRIES one who stands guard

SEPAL n pl. -S one of the individual leaves of a calyx SEPALED, SEPALINE, SEPALLED, SEPALOID, SEPALOUS adj

SEPARATE v -RATED, -RATING, -RATES to set or keep apart

SEPIA n pl. -S a brown pigment **SEPIC** adj

SEPOY n pl. -POYS a native of India serving in the British army

SEPPUKU n pl. -S a Japanese form of suicide

SEPSIS n pl. SEPSES bacterial invasion of the body

SEPT n pl. -S a clan

SEPTA pl. of septum

SEPTAL adj pertaining to a septum

SEPTARIA n/pl limestone nodules

SEPTATE adj having a septum

SEPTET n pl. -S a group of seven

SEPTETTE n pl. -S septet

SEPTIC *n* pl. -S an agent producing sepsis **SEPTICAL** *adj*

SEPTIME *n* pl. -S a position in fencing

SEPTUM *n* pl. -TA a dividing membrane or partition

SEPTUPLE *v* -PLED, -PLING, -PLES to make seven times as great

SEQUEL *n* pl. -S something that follows and serves as a continuation

SEQUELA *n* pl. -QUELAE an abnormal condition resulting from a preceding disease

SEQUENCE *v* -QUENCED, -QUENCING, -QUENCES to arrange in consecutive order

SEQUENCY *n* pl. -CIES the following of one thing after another

SEQUENT *n* pl. -S something that follows

SEQUIN *n* pl. -S a shiny ornamental disk **SEQUINED** *adj*

SEQUITUR *n* pl. -S the conclusion of an inference

SEQUOIA *n* pl. -S a large evergreen tree

SER *n* pl. -S a unit of weight of India

SERA a pl. of serum

SERAC *n* pl. -S a large mass of ice broken off of a glacier

SERAGLIO *n* pl. -GLIOS a harem

SERAI *n* pl. -S a Turkish palace

SERAIL *n* pl. -S a seraglio

SERAL *adj* pertaining to a series of ecological changes

SERAPE *n* pl. -S a colorful woolen shawl

SERAPH *n* pl. -APHS, -APHIM, or -APHIN a winged celestial being **SERAPHIC** *adj*

SERAPHIM *n* pl. -S seraph

SERDAB *n* pl. -S a chamber within an ancient Egyptian tomb

SERE *adj* SERER, SEREST withered; dry

SERE *v* SERED, SERING, SERES to sear

SEREIN *n* pl. -S a fine rain falling from an apparently clear sky

SERENADE *v* -NADED, -NADING, -NADES to perform an honorific evening song for

SERENATA *n* pl. -TAS or -TE a dramatic cantata

SERENE *adj* SERENER, SERENEST calm; tranquil **SERENELY** *adv*

SERENE *n* pl. -S a serene condition or expanse

SERENITY *n* pl. -TIES the state of being serene

SERER comparative of sere

SEREST superlative of sere

SERF *n* pl. -S a feudal slave

SERFAGE *n* pl. -S serfdom

SERFDOM *n* pl. -S the state of being a serf

SERFHOOD *n* pl. -S serfdom

SERFISH *adj* characteristic of a serf

SERFLIKE *adj* serfish

SERGE *n* pl. -S a twilled fabric

SERGEANT *n* pl. -S a noncommissioned military officer

SERGING *n* pl. -S a process of finishing the raw edges of a fabric

SERIAL *n* pl. -S a literary or dramatic work presented in successive installments

SERIALLY *adv* in the manner or form of a serial

SERIATE *v* -ATED, -ATING, -ATES to put into a series

SERIATIM *adv* serially

SERICIN *n* pl. -S a kind of protein

SERIEMA *n* pl. -S a Brazilian bird

SERIES *n* pl. SERIES an arrangement of one after another

SERIF *n* pl. -S a fine line used to finish off the main stroke of a letter

SERIN *n* pl. -S a European finch

SERINE *n* pl. -S an amino acid

SERING present participle of sere

SERINGA *n* pl. -S a Brazilian tree

SERIOUS *adj* thoughtful or subdued in appearance or manner

SERJEANT *n* pl. -S sergeant

SERMON *n* pl. -S a religious discourse **SERMONIC** *adj*

SEROLOGY *n* pl. -GIES the science of serums

SEROSA *n* pl. -SAS or -SAE a thin membrane lining certain bodily cavities **SEROSAL** *adj*

SEROSITY *n* pl. -TIES the quality or state of being serous

SEROTINE *n* pl. -S a European bat

EROTYPE — n pl. -S a group of closely related organisms distinguished by a common set of antigens

EROUS — adj of or resembling serum

EROW — n pl. -S an Asian antelope

ERPENT — n pl. -S a snake

ERPIGO — n pl. -GOES or -GINES a spreading skin eruption

ERRANID — n pl. -S a marine fish

ERRATE — v -RATED, -RATING, -RATES to furnish with toothlike projections

ERRY — v -RIED, -RYING, -RIES to crowd together

ERUM — n pl. -RUMS or -RA the watery portion of whole blood SERUMAL adj

ERVABLE — adj capable of serving or being served

ERVAL — n pl. -S an African wildcat

ERVANT — n pl. -S one that serves others

ERVE — v SERVED, SERVING, SERVES to work for

ERVER — n pl. -S one that serves another

ERVICE — v -VICED, -VICING, -VICES to repair

ERVICER — n pl. -S one that services

ERVILE — adj slavishly submissive

ERVING — n pl. -S a portion of food

ERVITOR — n pl. -S a male servant

ERVO — n pl. -VOS an automatic device used to control another mechanism

ESAME — n pl. -S an East Indian plant

ESAMOID — n pl. -S a nodular mass of bone or cartilage

ESSILE — adj permanently attached

ESSION — n pl. -S a meeting of a legislative or judicial body for the transaction of business

ESSPOOL — n pl. -S cesspool

ESTERCE — n pl. -S a coin of ancient Rome

ESTET — n pl. -S a stanza of six lines

ESTINA — n pl. -S a type of verse form

ESTINE — n pl. -S sestina

ET — v SET, SETTING, SETS to put in a particular position

ETA — n pl. -TAE a coarse, stiff hair SETAL adj

ETBACK — n pl. -S a defeat

ETIFORM — adj having the form of a seta

SETLINE — n pl. -S a strong fishing line

SETOFF — n pl. -S something that offsets something else

SETON — n pl. -S a type of surgical thread

SETOSE — adj covered with setae

SETOUS — adj setose

SETOUT — n pl. -S a display

SETSCREW — n pl. -S a type of screw

SETTEE — n pl. -S a long seat with a high back

SETTER — n pl. -S one that sets

SETTING — n pl. -S the scenery used in a dramatic production

SETTLE — v -TLED, -TLING, -TLES to place in a desired state or order

SETTLER — n pl. -S one that settles

SETTLING — n pl. -S sediment

SETTLOR — n pl. -S one that makes a legal settlement

SETULOSE — adj covered with seta

SETULOUS — adj setulose

SETUP — n pl. -S the way something is arranged

SEVEN — n pl. -S a number

SEVENTH — n pl. -S one of seven equal parts

SEVENTY — n pl. -TIES a number

SEVER — v -ED, -ING, -S to divide or cut into parts

SEVERAL — n pl. -S a few persons or things

SEVERE — adj -VERER, -VEREST unsparing in the treatment of others SEVERELY adv

SEVERITY — n pl. -TIES the quality or state of being severe

SEW — v SEWED, SEWN, SEWING, SEWS to mend or fasten with a needle and thread

SEWAGE — n pl. -S the waste matter carried off by sewers

SEWAN — n pl. -S seawan

SEWAR — n pl. -S a medieval servant

SEWER — n pl. -S an underground conduit for carrying off liquid and solid waste

SEWERAGE — n pl. -S sewage

SEWING — n pl. -S material that has been or is to be sewed

SEWN — a past participle of sew

SEX v -ED, -ING, -ES to determine the sex (the property by which organisms are classified according to reproductive functions) of

SEXIER comparative of sexy

SEXIEST superlative of sexy

SEXILY adv in a sexy manner

SEXINESS n pl. -ES the quality or state of being sexy

SEXISM n pl. -S prejudice or discrimination against women

SEXIST n pl. -S one that practices sexism

SEXLESS adj lacking sexual characteristics

SEXOLOGY n pl. -GIES the study of human sexual behavior

SEXPOT n pl. -S a sexually attractive woman

SEXT n pl. -S one of seven canonical daily periods for prayer and devotion

SEXTAIN n pl. -S a stanza of six lines

SEXTAN n pl. -S a recurrent malarial fever

SEXTANT n pl. -S an instrument for measuring angular distances

SEXTARII n/pl ancient Roman units of liquid measure

SEXTET n pl. -S a group of six

SEXTETTE n pl. -S sextet

SEXTILE n pl. -S the position of two celestial bodies when they are sixty degrees apart

SEXTO n pl. -TOS sixmo

SEXTON n pl. -S a maintenance worker of a church

SEXTUPLE v -PLED, -PLING, -PLES to make six times as great

SEXTUPLY adv to six times as much or as many

SEXUAL adj pertaining to sex SEXUALLY adv

SEXY adj SEXIER, SEXIEST arousing sexual desire

SFERICS n/pl an electronic detector of storms

SFORZATO n pl. -TOS the playing of a tone or chord with sudden force

SFUMATO n pl. -TOS a technique used in painting

SH interj — used to urge silence

SHABBY adj -BIER, -BIEST ragged SHABBILY adv

SHACK n pl. -S a shanty

SHACKLE v -LED, -LING, -LES to confine with metal fastenings placed around the wrists or ankles

SHACKLER n pl. -S one that shackles

SHACKO n pl. -KOS or -KOES shako

SHAD n pl. -S a food fish

SHADBLOW n pl. -S a shadbush

SHADBUSH n pl. -ES a flowering tree or shrub

SHADCHAN n pl. -CHANIM or -CHANS a Jewish marriage broker

SHADDOCK n pl. -S a citrus fruit

SHADE v SHADED, SHADING, SHADES to screen from light or heat

SHADER n pl. -S one that shades

SHADFLY n pl. -FLIES a winged insect

SHADIER comparative of shady

SHADIEST superlative of shady

SHADILY adv in a shady manner

SHADING n pl. -S protection against light or heat

SHADOOF n pl. -S a device used in Egypt for raising water for irrigation

SHADOW v -ED, -ING, -S to make dark or gloomy

SHADOWER n pl. -S one that shadows

SHADOWY adj -OWIER, -OWIEST dark

SHADRACH n pl. -S a mass of unfused material in the hearth of a blast furnace

SHADUF n pl. -S shadoof

SHADY adj SHADIER, SHADIEST shaded

SHAFT v -ED, -ING, -S to push or propel with a pole

SHAFTING n pl. -S a system of rods for transmitting motion or power

SHAG v SHAGGED, SHAGGING, SHAGS to make shaggy

SHAGBARK n pl. -S a hardwood tree

SHAGGY adj -GIER, -GIEST covered with long, coarse hair SHAGGILY adv

SHAGREEN n pl. -S the rough skin of certain sharks

SHAH n pl. -S an Iranian ruler

SHAHDOM n pl. -S the territory ruled by a shah

SHAIRD n pl. -S shard

SHAIRN n pl. -S sharn

SHAITAN n pl. -S an evil spirit

SHAKE v SHOOK, SHAKEN, SHAKING, SHAKES to move to and fro with short, rapid movements **SHAKABLE** adj

SHAKEOUT n pl. -S a minor economic recession

SHAKER n pl. -S one that shakes

SHAKEUP n pl. -S a total reorganization

SHAKIER comparative of shaky

SHAKIEST superlative of shaky

SHAKILY adv in a shaky manner

SHAKING present participle of shake

SHAKO n pl. -KOS or -KOES a type of military hat

SHAKY adj SHAKIER, SHAKIEST shaking

SHALE n pl. -S a fissile rock

SHALED adj having a shell or husk

SHALIER comparative of shaly

SHALIEST superlative of shaly

SHALL v present sing. 2d person SHALL or SHALT, past sing. 2d person SHOULD, SHOULDST, or SHOULDEST — used as an auxiliary to express futurity, inevitability, or command

SHALLOON n pl. -S a woolen fabric

SHALLOP n pl. -S a small, open boat

SHALLOT n pl. -S a plant resembling an onion

SHALLOW adj -LOWER, -LOWEST having little depth

SHALLOW v -ED, -ING, -S to make shallow

SHALOM interj peace — used as a Jewish greeting and farewell

SHALT a present 2d person sing. of shall

SHALY adj SHALIER, SHALIEST resembling shale

SHAM v SHAMMED, SHAMMING, SHAMS to feign

SHAMABLE adj capable of being shamed

SHAMAN n pl. -S a medicine man among certain North American Indians **SHAMANIC** adj

SHAMBLE v -BLED, -BLING, -BLES to walk awkwardly

SHAME v SHAMED, SHAMING, SHAMES to cause to feel a painful sense of guilt or degradation

SHAMEFUL adj disgraceful

SHAMES n pl. -MOSIM shammes

SHAMING present participle of shame

SHAMMAS n pl. -MASIM shammes

SHAMMASH n pl. -MASHIM shammes

SHAMMED past tense of sham

SHAMMER n pl. -S one that shams

SHAMMES n pl. -MOSIM a minor official of a synagogue

SHAMMIED past tense of shammy

SHAMMIES present 3d person sing. of shammy

SHAMMING present participle of sham

SHAMMOS n pl. -MOSIM shammes

SHAMMOSIM pl. of shammes

SHAMMY v -MIED, -MYING, -MIES to chamois

SHAMOIS n pl. SHAMOIS chamois

SHAMOSIM pl. of shames

SHAMOY v -ED, -ING, -S to chamois

SHAMPOO v -ED, -ING, -S to cleanse with a special preparation

SHAMROCK n pl. -S a three-leaved plant

SHAMUS n pl. -ES a private detective

SHANDY n pl. -DIES an alcoholic drink

SHANGHAI v -ED, -ING, -S to kidnap for service aboard a ship

SHANK v -ED, -ING, -S to hit sharply to the right, as a golf ball

SHANTEY n pl. -TEYS chantey

SHANTI n pl. -S peace

SHANTIES pl. of shanty

SHANTIH n pl. -S shanti

SHANTUNG n pl. -S a silk fabric

SHANTY n pl. -TIES a small, crudely built dwelling

SHAPE v SHAPED, SHAPEN, SHAPING, SHAPES to give shape (outward form) to **SHAPABLE** adj

SHAPELY adj -LIER, -LIEST having a pleasing shape

SHAPER n pl. -S one that shapes

SHAPEUP n pl. -S a system of hiring a work crew

SHAPING present participle of shape

SHARD n pl. -S a fragment of broken pottery

SHARE v SHARED, SHARING, SHARES to have, get, or use in common with another or others SHARABLE adj

SHARER n pl. -S one that shares

SHARIF n pl. -S sherif

SHARING present participle of share

SHARK v -ED, -ING, -S to live by trickery

SHARKER n pl. -S one that sharks

SHARN n pl. -S cow dung SHARNY adj

SHARP adj SHARPER, SHARPEST suitable for or capable of cutting or piercing

SHARP v -ED, -ING, -S to raise in pitch, as a musical tone

SHARPEN v -ED, -ING, -S to make or become sharp

SHARPER n pl. -S a swindler

SHARPIE n pl. -S a very alert person

SHARPLY adv in a sharp manner

SHARPY n pl. SHARPIES sharpie

SHASHLIK n pl. -S kabob

SHASLIK n pl. -S shashlik

SHAT a past tense of shit

SHATTER v -ED, -ING, -S to break into pieces

SHAUGH n pl. -S a thicket

SHAUL v -ED, -ING, -S to shoal

SHAVE v SHAVED, SHAVEN, SHAVING, SHAVES to sever the hair close to the roots SHAVABLE adj

SHAVER n pl. -S one that shaves

SHAVIE n pl. -S a trick or prank

SHAVING n pl. -S something shaved off

SHAW v SHAWED, SHAWN, SHAWING, SHAWS to show

SHAWL v -ED, -ING, -S to wrap in a shawl (a piece of cloth worn as a covering)

SHAWM n pl. -S an early woodwind instrument

SHAWN past participle of shaw

SHAY n pl. SHAYS a chaise

SHE n pl. -S a female person

SHEA n pl. -S an African tree

SHEAF v -ED, -ING, -S to sheave

SHEAL n pl. -S shealing

SHEALING n pl. -S a shepherd's hut

SHEAR v SHEARED or SHORE, SHORN, SHEARING, SHEARS to cut the hair from

SHEARER n pl. -S one that shears

SHEATH v -ED, -ING, -S to sheathe

SHEATHE v SHEATHED, SHEATHING, SHEATHES to put into a protective case

SHEATHER n pl. -S one that sheathes

SHEAVE v SHEAVED, SHEAVING, SHEAVES to gather into a bundle

SHEBANG n pl. -S a situation, organization, or matter

SHEBEAN n pl. -S shebeen

SHEBEEN n pl. -S a place where liquor is sold illegally

SHED v SHEDDED, SHEDDING, SHEDS to house in a shed (a small, low structure)

SHEDABLE adj capable of being cast off

SHEDDER n pl. -S one that casts off something

SHEDDING present participle of shed

SHEEN v -ED, -ING, -S to shine

SHEENEY n pl. -NEYS sheenie

SHEENFUL adj shining

SHEENIE n pl. -S a Jew — an offensive term

SHEENY adj SHEENIER, SHEENIEST shining

SHEEP n pl. SHEEP a ruminant mammal

SHEEPDOG n pl. -S a dog trained to guard and herd sheep

SHEEPISH adj embarrassed

SHEEPMAN n pl. -MEN a person who raises sheep

SHEER v -ED, -ING, -S to deviate from a course

SHEER adj SHEERER, SHEEREST of very thin texture SHEERLY adv

SHEET v -ED, -ING, -S to cover with a sheet (a thin, rectangular piece of material)

SHEETER n pl. -S one that sheets

SHEETFED adj pertaining to a type of printing press

SHEETING n pl. -S material in the form of sheets

SHEEVE n pl. -S a grooved pulley wheel

SHEGETZ n pl. SHKOTZIM a non-Jewish boy or young man

SHEIK n pl. -S an Arab chief

SHEIKDOM n pl. -S the area ruled by a sheik

SHEIKH n pl. -S sheik

SHEITAN n pl. -S shaitan

SHEKEL n pl. -S an ancient unit of weight and money

SHELDUCK n pl. -S a European duck

SHELF n pl. SHELVES a flat rigid structure used to support articles

SHELFFUL n pl. -S as much as a shelf can hold

SHELL v -ED, -ING, -S to divest of a shell (a hard outer covering)

SHELLAC v -LACKED, -LACKING, -LACS to cover with a thin varnish

SHELLACK v -ED, -ING, -S to shellac

SHELLER n pl. -S one that shells

SHELLY adj SHELLIER, SHELLIEST abounding in seashells

SHELTER v -ED, -ING, -S to provide cover or protection for

SHELTIE n pl. -S a small, shaggy pony

SHELTY n pl. -TIES sheltie

SHELVE v SHELVED, SHELVING, SHELVES to place on a shelf

SHELVER n pl. -S one that shelves

SHELVES pl. of shelf

SHELVING n pl. -S material for shelves

SHELVY adj SHELVIER, SHELVIEST inclining gradually

SHEND v SHENT, SHENDING, SHENDS to disgrace

SHEOL n pl. -S hell

SHEPHERD v -ED, -ING, -S to watch over carefully

SHERBERT n pl. -S sherbet

SHERBET n pl. -S a frozen fruit-flavored mixture

SHERD n pl. -S shard

SHEREEF n pl. -S sherif

SHERIF n pl. -S an Arab ruler

SHERIFF n pl. -S a law-enforcement officer of a county

SHERLOCK n pl. -S a detective

SHEROOT n pl. -S cheroot

SHERRIS n pl. -RISES sherry

SHERRY n pl. -RIES a type of wine

SHETLAND n pl. -S a wool yarn

SHEUCH n pl. -S sheugh

SHEUGH n pl. -S a ditch

SHEW v SHEWED, SHEWN, SHEWING, SHEWS to show

SHEWER n pl. -S one that shews

SHH interj sh

SHIBAH n pl. -S shiva

SHICKSA n pl. -S shiksa

SHIED past tense of shy

SHIEL n pl. -S shieling

SHIELD v -ED, -ING, -S to provide with a protective cover or shelter

SHIELDER n pl. -S one that shields

SHIELING n pl. -S shealing

SHIER n pl. -S a horse having a tendency to shy

SHIES present 3d person sing. of shy

SHIEST a superlative of shy

SHIFT v -ED, -ING, -S to move from one position to another

SHIFTER n pl. -S one that shifts

SHIFTY adj SHIFTIER, SHIFTIEST tricky SHIFTILY adv

SHIGELLA n pl. -LAE or -LAS any of a genus of aerobic bacteria

SHIKAR v -KARRED, -KARRING, -KARS to hunt

SHIKAREE n pl. -S a big game hunter

SHIKARI n pl. -S shikaree

SHIKARRED past tense of shikar

SHIKARRING present participle of shikar

SHIKSA n pl. -S a non-Jewish girl or young woman

SHIKSE n pl. -S shiksa

SHILINGI n pl. SHILINGI a monetary unit of Tanzania

SHILL v -ED, -ING, -S to act as a decoy

SHILLALA n pl. -S a short, thick club

SHILLING n pl. -S a former monetary unit of Great Britain

SHILPIT adj sickly

SHILY adv in a shy manner

SHIM *v* SHIMMED, SHIMMING, SHIMS to fill out or level by inserting a thin wedge

SHIMMER *v* -ED, -ING, -S to glimmer

SHIMMERY *adj* shimmering

SHIMMING present participle of shim

SHIMMY *v* -MIED, -MYING, -MIES to vibrate or wobble

SHIN *v* SHINNED, SHINNING, SHINS to climb by gripping and pulling alternately with the hands and legs

SHINBONE *n pl.* -S the tibia

SHINDIG *n pl.* -S an elaborate dance or party

SHINDY *n pl.* -DYS or -DIES a shindig

SHINE *v* SHONE or SHINED, SHINING, SHINES to emit light

SHINER *n pl.* -S one that shines

SHINGLE *v* -GLED, -GLING, -GLES to cover with shingles (thin, oblong pieces of building material)

SHINGLER *n pl.* -S one that shingles

SHINGLY *adj* covered with small, loose stones

SHINIER comparative of shiny

SHINIEST superlative of shiny

SHINILY *adv* in a shiny manner

SHINING *adj* emitting or reflecting light

SHINLEAF *n pl.* -LEAFS or -LEAVES a perennial herb

SHINNED past of shin

SHINNERY *n pl.* -NERIES a dense growth of small trees

SHINNEY *n pl.* -NEYS a form of hockey

SHINNING present participle of shin

SHINNY *v* -NIED, -NYING, -NIES to shin

SHINY *adj* SHINIER, SHINIEST filled with light

SHIP *v* SHIPPED, SHIPPING, SHIPS to transport by ship (a vessel suitable for navigation in deep water)

SHIPLAP *n pl.* -S an overlapping joint used in carpentry

SHIPLOAD *n pl.* -S as much as a ship can carry

SHIPMAN *n pl.* -MEN a sailor

SHIPMATE *n pl.* -S a fellow sailor

SHIPMENT *n pl.* -S something that is shipped

SHIPPED past tense of ship

SHIPPEN *n pl.* -S a cowshed

SHIPPER *n pl.* -S one that ships

SHIPPING *n pl.* -S the business of one that ships

SHIPPON *n pl.* -S shippen

SHIPSIDE *n pl.* -S the area alongside a ship

SHIPWAY *n pl.* -WAYS a canal deep enough to serve ships

SHIPWORM *n pl.* -S a wormlike marine mollusk

SHIPYARD *n pl.* -S a place where ships are built or repaired

SHIRE *n pl.* -S a territorial division of Great Britain

SHIRK *v* -ED, -ING, -S to avoid work or duty

SHIRKER *n pl.* -S one that shirks

SHIRR *v* -ED, -ING, -S to draw into three or more parallel rows, as cloth

SHIRRING *n pl.* -S a shirred arrangement of cloth

SHIRT *n pl.* -S a garment for the upper part of the body

SHIRTING *n pl.* -S fabric used for making shirts

SHIRTY *adj* SHIRTIER, SHIRTIEST angry

SHIST *n pl.* -S schist

SHIT *v* SHITTED or SHAT, SHITTING, SHITS to defecate — usually considered vulgar

SHITTAH *n pl.* -S a hardwood tree

SHITTIM *n pl.* -S the wood of the shittah

SHITTING present participle of shit

SHIV *n pl.* -S a knife

SHIVA *n pl.* -S a period of mourning

SHIVAH *n pl.* -S shiva

SHIVAREE *v* -REED, -REEING, -REES to chivaree

SHIVE *n pl.* -S a thin fragment

SHIVER *v* -ED, -ING, -S to tremble with fear or cold

SHIVERER *n pl.* -S one that shivers

SHIVERY *adj* shivering

SHKOTZIM pl. of shegetz

SHLEMIEL *n pl.* -S an unlucky bungler

SHLOCK *n pl.* -S schlock

SHMO *n pl.* SHMOES schmo

SHNAPS *n pl.* SHNAPS schnapps

SHOAL *adj* SHOALER, SHOALEST shallow

SHOAL *v* -ED, -ING, -S to become shallow

SHOALY *adj* SHOALIER, SHOALIEST full of shallow areas

SHOAT *n pl.* -S a young hog

SHOCK *v* -ED, -ING, -S to strike with great surprise, horror, or disgust

SHOCKER *n pl.* -S one that shocks

SHOD a past tense of shoe

SHODDEN a past participle of shoe

SHODDY *adj* -DIER, -DIEST of inferior quality SHODDILY *adv*

SHODDY *n pl.* -DIES a low-quality wool

SHOE *n pl.* SHOES or SHOON a covering for the foot

SHOE *v* SHOD or SHOED, SHODDEN, SHOEING, SHOES to provide with shoes

SHOEBILL *n pl.* -S a wading bird

SHOEHORN *v* -ED, -ING, -S to force into a small space

SHOELACE *n pl.* -S a lace for fastening a shoe

SHOEPAC *n pl.* -S a waterproof boot

SHOEPACK *n pl.* -S shoepac

SHOER *n pl.* -S one that shoes horses

SHOETREE *n pl.* -S a device shaped like a foot that is inserted into a shoe to preserve its shape

SHOFAR *n pl.* SHOFARS or SHOFROTH a ram's-horn trumpet blown in certain Jewish rituals

SHOG *v* SHOGGED, SHOGGING, SHOGS to move along

SHOGUN *n pl.* -S a former military leader of Japan SHOGUNAL *adj*

SHOJI *n pl.* -S a paper screen used as a partition or door in a Japanese house

SHOLOM *interj* shalom

SHONE a past tense of shine

SHOO *v* -ED, -ING, -S to drive away

SHOOFLY *n pl.* -FLIES a child's rocker

SHOOK *n pl.* -S a set of parts for assembling a barrel or packing

SHOOL *v* -ED, -ING, -S to shovel

SHOON a pl. of shoe

SHOOT *v* SHOT, SHOOTING, SHOOTS to hit, wound, or kill with a missile discharged from a weapon

SHOOTER *n pl.* -S one that shoots

SHOOTING *n pl.* -S the act of one that shoots

SHOP *v* SHOPPED, SHOPPING, SHOPS to examine goods with intent to buy

SHOPBOY *n pl.* -BOYS a salesclerk

SHOPGIRL *n pl.* -S a salesgirl

SHOPHAR *n pl.* -PHARS or -PHROTH shofar

SHOPLIFT *v* -ED, -ING, -S to steal goods from a store

SHOPMAN *n pl.* -MEN one who owns or operates a small store

SHOPPE *n pl.* -S a small store

SHOPPED past tense of shop

SHOPPER *n pl.* -S one that shops

SHOPPING *n pl.* -S the act of one that shops

SHOPTALK *n pl.* -S conversation concerning one's business or occupation

SHOPWORN *adj* worn out from being on display in a store

SHORAN *n pl.* -S a type of navigational system

SHORE *v* SHORED, SHORING, SHORES to prop with a supporting timber

SHORING *n pl.* -S a system of supporting timbers

SHORL *n pl.* -S schorl

SHORN a past participle of shear

SHORT *adj* SHORTER, SHORTEST having little length

SHORT *v* -ED, -ING, -S to cause a type of electrical malfunction in

SHORTAGE *n pl.* -S an insufficient supply or amount

SHORTCUT *n pl.* -S a shorter or quicker way

SHORTEN *v* -ED, -ING, -S to make or become shorter

SHORTIA *n pl.* -S a perennial herb

SHORTIE *n pl.* -S shorty

SHORTIES pl. of shorty

SHORTISH *adj* somewhat short

SHORTLY *adv* in a short time

SHORTY n pl. SHORTIES one that is short

SHOT v SHOTTED, SHOTTING, SHOTS to load with shot (small lead or steel pellets)

SHOTE n pl. -S shoat

SHOTGUN v -GUNNED, -GUNNING, -GUNS to shoot with a type of gun

SHOTT n pl. -S chott

SHOTTED past tense of shot

SHOTTEN adj having spawned — used of a fish

SHOTTING present participle of shot

SHOULD past tense of shall

SHOULDER v -ED, -ING, -S to assume the burden or responsibility of

SHOULDEST a 2d person sing. past tense of shall

SHOULDST a 2d person sing. past tense of shall

SHOUT v -ED, -ING, -S to utter loudly

SHOUTER n pl. -S one that shouts

SHOVE v SHOVED, SHOVING, SHOVES to push roughly

SHOVEL v -ELED, -ELING, -ELS or -ELLED, -ELLING, -ELS to take up with a shovel (a digging implement)

SHOVELER n pl. -S one that shovels

SHOVER n pl. -S one that shoves

SHOVING present participle of shove

SHOW v SHOWED, SHOWN, SHOWING, SHOWS to cause or permit to be seen

SHOWBOAT n pl. -S a boat on which theatrical performances are given

SHOWCASE v -CASED, -CASING, -CASES to exhibit

SHOWDOWN n pl. -S an event that forces the conclusion of an issue

SHOWER v -ED, -ING, -S to fall in a brief, heavy rain

SHOWERY adj showering

SHOWGIRL n pl. -S a chorus girl

SHOWIER comparative of showy

SHOWIEST superlative of showy

SHOWILY adv in a showy manner

SHOWING n pl. -S an exhibition or display

SHOWMAN n pl. -MEN a theatrical producer

SHOWN past participle of show

SHOWOFF n pl. -S one given to pretentious display

SHOWROOM n pl. -S a room used for the display of merchandise

SHOWY adj SHOWIER, SHOWIEST making a great or brilliant display

SHRANK past tense of shrink

SHRAPNEL n pl. SHRAPNEL fragments from an exploding bomb, mine, or shell

SHRED v SHREDDED, SHREDDING, SHREDS to tear into small strips

SHREDDER n pl. -S one that shreds

SHREW v -ED, -ING, -S to curse

SHREWD adj SHREWDER, SHREWDEST having keen insight SHREWDLY adv

SHREWISH adj ill-tempered

SHRI n pl. -S sri

SHRIEK v -ED, -ING, -S to utter a shrill cry

SHRIEKER n pl. -S one that shrieks

SHRIEKY adj SHRIEKIER, SHRIEKIEST shrill

SHRIEVAL adj pertaining to a sheriff

SHRIEVE v SHRIEVED, SHRIEVING, SHRIEVES to shrive

SHRIFT n pl. -S the act of shriving

SHRIKE n pl. -S a predatory bird

SHRILL adj SHRILLER, SHRILLEST having a high-pitched and piercing quality SHRILLY adv

SHRILL v -ED, -ING, -S to utter a shrill sound

SHRIMP v -ED, -ING, -S to catch shrimps (small marine decapods)

SHRIMPER n pl. -S a shrimp fisher

SHRIMPY adj SHRIMPIER, SHRIMPIEST abounding in shrimp

SHRINE v SHRINED, SHRINING, SHRINES to place in a shrine (a receptacle for sacred relics)

SHRINK v SHRANK, SHRUNK or SHRUNKEN, SHRINKING, SHRINKS to contract or draw back

SHRINKER n pl. -S one that shrinks

SHRIVE — v SHROVE or SHRIVED, SHRIVEN, SHRIVING, SHRIVES to hear the confession of and grant absolution to

SHRIVEL — v -ELED, -ELING, -ELS or -ELLED, -ELLING, -ELS to contract into wrinkles

SHRIVER — n pl. -S one that shrives

SHRIVING — present participle of shrive

SHROFF — v -ED, -ING, -S to test the genuineness of, as a coin

SHROUD — v -ED, -ING, -S to wrap in burial clothing

SHROVE — a past tense of shrive

SHRUB — n pl. -S a low, woody plant

SHRUBBY — adj -BIER, -BIEST covered with shrubs

SHRUG — v SHRUGGED, SHRUGGING, SHRUGS to raise and contract the shoulders

SHRUNK — a past tense of shrink

SHRUNKEN — a past participle of shrink

SHTETEL — n pl. SHTETLACH a Jewish village

SHTETL — n pl. SHTETLACH shtetel

SHTICK — n pl. -S an entertainment routine

SHUCK — v -ED, -ING, -S to remove the husk or shell from

SHUCKER — n pl. -S one that shucks

SHUCKING — n pl. -S the act of one that shucks

SHUDDER — v -ED, -ING, -S to tremble

SHUDDERY — adj shuddering

SHUFFLE — v -FLED, -FLING, -FLES to walk without lifting the feet

SHUFFLER — n pl. -S one that shuffles

SHUL — n pl. SHULN or SHULS a synagogue

SHUN — v SHUNNED, SHUNNING, SHUNS to avoid

SHUNNER — n pl. -S one that shuns

SHUNPIKE — n pl. -S a side road taken to avoid paying tolls

SHUNT — v -ED, -ING, -S to turn aside

SHUNTER — n pl. -S one that shunts

SHUSH — v -ED, -ING, -ES to silence

SHUT — v SHUT, SHUTTING, SHUTS to close

SHUTDOWN — n pl. -S a temporary closing of an industrial plant

SHUTE — v SHUTED, SHUTING, SHUTES to chute

SHUTEYE — n pl. -S sleep

SHUTOFF — n pl. -S a device that shuts something off

SHUTOUT — n pl. -S a game in which one team fails to score

SHUTTER — v -ED, -ING, -S to provide with shutters (hinged window covers)

SHUTTING — present participle of shut

SHUTTLE — v -TLED, -TLING, -TLES to move or travel back and forth

SHWANPAN — n pl. -S swanpan

SHY — adj SHIER, SHIEST or SHYER, SHYEST timid

SHY — v SHIED, SHYING, SHIES to move suddenly back or aside, as in fear

SHYER — n pl. -S shier

SHYLOCK — v -ED, -ING, -S to lend money at high interest rates

SHYLY — adv in a shy manner

SHYNESS — n pl. -ES the state of being shy

SHYSTER — n pl. -S an unscrupulous lawyer or politician

SI — n pl. -S ti

SIAL — n pl. -S a type of rock formation SIALIC adj

SIALOID — adj resembling saliva

SIAMANG — n pl. -S a large, black gibbon

SIAMESE — n pl. -S a water pipe with a connection for two hoses

SIB — n pl. -S a sibling

SIBB — n pl. -S sib

SIBILANT — n pl. -S a speech sound produced by the fricative passage of breath through a narrow orifice

SIBILATE — v -LATED, -LATING, -LATES to hiss

SIBLING — n pl. -S one having the same parents as another

SIBYL — n pl. -S a female prophet SIBYLIC, SIBYLLIC adj

SIC — v SICCED, SICCING, SICS to urge to attack

SICCAN — adj such

SICE — n pl. -S syce

SICK   *adj* SICKER, SICKEST affected with disease or ill health

SICK   *v* -ED, -ING, -S to sic

SICKBAY   *n pl.* -BAYS a ship's hospital

SICKBED   *n pl.* -S a sick person's bed

SICKEN   *v* -ED, -ING, -S to make sick

SICKENER   *n pl.* -S one that sickens

SICKERLY   *adv* securely

SICKISH   *adj* somewhat sick

SICKLE   *v* -LED, -LING, -LES to cut with an agricultural implement having a single blade

SICKLY   *adj* -LIER, -LIEST appearing as if sick SICKLILY *adv*

SICKLY   *v* -LIED, -LYING, -LIES to make sickly

SICKNESS   *n pl.* -ES the state of being sick

SICKROOM   *n pl.* -S a room occupied by a sick person

SIDDUR   *n pl.* -DURIM or -DURS a Jewish prayer book

SIDE   *v* SIDED, SIDING, SIDES to agree with or support

SIDEARM   *adj* thrown with a sideways sweep of the arm

SIDEBAND   *n pl.* -S a band of radio frequencies

SIDECAR   *n pl.* -S a passenger car attached to a motorcycle

SIDED   past tense of side

SIDEHILL   *n pl.* -S a hillside

SIDEKICK   *n pl.* -S a close friend

SIDELINE   *v* -LINED, -LINING, -LINES to put out of action

SIDELING   *adj* sloping

SIDELONG   *adj* directed to one side

SIDEMAN   *n pl.* -MEN a member of a jazz band

SIDEREAL   *adj* pertaining to the stars

SIDERITE   *n pl.* -S a mineral

SIDESHOW   *n pl.* -S a small show offered in addition to a main attraction

SIDESLIP   *v* -SLIPPED, -SLIPPING, -SLIPS to slip to one side

SIDESPIN   *n pl.* -S a type of spin imparted to a ball

SIDESTEP   *v* -STEPPED, -STEPPING, -STEPS to step to one side

SIDEWALK   *n pl.* -S a paved walk for pedestrians

SIDEWALL   *n pl.* -S a side surface of a tire

SIDEWARD   *adv* toward one side

SIDEWAY   *adv* sideways

SIDEWAYS   *adv* toward or from one side

SIDEWISE   *adv* sideways

SIDING   *n pl.* -S material used for surfacing a frame building

SIDLE   *v* -DLED, -DLING, -DLES to move sideways

SIDLER   *n pl.* -S one that sidles

SIEGE   *v* SIEGED, SIEGING, SIEGES to attempt to capture or gain

SIEMENS   *n pl.* SIEMENS a unit of electrical conductance

SIENITE   *n pl.* -S syenite

SIENNA   *n pl.* -S a brown pigment

SIEROZEM   *n pl.* -S a type of soil

SIERRA   *n pl.* -S a mountain range SIERRAN *adj*

SIESTA   *n pl.* -S an afternoon nap or rest

SIEUR   *n pl.* -S an old French title of respect for a man

SIEVE   *v* SIEVED, SIEVING, SIEVES to pass through a sieve (a utensil for separating the coarse parts from the fine parts of loose matter)

SIFFLEUR   *n pl.* -S an animal that makes a whistling noise

SIFT   *v* -ED, -ING, -S to sieve

SIFTER   *n pl.* -S one that sifts

SIFTING   *n pl.* -S the work of a sifter

SIGANID   *n pl.* -S any of a family of fishes

SIGH   *v* -ED, -ING, -S to let out a sigh (a deep, audible breath)

SIGHER   *n pl.* -S one that sighs

SIGHLESS   *adj* uttering no sigh

SIGHLIKE   *adj* resembling a sigh

SIGHT   *v* -ED, -ING, -S to observe or notice

SIGHTER   *n pl.* -S one that sights

SIGHTLY   *adj* -LIER, -LIEST pleasing to look at

SIGHTSEE   *v* -SAW, -SEEN, -SEEING, -SEES to visit and view places of interest

SIGIL   *n pl.* -S an official seal

SIGLOS   *n pl.* -LOI an ancient Persian coin

SIGMA *n pl.* -S a Greek letter **SIGMATE** *adj*

SIGMOID *n pl.* -S an S-shaped curve in a bodily part

SIGN *v* -ED, -ING, -S to write one's name on

SIGNAL *v* -NALED, -NALING, -NALS or -NALLED, -NALLING, -NALS to notify by a means of communication

SIGNALER *n pl.* -S one that signals

SIGNALLY *adv* notably

SIGNER *n pl.* -S one that signs

SIGNET *v* -ED, -ING, -S to mark with an official seal

SIGNIFY *v* -FIED, -FYING, -FIES to make known

SIGNIOR *n pl.* -GNIORI or -GNIORS signor

SIGNIORY *n pl.* -GNIORIES signory

SIGNOR *n pl.* -GNORI or -GNORS an Italian title of courtesy for a man

SIGNORA *n pl.* -GNORE or -GNORAS an Italian title of courtesy for a married woman

SIGNORE *n pl.* -GNORI signor

SIGNORY *n pl.* -GNORIES seignory

SIGNPOST *v* -ED, -ING, -S to provide with signposts (posts bearing signs)

SIKE *n pl.* -S syke

SIKER *adj* secure

SILAGE *n pl.* -S fodder that has been preserved in a silo

SILANE *n pl.* -S a chemical compound

SILD *n pl.* -S a young herring

SILENCE *v* -LENCED, -LENCING, -LENCES to make silent

SILENCER *n pl.* -S one that silences

SILENI *pl.* of silenus

SILENT *adj* -LENTER, -LENTEST making no sound or noise **SILENTLY** *adv*

SILENTS *n/pl* silent movies

SILENUS *n pl.* -NI a woodland deity of Greek mythology

SILESIA *n pl.* -S a cotton fabric

SILEX *n pl.* -ES silica

SILICA *n pl.* -S a form of silicon

SILICATE *n pl.* -S a chemical salt

SILICIC *adj* pertaining to silicon

SILICIDE *n pl.* -S a silicon compound

SILICIFY *v* -FIED, -FYING, -FIES to convert into silica

SILICIUM *n pl.* -S silicon

SILICLE *n pl.* -S a short, flat silique

SILICON *n pl.* -S a nonmetallic element

SILICONE *n pl.* -S a silicon compound

SILIQUA *n pl.* -QUAE silique

SILIQUE *n pl.* -LIQUES a type of seed vessel

SILK *v* -ED, -ING, -S to cover with silk (a soft, lustrous fabric)

SILKEN *adj* made of silk

SILKIER comparative of silky

SILKIEST superlative of silky

SILKILY *adv* in a silky manner

SILKLIKE *adj* resembling silk

SILKWEED *n pl.* -S milkweed

SILKWORM *n pl.* -S a caterpillar that spins a cocoon of silk fibers

SILKY *adj* SILKIER, SILKIEST resembling silk

SILL *n pl.* -S the horizontal piece that bears the upright portion of a frame

SILLABUB *n pl.* -S an alcoholic beverage or dessert

SILLER *n pl.* -S silver

SILLIBUB *n pl.* -S sillabub

SILLY *adj* -LIER, -LIEST showing a lack of good sense **SILLILY** *adv*

SILLY *n pl.* -LIES a silly person

SILO *v* -ED, -ING, -S to store in a silo (a tall, cylindrical structure)

SILOXANE *n pl.* -S a chemical compound

SILT *v* -ED, -ING, -S to fill with silt (a sedimentary material)

SILTY *adj* SILTIER, SILTIEST full of silt

SILURID *n pl.* -S any of a family of catfishes

SILUROID *n pl.* -S a silurid

SILVA *n pl.* -VAS or -VAE sylva

SILVAN *n pl.* -S sylvan

SILVER *v* -ED, -ING, -S to cover with silver (a metallic element)

SILVERER *n pl.* -S one that silvers

SILVERLY *adv* with a silvery appearance

SILVERN *adj* silvery

SILVERY *adj* resembling silver

SILVICAL   adj pertaining to silvics

SILVICS   n/pl the study of forest trees

SIM   n pl. -S simulation

SIMA   n pl. -S an igneous rock

SIMAR   n pl. -S a woman's light jacket or robe

SIMARUBA   n pl. -S a tropical tree

SIMAZINE   n pl. -S an herbicide

SIMIAN   n pl. -S an ape or monkey

SIMILAR   adj being like but not completely identical to

SIMILE   n pl. -S a figure of speech

SIMIOID   adj simious

SIMIOUS   adj pertaining to simians

SIMITAR   n pl. -S scimitar

SIMLIN   n pl. -S cymling

SIMMER   v -ED, -ING, -S to cook below or just at the boiling point

SIMNEL   n pl. -S a crisp bread

SIMOLEON   n pl. -S a dollar

SIMONIAC   n pl. -S one who practices simony

SIMONIES   pl. of simony

SIMONIST   n pl. -S a simoniac

SIMONIZE   v -NIZED, -NIZING, -NIZES to polish with wax

SIMONY   n pl. -NIES the buying or selling of a church office

SIMOOM   n pl. -S a hot, dry desert wind

SIMOON   n pl. -S a simoom

SIMP   n pl. -S a foolish person

SIMPER   v -ED, -ING, -S to smile in a silly manner

SIMPERER   n pl. -S one that simpers

SIMPLE   adj SIMPLER, SIMPLEST not complex or complicated

SIMPLE   n pl. -S something that is simple

SIMPLEX   n pl. -PLEXES, -PLICES, or -PLICIA a simple word

SIMPLIFY   v -FIED, -FYING, -FIES to make simple

SIMPLISM   n pl. -S the tendency to oversimplify an issue or problem

SIMPLY   adv in a simple manner

SIMULANT   n pl. -S one that simulates

SIMULAR   n pl. -S a simulant

SIMULATE   v -LATED, -LATING, -LATES to take on the appearance of

SIN   v SINNED, SINNING, SINS to commit a sin (an offense against religious or moral law)

SINAPISM   n pl. -S a pasty mixture applied to an irritated part of the body

SINCE   adv from then until now

SINCERE   adj -CERER, -CEREST free from hypocrisy or falseness

SINCIPUT   n pl. -CIPUTS or -CIPITA the forehead

SINE   n pl. -S a trigonometric function of an angle

SINECURE   n pl. -S an office or position requiring little or no work

SINEW   v -ED, -ING, -S to strengthen

SINEWY   adj lean and muscular

SINFONIA   n pl. -NIE a symphony

SINFUL   adj marked by sin SINFULLY adv

SING   v SANG, SUNG, SINGING, SINGS to utter with musical inflections of the voice SINGABLE adj

SINGE   v SINGED, SINGEING, SINGES to burn slightly

SINGER   n pl. -S one that sings

SINGLE   v -GLED, -GLING, -GLES to select from a group

SINGLET   n pl. -S a man's undershirt or jersey

SINGLY   adv without the company of others

SINGSONG   n pl. -S monotonous cadence in speaking or reading

SINGULAR   n pl. -S a word form that denotes one person or thing

SINH   n pl. -S a hyperbolic function of an angle

SINICIZE   v -CIZED, -CIZING, -CIZES to modify by Chinese influence

SINISTER   adj threatening or portending evil

SINK   v SANK, SUNK or SUNKEN, SINKING, SINKS to move to a lower level SINKABLE adj

SINKAGE   n pl. -S the act, process, or degree of sinking

SINKER   n pl. -S one that sinks

SINKHOLE   n pl. -S a natural depression in a land surface

SINLESS   adj free from sin

SINNED   past tense of sin

SINNER	n pl. -S one that sins
SINNING	present participle of sin
SINOLOGY	n pl. -GIES the study of the Chinese
SINOPIA	n pl. -PIAS or -PIE a red pigment
SINSYNE	adv since
SINTER	v -ED, -ING, -S to make cohesive by the combined action of heat and pressure
SINUATE	v -ATED, -ATING, -ATES to curve in and out
SINUOUS	adj characterized by curves, bends, or turns
SINUS	n pl. -ES a cranial cavity
SINUSOID	n pl. -S a mathematical curve
SIP	v SIPPED, SIPPING, SIPS to drink in small quantities
SIPE	v SIPED, SIPING, SIPES to seep
SIPHON	v -ED, -ING, -S to draw off through a siphon (a type of tube)
SIPHONAL	adj of or pertaining to a siphon
SIPHONIC	adj siphonal
SIPING	present participle of sipe
SIPPED	past tense of sip
SIPPER	n pl. -S one that sips
SIPPET	n pl. -S a small piece of bread soaked in gravy
SIPPING	present participle of sip
SIR	n pl. -S a respectful form of address used to a man
SIRDAR	n pl. -S a person of rank in India
SIRE	v SIRED, SIRING, SIRES to beget
SIREE	n pl. -S sirree
SIREN	n pl. -S a device that produces a penetrating warning sound
SIRENIAN	n pl. -S any of an order of aquatic mammals
SIRING	present participle of sire
SIRLOIN	n pl. -S a cut of beef
SIROCCO	n pl. -COS a hot, dry wind
SIRRA	n pl. -S sirrah
SIRRAH	n pl. -S a form of address used to inferiors
SIRREE	n pl. -S sir
SIRUP	n pl. -S syrup **SIRUPY** adj
SIRVENTE	n pl. -S a satirical medieval song or poem
SIS	n pl. SISES sister
SISAL	n pl. -S a strong fiber used for rope
SISKIN	n pl. -S a Eurasian finch
SISSY	n pl. -SIES an effeminate man or boy
SISSY	adj SISSIER, SISSIEST sissyish
SISSYISH	adj resembling a sissy
SISTER	v -ED, -ING, -S to treat like a sister (a female sibling)
SISTERLY	adj of or resembling a sister
SISTRA	a pl. of sistrum
SISTROID	adj included between the convex sides of two intersecting curves
SISTRUM	n pl. -TRUMS or -TRA an ancient Egyptian percussion instrument
SIT	v SAT, SITTEN, SITTING, SITS to rest on the buttocks
SITAR	n pl. -S a lute of India
SITARIST	n pl. -S one who plays the sitar
SITE	v SITED, SITING, SITES to place in position for operation
SITH	adv since
SITHENCE	adv since
SITHENS	adv since
SITI	a pl. of situs
SITING	present participle of site
SITOLOGY	n pl. -GIES the science of nutrition and diet
SITTEN	a past participle of sit
SITTER	n pl. -S one that sits
SITTING	n pl. -S a meeting or session
SITUATE	v -ATED, -ATING, -ATES to place in a certain position
SITUS	n pl. -TI or -TUSES a position or location
SITZMARK	n pl. -S a mark left in the snow by a skier who has fallen backward
SIVER	n pl. -S a sewer
SIX	n pl. -ES a number
SIXFOLD	adj being six times as great as
SIXMO	n pl. -MOS a paper size
SIXPENCE	n pl. -S a British coin worth six pennies

SIXPENNY *adj* worth sixpence

SIXTE *n pl.* -S a fencing parry

SIXTEEN *n pl.* -S a number

SIXTH *n pl.* -S one of six equal parts

SIXTHLY *adv* in the sixth place

SIXTIETH *n pl.* -S one of sixty equal parts

SIXTY *n pl.* -TIES a number

SIZABLE *adj* of considerable size SIZABLY *adv*

SIZAR *n pl.* -S a British student who receives financial assistance from his college

SIZE *v* SIZED, SIZING, SIZES to arrange according to size (physical proportions)

SIZEABLE *adj* sizable SIZEABLY *adv*

SIZER *n pl.* -S sizar

SIZIER comparative of sizy

SIZIEST superlative of sizy

SIZINESS *n pl.* -ES the quality or state of being sizy

SIZING *n pl.* -S a substance used as a glaze or filler for porous materials

SIZY *adj* SIZIER, SIZIEST viscid

SIZZLE *v* -ZLED, -ZLING, -ZLES to burn or fry with a hissing sound

SIZZLER *n pl.* -S a very hot day

SKAG *n pl.* -S heroin

SKALD *n pl.* -S an ancient Scandinavian poet SKALDIC *adj*

SKAT *n pl.* -S a card game

SKATE *v* SKATED, SKATING, SKATES to glide over ice or the ground on skates (shoes fitted with runners or wheels)

SKATER *n pl.* -S one that skates

SKATING *n pl.* -S the sport of gliding on skates

SKATOL *n pl.* -S skatole

SKATOLE *n pl.* -S a chemical compound

SKEAN *n pl.* -S a type of dagger

SKEANE *n pl.* -S a length of yarn wound in a loose coil

SKEE *v* SKEED, SKEEING, SKEES to ski

SKEEN *n pl.* -S skean

SKEET *n pl.* -S the sport of shooting at clay pigeons hurled in the air by spring traps

SKEETER *n pl.* -S a skeet shooter

SKEG *n pl.* -S a timber that connects the keel and sternpost of a ship

SKEIGH *adj* proud

SKEIN *v* -ED, -ING, -S to wind into long, loose coils

SKELETON *n pl.* -S the supporting or protective framework of a human or animal body SKELETAL *adj*

SKELLUM *n pl.* -S a rascal

SKELP *v* SKELPED or SKELPIT, SKELPING, SKELPS to slap

SKELTER *v* -ED, -ING, -S to scurry

SKENE *n pl.* -S skean

SKEP *n pl.* -S a beehive

SKEPSIS *n pl.* -SISES the attitude or outlook of a skeptic

SKEPTIC *n pl.* -S a person who doubts generally accepted ideas

SKERRY *n pl.* -RIES a small, rocky island

SKETCH *v* -ED, -ING, -ES to make a rough, hasty drawing of

SKETCHER *n pl.* -S one that sketches

SKETCHY *adj* SKETCHIER, SKETCHIEST lacking in completeness or clearness

SKEW *v* -ED, -ING, -S to turn aside

SKEWBACK *n pl.* -S a sloping surface against which the end of an arch rests

SKEWBALD *n pl.* -S a horse having patches of brown and white

SKEWER *v* -ED, -ING, -S to pierce with a long pin, as meat

SKEWNESS *n pl.* -ES lack of symmetry

SKI *v* -ED, -ING, -S to travel on skis (long, narrow strips of wood or metal)

SKIABLE *adj* capable of being skied over

SKIAGRAM *n pl.* -S a picture made up of shadows or outlines

SKIBOB *n pl.* -S a vehicle used for traveling over snow

SKID *v* SKIDDED, SKIDDING, SKIDS to slide sideways as a result of a loss of traction

SKIDDER *n pl.* -S one that skids

SKIDDOO *v* -ED, -ING, -S to go away

SKIDDY *adj* -DIER, -DIEST likely to cause skidding

SKIDOO *v* -ED, -ING, -S to skiddoo

SKIDWAY *n pl.* -WAYS a platform on which logs are piled for loading or sawing

SKIED past tense of ski and sky

SKIER *n pl.* -S one that skis

SKIES present 3d person sing. of sky

SKIEY *adj* skyey

SKIFF *n pl.* -S a small, open boat

SKIFFLE *v* -FLED, -FLING, -FLES to play a particular style of music

SKIING *n pl.* -S the sport of traveling on skis

SKIJORER *n pl.* -S a skier who is drawn over snow by a horse or vehicle

SKILFUL *adj* skillful

SKILL *n pl.* -S the ability to do something well **SKILLED** *adj*

SKILLESS *adj* having no skill

SKILLET *n pl.* -S a frying pan

SKILLFUL *adj* having skill

SKILLING *n pl.* -S a former coin of Scandinavian countries

SKIM *v* SKIMMED, SKIMMING, SKIMS to remove floating matter from the surface of

SKIMMER *n pl.* -S one that skims

SKIMMING *n pl.* -S something that is skimmed from a liquid

SKIMO *n pl.* -MOS an Eskimo

SKIMP *v* -ED, -ING, -S to scrimp

SKIMPY *adj* SKIMPIER, SKIMPIEST scanty **SKIMPILY** *adv*

SKIN *v* SKINNED, SKINNING, SKINS to strip or deprive of skin (the membranous tissue covering the body of an animal)

SKINFUL *n pl.* -S as much as a skin container can hold

SKINHEAD *n pl.* -S one whose hair is cut very short

SKINK *v* -ED, -ING, -S to pour out or serve, as liquor

SKINKER *n pl.* -S one that skinks

SKINLESS *adj* having no skin

SKINLIKE *adj* resembling skin

SKINNED past tense of skin

SKINNER *n pl.* -S one that skins

SKINNING present participle of skin

SKINNY *adj* -NIER, -NIEST very thin

SKINT *adj* having no money

SKIORING *n pl.* -S a form of skiing

SKIP *v* SKIPPED, SKIPPING, SKIPS to move with light springing steps

SKIPJACK *n pl.* -S a marine fish

SKIPLANE *n pl.* -S an airplane designed to take off from or land on snow

SKIPPED past tense of skip

SKIPPER *v* -ED, -ING, -S to act as master or captain of

SKIPPET *n pl.* -S a small box for protecting an official seal

SKIPPING present participle of skip

SKIRL *v* -ED, -ING, -S to produce a shrill sound

SKIRMISH *v* -ED, -ING, -ES to engage in a minor battle

SKIRR *v* -ED, -ING, -S to move rapidly

SKIRRET *n pl.* -S an Asian herb

SKIRT *v* -ED, -ING, -S to go or pass around

SKIRTER *n pl.* -S one that skirts

SKIRTING *n pl.* -S a board at the base of a wall

SKIT *n pl.* -S a short dramatic scene

SKITE *v* SKITED, SKITING, SKITES to move away quickly

SKITTER *v* -ED, -ING, -S to move lightly or rapidly along a surface

SKITTERY *adj* -TERIER, -TERIEST skittish

SKITTISH *adj* easily frightened

SKITTLE *n pl.* -S a wooden pin used in a bowling game

SKIVE *v* SKIVED, SKIVING, SKIVES to pare

SKIVER *n pl.* -S one that skives

SKIVVY *n pl.* -VIES a female servant

SKIWEAR *n pl.* -S clothing suitable for wear while skiing

SKLENT *v* -ED, -ING, -S to slant

SKOAL *v* -ED, -ING, -S to drink to the health of

SKOOKUM *adj* excellent

SKREEGH *v* -ED, -ING, -S to screech

SKREIGH *v* -ED, -ING, -S to screech

SKUA *n pl.* -S a predatory seabird

SKULK *v* -ED, -ING, -S to move about stealthily

SKULKER *n pl.* -S one that skulks

SKULL	*n* pl. -S the framework of the head **SKULLED** *adj*	**SLAGGY**	*adj* -GIER, -GIEST resembling slag
SKULLCAP	*n* pl. -S a close-fitting cap	**SLAIN**	past participle of slay
SKUNK	*v* -ED, -ING, -S to defeat overwhelmingly	**SLAKE**	*v* SLAKED, SLAKING, SLAKES to quench **SLAKABLE** *adj*
SKY	*v* SKIED or SKYED, SKYING, SKIES to hit or throw toward the sky (the upper atmosphere)	**SLAKER**	*n* pl. -S one that slakes
		SLALOM	*v* -ED, -ING, -S to ski in a zigzag course
SKYBORNE	*adj* airborne	**SLAM**	*v* SLAMMED, SLAMMING, SLAMS to shut forcibly and noisily
SKYCAP	*n* pl. -S a porter at an airport		
SKYDIVE	*v* -DIVED or -DOVE, -DIVING, -DIVES to parachute from an airplane for sport	**SLANDER**	*v* -ED, -ING, -S to defame
		SLANG	*v* -ED, -ING, -S to assail with harsh or coarse language
SKYDIVER	*n* pl. -S one that skydives		
SKYEY	*adj* resembling the sky	**SLANGY**	*adj* SLANGIER, SLANGIEST given to vulgarity **SLANGILY** *adv*
SKYHOOK	*n* pl. -S a hook conceived as being suspended from the sky		
		SLANK	a past tense of slink
SKYJACK	*v* -ED, -ING, -S to hijack an airplane	**SLANT**	*v* -ED, -ING, -S to deviate from the horizontal or vertical
SKYLARK	*v* -ED, -ING, -S to frolic	**SLAP**	*v* SLAPPED, SLAPPING, SLAPS to strike with the open hand
SKYLIGHT	*n* pl. -S a window in a roof or ceiling		
		SLAPDASH	*n* pl. -ES careless work
SKYLINE	*n* pl. -S the horizon	**SLAPJACK**	*n* pl. -S a pancake
SKYMAN	*n* pl. -MEN an aviator	**SLAPPED**	past tense of slap
SKYPHOS	*n* pl. -PHOI a drinking vessel used in ancient Greece	**SLAPPER**	*n* pl. -S one that slaps
		SLAPPING	present participle of slap
SKYSAIL	*n* pl. -S a type of sail	**SLASH**	*v* -ED, -ING, -ES to cut with violent sweeping strokes
SKYWARD	*adv* toward the sky		
SKYWARDS	*adv* skyward	**SLASHER**	*n* pl. -S one that slashes
SKYWAY	*n* pl. -WAYS an elevated highway	**SLASHING**	*n* pl. -S the act of one that slashes
SKYWRITE	*v* -WROTE, -WRITTEN, -WRITING, -WRITES to write in the sky by releasing a visible vapor from an airplane	**SLAT**	*v* SLATTED, SLATTING, SLATS to provide with slats (narrow strips of wood or metal)
		SLATCH	*n* pl. -ES a calm between breaking waves
SLAB	*v* SLABBED, SLABBING, SLABS to cover with slabs (broad, flat pieces of solid material)	**SLATE**	*v* SLATED, SLATING, SLATES to cover with slate (a roofing material)
SLABBER	*v* -ED, -ING, -S to slobber	**SLATER**	*n* pl. -S one that slates
SLABBERY	*adj* slobbery	**SLATHER**	*v* -ED, -ING, -S to spread thickly
SLABBING	present participle of slab	**SLATIER**	comparative of slaty
SLACK	*adj* SLACKER, SLACKEST not tight or taut	**SLATIEST**	superlative of slaty
SLACK	*v* -ED, -ING, -S to slacken	**SLATING**	*n* pl. -S the act of one that slates
SLACKEN	*v* -ED, -ING, -S to make less tight or taut	**SLATTED**	past tense of slat
SLACKER	*n* pl. -S a shirker	**SLATTERN**	*n* pl. -S a slovenly woman
SLACKLY	*adv* in a slack manner	**SLATTING**	present participle of slat
SLAG	*v* SLAGGED, SLAGGING, SLAGS to convert into slag (the fused residue of a smelted ore)	**SLATY**	*adj* SLATIER, SLATIEST resembling slate

SLAVE   *v* SLAVED, SLAVING, SLAVES to work like a slave (one who is owned by another)

SLAVER   *v* -ED, -ING, -S to drool

SLAVERER   *n* pl. -S one that slavers

SLAVERY   *n* pl. -ERIES ownership of one person by another

SLAVEY   *n* pl. -EYS a female servant

SLAVING   present participle of slave

SLAVISH   *adj* pertaining to or characteristic of a slave

SLAW   *n* pl. -S coleslaw

SLAY   *v* SLEW, SLAIN, SLAYING, SLAYS to kill violently

SLAYER   *n* pl. -S one that slays

SLEAVE   *v* SLEAVED, SLEAVING, SLEAVES to separate into filaments

SLEAZY   *adj* SLEAZIER, SLEAZIEST shoddy **SLEAZILY** *adv*

SLED   *v* SLEDDED, SLEDDING, SLEDS to convey on a sled (a vehicle for carrying people or loads over snow or ice)

SLEDDER   *n* pl. -S one that sleds

SLEDDING   *n* pl. -S the act of one that sleds

SLEDGE   *v* SLEDGED, SLEDGING, SLEDGES to convey on a type of sled

SLEEK   *adj* SLEEKER, SLEEKEST smooth and glossy

SLEEK   *v* -ED, -ING, -S to make sleek

SLEEKEN   *v* -ED, -ING, -S to sleek

SLEEKIER   comparative of sleeky

SLEEKIEST   superlative of sleeky

SLEEKIT   *adj* sleek

SLEEKLY   *adv* in a sleek manner

SLEEKY   *adj* SLEEKIER, SLEEKIEST sleek

SLEEP   *v* SLEPT, SLEEPING, SLEEPS to be in a natural, periodic state of rest

SLEEPER   *n* pl. -S one that sleeps

SLEEPING   *n* pl. -S the act of one that sleeps

SLEEPY   *adj* SLEEPIER, SLEEPIEST ready or inclined to sleep **SLEEPILY** *adv*

SLEET   *v* -ED, -ING, -S to shower sleet (frozen rain)

SLEETY   *adj* SLEETIER, SLEETIEST resembling sleet

SLEEVE   *v* SLEEVED, SLEEVING, SLEEVES to furnish with a sleeve (the part of a garment covering the arm)

SLEIGH   *v* -ED, -ING, -S to ride in a sled

SLEIGHER   *n* pl. -S one that sleighs

SLEIGHT   *n* pl. -S deftness

SLENDER   *adj* -DERER, -DEREST thin

SLEPT   past tense of sleep

SLEUTH   *v* -ED, -ING, -S to act as a detective

SLEW   *v* -ED, -ING, -S to slue

SLICE   *v* SLICED, SLICING, SLICES to cut into thin, flat pieces

SLICER   *n* pl. -S one that slices

SLICK   *adj* SLICKER, SLICKEST smooth and slippery

SLICK   *v* -ED, -ING, -S to make slick

SLICKER   *n* pl. -S an oilskin raincoat

SLICKLY   *adv* in a slick manner

SLIDE   *v* SLID, SLIDDEN, SLIDING, SLIDES to move smoothly along a surface **SLIDABLE** *adj*

SLIDER   *n* pl. -S one that slides

SLIDEWAY   *n* pl. -WAYS a route along which something slides

SLIDING   present participle of slide

SLIER   a comparative of sly

SLIEST   a superlative of sly

SLIGHT   *adj* SLIGHTER, SLIGHTEST small in size or amount **SLIGHTLY** *adv*

SLIGHT   *v* -ED, -ING, -S to treat with disregard

SLILY   *adv* in a sly manner

SLIM   *adj* SLIMMER, SLIMMEST slender

SLIM   *v* SLIMMED, SLIMMING, SLIMS to make slim

SLIME   *v* SLIMED, SLIMING, SLIMES to cover with slime (viscous mud)

SLIMIER   comparative of slimy

SLIMIEST   superlative of slimy

SLIMILY   *adv* in a slimy manner

SLIMING   present participle of slime

SLIMLY   *adv* in a slim manner

SLIMMED   past tense of slim

SLIMMER	comparative of slim	**SLITHER**	v -ED, -ING, -S to slide from side to side
SLIMMEST	superlative of slim		
SLIMMING	present participle of slim	**SLITHERY**	adj slippery
SLIMNESS	n pl. -ES the state of being slim	**SLITLESS**	adj having no slits
SLIMPSY	adj -SIER, -SIEST slimsy	**SLITTED**	past tense of slit
SLIMSY	adj -SIER, -SIEST flimsy	**SLITTER**	n pl. -S one that slits
SLIMY	adj SLIMIER, SLIMIEST resembling slime	**SLITTING**	present participle of slit
SLING	v SLUNG, SLINGING, SLINGS to throw with a sudden motion	**SLIVER**	v -ED, -ING, -S to cut into long, thin pieces
SLINGER	n pl. -S one that slings	**SLIVERER**	n pl. -S one that slivers
SLINK	v SLUNK or SLANK, SLINKING, SLINKS to move stealthily	**SLIVOVIC**	n pl. -S a plum brandy
		SLOB	n pl. -S a slovenly or boorish person
SLINKY	adj SLINKIER, SLINKIEST stealthily SLINKILY adv	**SLOBBER**	v -ED, -ING, -S to drool
SLIP	v SLIPPED or SLIPT, SLIPPING, SLIPS to slide suddenly and accidentally	**SLOBBERY**	adj slobbering
		SLOBBISH	adj resembling a slob
		SLOE	n pl. -S a plumlike fruit
SLIPCASE	n pl. -S a protective box for a book	**SLOG**	v SLOGGED, SLOGGING, SLOGS to plod
SLIPE	v SLIPED, SLIPING, SLIPES to peel	**SLOGAN**	n pl. -S a motto adopted by a group
SLIPFORM	v -ED, -ING, -S to construct with the use of a mold in which concrete is placed to set	**SLOGGER**	n pl. -S one that slogs
		SLOGGING	present participle of slog
SLIPKNOT	n pl. -S a type of knot	**SLOID**	n pl. -S sloyd
SLIPLESS	adj free from errors	**SLOJD**	n pl. -S sloyd
SLIPOUT	n pl. -S an insert in a newspaper	**SLOOP**	n pl. -S a type of sailing vessel
SLIPOVER	n pl. -S a pullover	**SLOP**	v SLOPPED, SLOPPING, SLOPS to spill or splash
SLIPPAGE	n pl. -S a falling off from a standard or level	**SLOPE**	v SLOPED, SLOPING, SLOPES to slant
SLIPPED	a past tense of slip	**SLOPER**	n pl. -S one that slopes
SLIPPER	n pl. -S a light, low shoe	**SLOPPED**	past tense of slop
SLIPPERY	adj -PERIER, -PERIEST causing or tending to cause slipping	**SLOPPING**	present participle of slop
		SLOPPY	adj -PIER, -PIEST messy SLOPPILY adv
SLIPPING	present participle of slip		
SLIPPY	adj -PIER, -PIEST slippery	**SLOPWORK**	n pl. -S the manufacture of cheap clothing
SLIPSHOD	adj carelessly done or made		
SLIPSLOP	n pl. -S watery food	**SLOSH**	v -ED, -ING, -ES to move with a splashing motion
SLIPSOLE	n pl. -S a thin insole		
SLIPT	a past tense of slip	**SLOSHY**	adj SLOSHIER, SLOSHIEST slushy
SLIPUP	n pl. -S a mistake		
SLIPWARE	n pl. -S a type of pottery	**SLOT**	v SLOTTED, SLOTTING, SLOTS to cut a long, narrow opening in
SLIPWAY	n pl. -WAYS an area sloping toward the water in a shipyard		
		SLOTBACK	n pl. -S a type of football player
SLIT	v SLITTED, SLITTING, SLITS to make a slit (a long, narrow cut) in	**SLOTH**	n pl. -S a slow-moving arboreal mammal
		SLOTHFUL	adj sluggish
		SLOTTED	past tense of slot

SLOTTING present participle of slot

SLOUCH v -ED, -ING, -ES to sit, stand, or move with a drooping posture

SLOUCHER n pl. -S one that slouches

SLOUCHY adj SLOUCHIER, SLOUCHIEST slouching

SLOUGH v -ED, -ING, -S to cast off

SLOUGHY adj SLOUGHIER, SLOUGHIEST miry

SLOVEN n pl. -S a slovenly person

SLOVENLY adj -LIER, -LIEST habitually untidy or unclean

SLOW adj SLOWER, SLOWEST moving with little speed

SLOW v -ED, -ING, -S to lessen the speed of

SLOWDOWN n pl. -S a lessening of pace

SLOWISH adj somewhat slow

SLOWLY adv in a slow manner

SLOWNESS n pl. -ES the state of being slow

SLOWPOKE n pl. -S a slow individual

SLOWWORM n pl. -S a European lizard having no legs

SLOYD n pl. -S a Swedish system of manual training

SLUB v SLUBBED, SLUBBING, SLUBS to draw out and twist slightly

SLUBBER v -ED, -ING, -S to stain or dirty

SLUBBING n pl. -S a slightly twisted roll of textile fibers

SLUDGE n pl. -S a muddy deposit

SLUDGY adj SLUDGIER, SLUDGIEST covered with sludge

SLUE v SLUED, SLUING, SLUES to cause to move sideways

SLUFF v -ED, -ING, -S to discard a card or cards

SLUG v SLUGGED, SLUGGING, SLUGS to strike heavily

SLUGABED n pl. -S one inclined to stay in bed out of laziness

SLUGFEST n pl. -S a vigorous fight

SLUGGARD n pl. -S an habitually lazy person

SLUGGED past tense of slug

SLUGGER n pl. -S one that slugs

SLUGGING present participle of slug

SLUGGISH adj displaying little movement or activity

SLUICE v SLUICED, SLUICING, SLUICES to wash with a sudden flow of water

SLUICY adj falling in streams

SLUING present participle of slue

SLUM v SLUMMED, SLUMMING, SLUMS to visit slums (squalid urban areas)

SLUMBER v -ED, -ING, -S to sleep

SLUMBERY adj sleepy

SLUMGUM n pl. -S the residue remaining after honey is extracted from a honeycomb

SLUMLORD n pl. -S a landlord of slum property

SLUMMED past tense of slum

SLUMMER n pl. -S one that slums

SLUMMING present participle of slum

SLUMMY adj -MIER, -MIEST resembling a slum

SLUMP v -ED, -ING, -S to fall or sink suddenly

SLUNG past tense of sling

SLUNK a past tense of slink

SLUR v SLURRED, SLURRING, SLURS to pass over lightly or carelessly

SLURB n pl. -S a poorly planned suburban area SLURBAN adj

SLURP v -ED, -ING, -S to eat or drink noisily

SLURRED past tense of slur

SLURRING present participle of slur

SLURRY v -RIED, -RYING, -RIES to convert into a type of watery mixture

SLUSH v -ED, -ING, -ES to splash with slush (partly melted snow)

SLUSHY adj SLUSHIER, SLUSHIEST resembling slush SLUSHILY adv

SLUT n pl. -S a slovenly woman SLUTTISH adj

SLY adj SLIER, SLIEST or SLYER, SLYEST crafty SLYLY adv

SLYBOOTS n pl. SLYBOOTS a sly person

SLYNESS n pl. -ES the quality or state of being sly

SLYPE n pl. -S a narrow passage in an English cathedral

SMACK v -ED, -ING, -S to strike sharply

SMACKER n pl. -S one that smacks

SMALL *adj* SMALLER, SMALLEST of limited size or quantity

SMALL *n pl.* -S a small part

SMALLAGE *n pl.* -S a wild celery

SMALLISH *adj* somewhat small

SMALLPOX *n pl.* -ES a virus disease

SMALT *n pl.* -S a blue pigment

SMALTI a *pl.* of smalto

SMALTINE *n pl.* -S smaltite

SMALTITE *n pl.* -S a mineral

SMALTO *n pl.* -TOS or -TI colored glass used in mosaics

SMARAGD *n pl.* -S an emerald

SMARAGDE *n pl.* -S smaragd

SMARM *n pl.* -S trite sentimentality

SMARMY *adj* SMARMIER, SMARMIEST marked by excessive flattery

SMART *v* -ED, -ING, -S to cause a sharp, stinging pain

SMART *adj* SMARTER, SMARTEST characterized by mental acuity

SMARTEN *v* -ED, -ING, -S to improve in appearance

SMARTIE *n pl.* -S smarty

SMARTLY *adv* in a smart manner

SMARTY *n pl.* SMARTIES an obnoxiously conceited person

SMASH *v* -ED, -ING, -ES to shatter violently

SMASHER *n pl.* -S one that smashes

SMASHUP *n pl.* -S a collision of motor vehicles

SMATTER *v* -ED, -ING, -S to speak with little knowledge

SMAZE *n pl.* -S an atmospheric mixture of smoke and haze

SMEAR *v* -ED, -ING, -S to spread with a sticky, greasy, or dirty substance

SMEARER *n pl.* -S one that smears

SMEARY *adj* SMEARIER, SMEARIEST smeared

SMECTIC *adj* pertaining to a phase of a liquid crystal

SMEDDUM *n pl.* -S ground malt powder

SMEEK *v* -ED, -ING, -S to smoke

SMEGMA *n pl.* -S sebum

SMELL *v* SMELLED or SMELT, SMELLING, SMELLS to perceive by means of the olfactory nerves

SMELLER *n pl.* -S one that smells

SMELLY *adj* SMELLIER, SMELLIEST having an unpleasant odor

SMELT *v* -ED, -ING, -S to melt or fuse, as ores

SMELTER *n pl.* -S one that smelts

SMELTERY *n pl.* -ERIES a place for smelting

SMERK *v* -ED, -ING, -S to smirk

SMEW *n pl.* -S a Eurasian duck

SMIDGEN *n pl.* -S a very small amount

SMIDGEON *n pl.* -S smidgen

SMIDGIN *n pl.* -S smidgen

SMILAX *n pl.* -ES a twining plant

SMILE *v* SMILED, SMILING, SMILES to upturn the corners of the mouth in pleasure

SMILER *n pl.* -S one that smiles

SMIRCH *v* -ED, -ING, -ES to soil

SMIRK *v* -ED, -ING, -S to smile in an affected or smug manner

SMIRKER *n pl.* -S one that smirks

SMIRKY *adj* SMIRKIER, SMIRKIEST smirking

SMITE *v* SMOTE, SMIT or SMITTEN, SMITING, SMITES to strike heavily

SMITER *n pl.* -S one that smites

SMITH *n pl.* -S a worker in metals

SMITHERY *n pl.* -ERIES the trade of a smith

SMITHY *n pl.* SMITHIES the workshop of a smith

SMITING present participle of smite

SMITTEN a past participle of smite

SMOCK *v* -ED, -ING, -S to furnish with a smock (a loose outer garment)

SMOCKING *n pl.* -S a type of embroidery

SMOG *n pl.* -S an atmospheric mixture of smoke and fog **SMOGLESS** *adj*

SMOGGY *adj* -GIER, -GIEST filled with smog

SMOKE *v* SMOKED, SMOKING, SMOKES to emit smoke (the gaseous product of burning materials) **SMOKABLE** *adj*

SMOKEPOT *n* pl. -S a container for giving off smoke

SMOKER *n* pl. -S one that smokes

SMOKEY *adj* SMOKIER, SMOKIEST smoky

SMOKING present participle of smoke

SMOKY *adj* SMOKIER, SMOKIEST filled with smoke **SMOKILY** *adv*

SMOLDER *v* -ED, -ING, -S to burn with no flame

SMOLT *n* pl. -S a young salmon

SMOOCH *v* -ED, -ING, -ES to kiss

SMOOCHY *adj* smudgy

SMOOTH *adj* SMOOTHER, SMOOTHEST having a surface that is free from irregularities

SMOOTH *v* -ED, -ING, -S to make smooth

SMOOTHEN *v* -ED, -ING, -S to smooth

SMOOTHER *n* pl. -S one that smooths

SMOOTHIE *n* pl. -S a person with polished manners

SMOOTHLY *adv* in a smooth manner

SMOOTHY *n* pl. SMOOTHIES smoothie

SMOTE past tense of smite

SMOTHER *v* -ED, -ING, -S to prevent from breathing

SMOTHERY *adj* tending to smother

SMOULDER *v* -ED, -ING, -S to smolder

SMUDGE *v* SMUDGED, SMUDGING, SMUDGES to smear or dirty

SMUDGY *adj* SMUDGIER, SMUDGIEST smudged **SMUDGILY** *adv*

SMUG *adj* SMUGGER, SMUGGEST highly self-satisfied

SMUGGLE *v* -GLED, -GLING, -GLES to import or export illicitly

SMUGGLER *n* pl. -S one that smuggles

SMUGLY *adv* in a smug manner

SMUGNESS *n* pl. -ES the quality or state of being smug

SMUT *v* SMUTTED, SMUTTING, SMUTS to soil

SMUTCH *v* -ED, -ING, -ES to smudge

SMUTCHY *adj* SMUTCHIER, SMUTCHIEST smudgy

SMUTTED past tense of smut

SMUTTING present participle of smut

SMUTTY *adj* -TIER, -TIEST obscene **SMUTTILY** *adv*

SNACK *v* -ED, -ING, -S to eat a light meal

SNAFFLE *v* -FLED, -FLING, -FLES to obtain by devious means

SNAFU *v* -ED, -ING, -S to bring into a state of confusion

SNAG *v* SNAGGED, SNAGGING, SNAGS to catch on a snag (a jagged protuberance)

SNAGGY *adj* -GIER, -GIEST full of snags

SNAGLIKE *adj* resembling a snag

SNAIL *v* -ED, -ING, -S to move slowly

SNAKE *v* SNAKED, SNAKING, SNAKES to move like a snake (a limbless reptile)

SNAKY *adj* SNAKIER, SNAKIEST resembling a snake **SNAKILY** *adv*

SNAP *v* SNAPPED, SNAPPING, SNAPS to make a sharp cracking sound

SNAPBACK *n* pl. -S a sudden rebound or recovery

SNAPLESS *adj* lacking a snap (a type of fastening device)

SNAPPED past tense of snap

SNAPPER *n* pl. -S one that snaps

SNAPPIER comparative of snappy

SNAPPIEST superlative of snappy

SNAPPILY *adv* in a snappy manner

SNAPPING present participle of snap

SNAPPISH *adj* tending to speak in an impatient or irritable manner

SNAPPY *adj* -PIER, -PIEST snappish

SNAPSHOT *v* -SHOTTED, -SHOTTING, -SHOTS to photograph informally and quickly

SNAPWEED *n* pl. -S a flowering plant

SNARE *v* SNARED, SNARING, SNARES to trap

SNARER *n* pl. -S one that snares

SNARK *n* pl. -S an imaginary animal

SNARL *v* -ED, -ING, -S to growl viciously

SNARLER *n* pl. -S one that snarls

SNARLY *adj* SNARLIER, SNARLIEST tangled

SNASH *n* pl. -ES abusive language

SNATCH *v* -ED, -ING, -ES to seize suddenly

SNATCHER *n* pl. -S one that snatches

SNATCHY *adj* SNATCHIER, SNATCHIEST occurring irregularly

SNATH *n pl.* -S the handle of a scythe

SNATHE *n pl.* -S snath

SNAW *v* -ED, -ING, -S to snow

SNAZZY *adj* -ZIER, -ZIEST very stylish

SNEAK *v* SNEAKED or SNUCK, SNEAKING, SNEAKS to move stealthily

SNEAKER *n pl.* -S one that sneaks

SNEAKY *adj* SNEAKIER, SNEAKIEST deceitful **SNEAKILY** *adv*

SNEAP *v* -ED, -ING, -S to chide

SNECK *n pl.* -S a latch

SNED *v* SNEDDED, SNEDDING, SNEDS to prune

SNEER *v* -ED, -ING, -S to curl the lip in contempt

SNEERER *n pl.* -S one that sneers

SNEERFUL *adj* given to sneering

SNEESH *n pl.* -ES snuff

SNEEZE *v* SNEEZED, SNEEZING, SNEEZES to make a sudden, involuntary expiration of breath

SNEEZER *n pl.* -S one that sneezes

SNEEZY *adj* SNEEZIER, SNEEZIEST tending to sneeze

SNELL *n pl.* -S a short line by which a fishhook is attached to a longer line

SNELL *adj* SNELLER, SNELLEST keen

SNIB *v* SNIBBED, SNIBBING, SNIBS to latch

SNICK *v* -ED, -ING, -S to nick

SNICKER *v* -ED, -ING, -S to utter a partly stifled laugh

SNICKERY *adj* tending to snicker

SNIDE *adj* SNIDER, SNIDEST maliciously derogatory **SNIDELY** *adv*

SNIFF *v* -ED, -ING, -S to inhale audibly through the nose

SNIFFER *n pl.* -S one that sniffs

SNIFFIER comparative of sniffy

SNIFFIEST superlative of sniffy

SNIFFILY *adv* in a sniffy manner

SNIFFISH *adj* haughty

SNIFFLE *v* -FLED, -FLING, -FLES to sniff repeatedly

SNIFFLER *n pl.* -S one that sniffles

SNIFFY *adj* -FIER, -FIEST sniffish

SNIFTER *n pl.* -S a pear-shaped liquor glass

SNIGGER *v* -ED, -ING, -S to snicker

SNIGGLE *v* -GLED, -GLING, -GLES to fish for eels

SNIGGLER *n pl.* -S one that sniggles

SNIP *v* SNIPPED, SNIPPING, SNIPS to cut with a short, quick stroke

SNIPE *v* SNIPED, SNIPING, SNIPES to shoot at individuals from a concealed place

SNIPER *n pl.* -S one that snipes

SNIPPED past tense of snip

SNIPPER *n pl.* -S one that snips

SNIPPET *n pl.* -S a small piece snipped off

SNIPPETY *adj* -PETIER, -PETIEST snippy

SNIPPING present participle of snip

SNIPPY *adj* -PIER, -PIEST snappish **SNIPPILY** *adv*

SNIT *n pl.* -S a state of agitation

SNITCH *v* -ED, -ING, -ES to tattle

SNITCHER *n pl.* -S one that snitches

SNIVEL *v* -ELED, -ELING, -ELS or -ELLED, -ELLING, -ELS to cry or whine with sniffling

SNIVELER *n pl.* -S one that snivels

SNOB *n pl.* -S one who tends to avoid or rebuff those regarded as inferior

SNOBBERY *n pl.* -BERIES snobbish behavior

SNOBBIER comparative of snobby

SNOBBIEST superlative of snobby

SNOBBILY *adv* in a snobby manner

SNOBBISH *adj* characteristic of a snob

SNOBBISM *n pl.* -S snobbery

SNOBBY *adj* -BIER, -BIEST snobbish

SNOOD *v* -ED, -ING, -S to secure with a snood (a net or fabric cap for the hair)

SNOOK *v* -ED, -ING, -S to sniff

SNOOKER *n pl.* -S a pocket billiards game

SNOOL *v* -ED, -ING, -S to yield meekly

SNOOP *v* -ED, -ING, -S to pry about

SNOOPER *n pl.* -S one that snoops

SNOOPY *adj* SNOOPIER, SNOOPIEST given to snooping **SNOOPILY** *adv*

SNOOT   v -ED, -ING, -S to treat with disdain

SNOOTY   adj SNOOTIER, SNOOTIEST snobbish **SNOOTILY** adv

SNOOZE   v SNOOZED, SNOOZING, SNOOZES to sleep lightly

SNOOZER   n pl. -S one that snoozes

SNOOZLE   v -ZLED, -ZLING, -ZLES to nuzzle

SNOOZY   adj SNOOZIER, SNOOZIEST drowsy

SNORE   v SNORED, SNORING, SNORES to breathe loudly while sleeping

SNORER   n pl. -S one that snores

SNORKEL   v -ED, -ING, -S to swim underwater with a type of breathing device

SNORT   v -ED, -ING, -S to exhale noisily through the nostrils

SNORTER   n pl. -S one that snorts

SNOT   n pl. -S nasal mucus

SNOTTY   adj -TIER, -TIEST arrogant **SNOTTILY** adv

SNOUT   v -ED, -ING, -S to provide with a nozzle

SNOUTISH   adj snouty

SNOUTY   adj SNOUTIER, SNOUTIEST resembling a long, projecting nose

SNOW   v -ED, -ING, -S to fall as snow (precipitation in the form of ice crystals)

SNOWBALL   v -ED, -ING, -S to increase at a rapidly accelerating rate

SNOWBANK   n pl. -S a mound of snow

SNOWBELL   n pl. -S a flowering shrub

SNOWBIRD   n pl. -S a small bird

SNOWBUSH   n pl. -ES a flowering shrub

SNOWCAP   n pl. -S a covering of snow

SNOWDROP   n pl. -S a European herb

SNOWFALL   n pl. -S a fall of snow

SNOWIER   comparative of snowy

SNOWIEST   superlative of snowy

SNOWILY   adv in a snowy manner

SNOWLAND   n pl. -S an area marked by a great amount of snow

SNOWLESS   adj having no snow

SNOWLIKE   adj resembling snow

SNOWMAN   n pl. -MEN a figure of a person that is made of snow

SNOWMELT   n pl. -S water produced by the melting of snow

SNOWPACK   n pl. -S an accumulation of packed snow

SNOWPLOW   v -ED, -ING, -S to execute a type of skiing maneuver

SNOWSHED   n pl. -S a structure built to provide protection against snow

SNOWSHOE   v -SHOED, -SHOEING, -SHOES to walk on snowshoes (oval frames that allow a person to walk on deep snow)

SNOWSUIT   n pl. -S a child's garment for winter wear

SNOWY   adj SNOWIER, SNOWIEST abounding in snow

SNUB   v SNUBBED, SNUBBING, SNUBS to treat with contempt or neglect

SNUBBER   n pl. -S one that snubs

SNUBBY   adj -BIER, -BIEST blunt

SNUBNESS   n pl. -ES bluntness

SNUCK   a past tense of sneak

SNUFF   v -ED, -ING, -S to use or inhale snuff (powdered tobacco)

SNUFFBOX   n pl. -ES a box for holding snuff

SNUFFER   n pl. -S one that snuffs

SNUFFIER   comparative of snuffy

SNUFFIEST   superlative of snuffy

SNUFFILY   adv in a snuffy manner

SNUFFLE   v -FLED, -FLING, -FLES to sniffle

SNUFFLER   n pl. -S one that snuffles

SNUFFLY   adj -FLIER, -FLIEST tending to snuffle

SNUFFY   adj SNUFFIER, SNUFFIEST dingy

SNUG   adj SNUGGER, SNUGGEST warmly comfortable

SNUG   v SNUGGED, SNUGGING, SNUGS to make snug

SNUGGERY   n pl. -GERIES a snug place

SNUGGEST   superlative of snug

SNUGGING   present participle of snug

SNUGGLE   v -GLED, -GLING, -GLES to lie or press closely

SNUGLY   adv in a snug manner

SNUGNESS   n pl. -ES the quality or state of being snug

SNYE   n pl. -S a side channel in a river or creek

SO   *n pl.* SOS sol

SOAK   *v* -ED, -ING, -S to saturate thoroughly in liquid

SOAKAGE   *n pl.* -S the act of soaking

SOAKER   *n pl.* -S one that soaks

SOAP   *v* -ED, -ING, -S to treat with soap (a cleansing agent)

SOAPBARK   *n pl.* -S a tropical tree

SOAPBOX   *n pl.* -ES a box for soap

SOAPIER   comparative of soapy

SOAPIEST   superlative of soapy

SOAPILY   *adv* in a soapy manner

SOAPLESS   *adj* having no soap

SOAPLIKE   *adj* resembling soap

SOAPSUDS   *n/pl* suds (soapy water)

SOAPWORT   *n pl.* -S a perennial herb

SOAPY   *adj* SOAPIER, SOAPIEST containing or resembling soap

SOAR   *v* -ED, -ING, -S to fly at a great height

SOARER   *n pl.* -S one that soars

SOARING   *n pl.* -S the sport of flying in a heavier-than-air craft without power

SOAVE   *n pl.* -S an Italian wine

SOB   *v* SOBBED, SOBBING, SOBS to cry with a convulsive catching of the breath

SOBBER   *n pl.* -S one that sobs

SOBEIT   *conj* provided that

SOBER   *adj* SOBERER, SOBEREST having control of one's faculties

SOBER   *v* -ED, -ING, -S to make sober

SOBERIZE   *v* -IZED, -IZING, -IZES to sober

SOBERLY   *adv* in a sober manner

SOBFUL   *adj* given to sobbing

SOBRIETY   *n pl.* -ETIES the quality or state of being sober

SOCAGE   *n pl.* -S a form of feudal land tenure

SOCAGER   *n pl.* -S a tenant by socage

SOCCAGE   *n pl.* -S socage

SOCCER   *n pl.* -S a type of ball game

SOCIABLE   *n pl.* -S a social

SOCIABLY   *adv* in a friendly manner

SOCIAL   *n pl.* -S a friendly gathering

SOCIALLY   *adv* with respect to society

SOCIETY   *n pl.* -ETIES an organized group of persons SOCIETAL *adj*

SOCK   *n pl.* SOCKS or SOX a knitted or woven covering for the foot

SOCK   *v* -ED, -ING, -S to strike forcefully

SOCKET   *v* -ED, -ING, -S to furnish with a socket (an opening for receiving something)

SOCKEYE   *n pl.* -S a food fish

SOCKMAN   *n pl.* -MEN socman

SOCLE   *n pl.* -S a block used as a base for a column or pedestal

SOCMAN   *n pl.* -MEN a socager

SOD   *v* SODDED, SODDING, SODS to cover with sod (turf)

SODA   *n pl.* -S a type of chemical compound SODALESS *adj*

SODALIST   *n pl.* -S a member of a sodality

SODALITE   *n pl.* -S a mineral

SODALITY   *n pl.* -TIES a society

SODAMIDE   *n pl.* -S a chemical compound

SODDED   past tense of sod

SODDEN   *v* -ED, -ING, -S to make soggy

SODDENLY   *adv* in a soggy manner

SODDING   present participle of sod

SODDY   *n pl.* -DIES a house built of sod

SODIUM   *n pl.* -S a metallic element SODIC *adj*

SODOMITE   *n pl.* -S one who practices sodomy

SODOMY   *n pl.* -OMIES unnatural copulation

SOEVER   *adv* at all

SOFA   *n pl.* -S a long, upholstered seat

SOFAR   *n pl.* -S a system for locating underwater explosions

SOFFIT   *n pl.* -S the underside of an architectural structure

SOFT   *adj* SOFTER, SOFTEST yielding readily to pressure

SOFT   *n pl.* -S a soft object or part

SOFTA   *n pl.* -S a Muslim theological student

SOFTBACK   *n pl.* -S a book bound in a flexible paper cover

SOFTBALL   *n pl.* -S a type of ball

SOFTEN   *v* -ED, -ING, -S to make soft

SOFTENER   *n pl.* -S one that softens

SOFTHEAD *n* pl. -S a foolish person

SOFTIE *n* pl. -S softy

SOFTIES pl. of softy

SOFTLY *adv* in a soft manner

SOFTNESS *n* pl. -ES the quality or state of being soft

SOFTWARE *n* pl. -S written or printed data used in computer operations

SOFTWOOD *n* pl. -S the soft wood of various trees

SOFTY *n* pl. SOFTIES a sentimental person

SOGGED *adj* soggy

SOGGY *adj* -GIER, -GIEST heavy with moisture SOGGILY *adv*

SOIGNE *adj* carefully done

SOIGNEE *adj* soigne

SOIL *v* -ED, -ING, -S to make dirty

SOILAGE *n* pl. -S green crops for feeding animals

SOILLESS *adj* carried on without soil (finely divided rock mixed with organic matter)

SOILURE *n* pl. -S a stain or smudge

SOIREE *n* pl. -S an evening party

SOJA *n* pl. -S the soybean

SOJOURN *v* -ED, -ING, -S to stay temporarily

SOKE *n* pl. -S a feudal right to administer justice within a certain territory

SOKEMAN *n* pl. -MEN socman

SOL *n* pl. -S the fifth tone of the diatonic musical scale

SOLA *a* pl. of solum

SOLACE *v* -LACED, -LACING, -LACES to console

SOLACER *n* pl. -S one that solaces

SOLAN *n* pl. -S a gannet

SOLAND *n* pl. -S solan

SOLANDER *n* pl. -S a protective box for library materials

SOLANIN *n* pl. -S solanine

SOLANINE *n* pl. -S a poisonous alkaloid

SOLANO *n* pl. -NOS a strong, hot wind

SOLANUM *n* pl. -S any of a genus of herbs and shrubs

SOLAR *adj* pertaining to the sun

SOLARIA *a* pl. of solarium

SOLARISE *v* -ISED, -ISING, -ISES to solarize

SOLARISM *n* pl. -S an interpretation of folk tales as concepts of the nature of the sun

SOLARIUM *n* pl. -IA or -IUMS a room exposed to the sun

SOLARIZE *v* -IZED, -IZING, -IZES to expose to sunlight

SOLATE *v* -ATED, -ATING, -ATES to change to a fluid colloidal system

SOLATIA pl. of solatium

SOLATION *n* pl. -S the act of solating

SOLATIUM *n* pl. -TIA a compensation given for damage to the feelings

SOLD past tense of sell

SOLDAN *n* pl. -S a Muslim ruler

SOLDER *v* -ED, -ING, -S to join closely together

SOLDERER *n* pl. -S one that solders

SOLDI pl. of soldo

SOLDIER *v* -ED, -ING, -S to perform military service

SOLDIERY *n* pl. -DIERIES the military profession

SOLDO *n* pl. -DI a former coin of Italy

SOLE *v* SOLED, SOLING, SOLES to furnish with a sole (the bottom surface of a shoe or boot)

SOLECISE *v* -CISED, -CISING, -CISES to solecize

SOLECISM *n* pl. -S an ungrammatical combination of words in a sentence

SOLECIST *n* pl. -S one who solecizes

SOLECIZE *v* -CIZED, -CIZING, -CIZES to use solecisms

SOLED past tense of sole

SOLELESS *adj* having no sole

SOLELY *adv* singly

SOLEMN *adj* -EMNER, -EMNEST serious SOLEMNLY *adv*

SOLENESS *n* pl. -ES the state of being the only one

SOLENOID *n* pl. -S a type of electric coil

SOLERET *n* pl. -S solleret

SOLFEGE *n* pl. -S a type of singing exercise

SOLFEGGI *n/pl* solfeges

SOLGEL *adj* involving some changes in the state of a colloidal system

SOLI a pl. of solo

SOLICIT *v* -ED, -ING, -S to ask for earnestly

SOLID *adj* -IDER, -IDEST having definite shape and volume

SOLID *n* pl. -S a solid substance

SOLIDAGO *n* pl. -GOS a flowering plant

SOLIDARY *adj* united

SOLIDI pl. of solidus

SOLIDIFY *v* -FIED, -FYING, -FIES to make solid

SOLIDITY *n* pl. -TIES the quality or state of being solid

SOLIDLY *adv* in a solid manner

SOLIDUS *n* pl. -DI a coin of ancient Rome

SOLING present participle of sole

SOLION *n* pl. -S an electronic detecting and amplifying device

SOLIQUID *n* pl. -S a fluid colloidal system

SOLITARY *n* pl. -TARIES one who lives alone

SOLITUDE *n* pl. -S the state of being alone

SOLLERET *n* pl. -S a sabaton

SOLO *n* pl. -LOS or -LI a musical composition for a single voice or instrument

SOLO *v* -ED, -ING, -S to perform alone

SOLOIST *n* pl. -S one that performs a solo

SOLON *n* pl. -S a wise lawgiver

SOLONETS *n* pl. -ES solonetz

SOLONETZ *n* pl. -ES a type of soil

SOLSTICE *n* pl. -S the time of the year when the sun is at its greatest distance from the celestial equator

SOLUBLE *n* pl. -S something that is soluble (capable of being dissolved)

SOLUBLY *adv* in a soluble manner

SOLUM *n* pl. -LA or -LUMS a soil layer

SOLUS *adj* alone

SOLUTE *n* pl. -S a dissolved substance

SOLUTION *n* pl. -S a homogenous liquid mixture

SOLVABLE *adj* capable of being solved

SOLVATE *v* -VATED, -VATING, -VATES to convert into a type of ion

SOLVE *v* SOLVED, SOLVING, SOLVES to find the answer or explanation for

SOLVENCY *n* pl. -CIES the ability to pay all debts

SOLVENT *n* pl. -S a substance capable of dissolving others

SOLVER *n* pl. -S one that solves

SOLVING present participle of solve

SOMA *n* pl. -MATA or -MAS the body of an organism **SOMATIC** *adj*

SOMBER *adj* gloomy **SOMBERLY** *adv*

SOMBRE *adj* somber **SOMBRELY** *adv*

SOMBRERO *n* pl. -ROS a broad-brimmed hat

SOMBROUS *adj* somber

SOME *adj* being an unspecified number or part

SOMEBODY *n* pl. -BODIES an important person

SOMEDAY *adv* at some future time

SOMEDEAL *adv* to some degree

SOMEHOW *adv* by some means

SOMEONE *n* pl. -S a somebody

SOMERSET *v* -SETED, -SETING, -SETS or -SETTED, -SETTING, -SETS to roll the body in a complete circle, head over heels

SOMETIME *adv* at some future time

SOMEWAY *adv* somehow

SOMEWAYS *adv* someway

SOMEWHAT *n* pl. -S an unspecified number or part

SOMEWHEN *adv* sometime

SOMEWISE *adv* somehow

SOMITE *n* pl. -S a longitudinal segment of the body of some animals **SOMITAL, SOMITIC** *adj*

SON *n* pl. -S a male child

SONANCE *n* pl. -S sound

SONANT *n* pl. -S a sound uttered with vibration of the vocal cords **SONANTAL, SONANTIC** *adj*

SONAR *n* pl. -S an underwater locating device

SONARMAN *n* pl. -MEN a person who operates sonar equipment

SONATA *n* pl. -S a type of musical composition

SONATINA *n* pl. -TINAS or -TINE a short sonata

SONDE   *n* pl. -S a device for observing atmospheric phenomena

SONDER   *n* pl. -S a class of small yachts

SONE   *n* pl. -S a unit of loudness

SONG   *n* pl. -S a musical composition written or adapted for singing

SONGBIRD   *n* pl. -S a bird that utters a musical call

SONGBOOK   *n* pl. -S a book of songs

SONGFEST   *n* pl. -S an informal gathering for group singing

SONGFUL   *adj* melodious

SONGLESS   *adj* incapable of singing

SONGLIKE   *adj* resembling a song

SONGSTER   *n* pl. -S a singer

SONIC   *adj* pertaining to sound

SONICATE   *v* -CATED, -CATING, -CATES to disrupt with sound waves

SONICS   *n/pl* the science dealing with the practical applications of sound

SONLESS   *adj* having no son

SONLIKE   *adj* resembling a son

SONLY   *adj* pertaining to a son

SONNET   *v* -NETED, -NETING, -NETS or -NETTED, -NETTING, -NETS to compose a sonnet (a type of poem)

SONNY   *n* pl. -NIES a small boy

SONORANT   *n* pl. -S a type of voiced sound

SONORITY   *n* pl. -TIES the quality or state of being sonorous

SONOROUS   *adj* characterized by a full and loud sound

SONOVOX   *n* pl. -ES a sound effects device

SONSHIP   *n* pl. -S the state of being a son

SONSIE   *adj* -SIER, -SIEST sonsy

SONSY   *adj* -SIER, -SIEST comely

SOOCHONG   *n* pl. -S souchong

SOOEY   *interj* — used in calling pigs

SOON   *adv* SOONER, SOONEST in the near future

SOONER   *n* pl. -S one who settles on government land before it is officially opened for settlement

SOOT   *v* -ED, -ING, -S to cover with soot (a black substance produced by combustion)

SOOTH   *adj* SOOTHER, SOOTHEST true

SOOTH   *n* pl. -S truth

SOOTHE   *v* SOOTHED, SOOTHING, SOOTHES to restore to a quiet or normal state

SOOTHER   *n* pl. -S one that soothes

SOOTHEST   superlative of sooth

SOOTHING   present participle of soothe

SOOTHLY   *adv* in truth

SOOTHSAY   *v* -SAID, -SAYING, -SAYS to predict

SOOTY   *adj* SOOTIER, SOOTIEST covered with soot **SOOTILY** *adv*

SOP   *v* SOPPED, SOPPING, SOPS to dip or soak in a liquid

SOPH   *n* pl. -S a sophomore

SOPHIES   pl. of sophy

SOPHISM   *n* pl. -S a plausible but fallacious argument

SOPHIST   *n* pl. -S one that uses sophisms

SOPHY   *n* pl. -PHIES a ruler of Persia

SOPITE   *v* -PITED, -PITING, -PITES to put to sleep

SOPOR   *n* pl. -S an abnormally deep sleep

SOPPED   past tense of sop

SOPPING   *adj* very wet

SOPPY   *adj* -PIER, -PIEST very wet

SOPRANO   *n* pl. -NOS or -NI the highest singing voice

SORA   *n* pl. -S a marsh bird

SORB   *v* -ED, -ING, -S to take up and hold by absorption or adsorption **SORBABLE** *adj*

SORBATE   *n* pl. -S a sorbed substance

SORBENT   *n* pl. -S a substance that sorbs

SORBET   *n* pl. -S sherbet

SORBIC   *adj* pertaining to a type of fruit

SORBITOL   *n* pl. -S a chemical compound

SORBOSE   *n* pl. -S a type of sugar

SORCERER   *n* pl. -S one who practices sorcery

SORCERY   *n* pl. -CERIES alleged use of supernatural powers

SORD   *n* pl. -S a flight of mallards

SORDID   *adj* filthy **SORDIDLY** *adv*

SORDINE   *n* pl. -S a device used to muffle the tone of a musical instrument

SORDINO   *n* pl. -NI sordine

SORE   *adj* SORER, SOREST painfully sensitive to the touch

SORE	*n* pl. -S a sore area on the body	**SOTH**	*n* pl. -S sooth
SOREHEAD	*n* pl. -S a person who is easily angered or offended	**SOTOL**	*n* pl. -S a flowering plant
		SOTTISH	*adj* resembling a sot
SOREL	*n* pl. -S sorrel	**SOU**	*n* pl. -S a former French coin
SORELY	*adv* in a sore manner	**SOUARI**	*n* pl. -S a tropical tree
SORENESS	*n* pl. -ES the quality or state of being sore	**SOUBISE**	*n* pl. -S a sauce of onions and butter
SORER	comparative of sore	**SOUCAR**	*n* pl. -S a Hindu banker
SOREST	superlative of sore	**SOUCHONG**	*n* pl. -S a Chinese tea
SORGHO	*n* pl. -GHOS sorgo	**SOUDAN**	*n* pl. -S soldan
SORGHUM	*n* pl. -S a cereal grass	**SOUFFLE**	*n* pl. -S a light, baked dish
SORGO	*n* pl. -GOS a variety of sorghum	**SOUGH**	*v* -ED, -ING, -S to make a moaning or sighing sound
SORI	pl. of sorus		
SORICINE	*adj* belonging to the shrew family of mammals	**SOUGHT**	past tense of seek
SORITES	*n* pl. SORITES a type of argument used in logic **SORITIC** *adj*	**SOUL**	*n* pl. -S the spiritual aspect of human beings **SOULED, SOULLESS, SOULLIKE** *adj*
SORN	*v* -ED, -ING, -S to force oneself on others for food and lodging	**SOULFUL**	*adj* full of emotion
SORNER	*n* pl. -S one that sorns	**SOUND**	*adj* **SOUNDER, SOUNDEST** being in good health or condition
SOROCHE	*n* pl. -S mountain sickness		
SORORAL	*adj* sisterly	**SOUND**	*v* -ED, -ING, -S to make a sound (something that stimulates the auditory receptors)
SORORATE	*n* pl. -S the marriage of a man usually with his deceased wife's sister		
		SOUNDBOX	*n* pl. -ES a resonant cavity in a musical instrument
SORORITY	*n* pl. -TIES a social club for women	**SOUNDER**	*n* pl. -S one that sounds
		SOUNDING	*n* pl. -S a sampling or test of opinions
SOROSIS	*n* pl. -ROSES or -ROSISES a women's club or society		
SORPTION	*n* pl. -S the act or process of sorbing **SORPTIVE** *adj*	**SOUNDLY**	*adv* in a sound manner
		SOUP	*v* -ED, -ING, -S to increase the power or efficiency of
SORREL	*n* pl. -S a reddish brown color		
SORRIER	comparative of sorry	**SOUPCON**	*n* pl. -S a minute amount
SORRIEST	superlative of sorry	**SOUPY**	*adj* **SOUPIER, SOUPIEST** foggy
SORRILY	*adv* in a sorry manner	**SOUR**	*adj* **SOURER, SOUREST** sharp or biting to the taste
SORROW	*v* -ED, -ING, -S to grieve		
SORROWER	*n* pl. -S one that sorrows	**SOUR**	*v* -ED, -ING, -S to make or become sour
SORRY	*adj* -RIER, -RIEST feeling grief or penitence		
		SOURBALL	*n* pl. -S a sour candy
SORT	*v* -ED, -ING, -S to arrange according to kind, class, or size **SORTABLE** *adj* **SORTABLY** *adv*	**SOURCE**	*n* pl. -S a point of origin
		SOURDINE	*n* pl. -S sordine
SORTER	*n* pl. -S one that sorts	**SOURISH**	*adj* somewhat sour
SORTIE	*v* -TIED, -TIEING, -TIES to attack suddenly from a defensive position	**SOURLY**	*adv* in a sour manner
		SOURNESS	*n* pl. -ES the quality or state of being sour
SORUS	*n* pl. -RI a cluster of plant reproductive bodies	**SOURPUSS**	*n* pl. -ES a grouchy person
		SOURSOP	*n* pl. -S a tropical tree
SOT	*n* pl. -S an habitual drunkard	**SOURWOOD**	*n* pl. -S a flowering tree

SOUSE   *v* SOUSED, SOUSING, SOUSES to immerse

SOUTACHE   *n pl.* -S a flat, narrow braid

SOUTANE   *n pl.* -S a cassock

SOUTER   *n pl.* -S a shoemaker

SOUTH   *v* -ED, -ING, -S to move toward the south (a cardinal point of the compass)

SOUTHER   *n pl.* -S a wind or storm from the south

SOUTHERN   *n pl.* -S a person living in the south

SOUTHING   *n pl.* -S movement toward the south

SOUTHPAW   *n pl.* -S a left-handed person

SOUTHRON   *n pl.* -S a southern

SOUVENIR   *n pl.* -S a memento

SOVIET   *n pl.* -S a legislative body in a Communist country

SOVKHOZ   *n pl.* -KHOZES or -KHOZY a state-owned farm in the Soviet Union

SOVRAN   *n pl.* -S a monarch

SOVRANLY   *adv* supremely

SOVRANTY   *n pl.* -TIES a monarchy

SOW   *v* SOWED, SOWN, SOWING, SOWS to scatter over land for growth, as seed **SOWABLE** *adj*

SOWANS   *n pl.* SOWANS sowens

SOWAR   *n pl.* -S a mounted native soldier in India

SOWBELLY   *n pl.* -LIES pork cured in salt

SOWBREAD   *n pl.* -S a flowering plant

SOWCAR   *n pl.* -S soucar

SOWENS   *n pl.* SOWENS porridge made from oat husks

SOWER   *n pl.* -S one that sows

SOWN   past participle of sow

SOX   a *pl.* of sock

SOY   *n pl.* SOYS the soybean

SOYA   *n pl.* -S soy

SOYBEAN   *n pl.* -S the seed of a cultivated Asian herb

SOZIN   *n pl.* -S a type of protein

SOZINE   *n pl.* -S sozin

SPA   *n pl.* -S a mineral spring

SPACE   *v* SPACED, SPACING, SPACES to set some distance apart

SPACEMAN   *n pl.* -MEN an astronaut

SPACER   *n pl.* -S one that spaces

SPACIAL   *adj* spatial

SPACING   *n pl.* -S the distance between any two objects

SPACIOUS   *adj* vast or ample in extent

SPADE   *v* SPADED, SPADING, SPADES to take up with a spade (a digging implement)

SPADEFUL   *n pl.* -S as much as a spade can hold

SPADER   *n pl.* -S one that spades

SPADICES   *pl.* of spadix

SPADILLE   *n pl.* -S the highest trump in certain card games

SPADING   present participle of spade

SPADIX   *n pl.* -DICES a flower cluster

SPADO   *n pl.* -DONES a castrated man or animal

SPAE   *v* SPAED, SPAEING, SPAES to foretell

SPAEING   *n pl.* -S the act of foretelling

SPAGYRIC   *n pl.* -S a person skilled in alchemy

SPAHEE   *n pl.* -S spahi

SPAHI   *n pl.* -S a Turkish cavalryman

SPAIL   *n pl.* -S spale

SPAIT   *n pl.* -S spate

SPAKE   a past tense of speak

SPALE   *n pl.* -S a splinter or chip

SPALL   *v* -ED, -ING, -S to break up into fragments

SPALLER   *n pl.* -S one that spalls

SPALPEEN   *n pl.* -S a rascal

SPAN   *v* SPANNED, SPANNING, SPANS to extend over or across

SPANCEL   *v* -CELED, -CELING, -CELS or -CELLED, -CELLING, -CELS to bind or fetter with a rope

SPANDREL   *n pl.* -S a space between two adjoining arches

SPANDRIL   *n pl.* -S spandrel

SPANG   *adv* directly

SPANGLE   *v* -GLED, -GLING, -GLES to adorn with spangles (bits of sparkling metal)

SPANGLY   *adj* -GLIER, -GLIEST covered with spangles

SPANIEL   *n pl.* -S a dog with silky hair

SPANK v -ED, -ING, -S to slap on the buttocks

SPANKER n pl. -S one that spanks

SPANKING n pl. -S the act of one that spanks

SPANLESS adj having no extent

SPANNED past tense of span

SPANNER n pl. -S one that spans

SPANNING present participle of span

SPANWORM n pl. -S an inchworm

SPAR v SPARRED, SPARRING, SPARS to provide with spars (stout poles used to support rigging)

SPARABLE n pl. -S a type of nail

SPARE v SPARED, SPARING, SPARES to refrain from punishing, harming, or destroying

SPARE adj SPARER, SPAREST meager SPARELY adv

SPARER n pl. -S one that spares

SPARERIB n pl. -S a cut of pork

SPAREST adj superlative of spare

SPARGE v SPARGED, SPARGING, SPARGES to sprinkle

SPARGER n pl. -S one that sparges

SPARID n pl. -S any of a family of marine fishes

SPARING present participle of spare

SPARK v -ED, -ING, -S to give off sparks (small fiery particles)

SPARKER n pl. -S something that sparks

SPARKIER comparative of sparky

SPARKIEST superlative of sparky

SPARKILY adv in a lively manner

SPARKISH adj jaunty

SPARKLE v -KLED, -KLING, -KLES to give off or reflect flashes of light

SPARKLER n pl. -S something that sparkles

SPARKY adj SPARKIER, SPARKIEST lively

SPARLIKE adj resembling a spar

SPARLING n pl. -S a young herring

SPAROID n pl. -S a sparid

SPARRED past tense of spar

SPARRIER comparative of sparry

SPARRIEST superlative of sparry

SPARRING present participle of spar

SPARROW n pl. -S a small bird

SPARRY adj -RIER, -RIEST resembling spar (a lustrous mineral)

SPARSE adj SPARSER, SPARSEST thinly distributed SPARSELY adv

SPARSITY n pl. -S the quality or state of being sparse

SPASM n pl. -S an abnormal, involuntary muscular contraction

SPASTIC n pl. -S one suffering from spastic paralysis (a paralysis with muscle spasms)

SPAT v SPATTED, SPATTING, SPATS to strike lightly

SPATE n pl. -S a freshet

SPATHE n pl. -S a leaflike organ of certain plants SPATHAL, SPATHED, SPATHOSE adj

SPATHIC adj sparry

SPATIAL adj of or pertaining to space

SPATTED past tense of spat

SPATTER v -ED, -ING, -S to scatter in drops

SPATTING present participle of spat

SPATULA n pl. -S a mixing implement SPATULAR adj

SPAVIE n pl. -S spavin SPAVIET adj

SPAVIN n pl. -S a disease of horses SPAVINED adj

SPAWN v -ED, -ING, -S to deposit eggs

SPAWNER n pl. -S one that spawns

SPAY v -ED, -ING, -S to remove the ovaries of

SPEAK v SPOKE or SPAKE, SPOKEN, SPEAKING, SPEAKS to utter words

SPEAKER n pl. -S one that speaks

SPEAKING n pl. -S a speech or discourse

SPEAN v -ED, -ING, -S to wean

SPEAR v -ED, -ING, -S to pierce with a spear (a long, pointed weapon)

SPEARER n pl. -S one that spears

SPEARMAN n pl. -MEN a person armed with a spear

SPECIAL adj -CIALER, -CIALEST of a distinct or particular kind or character

SPECIAL n pl. -S a special person or thing

SPECIATE v -ATED, -ATING, -ATES to undergo a type of evolutionary process

SPECIE   n pl. -S coined money

SPECIFIC   n pl. -S a remedy intended for a particular disease

SPECIFY   v -FIED, -FYING, -FIES to state in detail

SPECIMEN   n pl. -S a part or individual representative of a group or whole

SPECIOUS   adj having a false look of truth or authenticity

SPECK   v -ED, -ING, -S to mark with small spots

SPECKLE   v -LED, -LING, -LES to speck

SPECS   n/pl eyeglasses

SPECTATE   v -TATED, -TATING, -TATES to attend and view

SPECTER   n pl. -S a visible disembodied spirit

SPECTRA   a pl. of spectrum

SPECTRAL   adj resembling a specter

SPECTRE   n pl. -S specter

SPECTRUM   n pl. -TRA or -TRUMS an array of the components of a light wave

SPECULUM   n pl. -LA or -LUMS a medical instrument SPECULAR adj

SPED   a past tense of speed

SPEECH   n pl. -ES the faculty or act of speaking

SPEED   v SPED or SPEEDED, SPEEDING, SPEEDS to move swiftly

SPEEDER   n pl. -S one that speeds

SPEEDIER   comparative of speedy

SPEEDIEST   superlative of speedy

SPEEDILY   adv in a speedy manner

SPEEDING   n pl. -S the act of driving faster than the law allows

SPEEDUP   n pl. -S an acceleration of production without an increase in pay

SPEEDWAY   n pl. -WAYS a road designed for rapid travel

SPEEDY   adj SPEEDIER, SPEEDIEST swift

SPEEL   v -ED, -ING, -S to climb

SPEER   v -ED, -ING, -S to inquire

SPEERING   n pl. -S inquiry

SPEIL   v -ED, -ING, -S to speel

SPEIR   v -ED, -ING, -S to speer

SPEISE   n pl. -S speiss

SPEISS   n pl. -ES a metallic mixture obtained in smelting certain ores

SPELAEAN   adj spelean

SPELEAN   adj living in caves

SPELL   v SPELLED or SPELT, SPELLING, SPELLS to name or write the letters of in order

SPELLER   n pl. -S one that spells words

SPELLING   n pl. -S a sequence of letters composing a word

SPELT   n pl. -S a variety of wheat

SPELTER   n pl. -S zinc in the form of ingots

SPELTZ   n pl. -ES spelt

SPELUNK   v -ED, -ING, -S to explore caves

SPENCE   n pl. -S a pantry

SPENCER   n pl. -S a trysail

SPEND   v SPENT, SPENDING, SPENDS to pay out

SPENDER   n pl. -S one that spends

SPENT   past tense of spend

SPERM   n pl. -S a male gamete SPERMIC adj

SPERMARY   n pl. -RIES an organ in which sperms are formed

SPERMINE   n pl. -S a chemical compound

SPERMOUS   adj resembling or made up of sperms

SPEW   v -ED, -ING, -S to vomit

SPEWER   n pl. -S one that spews

SPHAGNUM   n pl. -S a grayish moss

SPHENE   n pl. -S a mineral

SPHENIC   adj shaped like a wedge

SPHENOID   n pl. -S a bone of the skull

SPHERAL   adj of, pertaining to, or having the form of a sphere

SPHERE   v SPHERED, SPHERING, SPHERES to form into a sphere (a type of geometric solid)

SPHERIC   adj spheral

SPHERICS   n/pl the geometry of figures on the surface of a sphere

SPHERIER   comparative of sphery

SPHERIEST   superlative of sphery

SPHERING   present participle of sphere

SPHEROID   n pl. -S a type of geometric solid

SPHERULE   n pl. -S a small sphere

SPHERY *adj* SPHERIER, SPHERIEST resembling a sphere

SPHINGES a pl. of sphinx

SPHINGID *n* pl. -S the hawkmoth

SPHINX *n* pl. SPHINXES or SPHINGES a figure of a creature of Egyptian mythology

SPHYGMUS *n* pl. -ES the pulse SPHYGMIC *adj*

SPIC *n* pl. -S a Spanish-American person — an offensive term

SPICA *n* pl. -CAE or -CAS an ear of grain SPICATE, SPICATED *adj*

SPICCATO *n* pl. -TOS a method of playing a stringed instrument

SPICE *v* SPICED, SPICING, SPICES to season with a spice (an aromatic vegetable substance)

SPICER *n* pl. -S one that spices

SPICERY *n* pl. -ERIES a spicy quality

SPICEY *adj* SPICIER, SPICIEST spicy

SPICIER comparative of spicy

SPICIEST superlative of spicy

SPICILY *adv* in a spicy manner

SPICING present participle of spice

SPICK *n* pl. -S spic

SPICULA *n* pl. -LAE spicule SPICULAR *adj*

SPICULE *n* pl. -S a small, needlelike structure

SPICULUM *n* pl. -LA spicule

SPICY *adj* SPICIER, SPICIEST containing spices

SPIDER *n* pl. -S a type of arachnid

SPIDERY *adj* -DERIER, -DERIEST resembling a spider

SPIED past tense of spy

SPIEGEL *n* pl. -S a type of cast iron

SPIEL *v* -ED, -ING, -S to talk at length

SPIELER *n* pl. -S one that spiels

SPIER *v* -ED, -ING, -S to speer

SPIES present 3d person sing. of spy

SPIFFING *adj* spiffy

SPIFFY *adj* -FIER, -FIEST stylish SPIFFILY *adv*

SPIGOT *n* pl. -S a faucet

SPIK *n* pl. -S spic

SPIKE *v* SPIKED, SPIKING, SPIKES to fasten with a spike (a long, thick nail)

SPIKELET *n* pl. -S a type of flower cluster

SPIKER *n* pl. -S one that spikes

SPIKING present participle of spike

SPIKY *adj* SPIKIER, SPIKIEST resembling a spike SPIKILY *adv*

SPILE *v* SPILED, SPILING, SPILES to stop up with a wooden plug

SPILIKIN *n* pl. -S a strip of wood used in a game

SPILING *n* pl. -S a piling

SPILL *v* SPILLED or SPILT, SPILLING, SPILLS to cause to run out of a container

SPILLAGE *n* pl. -S something that is spilled

SPILLER *n* pl. -S one that spills

SPILLWAY *n* pl. -WAYS a channel for surplus water in a reservoir

SPILT a past tense of spill

SPILTH *n* pl. -S spillage

SPIN *v* SPUN, SPINNING, SPINS to draw out and twist into threads

SPINACH *n* pl. -ES a cultivated herb

SPINAGE *n* pl. -S spinach

SPINAL *n* pl. -S an injection of an anesthetic into the spinal cord

SPINALLY *adv* with respect to the spine

SPINATE *adj* bearing thorns

SPINDLE *v* -DLED, -DLING, -DLES to impale on a slender rod

SPINDLER *n* pl. -S one that spindles

SPINDLY *adj* -DLIER, -DLIEST long and slender

SPINE *n* pl. -S the vertebral column SPINED *adj*

SPINEL *n* pl. -S a mineral

SPINELLE *n* pl. -S spinel

SPINET *n* pl. -S a small piano

SPINIER comparative of spiny

SPINIEST superlative of spiny

SPINIFEX *n* pl. -ES an Australian grass

SPINLESS *adj* having no rotation

SPINNER *n* pl. -S one that spins

SPINNERY *n* pl. -NERIES a spinning mill

SPINNEY *n* pl. -NEYS a thicket

SPINNING n pl. -S the act of one that spins

SPINNY n pl. -NIES spinney

SPINOFF n pl. -S a new application or incidental result

SPINOR n pl. -S a type of mathematical vector

SPINOSE adj spiny

SPINOUS adj spiny

SPINOUT n pl. -S a rotational skid by an automobile

SPINSTER n pl. -S an unmarried woman who is past the usual age for marrying

SPINULA n pl. -LAE spinule

SPINULE n pl. -S a small thorn

SPINY adj SPINIER, SPINIEST bearing or covered with thorns

SPIRACLE n pl. -S an orifice through which breathing occurs

SPIRAEA n pl. -S spirea

SPIRAL v -RALED, -RALING, -RALS or -RALLED, -RALLING, -RALS to move like a spiral (a type of plane curve)

SPIRALLY adv in a spiral manner

SPIRANT n pl. -S a speech sound produced by the forcing of breath through a narrow passage

SPIRE v SPIRED, SPIRING, SPIRES to rise in a tapering manner

SPIREA n pl. -S a flowering shrub

SPIREM n pl. -S spireme

SPIREME n pl. -S a filament forming part of a cell nucleus during mitosis

SPIRILLA n/pl spirally twisted, aerobic bacteria

SPIRING present participle of spire

SPIRIT v -ED, -ING, -S to carry off secretly

SPIROID adj resembling a spiral

SPIRT v -ED, -ING, -S to spurt

SPIRULA n pl. -LAE or -LAS a spiral-shelled mollusk

SPIRY adj tall, slender, and tapering

SPIT v SPITTED, SPITTING, SPITS to impale on a spit (a pointed rod on which meat is turned)

SPITAL n pl. -S a hospital

SPITBALL n pl. -S a type of pitch in baseball

SPITE v SPITED, SPITING, SPITES to treat with malice

SPITEFUL adj -FULLER, -FULLEST malicious

SPITFIRE n pl. -S a quick-tempered person

SPITING present participle of spite

SPITTED past tense of spit

SPITTER n pl. -S a spitball

SPITTING present participle of spit

SPITTLE n pl. -S saliva

SPITTOON n pl. -S a receptacle for saliva

SPITZ n pl. -ES a dog having a heavy coat

SPIV n pl. -S a petty criminal

SPLAKE n pl. -S a freshwater fish

SPLASH v -ED, -ING, -ES to scatter a liquid about

SPLASHER n pl. -S one that splashes

SPLASHY adj SPLASHIER, SPLASHIEST showy

SPLAT n pl. -S a piece of wood forming the middle of a chair back

SPLATTER v -ED, -ING, -S to spatter

SPLAY v -ED, -ING, -S to spread out

SPLEEN n pl. -S a ductless organ of the body

SPLEENY adj SPLEENIER, SPLEENIEST peevish

SPLENDID adj -DIDER, -DIDEST magnificent

SPLENDOR n pl. -S magnificence

SPLENIA pl. of splenium

SPLENIAL adj pertaining to the splenius

SPLENIC adj pertaining to the spleen

SPLENIUM n pl. -NIA a surgical bandage

SPLENIUS n pl. -NII a muscle of the neck

SPLENT n pl. -S a splint

SPLICE v SPLICED, SPLICING, SPLICES to join at the ends

SPLICER n pl. -S one that splices

SPLINE v SPLINED, SPLINING, SPLINES to provide with a spline (a key that connects two rotating mechanical parts)

SPLINT v -ED, -ING, -S to brace with a splint (a thin piece of wood)

SPLINTER v -ED, -ING, -S to split into sharp, slender pieces

SPLIT v SPLIT, SPLITTING, SPLITS to separate lengthwise

SPLITTER n pl. -S one that splits

SPLORE n pl. -S a carousal

SPLOSH v -ED, -ING, -ES to splash

SPLOTCH v -ED, -ING, -ES to mark with large, irregular spots

SPLOTCHY adj SPLOTCHIER, SPLOTCHIEST splotched

SPLURGE v SPLURGED, SPLURGING, SPLURGES to spend money lavishly

SPLURGY adj SPLURGIER, SPLURGIEST tending to splurge

SPLUTTER v -ED, -ING, -S to speak rapidly and confusedly

SPODE n pl. -S a fine china

SPOIL v SPOILED or SPOILT, SPOILING, SPOILS to impair the value or quality of

SPOILAGE n pl. -S something that is spoiled or wasted

SPOILER n pl. -S one that spoils

SPOILT a past tense of spoil

SPOKE v SPOKED, SPOKING, SPOKES to provide with spokes (rods that support the rim of a wheel)

SPOKEN past participle of speak

SPOLIATE v -ATED, -ATING, -ATES to plunder

SPONDAIC n pl. -S a spondee

SPONDEE n pl. -S a type of metrical foot

SPONGE v SPONGED, SPONGING, SPONGES to wipe with a sponge (a mass of absorbent material)

SPONGER n pl. -S one that sponges

SPONGIER comparative of spongy

SPONGIEST superlative of spongy

SPONGILY adv in a spongy manner

SPONGIN n pl. -S a fibrous material

SPONGING present participle of sponge

SPONGY adj SPONGIER, SPONGIEST resembling a sponge

SPONSAL adj pertaining to marriage

SPONSION n pl. -S the act of sponsoring

SPONSON n pl. -S a projection from the side of a ship

SPONSOR v -ED, -ING, -S to make oneself responsible for

SPONTOON n pl. -S a spear-like weapon

SPOOF v -ED, -ING, -S to hoax

SPOOK v -ED, -ING, -S to scare

SPOOKISH adj spooky

SPOOKY adj SPOOKIER, SPOOKIEST scary SPOOKILY adv

SPOOL v -ED, -ING, -S to wind on a small cylinder

SPOON v -ED, -ING, -S to take up with a spoon (a type of eating utensil)

SPOONEY adj SPOONIER, SPOONIEST spoony

SPOONEY n pl. -EYS a spoony

SPOONFUL n pl. SPOONFULS or SPOONSFUL as much as a spoon will hold

SPOONIER comparative of spooney

SPOONIES pl. of spooney

SPOONIEST superlative of spooney

SPOONING present participle of spoon

SPOONY adj SPOONIER, SPOONIEST overly sentimental SPOONILY adv

SPOONY n pl. SPOONIES a spoony person

SPOOR v -ED, -ING, -S to track

SPORADIC adj occurring at irregular intervals

SPORAL adj of, pertaining to, or resembling a spore

SPORE v SPORED, SPORING, SPORES to produce spores (asexual, usually single-celled reproductive bodies)

SPOROID adj resembling a spore

SPORRAN n pl. -S a large purse worn by Scottish Highlanders

SPORT v -ED, -ING, -S to frolic

SPORTER n pl. -S one that sports

SPORTFUL adj sportive

SPORTIVE adj playful

SPORTY adj SPORTIER, SPORTIEST showy SPORTILY adv

SPORULE n pl. -S a small spore SPORULAR adj

SPOT v SPOTTED, SPOTTING, SPOTS to mark with spots (small, roundish discolorations)

SPOTLESS adj perfectly clean

SPOTTER   n pl. -S one that spots

SPOTTING   present participle of spot

SPOTTY   adj -TIER, -TIEST marked with spots **SPOTTILY** adv

SPOUSAL   n pl. -S marriage

SPOUSE   v SPOUSED, SPOUSING, SPOUSES to marry

SPOUT   v -ED, -ING, -S to eject in a rapid stream

SPOUTER   n pl. -S one that spouts

SPRADDLE   v -DLED, -DLING, -DLES to straddle

SPRAG   n pl. -S a device used to prevent a vehicle from rolling backward

SPRAIN   v -ED, -ING, -S to weaken by a sudden and violent twisting or wrenching

SPRANG   a past tense of spring

SPRAT   n pl. -S a small herring

SPRATTLE   v -TLED, -TLING, -TLES to struggle

SPRAWL   v -ED, -ING, -S to stretch out ungracefully

SPRAWLER   n pl. -S one that sprawls

SPRAWLY   adj SPRAWLIER, SPRAWLIEST tending to sprawl

SPRAY   v -ED, -ING, -S to disperse in fine particles

SPRAYER   n pl. -S one that sprays

SPREAD   v SPREAD, SPREADING, SPREADS to open or expand over a larger area

SPREADER   n pl. -S one that spreads

SPREE   n pl. -S an unrestrained indulgence in an activity

SPRENT   adj sprinkled over

SPRIER   a comparative of spry

SPRIEST   a superlative of spry

SPRIG   v SPRIGGED, SPRIGGING, SPRIGS to fasten with small, thin nails

SPRIGGER   n pl. -S one that sprigs

SPRIGGY   adj -GIER, -GIEST having small branches

SPRIGHT   n pl. -S sprite

SPRING   v SPRANG or SPRUNG, SPRINGING, SPRINGS to move upward suddenly and swiftly

SPRINGAL   n pl. -S a young man

SPRINGE   v SPRINGED, SPRINGEING, SPRINGES to catch with a type of snare

SPRINGER   n pl. -S one that springs

SPRINGY   adj SPRINGIER, SPRINGIEST resilient

SPRINKLE   v -KLED, -KLING, -KLES to scatter drops or particles on

SPRINT   v -ED, -ING, -S to run at top speed

SPRINTER   n pl. -S one that sprints

SPRIT   n pl. -S a ship's spar

SPRITE   n pl. -S an elf or fairy

SPROCKET   n pl. -S a toothlike projection that engages with the links of a chain

SPROUT   v -ED, -ING, -S to begin to grow

SPRUCE   adj SPRUCER, SPRUCEST neat and trim in appearance **SPRUCELY** adv

SPRUCE   v SPRUCED, SPRUCING, SPRUCES to make spruce

SPRUCY   adj SPRUCIER, SPRUCIEST spruce

SPRUE   n pl. -S a tropical disease

SPRUG   n pl. -S a sparrow

SPRUNG   a past tense of spring

SPRY   adj SPRYER, SPRYEST or SPRIER, SPRIEST nimble **SPRYLY** adv

SPRYNESS   n pl. -ES the quality or state of being spry

SPUD   v SPUDDED, SPUDDING, SPUDS to remove with a spade-like tool

SPUDDER   n pl. -S a tool for removing bark from trees

SPUE   v SPUED, SPUING, SPUES to spew

SPUME   v SPUMED, SPUMING, SPUMES to foam

SPUMIER   comparative of spumy

SPUMIEST   superlative of spumy

SPUMING   present participle of spume

SPUMONE   n pl. -S an Italian ice cream

SPUMONI   n pl. -S spumone

SPUMOUS   adj spumy

SPUMY   adj SPUMIER, SPUMIEST foamy

SPUN   past tense of spin

SPUNK   v -ED, -ING, -S to begin to burn

SPUNKIE   n pl. -S a light caused by the combustion of marsh gas

SPUNKY   adj SPUNKIER, SPUNKIEST plucky **SPUNKILY** adv

SPUR   v SPURRED, SPURRING, SPURS to urge on with a spur (a horseman's goad)

SPURGALL   v -ED, -ING, -S to injure with a spur

SPURGE   n pl. -S a tropical plant

SPURIOUS   adj not genuine

SPURN   v -ED, -ING, -S to reject with contempt

SPURNER   n pl. -S one that spurns

SPURRED   past tense of spur

SPURRER   n pl. -S one that spurs

SPURREY   n pl. -REYS spurry

SPURRIER   n pl. -S one that makes spurs

SPURRING   present participle of spur

SPURRY   n pl. -RIES a European weed

SPURT   v -ED, -ING, -S to gush forth

SPURTLE   n pl. -S a stick for stirring porridge

SPUTA   pl. of sputum

SPUTNIK   n pl. -S a Soviet artificial earth satellite

SPUTTER   v -ED, -ING, -S to eject particles in short bursts

SPUTUM   n pl. -TA saliva

SPY   v SPIED, SPYING, SPIES to watch secretly

SPYGLASS   n pl. -ES a small telescope

SQUAB   n pl. -S a young pigeon

SQUABBLE   v -BLED, -BLING, -BLES to quarrel

SQUABBY   adj -BIER, -BIEST short and fat

SQUAD   v SQUADDED, SQUADDING, SQUADS to form into squads (small, organized groups)

SQUADRON   v -ED, -ING, -S to arrange in squadrons (units of military organization)

SQUALENE   n pl. -S a chemical compound

SQUALID   adj -IDER, -IDEST marked by filthiness caused by neglect or poverty

SQUALL   v -ED, -ING, -S to cry or scream loudly

SQUALLER   n pl. -S one that squalls

SQUALLY   adj SQUALLIER, SQUALLIEST gusty

SQUALOR   n pl. -S the quality or state of being squalid

SQUAMA   n pl. -MAE a scale **SQUAMATE, SQUAMOSE, SQUAMOUS** adj

SQUANDER   v -ED, -ING, -S to spend wastefully

SQUARE   adj SQUARER, SQUAREST having four equal sides and four right angles

SQUARE   v SQUARED, SQUARING, SQUARES to make square

SQUARELY   adv in a direct manner

SQUARER   n pl. -S one that squares

SQUAREST   superlative of square

SQUARING   present participle of square

SQUARISH   adj somewhat square

SQUASH   v -ED, -ING, -ES to press into a pulp or flat mass

SQUASHER   n pl. -S one that squashes

SQUASHY   adj SQUASHIER, SQUASHIEST soft and moist

SQUAT   v SQUATTED, SQUATTING, SQUATS to sit on one's heels

SQUAT   adj SQUATTER, SQUATTEST short and thick **SQUATLY** adv

SQUATTER   v -ED, -ING, -S to move through water

SQUATTING   present participle of squat

SQUATTY   adj -TIER, -TIEST squat

SQUAW   n pl. -S an American Indian woman

SQUAWK   v -ED, -ING, -S to utter a loud, harsh cry

SQUAWKER   n pl. -S one that squawks

SQUEAK   v -ED, -ING, -S to make a sharp, high-pitched sound

SQUEAKER   n pl. -S one that squeaks

SQUEAKY   adj SQUEAKIER, SQUEAKIEST tending to squeak

SQUEAL   v -ED, -ING, -S to utter a sharp, shrill cry

SQUEALER   n pl. -S one that squeals

SQUEEGEE   v -GEED, -GEEING, -GEES to wipe with a squeegee (an implement for removing water from a surface)

SQUEEZE   v SQUEEZED, SQUEEZING, SQUEEZES to press hard upon

SQUEEZER	n pl. -S one that squeezes
SQUEG	v SQUEGGED, SQUEGGING, SQUEGS to oscillate in an irregular manner
SQUELCH	v -ED, -ING, -ES to squash
SQUELCHY	adj SQUELCHIER, SQUELCHIEST squashy
SQUIB	v SQUIBBED, SQUIBBING, SQUIBS to lampoon
SQUID	v SQUIDDED, SQUIDDING, SQUIDS to fish for squid (ten-armed marine mollusks)
SQUIFFED	adj drunk
SQUIFFY	adj squiffed
SQUIGGLE	v -GLED, -GLING, -GLES to wriggle
SQUIGGLY	adj -GLIER, -GLIEST wriggly
SQUILGEE	v -GEED, -GEEING, -GEES to squeegee
SQUILL	n pl. -S a Eurasian herb
SQUILLA	n pl. -LAS or -LAE a burrowing crustacean
SQUINCH	v -ED, -ING, -ES to squint
SQUINNY	v -NIED, -NYING, -NIES to squint
SQUINNY	adj -NIER, -NIEST squinty
SQUINT	adj SQUINTER, SQUINTEST cross-eyed
SQUINT	v -ED, -ING, -S to look with the eyes partly closed
SQUINTER	n pl. -S one that squints
SQUINTY	adj SQUINTIER, SQUINTIEST marked by squinting
SQUIRE	v SQUIRED, SQUIRING, SQUIRES to serve as a squire (an escort)
SQUIREEN	n pl. -S an owner of a small estate
SQUIRISH	adj of, resembling, or befitting a squire
SQUIRM	v -ED, -ING, -S to wriggle
SQUIRMER	n pl. -S one that squirms
SQUIRMY	adj SQUIRMIER, SQUIRMIEST wriggly
SQUIRREL	v -RELED, -RELING, -RELS or -RELLED, -RELLING, -RELS to store up for future use
SQUIRT	v -ED, -ING, -S to eject in a thin, swift stream
SQUIRTER	n pl. -S one that squirts
SQUISH	v -ED, -ING, -ES to squash

SQUISHY	adj SQUISHIER, SQUISHIEST squashy
SQUOOSH	v -ED, -ING, -ES to squash
SQUUSH	v -ED, -ING, -ES to squash
SRADDHA	n pl. -S sradha
SRADHA	n pl. -S a Hindu ceremonial offering
SRI	n pl. -S mister; sir — used as a Hindu title of respect
STAB	v STABBED, STABBING, STABS to pierce with a pointed weapon
STABBER	n pl. -S one that stabs
STABILE	n pl. -S a stationary abstract sculpture
STABLE	adj -BLER, -BLEST resistant to sudden change or position or condition
STABLE	v -BLED, -BLING, -BLES to put in a stable (a shelter for domestic animals)
STABLER	n pl. -S one that keeps a stable
STABLEST	superlative of stable
STABLING	n pl. -S accommodation for animals in a stable
STABLISH	v -ED, -ING, -ES to establish
STABLY	adv in a stable manner
STACCATO	n pl. -TOS or -TI a musical passage marked by the short, clear-cut playing of tones
STACK	v -ED, -ING, -S to pile
STACKER	n pl. -S one that stacks
STACTE	n pl. -S a spice used by the ancient Jews in making incense
STADDLE	n pl. -S a platform on which hay is stacked
STADE	n pl. -S an ancient Greek unit of length
STADIA	n pl. -S a method of surveying distances
STADIUM	n pl. -S a structure in which athletic events are held
STAFF	v -ED, -ING, -S to provide with a staff (a body of assistants)
STAFFER	n pl. -S a member of a staff
STAG	v STAGGED, STAGGING, STAGS to attend a social function without a female companion
STAGE	v STAGED, STAGING, STAGES to produce for public view
STAGER	n pl. -S an experienced person
STAGEY	adj STAGIER, STAGIEST stagy

STAGGARD *n* pl. -S a full-grown male red deer

STAGGART *n* pl. -S staggard

STAGGED past tense of stag

STAGGER *v* -ED, -ING, -S to walk or stand unsteadily

STAGGERY *adj* unsteady

STAGGIE *n* pl. -S a colt

STAGGING present participle of stag

STAGGY *adj* -GIER, -GIEST having the appearance of a mature male

STAGIER comparative of stagey and stagy

STAGIEST superlative of stagey and stagy

STAGILY *adv* in a stagy manner

STAGING *n* pl. -S a temporary platform

STAGNANT *adj* not moving or flowing

STAGNATE *v* -NATED, -NATING, -NATES to become stagnant

STAGY *adj* STAGIER, STAGIEST having a theatrical quality

STAID *adj* STAIDER, STAIDEST sober and sedate **STAIDLY** *adv*

STAIG *n* pl. -S a colt

STAIN *v* -ED, -ING, -S to discolor or dirty

STAINER *n* pl. -S one that stains

STAIR *n* pl. -S a rest for the foot used in going from one level to another

STAIRWAY *n* pl. -WAYS a flight of stairs

STAKE *v* STAKED, STAKING, STAKES to fasten with a stake (a pointed piece of wood or metal)

STAKEOUT *n* pl. -S a surveillance of an area especially by the police

STALAG *n* pl. -S a German prisoner-of-war camp

STALE *adj* STALER, STALEST not fresh **STALELY** *adv*

STALE *v* STALED, STALING, STALES to become stale

STALK *v* -ED, -ING, -S to pursue stealthily

STALKER *n* pl. -S one that stalks

STALKY *adj* STALKIER, STALKIEST long and slender **STALKILY** *adv*

STALL *v* -ED, -ING, -S to stop the progress of

STALLION *n* pl. -S an uncastrated male horse

STALWART *n* pl. -S an unwavering partisan

STAMEN *n* pl. -S the pollen-bearing organ of flowering plants

STAMINA *n* pl. -S endurance **STAMINAL** *adj*

STAMMEL *n* pl. -S a red color

STAMMER *v* -ED, -ING, -S to speak with involuntary breaks and pauses

STAMP *v* -ED, -ING, -S to bring the foot down heavily

STAMPEDE *v* -PEDED, -PEDING, -PEDES to cause to run away in headlong panic

STAMPER *n* pl. -S one that stamps

STANCE *n* pl. -S a manner of standing

STANCH *adj* STANCHER, STANCHEST staunch

STANCH *v* -ED, -ING, -ES to stop the flow of blood from

STANCHER *n* pl. -S one that stanches

STANCHLY *adv* in a stanch manner

STAND *v* STOOD, STANDING, STANDS to assume or maintain an upright position

STANDARD *n* pl. -S an established measure of comparison

STANDBY *n* pl. -BYS one that can be relied on

STANDEE *n* pl. -S one who stands because of the lack of seats

STANDER *n* pl. -S one that stands

STANDING *n* pl. -S a position or condition in society

STANDISH *n* pl. -ES a receptacle for pens and ink

STANDOFF *n* pl. -S a tie or draw, as in a game

STANDOUT *n* pl. -S one that shows marked superiority

STANDPAT *adj* resisting or opposing change

STANDUP *adj* having an upright position

STANE *v* STANED, STANING, STANES to stone

STANG *v* -ED, -ING, -S to sting

STANHOPE *n* pl. -S a light, open carriage

STANING present participle of stane

STANK *n* pl. -S a pond

STANNARY *n* pl. -RIES a tin-mining region

STANNIC *adj* pertaining to tin

STANNITE n pl. -S an ore of tin

STANNOUS adj pertaining to tin

STANNUM n pl. -S tin

STANZA n pl. -S a division of a poem **STANZAED, STANZAIC** adj

STAPEDES pl. of stapes

STAPELIA n pl. -S an African plant

STAPES n pl. -PEDES a bone of the middle ear

STAPH n pl. -S any of various spherical bacteria

STAPLE v -PLED, -PLING, -PLES to fasten by means of a U-shaped metal loop

STAPLER n pl. -S a stapling device

STAR v STARRED, STARRING, STARS to shine as a star (a natural luminous body visible in the sky)

STARCH v -ED, -ING, -ES to treat with starch (a solid carbohydrate)

STARCHY adj STARCHIER, STARCHIEST containing starch

STARDOM n pl. -S the status of a preeminent performer

STARDUST n pl. -S a romantic quality

STARE v STARED, STARING, STARES to gaze fixedly

STARER n pl. -S one that stares

STARETS n pl. STARTSY a spiritual adviser in the Eastern Orthodox Church.

STARFISH n pl. -ES a star-shaped marine animal

STARGAZE v -GAZED, -GAZING, -GAZES to gaze at the stars

STARING present participle of stare

STARK adj STARKER, STARKEST harsh in appearance **STARKLY** adv

STARLESS adj having no stars

STARLET n pl. -S a small star

STARLIKE adj resembling a star

STARLING n pl. -S a European bird

STARLIT adj lighted by the stars

STARNOSE n pl. -S a burrowing mammal

STARRED past tense of star

STARRING present participle of star

STARRY adj -RIER, -RIEST abounding with stars

START v -ED, -ING, -S to set out

STARTER n pl. -S one that starts

STARTLE v -TLED, -TLING, -TLES to frighten or surprise suddenly

STARTLER n pl. -S one that startles

STARTSY pl. of starets

STARVE v STARVED, STARVING, STARVES to die from lack of food

STARVER n pl. -S one that starves

STARWORT n pl. -S a flowering plant

STASES pl. of stasis

STASH v -ED, -ING, -ES to store in a secret place

STASIMON n pl. -MA a choral ode in ancient Greek drama

STASIS n pl. STASES a stoppage of the normal flow of bodily fluids

STATABLE adj capable of being stated

STATAL adj pertaining to a national government

STATANT adj standing with all feet on the ground — used of a heraldic animal

STATE v STATED, STATING, STATES to set forth in words

STATEDLY adv regularly

STATELY adj -LIER, -LIEST dignified

STATER n pl. -S one that states

STATIC n pl. -S random noise produced in a radio or television receiver **STATICAL** adj

STATICE n pl. -S a flowering plant

STATING present participle of state

STATION v -ED, -ING, -S to assign to a position

STATISM n pl. -S a theory of government

STATIST n pl. -S an adherent of statism

STATIVE n pl. -S a verb that expresses a condition

STATOR n pl. -S the part of a machine about which the rotor revolves

STATUARY n pl. -ARIES a group of statues

STATUE n pl. -S a three-dimensional work of art **STATUED** adj

STATURE n pl. -S the natural height of a human or animal body

STATUS n pl. -ES relative position

STATUTE n pl. -S a law enacted by the legislative branch of a government

STAUMREL n pl. -S a dolt

STAUNCH	adj STAUNCHER, STAUNCHEST firm and dependable	**STEEL**	v -ED, -ING, -S to cover with steel (a tough iron alloy)
STAUNCH	v -ED, -ING, -ES to stanch	**STEELIE**	n pl. -S a steel playing marble
STAVE	v STAVED or STOVE, STAVING, STAVES to drive or thrust away	**STEELY**	adj STEELIER, STEELIEST resembling steel
STAW	a past tense of steal	**STEENBOK**	n pl. -S an African antelope
STAY	v STAYED or STAID, STAYING, STAYS to continue in a place or condition	**STEEP**	adj STEEPER, STEEPEST inclined sharply
		STEEP	v -ED, -ING, -S to soak in a liquid
STAYER	n pl. -S one that stays		
STAYSAIL	n pl. -S a type of sail	**STEEPEN**	v -ED, -ING, -S to make steep
STEAD	v -ED, -ING, -S to be of advantage to	**STEEPER**	n pl. -S one that steeps
STEADIED	past tense of steady	**STEEPLE**	n pl. -S a tapering structure on a church tower STEEPLED adj
STEADIER	n pl. -S one that steadies	**STEEPLY**	adv in a steep manner
STEADIES	present 3d person sing. of steady	**STEER**	v -ED, -ING, -S to direct the course of
STEADING	n pl. -S a small farm		
STEADY	adj STEADIER, STEADIEST firm in position STEADILY adv	**STEERAGE**	n pl. -S the act of steering
		STEERER	n pl. -S one that steers
STEADY	v STEADIED, STEADYING, STEADIES to make steady	**STEEVE**	v STEEVED, STEEVING, STEEVES to stow in the hold of a ship
STEAK	n pl. -S a slice of meat		
STEAL	v STOLE or STAW, STOLEN, STEALING, STEALS to take without right or permission	**STEEVING**	n pl. -S the angular elevation of a bowsprit from a ship's keel
		STEGODON	n pl. -S an extinct elephant-like mammal
STEALAGE	n pl. -S theft		
STEALER	n pl. -S one that steals	**STEIN**	n pl. -S a beer mug
STEALING	n pl. -S the act of one that steals	**STEINBOK**	n pl. -S steenbok
		STELA	n pl. -LAE or -LAI an inscribed slab used as a monument STELAR, STELENE adj
STEALTH	n pl. -S stealthy procedure		
STEALTHY	adj STEALTHIER, STEALTHIEST intended to escape observation	**STELE**	n pl. -S the central portion of vascular tissue in a plant stem STELIC adj
STEAM	v -ED, -ING, -S to expose to steam (water in the form of vapor)		
		STELLA	n pl. -S a former coin of the United States
STEAMER	v -ED, -ING, -S to travel by steamship	**STELLAR**	adj pertaining to the stars
		STELLATE	adj shaped like a star
STEAMY	adj STEAMIER, STEAMIEST marked by steam STEAMILY adv	**STELLIFY**	v -FIED, -FYING, -FIES to convert into a star
STEAPSIN	n pl. -S an enzyme	**STEM**	v STEMMED, STEMMING, STEMS to remove stems (ascending axes of a plant) from
STEARATE	n pl. -S a chemical salt		
STEARIN	n pl. -S the solid portion of a fat STEARIC adj	**STEMLESS**	adj having no stem
STEARINE	n pl. -S stearin	**STEMLIKE**	adj resembling a stem
STEATITE	n pl. -S a variety of talc	**STEMMA**	n pl. -MAS or -MATA a scroll recording the genealogy of a family in ancient Rome
STEDFAST	adj staunch		
STEED	n pl. -S a horse	**STEMMED**	past tense of stem
STEEK	v -ED, -ING, -S to shut	**STEMMER**	n pl. -S one that removes stems

STEMMERY n pl. -MERIES a place where tobacco leaves are stripped

STEMMING present participle of stem

STEMMY adj -MIER, -MIEST abounding in stems

STEMSON n pl. -S a supporting timber of a ship

STEMWARE n pl. -S a type of glassware

STENCH n pl. -ES a foul odor

STENCHY adj STENCHIER, STENCHIEST having a stench

STENCIL v -CILED, -CILING, -CILS or -CILLED, -CILLING, -CILS to merk by means of a perforated sheet of material

STENGAH n pl. -S a mixed drink

STENO n pl. STENOS a stenographer

STENOSED adj affected with stenosis

STENOSIS n pl. -NOSES a narrowing of a bodily passage **STENOTIC** adj

STENTOR n pl. -S a person having a very loud voice

STEP v STEPPED, STEPPING, STEPS to move by lifting the foot and setting it down in another place

STEPDAME n pl. -S a stepmother

STEPLIKE adj resembling a stair

STEPPE n pl. -S a vast treeless plain

STEPPED past tense of step

STEPPER n pl. -S one that steps

STEPPING present participle of step

STEPSON n pl. -S a son of one's spouse by a former marriage

STEPWISE adj marked by a gradual progression

STERE n pl. -S a unit of volume

STEREO v -ED, -ING, -S to make a type of printing plate

STERIC adj pertaining to the spatial relationships of the atoms in a molecule

STERICAL adj steric

STERIGMA n pl. -MAS or -MATA a spore-bearing stalk of certain fungi

STERILE adj incapable of producing offspring

STERLET n pl. -S a small sturgeon

STERLING n pl. -S British money

STERN adj STERNER, STERNEST unyielding

STERN n pl. -S the rear part of a ship

STERNA a pl. of sternum

STERNAL adj pertaining to the sternum

STERNITE n pl. -S a somitic sclerite

STERNLY adv in a stern manner

STERNSON n pl. -S a reinforcing post of a ship

STERNUM n pl. -NA or -NUMS a long, flat supporting bone of most vertebrates

STERNWAY n pl. -WAYS the backward movement of a vessel

STEROID n pl. -S a type of chemical compound

STEROL n pl. -S a type of solid alcohol

STERTOR n pl. -S a deep snoring sound

STET v STETTED, STETTING, STETS to cancel a previously made printing correction

STETSON n pl. -S a broad-brimmed hat

STEW v -ED, -ING, -S to cook by boiling slowly

STEWARD v -ED, -ING, -S to manage

STEWBUM n pl. -S a drunken bum

STEWPAN n pl. -S a pan used for stewing

STEY adj steep

STHENIA n pl. -S excessive energy **STHENIC** adj

STIBIAL adj pertaining to stibium

STIBINE n pl. -S a poisonous gas

STIBIUM n pl. -S antimony

STIBNITE n pl. -S an ore of antimony

STICH n pl. -S a line of poetry **STICHIC** adj

STICK v -ED, -ING, -S to support with slender pieces of wood

STICK v STUCK, STICKING, STICKS to pierce with a pointed object

STICKER n pl. -S an adhesive label

STICKFUL n pl. -S an amount of set type

STICKIER comparative of sticky

STICKIEST superlative of sticky

STICKILY adv in a sticky manner

STICKIT adj unsuccessful

STICKLE v -LED, -LING, -LES to argue stubbornly

STICKLER n pl. -S one that stickles

STICKMAN n pl. -MEN one who supervises the play at a dice table

STICKOUT *n* pl. -S one that is conspicuous

STICKPIN *n* pl. -S a decorative tiepin

STICKUM *n* pl. -S a substance that causes adhesion

STICKUP *n* pl. -S a robbery at gunpoint

STICKY *adj* STICKIER, STICKIEST tending to adhere

STIED a past tense of sty

STIES present 3d person sing. of sty

STIFF *adj* STIFFER, STIFFEST difficult to bend or stretch

STIFF *n* pl. -S a corpse

STIFFEN *v* -ED, -ING, -S to make stiff

STIFFISH *adj* somewhat stiff

STIFFLY *adv* in a stiff manner

STIFLE *v* -FLED, -FLING, -FLES to smother

STIFLER *n* pl. -S one that stifles

STIGMA *n* pl. -MAS or -MATA a mark of disgrace STIGMAL *adj*

STILBENE *n* pl. -S a chemical compound

STILBITE *n* pl. -S a mineral

STILE *n* pl. -S a series of steps for passing over a fence or wall

STILETTO *v* -ED, -ING, -S or -ES to stab with a short dagger

STILL *adj* STILLER, STILLEST free from sound or motion

STILL *v* -ED, -ING, -S to make still

STILLMAN *n* pl. -MEN one who operates a distillery

STILLY *adj* STILLIER, STILLIEST still

STILT *v* -ED, -ING, -S to raise on stilts (long, slender poles)

STIME *n* pl. -S a glimpse

STIMULUS *n* pl. -LI something that causes a response

STIMY *v* -MIED, -MYING, -MIES to stymie

STING *v* STUNG, STINGING, STINGS to prick painfully

STINGER *n* pl. -S one that stings

STINGIER comparative of stingy

STINGIEST superlative of stingy

STINGILY *adv* in a stingy manner

STINGO *n* pl. -GOS a strong ale or beer

STINGRAY *n* pl. -RAYS a flat-bodied marine fish

STINGY *adj* -GIER, -GIEST unwilling to spend or give

STINK *v* STANK or STUNK, STINKING, STINKS to emit a foul odor

STINKARD *n* pl. -S a despicable person

STINKBUG *n* pl. -S an insect that emits a foul odor

STINKER *n* pl. -S one that stinks

STINKIER comparative of stinky

STINKIEST superlative of stinky

STINKO *adj* drunk

STINKPOT *n* pl. -S a jar containing foul-smelling combustibles formerly used in warfare

STINKY *adj* STINKIER, STINKIEST emitting a foul odor

STINT *v* -ED, -ING, -S to limit

STINTER *n* pl. -S one that stints

STIPE *n* pl. -S a slender supporting part of a plant STIPED *adj*

STIPEL *n* pl. -S a small stipule

STIPEND *n* pl. -S a fixed sum of money paid periodically

STIPES *n* pl. STIPITES a stipe

STIPPLE *v* -PLED, -PLING, -PLES to draw, paint, or engrave by means of dots or short touches

STIPPLER *n* pl. -S one that stipples

STIPULE *n* pl. -S an appendage at the base of a leaf in certain plants STIPULAR, STIPULED *adj*

STIR *v* STIRRED, STIRRING, STIRS to pass an implement through in circular motions

STIRK *n* pl. -S a young cow

STIRP *n* pl. -S lineage

STIRPS *n* pl. STIRPES a family or branch of a family

STIRRED past tense of stir

STIRRER *n* pl. -S one that stirs

STIRRING present participle of stir

STIRRUP *n* pl. -S a support for the foot of a horseman

STITCH *v* -ED, -ING, -ES to join by making in-and-out movements with a threaded needle

STITCHER *n* pl. -S one that stitches

STITHY *v* STITHIED, STITHYING, STITHIES to forge on an anvil

STIVER *n* pl. -S a former Dutch coin

STOA   n pl. STOAE, STOAI, or STOAS an ancient Greek covered walkway

STOAT   n pl. -S a weasel with a black-tipped tail

STOB   v STOBBED, STOBBING, STOBS to stab

STOCCADO   n pl. -DOS a thrust with a rapier

STOCCATA   n pl. -S stoccado

STOCK   v -ED, -ING, -S to keep for future sale or use

STOCKADE   v -ADED, -ADING, -ADES to build a type of protective fence around

STOCKCAR   n pl. -S a boxcar for carrying livestock

STOCKER   n pl. -S a young animal suitable for being fattened for market

STOCKIER   comparative of stocky

STOCKIEST   superlative of stocky

STOCKILY   adv in a stocky manner

STOCKING   n pl. -S a knitted or woven covering for the foot and leg

STOCKISH   adj stupid

STOCKIST   n pl. -S one who stocks goods

STOCKMAN   n pl. -MEN one who owns or raises livestock

STOCKPOT   n pl. -S a pot in which broth is prepared

STOCKY   adj STOCKIER, STOCKIEST having a short, thick body

STODGE   v STODGED, STODGING, STODGES to stuff full with food

STODGY   adj STODGIER, STODGIEST boring STODGILY adv

STOGEY   n pl. -GEYS stogy

STOGIE   n pl. -S stogy

STOGY   n pl. -GIES a long, slender cigar

STOIC   n pl. -S one who is indifferent to pleasure or pain STOICAL adj

STOICISM   n pl. -S indifference to pleasure or pain

STOKE   v STOKED, STOKING, STOKES to supply a furnace with fuel

STOKER   n pl. -S one that stokes

STOKESIA   n pl. -S a perennial herb

STOKING   present participle of stoke

STOLE   n pl. -S a long-wide scarf STOLED adj

STOLEN   past participle of steal

STOLID   adj -IDER, -IDEST showing little or no emotion STOLIDLY adv

STOLLEN   n pl. -S a sweet bread

STOLON   n pl. -S a type of plant stem STOLONIC adj

STOMA   n pl. -MAS or -MATA a minute opening in the epidermis of a plant organ

STOMACH   v -ED, -ING, -S to tolerate

STOMACHY   adj paunchy

STOMAL   adj stomatal

STOMATA   a pl. of stoma

STOMATAL   adj pertaining to a stoma

STOMATE   n pl. -S a stoma

STOMATIC   adj pertaining to the mouth

STOMODEA   n/pl embryonic oral cavities

STOMP   v -ED, -ING, -S to tread heavily

STOMPER   n pl. -S one that stomps

STONE   v STONED, STONING, STONES to pelt with stones (pieces of concreted earthy or mineral matter) STONABLE adj

STONEFLY   n pl. -FLIES a winged insect

STONER   n pl. -S one that stones

STONEY   adj STONIER, STONIEST stony

STONIER   comparative of stony

STONIEST   superlative of stony

STONILY   adv in a stony manner

STONING   present participle of stone

STONISH   v -ED, -ING, -ES to astonish

STONY   adj STONIER, STONIEST abounding in stones

STOOD   past tense of stand

STOOGE   v STOOGED, STOOGING, STOOGES to act as a comedian's straight man

STOOK   v -ED, -ING, -S to stack upright in a field for drying, as bundles of grain

STOOKER   n pl. -S one that stooks

STOOL   v -ED, -ING, -S to defecate

STOOLIE   n pl. -S an informer

STOOP   v -ED, -ING, -S to bend the body forward and down

STOOPER   n pl. -S one that stoops

STOP   v STOPPED or STOPT, STOPPING, STOPS to discontinue the progress or motion of

STOPCOCK   *n pl.* -S a type of faucet

STOPE   *v* STOPED, STOPING, STOPES to excavate in layers, as ore

STOPER   *n pl.* -S one that stopes

STOPGAP   *n pl.* -S a temporary substitute

STOPING   present participle of stope

STOPOVER   *n pl.* -S a brief stop in the course of a journey

STOPPAGE   *n pl.* -S the act of stopping

STOPPED   a past tense of stop

STOPPER   *v* -ED, -ING, -S to plug

STOPPING   present participle of stop

STOPPLE   *v* -PLED, -PLING, -PLES to stopper

STOPT   a past tense of stop

STORABLE   *n pl.* -S something that can be stored

STORAGE   *n pl.* -S a place for storing

STORAX   *n pl.* -ES a fragrant resin

STORE   *v* STORED, STORING, STORES to put away for future use

STOREY   *n pl.* -REYS a horizontal division of a building STOREYED *adj*

STORIED   past tense of story

STORIES   present 3d person sing. of story

STORING   present participle of store

STORK   *n pl.* -S a wading bird

STORM   *v* -ED, -ING, -S to blow violently

STORMY   *adj* STORMIER, STORMIEST storming STORMILY *adv*

STORY   *v* -RIED, -RYING, -RIES to relate as a story (an account of an event or series of events)

STOSS   *adj* facing the direction from which a glacier moves

STOTINKA   *n pl.* -KI a monetary unit of Bulgaria

STOUND   *v* -ED, -ING, -S to ache

STOUP   *n pl.* -S a basin for holy water

STOUR   *n pl.* -S dust

STOURE   *n pl.* -S atour

STOURIE   *adj* stoury

STOURY   *adj* dusty

STOUT   *adj* STOUTER, STOUTEST fat

STOUT   *n pl.* -S a strong, dark ale

STOUTEN   *v* -ED, -ING, -S to make stout

STOUTISH   *adj* somewhat stout

STOUTLY   *adv* in a stout manner

STOVE   *n pl.* -S a heating apparatus

STOVER   *n pl.* -S coarse food for cattle

STOW   *v* -ED, -ING, -S to pack STOWABLE *adj*

STOWAGE   *n pl.* -S goods in storage

STOWAWAY   *n pl.* -AWAYS one who hides aboard a conveyance to obtain free passage

STOWP   *n pl.* -S stoup

STRADDLE   *v* -DLED, -DLING, -DLES to sit, stand, or walk with the legs wide apart

STRAFE   *v* STRAFED, STRAFING, STRAFES to attack with machine-gun fire from an airplane

STRAFER   *n pl.* -S one that strafes

STRAGGLE   *v* -GLED, -GLING, -GLES to stray

STRAGGLY   *adj* -GLIER, -GLIEST irregularly spread out

STRAIGHT   *adj* STRAIGHTER, STRAIGHTEST extending uniformly in one direction without bends or irregularities

STRAIGHT   *v* -ED, -ING, -S to make straight

STRAIN   *v* -ED, -ING, -S to exert to the utmost

STRAINER   *n pl.* -S a utensil used to separate liquids from solids

STRAIT   *n pl.* -S a narrow waterway connecting two larger bodies of water

STRAIT   *adj* STRAITER, STRAITEST narrow STRAITLY *adv*

STRAITEN   *v* -ED, -ING, -S to make strait

STRAKE   *n pl.* -S a line of planking extending along a ship's hull STRAKED *adj*

STRAMASH   *n pl.* -ES an uproar

STRAMONY   *n pl.* -NIES a poisonous weed

STRAND   *v* -ED, -ING, -S to leave in an unfavorable situation

STRANDER   *n pl.* -S a machine that twists fibers into rope

STRANG   *adj* strong

STRANGE   *adj* STRANGER, STRANGEST unusual or unfamiliar

STRANGER   *v* -ED, -ING, -S to estrange

STRANGLE   *v* -GLED, -GLING, -GLES to choke to death

STRAP *v* STRAPPED, STRAPPING, STRAPS to fasten with a strap (a narrow strip of flexible material)

STRAPPER *n pl.* -S one that straps

STRASS *n pl.* -ES a brilliant glass used in making imitation gems

STRATA *n pl.* -S a stratum

STRATAL *adj* pertaining to a stratum

STRATEGY *n pl.* -GIES a plan for obtaining a specific goal

STRATH *n pl.* -S a wide river valley

STRATI pl. of stratus

STRATIFY *v* -FIED, -FYING, -FIES to form or arrange in layers

STRATOUS *adj* stratal

STRATUM *n pl.* -TA or -TUMS a layer of material

STRATUS *n pl.* -TI a type of cloud

STRAVAGE *v* -VAGED, -VAGING, -VAGES to stroll

STRAVAIG *v* -ED, -ING, -S to stravage

STRAW *v* -ED, -ING, -S to cover with straw (stalks of threshed grain)

STRAWHAT *adj* pertaining to a summer theater situated in a resort area

STRAWY *adj* STRAWIER, STRAWIEST resembling straw

STRAY *v* -ED, -ING, -S to wander from the proper area or course

STRAYER *n pl.* -S one that strays

STREAK *v* -ED, -ING, -S to cover with streaks (long, narrow marks)

STREAKER *n pl.* -S one that streaks

STREAKY *adj* STREAKIER, STREAKIEST covered with streaks

STREAM *v* -ED, -ING, -S to flow in a steady current

STREAMER *n pl.* -S a long, narrow flag

STREAMY *adj* STREAMIER, STREAMIEST streaming

STREEK *v* -ED, -ING, -S to stretch

STREEKER *n pl.* -S one that streeks

STREET *n pl.* -S a public thoroughfare

STRENGTH *n pl.* -S capacity for exertion or endurance

STREP *n pl.* -S any of various spherical or oval bacteria

STRESS *v* -ED, -ING, -ES to place emphasis on

STRESSOR *n pl.* -S a type of stimulus

STRETCH *v* -ED, -ING, -ES to draw out or open to full length

STRETCHY *adj* STRETCHIER, STRETCHIEST having a tendency to stretch

STRETTA *n pl.* -TE or -TAS stretto

STRETTO *n pl.* -TI or -TOS a concluding musical passage played at a faster tempo

STREUSEL *n pl.* -S a topping for coffee cakes

STREW *v* STREWED, STREWN, STREWING, STREWS to scatter about

STREWER *n pl.* -S one that strews

STRIA *n pl.* STRIAE a thin groove, stripe, or streak

STRIATE *v* -ATED, -ATING, -ATES to mark with striae

STRICK *n pl.* -S a bunch of flax fibers

STRICKEN *adj* strongly affected or afflicted

STRICKLE *v* -LED, -LING, -LES to shape or smooth with a strickle (an instrument for leveling off grain)

STRICT *adj* STRICTER, STRICTEST kept within narrow and specific limits **STRICTLY** *adv*

STRIDE *v* STRODE or STRID, STRIDDEN, STRIDING, STRIDES to walk with long steps

STRIDENT *adj* shrill

STRIDER *n pl.* -S one that strides

STRIDING present participle of stride

STRIDOR *n pl.* -S a strident sound

STRIFE *n pl.* -S bitter conflict or dissension

STRIGIL *n pl.* -S a scraping instrument

STRIGOSE *adj* covered with short, stiff hairs

STRIKE *v* STRUCK or STROOK, STRICKEN or STRUCKEN, STRIKING, STRIKES to come or cause to come into contact with

STRIKER *n pl.* -S one that strikes

STRING *v* STRUNG or STRINGED, STRINGING, STRINGS to provide with strings (slender cords)

STRINGER *n pl.* -S one that strings

STRINGY *adj* STRINGIER, STRINGIEST resembling a string or strings

STRIP v STRIPPED or STRIPT, STRIPPING, STRIPS to remove the outer covering from

STRIPE v STRIPED, STRIPING, STRIPES to mark with stripes (long, distinct bands)

STRIPER n pl. -S a food and game fish

STRIPIER comparative of stripy

STRIPIEST superlative of stripy

STRIPING n pl. -S the stripes marked or painted on something

STRIPPED a past tense of strip

STRIPPER n pl. -S one that strips

STRIPPING present participle of strip

STRIPT a past tense of strip

STRIPY adj STRIPIER, STRIPIEST marked with stripes

STRIVE v STROVE or STRIVED, STRIVEN, STRIVING, STRIVES to exert much effort or energy

STRIVER n pl. -S one that strives

STROBE n pl. -S a device that produces brief, high-intensity flashes of light

STROBIC adj spinning

STROBIL n pl. -S a strobile

STROBILA n pl. -LAE the entire body of a tapeworm

STROBILE n pl. -S the conical, multiple fruit of certain trees

STROBILI n/pl strobiles

STRODE a past tense of stride

STROKE v STROKED, STROKING, STROKES to rub gently

STROKER n pl. -S one that strokes

STROLL v -ED, -ING, -S to walk in a leisurely manner

STROLLER n pl. -S one that strolls

STROMA n pl. -MATA the substance that forms the framework of an organ or cell STROMAL adj

STRONG adj STRONGER, STRONGEST having great strength STRONGLY adv

STRONGYL n pl. -S a parasitic worm

STRONTIA n pl. -S a chemical compound STRONTIC adj

STROOK a past tense of strike

STROP v STROPPED, STROPPING, STROPS to sharpen on a strip of leather

STROPHE n pl. -S a part of an ancient Greek choral ode STROPHIC adj

STROUD n pl. -S a coarse woolen blanket

STROVE a past tense of strive

STROW v STROWED, STROWN, STROWING, STROWS to strew

STROY v -ED, -ING, -S to destroy

STROYER n pl. -S one that stroys

STRUCK a past tense of strike

STRUCKEN a past participle of strike

STRUDEL n pl. -S a type of pastry

STRUGGLE v -GLED, -GLING, -GLES to make strenuous efforts against opposition

STRUM v STRUMMED, STRUMMING, STRUMS to play a stringed instrument by running the fingers lightly across the strings

STRUMA n pl. -MAE or -MAS scrofula

STRUMMER n pl. -S one that strums

STRUMMING present participle of strum

STRUMOSE adj having a struma

STRUMOUS adj having or pertaining to a struma

STRUMPET n pl. -S a prostitute

STRUNG a past tense of string

STRUNT v -ED, -ING, -S to strut

STRUT v STRUTTED, STRUTTING, STRUTS to walk with a pompous air

STRUTTER n pl. -S one that struts

STUB v STUBBED, STUBBING, STUBS to strike accidentally against a projecting object

STUBBIER comparative of stubby

STUBBIEST superlative of stubby

STUBBILY adv in a stubby manner

STUBBING present participle of stub

STUBBLE n pl. -S a short, rough growth of beard STUBBLED adj

STUBBLY adj -BLIER, -BLIEST covered with stubble

STUBBORN adj unyielding

STUBBY adj -BIER, -BIEST short and thick

STUCCO v -ED, -ING, -ES or -S to coat with a type of plaster

STUCCOER n pl. -S one that stuccoes

STUCK past tense of stick

STUD   v STUDDED, STUDDING, STUDS to set thickly with small projections

STUDBOOK   n pl. -S a record of the pedigree of purebred animals

STUDDIE   n pl. -S an anvil

STUDDING   n pl. -S the framework of a wall

STUDENT   n pl. -S a person formally engaged in learning

STUDFISH   n pl. -ES a freshwater fish

STUDIED   past tense of study

STUDIER   n pl. -S one that studies

STUDIES   present 3d person sing. of study

STUDIO   n pl. -DIOS an artist's workroom

STUDIOUS   adj given to study

STUDWORK   n pl. -S studding

STUDY   v STUDIED, STUDYING, STUDIES to apply the mind to the acquisition of knowledge

STUFF   v -ED, -ING, -S to fill or pack tightly

STUFFER   n pl. -S one that stuffs

STUFFING   n pl. -S material with which something is stuffed

STUFFY   adj STUFFIER, STUFFIEST poorly ventilated STUFFILY adv

STUIVER   n pl. -S a stiver

STULL   n pl. -S a supporting timber in a mine

STULTIFY   v -FIED, -FYING, -FIES to cause to appear absurd

STUM   v STUMMED, STUMMING, STUMS to increase the fermentation of by adding grape juice

STUMBLE   v -BLED, -BLING, -BLES to miss one's step in walking or running

STUMBLER   n pl. -S one that stumbles

STUMMED   past tense of stum

STUMMING   present participle of stum

STUMP   v -ED, -ING, -S to baffle

STUMPAGE   n pl. -S uncut marketable timber

STUMPER   n pl. -S a baffling question

STUMPY   adj STUMPIER, STUMPIEST short and thick

STUN   v STUNNED, STUNNING, STUNS to render senseless or incapable of action

STUNG   past tense of sting

STUNK   a past tense of stink

STUNNED   past tense of stun

STUNNER   n pl. -S one that stuns

STUNNING   adj strikingly beautiful or attractive

STUNSAIL   n pl. -S a type of sail

STUNT   v -ED, -ING, -S to hinder the normal growth of

STUPA   n pl. -S a Buddhist shrine

STUPE   n pl. -S a medicated cloth to be applied to a wound

STUPEFY   v -FIED, -FYING, -FIES to dull the senses of

STUPID   adj -PIDER, -PIDEST mentally slow STUPIDLY adv

STUPID   n pl. -S a stupid person

STUPOR   n pl. -S a state of reduced sensibility

STURDY   adj -DIER, -DIEST strong and durable STURDILY adv

STURDY   n pl. -DIES a disease of sheep STURDIED adj

STURGEON   n pl. -S an edible fish

STURT   n pl. -S contention

STUTTER   v -ED, -ING, -S to speak with spasmodic repetition

STY   v STIED or STYED, STYING, STIES to keep in a pigpen

STYE   n pl. -S an inflamed swelling of the eyelid

STYGIAN   adj gloomy

STYLAR   adj pertaining to a stylus

STYLATE   adj bearing a stylet

STYLE   v STYLED, STYLING, STYLES to name

STYLER   n pl. -S one that styles

STYLET   n pl. -S a small, stiff organ or appendage of certain animals

STYLI   a pl. of stylus

STYLING   n pl. -S the way in which something is styled

STYLISE   v -ISED, -ISING, -ISES to stylize

STYLISER   n pl. -S one that stylises

STYLISH   adj fashionable

STYLISING   present participle of stylise

STYLIST   n pl. -S one who is a master of a literary or rhetorical style

STYLITE   n pl. -S an early Christian ascetic STYLITIC adj

STYLIZE v -IZED, -IZING, -IZES to make conventional

STYLIZER n pl. -S one that stylizes

STYLOID adj slender and pointed

STYLUS n pl. -LI or -LUSES a pointed instrument for writing, marking, or engraving

STYMIE v -MIED, -MIEING, -MIES to thwart

STYMY v -MIED, -MYING, -MIES to stymie

STYPSIS n pl. -SISES the use of a styptic

STYPTIC n pl. -S a substance used to check bleeding

STYRAX n pl. -ES storax

STYRENE n pl. -S a liquid hydrocarbon

SUABLE adj capable of being sued SUABLY adv

SUASION n pl. -S persuasion SUASIVE, SUASORY adj

SUAVE adj SUAVER, SUAVEST smoothly affable and polite SUAVELY adv

SUAVITY n pl. -TIES the state of being suave

SUB v SUBBED, SUBBING, SUBS to act as a substitute

SUBA n pl. -S subah

SUBABBOT n pl. -S a subordinate abbot

SUBACID adj slightly sour

SUBACRID adj somewhat acrid

SUBACUTE adj somewhat acute

SUBADAR n pl. -S subahdar

SUBADULT n pl. -S an individual approaching adulthood

SUBAGENT n pl. -S a subordinate agent

SUBAH n pl. -S a province of India

SUBAHDAR n pl. -S a governor of a subah

SUBALAR adj somewhat alar

SUBAREA n pl. -S a subdivision of an area

SUBARID adj somewhat arid

SUBATOM n pl. -S a component of an atom

SUBAXIAL adj somewhat axial

SUBBASE n pl. -S the lowest part of a base

SUBBASS n pl. -ES a pedal stop producing the lowest tones of an organ

SUBBED past tense of sub

SUBBING n pl. -S a thin coating on the support of a photographic film

SUBBREED n pl. -S a distinguishable strain within a breed

SUBCAUSE n pl. -S a subordinate cause

SUBCELL n pl. -S a subdivision of a cell

SUBCHIEF n pl. -S a subordinate chief

SUBCLAN n pl. -S a subdivision of a clan

SUBCLASS v -ED, -ING, -ES to place in a subdivision of a class

SUBCLERK n pl. -S a subordinate clerk

SUBCOOL v -ED, -ING, -S to cool below the freezing point without solidification

SUBCUTIS n pl. -CUTES or -CUTISES the deeper part of the dermis

SUBDEAN n pl. -S a subordinate dean

SUBDEB n pl. -S a girl the year before she becomes a debutante

SUBDEPOT n pl. -S a military depot that operates under the jurisdiction of another depot

SUBDUAL n pl. -S the act of subduing

SUBDUCE v -DUCED, -DUCING, -DUCES to take away

SUBDUCT v -ED, -ING, -S to subduce

SUBDUE v -DUED, -DUING, -DUES to bring under control

SUBDUER n pl. -S one that subdues

SUBECHO n pl. -ECHOES an inferior echo

SUBEDIT v -ED, -ING, -S to act as the assistant editor of

SUBENTRY n pl. -TRIES an entry made under a more general entry

SUBEPOCH n pl. -S a subdivision of an epoch

SUBER n pl. -S phellem

SUBERECT adj nearly erect

SUBERIC adj pertaining to cork

SUBERIN n pl. -S a substance found in cork cells

SUBERISE v -ISED, -ISING, -ISES to suberize

SUBERIZE v -IZED, -IZING, -IZES to convert into cork tissue

SUBEROSE adj corky

SUBEROUS adj suberose

SUBFIELD n pl. -S a subset of a mathematical field that is itself a field

SUBFIX   *n* pl. -ES a distinguishing symbol or letter written below another character

SUBFLOOR   *n* pl. -S a rough floor laid as a base for a finished floor

SUBFLUID   *adj* somewhat fluid

SUBFUSC   *adj* dark in color

SUBGENUS   *n* pl. -GENERA or -GENUSES a subdivision of a genus

SUBGRADE   *n* pl. -S a surface on which a pavement is placed

SUBGROUP   *n* pl. -S a distinct group within a group

SUBGUM   *adj* prepared with mixed vegetables

SUBHEAD   *n* pl. -S the heading of a subdivision

SUBHUMAN   *n* pl. -S one that is less than human

SUBHUMID   *adj* somewhat humid

SUBIDEA   *n* pl. -S an inferior idea

SUBINDEX   *n* pl. -DEXES or -DICES a subfix

SUBITEM   *n* pl. -S an item that forms a subdivision of a larger topic

SUBITO   *adv* quickly — used as a musical direction

SUBJECT   *v* -ED, -ING, -S to cause to experience

SUBJOIN   *v* -ED, -ING, -S to add at the end

SUBLATE   *v* -LATED, -LATING, -LATES to cancel

SUBLEASE   *v* -LEASED, -LEASING, -LEASES to sublet

SUBLET   *v* -LET, -LETTING, -LETS to rent leased property to another

SUBLEVEL   *n* pl. -S a lower level

SUBLIME   *adj* -LIMER, -LIMEST of elevated or noble quality

SUBLIME   *v* -LIMED, -LIMING, -LIMES to make sublime

SUBLIMER   *n* pl. -S one that sublimes

SUBLIMEST   superlative of sublime

SUBLIMING   present participle of sublime

SUBMERGE   *v* -MERGED, -MERGING, -MERGES to place below the surface of a liquid

SUBMERSE   *v* -MERSED, -MERSING, -MERSES to submerge

SUBMISS   *adj* inclined to submit

SUBMIT   *v* -MITTED, -MITTING, -MITS to yield to the power of another

SUBNASAL   *adj* situated under the nose

SUBNODAL   *adj* situated under a node

SUBOPTIC   *adj* situated under the eyes

SUBORAL   *adj* situated under the mouth

SUBORDER   *n* pl. -S a category of related families within an order

SUBORN   *v* -ED, -ING, -S to induce to commit perjury

SUBORNER   *n* pl. -S one that suborns

SUBOVAL   *adj* nearly oval

SUBOVATE   *adj* nearly ovate

SUBOXIDE   *n* pl. -S an oxide containing relatively little oxygen

SUBPAR   *adj* below par

SUBPART   *n* pl. -S a subdivision of a part

SUBPENA   *v* -ED, -ING, -S to subpoena

SUBPHYLA   *n/pl* divisions within a phylum

SUBPLOT   *n* pl. -S a secondary literary plot

SUBPOENA   *v* -ED, -ING, -S to summon with a type of judicial writ

SUBPOLAR   *adj* situated just outside the polar circles

SUBPUBIC   *adj* situated under the pubis

SUBRACE   *n* pl. -S a subdivision of a race

SUBRENT   *n* pl. -S rent from a subtenant

SUBRING   *n* pl. -S a subset of a mathematical ring that is itself a ring

SUBRULE   *n* pl. -S a subordinate rule

SUBSALE   *n* pl. -S a resale of purchased goods

SUBSECT   *n* pl. -S a sect directly derived from another

SUBSERE   *n* pl. -S a type of ecological succession

SUBSERVE   *v* -SERVED, -SERVING, -SERVES to serve to promote

SUBSET   *n* pl. -S a mathematical set contained within a larger set

SUBSHAFT   *n* pl. -S a shaft that is beneath another shaft

SUBSHRUB   *n* pl. -S a low shrub

SUBSIDE   *v* -SIDED, -SIDING, -SIDES to sink to a lower or normal level

SUBSIDER   *n* pl. -S one that subsides

SUBSIDY   *n* pl. -DIES a grant or contribution of money

SUBSIST v -ED, -ING, -S to continue to exist

SUBSOIL v -ED, -ING, -S to plow so as to turn up the subsoil (the layer of earth beneath the surface soil)

SUBSOLAR adj situated directly beneath the sun

SUBSONIC adj moving at a speed less than that of sound

SUBSPACE n pl. -S a subset of a mathematical space

SUBSTAGE n pl. -S a part of a microscope for supporting accessories

SUBSUME v -SUMED, -SUMING, -SUMES to classify within a larger category

SUBTEEN n pl. -S a person approaching the teenage years

SUBTEND v -ED, -ING, -S to extend under or opposite to

SUBTEXT n pl. -S written or printed matter under a more general text

SUBTILE adj -TILER, -TILEST subtle

SUBTILTY n pl. -TIES subtlety

SUBTITLE v -TLED, -TLING, -TLES to give a secondary title to

SUBTLE adj -TLER, -TLEST so slight as to be difficult to detect **SUBTLY** adj

SUBTLETY n pl. -TIES the state of being subtle

SUBTONE n pl. -S a low or subdued tone

SUBTONIC n pl. -S a type of musical tone

SUBTOPIC n pl. -S a secondary topic

SUBTOTAL v -TALED, -TALING, -TALS or -TALLED, -TALLING, -TALS to total a portion of

SUBTRACT v -ED, -ING, -S to take away

SUBTRIBE n pl. -S a subdivision of a tribe

SUBTUNIC n pl. -S a tunic worn under another tunic

SUBTYPE n pl. -S a type that is subordinate to or included in another type

SUBULATE adj slender and tapering to a point

SUBUNIT n pl. -S a unit that is a part of a larger unit

SUBURB n pl. -S a residential area adjacent to a city **SUBURBED** adj

SUBURBAN n pl. -S one who lives in a suburb

SUBURBIA n pl. -S the suburbs of a city

SUBVENE v -VENED, -VENING, -VENES to arrive or occur as a support or relief

SUBVERT v -ED, -ING, -S to destroy completely

SUBVICAR n pl. -S a subordinate vicar

SUBVIRAL adj pertaining to a part of a virus

SUBVOCAL adj mentally formulated as words

SUBWAY n pl. -WAYS an underground railroad

SUBZONE n pl. -S a subdivision of a zone

SUCCAH n pl. -CAHS or -COTH sukkah

SUCCEED v -ED, -ING, -S to accomplish something desired or intended

SUCCESS n pl. -ES the attainment of something desired or intended

SUCCINCT adj -CINCTER, -CINCTEST clearly expressed in few words

SUCCINIC adj pertaining to amber

SUCCINYL n pl. -S a univalent radical

SUCCOR v -ED, -ING, -S to go to the aid of

SUCCORER n pl. -S one that succors

SUCCORY n pl. -RIES chicory

SUCCOTH a pl. of succah

SUCCOUR v -ED, -ING, -S to succor

SUCCUBA n pl. -BAE a succubus

SUCCUBUS n pl. -BI or -BUSES a female demon

SUCCUMB v -ED, -ING, -S to yield to superior force

SUCCUSS v -ED, -ING, -ES to shake violently

SUCH adj of that kind

SUCHLIKE adj of a similar kind

SUCHNESS n pl. -ES essential or characteristic quality

SUCK v -ED, -ING, -S to draw in by establishing a partial vacuum

SUCKER v -ED, -ING, -S to strip of lower shoots or branches

SUCKFISH n pl. -ES a remora

SUCKLE v -LED, -LING, -LES to give milk from the breast

SUCKLER n pl. -S one that suckles

SUCKLESS adj having no juice

SUCKLING n pl. -S a young mammal that has not been weaned

SUCRASE n pl. -S an enzyme

SUCRE n pl. -S a monetary unit of Ecuador

SUCROSE n pl. -S a type of sugar

SUCTION n pl. -S the act of sucking

SUDARIUM n pl. -IA a cloth for wiping the face

SUDARY n pl. -RIES sudarium

SUDATION n pl. -S excessive sweating

SUDATORY n pl. -RIES a hot-air bath for inducing sweating

SUDD n pl. -S a floating mass of vegetation

SUDDEN adj happening quickly and without warning **SUDDENLY** adv

SUDDEN n pl. -S a sudden occurrence

SUDOR n pl. -S sweat **SUDORAL** adj

SUDS v -ED, -ING, -ES to wash in soapy water

SUDSER n pl. -S one that sudses

SUDSLESS adj having no suds

SUDSY adj SUDSIER, SUDSIEST foamy

SUE v SUED, SUING, SUES to institute legal proceedings against

SUEDE v SUEDED, SUEDING, SUEDES to finish leather with a soft, napped surface

SUER n pl. -S one that sues

SUET n pl. -S the hard, fatty tissue around the kidneys of cattle and sheep **SUETY** adj

SUFFARI n pl. -S a safari

SUFFER v -ED, -ING, -S to feel pain or distress

SUFFERER n pl. -S one that suffers

SUFFICE v -FICED, -FICING, -FICES to be adequate

SUFFICER n pl. -S one that suffices

SUFFIX v -ED, -ING, -ES to add as a suffix (a form affixed to the end of a root word)

SUFFIXAL adj pertaining to or being a suffix

SUFFLATE v -FLATED, -FLATING, -FLATES to inflate

SUFFRAGE n pl. -S the right to vote

SUFFUSE v -FUSED, -FUSING, -FUSES to spread through or over

SUGAR v -ED, -ING, -S to cover with sugar (a sweet carbohydrate)

SUGARY adj -ARIER, -ARIEST containing or resembling sugar

SUGGEST v -ED, -ING, -S to bring or put forward for consideration

SUGH v -ED, -ING, -S to sough

SUICIDAL adj self-destructive

SUICIDE v -CIDED, -CIDING, -CIDES to kill oneself intentionally

SUING present participle of sue

SUINT n pl. -S a natural grease found in the wool of sheep

SUIT v -ED, -ING, -S to be appropriate to

SUITABLE adj appropriate **SUITABLY** adv

SUITCASE n pl. -S a flat, rectangular piece of luggage

SUITE n pl. -S a series of things forming a unit

SUITING n pl. -S fabric for making suits

SUITLIKE adj resembling a suit (a set of garments)

SUITOR n pl. -S one that is courting a woman

SUKIYAKI n pl. -S a Japanese dish

SUKKAH n pl. -KAHS or -KOTH a temporary shelter in which meals are eaten during a Jewish festival

SULCATE adj having long, narrow furrows

SULCATED adj sulcate

SULCUS n pl. -CI furrow

SULDAN n pl. -S soldan

SULFA n pl. -S a bacteria-inhibiting drug

SULFATE v -FATED, -FATING, -FATES to treat with sulfuric acid

SULFID n pl. -S sulfide

SULFIDE n pl. -S a sulfur compound

SULFINYL n pl. -S a bivalent radical

SULFITE n pl. -S a chemical salt **SULFITIC** adj

SULFO adj sulfonic

SULFONAL n pl. -S a sulfone used as a sedative

SULFONE n pl. -S a sulfur compound

SULFONIC adj containing a certain univalent radical

SULFONYL n pl. -S a bivalent radical

SULFUR *v* -ED, -ING, -S to treat with sulfur (a nonmetallic element)

SULFURET *v* -RETED, -RETING, -RETS or -RETTED, -RETTING, -RETS to treat with sulfur

SULPURIC *adj* pertaining to sulfur

SULFURY *adj* resembling sulfur

SULFURYL *n pl.* -S sulfonyl

SULK *v* -ED, -ING, -S to be sulky

SULKER *n pl.* -S one that sulks

SULKY *adj* SULKIER, SULKIEST sullenly aloof or withdrawn **SULKILY** *adv*

SULKY *n pl.* SULKIES a light horse-drawn vehicle

SULLAGE *n pl.* -S sewage

SULLEN *adj* -LENER, -LENEST showing a brooding ill humor or resentment **SULLENLY** *adv*

SULLY *v* -LIED, -LYING, -LIES to soil

SULPHA *n pl.* -S sulfa

SULPHATE *v* -PHATED, -PHATING, -PHATES to sulfate

SULPHID *n pl.* -S sulfide

SULPHIDE *n pl.* -S sulfide

SULPHITE *n pl.* -S sulfite

SULPHONE *n pl.* -S sulfone

SULPHUR *v* -ED, -ING, -S to sulfor

SULPHURY *adj* sulfury

SULTAN *n pl.* -S the ruler of a Muslim country **SULTANIC** *adj*

SULTANA *n pl.* -S a sultan's wife

SULTRY *adj* -TRIER, -TRIEST very hot and humid **SULTRILY** *adv*

SUM *v* SUMMED, SUMMING, SUMS to add into one total

SUMAC *n pl.* -S a flowering tree or shrub

SUMACH *n pl.* -S sumac

SUMLESS *adj* too large for calculation

SUMMA *n pl.* -MAE or -MAS a comprehensive work covering a specific subject

SUMMABLE *adj* capable of being summed

SUMMAND *n pl.* -S an addend

SUMMARY *n pl.* -RIES a condensation of the substance of a larger work

SUMMATE *v* -MATED, -MATING, -MATES to sum

SUMMED past tense of sum

SUMMER *v* -ED, -ING, -S to pass the summer (the warmest season of the year)

SUMMERLY *adj* summery

SUMMERY *adj* -MERIER, -MERIEST characteristic of summer

SUMMING present participle of sum

SUMMIT *n pl.* -S the highest point **SUMMITAL** *adj*

SUMMITRY *n pl.* -RIES the use of conferences between chiefs of state for international negotiation

SUMMON *v* -ED, -ING, -S to order to appear

SUMMONER *n pl.* -S one that summons

SUMMONS *v* -ED, -ING, -ES to summon with a court order

SUMO *n pl.* -MOS a Japanese form of wrestling

SUMP *n pl.* -S a low area serving as a drain or receptacle for liquids

SUMPTER *n pl.* -S a pack animal

SUMPWEED *n pl.* -S a marsh plant

SUN *v* SUNNED, SUNNING, SUNS to expose to the sun (the star around which the earth revolves)

SUNBACK *adj* cut low to expose the back to sunlight

SUNBAKED *adj* baked by the sun

SUNBATH *n pl.* -S an exposure to sunlight

SUNBATHE *v* -BATHED, -BATHING, -BATHES to take a sunbath

SUNBEAM *n pl.* -S a beam of sunlight

SUNBIRD *n pl.* -S a tropical bird

SUNBOW *n pl.* -S an arc of spectral colors formed by the sun shining through a mist

SUNBURN *v* -BURNED or -BURNT, -BURNING, -BURNS to burn or discolor from exposure to the sun

SUNBURST *n pl.* -S a burst of sunlight

SUNDAE *n pl.* -S a dish of ice cream served with a topping

SUNDER *v* -ED, -ING, -S to break apart

SUNDERER *n pl.* -S one that sunders

SUNDEW *n pl.* -S a marsh plant

SUNDIAL *n pl.* -S a type of time-telling device

SUNDOG *n pl.* -S a small rainbow

SUNDOWN   n pl. -S sunset

SUNDRIES   n/pl miscellaneous items

SUNDROPS   n pl. SUNDROPS a flowering plant

SUNDRY   adj miscellaneous

SUNFAST   adj resistant to fading by the sun

SUNFISH   n pl. -ES a marine fish

SUNG   past participle of sing

SUNGLASS   n pl. -ES a lens for concentrating the sun's rays in order to produce heat

SUNGLOW   n pl. -S a glow in the sky caused by the sun

SUNK   a past participle of sink

SUNKEN   a past participle of sink

SUNKET   n pl. -S a tidbit

SUNLAMP   n pl. -S a lamp that radiates ultraviolet rays

SUNLAND   n pl. -S an area marked by a great amount of sunshine

SUNLESS   adj having no sunlight

SUNLIGHT   n pl. -S the light of the sun

SUNLIKE   adj resembling the sun

SUNLIT   adj lighted by the sun

SUNN   n pl. -S an East Indian shrub

SUNNA   n pl. -S the body of traditional Muslim law

SUNNED   past tense of sun

SUNNING   present participle of sun

SUNNY   adj -NIER, -NIEST filled with sunlight SUNNILY adv

SUNRISE   n pl. -S the ascent of the sun above the horizon in the morning

SUNROOF   n pl. -S an automobile roof having an openable panel

SUNROOM   n pl. -S a room built to admit a great amount of sunlight

SUNSCALD   n pl. -S an injury of woody plants caused by the sun

SUNSET   n pl. -S the descent of the sun below the horizon in the evening

SUNSHADE   n pl. -S something used as a protection from the sun

SUNSHINE   n pl. -S the light of the sun SUNSHINY adj

SUNSPOT   n pl. -S a dark spot on the surface of the sun

SUNSTONE   n pl. -S a variety of quartz

SUNSUIT   n pl. -S an outfit worn for sunbathing

SUNTAN   n pl. -S a brown color on the skin produced by exposure to the sun

SUNUP   n pl. -S sunrise

SUNWARD   adv toward the sun

SUNWARDS   adv sunward

SUNWISE   adv from left to right

SUP   v SUPPED, SUPPING, SUPS to eat supper

SUPE   n pl. -S an actor without a speaking part

SUPER   v -ED, -ING, -S to reinforce with a thin cotton mesh, as a book

SUPERADD   n pl. -ED, -ING, -S to add further

SUPERB   adj -PERBER, -PERBEST of excellent quality SUPERBLY adv

SUPEREGO   n pl -EGOS a part of the psyche

SUPERFIX   n pl -ES a recurrent pattern of stress in speech

SUPERIOR   n pl. -S one of higher rank, quality, or authority than another

SUPERJET   n pl -S a type of jet airplane

SUPERLIE   v -LAY, -LAIN, -LYING, -LIES to lie above

SUPERMAN   n pl -MEN a hypothetical superior man

SUPERNAL   adj pertaining to the sky

SUPERSEX   n pl -ES a type of sterile organism

SUPERTAX   n pl -ES an additional tax

SUPINATE   v -NATED, -NATING, -NATES to turn so that the palm is facing upward

SUPINE   n pl -S a Latin verbal noun

SUPINELY   adv in an inactive manner

SUPPED   past tense of sup

SUPPER   n pl -S an evening meal

SUPPING   present participle of sup

SUPPLANT   v -ED, -ING, -S to take the place of

SUPPLE   adj -PLER, -PLEST pliant SUPPLELY adv

SUPPLE   v -PLED, -PLING -PLES to make supple

SUPPLIER   n pl -S one that supplies

SUPPLY   v -PLIED, -PLYING -PLIES to furnish with what is needed

SUPPORT *v* -ED, -ING, -S to hold up or add strength to

SUPPOSAL *n* pl. -S something supposed

SUPPOSE *v* -POSED, -POSING, -POSES to assume to be true

SUPPOSER *n* pl. -S one that supposes

SUPPRESS *v* -ED, -ING, -ES to put an end to forcibly

SUPRA *adv* above

SUPREME *adj* -PREMER, -PREMEST highest in power or authority

SURA *n* pl. -S a chapter of the Koran

SURAH *n* pl. -S a silk fabric

SURAL *adj* pertaining to the calf of the leg

SURBASE *n* pl. -S a molding or border above the base of a structure SURBASED *adj*

SURCEASE *v* -CEASED, -CEASING, -CEASES to cease

SURCOAT *n* pl. -S an outer coat or cloak

SURD *n* pl. -S a voiceless speech sound

SURE *adj* SURER, SUREST free from doubt

SUREFIRE *adj* sure to meet expectations

SURELY *adv* certainly

SURENESS *n* pl. -ES the state of being sure

SURER comparative of sure

SUREST superlative of sure

SURETY *n* pl. -TIES sureness

SURF *v* -ED, -ING, -S to ride breaking waves on a long, narrow board SURFABLE *adj*

SURFACE *v* -FACED, -FACING, -FACES to apply an outer layer to

SURFACER *n* pl. -S one that surfaces

SURFBIRD *n* pl. -S a shore bird

SURFBOAT *n* pl. -S a strong rowboat

SURFEIT *v* -ED, -ING, -S to supply to excess

SURFER *n* pl. -S one that surfs

SURFFISH *n* pl. -ES a marine fish

SURFIER comparative of surfy

SURFIEST superlative of surfy

SURFING *n* pl. -S the act or sport of riding the surf (breaking waves)

SURFLIKE *adj* resembling breaking waves

SURFY *adj* SURFIER, SURFIEST abounding in breaking waves

SURGE *v* SURGED, SURGING, SURGES to move in a swelling manner

SURGEON *n* pl. -S one who practices surgery

SURGER *n* pl. -S one that surges

SURGERY *n* pl. -GERIES the treatment of medical problems by operation

SURGICAL *adj* pertaining to surgery

SURGING present participle of surge

SURGY *adj* surging

SURICATE *n* pl. -S a burrowing mammal

SURLY *adj* -LIER, -LIEST sullenly rude SURLILY *adv*

SURMISE *v* -MISED, -MISING, -MISES to infer with little evidence

SURMISER *n* pl. -S one that surmises

SURMOUNT *v* -ED, -ING, -S to get over or across

SURNAME *v* -NAMED, -NAMING, -NAMES to give a family name to

SURNAMER *n* pl. -S one that surnames

SURPASS *v* -ED, -ING, -ES to go beyond

SURPLICE *n* pl. -S a loose-fitting vestment

SURPLUS *n* pl. -ES an excess

SURPRINT *v* -ED, -ING, -S to print over something already printed

SURPRISE *v* -PRISED, -PRISING, -PRISES to come upon suddenly and unexpectedly

SURPRIZE *v* -PRIZED, -PRIZING, -PRIZES to surprise

SURRA *n* pl. -S a disease of domestic animals

SURREAL *adj* having dreamlike qualities

SURREY *n* pl. -REYS a light carriage

SURROUND *v* -ED, -ING, -S to extend completely around

SURROYAL *n* pl. -S the topmost prong of a stag's antler

SURTAX *v* -ED, -ING, -ES to assess with an extra tax

SURTOUT *n* pl. -S a close-fitting overcoat

SURVEIL *v* -ED, -ING, -S to watch closely

SURVEY *v* -ED, -ING, -S to determine the boundaries, area, or elevations of by measuring angles and distances

SURVEYOR *n* pl. -S one that surveys land

SURVIVAL	n pl. -S a living or continuing longer than another person or thing
SURVIVE	v -VIVED, -VIVING, -VIVES to remain in existence
SURVIVER	n pl. -S survivor
SURVIVOR	n pl. -S one that survives
SUSLIK	n pl. -S a Eurasian rodent
SUSPECT	v -ED, -ING, -S to think guilty on slight evidence
SUSPEND	v -ED, -ING, -S to cause to stop for a period
SUSPENSE	n pl. -S a state of mental uncertainty or excitement
SUSPIRE	v -PIRED, -PIRING, -PIRES to sigh
SUSTAIN	v -ED, -ING, -S to maintain by providing with food and drink
SUSURRUS	n pl. -ES a soft rustling sound
SUTLER	n pl. -S one that peddles goods to soldiers
SUTRA	n pl. -S a Hindu aphorism
SUTTA	n pl. -S sutra
SUTTEE	n pl. -S a Hindu widow cremated on her husband's funeral pile to show her devotion to him
SUTURAL	adj pertaining to the line of junction between two bones
SUTURE	v -TURED, -TURING, -TURES to unite by sewing
SUZERAIN	n pl. -S a feudal lord
SVARAJ	n pl. -ES swaraj
SVEDBERG	n pl. -S a unit of time
SVELTE	adj SVELTER, SVELTEST gracefully slender SVELTELY adv
SWAB	v SWABBED, SWABBING, SWABS to clean with a large mop
SWABBER	n pl. -S one that swabs
SWABBIE	n pl. -S a sailor
SWABBING	present participle of swab
SWABBY	n pl. -BIES swabbie
SWADDLE	v -DLED, -DLING, -DLES to wrap in bandages
SWAG	v SWAGGED, SWAGGING, SWAGS to sway
SWAGE	v SWAGED, SWAGING, SWAGES to shape with a hammering tool

SWAGER	n pl. -S one that swages
SWAGGED	past tense of swag
SWAGGER	v -ED, -ING, -S to walk with a pompous air
SWAGGING	present participle of swag
SWAGING	present participle of swage
SWAGMAN	n pl. -MEN a hobo
SWAIL	n pl. -S swale
SWAIN	n pl. -S a country boy SWAINISH adj
SWALE	n pl. -S a tract of low, marshy ground
SWALLOW	v -ED, -ING, -S to take through the mouth and esophagus into the stomach
SWAM	past tense of swim
SWAMI	n pl. -S a Hindu religious teacher
SWAMIES	pl. of swamy
SWAMP	v -ED, -ING, -S to inundate
SWAMPER	n pl. -S one that lives in a swampy area
SWAMPISH	adj swampy
SWAMPY	adj SWAMPIER, SWAMPIEST marshy
SWAMY	n pl. -MIES swami
SWAN	v SWANNED, SWANNING, SWANS to swear
SWANG	a past tense of swing
SWANHERD	n pl. -S one who tends swans (large aquatic birds)
SWANK	adj SWANKER, SWANKEST imposingly elegant
SWANK	v -ED, -ING, -S to swagger
SWANKY	adj SWANKIER, SWANKIEST swank SWANKILY adv
SWANLIKE	adj resembling a swan
SWANNED	past tense of swan
SWANNERY	n pl. -NERIES a place where swans are raised
SWANNING	present participle of swan
SWANPAN	n pl. -S a Chinese abacus
SWANSKIN	n pl. -S the skin of a swan
SWAP	v SWAPPED, SWAPPING, SWAPS to trade
SWAPPER	n pl. -S one that swaps
SWARAJ	n pl. -ES self-government in British India
SWARD	v -ED, -ING, -S to cover with turf

SWARE	a past tense of swear
SWARF	n pl. -S material removed by a cutting tool
SWARM	v -ED, -ING, -S to move in a large group
SWARMER	n pl. -S one that swarms
SWART	adj swarthy
SWARTH	n pl. -S turf
SWARTHY	adj -THIER, -THIEST having a dark complexion
SWARTY	adj swarthy
SWASH	v -ED, -ING, -ES to swagger
SWASHER	n pl. -S one that swashes
SWASTICA	n pl. -S swastika
SWASTIKA	n pl. -S a geometrical figure used as a symbol or ornament
SWAT	v SWATTED, SWATTING, SWATS to hit sharply
SWATCH	n pl. -ES a sample piece of cloth
SWATH	n pl. -S a row of cut grass or grain
SWATHE	v SWATHED, SWATHING, SWATHES to wrap in bandages
SWATHER	n pl. -S one that swathes
SWATTED	past tense of swat
SWATTER	n pl. -S one that swats
SWATTING	present participle of swat
SWAY	v -ED, -ING, -S to move slowly back and forth SWAYABLE adj
SWAYBACK	n pl. -S an abnormal sagging of the back
SWAYER	n pl. -S one that sways
SWAYFUL	adj capable of influencing
SWEAR	v SWORE or SWARE, SWORN, SWEARING, SWEARS to utter a solemn oath
SWEARER	n pl. -S one that swears
SWEAT	v -ED, -ING, -S to perspire
SWEATBOX	n pl. -ES a small enclosure in which one is made to sweat
SWEATER	n pl. -S a knitted outer garment
SWEATY	adj SWEATIER, SWEATIEST covered with perspiration SWEATILY adv
SWEDE	n pl. -S a rutabaga
SWEENY	n pl. -NIES atrophy of the shoulder muscles in horses

SWEEP	v SWEPT, SWEEPING, SWEEPS to clear or clean with a brush or broom
SWEEPER	n pl. -S one that sweeps
SWEEPING	n pl. -S the act of one that sweeps
SWEEPY	adj SWEEPIER, SWEEPIEST of wide range or scope
SWEER	adj lazy
SWEET	adj SWEETER, SWEETEST pleasing to the taste
SWEET	n pl. -S something that is sweet
SWEETEN	v -ED, -ING, -S to make sweet
SWEETIE	n pl. -S darling
SWEETING	n pl. -S a sweet apple
SWEETISH	adj somewhat sweet
SWEETLY	adv in a sweet manner
SWEETSOP	n pl. -S a tropical tree
SWELL	v SWELLED, SWOLLEN, SWELLING, SWELLS to increase in size or volume
SWELL	adj SWELLER, SWELLEST stylish
SWELLING	n pl. -S something that is swollen
SWELTER	v -ED, -ING, -S to suffer from oppressive heat
SWELTRY	adj -TRIER, -TRIEST oppressively hot
SWEPT	past tense of sweep
SWERVE	v SWERVED, SWERVING, SWERVES to turn aside suddenly from a straight course
SWERVER	n pl. -S one that swerves
SWEVEN	n pl. -S a dream or vision
SWIFT	adj SWIFTER, SWIFTEST moving with a great rate of motion
SWIFT	n pl. -S a fast-flying bird
SWIFTER	n pl. -S a rope on a ship
SWIFTLY	adv in a swift manner
SWIG	v SWIGGED, SWIGGING, SWIGS to drink deeply or rapidly
SWIGGER	n pl. -S one that swigs
SWILL	v -ED, -ING, -S to swig
SWILLER	n pl. -S one that swills
SWIM	v SWAM, SWUM, SWIMMING, SWIMS to propel oneself in water by natural means
SWIMMER	n pl. -S one that swims

SWIMMING   *n* pl. -S the act of one that swims

SWIMMY   *adj* -MIER, -MIEST dizzy **SWIMMILY** *adv*

SWIMSUIT   *n* pl. -S a bathing suit

SWINDLE   *v* -DLED, -DLING, -DLES to take money or property from by fraudulent means

SWINDLER   *n* pl. -S one that swindles

SWINE   *n* pl. SWINE a domestic pig

SWINEPOX   *n* pl. -ES a disease of swine

SWING   *v* SWUNG or SWANG, SWINGING, SWINGS to move freely back and forth

SWINGE   *v* SWINGED, SWINGEING, SWINGES to flog

SWINGER   *n* pl. -S one that swings

SWINGLE   *v* -GLED, -GLING, -GLES to scutch

SWINGY   *adj* SWINGIER, SWINGIEST marked by swinging

SWINISH   *adj* resembling or befitting swine

SWINK   *v* -ED, -ING, -S to toil

SWINNEY   *n* pl. -NEYS sweeny

SWIPE   *v* SWIPED, SWIPING, SWIPES to strike with a sweeping blow

SWIPLE   *n* pl. -S a part of a threshing device

SWIPPLE   *n* pl. -S swiple

SWIRL   *v* -ED, -ING, -S to move with a whirling motion

SWIRLY   *adj* SWIRLIER, SWIRLIEST swirling

SWISH   *v* -ED, -ING, -ES to move with a prolonged hissing sound

SWISHER   *n* pl. -S one that swishes

SWISHY   *adj* SWISHIER, SWISHIEST swishing

SWISS   *n* pl. -ES a cotton fabric

SWITCH   *v* -ED, -ING, -ES to beat with a flexible rod

SWITCHER   *n* pl. -S one that switches

SWITH   *adv* quickly

SWITHE   *adv* swith

SWITHER   *v* -ED, -ING, -S to doubt

SWITHLY   *adv* swith

SWIVE   *v* SWIVED, SWIVING, SWIVES to copulate with

SWIVEL   *v* -ELED, -ELING, -ELS or -ELLED, -ELLING, -ELS to turn on a pivoted support

SWIVET   *n* pl. -S a state of nervous excitement

SWIVING   present participle of swive

SWIZZLE   *v* -ZLED, -ZLING, -ZLES to drink excessively

SWIZZLER   *n* pl. -S one that swizzles

SWOB   *v* SWOBBED, SWOBBING, SWOBS to swab

SWOBBER   *n* pl. -S swabber

SWOLLEN   past participle of swell

SWOON   *v* -ED, -ING, -S to faint

SWOONER   *n* pl. -S one that swoons

SWOOP   *v* -ED, -ING, -S to make a sudden descent

SWOOPER   *n* pl. -S one that swoops

SWOOSH   *v* -ED, -ING, -ES to move with a rustling sound

SWOP   *v* SWOPPED, SWOPPING, SWOPS to swap

SWORD   *n* pl. -S a weapon having a long blade for cutting or thrusting

SWORDMAN   *n* pl. -MEN one skilled in the use of a sword

SWORE   a past tense of swear

SWORN   past participle of swear

SWOT   *v* SWOTTED, SWOTTING, SWOTS to swat

SWOTTER   *n* pl. -S one that swots

SWOUN   *v* -ED, -ING, -S to swoon

SWOUND   *v* -ED, -ING, -S to swoon

SWUM   past participle of swim

SWUNG   a past tense of swing

SYBARITE   *n* pl. -S a person devoted to pleasure and luxury

SYBO   *n* pl. -BOES the cibol

SYCAMINE   *n* pl. -S the mulberry tree

SYCAMORE   *n* pl. -S a North American tree

SYCE   *n* pl. -S a male servant in India

SYCEE   *n* pl. -S fine uncoined silver formerly used in China as money

SYCOMORE   *n* pl. -S sycamore

SYCONIUM   *n* pl. -NIA a fleshy multiple fruit

SYCOSIS   *n* pl. -COSES an inflammatory disease of the hair follicles

SYENITE   *n* pl. -S an igneous rock **SYENITIC** *adj*

SYKE	n pl. -S a small stream
SYLLABI	a pl. of syllabus
SYLLABIC	n pl. -S a speech sound of high sonority
SYLLABLE	v -BLED, -BLING, -BLES to pronounce syllables (units of spoken language)
SYLLABUB	n pl. -S sillabub
SYLLABUS	n pl. -BI or -BUSES an outline of a course of study
SYLPH	n pl. -S a slender, graceful girl or woman SYLPHIC, SYLPHISH, SYLPHY adj
SYLPHID	n pl. -S a young sylph
SYLVA	n pl. -VAS or -VAE the forest trees of an area
SYLVAN	n pl. -S one that lives in a forest
SYLVATIC	adj pertaining to a forest
SYLVIN	n pl. -S sylvite
SYLVINE	n pl. -S sylvite
SYLVITE	n pl. -S an ore of potassium
SYMBION	n pl. -S symbiont
SYMBIONT	n pl. -S an organism living in close association with another
SYMBIOT	n pl. -S symbiont
SYMBIOTE	n pl. -S symbiont
SYMBOL	v -BOLED, -BOLING, -BOLS or -BOLLED, -BOLLING, -BOLS to serve as a symbol (a representation) of
SYMBOLIC	adj pertaining to a symbol
SYMMETRY	n pl. -TRIES an exact correspondence between the opposite halves of a figure
SYMPATHY	n pl. -THIES a feeling of compassion for another's suffering
SYMPATRY	n pl. -RIES the state of occupying the same area without loss of identity from interbreeding
SYMPHONY	n pl. -NIES an orchestral composition
SYMPODIA	n/pl plant stems made up of a series of superposed branches
SYMPOSIA	n/pl conferences for the purpose of discussion
SYMPTOM	n pl. -S an indication of something
SYN	adv syne

SYNAGOG	n pl. -S a building for Jewish worship
SYNAPSE	v -APSED, -APSING, -APSES to come together in synapsis
SYNAPSIS	n pl. -APSES the point at which a nervous impulse passes from one neuron to another SYNAPTIC adj
SYNC	v -ED, -ING, -S to cause to operate in unison
SYNCARP	n pl. -S a fleshy multiple fruit
SYNCARPY	n pl. -PIES the state of being a syncarp
SYNCH	v -ED, -ING, -S to sync
SYNCHRO	n pl. -CHROS a selsyn
SYNCLINE	n pl. -S a type of rock formation
SYNCOM	n pl. -S a type of communications satellite
SYNCOPE	n pl. -S the contraction of a word by omitting one or more sounds from the middle SYNCOPAL, SYNCOPIC adj
SYNCYTIA	n/pl masses of protoplasm resulting from cell fusion
SYNDESIS	n pl. -DESES or -DESISES synapsis
SYNDET	n pl. -S a synthetic detergent
SYNDETIC	adj serving to connect
SYNDIC	n pl. -S a business agent SYNDICAL adj
SYNDROME	n pl. -S a group of symptoms that characterize a particular disorder
SYNE	adv since
SYNECTIC	adj pertaining to a system of problem solving
SYNERGIA	n pl. -S synergy
SYNERGID	n pl. -S a cell found in the embryo sac of a seed plant
SYNERGY	n pl. -GIES combined action SYNERGIC adj
SYNESIS	n pl. -SISES a type of grammatical construction
SYNGAMY	n pl. -MIES the union of two gametes SYNGAMIC adj
SYNOD	n pl. -S a church council SYNODAL, SYNODIC adj
SYNONYM	n pl. -S a word having the same meaning as another
SYNONYME	n pl. -S synonym
SYNONYMY	n pl. -MIES equivalence of meaning

SYNOPSIS	*n* pl. -OPSES a summary **SYNOPTIC** *adj*
SYNOVIA	*n* pl. -S a lubricating fluid secreted by certain membranes **SYNOVIAL** *adj*
SYNTAX	*n* pl. -ES the way in which words are put together to form phrases and sentences
SYNTONY	*n* pl. -NIES the tuning of transmitters and receivers with each other **SYNTONIC** *adj*
SYNURA	*n* pl. -RAE any of a genus of protozoa
SYPHER	*v* -ED, -ING, -S to overlap so as to make an even surface, as beveled plank edges
SYPHILIS	*n* pl. -LISES a venereal disease
SYPHON	*v* -ED, -ING, -S to siphon
SYREN	*n* pl. -S siren
SYRINGA	*n* pl. -S an ornamental shrub
SYRINGE	*v* -RINGED, -RINGING, -RINGES to cleanse or treat with injected fluid
SYRINX	*n* pl. -INGES or -INXES the vocal organ of a bird
SYRPHIAN	*n* pl. -S syrphid
SYRPHID	*n* pl. -S a winged insect
SYRUP	*n* pl. -S a thick, sweet liquid **SYRUPY** *adj*
SYSTEM	*n* pl. -S a group of interacting elements forming a unified whole
SYSTEMIC	*n* pl. -S a type of pesticide
SYSTOLE	*n* pl. -S the normal rhythmic contraction of the heart **SYSTOLIC** *adj*
SYZYGY	*n* pl. -GIES the configuration of the earth, moon, and sun lying in a straight line **SYZYGAL**, **SYZYGIAL** *adj*

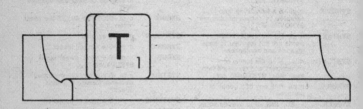

TA	*n* pl. -S an expression of gratitude	**TABLOID**	*n* pl. -S a small newspaper
TAB	*v* TABBED, TABBING, TABS to name or designate	**TABOO**	*v* -ED, -ING, -S to exclude from use, approach, or mention
TABANID	*n* pl. -S a bloodsucking insect	**TABOR**	*v* -ED, -ING, -S to beat on a small drum
TABARD	*n* pl. -S a sleeveless outer garment **TABARDED** *adj*	**TABORER**	*n* pl. -S one that tabors
TABARET	*n* pl. -S a silk fabric	**TABORET**	*n* pl. -S a small drum
TABBED	past tense of tab	**TABORIN**	*n* pl. -S taborine
TABBIED	past tense of tabby	**TABORINE**	*n* pl. -S a taboret
TABBIES	present 3d person sing. of tabby	**TABOUR**	*v* -ED, -ING, -S to tabor
TABBING	present participle of tab	**TABOURER**	*n* pl. -S taborer
TABBIS	*n* pl. -BISES a silk fabric	**TABOURET**	*n* pl. -S taboret
TABBY	*v* -BIED, -BYING, -BIES to give a wavy appearance to	**TABU**	*v* -ED, -ING, -S to taboo
TABER	*v* -ED, -ING, -S to tabor	**TABULAR**	*adj* of or pertaining to a list
TABES	*n* pl. TABES a syphilitic disease	**TABULATE**	*v* -LATED, -LATING, -LATES to arrange in a list
TABETIC	*n* pl. -S one affected with tabes	**TACE**	*n* pl. -S taasse
TABID	*adj* affected with tabes	**TACET**	*interj* be silent — used as a musical direction
TABLA	*n* pl. -S a small drum	**TACH**	*n* pl. -S a device for indicating speed of rotation
TABLE	*v* -BLED, -BLING, -BLES to place on a table (a piece of furniture having a flat upper surface)		
TABLEAU	*n* pl. -LEAUX or -LEAUS a picture	**TACHE**	*n* pl. -S a clasp or buckle
		TACHINID	*n* pl. -S a grayish fly
		TACHISM	*n* pl. -S action painting
TABLEFUL	*n* pl. TABLEFULS or TABLESFUL as much as a table can hold	**TACHIST**	*n* pl. -S an action painter
		TACHISTE	*n* pl. -S tachist
		TACIT	*adj* unspoken **TACITLY** *adv*
TABLET	*v* -LETED, -LETING, -LETS or -LETTED, -LETTING, -LETS to inscribe on a small, flat surface	**TACITURN**	*adj* habitually silent
		TACK	*v* -ED, -ING, -S to fasten with tacks (short, sharp-pointed nails)
TABLETOP	*n* pl. -S the top of a table	**TACKER**	*n* pl. -S one that tacks
TABLING	present participle of table	**TACKET**	*n* pl. -S a hobnail

TACKEY adj TACKIER, TACKIEST tacky

TACKIER comparative of tacky

TACKIEST superlative of tacky

TACKIFY v -FIED, -FYING, -FIES to make tacky

TACKILY adv in a tacky manner

TACKLE v -LED, -LING, -LES to seize and throw to the ground

TACKLER n pl. -S one that tackles

TACKLESS adj having no tacks

TACKLING n pl. -S equipment

TACKY adj TACKIER, TACKIEST adhesive

TACNODE n pl. -S a point of contact between two curves

TACO n pl. -COS a tortilla folded around a filling

TACONITE n pl. -S a low-grade iron ore

TACT n pl. -S skill in dealing with delicate situations

TACTFUL adj having tact

TACTIC n pl. -S a maneuver for gaining an objective TACTICAL adj

TACTILE adj pertaining to the sense of touch

TACTION n pl. -S the act of touching

TACTLESS adj lacking tact

TACTUAL adj tactile

TAD n pl. -S a small boy

TADPOLE n pl. -S the aquatic larva of an amphibian

TAE prep to

TAEL n pl. -S a Chinese unit of weight

TAENIA n pl. -NIAE or -NIAS a headband worn in ancient Greece

TAFFAREL n pl. -S taffrail

TAFFEREL n pl. -S taffrail

TAFFETA n pl. -S a lustrous fabric

TAFFIA n pl. -S tafia

TAFFRAIL n pl. -S a rail around the stern of a ship

TAFFY n pl. -FIES a chewy candy

TAFIA n pl. -S an inferior rum

TAG v TAGGED, TAGGING, TAGS to provide with a tag (an identifying marker)

TAGALONG n pl. -S one that follows another

TAGBOARD n pl. -S a material for making shipping tags

TAGGED past tense of tag

TAGGER n pl. -S one that tags

TAGGING present participle of tag

TAGLIKE adj resembling a tag

TAGMEME n pl. -S the smallest unit of meaningful grammatical relation

TAGRAG n pl. -S riffraff

TAHR n pl. -S a goatlike mammal

TAHSIL n pl. -S a district in India

TAIGA n pl. -S a subarctic evergreen forest

TAIGLACH n pl. TAIGLACH teiglach

TAIL v -ED, -ING, -S to provide with a tail (a hindmost part)

TAILBACK n pl. -S a member of the backfield in some football formations

TAILBONE n pl. -S the coccyx

TAILCOAT n pl. -S a man's coat

TAILER n pl. -S one that secretly follows another

TAILGATE v -GATED, -GATING, -GATES to drive dangerously close behind another vehicle

TAILING n pl. -S the part of a projecting stone or brick that is inserted into a wall

TAILLE n pl. -S a former French tax

TAILLESS adj having no tail

TAILLIKE adj resembling a tail

TAILOR v -ED, -ING, -S to fit with clothes

TAILPIPE n pl. -S an exhaust pipe

TAILRACE n pl. -S a part of a millrace

TAILSKID n pl. -S a support on which the tail of an airplane rests

TAILSPIN n pl. -S the spiral descent of a stalled airplane

TAILWIND n pl. -S a wind coming from behind a moving vehicle

TAIN n pl. -S a thin plate

TAINT v -ED, -ING, -S to touch or affect slightly with something bad

TAIPAN n pl. -S a venomous snake

TAJ n pl. -ES a tall, conical cap worn in Muslim countries

TAKAHE n pl. -S a flightless bird

TAKE	v TOOK, TAKEN, TAKING, TAKES to get possession of TAKABLE, TAKEABLE adj	**TALKY**	adj TALKIER, TALKIEST tending to talk a great deal
TAKEDOWN	n pl. -S an article that can be taken apart easily	**TALL**	adj TALLER, TALLEST having great height
TAKEOFF	n pl. -S the act of rising in flight	**TALLAGE**	v -LAGED, -LAGING, -LAGES to tax
TAKEOUT	n pl. -S the act of removing	**TALLAISIM**	a pl. of tallith
TAKEOVER	n pl. -S the act of assuming control	**TALLBOY**	n pl. -BOYS a highboy
		TALLIED	past tense of tally
TAKER	n pl. -S one that takes	**TALLIER**	n pl. -S one that tallies
TAKIN	n pl. -S a goatlike mammal	**TALLIES**	present 3d person sing. of tally
TAKING	n pl. -S a seizure	**TALLISH**	adj somewhat tall
TAKINGLY	adv in an attractive manner	**TALLITH**	n pl. TALLITHES, TALLITHIM, TALLITOTH, TALEYSIM, or TALLAISIM a Jewish prayer shawl
TALA	n pl. -S a traditional rhythmic pattern of music in India		
TALAPOIN	n pl. -S a small African monkey	**TALLNESS**	n pl. -ES the state of being tall
TALAR	n pl. -S a long cloak	**TALLOL**	n pl. -S a resinous liquid
TALARIA	n/pl winged sandals worn by various figures of classical mythology	**TALLOW**	v -ED, -ING, -S to smear with tallow (a mixture of animal fats)
		TALLOWY	adj resembling tallow
TALC	v TALCKED, TALCKING, TALCS or TALCED, TALCING, TALCS to treat with talc (a soft mineral with a soapy texture) TALCKY, TALCOSE, TALCOUS adj	**TALLY**	v -LIED, -LYING, -LIES to count
		TALLYHO	v -ED, -ING, -S to make an encouraging shout to hunting hounds
		TALLYMAN	n pl. -MEN a person who tallies
TALCUM	n pl. -S a powder made from talc	**TALMUDIC**	adj pertaining to the body of Jewish civil and religious law
TALE	n pl. -S a story	**TALON**	n pl. -S a claw of a bird of prey TALONED adj
TALENT	n pl. -S a special natural ability TALENTED adj		
TALER	n pl. -S a former German coin	**TALOOKA**	n pl. -S taluk
TALESMAN	n pl. -MEN a person summoned to fill a vacancy on a jury	**TALUK**	n pl. -S an estate in India
		TALUKA	n pl. -S taluk
TALEYSIM	a pl. of tallith	**TALUS**	n pl. -LI a bone of the foot
TALI	pl. of talus	**TALUS**	n pl. -ES a slope formed by an accumulation of rock debris
TALION	n pl. -S a retaliation for a crime		
TALIPED	n pl. -S a person afflicted with clubfoot	**TAM**	n pl. -S a tight-fitting Scottish cap
TALIPES	n pl. TALIPES clubfoot	**TAMABLE**	adj capable of being tamed
TALIPOT	n pl. -S a tall palm tree	**TAMAL**	n pl. -S tamale
TALISMAN	n pl. -S an object believed to possess magical powers	**TAMALE**	n pl. -S a Mexican dish
		TAMANDU	n pl. -S tamandua
TALK	v -ED, -ING, -S to communicate by speaking	**TAMANDUA**	n pl. -S an arboreal anteater
		TAMARACK	n pl. -S a timber tree
TALKABLE	adj able to be talked about	**TAMARAO**	n pl. -RAOS tamarau
TALKER	n pl. -S one that talks	**TAMARAU**	n pl. -S a small buffalo of the Philippines
TALKIE	n pl. -S a moving picture with synchronized sound		
TALKING	n pl. -S conversation	**TAMARIN**	n pl. -S a South American monkey

TAMARIND *n* pl. -S a tropical tree

TAMARISK *n* pl. -S an evergreen shrub

TAMASHA *n* pl. -S a public entertainment in India

TAMBAC *n* pl. -S tombac

TAMBALA *n* pl. -S a monetary unit of Malawi

TAMBOUR *v* -ED, -ING, -S to embroider on a round wooden frame

TAMBOURA *n* pl. -S tambura

TAMBUR *n* pl. -S tambura

TAMBURA *n* pl. -S a stringed instrument

TAME *adj* TAMER, TAMEST gentle or docile

TAME *v* TAMED, TAMING, TAMES to make tame

TAMEABLE *adj* tamable

TAMEIN *n* pl. -S a garment worn by Burmese women

TAMELESS *adj* not capable of being tamed

TAMELY *adv* in a tame manner

TAMENESS *n* pl. -ES the state of being tame

TAMER *n* pl. -S one that tames

TAMEST superlative of tame

TAMING present participle of tame

TAMIS *n* pl. -ISES a strainer made of cloth mesh

TAMMIE *n* pl. -S tammy

TAMMY *n* pl. -MIES a fabric of mixed fibers

TAMP *v* -ED, -ING, -S to pack down by tapping

TAMPALA *n* pl. -S an annual herb

TAMPAN *n* pl. -S a biting insect

TAMPER *v* -ED, -ING, -S to interfere in a harmful manner

TAMPERER *n* pl. -S one that tampers

TAMPION *n* pl. -S a plug for the muzzle of a cannon

TAMPON *v* -ED, -ING, -S to plug with a cotton pad

TAN *v* TANNED, TANNING, TANS to convert hide into leather by soaking in chemicals

TAN *adj* TANNER, TANNEST brown from the sun's rays

TANAGER *n* pl. -S a brightly colored bird

TANBARK *n* pl. -S a tree bark used as a source of tannin

TANDEM *n* pl. -S a bicycle built for two

TANG *v* -ED, -ING, -S to provide with a pungent flavor

TANGELO *n* pl. -LOS a citrus fruit

TANGENCE *n* pl. -S tangency

TANGENCY *n* pl. -CIES the state of being in immediate physical contact

TANGENT *n* pl. -S a straight line in contact with a curve at one point

TANGIBLE *n* pl. -S something palpable

TANGIBLY *adv* palpably

TANGIER comparative of tangy

TANGIEST superlative of tangy

TANGLE *v* -GLED, -GLING, -GLES to bring together in intricate confusion

TANGLER *n* pl. -S one that tangles

TANGLY *adj* -GLIER, -GLIEST tangled

TANGO *v* -ED, -ING, -S to perform a Latin-American dance

TANGRAM *n* pl. -S a Chinese puzzle

TANGY *adj* TANGIER, TANGIEST pungent

TANIST *n* pl. -S the heir apparent to a Celtic chief

TANISTRY *n* pl. -RIES the system of electing a tanist

TANK *v* -ED, -ING, -S to store in a tank (a container usually for liquids)

TANKA *n* pl. -S a Japanese verse form

TANKAGE *n* pl. -S the capacity of a tank

TANKARD *n* pl. -S a tall drinking vessel

TANKER *n* pl. -S a ship designed to transport liquids

TANKFUL *n* pl. -S the amount a tank can hold

TANKSHIP *n* pl. -S a tanker

TANNABLE *adj* capable of being tanned

TANNAGE *n* pl. -S the process of tanning

TANNATE *n* pl. -S a chemical salt

TANNED past tense of tan

TANNER *n* pl. -S one that tans

TANNERY *n* pl. -NERIES a place where hides are tanned

TANNEST superlative of tan

TANNIC *adj* pertaining to tannin

TANNIN *n* pl. -S a chemical compound used in tanning

TANNING   *n* pl. -S the process of converting hides into leather

TANNISH   *adj* somewhat tan

TANREC   *n* pl. -S tenrec

TANSY   *n* pl. -SIES a perennial herb

TANTALUM   *n* pl. -S a metallic element **TANTALIC** *adj*

TANTALUS   *n* pl. -ES a case for wine bottles

TANTARA   *n* pl. -S the sound of a trumpet or horn

TANTIVY   *n* pl. -TIVIES a hunting cry

TANTO   *adv* so much — used as a musical direction

TANTRA   *n* pl. -S one of a class of Hindu religious writings **TANTRIC** *adj*

TANTRUM   *n* pl. -S a fit of rage

TANYARD   *n* pl. -S the section of a tannery containing the vats

TAO   *n* pl. -S the path of virtuous conduct according to a Chinese philosophy

TAP   *v* TAPPED, TAPPING, TAPS to strike gently

TAPA   *n* pl. -S a cloth made from tree bark

TAPADERA   *n* pl. -S a part of a saddle

TAPADERO   *n* pl. -ROS tapadera

TAPALO   *n* pl. -LOS a scarf worn in Latin-American countries

TAPE   *v* TAPED, TAPING, TAPES to fasten with tape (a long, narrow strip or band)

TAPELESS   *adj* being without tape

TAPELIKE   *adj* resembling tape

TAPELINE   *n* pl. -S a tape for measuring distances

TAPER   *v* -ED, -ING, -S to become gradually narrower toward one end

TAPERER   *n* pl. -S one that carries a candle in a religious procession

TAPESTRY   *v* -TRIED, -TRYING, -TRIES to decorate with woven wall hangings

TAPETUM   *n* pl. -TA a layer of cells in some plants **TAPETAL** *adj*

TAPEWORM   *n* pl. -S a parasitic worm

TAPHOLE   *n* pl. -S a hole in a blast furnace

TAPHOUSE   *n* pl. -S a tavern

TAPING   present participle of tape

TAPIOCA   *n* pl. -S a starchy food

TAPIR   *n* pl. -S a hoofed mammal

TAPIS   *n* pl. -PISES material used for wall hangings and floor coverings

TAPPED   past tense of tap

TAPPER   *n* pl. -S one that taps

TAPPET   *n* pl. -S a sliding rod that causes another part of a mechanism to move

TAPPING   *n* pl. -S the process or means by which something is tapped

TAPROOM   *n* pl. -S a barroom

TAPROOT   *n* pl. -S the main root of a plant

TAPSTER   *n* pl. -S one that dispenses liquor in a barroom

TAR   *v* TARRED, TARRING, TARS to cover with tar (a black viscous liquid)

TARANTAS   *n* pl. -ES a Russian carriage

TARBOOSH   *n* pl. -ES a cap worn by Muslim men

TARBUSH   *n* pl. -ES tarboosh

TARDIER   comparative of tardy

TARDIES   pl. of tardy

TARDO   *adj* slow — used as a musical direction

TARDY   *adj* TARDIER, TARDIEST late **TARDILY** *adv*

TARDY   *n* pl. -DIES an instance of being late

TARE   *v* TARED, TARING, TARES to determine the weight of a container holding goods

TARGE   *n* pl. -S a small, round shield

TARGET   *v* -ED, -ING, -S to make a goal of

TARIFF   *v* -ED, -ING, -S to tax imported or exported goods

TARING   present participle of tare

TARLATAN   *n* pl. -S a cotton fabric

TARLETAN   *n* pl. -S tarlatan

TARMAC   *n* pl. -S an asphalt road

TARN   *n* pl. -S a small mountain lake

TARNAL   *adj* damned **TARNALLY** *adv*

TARNISH   *v* -ED, -ING, -ES to dull the luster of

TARO   *n* pl. -ROS a tropical plant

TAROC   *n* pl. -S tarok

TAROK   *n* pl. -S a card game

TAROT *n* pl. -S any of a set of playing cards used for fortune-telling

TARP *n* pl. -S a protective canvas covering

TARPAN *n* pl. -S an Asian wild horse

TARPAPER *n* pl. -S a heavy paper coated with tar

TARPON *n* pl. -S a marine game fish

TARRAGON *n* pl. -S a perennial herb

TARRE *v* TARRED, TARRING, TARRES to urge to action

TARRED past tense of tar

TARRIED past tense of tarry

TARRIER *n* pl. -S one that tarries

TARRIES present 3d person sing. of tarry

TARRIEST superlative of tarry

TARRING present participle of tar and tarre

TARRY *v* -RIED, -RYING, -RIES to delay or be slow in acting or doing

TARRY *adj* -RIER, -RIEST resembling tar

TARSAL *n* pl. -S a bone of the foot

TARSI pl. of tarsus

TARSIA *n* pl. -S intarsia

TARSIER *n* pl. -S a nocturnal primate

TARSUS *n* pl. TARSI a part of the foot

TART *adj* TARTER, TARTEST having a sharp, sour taste

TART *v* -ED, -ING, -S to dress up

TARTAN *n* pl. -S a patterned woolen fabric

TARTANA *n* pl. -S a Mediterranean sailing vessel

TARTAR *n* pl. -S a crust on the teeth **TARTARIC** *adj*

TARTISH *adj* somewhat tart

TARTLET *n* pl. -S a small pie

TARTLY *adv* in a tart manner

TARTNESS *n* pl. -ES the state of being tart

TARTRATE *n* pl. -S a chemical salt

TARTUFE *n* pl. -S tartuffe

TARTUFFE *n* pl. -S a hypocrite

TARWEED *n* pl. -S a flowering plant

TARZAN *n* pl. -S a person of superior strength and agility

TASK *v* -ED, -ING, -S to assign a job to

TASKWORK *n* pl. -S hard work

TASS *n* pl. -ES a drinking cup

TASSE *n* pl. -S tasset

TASSEL *v* -SELED, -SELING, -SELS or -SELLED, -SELLING, -SELS to adorn with dangling ornaments

TASSET *n* pl. -S a piece of plate armor for the upper thigh

TASSIE *n* pl. -S tass

TASTE *v* TASTED, TASTING, TASTES to perceive the flavor of by taking into the mouth **TASTABLE** *adj*

TASTEFUL *adj* tasty

TASTER *n* pl. -S one that tastes

TASTING present participle of taste

TASTY *adj* TASTIER, TASTIEST pleasant to the taste **TASTILY** *adv*

TAT *v* TATTED, TATTING, TATS to make tatting

TATAMI *n* pl. -S straw matting used as a floor covering

TATE *n* pl. -S a tuft of hair

TATER *n* pl. -S a potato

TATOUAY *n* pl. -AYS a South American armadillo

TATTED past tense of tat

TATTER *v* -ED, -ING, -S to become torn and worn

TATTIER comparative of tatty

TATTIEST superlative of tatty

TATTING *n* pl. -S delicate handmade lace

TATTLE *v* -TLED, -TLING, -TLES to reveal the activities of another

TATTLER *n* pl. -S one that tattles

TATTOO *v* -ED, -ING, -S to mark the skin with indelible pigments

TATTOOER *n* pl. -S one that tattoos

TATTY *adj* -TIER, -TIEST shabby

TAU *n* pl. -S a Greek letter

TAUGHT past tense of teach

TAUNT *v* -ED, -ING, -S to challenge or reproach sarcastically

TAUNTER *n* pl. -S one that taunts

TAUPE *n* pl. -S a dark gray color

TAURINE *n* pl. -S a chemical compound

TAUT *adj* TAUTER, TAUTEST fully stretched, so as not to be slack

TAUT *v* -ED, -ING, -S to tangle

TAUTAUG n pl. -S tautog

TAUTEN v -ED, -ING, -S to make taut

TAUTLY adv in a taut manner

TAUTNESS n pl. -ES the state of being taut

TAUTOG n pl. -S a marine fish

TAUTOMER n pl. -S a type of chemical compound

TAUTONYM n pl. -S a type of taxonomic designation

TAV n pl. -S a Hebrew letter

TAVERN n pl. -S a place where liquor is sold to be drunk on the premises

TAVERNER n pl. -S one that runs a tavern

TAW v -ED, -ING, -S to convert into white leather by the application of minerals

TAWDRY adj -DRIER, -DRIEST gaudy TAWDRILY adv

TAWDRY n pl. -DRIES gaudy finery

TAWER n pl. -S one that taws

TAWIE adj docile

TAWNEY n pl. -NEYS tawny

TAWNY adj -NIER, -NIEST light brown TAWNILY adv

TAWNY n pl. -NIES a light brown color

TAWPIE n pl. -S a foolish young person

TAWSE v TAWSED, TAWSING, TAWSES to flog

TAX v -ED, -ING, -ES to place a tax (a charge imposed by authority for public purposes) on

TAXA a pl. of taxon

TAXABLE adj subject to tax TAXABLY adv

TAXABLE n pl. -S a taxable item

TAXATION n pl. -S the process of taxing

TAXEME n pl. -S a minimum grammatical feature of selection TAXEMIC adj

TAXER n pl. -S one that taxes

TAXI v TAXIED, TAXIING or TAXYING, TAXIS or TAXIES to travel in a taxicab

TAXICAB n pl. -S an automobile for hire

TAXIMAN n pl. -MEN the operator of a taxicab

TAXINGLY adv in an onerous manner

TAXITE n pl. -S a volcanic rock TAXITIC adj

TAXIWAY n pl. -WAYS a paved strip at an airport

TAXLESS adj free from taxation

TAXMAN n pl. -MEN one who collects taxes

TAXON n pl. TAXA or TAXONS a unit of scientific classification

TAXONOMY n pl. -MIES the study of scientific classification

TAXPAID adj paid for by taxes

TAXPAYER n pl. -S one that pays taxes

TAXUS n pl. TAXUS an evergreen tree or shrub

TAXWISE adj pertaining to taxes

TAXYING a present participle of taxi

TAZZA n pl. -ZAS or -ZE an ornamental bowl

TEA n pl. -S a beverage made by infusing dried leaves in boiling water

TEABERRY n pl. -RIES a North American shrub

TEABOARD n pl. -S a tray for serving tea

TEABOWL n pl. -S a teacup having no handle

TEABOX n pl. -ES a box for tea leaves

TEACAKE n pl. -S a small cake served with tea

TEACART n pl. -S a wheeled table used in serving tea

TEACH v TAUGHT, TEACHING, TEACHES to impart knowledge or skill to

TEACHER n pl. -S one that teaches

TEACHING n pl. -S a doctrine

TEACUP n pl. -S a cup in which tea is served

TEAHOUSE n pl. -S a public establishment serving tea

TEAK n pl. -S an East Indian tree

TEAKWOOD n pl. -S the wood of the teak

TEAL n pl. -S a river duck

TEAM v -ED, -ING, -S to form a team (a group of persons associated in a joint action)

TEAMAKER n pl. -S one that makes tea

TEAMMATE n pl. -S a member of the same team

TEAMSTER n pl. -S a truck driver

TEAMWORK n pl. -S cooperative effort to achieve a common goal

TEAPOT n pl. -S a vessel used in making and serving tea

TEAPOY n pl. -POYS a small table used in serving tea

TEAR v -ED, -ING, -S to emit tears (drops of saline liquid secreted by a gland of the eye)

TEAR v TORE, TORN, TEARING, TEARS to pull apart or into pieces TEARABLE adj

TEARDOWN n pl. -S the process of disassembling

TEARDROP n pl. -S a tear

TEARER n pl. -S one that tears or rips

TEARFUL adj full of tears

TEARGAS v -GASSED, -GASSING, -GASES or -GASSES to subject to a gas that irritates the eyes

TEARIER comparative of teary

TEARIEST superlative of teary

TEARILY adv in a teary manner

TEARLESS adj being without tears

TEAROOM n pl. -S a restaurant serving tea

TEARY adj TEARIER, TEARIEST tearful

TEASE v TEASED, TEASING, TEASES to make fun of

TEASEL v -SELED, -SELING, -SELS or -SELLED, -SELLING, -SELS to raise a soft surface on fabric with a bristly flower head

TEASELER n pl. -S one that teasels

TEASER n pl. -S one that teases

TEASHOP n pl. -S a tearoom

TEASING present participle of tease

TEASPOON n pl. -S a small spoon

TEAT n pl. -S a mammary gland TEATED adj

TEATIME n pl. -S the customary time for tea

TEAWARE n pl. -S a tea service

TEAZEL v -ZELED, -ZELING, -ZELS or -ZELLED, -ZELLING, -ZELS to teasel

TEAZLE v -ZLED, -ZLING, -ZLES to teasel

TECHED adj crazy

TECHNIC n pl. -S technique

TECHY adj TECHIER, TECHIEST tetchy TECHILY adv

TECTA pl. of tectum

TECTAL adj pertaining to a tectum

TECTONIC adj pertaining to construction

TECTRIX n pl. -TRICES a small feather of a bird's wing

TECTUM n pl. -TA a bodily structure resembling or serving as a roof

TED v TEDDED, TEDDING, TEDS to spread for drying

TEDDER n pl. -S one that teds

TEDDY n pl. -DIES a woman's undergarment

TEDIOUS adj causing weariness

TEDIUM n pl. -S the state of being tedious

TEE v TEED, TEEING, TEES to place a golf ball on a small peg

TEEM v -ED, -ING, -S to be full to overflowing

TEEMER n pl. -S one that teems

TEEN n pl. -S a teenager

TEENAGE adj pertaining to teenagers

TEENAGED adj teenage

TEENAGER n pl. -S a person between the ages of thirteen and nineteen

TEENER n pl. -S a teenager

TEENFUL adj filled with grief

TEENSY adj -SIER, -SIEST tiny

TEENTSY adj -SIER, -SIEST tiny

TEENY adj -NIER, -NIEST tiny

TEEPEE n pl. -S tepee

TEETER v -ED, -ING, -S to move unsteadily

TEETH pl. of tooth

TEETHE v TEETHED, TEETHING, TEETHES to cut teeth

TEETHER n pl. -S an object for a baby to bite on during teething

TEETHING n pl. -S the first growth of teeth

TEETOTAL v -TALED, -TALING, -TALS or -TALLED, -TALLING, -TALS to abstain completely from alcoholic beverages

TEETOTUM n pl. -S a spinning toy

TEFF n pl. -S a cereal grass

TEG n pl. -S a yearling sheep

TEGMEN n pl. -MINA a covering

TEGMENTA n/pl anatomical coverings

TEGMINAL adj pertaining to a tegmen

TEGUA n pl. -S a type of moccasin

TEGULAR *adj* resembling a tile

TEGUMEN *n pl.* -MINA tegmen

TEGUMENT *n pl.* -S a covering

TEIGLACH *n pl.* TEIGLACH a confection consisting of balls of dough boiled in honey

TEIID *n pl.* -S a tropical American lizard

TEIND *n pl.* -S a tithe

TEKTITE *n pl.* -S a glassy body believed to be of meteoritic origin **TEKTITIC** *adj*

TELA *n pl.* -LAE an anatomical tissue

TELAMON *n pl.* -ES a male figure used as a supporting column

TELE *n pl.* -S a television set

TELECAST *v* -ED, -ING, -S to broadcast by television

TELEDU *n pl.* -S a carnivorous mammal

TELEFILM *n pl.* -S a motion picture made for television

TELEGA *n pl.* -S a Russian wagon

TELEGONY *n pl.* -NIES the supposed influence of a previous sire on the offspring of later matings of the mother with other males

TELEGRAM *v* -GRAMMED, -GRAMMING, -GRAMS to send a message by telegraph

TELEMAN *n pl.* -MEN a naval officer

TELEMARK *n pl.* -S a type of turn in skiing

TELEOST *n pl.* -S a bony fish

TELEPLAY *n pl.* -PLAYS a play written for television

TELEPORT *v* -ED, -ING, -S to transport by a process that involves no physical means

TELERAN *n pl.* -S a system of air navigation

TELESIS *n pl.* TELESES planned progress

TELETHON *n pl.* -S a fund-raising television program

TELEVIEW *v* -ED, -ING, -S to observe by means of television

TELEVISE *v* -VISED, -VISING, -VISES to broadcast by television (an electronic system of transmitting images and sound)

TELEX *v* -ED, -ING, -ES to send a message by a type of telegraphic system

TELFER *v* -ED, -ING, -S to telpher

TELFORD *n pl.* -S a road made of stones

TELIA *pl.* of telium

TELIAL *adj* pertaining to a telium

TELIC *adj* directed toward a goal

TELIUM *n pl.* -LIA a sorus on the host plant of a rust fungus

TELL *v* TOLD, TELLING, TELLS to give a detailed account of **TELLABLE** *adj*

TELLER *n pl.* -S a bank employee who receives and pays out money

TELLIES *pl.* of telly

TELLTALE *n pl.* -S a tattler

TELLURIC *adj* pertaining to the earth

TELLY *n pl.* -LIES a television set

TELOME *n pl.* -S a structural unit of a vascular plant **TELOMIC** *adj*

TELOS *n pl.* TELOI an ultimate end

TELPHER *v* -ED, -ING, -S to transport by a system of aerial cable cars

TELSON *n pl.* -S the terminal segment of an arthropod **TELSONIC** *adj*

TEMBLOR *n pl.* -S or -ES an earthquake

TEMERITY *n pl.* -TIES foolish boldness

TEMPEH *n pl.* -S an Asian food

TEMPER *v* -ED, -ING, -S to moderate by adding a counterbalancing agent

TEMPERA *n pl.* -S a technique of painting

TEMPERER *n pl.* -S one that tempers

TEMPEST *v* -ED, -ING, -S to agitate violently

TEMPI *a pl.* of tempo

TEMPLAR *n pl.* -S a lawyer or student of law in London

TEMPLATE *n pl.* -S a pattern used as a guide in making something

TEMPLE *n pl.* -S a house of worship **TEMPLED** *adj*

TEMPLET *n pl.* -S template

TEMPO *n pl.* -PI or -POS the rate of speed of a musical piece

TEMPORAL *n pl.* -S a bone of the skull

TEMPT *v* -ED, -ING, -S to entice to commit an unwise or immoral act

TEMPTER *n pl.* -S one that tempts

TEMPURA *n pl.* -S a Japanese dish

TEN *n pl.* -S a number

TENABLE *adj* capable of being held TENABLY *adv*

TENACE *n pl.* -S a combination of two high cards in some card games

TENACITY *n pl.* -TIES perseverance or persistence

TENACULA *n/pl* hooked surgical instruments

TENAIL *n pl.* -S tenaille

TENAILLE *n pl.* -S an outer defense

TENANCY *n pl.* -CIES the temporary occupancy of something that belongs to another

TENANT *v* -ED, -ING, -S to inhabit

TENANTRY *n pl.* -RIES tenancy

TENCH *n pl.* -ES a freshwater fish

TEND *v* -ED, -ING, -S to be disposed or inclined

TENDANCE *n pl.* -S watchful care

TENDENCE *n pl.* -S tendance

TENDENCY *n pl.* -CIES an inclination to act or think in a particular way

TENDER *adj* -DERER, -DEREST soft or delicate

TENDER *v* -ED, -ING, -S to present for acceptance

TENDERER *n pl.* -S one that tenders

TENDERLY *adv* in a tender manner

TENDON *n pl.* -S a band of tough, fibrous tissue

TENDRIL *n pl.* -S a leafless organ of climbing plants

TENEBRAE *n/pl* a religious service

TENEMENT *n pl.* -S an apartment house

TENESMUS *n pl.* -ES an urgent but ineffectual effort to defecate or urinate TENESMIC *adj*

TENET *n pl.* -S a principle, belief, or doctrine held to be true

TENFOLD *n pl.* -S an amount ten times as great as a given unit

TENIA *n pl.* -NIAE or -NIAS a tapeworm

TENIASIS *n pl.* -SISES infestation with tapeworms

TENNER *n pl.* -S a ten-dollar bill

TENNIS *n pl.* -NISES an outdoor ball game

TENNIST *n pl.* -S a tennis player

TENON *v* -ED, -ING, -S to unite by means of a tenon (a projection on the end of a piece of wood)

TENONER *n pl.* -S one that tenons

TENOR *n pl.* -S a high male singing voice

TENORITE *n pl.* -S a mineral

TENOTOMY *n pl.* -MIES the surgical division of a tendon

TENOUR *n pl.* -S tenor

TENPENCE *n pl.* -S the sum of ten pennies

TENPENNY *adj* worth tenpence

TENPIN *n pl.* -S a bowling pin

TENREC *n pl.* -S a mammal that feeds on insects

TENSE *adj* TENSER, TENSEST taut TENSELY *adv*

TENSE *v* TENSED, TENSING, TENSES to make tense

TENSIBLE *adj* capable of being stretched TENSIBLY *adv*

TENSILE *adj* tensible

TENSING present participle of tense

TENSION *v* -ED, -ING, -S to make tense

TENSITY *n pl.* -TIES the state of being tense

TENSIVE *adj* causing tensity

TENSOR *n pl.* -S a muscle that stretches a body part

TENT *v* -ED, -ING, -S to live in a tent (a type of portable shelter)

TENTACLE *n pl.* -S an elongated, flexible appendage of some animals

TENTAGE *n pl.* -S a supply of tents

TENTER *v* -ED, -ING, -S to stretch on a type of frame

TENTH *n pl.* -S one of ten equal parts

TENTHLY *adv* in the tenth place

TENTIE *adj* TENTIER, TENTIEST tenty

TENTIER comparative of tenty

TENTIEST superlative of tenty

TENTLESS *adj* having no tent

TENTLIKE *adj* resembling a tent

TENTY *adj* TENTIER, TENTIEST watchful

TENUIS *n pl.* -UES a voiceless phonetic stop

TENUITY *n pl.* -ITIES lack of substance or strength

TENUOUS	*adj* having little substance or strength
TENURE	*n pl.* -S the holding of something TENURED, TENURIAL *adj*
TENUTO	*n pl.* -TI or -TOS a musical note or chord held longer than its normal duration
TEOCALLI	*n pl.* -S an Aztec temple
TEOPAN	*n pl.* -S a teocalli
TEOSINTE	*n pl.* -S an annual grass
TEPA	*n pl.* -S a chemical compound
TEPAL	*n pl.* -S a division of a perianth
TEPEE	*n pl.* -S a conical tent of some North American Indians
TEPEFY	*v* -FIED, -FYING, -FIES to make tepid
TEPHRA	*n pl.* -S solid material ejected from a volcano
TEPHRITE	*n pl.* -S a volcanic rock
TEPID	*adj* moderately warm TEPIDLY *adv*
TEPIDITY	*n pl.* -TIES the state of being tepid
TEQUILA	*n pl.* -S a Mexican liquor
TERAI	*n pl.* -S a sun hat with a wide brim
TERAOHM	*n pl.* -S one trillion ohms
TERAPH	*n pl.* -APHIM an image of a Semitic household god
TERATISM	*n pl.* -S a malformed fetus TERATOID *adj*
TERATOMA	*n pl.* -MAS or -MATA a type of tumor
TERBIA	*n pl.* -S an oxide of terbium
TERBIUM	*n pl.* -S a metallic element TERBIC *adj*
TERCE	*n pl.* -S tierce
TERCEL	*n pl.* -S a male falcon
TERCELET	*n pl.* -S a tercel
TERCET	*n pl.* -S a group of three lines of verse
TEREBENE	*n pl.* -S a mixture of terpenes
TEREBIC	*adj* pertaining to an acid derived from oil of turpentine
TEREDO	*n pl.* -DOS or -DINES a bivalve mollusk
TEREFAH	*adj* tref
TERETE	*adj* cylindrical and slightly tapering
TERGA	*pl.* of tergum
TERGAL	*adj* pertaining to a tergum
TERGITE	*n pl.* -S a tergum
TERGUM	*n pl.* -GA a back part of a segment of an arthropod
TERIYAKI	*n pl.* -S a Japanese food
TERM	*v* -ED, -ING, -S to give a name to
TERMER	*n pl.* -S a prisoner serving a specified sentence
TERMINAL	*n pl.* -S an end or extremity
TERMINUS	*n pl.* -NI or -NUSES a terminal
TERMITE	*n pl.* -S an insect resembling an ant TERMITIC *adj*
TERMLESS	*adj* having no limits
TERMLY	*adv* periodically
TERMOR	*n pl.* -S one that holds land for a certain number of years
TERMTIME	*n pl.* -S the time when a school or court is in session
TERN	*n pl.* -S a seabird
TERNARY	*n pl.* -RIES a group of three
TERNATE	*adj* arranged in groups of three
TERNE	*n pl.* -S an alloy of lead and tin
TERNION	*n pl.* -S a group of three
TERPENE	*n pl.* -S a chemical compound TERPENIC *adj*
TERPINOL	*n pl.* -S a fragrant liquid
TERRA	*n pl.* -RAE earth; land
TERRACE	*v* -RACED, -RACING, -RACES to provide with a terrace (a raised embankment)
TERRAIN	*n pl.* -S a tract of land
TERRANE	*n pl.* -S a rock formation
TERRAPIN	*n pl.* -S a North American tortoise
TERRARIA	*n/pl* glass enclosures for plants or small animals
TERRAS	*n pl.* -ES trass
TERRAZZO	*n pl.* -ZOS a mosaic flooring
TERREEN	*n pl.* -S terrine
TERRELLA	*n pl.* -S a spherical magnet
TERRENE	*n pl.* -S a land area
TERRET	*n pl.* -S a metal ring on a harness
TERRIBLE	*adj* very bad TERRIBLY *adv*
TERRIER	*n pl.* -S a small, active dog
TERRIES	*pl.* of terry

TERRIFIC *adj* very good; fine

TERRIFY *v* -FIED, -FYING, -FIES to fill with terror

TERRINE *n pl.* -S an earthenware jar

TERRIT *n pl.* -S terret

TERROR *n pl.* -S intense fear

TERRY *n pl.* -RIES an absorbent fabric

TERSE *adj* TERSER, TERSEST succinct TERSELY *adv*

TERTIAL *n pl.* -S a flight feather of a bird's wing

TERTIAN *n pl.* -S a recurrent fever

TERTIARY *n pl.* -ARIES a tertial

TESLA *n pl.* -S a unit of magnetic induction

TESSERA *n pl.* -SERAE a small square used in mosaic work

TEST *v* -ED, -ING, -S to subject to an examination TESTABLE *adj*

TESTA *n pl.* -TAE the hard outer coating of a seed

TESTACY *n pl.* -CIES the state of being testate

TESTATE *adj* having made a valid will before death

TESTATOR *n pl.* -S one that makes a will

TESTEE *n pl.* -S one that is tested

TESTER *n pl.* -S one that tests

TESTES pl. of testis

TESTICLE *n pl.* -S a testis

TESTIER comparative of testy

TESTIEST superlative of testy

TESTIFY *v* -FIED, -FYING, -FIES to make a declaration of truth under oath

TESTILY *adv* in a testy manner

TESTING present participle of test

TESTIS *n pl.* TESTES a male reproductive gland

TESTON *n pl.* -S a former French coin

TESTOON *n pl.* -S a teston

TESTUDO *n pl.* -DINES or -DOS a portable screen used as a shield by the ancient Romans

TESTY *adj* TESTIER, TESTIEST irritable

TETANAL *adj* pertaining to tetanus

TETANIC *n pl.* -S a drug capable of causing convulsions

TETANIES pl. of tetany

TETANISE *v* -NISED, -NISING, -NISES to tetanize

TETANIZE *v* -NIZED, -NIZING, -NIZES to affect with convulsions

TETANUS *n pl.* -ES an infectious disease TETANOID *adj*

TETANY *n pl.* -NIES a condition marked by painful muscular spasms

TETCHED *adj* crazy

TETCHY *adj* TETCHIER, TETCHIEST irritable TETCHILY *adv*

TETH *n pl.* -S a Hebrew letter

TETHER *v* -ED, -ING, -S to fasten to a fixed object with a rope

TETOTUM *n pl.* -S teetotum

TETRA *n pl.* -S a tropical fish

TETRACID *n pl.* -S a type of acid

TETRAD *n pl.* -S a group of four TETRADIC *adj*

TETRAGON *n pl.* -S a four-sided polygon

TETRAMER *n pl.* -S a type of polymer

TETRAPOD *n pl.* -S a four-footed animal

TETRARCH *n pl.* -S one of four joint rulers

TETRODE *n pl.* -S a type of electron tube

TETROXID *n pl.* -S a type of oxide

TETRYL *n pl.* -S a chemical compound

TETTER *n pl.* -S a skin disease

TEUCH *adj* teugh

TEUGH *adj* tough TEUGHLY *adv*

TEW *v* -ED, -ING, -S to work hard

TEXAS *n pl.* -ES the uppermost structure on a steamboat

TEXT *n pl.* -S the main body of a written or printed work

TEXTBOOK *n pl.* -S a book used in the study of a subject

TEXTILE *n pl.* -S a woven fabric

TEXTLESS *adj* having no text

TEXTUAL *adj* pertaining to a text

TEXTUARY *n pl.* -ARIES a specialist in the study of the Scriptures

TEXTURE *v* -TURED, -TURING, -TURES to make by weaving

TEXTURAL *adj* pertaining to the surface characteristics of something

THACK *v* -ED, -ING, -S to thatch

THAE *adj* these; those

THAIRM *n pl.* -S tharm

THALAMUS *n* pl. -MI a part of the brain THALAMIC *adj*

THALER *n* pl. -S taler

THALLIUM *n* pl. -S a metallic element THALLIC, THALLOUS *adj*

THALLUS *n* pl. -LI or -LUSES a plant body without true root, stem, or leaf THALLOID *adj*

THAN *conj* — used to introduce the second element of a comparison

THANAGE *n* pl. -S the land held by a thane

THANATOS *n* pl. -ES an instinctual desire for death

THANE *n* pl. -S a man holding land by military service in Anglo-Saxon England

THANK *v* -ED, -ING, -S to express gratitude to

THANKER *n* pl. -S one that thanks

THANKFUL *adj* -FULLER, -FULLEST feeling gratitude

THARM *n* pl. -S the belly

THAT *pron* pl. THOSE the one indicated

THATAWAY *adv* in that direction

THATCH *v* -ED, -ING, -ES to cover with thatch (plant stalks or foliage)

THATCHER *n* pl. -S one that thatches

THATCHY *adj* resembling thatch

THAW *v* -ED, -ING, -S to melt

THAWER *n* pl. -S one that thaws

THAWLESS *adj* never thawing

THE *definite article* — used to specify or make particular

THEARCHY *n* pl. -CHIES rule by a god

THEATER *n* pl. -S a building for dramatic presentations THEATRIC *adj*

THEATRE *n* pl. -S theater

THEBAINE *n* pl. -S a poisonous alkaloid

THECA *n* pl. -CAE a protective anatomical covering THECAL, THECATE *adj*

THEE *pron* the objective case of the pronoun thou

THEELIN *n* pl. -S estrone

THEELOL *n* pl. -S estriol

THEFT *n* pl. -S the act of stealing

THEGN *n* pl. -S thane THEGNLY *adj*

THEIN *n* pl. -S theine

THEINE *n* pl. -S caffeine

THEIR *pron* a possessive form of the pronoun they

THEIRS *pron* a possessive form of the pronoun they

THEISM *n* pl. -S belief in the existence of a god

THEIST *n* pl. -S one who belives in the existence of a god THEISTIC *adj*

THELITIS *n* pl. -TISES inflammation of the nipple

THEM *pron* the objective case of the pronoun they

THEMATIC *adj* pertaining to a theme

THEME *n* pl. -S a subject discussed in speech or writing

THEN *n* pl. -S that time

THENAGE *n* pl. -S thanage

THENAL *adj* pertaining to the palm of the hand

THENAR *n* pl. -S the palm of the hand

THENCE *adv* from that place

THEOCRAT *n* pl. -S a person who rules as a representative of a god

THEODICY *n* pl. -CIES a defense of God's goodness in respect to the existence of evil

THEOGONY *n* pl. -NIES an account of the origin of the gods

THEOLOG *n* pl. -S a student of theology

THEOLOGY *n* pl. -GIES the study of religion

THEONOMY *n* pl. -MIES rule by a god

THEORBO *n* pl. -BOS an ancient lute

THEOREM *n* pl. -S a proposition that is demonstrably true or is assumed to be so

THEORIES pl. of theory

THEORISE *v* -RISED, -RISING, -RISES to theorize

THEORIST *n* pl. -S one that theorizes

THEORIZE *v* -RIZED, -RIZING, -RIZES to form theories

THEORY *n* pl. -RIES a group of propositions used to explain a class of phenomena

THERAPY *n* pl. -PIES the treatment of illness or disability

THERE *n* pl. -S that place

THEREAT *adv* at that place or time

THEREBY *adv* by that means

THEREFOR *adv* for that

THEREIN *adv* in that place

THEREMIN *n* pl. -S a musical instrument

THEREOF *adv* of that

THEREON *adv* on that

THERETO *adv* to that

THERIAC *n* pl. -S molasses

THERIACA *n* pl. -S theriac

THERM *n* pl. -S a unit of quantity of heat

THERMAE *n/pl* hot springs

THERMAL *n* pl. -S a rising mass of warm air

THERME *n* pl. -S therm

THERMEL *n* pl. -S a device for temperature measurement

THERMIC *adj* pertaining to heat

THERMION *n* pl. -S an ion emitted by a heated body

THERMIT *n* pl. -S thermite

THERMITE *n* pl. -S a metallic mixture that produces intense heat when ignited

THERMOS *n* pl. -ES a container used to keep liquids either hot or cold

THEROID *adj* resembling a beast

THEROPOD *n* pl. -S a carnivorous dinosaur

THESAURI *n/pl* dictionaries of synonyms and antonyms

THESE pl. of this

THESIS *n* pl. THESES a proposition put forward for discussion

THESPIAN *n* pl. -S an actor or actress

THETA *n* pl. -S a Greek letter

THETIC *adj* arbitrary

THETICAL *adj* thetic

THEURGY *n* pl. -GIES divine intervention in human affairs **THEURGIC** *adj*

THEW *n* pl. -S a well-developed muscle **THEWY** *adj*

THEWLESS *adj* weak

THEY pron the 3d person pl. pronoun in the nominative case

THIAMIN *n* pl. -S thiamine

THIAMINE *n* pl. -S a B vitamin

THIAZIDE *n* pl. -S a drug used to treat high blood pressure

THIAZIN *n* pl. -S thiazine

THIAZINE *n* pl. -S a chemical compound

THIAZOL *n* pl. -S thiazole

THIAZOLE *n* pl. -S a chemical compound

THICK *adj* THICKER, THICKEST having relatively great extent from one surface to its opposite

THICK *n* pl. -S the thickest part

THICKEN *v* -ED, -ING, -S to make thick

THICKET *n* pl. -S a dense growth of shrubs or small trees **THICKETY** *adj*

THICKISH *adj* somewhat thick

THICKLY *adv* in a thick manner

THICKSET *n* pl. -S a thicket

THIEF *n* pl. THIEVES one that steals

THIEVE *v* THIEVED, THIEVING, THIEVES to steal

THIEVERY *n* pl. -ERIES the act or practice of stealing

THIEVES pl. of thief

THIEVING present participle of thieve

THIEVISH *adj* given to stealing

THIGH *n* pl. -S a part of the leg **THIGHED** *adj*

THILL *n* pl. -S a shaft of a vehicle

THIMBLE *n* pl. -S a cap used to protect the fingertip during sewing

THIN *adj* THINNER, THINNEST having relatively little density or thickness

THIN *v* THINNED, THINNING, THINS to make thin

THINCLAD *n* pl. -S a runner on a track team

THINDOWN *n* pl. -S a lessening in the number of atomic particles and cosmic rays passing through the earth's atmosphere

THINE pron a possessive form of the pronoun thou

THING *n* pl. -S an inanimate object

THINK *v* THOUGHT, THINKING, THINKS to formulate in the mind

THINKER *n* pl. -S one that thinks

THINKING *n* pl. -S an opinion or judgment

THINLY *adv* in a thin manner

THINNED past tense of thin

THINNER *n* pl. -S one that thins

THINNESS *n* pl. -ES the quality or state of being thin

THINNEST superlative of thin

THINNING present participle of thin

THINNISH adj somewhat thin

THIO adj containing sulfur

THIOL n pl. -S a sulfur compound **THIOLIC** adj

THIONATE n pl. -S a chemical salt

THIONIC adj pertaining to sulfur

THIONIN n pl. -S a violet dye

THIONINE n pl. -S thionin

THIONYL n pl. -S sulfinyl

THIOPHEN n pl. -S a chemical compound

THIOTEPA n pl. -S a chemical compound

THIOUREA n pl. -S a chemical compound

THIR pron these

THIRAM n pl. -S a chemical compound

THIRD n pl. -S one of three equal parts

THIRDLY adv in the third place

THIRL v -ED, -ING, -S to thrill

THIRLAGE n pl. -S an obligation requiring feudal tenants to grind grain at a certain mill

THIRST v -ED, -ING, -S to feel a desire or need to drink

THIRSTER n pl. -S one that thirsts

THIRSTY adj THIRSTIER, THIRSTIEST feeling a desire or need to drink

THIRTEEN n pl. -S a number

THIRTY n pl. -TIES a number

THIS pron pl. THESE the person or thing just mentioned

THISTLE n pl. -S a prickly plant **THISTLY** adj

THITHER adv in that direction

THO conj though

THOLE v THOLED, THOLING, THOLES to endure

THOLEPIN n pl. -S a pin that serves as an oarlock

THOLOS n pl. -LOI a circular, underground tomb

THONG n pl. -S a narrow strip of leather used for binding **THONGED** adj

THORAX n pl. -RACES or -RAXES the part of the body between the neck and the abdomen **THORACAL, THORACIC** adj

THORIA n pl. -S an oxide of thorium

THORIC adj pertaining to thorium

THORITE n pl. -S a thorium ore

THORIUM n pl. -S a metallic element

THORN v -ED, -ING, -S to prick with a thorn (a sharp, rigid projection on a plant)

THORNY adj THORNIER, THORNIEST full of thorns **THORNILY** adv

THORO adj thorough

THORON n pl. -S a radioactive isotope of radon

THOROUGH adj -OUGHER, -OUGHEST complete in all respects

THORP n pl. -S a small village

THORPE n pl. -S thorp

THOSE pl. of that

THOU v -ED, -ING, -S to address as "thou" (the 2d person sing. pronoun in the nominative case)

THOUGH conj despite the fact that

THOUGHT n pl. -S a product of thinking

THOUSAND n pl. -S a number

THOWLESS adj listless

THRALDOM n pl. -S servitude

THRALL v -ED, -ING, -S to enslave

THRASH v -ED, -ING, -ES to beat

THRASHER n pl. -S one that thrashes

THRAVE n pl. -S a unit of measure for grain

THRAW v -ED, -ING, -S to twist

THRAWART adj stubborn

THRAWN adj twisted **THRAWNLY** adv

THREAD v -ED, -ING, -S to pass a thread (a very slender cord) through

THREADER n pl. -S one that threads

THREADY adj THREADIER, THREADIEST resembling a thread

THREAP v -ED, -ING, -S to dispute

THREAPER n pl. -S one that threaps

THREAT v -ED, -ING, -S to threaten

THREATEN v -ED, -ING, -S to be a source of danger to

THREE n pl. -S a number

THREEP v -ED, -ING, -S to threap

THRENODE n pl. -S a threnody

THRENODY n pl. -DIES a song of lamentation

THRESH v -ED, -ING, -ES to separate the grain or seeds from a plant mechanically

THRESHER *n* pl. -S one that threshes

THREW past tense of throw

THRICE *adv* three times

THRIFT *n* pl. -S care and wisdom in the management of one's resources

THRIFTY *adj* THRIFTIER, THRIFTIEST displaying thrift

THRILL *v* -ED, -ING, -S to excite greatly

THRILLER *n* pl. -S one that thrills

THRIP *n* pl. -S a British coin

THRIVE *v* THROVE or THRIVED, THRIVEN, THRIVING, THRIVES to grow vigorously

THRIVER *n* pl. -S one that thrives

THRO *prep* through

THROAT *v* -ED, -ING, -S to utter in a hoarse voice

THROATY *adj* THROATIER, THROATIEST hoarse

THROB *v* THROBBED, THROBBING, THROBS to pulsate

THROBBER *n* pl. -S one that throbs

THROE *n* pl. -S a violent spasm of pain

THROMBIN *n* pl. -S an enzyme

THROMBUS *n* pl. -BI a clot occluding a blood vessel

THRONE *v* THRONED, THRONING, THRONES to place on a throne (a royal chair)

THRONG *v* -ED, -ING, -S to crowd into

THROSTLE *n* pl. -S a songbird

THROTTLE *v* -TLED, -TLING, -TLES to strangle

THROUGH *prep* by way of

THROVE *a* past tense of thrive

THROW *v* THREW, THROWN, THROWING, THROWS to propel through the air with a movement of the arm

THROWER *n* pl. -S one that throws

THRU *prep* through

THRUM *v* THRUMMED, THRUMMING, THRUMS to play a stringed instrument idly or monotonously

THRUMMER *n* pl. -S one that thrums

THRUMMY *adj* -MIER, -MIEST shaggy

THRUPUT *n* pl. -S the amount of raw material processed within a given time

THRUSH *n* pl. -ES a songbird

THRUST *v* -ED, -ING, -S to push forcibly

THRUSTER *n* pl. -S one that thrusts

THRUSTOR *n* pl. -S thruster

THRUWAY *n* pl. -WAYS an express highway

THUD *v* THUDDED, THUDDING, THUDS to make a dull, heavy sound

THUG *n* pl. -S a brutal ruffian or assassin

THUGGEE *n* pl. -S thuggery in India

THUGGERY *n* pl. -GERIES thuggish behavior

THUGGISH *adj* characteristic of a thug

THUJA *n* pl. -S an evergreen tree or shrub

THULIA *n* pl. -S an oxide of thulium

THULIUM *n* pl. -S a metallic element

THUMB *v* -ED, -ING, -S to leaf through with the thumb (the short, thick digit of the human hand)

THUMBKIN *n* pl. -S a screw that is turned by the thumb and fingers

THUMBNUT *n* pl. -S a nut that is turned by the thumb and fingers

THUMP *v* -ED, -ING, -S to strike so as to make a dull, heavy sound

THUMPER *n* pl. -S one that thumps

THUNDER *v* -ED, -ING, -S to produce a loud, resounding sound

THUNDERY *adj* accompanied with thunder

THURIBLE *n* pl. -S a censer

THURIFER *n* pl. -S one who carries a thurible in a religious ceremony

THURL *n* pl. -S the hip joint in cattle

THUS *adv* in this manner

THUSLY *adv* thus

THUYA *n* pl. -S thuja

THWACK *v* -ED, -ING, -S to strike with something flat

THWACKER *n* pl. -S one that thwacks

THWART *v* -ED, -ING, -S to prevent the accomplishment of

THWARTER *n* pl. -S one that thwarts

THWARTLY *adv* athwart

THY *pron* a possessive form of the pronoun thou

THYME *n* pl. -S an aromatic herb

THYMEY *adj* THYMIER, THYMIEST thymy

THYMI *a* pl. of thymus

THYMIC *adj* pertaining to thyme

THYMIER comparative of thymey and thymy

THYMIEST superlative of thymey and thymy

THYMINE n pl. -S a chemical compound

THYMOL n pl. -S a chemical compound

THYMUS n pl. -MI or -MUSES a glandular structure in the body

THYMY adj THYMIER, THYMIEST abounding in thyme

THYREOID adj pertaining to the thyroid

THYROID n pl. -S an endocrine gland

THYROXIN n pl. -S an amino acid

THYRSE n pl. -S thyraus

THYRSUS n pl. -SI a type of flower cluster THYRSOID adj

THYSELF pron yourself

TI n pl. -S the seventh tone of the diatonic musical scale

TIARA n pl. -S a jeweled headpiece worn by women TIARAED adj

TIBIA n pl. -IAE or -IAS a bone of the leg TIBIAL adj

TIC n pl. -S an involuntary muscular contraction

TICAL n pl. -S a former Thai unit of weight

TICK v -ED, -ING, -S to make a recurrent clicking sound

TICKER n pl. -S one that ticks

TICKET v -ED, -ING, -S to attach a tag to

TICKING n pl. -S a strong cotton fabric

TICKLE v -LED, -LING, -LES to touch lightly so as to produce a tingling sensation

TICKLER n pl. -S one that tickles

TICKLISH adj sensitive to tickling

TICKSEED n pl. -S a flowering plant

TICKTACK v -ED, -ING, -S to ticktock

TICKTOCK v -ED, -ING, -S to make the ticking sound of a clock

TICTAC v -TACKED, -TACKING, -TACS to ticktock

TICTOC v -TOCKED, -TOCKING, -TOCS to ticktock

TIDAL adj pertaining to the tides TIDALLY adv

TIDBIT n pl. -S a choice bit of food

TIDDLY adj slightly drunk

TIDE v TIDED, TIDING, TIDES to flow like the tide (the rise and fall of the ocean's waters)

TIDELAND n pl. -S land alternately covered and uncovered by the tide

TIDELESS adj lacking a tide

TIDELIKE adj resembling a tide

TIDEMARK n pl. -S a mark showing the highest or lowest point of a tide

TIDERIP n pl. -S a riptide

TIDEWAY n pl. -WAYS a tidal channel

TIDIED past tense of tidy

TIDIER comparative of tidy

TIDIES present 3d person sing. of tidy

TIDIEST superlative of tidy

TIDILY adv in a tidy manner

TIDINESS n pl. -ES the state of being tidy

TIDING n pl. -S a piece of news

TIDY adj -DIER, -DIEST neat and orderly

TIDY v -DIED, -DYING, -DIES to make tidy

TIDYTIPS n pl. TIDYTIPS an annual herb

TIE v TIED, TYING or TIEING, TIES to fasten with a cord or rope

TIEBACK n pl. -S a loop for holding a curtain back to one side

TIECLASP n pl. -S a clasp for securing a necktie

TIED past tense of tie

TIEPIN n pl. -S a pin for securing a necktie

TIER v -ED, -ING, -S to arrange in tiers (rows placed one above another)

TIERCE n pl. -S one of seven canonical daily periods for prayer and devotion

TIERCED adj divided into three equal parts

TIERCEL n pl. -S tercel

TIFF v -ED, -ING, -S to have a petty quarrel

TIFFANY n pl. -NIES a thin, mesh fabric

TIFFIN v -ED, -ING, -S to lunch

TIGER n pl. -S a large feline mammal

TIGEREYE n pl. -S a gemstone

TIGERISH adj resembling a tiger

TIGHT   *adj* TIGHTER, TIGHTEST firmly or closely fixed in place **TIGHTLY** *adv*

TIGHTEN   *v* -ED, -ING, -S to make tight

TIGHTS   *n/pl* a close-fitting garment

TIGHTWAD   *n* pl. -S a miser

TIGLON   *n* pl. -S the offspring of a male tiger and a female lion

TIGON   *n* pl. -S tiglon

TIGRESS   *n* pl. -ES a female tiger

TIGRISH   *adj* tigerish

TIKE   *n* pl. -S tyke

TIKI   *n* pl. -S a wood or stone image of a Polynesian god

TIL   *n* pl. -S the sesame plant

TILAPIA   *n* pl. -S an African fish

TILBURY   *n* pl. -BURIES a carriage having two wheels

TILDE   *n* pl. -S a mark placed over a letter to indicate its sound

TILE   *v* TILED, TILING, TILES to cover with tiles (thin slabs of baked clay)

TILEFISH   *n* pl. -ES a marine food fish

TILELIKE   *adj* resembling a tile

TILER   *n* pl. -S one that tiles

TILING   *n* pl. -S a surface of tiles

TILL   *v* -ED, -ING, -S to prepare land for crops by plowing **TILLABLE** *adj*

TILLAGE   *n* pl. -S cultivated land

TILLER   *v* -ED, -ING, -S to put forth stems from a root

TILT   *v* -ED, -ING, -S to cause to slant **TILTABLE** *adj*

TILTER   *n* pl. -S one that tilts

TILTH   *n* pl. -S tillage

TILTYARD   *n* pl. -S an area for jousting contests

TIMARAU   *n* pl. -S tamarau

TIMBAL   *n* pl. -S a large drum

TIMBALE   *n* pl. -S a pastry shell shaped like a drum

TIMBER   *v* -ED, -ING, -S to furnish with timber (wood used as a building material)

TIMBRE   *n* pl. -S the quality given to a sound by its overtones

TIMBREL   *n* pl. -S a percussion instrument

TIME   *v* TIMED, TIMING, TIMES to determine the speed or duration of

TIMECARD   *n* pl. -S a card for recording an employee's times of arrival and departure

TIMELESS   *adj* having no beginning or end

TIMELY   *adj* -LIER, -LIEST occurring at the right moment

TIMEOUS   *adj* timely

TIMEOUT   *n* pl. -S a brief suspension of activity

TIMER   *n* pl. -S one that times

TIMEWORK   *n* pl. -S work paid for by the hour or by the day

TIMEWORN   *adj* showing the effects of long use or wear

TIMID   *adj* -IDER, -IDEST lacking courage or self-confidence **TIMIDLY** *adv*

TIMIDITY   *n* pl. -TIES the quality of being timid

TIMING   *n* pl. -S the selection of the proper moment for doing something

TIMOROUS   *adj* fearful

TIMOTHY   *n* pl. -THIES a European grass

TIMPANO   *n* pl. -NI a kettledrum

TIMPANUM   *n* pl. -NA or -NUMS tympanum

TIN   *v* TINNED, TINNING, TINS to coat with tin (a metallic element)

TINAMOU   *n* pl. -S a South American game bird

TINCAL   *n* pl. -S crude borax

TINCT   *v* -ED, -ING, -S to tinge

TINCTURE   *v* -TURED, -TURING, -TURES to tinge

TINDER   *n* pl. -S readily combustible material **TINDERY** *adj*

TINE   *v* TINED, TINING, TINES to lose

TINEA   *n* pl. -S a fungous skin disease **TINEAL** *adj*

TINEID   *n* pl. -S one of a family of moths

TINFOIL   *n* pl. -S a thin metal sheeting

TINFUL   *n* pl. -S as much as a tin container can hold

TING   *v* -ED, -ING, -S to emit a high-pitched metallic sound

TINGE   *v* TINGED, TINGEING or TINGING, TINGES to apply a trace of color to

TINGLE v -GLED, -GLING, -GLES to cause a prickly, stinging sensation

TINGLER n pl. -S one that tingles

TINGLY adj -GLIER, -GLIEST tingling

TINHORN n pl. -S a showily pretentious person

TINIER comparative of tiny

TINIEST superlative of tiny

TINILY adv in a tiny manner

TININESS n pl. -ES the quality of being tiny

TINING present participle of tine

TINKER v -ED, -ING, -S to repair in an unskilled or experimental manner

TINKERER n pl. -S one that tinkers

TINKLE v -KLED, -KLING, -KLES to make slight, sharp, metallic sounds

TINKLING n pl. -S the sound made by something that tinkles

TINKLY adj -KLIER, -KLIEST producing a tinkling sound

TINLIKE adj resembling tin

TINMAN n pl. -MEN a tinsmith

TINNED past tense of tin

TINNER n pl. -S a tin miner

TINNIER comparative of tinny

TINNIEST superlative of tinny

TINNILY adv in a tinny manner

TINNING present participle of tin

TINNITUS n pl. -ES a ringing sound in the ears

TINNY adj -NIER, -NIEST of or resembling tin

TINPLATE n pl. -S thin sheet iron coated with tin

TINSEL v -SELED, -SELING, -SELS or -SELLED, -SELLING, -SELS to give a showy or gaudy appearance to

TINSELLY adj cheaply gaudy

TINSMITH n pl. -S one who works with tin

TINSTONE n pl. -S a tin ore

TINT v -ED, -ING, -S to color slightly or delicately

TINTER n pl. -S one that tints

TINTING n pl. -S the process of one that tints

TINTLESS adj lacking color

TINTYPE n pl. -S a kind of photograph

TINWARE n pl. -S articles made of tinplate

TINWORK n pl. -S something made of tin

TINY adj TINIER, TINIEST very small

TIP v TIPPED, TIPPING, TIPS to tilt

TIPCART n pl. -S a type of cart

TIPCAT n pl. -S a game resembling baseball

TIPI n pl. -S tepee

TIPLESS adj having no point or extremity

TIPOFF n pl. -S a hint or warning

TIPPABLE adj capable of being tipped

TIPPED past tense of tip

TIPPER n pl. -S one that tips

TIPPET n pl. -S a covering for the shoulders

TIPPIER comparative of tippy

TIPPIEST superlative of tippy

TIPPING present participle of tip

TIPPLE v -PLED, -PLING, -PLES to drink alcoholic beverages

TIPPLER n pl. -S one that tipples

TIPPY adj -PIER, -PIEST unsteady

TIPSIER comparative of tipsy

TIPSIEST superlative of tipsy

TIPSILY adv in a tipsy manner

TIPSTAFF n pl. -STAFFS or -STAVES an attendant in a court of law

TIPSTER n pl. -S one that sells information to gamblers

TIPSTOCK n pl. -S a part of a gun

TIPSY adj -SIER, -SIEST slightly drunk

TIPTOE v -TOED, -TOEING, -TOES to walk on the tips of one's toes

TIPTOP n pl. -S the highest point

TIRADE n pl. -S a long, vehement speech

TIRE v TIRED, TIRING, TIRES to grow tired

TIRED adj TIREDER, TIREDEST sapped of strength TIREDLY adv

TIRELESS adj seemingly incapable of tiring

TIRESOME adj tedious

TIRING present participle of tire

TIRL v -ED, -ING, -S to make a vibrating sound

TIRO   n pl. -ROS tyro

TIRRIVEE   n pl. -S a tantrum

TISANE   n pl. -S a ptisan

TISSUAL   adj pertaining to tissue

TISSUE   v -SUED, -SUING, -SUES to weave into tissue (a fine sheer fabric)

TISSUEY   adj resembling tissue

TIT   n pl. -S a small bird

TITAN   n pl. -S a person of great size

TITANATE   n pl. -S a chemical salt

TITANESS   n pl. -ES a female titan

TITANIA   n pl. -S a mineral

TITANIC   adj of great size

TITANISM   n pl. -S revolt against social conventions

TITANITE   n pl. -S a mineral

TITANIUM   n pl. -S a metallic element

TITANOUS   adj pertaining to titanium

TITBIT   n pl. -S tidbit

TITER   n pl. -S the strength of a chemical solution

TITHABLE   adj subject to the payment of tithes

TITHE   v TITHED, TITHING, TITHES to pay a tithe (a small tax)

TITHER   n pl. -S one that tithes

TITHING   n pl. -S the act of levying tithes

TITHONIA   n pl. -S a tall herb

TITI   n pl. -S an evergreen shrub or tree

TITIAN   n pl. -S a reddish brown color

TITIVATE   v -VATED, -VATING, -VATES to dress smartly

TITLARK   n pl. -S a songbird

TITLE   v -TLED, -TLING, -TLES to furnish with a title (a distinctive appellation)

TITLIST   n pl. -S a sports champion

TITMAN   n pl. -MEN the smallest of a litter of pigs

TITMOUSE   n pl. -MICE a small bird

TITRABLE   adj capable of being titrated

TITRANT   n pl. -S the reagent used in titration

TITRATE   v -TRATED, -TRATING, -TRATES to determine the strength of a solution by adding a reagent until a desired reaction occurs

TITRATOR   n pl. -S one that titrates

TITRE   n pl. -S titer

TITTER   v -ED, -ING, -S to utter a restrained, nervous laugh

TITTERER   n pl. -S one that titters

TITTIE   n pl. -S a sister

TITTIES   pl. of titty

TITTLE   n pl. -S a very small mark in writing or printing

TITTUP   v -TUPED, -TUPING, -TUPS or -TUPPED, -TUPPING, -TUPS to move in a lively manner

TITTUPPY   adj shaky; unsteady

TITTY   n pl. -TIES a teat

TITULAR   n pl. -S one who holds a title

TITULARY   n pl. -LARIES a titular

TIVY   adv with great speed

TIZZY   n pl. -ZIES a state of nervous confusion

TMESIS   n pl. TMESES the separation of the parts of a compound word by an intervening word or words

TO   prep in the direction of

TOAD   n pl. -S a tailless, jumping amphibian

TOADFISH   n pl. -ES a marine fish

TOADFLAX   n pl. -ES a perennial herb

TOADIED   past tense of toady

TOADIES   present 3d person sing. of toady

TOADISH   adj resembling a toad

TOADLESS   adj having no toads

TOADLIKE   adj resembling a toad

TOADY   v TOADIED, TOADYING, TOADIES to engage in servile flattering

TOADYISH   adj characteristic of one that toadies

TOADYISM   n pl. -S toadyish behavior

TOAST   v -ED, -ING, -S to brown by exposure to heat

TOASTER   n pl. -S a device for toasting

TOASTY   adj TOASTIER, TOASTIEST comfortably warm

TOBACCO   n pl. -COS or -COES an annual herb cultivated for its leaves

TOBOGGAN   v -ED, -ING, -S to ride on a long, narrow sled

TOBY   n pl. -BIES a type of drinking mug

TOCCATA *n pl.* -TAS or -TE a musical composition usually for an organ

TOCHER *v* -ED, -ING, -S to give a dowry to

TOCOLOGY *n pl.* -GIES the branch of medicine dealing with childbirth

TOCSIN *n pl.* -S an alarm sounded on a bell

TOD *n pl.* -S a British unit of weight

TODAY *n pl.* -DAYS the present day

TODDIES *pl.* of toddy

TODDLE *v* -DLED, -DLING, -DLES to walk unsteadily

TODDLER *n pl.* -S one that toddles

TODDY *n pl.* -DIES an alcoholic beverage

TODY *n pl.* -DIES a West Indian bird

TOE *v* TOED, TOEING, TOES to touch with the toe (one of the terminal members of the foot)

TOECAP *n pl.* -S a covering for the tip of a shoe or boot

TOEHOLD *n pl.* -S a space that supports the toes in climbing

TOELESS *adj* having no toes

TOELIKE *adj* resembling a toe

TOENAIL *v* -ED, -ING, -S to fasten with obliquely driven nails

TOEPIECE *n pl.* -S a piece of a shoe designed to cover the toes

TOEPLATE *n pl.* -S a metal tab attached to the tip of a shoe

TOESHOE *n pl.* -S a dance slipper without a heel

TOFF *n pl.* -S a dandy

TOFFEE *n pl.* -S a chewy candy

TOFFY *n pl.* -FIES toffee

TOFT *n pl.* -S a hillock

TOFU *n pl.* -S a soft Oriental cheese made from soybean milk

TOG *v* TOGGED, TOGGING, TOGS to clothe

TOGA *n pl.* -GAS or -GAE an outer garment worn in ancient Rome **TOGAED** *adj*

TOGATE *adj* pertaining to ancient Rome

TOGATED *adj* wearing a toga

TOGETHER *adv* into a union or relationship

TOGGED past tense of tog

TOGGERY *n pl.* -GERIES clothing

TOGGING present participle of tog

TOGGLE *v* -GLED, -GLING, -GLES to fasten with a type of pin or short rod

TOGGLER *n pl.* -S one that toggles

TOGUE *n pl.* -S a freshwater fish

TOIL *v* -ED, -ING, -S to work strenuously

TOILE *n pl.* -S a sheer linen fabric

TOILER *n pl.* -S one that toils

TOILET *v* -ED, -ING, -S to dress and groom oneself

TOILETRY *n pl.* -TRIES an article used in dressing and grooming oneself

TOILETTE *n pl.* -S the act of dressing and grooming oneself

TOILFUL *adj* toilsome

TOILSOME *adj* demanding much exertion

TOILWORN *adj* worn by toil

TOIT *v* -ED, -ING, -S to saunter

TOKAY *n pl.* -KAYS a Malaysian gecko

TOKE *n pl.* -S a puff on a marijuana cigarette

TOKEN *v* -ED, -ING, -S to serve as a sign of

TOKENISM *n pl.* -S the policy of making a superficial effort

TOKOLOGY *n pl.* -GIES tocology

TOKONOMA *n pl.* -S a small alcove in a Japanese house

TOLA *n pl.* -S a unit of weight used in India

TOLAN *n pl.* -S a chemical compound

TOLANE *n pl.* -S tolan

TOLBOOTH *n pl.* -S a prison

TOLD past tense of tell

TOLE *v* TOLED, TOLING, TOLES to allure

TOLEDO *n pl.* -DOS a finely tempered sword

TOLERANT *adj* inclined to tolerate

TOLERATE *v* -ATED, -ATING, -ATES to allow without active opposition

TOLIDIN *n pl.* -S tolidine

TOLIDINE *n pl.* -S a chemical compound

TOLING present participle of tole

TOLL   v -ED, -ING, -S to collect or impose a toll (a fixed charge for a service or privilege)

TOLLAGE   n pl. -S a toll

TOLLBAR   n pl. -S a tollgate

TOLLER   n pl. -S a collector of tolls

TOLLGATE   n pl. -S a gate where a toll is collected

TOLLMAN   n pl. -MEN a toller

TOLLWAY   n pl. -WAYS a road on which tolls are collected

TOLU   n pl. -S a fragrant resin

TOLUATE   n pl. -S a chemical salt

TOLUENE   n pl. -S a flammable liquid

TOLUIC   adj pertaining to any of four isomeric acids derived from toluene

TOLUID   n pl. -S toluide

TOLUIDE   n pl. -S an amide

TOLUIDIN   n pl. -S an amine

TOLUOL   n pl. -S toluene

TOLUOLE   n pl. -S toluol

TOLUYL   n pl. -S a univalent chemical radical

TOLYL   n pl. -S a univalent chemical radical

TOM   n pl. -S the male of various animals

TOMAHAWK   v -ED, -ING, -S to strike with a light ax

TOMALLEY   n pl. -LEYS the liver of a lobster

TOMAN   n pl. -S a coin of Iran

TOMATO   n pl. -TOES the fleshy, edible fruit of a perennial plant

TOMB   v -ED, -ING, -S to place in a tomb (a burial vault or chamber)

TOMBAC   n pl. -S an alloy of copper and zinc

TOMBACK   n pl. -S tombac

TOMBAK   n pl. -S tombac

TOMBAL   adj pertaining to a tomb

TOMBLESS   adj having no tomb

TOMBLIKE   adj resembling a tomb

TOMBOLO   n pl. -LOS a sandbar connecting an island to the mainland

TOMBOY   n pl. -BOYS a girl who prefers boyish activities

TOMCAT   n pl. -S a male cat

TOMCOD   n pl. -S a marine fish

TOME   n pl. -S a large book

TOMENTUM   n pl. -TA a network of small blood vessels

TOMFOOL   n pl. -S a foolish person

TOMMY   n pl. -MIES a loaf of bread

TOMMYROT   n pl. -S nonsense

TOMOGRAM   n pl. -S a photograph made with X rays

TOMORROW   n pl. -S the day following today

TOMPION   n pl. -S tampion

TOMTIT   n pl. -S a small bird

TON   n pl. -S a unit of weight

TONAL   adj pertaining to tone **TONALLY** adv

TONALITY   n pl. TIES a system of tones

TONDO   n pl. -DI a circular painting

TONE   v TONED, TONING, TONES to give a particular tone (a sound of definite pitch and vibration) to

TONELESS   adj lacking in tone

TONEME   n pl. -S a tonal unit of speech **TONEMIC** adj

TONER   n pl. -S one that tones

TONETICS   n/pl the phonetic study of tone in language **TONETIC** adj

TONETTE   n pl. -S a simple flute

TONG   v -ED, -ING, -S to lift with a type of grasping device

TONGA   n pl. -S a light cart used in India

TONGER   n pl. -S one that tongs

TONGMAN   n pl. -MEN a member of a Chinese secret society

TONGUE   v TONGUED, TONGUING, TONGUES to touch with the tongue (an organ of the mouth)

TONGUING   n pl. -S the use of the tongue in articulating notes on a wind instrument

TONIC   n pl. -S something that invigorates or refreshes

TONICITY   n pl. -TIES normal, healthy bodily condition

TONIER   comparative of tony

TONIEST   superlative of tony

TONIGHT   n pl. -S the present night

TONING   present participle of tone

TONISH   adj stylish **TONISHLY** adv

TONLET   n pl. -S a skirt of plate armor

TONNAGE n pl. -S total weight in tons

TONNE n pl. -S a unit of weight

TONNEAU n pl. -NEAUS or -NEAUX the rear seating compartment of an automobile

TONNER n pl. -S an object having a specified tonnage

TONNISH adj tonish

TONSIL n pl. -S a lymphoid organ **TONSILAR** adj

TONSURE v -SURED, -SURING, -SURES to shave the head of

TONTINE n pl. -S a form of collective life insurance

TONUS n pl. -ES a normal state of tension in muscle tissue

TONY adj TONIER, TONIEST stylish

TOO adv in addition

TOOK past tense of take

TOOL v -ED, -ING, -S to form or finish with a tool (an implement used in manual work)

TOOLBOX n pl. -ES a box for tools

TOOLER n pl. -S one that tools

TOOLHEAD n pl. -S a part of a machine

TOOLING n pl. -S ornamentation done with tools

TOOLLESS adj having no tools

TOOLROOM n pl. -S a room where tools are stored

TOOLSHED n pl. -S a building where tools are stored

TOOM adj empty

TOON n pl. -S an East Indian tree

TOOT v -ED, -ING, -S to sound a horn or whistle in short blasts

TOOTER n pl. -S one that toots

TOOTH n pl. TEETH one of the hard structures attached in a row to each jaw

TOOTH v -ED, -ING, -S to furnish with toothlike projections

TOOTHY adj TOOTHIER, TOOTHIEST having or showing prominent teeth **TOOTHILY** adv

TOOTLE v -TLED, -TLING, -TLES to toot softly or repeatedly

TOOTLER n pl. -S one that tootles

TOOTS n pl. -ES a woman or girl — usually used as a form of address

TOOTSIE n pl. -S tootsy

TOOTSY n pl. -SIES a foot

TOP v TOPPED, TOPPING, TOPS to cut off the top (the highest part, point, or surface) of

TOPAZ n pl. -ES a mineral **TOPAZINE** adj

TOPCOAT n pl. -S a lightweight overcoat

TOPCROSS n pl. -ES a cross between a purebred male and inferior female stock

TOPE v TOPED, TOPING, TOPES to drink liquor to excess

TOPEE n pl. -S topi

TOPER n pl. -S one that topes

TOPFUL adj topfull

TOPFULL adj full to the top

TOPH n pl. -S tufa

TOPHE n pl. -S tufa

TOPHUS n pl. -PHI a deposit of urates in the tissue around a joint

TOPI n pl. -S a sun helmet

TOPIARY n pl. -ARIES the art of trimming shrubs into shapes

TOPIC n pl. -S a subject of discourse **TOPICAL** adj

TOPING present participle of tope

TOPKICK n pl. -S a first sergeant

TOPKNOT n pl. -S an ornament for the hair

TOPLESS adj having no top

TOPLOFTY adj -LOFTIER, -LOFTIEST haughty

TOPMAST n pl. -S a mast of a ship

TOPMOST adj highest

TOPNOTCH adj excellent

TOPOI pl. of topos

TOPOLOGY n pl. -GIES a branch of mathematics

TOPONYM n pl. -S the name of a place

TOPONYMY n pl. -MIES the study of toponyms

TOPOS n pl. -POI a stock rhetorical theme

TOPOTYPE n pl. -S a specimen selected from a locality typical of a species

TOPPED past tense of top

TOPPER n pl. -S one that tops

TOPPING *n* pl. -S something that forms a top

TOPPLE *v* -PLED, -PLING, -PLES to fall forward

TOPSAIL *n* pl. -S a sail of a ship

TOPSIDE *n* pl. -S the upper portion of a ship

TOPSOIL *v* -ED, -ING, -S to remove the surface layer of soil from

TOPSTONE *n* pl. -S the stone at the top of a structure

TOPWORK *v* -ED, -ING, -S to graft scions of another variety of plant on the main branches of

TOQUE *n* pl. -S a close-fitting woman's hat

TOQUET *n* pl. -S toque

TOR *n* pl. -S a high, craggy hill

TORA *n* pl. -S torah

TORAH *n* pl. -S the body of Jewish law

TORC *n* pl. -S a metal collar or necklace

TORCH *v* -ED, -ING, -ES to set on fire

TORCHERE *n* pl. -S a type of electric lamp

TORCHIER *n* pl. -S torchere

TORCHON *n* pl. -S a coarse lace

TORE *n* pl. -S a torus

TOREADOR *n* pl. -S a bullfighter

TORERO *n* pl. -ROS a bullfighter

TOREUTIC *adj* pertaining to a type of metalwork

TORI pl. of torus

TORIC *adj* pertaining to a torus

TORIES pl. of tory

TORII *n* pl. TORII the gateway of a Japanese temple

TORMENT *v* -ED, -ING, -S to inflict with great bodily or mental suffering

TORN past participle of tear

TORNADO *n* pl. -DOES or -DOS a violent windstorm **TORNADIC** *adj*

TORNILLO *n* pl. -LOS a flowering shrub

TORO *n* pl. -ROS a bull

TOROID *n* pl. -S a type of geometric surface **TOROIDAL** *adj*

TOROSE *adj* cylindrical and swollen at intervals

TOROSITY *n* pl. -TIES the quality or state of being torose

TOROUS *adj* torose

TORPEDO *v* -ED, -ING, -ES or -S to damage or sink with an underwater missile

TORPID *n* pl. -S a racing boat

TORPIDLY *adv* in a sluggish manner

TORPOR *n* pl. -S mental or physical inactivity

TORQUATE *adj* having a torques

TORQUE *v* TORQUED, TORQUING, TORQUES to cause to twist

TORQUER *n* pl. -S one that torques

TORQUES *n* pl. -QUESES a band of feathers, hair, or coloration around the neck

TORQUING present participle of torque

TORR *n* pl. TORR a unit of pressure

TORREFY *v* -FIED, -FYING, -FIES to subject to intense heat

TORRENT *n* pl. -S a rapid stream of water

TORRID *adj* -RIDER, -RIDEST extremely hot **TORRIDLY** *adv*

TORRIFY *v* -FIED, -FYING, -FIES to torrefy

TORSADE *n* pl. -S a twisted cord

TORSE *n* pl. -S a wreath of twisted silks

TORSI a pl. of torso

TORSION *n* pl. -S the act of twisting

TORSK *n* pl. -S a marine food fish

TORSO *n* pl. -SI or -SOS the trunk of the human body

TORT *n* pl. -S a civil wrong

TORTE *n* pl. TORTEN or TORTES a rich cake

TORTILE *adj* twisted; coiled

TORTILLA *n* pl. -S a round, flat cake of unleavened cornmeal

TORTIOUS *adj* of the nature of a tort

TORTOISE *n* pl. -S any of an order of reptiles having the body enclosed in a bony shell

TORTONI *n* pl. -S a type of ice cream

TORTRIX *n* pl. -ES a small moth

TORTUOUS *adj* marked by repeated turns or bends

TORTURE *v* -TURED, -TURING, -TURES to subject to severe physical pain

TORTURER *n* pl. -S one that tortures

TORULA *n* pl. -LAE or -LAS a type of fungus

TORUS *n pl.* -RI a large convex molding

TORY *n pl.* -RIES a political conservative

TOSH *n pl.* -ES nonsense

TOSS *v* TOSSED or TOST, TOSSING, TOSSES to throw lightly

TOSSER *n pl.* -S one that tosses

TOSSPOT *n pl.* -S a drunkard

TOSSUP *n pl.* -S an even choice or chance

TOST a past tense of toss

TOT *v* TOTTED, TOTTING, TOTS to total

TOTABLE *adj* capable of being toted

TOTAL *v* -TALED, -TALING, -TALS or -TALLED, -TALLING, -TALS to ascertain the entire amount of

TOTALISE *v* -ISED, -ISING, -ISES to totalize

TOTALISM *n pl.* -S centralized control by an autocratic authority

TOTALITY *n pl.* -TIES the quality or state of being complete

TOTALIZE *v* -IZED, -IZING, -IZES to make complete

TOTALLED a past tense of total

TOTALLING a present participle of total

TOTALLY *adv* completely

TOTE *v* TOTED, TOTING, TOTES to carry by hand

TOTEM *n pl.* -S a natural object serving as the emblem of a family or clan **TOTEMIC** *adj*

TOTEMISM *n pl.* -S a system of tribal division according to totems

TOTEMIST *n pl.* -S a specialist in totemism

TOTEMITE *n pl.* -S a totemist

TOTER *n pl.* -S one that totes

TOTHER *pron* the other

TOTING present participle of tote

TOTTED past tense of tot

TOTTER *v* -ED, -ING, -S to walk unsteadily

TOTTERER *n pl.* -S one that totters

TOTTERY *adj* shaky

TOTTING present participle of tot

TOUCAN *n pl.* -S a tropical bird

TOUCH *v* -ED, -ING, -ES to be in or come into contact with

TOUCHE *interj* — used to acknowledge a hit in fencing

TOUCHER *n pl.* -S one that touches

TOUCHUP *n pl.* -S an act of finishing by adding minor improvements

TOUCHY *adj* TOUCHIER, TOUCHIEST overly sensitive **TOUCHILY** *adv*

TOUGH *adj* TOUGHER, TOUGHEST strong and resilient

TOUGH *n pl.* -S a rowdy

TOUGHEN *v* -ED, -ING, -S to make tough

TOUGHIE *n pl.* -S a tough

TOUGHIES pl. of toughy

TOUGHISH *adj* somewhat tough

TOUGHLY *adv* in a tough manner

TOUGHY *n pl.* TOUGHIES toughie

TOUPEE *n pl.* -S a wig worn to cover a bald spot

TOUR *v* -ED, -ING, -S to travel from place to place

TOURACO *n pl.* -COS an African bird

TOURER *n pl.* -S a large, open automobile

TOURING *n pl.* -S cross-country skiing for pleasure

TOURISM *n pl.* -S the practice of touring for pleasure

TOURIST *n pl.* -S one who tours for pleasure **TOURISTY** *adj*

TOURNEY *v* -ED, -ING, -S to compete in a tournament

TOUSE *v* TOUSED, TOUSING, TOUSES to tousle

TOUSLE *v* -SLED, -SLING, -SLES to dishevel

TOUT *v* -ED, -ING, -S to solicit brazenly

TOUTER *n pl.* -S one that touts

TOUZLE *v* -ZLED, -ZLING, -ZLES to tousle

TOVARICH *n pl.* -ES comrade

TOVARISH *n pl.* -ES tovarich

TOW *v* -ED, -ING, -S to pull by means of a rope or chain

TOWAGE *n pl.* -S the price paid for towing

TOWARD *prep* in the direction of

TOWARDLY *adj* favorable

TOWARDS *prep* toward

TOWAWAY *n pl.* -AWAYS the act of towing away a vehicle

TOWBOAT   n pl. -S a tugboat

TOWEL   v -ELED, -ELING, -ELS or -ELLED, -ELLING, -ELS to wipe with a towel (an absorbent cloth)

TOWELING   n pl. -S material used for towels

TOWER   v -ED, -ING, -S to rise to a great height

TOWERY   adj -ERIER, -ERIEST very tall

TOWHEAD   n pl. -S a head of light blond hair

TOWHEE   n pl. -S a common finch

TOWIE   n pl. -S a form of contract bridge for three players

TOWLINE   n pl. -S a line used in towing

TOWMOND   n pl. -S a year

TOWMONT   n pl. -S towmond

TOWN   n pl. -S a center of population smaller than a city

TOWNEE   n pl. -S a townsman

TOWNFOLK   n/pl the inhabitants of a town

TOWNIE   n pl. -S a nonstudent who lives in a college town

TOWNIES   pl. of towny

TOWNISH   adj characteristic of a town

TOWNLESS   adj having no towns

TOWNLET   n pl. -S a small town

TOWNSHIP   n pl. -S an administrative division of a county

TOWNSMAN   n pl. -MEN a resident of a town

TOWNWEAR   n pl. -S apparel that is suitable for wear in the city

TOWNY   n pl. TOWNIES townie

TOWPATH   n pl. -S a path along a river that is used by animals towing boats

TOWROPE   n pl. -S a rope used in towing

TOWY   adj resembling coarse hemp or flax fiber

TOXAEMIA   n pl. -S toxemia TOXAEMIC adj

TOXEMIA   n pl. -S the condition of having toxins in the blood TOXEMIC adj

TOXIC   adj pertaining to a toxin

TOXICAL   adj toxic

TOXICANT   n pl. -S a poisonous substance

TOXICITY   n pl. -TIES the quality of being poisonous

TOXIN   n pl. -S a poisonous substance

TOXINE   n pl. -S toxin

TOXOID   n pl. -S a type of toxin

TOY   v -ED, -ING, -S to amuse oneself as if with a toy (a child's plaything)

TOYER   n pl. -S one that toys

TOYISH   adj frivolous

TOYLESS   adj having no toy

TOYLIKE   adj resembling a toy

TOYO   n pl. -YOS a smooth straw used in making hats

TOYON   n pl. -S an evergreen shrub

TRABEATE   adj constructed with horizontal beams

TRACE   v TRACED, TRACING, TRACES to follow the course of

TRACER   n pl. -S one that traces

TRACERY   n pl. -ERIES ornamental work of interlaced lines

TRACING   present participle of trace

TRACHEA   n pl. -CHEAE or -CHEAS the passage for conveying air to the lungs TRACHEAL adj

TRACHEID   n pl. -S a long, tubular plant cell

TRACHLE   v -LED, -LING, -LES to draggle

TRACHOMA   n pl. -S a disease of the eye

TRACHYTE   n pl. -S an igneous rock

TRACING   n pl. -S something that is traced

TRACK   v -ED, -ING, -S to follow the marks left by an animal, a person, or a vehicle

TRACKAGE   n pl. -S the track system of a railroad

TRACKER   n pl. -S one that tracks

TRACKING   n pl. -S the placement of students within a curriculum

TRACKMAN   n pl. -MEN a railroad worker

TRACT   n pl. -S an expanse of land

TRACTATE   n pl. -S a treatise

TRACTILE   adj capable of being drawn out in length

TRACTION   n pl. -S the act of pulling or drawing over a surface TRACTIVE adj

TRACTOR   n pl. -S a motor vehicle used in farming

TRAD   adj traditional

TRADE   v TRADED, TRADING, TRADES to give in exchange for another commodity TRADABLE adj

TRADER   n pl. -S one that trades

TRADITOR n pl. -ES a traitor among the early Christians

TRADUCE v -DUCED, -DUCING, -DUCES to defame

TRADUCER n pl. -S one that traduces

TRAFFIC v -FICKED, -FICKING, -FICS to engage in buying and selling

TRAGEDY n pl. -DIES a disastrous event

TRAGI pl. of tragus

TRAGIC adj of the nature of a tragedy

TRAGICAL adj tragic

TRAGOPAN n pl. -S an Asian pheasant

TRAGUS n pl. -GI a part of the external opening of the ear

TRAIK v -ED, -ING, -S to trudge

TRAIL v -ED, -ING, -S to drag along a surface

TRAILER v -ED, -ING, -S to transport by means of a trailer (a vehicle drawn by another)

TRAIN v -ED, -ING, -S to instruct systematically

TRAINEE n pl. -S a person receiving training

TRAINER n pl. -S one that trains

TRAINFUL n pl. -S as much as a railroad train will hold

TRAINING n pl. -S systematic instruction

TRAINMAN n pl. -MEN a railroad employee

TRAINWAY n pl. -WAYS a railway

TRAIPSE v TRAIPSED, TRAIPSING, TRAIPSES to walk about in an idle or aimless manner

TRAIT n pl. -S a distinguishing characteristic

TRAITOR n pl. -S one who betrays another

TRAJECT v -ED, -ING, -S to transmit

TRAM v TRAMMED, TRAMMING, TRAMS to convey in a tramcar

TRAMCAR n pl. -S a streetcar

TRAMEL v -ELED, -ELING, -ELS or -ELLED, -ELLING, -ELS to trammel

TRAMELL v -ED, -ING, -S to trammel

TRAMLESS adj having no tramcar

TRAMLINE n pl. -S a streetcar line

TRAMMED past tense of tram

TRAMMEL v -MELED, -MELING, -MELS or -MELLED, -MELLING, -MELS to hinder

TRAMMING present participle of tram

TRAMP v -ED, -ING, -S to walk with a firm, heavy step

TRAMPER n pl. -S one that tramps

TRAMPISH adj resembling a vagabond

TRAMPLE v -PLED, -PLING, -PLES to tread on heavily

TRAMPLER n pl. -S one that tramples

TRAMROAD n pl. -S a railway in a mine

TRAMWAY n pl. -WAYS a tramline

TRANCE v TRANCED, TRANCING, TRANCES to put into a trance (a semiconscious state)

TRANGAM n pl. -S a gewgaw

TRANQUIL adj -QUILER, -QUILEST or -QUILLER, -QUILLEST free from disturbance

TRANS adj characterized by the arrangement of different atoms on opposite sides of the molecule

TRANSACT v -ED, -ING, -S to carry out

TRANSECT v -ED, -ING, -S to cut across

TRANSEPT n pl. -S a major transverse part of the body of a church

TRANSFER v -FERRED, -FERRING, -FERS to convey from one source to another

TRANSFIX v -FIXED or -FIXT, -FIXING, -FIXES to impale

TRANSHIP v -SHIPPED, -SHIPPING, -SHIPS to transfer from one conveyance to another

TRANSIT v -ED, -ING, -S to pass across or through

TRANSMIT v -MITTED, -MITTING, -MITS to send from one place or person to another

TRANSOM n pl. -S a small window above a door or another window

TRANSUDE v -SUDED, -SUDING, -SUDES to pass through a membrane

TRAP v TRAPPED or TRAPT, TRAPPING, TRAPS to catch in a trap (a device for capturing and holding animals)

TRAPAN v -PANNED, -PANNING, -PANS to trepan

TRAPBALL n pl. -S a type of ball game

TRAPDOOR	*n pl.* -S a lifting or sliding door covering an opening	
TRAPES	*v* -ED, -ING, -ES to traipse	
TRAPEZE	*n pl.* -S a gymnastic apparatus	
TRAPEZIA	*n/pl* four-sided polygons having no parallel sides	
TRAPLIKE	*adj* resembling a trap	
TRAPNEST	*v* -ED, -ING, -S to determine the productivity of hens with a type of nest	
TRAPPEAN	*adj* pertaining to traprock	
TRAPPED	a past tense of trap	
TRAPPER	*n pl.* -S one that traps	
TRAPPING	*n pl.* -S a covering for a horse	
TRAPPOSE	*adj* trappean	
TRAPPOUS	*adj* trappean	
TRAPROCK	*n pl.* -S an igneous rock	
TRAPT	a past tense of trap	
TRAPUNTO	*n pl.* -TOS a decorative quilted design	
TRASH	*v* -ED, -ING, -ES to free from trash (worthless or waste matter)	
TRASHMAN	*n pl.* -MEN a person who removes trash	
TRASHY	*adj* TRASHIER, TRASHIEST resembling trash **TRASHILY** *adv*	
TRASS	*n pl.* -ES a volcanic rock	
TRAUCHLE	*v* -LED, -LING, -LES to trachle	
TRAUMA	*n pl.* -MAS or -MATA a severe emotional shock	
TRAVAIL	*v* -ED, -ING, -S to toil	
TRAVE	*n pl.* -S a frame for confining a horse	
TRAVEL	*v* -ELED, -ELING, -ELS or -ELLED, -ELLING, -ELS to go from one place to another	
TRAVELER	*n pl.* -S one that travels	
TRAVELOG	*n pl.* -S a lecture or film on traveling	
TRAVERSE	*v* -VERSED, -VERSING, -VERSES to pass across or through	
TRAVESTY	*v* -TIED, -TYING, -TIES to parody	
TRAVOIS	*n pl.* -ES a type of sled	
TRAVOISE	*n pl.* -S travois	
TRAWL	*v* -ED, -ING, -S to fish by dragging a net along the sea bottom	
TRAWLER	*n pl.* -S a boat used for trawling	
TRAWLEY	*n pl.* -LEYS a small truck or car for conveying material	
TRAY	*n pl.* TRAYS a flat, shallow receptacle	
TRAYFUL	*n pl.* -S as much as a tray will hold	
TREACLE	*n pl.* -S molasses **TREACLY** *adj*	
TREAD	*v* TROD, TRODE, or TREADED, TRODDEN, TREADING, TREADS to walk on, over, or along	
TREADER	*n pl.* -S one that treads	
TREADLE	*v* -LED, -LING, -LES to work a foot lever	
TREADLER	*n pl.* -S one that treadles	
TREASON	*n pl.* -S violation of allegiance toward one's country	
TREASURE	*v* -URED, -URING, -URES to value highly	
TREASURY	*n pl.* -URIES a place where funds are received, kept, and disbursed	
TREAT	*v* -ED, -ING, -S to behave in a particular way toward	
TREATER	*n pl.* -S one that treats	
TREATISE	*n pl.* -S a formal and systematic written account of a subject	
TREATY	*n pl.* -TIES a formal agreement between two or more nations	
TREBLE	*v* -BLED, -BLING, -BLES to triple	
TREBLY	*adv* triply	
TRECENTO	*n pl.* -TOS the fourteenth century	
TREDDLE	*v* -DLED, -DLING, -DLES to treadle	
TREE	*v* TREED, TREEING, TREES to drive up a tree (a tall, woody plant)	
TREELESS	*adj* having no tree	
TREELIKE	*adj* resembling a tree	
TREENAIL	*n pl.* -S a wooden peg used for fastening timbers	
TREETOP	*n pl.* -S the top of a tree	
TREF	*adj* unfit for use according to Jewish law	
TREFAH	*adj* tref	
TREFOIL	*n pl.* -S a plant having ternate leaves	
TREHALA	*n pl.* -S a sweet, edible substance forming the pupal case of certain weevils	

TREK *v* TREKKED, TREKKING, TREKS to make a slow or arduous journey

TREKKER *n* pl. -S one that treks

TRELLIS *v* -ED, -ING, -ES to provide with a trellis (a frame used as a support for climbing plants)

TREMBLE *v* -BLED, -BLING, -BLES to shake involuntarily

TREMBLER *n* pl. -S one that trembles

TREMBLY *adj* -BLIER, -BLIEST marked by trembling

TREMOLO *n* pl. -LOS a vibrating musical effect

TREMOR *n* pl. -S a shaking movement

TRENAIL *n* pl. -S treenail

TRENCH *v* -ED, -ING, -ES to dig a long, narrow excavation in the ground

TRENCHER *n* pl. -S a wooden platter for serving food

TREND *v* -ED, -ING, -S to take a particular course

TRENDY *adj* TRENDIER, TRENDIEST very fashionable TRENDILY *adv*

TREPAN *v* -PANNED, -PANNING, -PANS to trephine

TREPANG *n* pl. -S a marine animal

TREPHINE *v* -PHINED, -PHINING, -PHINES to operate on with a surgical saw

TREPID *adj* timorous

TRESPASS *v* -ED, -ING, -ES to enter upon the land of another unlawfully

TRESS *n* pl. -ES a long lock of hair TRESSED *adj*

TRESSEL *n* pl. -S trestle

TRESSIER comparative of tressy

TRESSIEST superlative of tressy

TRESSOUR *n* pl. -S tressure

TRESSURE *n* pl. -S a type of heraldic design

TRESSY *adj* TRESSIER, TRESSIEST abounding in tresses

TRESTLE *n* pl. -S a framework for supporting a bridge

TRET *n* pl. -S an allowance formerly paid to purchasers for waste incurred in transit

TREVET *n* pl. -S trivet

TREWS *n/pl* close-fitting tartan trousers

TREY *n* pl. TREYS a three in cards, dice, or dominoes

TRIABLE *adj* subject to judicial examination

TRIACID *n* pl. -S a type of acid

TRIAD *n* pl. -S a group of three

TRIADIC *n* pl. -S a member of a triad

TRIADISM *n* pl. -S the quality or state of being a triad

TRIAGE *n* pl. -S a system of treating disaster victims

TRIAL *n* pl. -S a judicial examination

TRIANGLE *n* pl. -S a polygon having three sides

TRIARCHY *n* pl. -CHIES government by three persons

TRIAXIAL *adj* having three axes

TRIAZIN *n* pl. -S triazine

TRIAZINE *n* pl. -S a chemical compound

TRIAZOLE *n* pl. -S a chemical compound

TRIBADE *n* pl. -S a lesbian TRIBADIC *adj*

TRIBAL *adj* pertaining to a tribe TRIBALLY *adv*

TRIBASIC *adj* having three replaceable hydrogen atoms

TRIBE *n* pl. -S a group of people sharing a common ancestry, language, and culture

TRIBRACH *n* pl. -S a type of metrical foot

TRIBUNAL *n* pl. -S a court of justice

TRIBUNE *n* pl. -S a defender of the rights of the people

TRIBUTE *n* pl. -S something given to show respect, gratitude, or admiration

TRICE *v* TRICED, TRICING, TRICES to haul up with a rope

TRICEPS *n* pl. -ES an arm muscle

TRICHINA *n* pl. -NAE or -NAS a parasitic worm

TRICHITE *n* pl. -S a minute mineral body found in volcanic rocks

TRICHOID *adj* hairlike

TRICHOME *n* pl. -S a hairlike outgrowth

TRICING present participle of trice

TRICK *v* -ED, -ING, -S to deceive

TRICKER *n* pl. -S one that tricks

TRICKERY *n* pl. -ERIES deception

TRICKIE *adj* TRICKIER, TRICKIEST tricky

TRICKIER	comparative of tricky
TRICKIEST	superlative of tricky
TRICKILY	*adv* in a tricky manner
TRICKISH	*adj* tricky
TRICKLE	*v* -LED, -LING, -LES to flow or fall in drops
TRICKLY	*adj* -LIER, -LIEST marked by trickling
TRICKSY	*adj* -SIER, -SIEST mischievous
TRICKY	*adj* TRICKIER, TRICKIEST characterized by deception
TRICLAD	*n* pl. -S an aquatic flatworm
TRICOLOR	*n* pl. -S a flag having three colors
TRICORN	*n* pl. -S a hat with the brim turned up on three sides
TRICORNE	*n* pl. -S tricorn
TRICOT	*n* pl. -S a knitted fabric
TRICTRAC	*n* pl. -S a form of backgammon
TRICYCLE	*n* pl. -S a vehicle having three wheels
TRIDENT	*n* pl. -S a spear having three prongs
TRIDUUM	*n* pl. -S a period of three days of prayer
TRIED	past tense of try
TRIENE	*n* pl. -S a type of chemical compound
TRIENNIA	*n/pl* periods of three years
TRIENS	*n* pl. -ENTES a coin of ancient Rome
TRIER	*n* pl. -S one that tries
TRIES	present 3d person sing. of try
TRIETHYL	*adj* containing three ethyl groups
TRIFID	*adj* divided into three parts
TRIFLE	*v* -FLED, -FLING, -FLES to waste time
TRIFLER	*n* pl. -S one that trifles
TRIFLING	*n* pl. -S a waste of time
TRIFOCAL	*n* pl. -S a type of lens
TRIFOLD	*adj* having three parts
TRIFORIA	*n/pl* galleries in a church
TRIFORM	*adj* having three forms
TRIG	*adj* TRIGGER, TRIGGEST neat
TRIG	*v* TRIGGED, TRIGGING, TRIGS to make trig
TRIGGER	*v* -ED, -ING, -S to actuate
TRIGGEST	superlative of trig
TRIGGING	present participle of trig
TRIGLY	*adv* in a trig manner
TRIGLYPH	*n* pl. -S an architectural ornament
TRIGNESS	*n* pl. -ES the quality or state of being trig
TRIGO	*n* pl. -GOS wheat
TRIGON	*n* pl. -S an ancient stringed instrument
TRIGONAL	*adj* shaped like a triangle
TRIGRAPH	*n* pl. -S a group of three letters representing one sound
TRIHEDRA	*n/pl* figures having three plane surfaces meeting at a point
TRIJET	*n* pl. -S an airplane powered by three jet engines
TRILBY	*n* pl. -BIES a soft felt hat
TRILL	*v* -ED, -ING, -S to sing or play with a vibrating effect
TRILLER	*n* pl. -S one that trills
TRILLION	*n* pl. -S a number
TRILLIUM	*n* pl. -S a flowering plant
TRILOBAL	*adj* trilobed
TRILOBED	*adj* having three lobes
TRILOGY	*n* pl. -GIES a group of three related literary works
TRIM	*adj* TRIMMER, TRIMMEST neat and orderly
TRIM	*v* TRIMMED, TRIMMING, TRIMS to make trim by cutting
TRIMARAN	*n* pl. -S a sailing vessel
TRIMER	*n* pl. -S a type of chemical compound
TRIMETER	*n* pl. -S a verse of three metrical feet
TRIMLY	*adv* in a trim manner
TRIMMED	past tense of trim
TRIMMER	*n* pl. -S one that trims
TRIMMEST	superlative of trim
TRIMMING	*n* pl. -S something added as a decoration
TRIMNESS	*n* pl. -ES the state of being trim
TRIMORPH	*n* pl. -S a substance existing in three forms
TRIMOTOR	*n* pl. -S en airplane powered by three engines
TRINAL	*adj* having three parts
TRINARY	*adj* consisting of three parts

TRINDLE	v -DLED, -DLING, -DLES to trundle	**TRIPPET**	n pl. -S a part of a mechanism designed to strike another part
TRINE	v TRINED, TRINING, TRINES to place in a particular astrological position	**TRIPPING**	n pl. -S the act of one that trips
		TRIPTANE	n pl. -S a chemical compound
TRINITY	n pl. -TIES a group of three	**TRIPTYCA**	n pl. -S a triptych
TRINKET	v -ED, -ING, -S to deal secretly	**TRIPTYCH**	n pl. -S an ancient writing tablet
TRINKUMS	n/pl small ornaments	**TRIREME**	n pl. -S an ancient Greek or Roman warship
TRINODAL	adj having three nodes		
TRIO	n pl. TRIOS a group of three	**TRISCELE**	n pl. -S triskele
TRIODE	n pl. -S a type of electron tube	**TRISECT**	v -ED, -ING, -S to divide into three equal parts
TRIOL	n pl. -S a type of chemical compound	**TRISEME**	n pl. -S a type of metrical foot TRISEMIC adj
TRIOLET	n pl. -S a short poem of fixed form	**TRISKELE**	n pl. -S a figure consisting of three branches radiating from a center
TRIOSE	n pl. -S a simple sugar		
TRIOXID	n pl. -S trioxide	**TRISMUS**	n pl. -ES lockjaw TRISMIC adj
TRIOXIDE	n pl. -S a type of oxide	**TRISOME**	n pl. -S an organism having one chromosome in addition to the usual diploid number
TRIP	v TRIPPED, TRIPPING, TRIPS to stumble		
TRIPACK	n pl. -S a type of film pack	**TRISOMIC**	n pl. -S a trisome
TRIPART	adj divided into three parts	**TRISOMY**	n pl. -MIES the condition of being a trisome
TRIPE	n pl. -S a part of the stomach of a ruminant that is used as food	**TRISTATE**	adj pertaining to an area made up of three adjoining states
TRIPEDAL	adj having three feet		
TRIPHASE	adj having three phases	**TRISTE**	adj sad
TRIPLANE	n pl. -S a type of airplane	**TRISTEZA**	n pl. -S a disease of citrus trees
TRIPLE	v -PLED, -PLING, -PLES to make three times as great	**TRISTFUL**	adj sad
TRIPLET	n pl. -S a group of three of one kind	**TRISTICH**	n pl. -S a stanza of three lines
TRIPLEX	n pl. -ES an apartment having three floors	**TRITE**	adj TRITER, TRITEST used so often as to be made commonplace TRITELY adv
TRIPLING	present participle of triple		
TRIPLITE	n pl. -S a mineral	**TRITHING**	n pl. -S an administrative division in England
TRIPLOID	n pl. -S a cell having a chromosome number that is three times the basic number	**TRITICUM**	n pl. -S a cereal grass
		TRITIUM	n pl. -S an isotope of hydrogen
TRIPLY	adv in a triple degree, manner, or number	**TRITOMA**	n pl. -S an African herb
TRIPOD	n pl. -S a stand having three legs TRIPODAL, TRIPODIC adj	**TRITON**	n pl. -S a marine mollusk
		TRITONE	n pl. -S a musical interval of three whole tones
TRIPODY	n pl. -DIES a verse of three metrical feet	**TRIUMPH**	v -ED, -ING, -S to be victorious
TRIPOLI	n pl. -S a soft, friable rock	**TRIUMVIR**	n pl. -VIRS or -VIRI one of a ruling body of three in ancient Rome
TRIPOS	n pl. -ES a tripod		
TRIPPED	past tense of trip	**TRIUNE**	n pl. -S a trinity
TRIPPER	n pl. -S one that trips	**TRIUNITY**	n pl. -TIES a trinity
		TRIVALVE	n pl. -S a type of shell
		TRIVET	n pl. -S a small stand having three legs

TRIVIA	*n/pl* Insignificant matters
TRIVIAL	*adj* insignificant
TRIVIUM	*n* pl. -IA a group of studies in medieval schools
TROAK	*v* -ED, -ING, -S to troke
TROCAR	*n* pl. -S a surgical instrument
TROCHAIC	*n* pl. -S a trochee
TROCHAL	*adj* shaped like a wheel
TROCHAR	*n* pl. -S trocar
TROCHE	*n* pl. -S a medicated lozenge
TROCHEE	*n* pl. -S a type of metrical foot
TROCHIL	*n* pl. -S an African bird
TROCHILI	*n/pl* trochils
TROCHLEA	*n* pl. -LEAE or -LEAS an anatomical structure resembling a pulley
TROCHOID	*n* pl. -S a type of geometric curve
TROCK	*v* -ED, -ING, -S to troke
TROD	a past tense of tread
TRODDEN	past participle of tread
TRODE	a past tense of tread
TROFFER	*n* pl. -S a fixture for fluorescent lighting
TROGON	*n* pl. -S a tropical bird
TROIKA	*n* pl. -S a Russian carriage
TROILITE	*n* pl. -S a mineral
TROILUS	*n* pl. -ES a large butterfly
TROIS	*n* pl. TROIS the number three
TROKE	*v* TROKED, TROKING, TROKES to exchange
TROLAND	*n* pl. -S a unit of measurement of retinal response to light
TROLL	*n* pl. -S a dwarf or giant of Teutonic folklore
TROLL	*v* -ED, -ING, -S to fish with a slowly trailing line
TROLLER	*n* pl. -S one that trolls
TROLLEY	*v* -ED, -ING, -S to convey by streetcar
TROLLIED	past tense of trolly
TROLLIES	present 3d person sing. of trolly
TROLLING	*n* pl. -S the act of one that trolls
TROLLOP	*n* pl. -S a prostitute **TROLLOPY** *adj*
TROLLY	*v* -LIED, -LYING, -LIES to trolley
TROMBONE	*n* pl. -S a brass wind instrument
TROMMEL	*n* pl. -S a screen used for sifting rock, ore, or coal
TROMP	*v* -ED, -ING, -S to tramp
TROMPE	*n* pl. -S a device used for supplying air to a furnace
TRONA	*n* pl. -S a mineral
TRONE	*n* pl. -S a weighing device
TROOP	*v* -ED, -ING, -S to move or gather in crowds
TROOPER	*n* pl. -S a cavalryman
TROOPIAL	*n* pl. -S troupial
TROOZ	*n/pl* trews
TROP	*adv* too much
TROPE	*n* pl. -S the figurative use of a word
TROPHIC	*adj* pertaining to nutrition
TROPHY	*v* -PHIED, -PHYING, -PHIES to honor with a trophy (a symbol of victory)
TROPIC	*n* pl. -S either of two circles of the celestial sphere on each side of the equator **TROPICAL** *adj*
TROPIN	*n* pl. -S tropine
TROPINE	*n* pl. -S a poisonous alkaloid
TROPISM	*n* pl. -S the involuntary response of an organism to an external stimulus
TROT	*v* TROTTED, TROTTING, TROTS to go at a gait between a walk and a run
TROTH	*v* -ED, -ING, -S to betroth
TROTLINE	*n* pl. -S a strong fishing line
TROTTED	past tense of trot
TROTTER	*n* pl. -S a horse that trots
TROTTING	present participle of trot
TROTYL	*n* pl. -S an explosive
TROUBLE	*v* -BLED, -BLING, -BLES to distress
TROUBLER	*n* pl. -S one that troubles
TROUGH	*n* pl. -S a long, narrow receptacle
TROUNCE	*v* TROUNCED, TROUNCING, TROUNCES to beat severely
TROUPE	*v* TROUPED, TROUPING, TROUPES to tour with a theatrical company
TROUPER	*n* pl. -S a member of a theatrical company
TROUPIAL	*n* pl. -S a tropical bird

TROUPING present participle of troupe

TROUSER *adj* pertaining to trousers

TROUSERS *n/pl* a garment for the lower part of the body

TROUT *n* pl. -S a freshwater fish

TROUTY *adj* TROUTIER, TROUTIEST abounding in trout

TROUVERE *n* pl. -S a medieval poet

TROUVEUR *n* pl. -S trouvere

TROVE *n* pl. -S a valuable discovery

TROVER *n* pl. -S a type of legal action

TROW *v* -ED, -ING, -S to suppose

TROWEL *v* -ELED, -ELING, -ELS or -ELLED, -ELLING, -ELS to smooth with a trowel (a hand tool having a flat blade)

TROWELER *n* pl. -S one that trowels

TROWSERS *n/pl* trousers

TROWTH *n* pl. -S truth

TROY *n* pl. TROYS a system of weights

TRUANCY *n* pl. -CIES an act of truanting

TRUANT *v* -ED, -ING, -S to stay out of school without permission

TRUANTRY *n* pl. -RIES truancy

TRUCE *v* TRUCED, TRUCING, TRUCES to suspend hostilities by mutual agreement

TRUCK *v* -ED, -ING, -S to transport by truck (an automotive vehicle designed to carry loads)

TRUCKAGE *n* pl. -S transportation of goods by trucks

TRUCKER *n* pl. -S a truck driver

TRUCKING *n* pl. -S truckage

TRUCKLE *v* -LED, -LING, -LES to yield weakly

TRUCKLER *n* pl. -S one that truckles

TRUCKMAN *n* pl. -MEN a trucker

TRUDGE *v* TRUDGED, TRUDGING, TRUDGES to walk tiredly

TRUDGEN *n* pl. -S a swimming stroke

TRUDGEON *n* pl. -S trudgen

TRUDGER *n* pl. -S one that trudges

TRUDGING present participle of trudge

TRUE *adj* TRUER, TRUEST consistent with fact or reality

TRUE *v* TRUED, TRUING or TRUEING, TRUES to bring to conformity with a standard or requirement

TRUEBLUE *n* pl. -S a person of unwavering loyalty

TRUEBORN *adj* genuinely such by birth

TRUED past tense of true

TRUELOVE *n* pl. -S a sweetheart

TRUENESS *n* pl. -ES the quality or state of being true

TRUER comparative of true

TRUEST superlative of true

TRUFFE *n* pl. -S truffle

TRUFFLE *n* pl. -S an edible fungus **TRUFFLED** *adj*

TRUING a present participle of true

TRUISM *n* pl. -S an obvious truth **TRUISTIC** *adj*

TRULL *n* pl. -S a prostitute

TRULY *adv* in conformity with fact or reality

TRUMEAU *n* pl. -MEAUX a column supporting part of a doorway

TRUMP *v* -ED, -ING, -S to outdo

TRUMPERY *n* pl. -ERIES worthless finery

TRUMPET *v* -ED, -ING, -S to sound on a trumpet (a brass wind instrument)

TRUNCATE *v* -CATED, -CATING, -CATES to shorten by cutting off a part

TRUNDLE *v* -DLED, -DLING, -DLES to propel by causing to rotate

TRUNDLER *n* pl. -S one that trundles

TRUNK *n* pl. -S the main stem of a tree **TRUNKED** *adj*

TRUNNEL *n* pl. -S treenail

TRUNNION *n* pl. -S a pin or pivot on which something can be rotated

TRUSS *v* -ED, -ING, -ES to secure tightly

TRUSSER *n* pl. -S one that trusses

TRUSSING *n* pl. -S the framework of a structure

TRUST *v* -ED, -ING, -S to place confidence in

TRUSTEE *v* -TEED, -TEEING, -TEES to commit to the care of an administrator

TRUSTER *n* pl. -S one that trusts

TRUSTFUL *adj* inclined to trust

TRUSTY *adj* TRUSTIER, TRUSTIEST worthy of trust **TRUSTILY** *adv*

TRUSTY   *n* pl. TRUSTIES one worthy of trust

TRUTH   *n* pl. -S conformity to fact or reality

TRUTHFUL   *adj* telling the truth

TRY   *v* TRIED, TRYING, TRIES to attempt

TRYINGLY   *adv* in a distressing manner

TRYMA   *n* pl. -MATA a type of nut

TRYOUT   *n* pl. -S a test of ability

TRYPSIN   *n* pl. -S an enzyme TRYPTIC *adj*

TRYSAIL   *n* pl. -S a type of sail

TRYST   *v* -ED, -ING, -S to agree to meet

TRYSTE   *n* pl. -S a market

TRYSTER   *n* pl. -S one that trysts

TRYWORKS   *n/pl* a type of furnace

TSADE   *n* pl. -S sade

TSADI   *n* pl. -S sade

TSAR   *n* pl. -S czar

TSARDOM   *n* pl. -S czardom

TSAREVNA   *n* pl. -S czarevna

TSARINA   *n* pl. -S czarina

TSARISM   *n* pl. -S czarism

TSARIST   *n* pl. -S czarist

TSARITZA   *n* pl. -S czaritza

TSETSE   *n* pl. -S an African fly

TSIMMES   *n* pl. TSIMMES tzimmes

TSK   *v* -ED, -ING, -S to utter an exclamation of annoyance

TSKTSK   *v* -ED, -ING, -S to tsk

TSUBA   *n* pl. TSUBA a part of a Japanese sword

TSUNAMI   *n* pl. -S a very large ocean wave TSUNAMIC *adj*

TSURIS   *n* pl. TSURIS a series of misfortunes

TUATARA   *n* pl. -S a large reptile

TUATERA   *n* pl. -S tuatara

TUB   *v* TUBBED, TUBBING, TUBS to wash in a tub (a round, open vessel)

TUBA   *n* pl. -BAS or -BAE a brass wind instrument

TUBAL   *adj* pertaining to a tube

TUBATE   *adj* tubular

TUBBABLE   *adj* suitable for washing in a tub

TUBBED   *past tense of tub*

TUBBER   *n* pl. -S one that tubs

TUBBING   *present participle of tub*

TUBBY   *adj* -BIER, -BIEST short and fat

TUBE   *v* TUBED, TUBING, TUBES to provide with a tube (a long, hollow cylinder)

TUBELESS   *adj* having no tube

TUBELIKE   *adj* resembling a tube

TUBER   *n* pl. -S a thick underground stem

TUBERCLE   *n* pl. -S a small, rounded swelling

TUBEROID   *adj* pertaining to a tuber

TUBEROSE   *n* pl. -S a Mexican herb

TUBEROUS   *adj* pertaining to a tuber

TUBEWORK   *n* pl. -S tubing

TUBFUL   *n* pl. -S as much as a tub will hold

TUBIFEX   *n* pl. -ES an aquatic worm

TUBIFORM   *adj* tubular

TUBING   *n* pl. -S material in the form of a tube

TUBLIKE   *adj* resembling a tub

TUBULAR   *adj* shaped like a tube

TUBULATE   *v* -LATED, -LATING, -LATES to form into a tube

TUBULE   *n* pl. -S a small tube

TUBULOSE   *adj* tubular

TUBULOUS   *adj* tubular

TUBULURE   *n* pl. -S a short tubular opening

TUCHUN   *n* pl. -S a Chinese military governor

TUCK   *v* -ED, -ING, -S to fold under

TUCKAHOE   *n* pl. -S the edible root of certain arums

TUCKER   *v* -ED, -ING, -S to weary

TUCKET   *n* pl. -S a trumpet fanfare

TUFA   *n* pl. -S a porous limestone

TUFF   *n* pl. -S a volcanic rock

TUFFET   *n* pl. -S a clump of grass

TUFT   *v* -ED, -ING, -S to form into tufts (clusters of flexible outgrowths attached at the base)

TUFTER   *n* pl. -S one that tufts

TUFTY   *adj* TUFTIER, TUFTIEST abounding in tufts TUFTILY *adv*

TUG   *v* TUGGED, TUGGING, TUGS to pull with force

TUGBOAT n pl. -S a boat built for towing

TUGGER n pl. -S one that tugs

TUGGING present participle of tug

TUGLESS adj being without a rope or chain with which to pull

TUGRIK n pl. -S a Mongolian unit of currency

TUI n pl. -S a bird of New Zealand

TUILLE n pl. -S a tasset

TUITION n pl. -S a fee for instruction

TULADI n pl. -S a freshwater fish

TULE n pl. -S a tall marsh plant

TULIP n pl. -S a flowering plant

TULLE n pl. -S a silk material

TULLIBEE n pl. -S a freshwater fish

TUMBLE v -BLED, -BLING, -BLES to fall or roll end over end

TUMBLER n pl. -S one that tumbles

TUMBLING n pl. -S the sport of gymnastics

TUMBREL n pl. -S a type of cart

TUMBRIL n pl. -S tumbrel

TUMEFY v -FIED, -FYING, -FIES to swell

TUMID adj swollen TUMIDLY adv

TUMIDITY n pl. -TIES the quality or state of being tumid

TUMMY n pl. -MIES the stomach

TUMOR n pl. -S an abnormal swelling TUMORAL, TUMOROUS adj

TUMOUR n pl. -S tumor

TUMP n pl. -S tumpline

TUMPLINE n pl. -S a strap for supporting a load on the back

TUMULAR adj having the form of a mound

TUMULI a pl. of tumulus

TUMULOSE adj full of mounds

TUMULOUS adj tumulose

TUMULT n pl. -S a great din and commotion

TUMULUS n pl. -LI or -LUSES a mound over a grave

TUN v TUNNED, TUNNING, TUNS to store in a large cask

TUNA n pl. -S a marine food fish

TUNABLE adj capable of being tuned TUNABLY adv

TUNDISH n pl. -ES a receptacle for molten metal

TUNDRA n pl. -S a level, treeless expanse of arctic land

TUNE v TUNED, TUNING, TUNES to put into the proper pitch

TUNEABLE adj tunable TUNEABLY adv

TUNEFUL adj melodious

TUNELESS adj not tuneful

TUNER n pl. -S one that tunes

TUNG n pl. -S a Chinese tree

TUNGSTEN n pl. -S a metallic element TUNGSTIC adj

TUNIC n pl. -S a loose-fitting garment

TUNICA n pl. -CAE an enveloping membrane or layer of body tissue

TUNICATE n pl. -S a small marine animal

TUNICLE n pl. -S a type of vestment

TUNING present participle of tune

TUNNAGE n pl. -S tonnage

TUNNED past tense of tun

TUNNEL v -NELED, -NELING, -NELS or -NELLED, -NELLING, -NELS to dig a tunnel (an underground passageway)

TUNNELER n pl. -S one that tunnels

TUNNING present participle of tun

TUNNY n pl. -NIES a tuna

TUP v TUPPED, TUPPING, TUPS to copulate with a ewe

TUPELO n pl. -LOS a softwood tree

TUPIK n pl. -S an Eskimo tent

TUPPED past tense of tup

TUPPENCE n pl. -S twopence

TUPPING present participle of tup

TUPPENNY adj twopenny

TUQUE n pl. -S a knitted woolen cap

TURACO n pl. -COS touraco

TURACOU n pl. -S touraco

TURBAN n pl. -S a head covering worn by Muslims TURBANED adj

TURBARY n pl. -RIES a place where peat can be dug

TURBETH n pl. -S turpeth

TURBID adj thick or opaque with roiled sediment TURBIDLY adv

TURBINAL n pl. -S a bone of the nasal passage

TURBINE n pl. -S a type of engine

TURBIT	n pl. -S a domestic pigeon
TURBITH	n pl. -S turpeth
TURBO	n pl. -BOS a turbine
TURBOCAR	n pl. -S an auto powered by a gas turbine
TURBOFAN	n pl. -S a type of jet engine
TURBOJET	n pl. -S a type of jet engine
TURBOT	n pl. -S a European flatfish
TURD	n pl. -S a piece of dung
TURDINE	adj belonging to a large family of singing birds
TUREEN	n pl. -S a large, deep bowl
TURF	n pl. TURFS or TURVES a surface layer of earth containing a dense growth of grass and its roots
TURF	v -ED, -ING, -S to cover with turf
TURFIER	comparative of turfy
TURFIEST	superlative of turfy
TURFLESS	adj having no turf
TURFLIKE	adj resembling turf
TURFMAN	n pl. -MEN a person who is devoted to horse racing
TURFSKI	n pl. -S a type of ski
TURFY	adj TURFIER, TURFIEST covered with turf
TURGENCY	n pl. -CIES turgor
TURGENT	adj turgid
TURGID	adj swollen TURGIDLY adv
TURGITE	n pl. -S an iron ore
TURGOR	n pl. -S the quality or state of being turgid
TURKEY	n pl. -KEYS a large American bird
TURKOIS	n pl. -ES turquois
TURMERIC	n pl. -S an East Indian herb
TURMOIL	v -ED, -ING, -S to throw into an uproar
TURN	v -ED, -ING, -S to move around a central point TURNABLE adj
TURNCOAT	n pl. -S a traitor
TURNDOWN	n pl. -S a rejection
TURNER	n pl. -S one that turns
TURNERY	n pl. -ERIES the process of shaping articles on a lathe
TURNHALL	n pl. -S a building where gymnasts practice
TURNING	n pl. -S a rotation about an axis

TURNIP	n pl. -S an edible plant root
TURNKEY	n pl. -KEYS a person who has charge of a prison's keys
TURNOFF	n pl. -S a road that branches off from a larger one
TURNOUT	n pl. -S an assemblage of people
TURNOVER	n pl. -S an upset or overthrow
TURNPIKE	n pl. -S a highway on which tolls are collected
TURNSOLE	n pl. -S a plant that turns with the sun
TURNSPIT	n pl. -S one that turns a roasting spit
TURNUP	n pl. -S a part of a garment that is turned up
TURPETH	n pl. -S a medicinal plant root
TURPS	n pl. TURPS turpentine
TURQUOIS	n pl. -ES a greenish blue gem
TURRET	n pl. -S a small tower TURRETED adj
TURRICAL	adj resembling a turret
TURTLE	v -TLED, -TLING, -TLES to catch turtles (tortoises)
TURTLER	n pl. -S one that turtles
TURTLING	n pl. -S the act of one that turtles
TURVES	a pl. of turf
TUSCHE	n pl. -S a liquid used in lithography
TUSH	v -ED, -ING, -ES to tusk
TUSK	v -ED, -ING, -S to gore with a tusk (a long, pointed tooth extending outside of the mouth)
TUSKER	n pl. -S an animal with tusks
TUSKLESS	adj having no tusk
TUSKLIKE	adj resembling a tusk
TUSSAH	n pl. -S an Asian silkworm
TUSSAL	adj pertaining to a cough
TUSSAR	n pl. -S tussah
TUSSEH	n pl. -S tussah
TUSSER	n pl. -S tussah
TUSSIS	n pl. -SISES a cough TUSSIVE adj
TUSSLE	v -SLED, -SLING, -SLES to struggle
TUSSOCK	n pl. -S a clump of grass TUSSOCKY adj
TUSSOR	n pl. -S tussah

TUSSORE n pl. -S tussah

TUSSUCK n pl. -S tussock

TUSSUR n pl. -S tussah

TUT v TUTTED, TUTTING, TUTS to utter an exclamation of impatience

TUTEE n pl. -S one who is being tutored

TUTELAGE n pl. -S the act of tutoring

TUTELAR n pl. -S a tutelary

TUTELARY n pl. -LARIES one who has the power to protect

TUTOR v -ED, -ING, -S to instruct privately

TUTORAGE n pl. -S tutelage

TUTORESS n pl. -ES a female who tutors

TUTORIAL n pl. -S a session of tutoring

TUTOYER v -TOYERED or -TOYED, -TOYERING, -TOYERS to address familiarly

TUTTED past tense of tut

TUTTI n pl. -S a musical passage performed by all the performers

TUTTING present participle of tut

TUTTY n pl. -TIES an impure zinc oxide

TUTU n pl. -S a short ballet skirt

TUX n pl. -ES a tuxedo

TUXEDO n pl. -DOES or -DOS a man's semiformal dinner coat

TUYER n pl. -S tuyere

TUYERE n pl. -S a pipe through which air is forced into a blast furnace

TWA n pl. -S two

TWADDLE v -DLED, -DLING, -DLES to talk foolishly

TWADDLER n pl. -S one that twaddles

TWAE n pl. -S two

TWAIN n pl. -S a set of two

TWANG v -ED, -ING, -S to make a sharp, vibrating sound

TWANGIER comparative of twangy

TWANGIEST superlative of twangy

TWANGLE v -GLED, -GLING, -GLES to twang

TWANGLER n pl. -S one that twangles

TWANGY adj TWANGIER, TWANGIEST twanging

TWANKY n pl. -KIES a variety of green tea

TWASOME n pl. -S twosome

TWAT n pl. -S the vulva — usually considered vulgar

TWATTLE v -TLED, -TLING, -TLES to twaddle

TWEAK v -ED, -ING, -S to pinch and twist sharply

TWEAKY adj TWEAKIER, TWEAKIEST twitchy

TWEED n pl. -S a coarse woolen fabric

TWEEDLE v -DLED, -DLING, -DLES to perform casually on a musical instrument

TWEEDY adj TWEEDIER, TWEEDIEST resembling tweed

TWEEN prep between

TWEET v -ED, -ING, -S to chirp

TWEETER n pl. -S a loudspeaker designed to reproduce high-pitched sounds

TWEEZE v TWEEZED, TWEEZING, TWEEZES to pluck with a tweezer

TWEEZER n pl. -S a pincerlike tool

TWELFTH n pl. -S the number twelve in a series

TWELVE n pl. -S a number

TWELVEMO n pl. -MOS a page size

TWENTY n pl. -TIES a number

TWERP n pl. -S a small, impudent person

TWIBIL n pl. -S a battle-ax with two cutting edges

TWIBILL n pl. -S twibil

TWICE adv two times

TWIDDLE v -DLED, -DLING, -DLES to play idly with something

TWIDDLER n pl. -S one that twiddles

TWIER n pl. -S tuyere

TWIG v TWIGGED, TWIGGING, TWIGS to observe

TWIGGEN adj made of twigs (small branches)

TWIGGY adj -GIER, -GIEST twiglike

TWIGLESS adj having no twigs

TWIGLIKE adj resembling a twig

TWILIGHT n pl. -S the early evening light

TWILIT adj lighted by twilight

TWILL v -ED, -ING, -S to weave so as to produce a diagonal pattern

TWILLING	n pl. -S a twilled fabric	**TWITTING**	present participle of twit
TWIN	v TWINNED, TWINNING, TWINS to bring together in close association	**TWIXT**	prep between
		TWO	n pl. TWOS a number
TWINBORN	adj born at the same birth	**TWOFER**	n pl. -S something sold at the rate of two for the price of one
TWINE	v TWINED, TWINING, TWINES to twist together	**TWOFOLD**	n pl. -S an amount twice as great as a given unit
TWINER	n pl. -S one that twines	**TWOPENCE**	n pl. -S a British coin worth two pennies
TWINGE	v TWINGED, TWINGING, TWINGES to affect with a sharp pain		
		TWOPENNY	adj worth twopence
TWINIER	comparative of twiny	**TWOSOME**	n pl. -S a group of two
TWINIEST	superlative of twiny	**TWYER**	n pl. -S tuyere
TWINIGHT	adj pertaining to a baseball doubleheader that begins in the late afternoon	**TYCOON**	n pl. -S a wealthy and powerful business person
		TYE	n pl. -S a chain on a ship
TWINING	present participle of twine	**TYEE**	n pl. -S a food fish
TWINKLE	v -KLED, -KLING, -KLES to shine with a flickering or sparkling light	**TYING**	a present participle of tie
		TYKE	n pl. -S a small child
		TYMBAL	n pl. -S timbal
TWINKLER	n pl. -S one that twinkles	**TYMPAN**	n pl. -S a drum
TWINKLY	adj twinkling	**TYMPANA**	a pl. of tympanum
TWINNED	past tense of twin	**TYMPANAL**	adj tympanic
TWINNING	n pl. -S the bearing of two children at the same birth	**TYMPANI**	n/pl kettledrums
		TYMPANIC	adj pertaining to the tympanum
TWINSHIP	n pl. -S close similarity or association	**TYMPANUM**	n pl. -NA or -NUMS the middle ear
TWINY	adj TWINIER, TWINIEST resembling twine (a strong string)	**TYMPANY**	n pl. -NIES a swelling of the abdomen
		TYNE	v TYNED, TYNING, TYNES to tine
TWIRL	v -ED, -ING, -S to rotate rapidly	**TYPAL**	adj typical
TWIRLER	n pl. -S one that twirls	**TYPE**	v TYPED, TYPING, TYPES to write with a typewriter TYPEABLE adj
TWIRLY	adj TWIRLIER, TWIRLIEST curved		
TWIRP	n pl. -S twerp	**TYPEBAR**	n pl. -S a part of a typewriter
TWIST	v -ED, -ING, -S to combine by winding together	**TYPECASE**	n pl. -S a tray for holding printing type
TWISTER	n pl. -S one that twists	**TYPECAST**	v -CAST, -CASTING, -CASTS to cast in an acting role befitting one's own nature
TWISTING	n pl. -S a form of trickery used in selling life insurance		
TWIT	v TWITTED, TWITTING, TWITS to ridicule	**TYPED**	past tense of type
		TYPEFACE	n pl. -S the face of printing type
TWITCH	v -ED, -ING, -ES to move or pull with a sudden motion	**TYPESET**	v -SET, -SETTING, -SETS to set in type
TWITCHER	n pl. -S one that twitches	**TYPEY**	adj TYPIER, TYPIEST typy
TWITCHY	adj TWITCHIER, TWITCHIEST fidgety	**TYPHOID**	n pl. -S an infectious disease
		TYPHON	n pl. -S a type of signal horn
TWITTED	past tense of twit	**TYPHOON**	n pl. -S a tropical hurricane TYPHONIC adj
TWITTER	v -ED, -ING, -S to utter a succession of chirping sounds		
TWITTERY	adj nervously agitated		

TYPHOSE	adj pertaining to typhoid	**TYRANT**	n pl. -S an absolute ruler
TYPHUS	n pl. -ES an infectious disease TYPHOUS adj	**TYRE**	v TYRED, TYRING, TYRES to furnish with a covering for a wheel
TYPIC	adj typical		
TYPICAL	adj having the nature of a representative specimen	**TYRO**	n pl. -ROS a beginner TYRONIC adj
TYPIER	comparative of typey and typy	**TYROSINE**	n pl. -S an amino acid
TYPIEST	superlative of typey and typy	**TYTHE**	v TYTHED, TYTHING, TYTHES to tithe
TYPIFIER	n pl. -S one that typifies		
TYPIFY	v -FIED, -FYING, -FIES to serve as a typical example of	**TZADDIK**	n pl. -DIKIM zaddik
		TZAR	n pl. -S czar
TYPING	present participle of type	**TZARDOM**	n pl. -S czardom
TYPIST	n pl. -S one who types	**TZAREVNA**	n pl. -S czarevna
TYPO	n pl. -POS a typographical error	**TZARINA**	n pl. -S czarina
TYPOLOGY	n pl. -GIES the study of classification according to common characteristics	**TZARISM**	n pl. -S czarism
		TZARIST	n pl. -S czarist
TYPP	n pl. -S a unit of yarn size	**TZARITZA**	n pl. -S czaritza
TYPY	adj TYPIER, TYPIEST characterized by strict conformance to the characteristics of a group	**TZETZE**	n pl. -S tsetse
		TZIGANE	n pl. -S a gypsy
		TZIMMES	n pl. TZIMMES a vegetable stew
TYRAMINE	n pl. -S a chemical compound	**TZITZIS**	n pl. TZITZIS zizith
TYRANNIC	adj characteristic of a tyrant	**TZITZITH**	n pl. TZITZITH zizith
TYRANNY	n pl. -NIES the rule of a tyrant	**TZURIS**	n pl. TZURIS tsuris

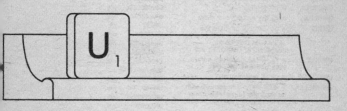

UBIETY   *n* pl. -ETIES the state of having a definite location

UBIQUE   *adv* everywhere

UBIQUITY   *n* pl. -TIES the state of being everywhere at the same time

UDDER   *n* pl. -S a mammary gland

UDO   *n* pl. UDOS a Japanese herb

UDOMETER   *n* pl. -S a rain gauge

UDOMETRY   *n* pl. -TRIES the measurement of rain

UGH   *n* pl. -S the sound of a cough or grunt

UGLIER   comparative of ugly

UGLIEST   superlative of ugly

UGLIFIER   *n* pl. -S one that uglifies

UGLIFY   *v* -FIED, -FYING, -FIES to make ugly

UGLINESS   *n* pl. -ES the state of being ugly

UGLY   *adj* -LIER, -LIEST displeasing to the sight UGLILY *adv*

UGSOME   *adj* disgusting

UHLAN   *n* pl. -S one of a body of Prussian cavalry

UINTAITE   *n* pl. -S a variety of asphalt

UIT   *prep* out of

UKASE   *n* pl. -S an edict

UKE   *n* pl. -S ukelele

UKELELE   *n* pl. -S ukulele

UKULELE   *n* pl. -S a small guitar-like instrument

ULAMA   *n* pl. -S ulema

ULAN   *n* pl. -S uhlan

ULCER   *v* -ED, -ING, -S to affect with an ulcer (a type of lesion)

ULCERATE   *v* -ATED, -ATING, -ATES to ulcer

ULCEROUS   *adj* being or affected with an ulcer

ULEMA   *n* pl. -S a Muslim scholar

ULEXITE   *n* pl. -S a mineral

ULLAGE   *n* pl. -S the amount that a container lacks of being full ULLAGED *adj*

ULNA   *n* pl. -NAE or -NAS a bone of the forearm ULNAR *adj*

ULSTER   *n* pl. -S a long, loose overcoat

ULTERIOR   *adj* more remote

ULTIMA   *n* pl. -S the last syllable of a word

ULTIMACY   *n* pl. -CIES an ultimate

ULTIMATA   *n/pl* final proposals

ULTIMATE   *n* pl. -S something final or fundamental

ULTIMO   *adj* of or occurring in the preceding month

ULTRA   *n* pl. -S an ultraist

ULTRAISM   *n* pl. -S advocacy of extreme measures

ULTRAIST   *n* pl. -S an advocate of extreme measures

ULTRARED   *n* pl. -S infrared

ULULANT   *adj* howling

ULULATE   *v* -LATED, -LATING, -LATES to howl

ULVA   *n* pl. -S an edible seaweed

UMBEL   *n* pl. -S a type of flower cluster UMBELED, UMBELLAR, UMBELLED *adj*

UMBELLET   *n* pl. -S a small umbel

UMBER	v -ED, -ING, -S to color with a brown pigment
UMBILICI	n/pl navels
UMBLES	n/pl the entrails of a deer
UMBO	n pl. -BONES or -BOS the rounded elevation at the center of a shield UMBONAL, UMBONATE, UMBONIC adj
UMBRA	n pl. -BRAE or -BRAS a dark area UMBRAL adj
UMBRAGE	n pl. -S resentment
UMBRELLA	v -ED, -ING, -S to provide with an umbrella (a portable cover for protection from rain or sun)
UMBRETTE	n pl. -S a wading bird
UMIAC	n pl. -S umiak
UMIACK	n pl. -S umiak
UMIAK	n pl. -S an open Eskimo boat
UMLAUT	v -ED, -ING, -S to modify a vowel sound by partial assimilation to a succeeding sound
UMP	v -ED, -ING, -S to umpire
UMPIRAGE	n pl. -S the function of an umpire
UMPIRE	v -PIRED, -PIRING, -PIRES to act as umpire (a person appointed to rule on the plays in a game)
UMPTEEN	adj indefinitely numerous
UMTEENTH	adj being the last in an indefinitely numerous series
UN	pron pl. -S one

U₁ N₁

Following is a list of self-explanatory adjectives and adverbs containing the prefix UN- (not):

UNABATED	adj
UNABLE	adj
UNABUSED	adj
UNACTED	adj
UNAFRAID	adj
UNAGED	adj
UNAGEING	adj
UNAGILE	adj
UNAGING	adj
UNAIDED	adj
UNAIMED	adj
UNAIRED	adj

UNALIKE	adj
UNALLIED	adj
UNAMUSED	adj
UNANELED	adj
UNAPT	adj
UNAPTLY	adv
UNARGUED	adj
UNARTFUL	adj
UNASKED	adj
UNATONED	adj
UNAVOWED	adj
UNAWAKED	adj
UNAWARE	adj
UNAWED	adj
UNBACKED	adj
UNBAKED	adj
UNBARBED	adj
UNBASED	adj
UNBEATEN	adj
UNBENIGN	adj
UNBIASED	adj
UNBITTED	adj
UNBLAMED	adj
UNBLEST	adj
UNBLOODY	adj
UNBONED	adj
UNBORN	adj
UNBOUGHT	adj
UNBOWED	adj
UNBRED	adj
UNBROKE	adj
UNBROKEN	adj
UNBURIED	adj
UNBURNED	adj
UNBURNT	adj
UNCALLED	adj
UNCANDID	adj
UNCARING	adj
UNCASHED	adj
UNCAUGHT	adj
UNCAUSED	adj
UNCHARY	adj
UNCHASTE	adj
UNCHEWED	adj
UNCHIC	adj
UNCHOSEN	adj
UNCIVIL	adj
UNCLEAN	adj -CLEANER, -CLEANEST
UNCLEAR	adj -CLEARER, -CLEAREST
UNCLOYED	adj
UNCOATED	adj
UNCOINED	adj
UNCOMBED	adj

UNCOMELY	adj		UNFORCED	adj
UNCOMIC	adj		UNFORGED	adj
UNCOMMON	adj -MONER, -MONEST		UNFORKED	adj
UNCOOKED	adj		UNFORMED	adj
UNCOOL	adj		UNFOUGHT	adj
UNCOUTH	adj		UNFOUND	adj
UNCURED	adj		UNFRAMED	adj
UNCURSED	adj		UNFUNDED	adj
UNCUT	adj		UNFUNNY	adj
UNDAMPED	adj		UNFUSED	adj
UNDARING	adj		UNFUSSY	adj
UNDATED	adj		UNGALLED	adj
UNDECKED	adj		UNGENIAL	adj
UNDENIED	adj		UNGENTLE	adj
UNDEVOUT	adj		UNGENTLY	adv
UNDIMMED	adj		UNGIFTED	adj
UNDREAMT	adj		UNGLAZED	adj
UNDRIED	adj		UNGOWNED	adj
UNDULLED	adj		UNGRACED	adj
UNDYED	adj		UNGRADED	adj
UNEAGER	adj		UNGREEDY	adj
UNEARNED	adj		UNGUIDED	adj
UNEATEN	adj		UNHAILED	adj
UNEDIBLE	adj		UNHALVED	adj
UNEDITED	adj		UNHAPPY	adj -PIER, -PIEST
UNENDED	adj		UNHARMED	adj
UNENDING	adj		UNHASTY	adj
UNENVIED	adj		UNHEALED	adj
UNERASED	adj		UNHEARD	adj
UNERRING	adj		UNHEATED	adj
UNEVADED	adj		UNHEEDED	adj
UNEVEN	adj -EVENER, -EVENEST		UNHELPED	adj
UNEVENLY	adv		UNHEROIC	adj
UNEXOTIC	adj		UNHEWN	adj
UNEXPERT	adj		UNHIP	adj
UNFADED	adj		UNHIRED	adj
UNFADING	adj		UNHOLILY	adv
UNFAIR	adj -FAIRER, -FAIREST		UNHOLY	adj -LIER, -LIEST
UNFAIRLY	adv		UNHUMAN	adj
UNFALLEN	adj		UNHUNG	adj
UNFANCY	adj		UNHURT	adj
UNFAZED	adj		UNIDEAL	adj
UNFEARED	adj		UNIMBUED	adj
UNFED	adj		UNIRONED	adj
UNFELT	adj		UNISSUED	adj
UNFILIAL	adj		UNJADED	adj
UNFILLED	adj		UNJOINED	adj
UNFILMED	adj		UNJOYFUL	adj
UNFIRED	adj		UNJUDGED	adj
UNFISHED	adj		UNJUST	adj
UNFLEXED	adj		UNJUSTLY	adv
UNFOILED	adj		UNKEPT	adj
UNFOND	adj		UNKIND	adj -KINDER, -KINDEST

UNKINDLY	adv -LIER, -LIEST	UNPARTED	adj	
UNKINGLY	adj	UNPAVED	adj	
UNKISSED	adj	UNPAYING	adj	
UNKOSHER	adj	UNPITIED	adj	
UNLAWFUL	adj	UNPLACED	adj	
UNLEASED	adj	UNPLAYED	adj	
UNLED	adj	UNPLIANT	adj	
UNLETHAL	adj	UNPLOWED	adj	
UNLETTED	adj	UNPOETIC	adj	
UNLEVIED	adj	UNPOISED	adj	
UNLICKED	adj	UNPOLITE	adj	
UNLIKE	adj	UNPOLLED	adj	
UNLIKELY	adj -LIER, -LIEST	UNPOSED	adj	
UNLINED	adj	UNPOSTED	adj	
UNLISTED	adj	UNPRETTY	adj	
UNLIT	adj	UNPRICED	adj	
UNLIVELY	adj	UNPRIMED	adj	
UNLOBED	adj	UNPRIZED	adj	
UNLOVED	adj	UNPROBED	adj	
UNLOVELY	adj -LIER, -LIEST	UNPROVED	adj	
UNLOVING	adj	UNPROVEN	adj	
UNLUCKY	adj -LUCKIER, -LUCKIEST	UNPRUNED	adj	
UNMANFUL	adj	UNPURE	adj	
UNMANLY	adj	UNPURGED	adj	
UNMAPPED	adj	UNQUIET	adj -ETER, -ETEST	
UNMARKED	adj	UNRAISED	adj	
UNMARRED	adj	UNRAKED	adj	
UNMATED	adj	UNRANKED	adj	
UNMATTED	adj	UNRATED	adj	
UNMEANT	adj	UNRAZED	adj	
UNMELLOW	adj	UNREAD	adj	
UNMELTED	adj	UNREADY	adj -READIER, -READIEST	
UNMENDED	adj	UNREAL	adj	
UNMET	adj	UNREALLY	adv	
UNMILLED	adj	UNRENTED	adj	
UNMIXED	adj	UNREPAID	adj	
UNMIXT	adj	UNRESTED	adj	
UNMODISH	adj	UNRHYMED	adj	
UNMOLTEN	adj	UNRIFLED	adj	
UNMOVED	adj	UNRIMED	adj	
UNMOVING	adj	UNRINSED	adj	
UNMOWN	adj	UNRISEN	adj	
UNNAMED	adj	UNROUGH	adj	
UNNEEDED	adj	UNRULED	adj	
UNNOISY	adj	UNRUSHED	adj	
UNNOTED	adj	UNSAFE	adj	
UNOILED	adj	UNSAFELY	adv	
UNOPEN	adj	UNSALTED	adj	
UNOPENED	adj	UNSATED	adj	
UNORNATE	adj	UNSAVED	adj	
UNOWNED	adj	UNSAVORY	adj	
UNPAID	adj	UNSAWED	adj	
UNPAIRED	adj	UNSAWN	adj	

UNSCALED	adj		UNSTUNG	adj
UNSEARED	adj		UNSUBTLE	adj
UNSEEDED	adj		UNSUITED	adj
UNSEEING	adj		UNSUNG	adj
UNSEEMLY	adj -LIER, -LIEST		UNSUNK	adj
UNSEEN	adj		UNSURE	adj
UNSEIZED	adj		UNSURELY	adv
UNSENT	adj		UNSWAYED	adj
UNSERVED	adj		UNSWEPT	adj
UNSEXUAL	adj		UNTAGGED	adj
UNSHADED	adj		UNTAKEN	adj
UNSHAKEN	adj		UNTAME	adj
UNSHAMED	adj		UNTAMED	adj
UNSHAPED	adj		UNTANNED	adj
UNSHAPEN	adj		UNTAPPED	adj
UNSHARED	adj		UNTASTED	adj
UNSHARP	adj		UNTAXED	adj
UNSHAVED	adj		UNTENDED	adj
UNSHAVEN	adj		UNTESTED	adj
UNSHED	adj		UNTHAWED	adj
UNSHOD	adj		UNTIDILY	adv
UNSHORN	adj		UNTIDY	adj -DIER, -DIEST
UNSHRUNK	adj		UNTILLED	adj
UNSHUT	adj		UNTILTED	adj
UNSIFTED	adj		UNTIMELY	adj -LIER, -LIEST
UNSIGNED	adj		UNTINGED	adj
UNSILENT	adj		UNTIRED	adj
UNSINFUL	adj		UNTIRING	adj
UNSIZED	adj		UNTITLED	adj
UNSLAKED	adj		UNTOLD	adj
UNSMOKED	adj		UNTRACED	adj
UNSOAKED	adj		UNTRIED	adj
UNSOBER	adj		UNTRUE	adj -TRUER, -TRUEST
UNSOCIAL	adj		UNTRULY	adv
UNSOILED	adj		UNTRUSTY	adj
UNSOLD	adj		UNTUFTED	adj
UNSOLID	adj		UNTURNED	adj
UNSOLVED	adj		UNUNITED	adj
UNSORTED	adj		UNURGED	adj
UNSOUGHT	adj		UNUSABLE	adj
UNSOUND	adj -SOUNDER, -SOUNDEST		UNUSED	adj
UNSOURED	adj		UNUSUAL	adj
UNSOWED	adj		UNVALUED	adj
UNSOWN	adj		UNVARIED	adj
UNSPENT	adj		UNVEINED	adj
UNSPILT	adj		UNVERSED	adj
UNSPLIT	adj		UNVEXED	adj
UNSPOILT	adj		UNVEXT	adj
UNSPRUNG	adj		UNVIABLE	adj
UNSPUN	adj		UNVOCAL	adj
UNSTABLE	adj -BLER, -BLEST		UNWALLED	adj
UNSTABLY	adv		UNWANTED	adj
UNSTEADY	adj -STEADIER, -STEADIEST		UNWARIER	comparative of unwary

UNWARIEST superlative of unwary
UNWARILY adv
UNWARMED adj
UNWARNED adj
UNWARPED adj
UNWARY adj -WARIER, -WARIEST
UNWASTED adj
UNWAXED adj
UNWEANED adj
UNWEARY adj
UNWED adj
UNWEDDED adj
UNWEEDED adj
UNWELDED adj
UNWELL adj
UNWEPT adj
UNWETTED adj
UNWIELDY adj -WIELDIER, -WIELDIEST
UNWIFELY adj
UNWILLED adj
UNWISE adj -WISER, -WISEST
UNWISELY adv
UNWON adj
UNWOODED adj
UNWOOED adj
UNWORKED adj
UNWORN adj
UNWORTHY adj -THIER, -THIEST
UNWRUNG adj
UNZONED adj

UNAI n pl. -S unau
UNANCHOR v -ED, -ING, -S to loosen from an anchor
UNARM v -ED, -ING, -S to disarm
UNARY adj consisting of a single element
UNAU n pl. -S a two-toed sloth
UNAWARES adv without warning
UNBAR v -BARRED, -BARRING, -BARS to remove a bar from
UNBATED adj unabated
UNBE v to cease to have being — UNBE is the only accepted form of this verb; it cannot be conjugated
UNBEAR v -BEARED, -BEARING, -BEARS to free from the pressure of a rein
UNBELIEF n pl. -S lack of belief

UNBELT v -ED, -ING, -S to remove the belt of
UNBEND v -BENT or -BENDED, -BENDING, -BENDS to make or allow to become straight
UNBID adj unbidden
UNBIDDEN adj not invited
UNBIND v -BOUND, -BINDING, -BINDS to free from bindings
UNBLOCK v -ED, -ING, -S to free from being blocked
UNBODIED adj having no body
UNBOLT v -ED, -ING, -S to open by withdrawing a bolt (a metal bar)
UNBONNET v -ED, -ING, -S to uncover the head
UNBOSOM v -ED, -ING, -S to reveal
UNBOUND past tense of unbind
UNBOX v -ED, -ING, -ES to remove from a box
UNBRACE v -BRACED, -BRACING, -BRACES to free from braces
UNBRAID v -ED, -ING, -S to separate the strands of
UNBREECH v -ED, -ING, -ES to remove the breeches of
UNBRIDLE v -DLED, -DLING, -DLES to set loose
UNBUCKLE v -LED, -LING, -LES to loosen a buckle
UNBUILD v -BUILT, -BUILDING, -BUILDS to demolish
UNBUNDLE v -DLED, -DLING, -DLES to price separately
UNBURDEN v -ED, -ING, -S to free from a burden
UNBUTTON v -ED, -ING, -S to unfasten the buttons of
UNCAGE v -CAGED, -CAGING, -CAGES to release from a cage
UNCAKE v -CAKED, -CAKING, -CAKES to break up a cake (a block of compacted matter)
UNCANNY adj -NIER, -NIEST strange and inexplicable
UNCAP v -CAPPED, -CAPPING, -CAPS to remove the cap from
UNCASE v -CASED, -CASING, -CASES to remove from a case
UNCHAIN v -ED, -ING, -S to free by removing a chain
UNCHANCY adj unlucky

UNCHARGE v -CHARGED, -CHARGING, -CHARGES to acquit

UNCHOKE v -CHOKED, -CHOKING, -CHOKES to free from obstruction

UNCHURCH v -ED, -ING, -ES to expel from a church

UNCI pl. of uncus

UNCIA n pl. -CIAE a coin of ancient Rome

UNCIAL n pl. -S a style of writing

UNCIALLY adv in the uncial style

UNCIFORM n pl. -S a bone of the wrist

UNCINAL adj uncinate

UNCINATE adj bent at the end like a hook

UNCINUS n pl. -NI an uncinate structure

UNCLAD a past tense of unclothe

UNCLAMP v -ED, -ING, -S to free from a clamp

UNCLASP v -ED, -ING, -S to free from a clasp

UNCLE n pl. -S the brother of one's father or mother

UNCLENCH v -ED, -ING, -ES to open from a clenched position

UNCLINCH v -ED, -ING, -ES to unclench

UNCLOAK v -ED, -ING, -S to remove a cloak from

UNCLOG v -CLOGGED, -CLOGGING, -CLOGS to free from a difficulty or obstruction

UNCLOSE v -CLOSED, -CLOSING, -CLOSES to open

UNCLOTHE v -CLOTHED or -CLAD, -CLOTHING, -CLOTHES to divest of clothing

UNCLOUD v -ED, -ING, -S to free from clouds

UNCO n pl. -COS a stranger

UNCOCK v -ED, -ING, -S to remove from a cocked position

UNCOFFIN v -ED, -ING, -S to remove from a coffin

UNCOIL v -ED, -ING, -S to release from a coiled position

UNCORK v -ED, -ING, -S to draw the cork from

UNCOUPLE v -PLED, -PLING, -PLES to disconnect

UNCOVER v -ED, -ING, -S to remove the covering from

UNCRATE v -CRATED, -CRATING, -CRATES to remove from a crate

UNCREATE v -ATED, -ATING, -ATES to deprive of existence

UNCROSS v -ED, -ING, -ES to change from a crossed position

UNCROWN v -ED, -ING, -S to deprive of a crown

UNCTION n pl. -S the act of anointing

UNCTUOUS adj greasy

UNCURB v -ED, -ING, -S to remove restraints from

UNCURL v -ED, -ING, -S to straighten the curls of

UNCUS n pl. -CI a hook-shaped anatomical part

UNDE adj wavy

UNDEE adj unde

UNDER prep in a lower position than

UNDERACT v -ED, -ING, -S to act subtly and with restraint

UNDERAGE n pl. -S a shortage

UNDERARM n pl. -S the armpit

UNDERATE past tense of undereat

UNDERBID v -BID, -BIDDING, -BIDS to bid lower than

UNDERBUD v -BUDDED, -BUDDING, -BUDS to bud from beneath

UNDERBUY v -BOUGHT, -BUYING, -BUYS to buy at a lower price than

UNDERCUT v -CUT, -CUTTING, -CUTS to cut under

UNDERDO v -DID, -DONE, -DOING, -DOES to do insufficiently

UNDERDOG n pl. -S one who is expected to lose

UNDEREAT v -ATE, -EATEN, -EATING, -EATS to eat an insufficient amount

UNDERFED adj fed an insufficient amount

UNDERFUR n pl. -S the thick, soft fur beneath the outer coat of certain mammals

UNDERGO v -WENT, -GONE, -GOING, -GOES to be subjected to

UNDERGOD n pl. -S a lesser god

UNDERJAW n pl. -S the lower jaw

UNDERLAIN past participle of underlie

UNDERLAP v -LAPPED, -LAPPING, -LAPS to extend partly under

UNDERLAY *v* -LAID, -LAYING, -LAYS to place under

UNDERLET *v* -LET, -LETTING, -LETS to lease at less than the usual value

UNDERLIE *v* -LAY, -LAIN, -LYING, -LIES to lie under

UNDERLIP *n* pl. -S the lower lip

UNDERLIT *adj* lacking adequate light

UNDERLYING present participle of underlie

UNDERPAY *v* -PAID, -PAYING, -PAYS to pay less than is deserved

UNDERPIN *v* -PINNED, -PINNING, -PINS to support from below

UNDERRUN *v* -RAN, -RUNNING, -RUNS to pass or extend under

UNDERSEA *adv* beneath the surface of the sea

UNDERSET *n* pl. -S a current below the surface of the ocean

UNDERTAX *v* -ED, -ING, -ES to tax less than the usual amount

UNDERTOW *n* pl. -S the seaward pull of receding waves breaking on a shore

UNDERWAY *adv* in progress

UNDERWENT past tense of undergo

UNDID past tense of undo

UNDIES *n/pl* underwear

UNDINE *n* pl. -S a female water spirit

UNDO *v* -DID, -DONE, -DOING, -DOES to bring to ruin

UNDOCK *v* -ED, -ING, -S to move away from a dock

UNDOER *n* pl. -S one that undoes

UNDOING *n* pl. -S a cause of ruin

UNDONE past participle of undo

UNDOUBLE *v* -BLED, -BLING, -BLES to unfold

UNDRAPE *v* -DRAPED, -DRAPING, -DRAPES to strip of drapery

UNDRAW *v* -DREW, -DRAWN, -DRAWING, -DRAWS to draw open

UNDRESS *v* -DRESSED or -DREST, -DRESSING, -DRESSES to remove one's clothing

UNDRUNK *adj* not swallowed

UNDUE *adj* exceeding what is appropriate or normal

UNDULANT *adj* undulating

UNDULATE *v* -LATED, -LATING, -LATES to move with a wavelike motion

UNDULY *adv* in an undue manner

UNDY *adj* unde

UNDYING *adj* not subject to death

UNEARTH *v* -ED, -ING, -S to dig up

UNEASE *n* pl. -S mental or physical discomfort

UNEASY *adj* -EASIER, -EASIEST marked by mental or physical discomfort
UNEASILY *adv*

UNEQUAL *n* pl. -S one that is not equal to another

UNFAITH *n* pl. -S lack of faith

UNFASTEN *v* -ED, -ING, -S to release from fastenings

UNFENCE *v* -FENCED, -FENCING, -FENCES to remove a fence from

UNFETTER *v* -ED, -ING, -S to free from fetters

UNFIT *v* -FITTED, -FITTING, -FITS to make unsuitable

UNFITLY *adv* in an unsuitable manner

UNFIX *v* -FIXED or -FIXT, -FIXING, -FIXES to unfasten

UNFOLD *v* -ED, -ING, -S to open something that is folded

UNFOLDER *n* pl. -S one that unfolds

UNFORGOT *adj* not forgotten

UNFREE *v* -FREED, -FREEING, -FREES to deprive of freedom

UNFREEZE *v* -FROZE, -FROZEN, -FREEZING, -FREEZES to cause to thaw

UNFROCK *v* -ED, -ING, -S to divest of ecclesiastical authority

UNFURL *v* -ED, -ING, -S to unroll

UNGAINLY *adj* -LIER, -LIEST awkward

UNGIRD *v* -GIRDED or -GIRT, -GIRDING, -GIRDS to remove a belt from

UNGLOVE *v* -GLOVED, -GLOVING, -GLOVES to uncover by removing a glove

UNGLUE *v* -GLUED, -GLUING, -GLUES to disjoin

UNGODLY *adj* -LIER, -LIEST impious

UNGOT *adj* ungotten

UNGOTTEN *adj* not obtained

UNGUAL *adj* pertaining to an unguis

UNGUARD v -ED, -ING, -S to leave unprotected

UNGUENT n pl. -S an ointment

UNGUIS n pl. -GUES a nail, claw, or hoof

UNGULA n pl. -LAE an unguis UNGULAR adj

UNGULATE n pl. -S a hoofed mammal

UNHAIR v -ED, -ING, -S to remove the hair from

UNHALLOW v -ED, -ING, -S to profane

UNHAND v -ED, -ING, -S to remove the hand from

UNHANDY adj -HANDIER, -HANDIEST difficult to handle

UNHANG v -HUNG or -HANGED, -HANGING, -HANGS to detach from a hanging support

UNHAT v -HATTED, -HATTING, -HATS to remove one's hat

UNHELM v -ED, -ING, -S to remove the helmet from

UNHINGE v -HINGED, -HINGING, -HINGES to remove from hinges

UNHITCH v -ED, -ING, -ES to free from being hitched

UNHOOD v -ED, -ING, -S to remove a hood from

UNHOOK v -ED, -ING, -S to remove from a hook

UNHOPED adj not hoped for or expected

UNHORSE v -HORSED, -HORSING, -HORSES to cause to fall from a horse

UNHOUSE v -HOUSED, -HOUSING, -HOUSES to deprive of a protective shelter

UNHUSK v -ED, -ING, -S to remove the husk from

UNIALGAL adj pertaining to a single algal cell

UNIAXIAL adj having one axis

UNICOLOR adj of one color

UNICORN n pl. -S a mythical horselike creature

UNICYCLE n pl. -S a one-wheeled vehicle

UNIDEAED adj lacking ideas

UNIFACE n pl. -S a coin having a design on only one side

UNIFIC adj unifying

UNIFIED past tense of unify

UNIFIER n pl. -S one that unifies

UNIFIES present 3d person sing. of unify

UNIFILAR adj having only one thread, wire, or fiber

UNIFORM adj -FORMER, -FORMEST unchanging

UNIFORM v -ED, -ING, -S to make uniform

UNIFY v -FIED, -FYING, -FIES to make into a coherent whole

UNILOBED adj having one lobe

UNION n pl. -S a number of persons, parties, or political entities united for a common purpose

UNIONISE v -ISED, -ISING, -ISES to unionize

UNIONISM n pl. -S the principle of forming a union

UNIONIST n pl. -S an advocate of unionism

UNIONIZE v -IZED, -IZING, -IZES to form into a union

UNIPOD n pl. -S a one-legged support

UNIPOLAR adj showing only one kind of polarity

UNIQUE adj UNIQUER, UNIQUEST existing as the only one of its kind; very unusual UNIQUELY adv

UNIQUE n pl. -S something that is unique

UNISEX n pl. -ES the condition of not being distinguishable as to sex

UNISON n pl. -S complete agreement UNISONAL adj

UNIT n pl. -S a specific quantity used as a standard of measurement

UNITAGE n pl. -S amount in units

UNITARY adj pertaining to a unit

UNITE v UNITED, UNITING, UNITES to bring together so as to form a whole UNITEDLY adv

UNITER n pl. -S one that unites

UNITIES pl. of unity

UNITIVE adj serving to unite

UNITIZE v -IZED, -IZING, -IZES to divide into units

UNITY n pl. -TIES the state of being one single entity

UNIVALVE n pl. -S a mollusk having a single shell

UNIVERSE n pl. -S the totality of all existing things

UNIVOCAL *n* pl. -S a word having only one meaning

UNKEMPT *adj* untidy

UNKEND *adj* unkenned

UNKENNED *adj* not known or recognized

UNKENNEL *v* -NELED, -NELING, -NELS or -NELLED, -NELLING, -NELS to release from a kennel

UNKENT *adj* unkenned

UNKNIT *v* -KNITTED, -KNITTING, -KNITS to unravel

UNKNOT *v* -KNOTTED, -KNOTTING, -KNOTS to undo a knot in

UNKNOWN *n* pl. -S one that is not known

UNLACE *v* -LACED, -LACING, -LACES to unfasten the laces of

UNLADE *v* -LADED, -LADEN, -LADING, -LADES to unload

UNLAID past tense of unlay

UNLASH *v* -ED, -ING, -ES to untie the lashing (a type of binding) of

UNLATCH *v* -ED, -ING, -ES to open by lifting the latch (a fastening device)

UNLAY *v* -LAID, -LAYING, -LAYS to untwist

UNLEAD *v* -ED, -ING, -S to remove the lead from

UNLEARN *v* -LEARNED or -LEARNT, -LEARNING, -LEARNS to put out of one's knowledge or memory

UNLEASH *v* -ED, -ING, -ES to free from a leash

UNLESS *conj* except on the condition that

UNLET *adj* not rented

UNLEVEL *v* -ELED, -ELING, -ELS or -ELLED, -ELLING, -ELS to make uneven

UNLIMBER *v* -ED, -ING, -S to prepare for action

UNLINK *v* -ED, -ING, -S to unfasten the links (connecting devices) of

UNLIVE *v* -LIVED, -LIVING, -LIVES to live so as to make amends for

UNLOAD *v* -ED, -ING, -S to remove the load or cargo from

UNLOADER *n* pl. -S one that unloads

UNLOCK *v* -ED, -ING, -S to unfasten the lock of

UNLOOSE *v* -LOOSED, -LOOSING, -LOOSES to set free

UNLOOSEN *v* -ED, -ING, -S to unloose

UNMAKE *v* -MADE, -MAKING, -MAKES to destroy

UNMAKER *n* pl. -S one that unmakes

UNMAN *v* -MANNED, -MANNING, -MANS to deprive of courage

UNMASK *v* -ED, -ING, -S to remove a mask from

UNMASKER *n* pl. -S one that unmasks

UNMEET *adj* improper **UNMEETLY** *adv*

UNMEW *v* -ED, -ING, -S to set free

UNMINGLE *v* -GLED, -GLING, -GLES to separate things that are mixed

UNMITER *v* -ED, -ING, -S to depose from the rank of bishop

UNMITRE *v* -TRED, -TRING, -TRES to unmiter

UNMOLD *v* -ED, -ING, -S to remove from a mold

UNMOOR *v* -ED, -ING, -S to release from moorings

UNMORAL *adj* amoral

UNMUFFLE *v* -FLED, -FLING, -FLES to free from something that muffles

UNMUZZLE *v* -ZLED, -ZLING, -ZLES to remove a muzzle from

UNNAIL *v* -ED, -ING, -S to remove the nails from

UNNERVE *v* -NERVED, -NERVING, -NERVES to deprive of courage

UNPACK *v* -ED, -ING, -S to remove the contents of

UNPACKER *n* pl. -S one that unpacks

UNPAGED *adj* having no page numbers

UNPEG *v* -PEGGED, -PEGGING, -PEGS to remove the pegs from

UNPEN *v* -PENNED or -PENT, -PENNING, -PENS to release from confinement

UNPEOPLE *v* -PLED, -PLING, -PLES to remove people from

UNPERSON *n* pl. -S one who is removed completely from recognition

UNPICK *v* -ED, -ING, -S to remove the stitches from

UNPILE *v* -PILED, -PILING, -PILES to take or disentangle from a pile

UNPIN *v* -PINNED, -PINNING, -PINS to remove the pins from

UNPLAIT *v* -ED, -ING, -S to undo the plaits of

UNPLUG v -PLUGGED, -PLUGGING, -PLUGS to take a plug out of

UNPUCKER v -ED, -ING, -S to remove the wrinkles from

UNPUZZLE v -ZLED, -ZLING, -ZLES to work out the obscured meaning of

UNQUIET n pl. -S a state of unrest

UNQUOTE v -QUOTED, -QUOTING, -QUOTES to close a quotation

UNRAVEL v -ELED, -ELING, -ELS or -ELLED, -ELLING, -ELS to separate the threads of

UNREASON v -ED, -ING, -S to disrupt the sanity of

UNREEL v -ED, -ING, -S to unwind from a reel

UNREELER n pl. -S one that unreels

UNREEVE v -REEVED or -ROVE, -ROVEN, -REEVING, -REEVES to withdraw a rope from an opening

UNRENT adj not torn

UNREPAIR n pl. -S lack of repair

UNREST n pl. -S a disturbed or uneasy state

UNRIDDLE v -DLED, -DLING, -DLES to solve

UNRIG v -RIGGED, -RIGGING, -RIGS to divest of rigging

UNRIP v -RIPPED, -RIPPING, -RIPS to rip open

UNRIPE adj -RIPER, -RIPEST not ripe **UNRIPELY** adv

UNROBE v -ROBED, -ROBING, -ROBES to undress

UNROLL v -ED, -ING, -S to open something that is rolled up

UNROOF v -ED, -ING, -S to strip off the roof of

UNROOT v -ED, -ING, -S to uproot

UNROUND v -ED, -ING, -S to articulate without rounding the lips

UNROVE a past tense of unreeve

UNROVEN a past participle of unreeve

UNRULY adj -LIER, -LIEST difficult to control

UNSADDLE v -DLED, -DLING, -DLES to remove the saddle from

UNSAFETY n pl. -TIES lack of safety

UNSAY v -SAID, -SAYING, -SAYS to retract something said

UNSCREW v -ED, -ING, -S to remove the screws from

UNSEAL v -ED, -ING, -S to remove the seal of

UNSEAM v -ED, -ING, -S to open the seams of

UNSEAT v -ED, -ING, -S to remove from a seat

UNSET v -SET, -SETTING, -SETS to unsettle

UNSETTLE v -TLED, -TLING, -TLES to make unstable

UNSEW v -SEWED, -SEWN, -SEWING, -SEWS to undo the sewing of

UNSEX v -ED, -ING, -ES to deprive of sexual power

UNSHELL v -ED, -ING, -S to remove the shell from

UNSHIFT v -ED, -ING, -S to release the shift key on a typewriter

UNSHIP v -SHIPPED, -SHIPPING, -SHIPS to unload from a ship

UNSICKER adj unreliable

UNSIGHT v -ED, -ING, -S to prevent from seeing

UNSLING v -SLUNG, -SLINGING, -SLINGS to remove from a slung position

UNSNAP v -SNAPPED, -SNAPPING, -SNAPS to undo the snaps (fastening devices) of

UNSNARL v -ED, -ING, -S to untangle

UNSOLDER v -ED, -ING, -S to separate

UNSONCY adj unsonsie

UNSONSIE adj unlucky

UNSONSY adj unsonsie

UNSPEAK v -SPOKE, -SPOKEN, -SPEAKING, -SPEAKS to unsay

UNSPHERE v -SPHERED, -SPHERING, -SPHERES to remove from a sphere

UNSTACK v -ED, -ING, -S to remove from a stack

UNSTATE v -STATED, -STATING, -STATES to deprive of status

UNSTEADY v -STEADIED, -STEADYING, -STEADIES to make unsteady

UNSTEEL v -ED, -ING, -S to make soft

UNSTEP v -STEPPED, -STEPPING, -STEPS to remove from a socket

UNSTICK v -ED, -ING, -S to disjoin

UNSTOP v -STOPPED, -STOPPING, -STOPS to remove a stopper from

UNSTRAP   v -STRAPPED, -STRAPPING, -STRAPS to remove a strap from

UNSTRESS   n pl. -ES a syllable having relatively weak stress

UNSTRING   v -STRUNG, -STRINGING, -STRINGS to remove from a string

UNSWATHE   v -SWATHED, -SWATHING, -SWATHES to unbind

UNSWEAR   v -SWORE, -SWORN, -SWEARING, -SWEARS to retract something sworn

UNTACK   v -ED, -ING, -S to remove a tack from

UNTANGLE   v -GLED, -GLING, -GLES to free from tangles

UNTEACH   v -TAUGHT, -TEACHING, -TEACHES to cause to unlearn something

UNTETHER   v -ED, -ING, -S to free from a tether

UNTHINK   v -THOUGHT, -THINKING, -THINKS to dismiss from the mind

UNTHREAD   v -ED, -ING, -S to remove the thread from

UNTHRONE   v -THRONED, -THRONING, -THRONES to remove from a throne

UNTIDY   v -DIED, -DYING, -DIES to make untidy

UNTIE   v -TIED, -TYING, -TIES to free from something that ties

UNTIL   prep up to the time of

UNTO   prep to

UNTOWARD   adj unruly

UNTREAD   v -TROD, -TRODDEN, -TREADING, -TREADS to retrace

UNTRIM   v -TRIMMED, -TRIMMING, -TRIMS to strip of trimming

UNTRUSS   v -ED, -ING, -ES to free from a truss

UNTRUTH   n pl. -S something that is untrue

UNTUCK   v -ED, -ING, -S to release from being tucked up

UNTUNE   v -TUNED, -TUNING, -TUNES to put out of tune

UNTWINE   v -TWINED, -TWINING, -TWINES to separate the twisted or tangled parts of

UNTWIST   v -ED, -ING, -S to untwine

UNTYING   present participle of untie

UNVEIL   v -ED, -ING, -S to remove a covering from

UNVOICE   v -VOICED, -VOICING, -VOICES to deprive of voice or vocal quality

UNWASHED   n pl. -S an ignorant or underprivileged group

UNWEAVE   v -WOVE, -WOVEN, -WEAVING, -WEAVES to undo something woven

UNWEIGHT   v -ED, -ING, -S to reduce the weight of

UNWIND   v -WOUND, -WINDING, -WINDS to reverse the winding of

UNWINDER   n pl. -S one that unwinds

UNWISDOM   n pl. -S lack of wisdom

UNWISH   v -ED, -ING, -ES to cease to wish for

UNWIT   v -WITTED, -WITTING, -WITS to make insane

UNWONTED   adj unusual

UNWORTHY   n pl. -THIES an unworthy person

UNWOUND   past tense of unwind

UNWOVE   past tense of unweave

UNWOVEN   past participle of unweave

UNWRAP   v -WRAPPED, -WRAPPING, -WRAPS to remove the wrapping from

UNYEANED   adj unborn

UNYOKE   v -YOKED, -YOKING, -YOKES to free from a yoke

UNZIP   v -ZIPPED, -ZIPPING, -ZIPS to open the zipper of

UP   v UPPED, UPPING, UPS to raise

UPAS   n pl. -ES an Asian tree

UPBEAR   v -BORE, -BORNE, -BEARING, -BEARS to raise aloft

UPBEARER   n pl. -S one that upbears

UPBEAT   n pl. -S an unaccented beat in a musical measure

UPBIND   v -BOUND, -BINDING, -BINDS to bind completely

UPBOIL   v -ED, -ING, -S to boil up

UPBORE   past tense of upbear

UPBORNE   past participle of upbear

UPBOUND   past tense of upbind

UPBRAID   v -ED, -ING, -S to reproach severely

UPBUILD   v -BUILT, -BUILDING, -BUILDS to build up

UPBY	*adv* upbye
UPBYE	*adv* a little farther on
UPCAST	*v* -CAST, -CASTING, -CASTS to cast up
UPCHUCK	*v* -ED, -ING, -S to vomit
UPCLIMB	*v* -ED, -ING, -S to climb up
UPCOIL	*v* -ED, -ING, -S to coil up
UPCOMING	*adj* about to happen or appear
UPCURL	*v* -ED, -ING, -S to curl up
UPCURVE	*v* -CURVED, -CURVING, -CURVES to curve upward
UPDART	*v* -ED, -ING, -S to dart up
UPDATE	*v* -DATED, -DATING, -DATES to bring up to date
UPDATER	*n pl.* -S one that updates
UPDIVE	*v* -DIVED or -DOVE, -DIVING, -DIVES to spring upward
UPDO	*n pl.* -DOS an upswept hairdo
UPDRAFT	*n pl.* -S an upward movement of air
UPDRY	*v* -DRIED, -DRYING, -DRIES to dry completely
UPEND	*v* -ED, -ING, -S to set or stand on end
UPFIELD	*adv* into the part of the field toward which the offensive team is going
UPFLING	*v* -FLUNG, -FLINGING, -FLINGS to fling up
UPFLOW	*v* -ED, -ING, -S to flow up
UPFOLD	*v* -ED, -ING, -S to fold up
UPGATHER	*v* -ED, -ING, -S to gather up
UPGAZE	*v* -GAZED, -GAZING, -GAZES to gaze up
UPGIRD	*v* -GIRDED or -GIRT, -GIRDING, -GIRDS to gird completely
UPGOING	*adj* going up
UPGRADE	*v* -GRADED, -GRADING, -GRADES to raise to a higher grade or standard
UPGROW	*v* -GREW, -GROWN, -GROWING, -GROWS to grow up
UPGROWTH	*n pl.* -S the process of growing up
UPHEAP	*v* -ED, -ING, -S to heap up
UPHEAVAL	*n pl.* -S the act of upheaving
UPHEAVE	*v* -HEAVED or -HOVE, -HEAVING, -HEAVES to heave up
UPHEAVER	*n pl.* -S one that upheaves
UPHELD	past tense of uphold
UPHILL	*n pl.* -S an upward slope
UPHOARD	*v* -ED, -ING, -S to hoard up
UPHOLD	*v* -HELD, -HOLDING, -HOLDS to hold aloft
UPHOLDER	*n pl.* -S one that upholds
UPHOVE	a past tense of upheave
UPHROE	*n pl.* -S euphroe
UPKEEP	*n pl.* -S the cost of maintaining something in good condition
UPLAND	*n pl.* -S the higher land of a region
UPLANDER	*n pl.* -S an inhabitant of an upland
UPLEAP	*v* -LEAPED or -LEAPT, -LEAPING, -LEAPS to leap up
UPLIFT	*v* -ED, -ING, -S to lift up
UPLIFTER	*n pl.* -S one that uplifts
UPLIGHT	*v* -LIGHTED or -LIT, -LIGHTING -LIGHTS to light to a higher degree
UPMOST	*adj* highest
UPO	*prep* upon
UPON	*prep* on
UPPED	past tense of up
UPPER	*n pl.* -S the part of a boot or shoe above the sole
UPPERCUT	*v* -CUT, -CUTTING, -CUTS to strike an upward blow
UPPILE	*v* -PILED, -PILING, -PILES to pile up
UPPING	*n pl.* -S the process of marking young swans for identification purposes
UPPISH	*adj* uppity UPPISHLY *adv*
UPPITY	*adj* tending to be snobbish and arrogant
UPPROP	*v* -PROPPED, -PROPPING, -PROPS to prop up
UPRAISE	*v* -RAISED, -RAISING, -RAISES to raise up
UPRAISER	*n pl.* -S one that upraises
UPREACH	*v* -ED, -ING, -ES to reach up
UPREAR	*v* -ED, -ING, -S to upraise
UPRIGHT	*v* -ED, -ING, -S to make vertical
UPRISE	*v* -ROSE, -RISEN, -RISING, -RISES to rise up
UPRISER	*n pl.* -S one that uprises
UPRISING	*n pl.* -S a revolt
UPRIVER	*n pl.* -S an area lying toward the source of a river

UPROAR *n pl.* -S a state of noisy excitement and confusion

UPROOT *v* -ED, -ING, -S to pull up by the roots

UPROOTAL *n pl.* -S the act of uprooting

UPROOTER *n pl.* -S one that uproots

UPROSE past tense of uprise

UPROUSE *v* -ROUSED, -ROUSING, -ROUSES to rouse up

UPRUSH *v* -ED, -ING, -ES to rush up

UPSEND *v* -SENT, -SENDING, -SENDS to send upward

UPSET *v* -SET, -SETTING, -SETS to overturn

UPSETTER *n pl.* -S one that upsets

UPSHIFT *v* -ED, -ING, -S to shift an automotive vehicle into a higher gear

UPSHOOT *v* -SHOT, -SHOOTING, -SHOOTS to shoot upward

UPSHOT *n pl.* -S the final result

UPSIDE *n pl.* -S the upper side

UPSILON *n pl.* -S a Greek letter

UPSOAR *v* -ED, -ING, -S to soar upward

UPSPRING *v* -SPRANG or -SPRUNG, -SPRINGING, -SPRINGS to spring up

UPSTAGE *v* -STAGED, -STAGING, -STAGES to outdo theatrically

UPSTAIR *adj* pertaining to an upper floor

UPSTAIRS *adv* up the stairs

UPSTAND *v* -STOOD, -STANDING, -STANDS to stand up on one's feet

UPSTARE *v* -STARED, -STARING, -STARES to stare upward

UPSTART *v* -ED, -ING, -S to spring up suddenly

UPSTATE *n pl.* -S the northern region of a state

UPSTATER *n pl.* -S an inhabitant of an upstate region

UPSTEP *v* -STEPPED, -STEPPING, -STEPS to step up

UPSTIR *v* -STIRRED, -STIRRING, -STIRS to stir up

UPSTOOD past tense of upstand

UPSTREAM *adv* toward the source of a stream

UPSTROKE *n pl.* -S an upward stroke

UPSURGE *v* -SURGED, -SURGING, -SURGES to surge up

UPSWEEP *v* -SWEPT, -SWEEPING, -SWEEPS to sweep upward

UPSWELL *v* -SWELLED, -SWOLLEN, -SWELLING, -SWELLS, to swell up

UPSWING *v* -SWUNG, -SWINGING, -SWINGS to swing upward

UPTAKE *n pl.* -S an upward ventilating shaft

UPTEAR *v* -TORE, -TORN, -TEARING, -TEARS to tear out by the roots

UPTHROW *v* -THREW, -THROWN, -THROWING, -THROWS to throw upward

UPTHRUST *v* -THRUST, -THRUSTING, -THRUSTS to thrust up

UPTIGHT *adj* nervous

UPTILT *v* -ED, -ING, -S to tilt upward

UPTIME *n pl.* -S the time during which machinery is functioning

UPTORE past tense of uptear

UPTORN past participle of uptear

UPTOSS *v* -ED, -ING, -ES to toss upward

UPTOWN *n pl.* -S the upper part of a city

UPTOWNER *n pl.* -S one that lives uptown

UPTREND *n pl.* -S a tendency upward or toward growth

UPTURN *v* -ED, -ING, -S to turn up or over

UPWAFT *v* -ED, -ING, -S to waft upward

UPWARD *adv* toward a higher place or position **UPWARDLY** *adv*

UPWARDS *adv* upward

UPWELL *v* -ED, -ING, -S to well up

UPWIND *n pl.* -S a wind that blows against one's course

URACIL *n pl.* -S a chemical compound

URAEI a pl. of uraeus

URAEMIA *n pl.* -S uremia **URAEMIC** *adj*

URAEUS *n pl.* URAEI or URAEUSES the figure of the sacred serpent on the headdress of ancient Egyptian rulers

URALITE *n pl.* -S a mineral **URALITIC** *adj*

URANIC *adj* pertaining to uranium

URANIDE *n pl.* -S uranium

URANISM *n pl.* -S homosexuality

URANITE *n pl.* -S a mineral **URANITIC** *adj*

URANIUM   n pl. -S a radioactive element

URANOUS   adj pertaining to uranium

URANYL   n pl. -S a bivalent radical **URANYLIC** adj

URARE   n pl. -S curare

URARI   n pl. -S curare

URASE   n pl. -S urease

URATE   n pl. -S a chemical salt **URATIC** adj

URBAN   adj pertaining to a city

URBANE   adj -BANER, -BANEST refined and elegant **URBANELY** adv

URBANISE   v -ISED, -ISING, -ISES to urbanize

URBANISM   n pl. -S the life-style of city dwellers

URBANIST   n pl. -S a specialist in city planning

URBANITE   n pl. -S one who lives in a city

URBANITY   n pl. -TIES the quality of being urbane

URBANIZE   v -IZED, -IZING, -IZES to cause to take on urban characteristics

URCHIN   n pl. -S a mischievous boy

URD   n pl. -S an annual bean grown in India

UREA   n pl. -S a chemical compound **UREAL** adj

UREASE   n pl. -S an enzyme

UREDIA   pl. of uredium

UREDIAL   adj pertaining to a uredium

UREDINIA   n/pl uredia

UREDIUM   n pl. -DIA a spore-producing organ of certain fungi

UREDO   n pl. -DOS a skin irritation

UREIC   adj pertaining to urea

UREIDE   n pl. -S a chemical compound

UREMIA   n pl. -S an abnormal condition of the blood **UREMIC** adj

URETER   n pl. -S the duct that conveys urine from the kidney to the bladder **URETERAL, URETERIC** adj

URETHAN   n pl. -S urethane

URETHANE   n pl. -S a chemical compound

URETHRA   n pl. -THRAE or -THRAS the duct through which urine is discharged from the bladder **URETHRAL** adj

URETIC   adj pertaining to urine

URGE   v URGED, URGING, URGES to force forward

URGENCY   n pl. -CIES the quality of being urgent

URGENT   adj requiring immediate attention **URGENTLY** adv

URGER   n pl. -S one that urges

URGING   present participle of urge

URGINGLY   adv in an urging manner

URIC   adj pertaining to urine

URIDINE   n pl. -S a chemical compound

URINAL   n pl. -S a fixture used for urinating

URINARY   n pl. -NARIES a urinal

URINATE   v -NATED, -NATING, -NATES to discharge urine

URINE   n pl. -S a liquid containing body wastes

URINEMIA   n pl. -S uremia **URINEMIC** adj

URINOSE   adj pertaining to urine

URINOUS   adj pertaining to urine

URN   n pl. -S a type of vase **URNLIKE** adj

UROCHORD   n pl. -S a rodlike structure in certain lower vertebrates

URODELE   n pl. -S a type of amphibian

UROLITH   n pl. -S a concretion in the urinary tract

UROLOGY   n pl. -GIES the branch of medicine dealing with the urinary tract **UROLOGIC** adj

UROPOD   n pl. -S an abdominal limb of an arthropod **UROPODAL** adj

UROSCOPY   n pl. -PIES analysis of the urine as a means of diagnosis

UROSTYLE   n pl. -S a part of the vertebral column of frogs and toads

URSA   n pl. -SAE a female bear

URSIFORM   adj having the form of a bear

URSINE   adj pertaining to a bear

URTICANT   n pl. -S an urticating substance

URTICATE   v -CATED, -CATING, -CATES to cause itching or stinging

URUS   n pl. -ES an extinct European ox

URUSHIOL   n pl. -S a toxic liquid

US   pron the objective case of the pronoun we

USABLE   adj capable of being used **USABLY** adv

USAGE *n* pl. -S a firmly established and generally accepted practice or procedure

USANCE *n* pl. -S usage

USAUNCE *n* pl. -S usance

USE *v* USED, USING, USES to put into service

USEABLE *adj* usable **USEABLY** *adv*

USEFUL *adj* serving a purpose **USEFULLY** *adv*

USELESS *adj* serving no purpose

USER *n* pl. -S one that uses

USHER *v* -ED, -ING, -S to conduct to a place

USING present participle of use

USNEA *n* pl. -S any of a genus of lichens

USQUABAE *n* pl. -S usquebae

USQUE *n* pl. -S usquebae

USQUEBAE *n* pl. -S whiskey

USTULATE *adj* scorched

USUAL *n* pl. -S something that is usual (ordinary)

USUALLY *adv* ordinarily

USUFRUCT *n* pl. -S the legal right to use another's property so long as it is not damaged or altered

USURER *n* pl. -S one that practices usury

USURIES pl. of usury

USURIOUS *adj* practicing usury

USURP *v* -ED, -ING, -S to seize and hold without legal authority

USURPER *n* pl. -S one that usurps

USURY *n* pl. -RIES the lending of money at an exorbitant interest rate

UT *n* pl. -S the musical tone C in the French solmization system now replaced by do

UTA *n* pl. -S any of a genus of large lizards

UTENSIL *n* pl. -S a useful implement

UTERUS *n* pl. UTERI or UTERUSES an organ of female mammals **UTERINE** *adj*

UTILE *adj* useful

UTILIDOR *n* pl. -S an insulated system of pipes for use in arctic regions

UTILISE *v* -LISED, -LISING, -LISES to utilize

UTILISER *n* pl. -S utilizer

UTILITY *n* pl. -TIES the quality of being useful

UTILIZE *v* -LIZED, -LIZING, -LIZES to make use of

UTILIZER *n* pl. -S one that utilizes

UTMOST *n* pl. -S the greatest degree or amount

UTOPIA *n* pl. -S a place of ideal perfection

UTOPIAN *n* pl. -S one who believes in the perfectibility of human society

UTOPISM *n* pl. -S the body of ideals or principles of a utopian

UTOPIST *n* pl. -S a utopian

UTRICLE *n* pl. -S a saclike cavity in the inner ear

UTRICULI *n/pl* utricles

UTTER *v* -ED, -ING, -S to give audible expression to

UTTERER *n* pl. -S one that utters

UTTERLY *adv* totally

UVEA *n* pl. -S a layer of the eye **UVEAL** *adj*

UVEITIS *n* pl. -ITISES inflammation of the uvea **UVEITIC** *adj*

UVEOUS *adj* pertaining to the uvea

UVULA *n* pl. -LAE or -LAS the pendent, fleshy portion of the soft palate

UVULAR *n* pl. -S a uvularly produced sound

UVULARLY *adv* with the use of the uvula

UVULITIS *n* pl. -TISES inflammation of the uvula

UXORIAL *adj* pertaining to a wife

UXORIOUS *adj* excessively submissive or devoted to one's wife

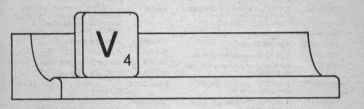

VACANCY	n pl. -CIES the quality or state of being vacant	**VAGINATE**	adj enclosed in a sheath
VACANT	adj empty **VACANTLY** adv	**VAGOTOMY**	n pl. -MIES surgical division of the vagus nerve
VACATE	v -CATED, -CATING, -CATES to make vacant	**VAGRANCY**	n pl. -CIES the state of being a vagrant
VACATION	v -ED, -ING, -S to take a vacation (a period of time devoted to rest and relaxation)	**VAGRANT**	n pl. -S a wanderer with no apparent means of support
		VAGROM	adj wandering
VACCINA	n pl. -S vaccinia	**VAGUE**	adj VAGUER, VAGUEST not clearly expressed or understood **VAGUELY** adv
VACCINE	n pl. -S a preparation given to produce immunity to a specific disease **VACCINAL** adj		
		VAGUS	n pl. -GI a cranial nerve
VACCINIA	n pl. -S cowpox	**VAHINE**	n pl. -S wahine
VACUA	a pl. of vacuum	**VAIL**	v -ED, -ING, -S to lower
VACUITY	n pl. -ITIES an empty	**VAIN**	adj VAINER, VAINEST filled with undue admiration for oneself **VAINLY** adv
VACUOLE	n pl. -S a small cavity in organic tissue **VACUOLAR** adj		
VACUOUS	adj empty	**VAINNESS**	n. -ES the quality or state of being vain
VACUUM	n pl. VACUUMS or VACUA a space entirely devoid of matter		
		VAIR	n pl. -S a fur used for lining and trimming medieval garments
VACUUM	v -ED, -ING, -S to use a device that cleans by suction	**VAKEEL**	n pl. -S a native lawyer in India
VADOSE	adj located above the permanent groundwater level	**VAKIL**	n pl. -S vakeel
VAGABOND	v -ED, -ING, -S to live like a vagabond (a vagrant)	**VALANCE**	v -LANCED, -LANCING, -LANCES to furnish with a short drapery
VAGAL	adj pertaining to the vagus nerve **VAGALLY** adv	**VALE**	n pl. -S a valley
		VALENCE	n pl. -S the degree of combining power of an element or radical
VAGARY	n pl. -RIES a whim		
VAGI	pl. of vagus	**VALENCIA**	n pl. -S a woven fabric
VAGILE	adj free to move about	**VALENCY**	n pl. -CIES valence
VAGILITY	n pl. -TIES freedom of movement	**VALERATE**	n pl. -S a chemical salt
VAGINA	n pl. -NAE or -NAS the passage leading from the uterus to the vulva **VAGINAL** adj	**VALERIAN**	n pl. -S a perennial herb **VALERIC** adj

VALET v -ED, -ING, -S to act as a personal servant to

VALGUS n pl. -ES the position of a joint that is abnormally turned outward **VALGOID** adj

VALIANCE n pl. -S valor

VALIANCY n pl. -CIES valor

VALIANT n pl. -S a courageous person

VALID adj based on evidence that can be supported

VALIDATE v -DATED, -DATING, -DATES to give legal force to

VALIDITY n pl. -TIES the quality or state of being valid

VALIDLY adv in a valid manner

VALINE n pl. -S an amino acid

VALISE n pl. -S a small piece of hand luggage

VALKYR n pl. -S valkyrie

VALKYRIE n pl. -S a maiden in Norse mythology

VALLATE adj bordered by a raised edge

VALLEY n pl. -LEYS a depression of the earth's surface

VALONIA n pl. -S a substance obtained from dried acorn cups and used in tanning and dyeing

VALOR n pl. -S courage

VALORISE v -ISED, -ISING, -ISES to valorize

VALORIZE v -IZED, -IZING, -IZES to establish and maintain the price of by governmental action

VALOROUS adj courageous

VALOUR n pl. -S valor

VALSE n pl. -S a concert waltz

VALUABLE n pl. -S a possession of value

VALUABLY adv with value

VALUATE v -ATED, -ATING, -ATES to appraise

VALUATOR n pl. -S one that valuates

VALUE v -UED, -UING, -UES to estimate the value (the quality that renders a thing useful or desirable) of

VALUER n pl. -S one that values

VALUTA n pl. -S the agreed or exchange value of a currency

VALVAL adj resembling or pertaining to a valve

VALVAR adj valval

VALVATE adj having valves or parts resembling valves

VALVE v VALVED, VALVING, VALVES to provide with a valve (a device for controlling the flow of a liquid or gas)

VALVELET n pl. -S a small valve

VALVULA n pl. -LAE valvule

VALVULAR adj pertaining to a valve

VALVULE n pl. -S a small valve

VAMBRACE n pl. -S a piece of armor for the forearm

VAMOOSE v -MOOSED, -MOOSING, -MOOSES to leave quickly

VAMOSE v -MOSED, -MOSING, -MOSES to vamoose

VAMP v -ED, -ING, -S to repair or patch

VAMPER n pl. -S one that vamps

VAMPIRE n pl. -S a reanimated corpse believed to feed on sleeping persons' blood **VAMPIRIC** adj

VAMPISH adj seductive

VAN n pl. -S a large motor vehicle

VANADATE n pl. -S a chemical salt

VANADIUM n pl. -S a metallic element **VANADIC, VANADOUS** adj

VANDA n pl. -S a tropical orchid

VANDAL n pl. -S one who willfully destroys or defaces property **VANDALIC** adj

VANDYKE n pl. -S a short, pointed beard **VANDYKED** adj

VANE n pl. -S a device for showing the direction of the wind **VANED** adj

VANG n pl. -S a rope on a ship

VANGUARD n pl. -S the forefront of a movement

VANILLA n pl. -S a flavoring extract **VANILLIC** adj

VANILLIN n pl. -S a chemical compound used in flavoring

VANISH v -ED, -ING, -ES to disappear

VANISHER n pl. -S one that vanishes

VANITY n pl. -TIES inflated pride in oneself **VANITIED** adj

VANMAN n pl. -MEN a person who drives a van

VANQUISH v -ED, -ING, -ES to defeat in battle

VANTAGE   *n* pl. -S superiority over a competitor

VANWARD   *adv* toward the front

VAPID   *adj* insipid **VAPIDLY** *adv*

VAPIDITY   *n* pl. -TIES the quality or state of being vapid

VAPOR   *v* -ED, -ING, -S to emit vapor (visible floating moisture)

VAPORER   *n* pl. -S one that vapors

VAPORING   *n* pl. -S boastful talk

VAPORISE   *v* -ISED, -ISING, -ISES to vaporize

VAPORISH   *adj* resembling vapor

VAPORIZE   *v* -IZED, -IZING, -IZES to convert into vapor

VAPOROUS   *adj* vaporish

VAPORY   *adj* vaporish

VAPOUR   *v* -ED, -ING, -S to vapor

VAPOURER   *n* pl. -S vaporer

VAPOURY   *adj* vapory

VAQUERO   *n* pl. -ROS a cowboy

VARA   *n* pl. -S a Spanish unit of length

VARIA   *n/pl* a collection of various literary works

VARIABLE   *n* pl. -S something that varies

VARIABLY   *adv* in a varying manner

VARIANCE   *n* pl. -S a license to perform an act contrary to the usual rule

VARIANT   *n* pl. -S a variable

VARIATE   *v* -ATED, -ATING, -ATES to vary

VARICES   pl. of varix

VARICOSE   *adj* abnormally swollen or dilated

VARIED   past tense of vary

VARIEDLY   *adv* in a varied manner

VARIER   *n* pl. -S one that varies

VARIES   present 3d person sing. of vary

VARIETY   *n* pl. -ETIES something differing from others of the same general kind **VARIETAL** *adj*

VARIFORM   *adj* having various forms

VARIOLA   *n* pl. -S smallpox **VARIOLAR** *adj*

VARIOLE   *n* pl. -S a foveola

VARIORUM   *n* pl. -S an edition containing various versions of a text

VARIOUS   *adj* of diverse kinds

VARISTOR   *n* pl. -S a type of electrical resistor

VARIX   *n* pl. VARICES a varicose vein

VARLET   *n* pl. -S a knave

VARLETRY   *n* pl. -RIES a group of common people

VARMENT   *n* pl. -S varmint

VARMINT   *n* pl. -S an animal considered to be a pest

VARNA   *n* pl. -S any of the four main Hindu social classes

VARNISH   *v* -ED, -ING, -ES to give a glossy appearance to

VARNISHY   *adj* glossy

VARSITY   *n* pl. -TIES the principal team representing a university, college, or school in any activity

VARUS   *n* pl. -ES a malformation of a bone or joint

VARVE   *n* pl. -S a deposit of sedimentary material **VARVED** *adj*

VARY   *v* VARIED, VARYING, VARIES to become or make different

VAS   *n* pl. VASA an anatomical duct **VASAL** *adj*

VASCULAR   *adj* pertaining to ducts that convey body liquids

VASCULUM   *n* pl. -LA or -LUMS a box used to hold plant specimens

VASE   *n* pl. -S a rounded, decorative container **VASELIKE** *adj*

VASIFORM   *adj* having the form of a vase

VASSAL   *n* pl. -S a person granted the use of land by a feudal lord in return for homage and allegiance

VAST   *adj* VASTER, VASTEST of great extent or size

VAST   *n* pl. -S a vast space

VASTIER   comparative of vasty

VASTIEST   superlative of vasty

VASTITY   *n* pl. -TIES vastness

VASTLY   *adv* to a vast extent or degree

VASTNESS   *n* pl. -ES the quality or state of being vast

VASTY   *adj* VASTIER, VASTIEST vast

VAT   *v* VATTED, VATTING, VATS to put into a vat (a large container for holding liquids)

VATFUL   *n* pl. -S as much as a vat will hold

VATIC   *adj* pertaining to a prophet

VATICAL	adj vatic	**VEGETANT**	adj characteristic of plant life
VATICIDE	n pl. -S the killing of a prophet	**VEGETATE**	v -TATED, -TATING, -TATES to grow in the manner of a plant
VATTED	past tense of vat		
VATTING	present participle of vat	**VEGETE**	adj healthy
VAU	n pl. -S vav	**VEGETIST**	n pl. -S one that eats only plant products
VAULT	v -ED, -ING, -S to provide with a vault (an arched ceiling)	**VEGETIVE**	adj growing or capable of growing
VAULTER	n pl. -S one that leaps	**VEHEMENT**	adj ardent
VAULTING	n pl. -S the structure forming a vault	**VEHICLE**	n pl. -S a device used as a means of conveyance
VAULTY	adj VAULTIER, VAULTIEST resembling a vault	**VEIL**	v -ED, -ING, -S to provide with a veil (a piece of sheer fabric worn over the face)
VAUNT	v -ED, -ING, -S to brag		
VAUNTER	n pl. -S one that vaunts	**VEILEDLY**	adv in a disguised manner
VAUNTFUL	adj boastful	**VEILER**	n pl. -S one that veils
VAUNTIE	adj boastful	**VEILING**	n pl. -S a veil
VAUNTY	adj vauntie	**VEILLIKE**	adj resembling a veil
VAV	n pl. -S a Hebrew letter	**VEIN**	v -ED, -ING, -S to fill with veins (tubular blood vessels)
VAVASOR	n pl. -S a high-ranking vassal		
VAVASOUR	n pl. -S vavasor	**VEINAL**	adj of or pertaining to the veins
VAVASSOR	n pl. -S vavasor	**VEINER**	n pl. -S a tool used in wood carving
VAW	n pl. -S vav		
VAWARD	n pl. -S the foremost part	**VEINIER**	comparative of veiny
VAWNTIE	adj vaunty	**VEINIEST**	superlative of veiny
VEAL	v -ED, -ING, -S to kill and prepare a calf for food	**VEINING**	n pl. -S a network of veins
		VEINLESS	adj having no veins
VEALER	n pl. -S a calf raised for food	**VEINLET**	n pl. -S a small vein
VEALY	adj VEALIER, VEALIEST immature	**VEINLIKE**	adj resembling a vein
		VEINULE	n pl. -S venule
VECTOR	v -ED, -ING, -S to guide in flight by means of radioed directions	**VEINULET**	n pl. -S venule
		VEINY	adj VEINIER, VEINIEST full of veins
VEDALIA	n pl. -S an Australian ladybug		
VEDETTE	n pl. -S a small boat used for scouting	**VELA**	pl. of velum
		VELAMEN	n pl. -MINA a velum
VEE	n pl. -S the letter V	**VELAR**	n pl. -S a kind of speech sound
VEENA	n pl. -S vina	**VELARIUM**	n pl. -IA an awning over an ancient Roman theater
VEEP	n pl. -S a vice-president		
VEEPEE	n pl. -S veep	**VELARIZE**	v -IZED, -IZING, -IZES to pronounce with the back of the tongue touching the soft palate
VEER	v -ED, -ING, -S to change direction		
VEERY	n pl. -RIES a songbird	**VELATE**	adj having a velum
VEG	n pl. VEG a vegetable	**VELD**	n pl. -S veldt
VEGAN	n pl. -S one that eats only plant products	**VELDT**	n pl. -S a grassland of southern Africa
VEGANISM	n pl. -S the practice of eating only plant products	**VELIGER**	n pl. -S a larval stage of certain mollusks
VEGETAL	adj pertaining to plants		

VELITES	*n/pl* foot soldiers of ancient Rome
VELLEITY	*n* pl. -ITIES a very low degree of desire
VELLUM	*n* pl. -S a fine parchment
VELOCE	*adv* rapidly — used as a musical direction
VELOCITY	*n* pl. -TIES rapidity of motion
VELOUR	*n* pl. -S a fabric resembling velvet
VELOUTE	*n* pl. -S a type of sauce
VELUM	*n* pl. -LA a thin membranous covering or partition
VELURE	*v* -LURED, -LURING, -LURES to smooth with a velvet or silk pad, as a hat
VELVERET	*n* pl. -S a fabric resembling velvet
VELVET	*n* pl. -S a soft, smooth fabric **VELVETED, VELVETY** *adj*
VENA	*n* pl. -NAE a vein
VENAL	*adj* open to bribery **VENALLY** *adv*
VENALITY	*n* pl. -TIES the quality or state of being venal
VENATIC	*adj* pertaining to hunting
VENATION	*n* pl. -S an arrangement of veins
VEND	*v* -ED, -ING, -S to sell **VENDABLE** *adj*
VENDACE	*n* pl. -S a European fish
VENDEE	*n* pl. -S a buyer
VENDER	*n* pl. -S a vendor
VENDETTA	*n* pl. -S a feud between two families
VENDIBLE	*n* pl. -S a salable article
VENDIBLY	*adv* salably
VENDOR	*n* pl. -S a seller
VENDUE	*n* pl. -S a public sale
VENEER	*v* -ED, -ING, -S to overlay with thin layers of material
VENEERER	*n* pl. -S one that veneers
VENENATE	*v* -NATED, -NATING, -NATES to poison
VENENOSE	*adj* poisonous
VENERATE	*v* -ATED, -ATING, -ATES to revere
VENEREAL	*adj* involving the genital organs
VENERY	*n* pl. -ERIES sexual intercourse
VENETIAN	*n* pl. -S a flexible window screen

VENGE	*v* VENGED, VENGING, VENGES to avenge
VENGEFUL	*adj* seeking to avenge
VENIAL	*adj* easily excused or forgiven **VENIALLY** *adv*
VENIN	*n* pl. -S a toxin found in snake venom
VENINE	*n* pl. -S venin
VENIRE	*n* pl. -S a type of judicial writ
VENISON	*n* pl. -S the edible flesh of a deer
VENOM	*v* -ED, -ING, -S to inject with venom (a poisonous secretion of certain animals)
VENOMER	*n* pl. -S one that venoms
VENOMOUS	*adj* poisonous
VENOSE	*adj* venous
VENOSITY	*n* pl. -TIES the quality of state of being venous
VENOUS	*adj* full of veins **VENOUSLY** *adv*
VENT	*v* -ED, -ING, -S to provide with a vent (an opening for the escape of gas or liquid)
VENTAGE	*n* pl. -S a small opening
VENTAIL	*n* pl. -S the adjustable front of a medieval helmet
VENTER	*n* pl. -S the abdomen
VENTLESS	*adj* having no vent
VENTRAL	*n* pl. -S a fin located on the underside of a fish
VENTURE	*v* -TURED, -TURING, -TURES to risk
VENTURER	*n* pl. -S one that ventures
VENTURI	*n* pl. -S a device for measuring the flow of a fluid
VENTURING	present participle of venture
VENUE	*n* pl. -S the locale of an event
VENULE	*n* pl. -S a small vein **VENULAR, VENULOSE, VENULOUS** *adj*
VERA	*adj* very
VERACITY	*n* pl. -TIES conformity to truth
VERANDA	*n* pl. -S a type of porch
VERANDAH	*n* pl. -S a veranda
VERATRIA	*n* pl. -S veratrin
VERATRIN	*n* pl. -S a poisonous mixture of alkaloids
VERATRUM	*n* pl. -S a poisonous herb
VERB	*n* pl. -S a word used to express an act, occurrence, or mode of being

VERBAL n pl. -S a word derived from a verb

VERBALLY adv in a spoken manner

VERBATIM adv word for word

VERBENA n pl. -S a flowering plant

VERBIAGE n pl. -S an excess of words

VERBID n pl. -S a verbal

VERBIFY v -FIED, -FYING, -FIES to use as a verb

VERBILE n pl. -S one whose mental imagery consists of words

VERBLESS adj lacking a verb

VERBOSE adj wordy

VERBOTEN adj forbidden

VERDANCY n pl. -CIES the quality or state of being verdant

VERDANT adj green with vegetation

VERDERER n pl. -S an officer in charge of the royal forests of England

VERDEROR n pl. -S verderer

VERDICT n pl. -S the decision of a jury at the end of a legal proceeding

VERDIN n pl. -S a small bird

VERDITER n pl. -S a blue or green pigment

VERDURE n pl. -S green vegetation **VERDURED** adj

VERECUND adj shy

VERGE v VERGED, VERGING, VERGES to come near

VERGENCE n pl. -S a movement of one eye in relation to the other

VERGER n pl. -S a church official

VERGING present participle of verge

VERGLAS n pl. -ES a thin coating of ice on rock

VERIDIC adj truthful

VERIER comparative of very

VERIEST superlative of very

VERIFIER n pl. -S one that verifies

VERIFY v -FIED, -FYING, -FIES to prove to be true

VERILY adv in truth

VERISM n pl. -S realism in art or literature

VERISMO n pl. -MOS verism

VERIST n pl. -S one who practices verism **VERISTIC** adj

VERITAS n pl. -TATES truth

VERITY n pl. -TIES truth

VERJUICE n pl. -S the juice of sour or unripe fruit

VERMEIL n pl. -S a red color

VERMES pl. of vermis

VERMIAN adj pertaining to worms

VERMIN n pl. VERMIN small, common, harmful, or objectionable animals

VERMIS n pl. -MES a part of the brain

VERMOULU adj eaten by worms

VERMOUTH n pl. -S a liqueur

VERMUTH n pl. -S vermouth

VERNACLE n pl. -S vernicle

VERNAL adj pertaining to spring **VERNALLY** adv

VERNICLE n pl. -S veronica

VERNIER n pl. -S an auxiliary scale used with a main scale to obtain fine measurements

VERNIX n pl. -ES a fatty substance covering the skin of a fetus

VERONICA n pl. -S a handkerchief bearing the image of Christ's face

VERRUCA n pl. -CAE a wart

VERSAL adj entire

VERSANT n pl. -S the slope of a mountain or mountain chain

VERSE v VERSED, VERSING, VERSES to versify

VERSEMAN n pl. -MEN one who versifies

VERSER n pl. -S a verseman

VERSET n pl. -S a versicle

VERSICLE n pl. -S a short line of metrical writing

VERSIFY v -FIED, -FYING, -FIES to change from prose into metrical form

VERSINE n pl. -S a trigonometric function of an angle

VERSING present participle of verse

VERSION n pl. -S an account or description from a particular point of view

VERSO n pl. -SOS a left-hand page of a book

VERST n pl. -S a Russian measure of distance

VERSTE n pl. -S verst

VERSUS prep against

VERT   n pl. -S the heraldic color green

VERTEBRA   n pl. -BRAE or -BRAS any of the bones or segments forming the spinal column

VERTEX   n pl. -TEXES or -TICES the highest point of something

VERTICAL   n pl. -S something that is vertical (extending up and down)

VERTICIL   n pl. -S a circular arrangement, as of flowers or leaves, about a point on an axis

VERTIGO   n pl. -GOES, -GOS, or -GINES a disordered state in which the individual or his surroundings seem to whirl dizzily

VERTU   n pl. -S virtu

VERVAIN   n pl. -S a flowering plant

VERVE   n pl. -S vivacity

VERVET   n pl. -S an African monkey

VERY   adj VERIER, VERIEST absolute

VESICA   n pl. -CAE a bladder VESICAL adj

VESICANT   n pl. -S a chemical warfare agent that induces blistering

VESICATE   v -CATED, -CATING, -CATES to blister

VESICLE   n pl. -S a small bladder

VESICULA   n pl. -LAE a vesicle

VESPER   n pl. -S an evening service, prayer, or song

VESPERAL   n pl. -S a covering for an altar cloth

VESPIARY   n pl. -ARIES a nest of wasps

VESPID   n pl. -S a wasp

VESPINE   adj pertaining to wasps

VESSEL   n pl. -S a craft for traveling on water VESSELED adj

VEST   v -ED, -ING, -S to place in the control of

VESTA   n pl. -S a short friction match

VESTAL   n pl. -S a chaste woman

VESTALLY   adv chastely

VESTEE   n pl. -S a garment worn under a woman's jacket or blouse

VESTIARY   n pl. -ARIES a dressing room

VESTIGE   n pl. -S a visible sign of something that is no longer in existence

VESTIGIA   n/pl vestiges

VESTING   n pl. -S the right of an employee to share in and withdraw from a pension fund without penalty

VESTLESS   adj being without a vest

VESTLIKE   adj resembling a vest (a short, sleeveless garment)

VESTMENT   n pl. -S one of the ceremonial garments of the clergy

VESTRY   n pl. -TRIES a room in which vestments are kept VESTRAL adj

VESTURAL   adj pertaining to clothing

VESTURE   v -TURED, -TURING, -TURES to clothe

VESUVIAN   n pl. -S a mineral

VET   v VETTED, VETTING, VETS to treat animals medically

VETCH   n pl. -ES a climbing plant

VETERAN   n pl. -S a former member of the armed forces

VETIVER   n pl. -S an Asian grass

VETO   v -ED, -ING, -ES to forbid or prevent authoritatively

VETOER   n pl. -S one that vetoes

VETTED   past tense of vet

VETTING   present participle of vet

VEX   v VEXED or VEXT, VEXING, VEXES to annoy

VEXATION   n pl. -S a cause of trouble

VEXEDLY   adv in a vexed manner

VEXER   n pl. -S one that vexes

VEXIL   n pl. -S vexillum

VEXILLUM   n pl. -LA the web or vane of a feather VEXILLAR adj

VEXINGLY   adv in a vexing manner

VEXT   a past tense of vex

VIA   prep by way of

VIABLE   adj capable of living VIABLY adv

VIADUCT   n pl. -S a type of bridge

VIAL   v VIALED, VIALING, VIALS or VIALLED, VIALLING, VIALS to put in a vial (a small container for liquids)

VIAND   n pl. -S an article of food

VIATIC   adj pertaining to traveling

VIATICAL   adj viatic

VIATICUM   n pl. -CA or -CUMS an allowance for traveling expenses

VIATOR n pl. -ES or -S a traveler

VIBES n/pl a percussion instrument

VIBIST n pl. -S one who plays the vibes

VIBRANCE n pl. -S vibrancy

VIBRANCY n pl. -CIES the quality or state of being vibrant

VIBRANT n pl. -S a sonant

VIBRATE v -BRATED, -BRATING, -BRATES to move back and forth rapidly

VIBRATO n pl. -TOS a tremulous or pulsating musical effect

VIBRATOR n pl. -S something that vibrates

VIBRIO n pl. -RIOS any of a genus of bacteria shaped like a comma VIBRIOID adj

VIBRION n pl. -S vibrio

VIBRISSA n pl. -SAE one of the stiff hairs growing about the mouth of certain mammals

VIBURNUM n pl. -S a flowering shrub

VICAR n pl. -S a church official

VICARAGE n pl. -S the office of a vicar

VICARATE n pl. -S vicarage

VICARIAL adj pertaining to a vicar

VICARLY adj vicarial

VICE v VICED, VICING, VICES to vise

VICELESS adj having no immoral habits

VICENARY adj pertaining to the number twenty

VICEROY n pl. -ROYS one who rules as the representative of a sovereign

VICHY n pl. -CHIES a type of mineral water

VICINAGE n pl. -S vicinity

VICINAL adj nearby

VICING present participle of vice

VICINITY n pl. -TIES the region near or about a place

VICIOUS adj dangerously aggressive

VICOMTE n pl. -S a French nobleman

VICTIM n pl. -S one who suffers from a destructive or injurious action

VICTOR n pl. -S one who defeats an adversary

VICTORIA n pl. -S a light carriage

VICTORY n pl. -RIES a successful outcome in a contest or struggle

VICTRESS n pl. -ES a female victor

VICTUAL v -UALED, -UALING; -UALS or -UALLED, -UALLING, -UALS to provide with food

VICUGNA n pl. -S vicuna

VICUNA n pl. -S a ruminant mammal

VIDE v see — used to direct a reader to another item; VIDE is the only form of this verb; it cannot be conjugated

VIDEO n pl. -EOS television

VIDETTE n pl. -S vedette

VIDICON n pl. -S a type of television camera tube

VIDUITY n pl. -ITIES the quality or state of being a widow

VIE v VIED, VYING, VIES to strive for superiority

VIER n pl. -S one that vies

VIEW v -ED, -ING, -S to look at VIEWABLE adj

VIEWER n pl. -S one that views

VIEWIER comparative of viewy

VIEWIEST superlative of viewy

VIEWING n pl. -S an act of seeing, watching, or looking

VIEWLESS adj having no opinions

VIEWY adj VIEWIER, VIEWIEST showy

VIGIL n pl. -S a period of watchfulness maintained during normal sleeping hours

VIGILANT adj watchful

VIGNETTE v -GNETTED, -GNETTING, -GNETTES to describe briefly

VIGOR n pl. -S active strength or force

VIGORISH n pl. -ES a charge paid to a bookie on a bet

VIGOROSO adv with emphasis and spirit — used as a musical direction

VIGOROUS adj full of vigor

VIGOUR n pl. -S vigor

VIKING n pl. -S a Scandinavian pirate

VILAYET n pl. -S an administrative division of Turkey

VILE adj VILER, VILEST physically repulsive VILELY adv

VILENESS n pl. -ES the state of being vile

VILIFIER n pl. -S one that vilifies

VILIFY v -FIED, -FYING, -FIES to defame

VILIPEND v -ED, -ING, -S to vilify

VILL — n pl. -S a village

VILLA — n pl. -LAE or -LAS an agricultural estate of ancient Rome

VILLADOM — n pl. -S the world constituted by suburban residences and their occupants

VILLAGE — n pl. -S a small community in a rural area

VILLAGER — n pl. -S one who lives in a village

VILLAIN — n pl. -S a cruelly malicious person

VILLAINY — n pl. -LAINIES conduct characteristic of a villain

VILLATIC — adj rural

VILLEIN — n pl. -S a type of serf

VILLUS — n pl. -LI one of the hairlike projections found on certain membranes VILLOSE, VILLOUS adj

VIM — n pl. -S energy

VIMEN — n pl. -MINA a long, flexible branch of a plant VIMINAL adj

VIN — n pl. -S wine

VINA — n pl. -S a stringed instrument of India

VINAL — n pl. -S a synthetic textile fiber

VINASSE — n pl. -S a residue left after the distillation of liquor

VINCA — n pl. -S a flowering plant

VINCIBLE — adj capable of being conquered

VINCULUM — n pl. -LA or -LUMS a unifying bond

VINE — v VINED, VINING, VINES to grow like a vine (a climbing plant)

VINEAL — adj vinous

VINEGAR — n pl. -S a sour liquid used as a condiment or preservative VINEGARY adj

VINERY — n pl. -ERIES a place in which grapevines are grown

VINEYARD — n pl. -S an area planted with grapevines

VINIC — adj derived from wine

VINIER — comparative of viny

VINIEST — superlative of viny

VINIFERA — n pl. -S a European grape

VINING — present participle of vine

VINO — n pl. -NOS wine

VINOSITY — n pl. -TIES the character of a wine

VINOUS — adj pertaining to wine VINOUSLY adv

VINTAGE — n pl. -S a season's yield of wine from a vineyard

VINTAGER — n pl. -S one that harvests wine grapes

VINTNER — n pl. -S a wine merchant

VINY — adj VINIER, VINIEST covered with vines

VINYL — n pl. -S a type of plastic VINYLIC adj

VIOL — n pl. -S a stringed instrument

VIOLA — n pl. -S a stringed instrument

VIOLABLE — adj capable of being violated VIOLABLY adv

VIOLATE — v -LATED, -LATING, -LATES to break or disregard the terms or requirements of

VIOLATER — n pl. -S violator

VIOLATOR — n pl. -S one that violates

VIOLENCE — n pl. -S violent action

VIOLENT — adj marked by intense physical force or roughness

VIOLET — n pl. -S a flowering plant

VIOLIN — n pl. -S a stringed instrument

VIOLIST — n pl. -S one who plays the viol or viola

VIOLONE — n pl. -S a stringed instrument

VIOMYCIN — n pl. -S an antibiotic

VIPER — n pl. -S a venomous snake VIPERINE, VIPERISH, VIPEROUS adj

VIRAGO — n pl. -GOES or -GOS a noisy, domineering woman

VIRAL — adj pertaining to or caused by a virus VIRALLY adv

VIRELAI — n pl. -S virelay

VIRELAY — n pl. -LAYS a medieval French verse form

VIREMIA — n pl. -S the presence of a virus in the blood VIREMIC adj

VIREO — n pl. -EOS a small bird

VIRES — pl. of vis

VIRGA — n pl. -S wisps of precipitation evaporating before reaching ground

VIRGATE — n pl. -S an early English measure of land area

VIRGIN	n pl. -S a person who has never had sexual intercourse
VIRGINAL	n pl. -S a musical instrument
VIRGULE	n pl. -S a diagonal printing mark used to separate alternatives
VIRICIDE	n pl. -S a substance that destroys viruses
VIRID	adj verdant
VIRIDIAN	n pl. -S a bluish-green pigment
VIRIDITY	n pl. -TIES verdancy
VIRILE	adj having masculine vigor
VIRILISM	n pl. -S the development of male secondary sex characteristics in a female
VIRILITY	n pl. -TIES the quality or state of being virile
VIRION	n pl. -S a virus particle
VIRL	n pl. -S a metal ring or cap put around a shaft to prevent splitting
VIROLOGY	n pl. -GIES the study of viruses
VIROSIS	n pl. -ROSES infection with a virus
VIRTU	n pl. -S a love or taste for the fine arts
VIRTUAL	adj having the effect but not the actual form of what is specified
VIRTUE	n pl. -S moral excellence
VIRTUOSA	n pl. -SAS or -SE a female virtuoso
VIRTUOSO	n pl. -SOS or -SI a highly skilled artistic performer
VIRTUOUS	adj characterized by virtue
VIRUCIDE	n pl. -S viricide
VIRULENT	adj extremely poisonous
VIRUS	n pl. -ES any of a class of submicroscopic pathogens
VIS	n pl. VIRES force or power
VISA	v -ED, -ING, -S to put an official endorsement on, as a passport
VISAGE	n pl. -S the face or facial expression of a person VISAGED adj
VISARD	n pl. -S vizard
VISCACHA	n pl. -S a burrowing rodent
VISCERA	pl. of viscus
VISCERAL	adj pertaining to the internal organs
VISCID	adj thick and adhesive VISCIDLY adv

VISCOID	adj somewhat viscid
VISCOSE	n pl. -S a viscous solution
VISCOUNT	n pl. -S a British nobleman
VISCOUS	adj having relatively high resistance to flow
VISCUS	n -CERA an internal organ
VISE	v VISED, VISING, VISES to hold in a vise (a clamping device)
VISE	v VISEED, VISEING, VISES to visa
VISELIKE	adj resembling a vice
VISIBLE	adj capable of being seen VISIBLY adv
VISING	present participle of vise
VISION	v -ED, -ING, -S to imagine
VISIONAL	adj imaginary
VISIT	v -ED, -ING, -S to go or come to see someone or something
VISITANT	n pl. -S a visitor
VISITER	n pl. -S visitor
VISITOR	n pl. -S one that visits
VISIVE	adj visible
VISOR	v -ED, -ING, -S to provide with a visor (a projecting brim)
VISTA	n pl. -S a distant view VISTAED adj
VISUAL	adj pertaining to the sense of sight VISUALLY adv
VITA	n pl. -TAE a brief, autobiographical sketch
VITAL	adj necessary to life
VITALISE	v -ISED, -ISING, -ISES to vitalize
VITALISM	n pl. -S a philosophical doctrine
VITALIST	n pl. -S an advocate of vitalism
VITALITY	n pl. -TIES exuberant physical strength or mental vigor
VITALIZE	v -IZED, -IZING, -IZES to give life to
VITALLY	adv in a vital manner
VITALS	n/pl vital organs
VITAMER	n pl. -S a type of chemical compound
VITAMIN	n pl. -S any of various organic substances essential to proper nutrition
VITAMINE	n pl. -S vitamin
VITELLIN	n pl. -S a protein found in egg yolk
VITELLUS	n pl. -ES the yolk of an egg

VITESSE   *n* pl. -S speed

VITIATE   *v* -ATED, -ATING, ATES to impair the value or quality of **VITIABLE** *adj*

VITIATOR   *n* pl. -S one that vitiates

VITILIGO   *n* pl. -GOS a skin disease

VITREOUS   *adj* resembling glass

VITRIC   *adj* pertaining to glass

VITRIFY   *v* -FIED, -FYING, -FIES to convert into glass

VITRINE   *n* pl. -S a glass showcase for art objects

VITRIOL   *v* -OLED, -OLING, -OLS or -OLLED, -OLLING, -OLS to treat with sulfuric acid

VITTA   *n* pl. -TAE a streak or band of color **VITTATE** *adj*

VITTLE   *v* -TLED, -TLING, -TLES to victual

VITULINE   *adj* pertaining to a calf

VIVA   *n* pl. -S a shout or cry used to express approval

VIVACE   *adj* lively — used as a musical direction

VIVACITY   *n* pl. -TIES the quality or state of being lively

VIVARIUM   *n* pl. -IA or -IUMS a place for raising and keeping live animals

VIVARY   *n* pl. -RIES vivarium

VIVE   *interj* — used as an exclamation of approval

VIVERRID   *n* pl. -S any of a family of small carnivorous mammals

VIVERS   *n/pl* food

VIVID   *adj* -IDER, -IDEST strikingly bright or intense **VIVIDLY** *adv*

VIVIFIC   *adj* vivifying

VIVIFIER   *n* pl. -S one that vivifies

VIVIFY   *v* -FIED, -FYING, -FIES to give life to

VIVIPARA   *n/pl* animals that bring forth living young

VIVISECT   *v* -ED, -ING, -S to dissect the living body of

VIXEN   *n* pl. -S a shrewish woman **VIXENISH, VIXENLY** *adj*

VIZARD   *n* pl. -S a mask **VIZARDED** *adj*

VIZCACHA   *n* pl. -S viscacha

VIZIER   *n* pl. -S a high official in some Muslim countries

VIZIR   *n* pl. -S vizier **VIZIRIAL** *adj*

VIZIRATE   *n* pl. -S the office of a vizir

VIZOR   *v* -ED, -ING, -S to visor

VIZSLA   *n* pl. -S a Hungarian breed of dog

VOCABLE   *n* pl. -S a word

VOCABLY   *adv* in a manner that may be voiced aloud

VOCAL   *n* pl. -S a sound produced with the voice

VOCALIC   *n* pl. -S a vowel sound

VOCALISE   *v* -ISED, -ISING, -ISES to vocalize

VOCALISM   *n* pl. -S the act of vocalizing

VOCALIST   *n* pl. -S a singer

VOCALITY   *n* pl. -TIES possession or exercise of vocal powers

VOCALIZE   *v* -IZED, -IZING, -IZES to produce with the voice

VOCALLY   *adv* with the voice

VOCATION   *n* pl. -S the work in which a person is regularly employed

VOCATIVE   *n* pl. -S a grammatical case used in some languages

VOCES   pl. of vox

VOCODER   *n* pl. -S an electronic device used in transmitting speech signals

VODKA   *n* pl. -S a liquor

VODUM   *n* pl. -S a primitive religion of the West Indies

VOE   *n* pl. -S a small bay, creek, or inlet

VOGIE   *adj* vain

VOGUE   *n* pl. -S the current trend or style **VOGUISH** *adj*

VOICE   *v* VOICED, VOICING, VOICES to express or utter

VOICEFUL   *adj* sonorous

VOICER   *n* pl. -S one that voices

VOICING   present participle of voice

VOID   *v* -ED, -ING, -S to make void (of no legal force or effect) **VOIDABLE** *adj*

VOIDANCE   *n* pl. -S the act or process of voiding

VOIDER   *n* pl. -S one that voids

VOIDNESS   *n* pl. -ES the quality or state of being void

VOILE   *n* pl. -S a sheer fabric

VOLANT   *adj* flying or capable of flying

VOLANTE adj moving with light rapidity — used as a musical direction

VOLAR adj pertaining to flight

VOLATILE n pl. -S a winged creature

VOLCANIC n pl. -S a rock produced by a volcano

VOLCANO n pl. -NOES or -NOS an opening in the earth's crust through which molten rock and gases are ejected

VOLE v VOLED, VOLING, VOLES to win all the tricks in a card game

VOLERY n pl. -ERIES a large birdcage

VOLITANT adj volant

VOLITION n pl. -S the power of choosing or determining

VOLITIVE adj pertaining to volition

VOLLEY v -ED, -ING, -S to return a tennis ball before it touches the ground

VOLLEYER n pl. -S one that volleys

VOLOST n pl. -S an administrative district in Russia

VOLPLANE v -PLANED, -PLANING, -PLANES to glide in an airplane

VOLT n pl. -S a unit of electromotive force

VOLTA n pl. -TE a turning

VOLTAGE n pl. -S electromotive force expressed in volts

VOLTAISM n pl. -S electricity produced by chemical action **VOLTAIC** adj

VOLTE n pl. -S a fencing movement

VOLTI interj — used to direct musicians to turn the page

VOLUBLE adj talkative **VOLUBLY** adv

VOLUME v -UMED, -UMING, -UMES to send or give out in large quantities

VOLUTE n pl. -S a spiral architectural ornament **VOLUTED** adj

VOLUTIN n pl. -S a granular substance that is common in microorganisms

VOLUTION n pl. -S a spiral

VOLVA n pl. -S a membranous sac that encloses certain immature mushrooms **VOLVATE** adj

VOLVOX n pl. -ES any of a genus of freshwater protozoa

VOLVULUS n pl. -LI or -LUSES a twisting of the intestine that causes obstruction

VOMER n pl. -S a bone of the skull **VOMERINE** adj

VOMICA n pl. -CAE a cavity in the body containing pus

VOMIT v -ED, -ING, -S to eject the contents of the stomach through the mouth

VOMITER n pl. -S one that vomits

VOMITIVE n pl. -S an emetic

VOMITO n pl. -TOS the black vomit of yellow fever

VOMITORY n pl. -RIES an emetic

VOMITOUS adj pertaining to vomiting

VOMITUS n pl. -ES vomited matter

VON prep of; from — used in some surnames

VOODOO v -ED, -ING, -S to hex

VORACITY n pl. -TIES the quality or state of being ravenous

VORLAGE n pl. -S a position in skiing

VORTEX n pl. -TEXES or -TICES a whirling mass of fluid **VORTICAL** adj

VOTABLE adj capable of being voted on

VOTARESS n pl. -ES a female votary

VOTARIST n pl. -S a votary

VOTARY n pl. -RIES a person who is bound by religious vows

VOTE v VOTED, VOTING, VOTES to cast a vote (a formal expression of will or opinion)

VOTEABLE adj votable

VOTELESS adj having no vote

VOTER n pl. -S one that votes

VOTING present participle of vote

VOTIVE adj performed in fullfillment of a vow **VOTIVELY** adv

VOTRESS n pl. -ES votaress

VOUCH v -ED, -ING, -ES to give one's personal assurance or guarantee

VOUCHEE n pl. -S one for whom another vouches

VOUCHER v -ED, -ING, -S to establish the authenticity of

VOUSSOIR n pl. -S a wedge-shaped building stone

VOW   *v* -ED, -ING, -S to make a vow (a solemn promise)

VOWEL   *n* pl. -S a type of speech sound

VOWELIZE   *v* -IZED, -IZING, -IZES to provide with symbols used to indicate vowels

VOWER   *n* pl. -S one that vows

VOWLESS   *adj* having made no vow

VOX   *n* pl. VOCES voice

VOYAGE   *v* -AGED, -AGING, -AGES to travel

VOYAGER   *n* pl. -S one that voyages

VOYAGEUR   *n* pl. -S a person employed by a fur company to transport goods between distant stations

VOYEUR   *n* pl. -S one who is sexually gratified by looking at sexual objects or acts

VROOM   *v* -ED, -ING, -S to run an engine at high speed

VROUW   *n* pl. -S a Dutch woman

VROW   *n* pl. -S vrouw

VUG   *n* pl. -S a small cavity in a rock or lode **VUGGY** *adj*

VUGG   *n* pl. -S vug

VUGH   *n* pl. -S vug

VULCANIC   *adj* pertaining to a volcano

VULGAR   *adj* -GARER, -GAREST crude **VULGARLY** *adv*

VULGAR   *n* pl. -S a common person

VULGATE   *n* pl. -S the common speech of a people

VULGO   *adv* commonly

VULGUS   *n* pl. -ES an exercise in Latin formerly required of pupils in some English public schools

VULPINE   *adj* pertaining to a fox

VULTURE   *n* pl. -S a bird of prey

VULVA   *n* pl. -VAE or -VAS the external genital organs of a female **VULVAL, VULVAR, VULVATE** *adj*

VULVITIS   *n* pl. -TISES inflammation of the vulva

VYING   present participle of vie

VYINGLY   *adv* in a vying manner

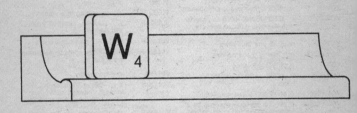

WAB *n* pl. -S a web

WABBLE *v* -BLED, -BLING, -BLES to wobble

WABBLER *n* pl. -S one that wabbles

WABBLY *adj* -BLIER, -BLIEST wobbly

WACK *n* pl. -S a wacky person

WACKE *n* pl. -S a type of basaltic rock

WACKY *adj* WACKIER, WACKIEST very irrational **WACKILY** *adv*

WAD *v* WADDED, WADDING, WADS to form into a wad (a small mass of soft material)

WADABLE *adj* wadeable

WADDER *n* pl. -S one that wads

WADDIE *n* pl. -S a cowboy

WADDIED past tense of waddy

WADDIES present 3d person sing. of waddy

WADDING *n* pl. -S a wad

WADDLE *v* -DLED, -DLING, -DLES to walk with short, swaying steps

WADDLER *n* pl. -S one that waddles

WADDLY *adj* having or being a waddling gait

WADDY *v* -DIED, -DYING, -DIES to strike with a thick club

WADE *v* WADED, WADING, WADES to walk through water

WADEABLE *adj* capable of being passed through by wading

WADER *n* pl. -S one that wades

WADI *n* pl. -S the bed of a usually dry watercourse

WADIES pl. of wady

WADING present participle of wade

WADMAAL *n* pl. -S wadmal

WADMAL *n* pl. -S a thick woolen fabric

WADMEL *n* pl. -S wadmal

WADMOL *n* pl. -S wadmal

WADMOLL *n* pl. -S wadmal

WADSET *v* -SETTED, -SETTING, -SETS to mortgage

WADY *n* pl. -DIES wadi

WAE *n* pl. -S woe

WAEFU *adj* waeful

WAEFUL *adj* woeful

WAENESS *n* pl. -ES woeness

WAESUCK *interj* waesucks

WAESUCKS *interj* — used to express pity

WAFER *v* -ED, -ING, -S to seal with an adhesive disk

WAFERY *adj* resembling a wafer (a thin, crisp biscuit)

WAFF *v* -ED, -ING, -S to wave

WAFFIE *n* pl. -S a vagabond

WAFFLE *v* -FLED, -FLING, -FLES to talk foolishly

WAFT *v* -ED, -ING, -S to carry lightly over air or water

WAFTAGE *n* pl. -S the act of wafting

WAFTER *n* pl. -S one that wafts

WAFTURE *n* pl. -S waftage

WAG *v* WAGGED, WAGGING, WAGS to move briskly up and down or to and fro

WAGE *v* WAGED, WAGING, WAGES to engage in or carry on

WAGELESS *adj* unpaid

WAGER *v* -ED, -ING, -S to risk on an uncertain outcome

WAGERER *n* pl. -S one that wagers

WAGGED past tense of wag

WAGGER *n* pl. -S one that wags

WAGGERY *n* pl. -GERIES waggish behavior

WAGGING present participle of wag

WAGGISH *adj* playfully humorous

WAGGLE *v* -GLED, -GLING, -GLES to wag

WAGGLY *adj* waggling

WAGGON *v* -ED, -ING, -S to wagon

WAGGONER *n* pl. -S wagoner

WAGING present participle of wage

WAGON *v* -ED, -ING, -S to convey by wagon (a four-wheeled, horse-drawn vehicle)

WAGONAGE *n* pl. -S conveyance by wagon

WAGONER *n* pl. -S one who drives a wagon

WAGSOME *adj* waggish

WAGTAIL *n* pl. -S a songbird

WAHCONDA *n* pl. -S wakanda

WAHINE *n* pl. -S a Hawaiian woman

WAHOO *n* pl. -HOOS a flowering shrub

WAIF *v* -ED, -ING, -S to throw away

WAIL *v* -ED, -ING, -S to utter a long, mournful cry

WAILER *n* pl. -S one that wails

WAILFUL *adj* mournful

WAILSOME *adj* wailful

WAIN *n* pl. -S a large, open wagon

WAINSCOT *v* -SCOTED, -SCOTING, -SCOTS or -SCOTTED, -SCOTTING, -SCOTS to line the walls of with wooden paneling

WAIR *v* -ED, -ING, -S to spend

WAIST *n* pl. -S the part of the body between the ribs and the hips **WAISTED** *adj*

WAISTER *n* pl. -S a seaman stationed in the middle section of a ship

WAISTING *n* pl. -S a type of dressmaking material

WAIT *v* -ED, -ING, -S to stay in expectation of

WAITER *n* pl. -S one who serves food in a restaurant

WAITING *n* pl. -S the act of one who waits

WAITRESS *n* pl. -ES a woman who serves food in a restaurant

WAIVE *v* WAIVED, WAIVING, WAIVES to give up intentionally

WAIVER *n* pl. -S the act of waiving something

WAKANDA *n* pl. -S a supernatural force in Sioux beliefs

WAKE *v* WAKED or WOKE, WOKEN, WAKING, WAKES to rouse from sleep

WAKEFUL *adj* not sleeping or able to sleep

WAKELESS *adj* unbroken — used of sleep

WAKEN *v* -ED, -ING, -S to wake

WAKENER *n* pl. -S one that wakens

WAKENING *n* pl. -S the act of one that wakens

WAKER *n* pl. -S one that wakes

WAKERIFE *adj* wakeful

WAKIKI *n* pl. -S shell money of the South Sea islands

WAKING present participle of wake

WALE *v* WALED, WALING, WALES to mark with welts

WALER *n* pl. -S an Australian-bred saddle horse

WALIES pl. of waly

WALING present participle of wale

WALK *v* -ED, -ING, -S to advance on foot **WALKABLE** *adj*

WALKAWAY *n* pl. -AWAYS an easy victory

WALKER *n* pl. -S one that walks

WALKING *n* pl. -S the act of one that walks

WALKOUT *n* pl. -S a strike by workers

WALKOVER *n* pl. -S a walkaway

WALKUP *n* pl. -S an apartment house having no elevator

WALKWAY *n* pl. -WAYS a passage for walking

WALKYRIE *n* pl. -S valkyrie

WALL *v* -ED, -ING, -S to provide with a wall (an upright structure built to enclose an area)

WALLA *n* pl. -S wallah

WALLABY *n* pl. -BIES a small kangaroo

WALLAH *n* pl. -S a person engaged in a particular occupation or activity

WALLAROO *n* pl. -ROOS a large kangaroo

WALLET   *n* pl. -S a flat folding case

WALLEYE   *n* pl. -S an eye having a white cornea **WALLEYED** *adj*

WALLIE   *n* pl. -S a valet

WALLIES   pl. of wally

WALLOP   *v* -ED, -ING, -S to beat soundly

WALLOPER   *n* pl. -S one that wallops

WALLOW   *v* -ED, -ING, -S to roll about

WALLOWER   *n* pl. -S one that wallows

WALLY   *n* pl. -LIES waly

WALNUT   *n* pl. -S an edible nut

WALRUS   *n* pl. -ES a marine mammal

WALTZ   *v* -ED, -ING, -ES to perform a ballroom dance

WALTZER   *n* pl. -S one that waltzes

WALY   *n* pl. WALIES something visually pleasing

WAMBLE   *v* -BLED, -BLING, -BLES to move unsteadily

WAMBLY   *adj* -BLIER, -BLIEST unsteady

WAME   *n* pl. -S the belly

WAMEFOU   *n* pl. -S a bellyful

WAMEFUL   *n* pl. -S wamefou

WAMMUS   *n* pl. -ES wamus

WAMPISH   *v* -ED, -ING, -ES to throw about

WAMPUM   *n* pl. -S a form of currency formerly used by North American Indians

WAMPUS   *n* pl. -ES wamus

WAMUS   *n* pl. -ES a heavy outer jacket

WAN   *adj* WANNER, WANNEST unnaturally pale

WAN   *v* WANNED, WANNING, WANS to become wan

WAND   *n* pl. -S a slender rod

WANDER   *v* -ED, -ING, -S to move about with no destination or purpose

WANDERER   *n* pl. -S one that wanders

WANDEROO   *n* pl. -ROOS an Asian monkey

WANDLE   *adj* supple

WANE   *v* WANED, WANING, WANES to decrease in size or extent

WANEY   *adj* WANIER, WANIEST wany

WANGAN   *n* pl. -S wanigan

WANGLE   *v* -GLED, -GLING, -GLES to obtain or accomplish by contrivance

WANGLER   *n* pl. -S one that wangles

WANGUN   *n* pl. -S wanigan

WANIER   comparative of waney and wany

WANIEST   superlative of waney and wany

WANIGAN   *n* pl. -S a supply chest used in a logging camp

WANING   present participle of wane

WANION   *n* pl. -S vengeance

WANLY   *adv* in a wan manner

WANNED   past tense of wan

WANNER   comparative of wan

WANNESS   *n* pl. -ES the quality of being wan

WANNEST   superlative of wan

WANNIGAN   *n* pl. -S wanigan

WANNING   present participle of wan

WANT   *v* -ED, -ING, -S to have a desire for

WANTAGE   *n* pl. -S something that is lacking

WANTER   *n* pl. -S one that wants

WANTON   *v* -ED, -ING, -S to behave immorally

WANTONER   *n* pl. -S one that wantons

WANTONLY   *adv* immorally

WANY   *adj* WANIER, WANIEST waning in some parts

WAP   *v* WAPPED, WAPPING, WAPS to wrap

WAPITI   *n* pl. -S a large deer

WAR   *v* WARRED, WARRING, WARS to engage in war (a state of open, armed conflict)

WARBLE   *v* -BLED, -BLING, -BLES to sing with melodic embellishments

WARBLER   *n* pl. -S one that warbles

WARCRAFT   *n* pl. -S the art of war

WARD   *v* -ED, -ING, -S to turn aside

WARDEN   *n* pl. -S the chief officer of a prison

WARDENRY   *n* pl. -RIES the office of a warden

WARDER   *n* pl. -S a person who guards something

WARDRESS   *n* pl. -ES a female warden

WARDROBE   *n* pl. -S a collection of garments

WARDROOM   *n* pl. -S a recreation area on a warship

WARDSHIP *n pl.* -S the state of being under a guardian

WARE *v* WARED, WARING, WARES to beware of

WAREROOM *n pl.* -S a room in which goods are displayed for sale

WARFARE *n pl.* -S the act of engaging in war

WARFARIN *n pl.* -S a chemical compound

WARHEAD *n pl.* -S the front part of a missile containing the explosive

WARIER comparative of wary

WARIEST superlative of wary

WARILY *adv* in a wary manner

WARINESS *n pl.* -ES the state of being wary

WARING present participle of ware

WARISON *n pl.* -S a call to attack

WARK *v* -ED, -ING, -S to endure pain

WARLESS *adj* free from war

WARLIKE *adj* disposed to engage in war

WARLOCK *n pl.* -S a sorcerer

WARLORD *n pl.* -S a military leader of a warlike nation

WARM *adj* WARMER, WARMEST moderately hot

WARM *v* -ED, -ING, -S to make warm

WARMAKER *n pl.* -S one that wars

WARMER *n pl.* -S one that warms

WARMISH *adj* somewhat warm

WARMLY *adv* in a warm manner

WARMNESS *n pl.* -ES the state of being warm

WARMOUTH *n* -S a freshwater fish

WARMTH *n pl.* -S warmness

WARMUP *n pl.* -S a preparatory exercise or procedure

WARN *v* -ED, -ING, -S to make aware of impending or possible danger

WARNER *n pl.* -S one that warns

WARNING *n pl.* -S something that warns

WARP *v* -ED, -ING, -S to turn or twist out of shape

WARPAGE *n pl.* -S the act of warping

WARPATH *n pl.* -S the route taken by attacking American Indians

WARPER *n pl.* -S one that warps

WARPLANE *n pl.* -S an airplane armed for combat

WARPOWER *n pl.* -S the power to make war

WARPWISE *adv* in a vertical direction

WARRAGAL *n pl.* -S warrigal

WARRANT *v* -ED, -ING, -S to give authority to

WARRANTY *n pl.* -TIES the act of warranting

WARRED past tense of war

WARREN *n pl.* -S a place where rabbits live and breed

WARRENER *n pl.* -S the keeper of a warren

WARRIGAL *n pl.* -S a dingo

WARRING present participle of war

WARRIOR *n pl.* -S one engaged or experienced in warfare

WARSAW *n pl.* -S a marine fish

WARSHIP *n pl.* -S a ship armed for combat

WARSLE *v* -SLED, -SLING, -SLES to wrestle

WARSLER *n pl.* -S a wrestler

WARSTLE *v* -TLED, -TLING, -TLES to wrestle

WARSTLER *n pl.* -S a wrestler

WART *n pl.* -S a protuberance on the skin WARTED *adj*

WARTHOG *n pl.* -S an African wild hog

WARTIER comparative of warty

WARTIEST superlative of warty

WARTIME *n pl.* -S a time of war

WARTLIKE *adj* resembling a wart

WARTY *adj* WARTIER, WARTIEST covered with warts

WARWORK *n pl.* -S work done during a war

WARWORN *adj* showing the effects of war

WARY *adj* WARIER, WARIEST watchful

WAS 1st and 3d person sing. past indicative of be

WASH *v* -ED, -ING, -ES to cleanse by immersing in or applying a liquid

WASHABLE *adj* capable of being washed without damage

WASHBOWL *n pl.* -S a bowl used for washing oneself

WASHDAY *n pl.* -DAYS a day set aside for washing clothes

WASHER *n pl.* -S one that washes

WASHIER comparative of washy

WASHIEST superlative of washy

WASHING n pl. -S articles washed or to be washed

WASHOUT n pl. -S an erosion of earth by the action of water

WASHRAG n pl. -S a small cloth used for washing oneself

WASHROOM n pl. -S a lavatory

WASHTUB n pl. -S a tub used for washing clothes

WASHY adj WASHIER, WASHIEST overly diluted

WASP n pl. -S a stinging insect WASPISH, WASPLIKE adj

WASPY adj WASPIER, WASPIEST resembling a wasp WASPILY adv

WASSAIL v -ED, -ING, -S to drink to the health of

WAST n pl. -S weet

WASTABLE adj capable of being wasted

WASTAGE n pl. -S something that is wasted

WASTE v WASTED, WASTING, WASTES to use thoughtlessly

WASTEFUL adj tending to waste

WASTELOT n pl. -S a vacant lot

WASTER n pl. -S one that wastes

WASTERIE n pl. -S wastry

WASTERY n pl. -RIES wastry

WASTEWAY n pl. -WAYS a channel for excess water

WASTING present participle of waste

WASTREL n pl. -S one that wastes

WASTRIE n pl. -S wastry

WASTRY n pl. -RIES reckless extravagance

WAT adj WATTER, WATTEST wet

WAT n pl. -S a hare

WATAP n pl. -S a thread made from the roots of various trees

WATAPE n pl. -S watap

WATCH v -ED, -ING, -ES to observe carefully

WATCHCRY n pl. -CRIES a password

WATCHDOG v -DOGGED, -DOGGING, -DOGS to act as a guardian for

WATCHER n pl. -S one that watches

WATCHEYE n pl. -S a walleye

WATCHFUL adj closely observant or alert

WATCHMAN n pl. -MEN a man employed to stand guard

WATCHOUT n pl. -S the act of looking out for something

WATER v -ED, -ING, -S to sprinkle with water (a transparent, odorless, tasteless liquid)

WATERAGE n pl. -S the conveyance of goods by water

WATERBED n pl. -S a bed whose mattress is a plastic bag filled with water

WATERDOG n pl. -S a large salamander

WATERER n pl. -S one that waters

WATERIER comparative of watery

WATERIEST superlative of watery

WATERILY adv in a watery manner

WATERING n pl. -S the act of one that waters

WATERISH adj watery

WATERLOG v -LOGGED, -LOGGING, -LOGS to soak with water

WATERLOO n pl. -LOOS a decisive defeat

WATERMAN n pl. -MEN a boatman

WATERWAY n pl. -WAYS a navigable body of water

WATERY adj -TERIER, -TERIEST containing water

WATT n pl. -S a unit of power

WATTAGE n pl. -S an amount of power in terms of watts

WATTAPE n pl. -S watap

WATTER comparative of wat

WATTEST superlative of wat

WATTHOUR n pl. -S a unit of energy

WATTLE v -TLED, -TLING, -TLES to weave into a network

WATTLESS adj denoting a type of electric current

WAUCHT v -ED, -ING, -S to waught

WAUGH adj damp

WAUGHT v -ED, -ING, -S to drink deeply

WAUK v -ED, -ING, -S to wake

WAUL v -ED, -ING, -S to cry like a cat

WAUR adj worse

WAVE v WAVED, WAVING, WAVES to move freely back and forth or up and down

WAVEBAND n pl. -S a range of radio frequencies

WAVEFORM	n pl. -S a type of mathematical graph	**WAXY**	adj WAXIER, WAXIEST resembling wax
WAVELESS	adj having no waves (moving ridges on the surface of a liquid)	**WAY**	n pl. WAYS a method of doing something
WAVELET	n pl. -S a small wave	**WAYBILL**	n pl. -S a list of goods relative to a shipment
WAVELIKE	adj resembling a wave	**WAYFARER**	n pl. -S a traveler
WAVEOFF	n pl. -S the act of denying landing permission to an approaching aircraft	**WAYGOING**	n pl. -S the act of leaving
WAVER	v -ED, -ING, -S to move back and forth	**WAYLAY**	v -LAID, -LAYING, -LAYS to ambush
WAVERER	n pl. -S one that wavers	**WAYLAYER**	n pl. -S one that waylays
WAVERY	adj wavering	**WAYLESS**	adj having no road or path
WAVEY	n pl. -VEYS the snow goose	**WAYSIDE**	n pl. -S the side of a road
WAVIER	comparative of wavy	**WAYWARD**	adj willful
WAVIES	present 3d person sing. of wavy	**WAYWORN**	adj fatigued by travel
WAVIEST	superlative of wavy	**WE**	pron 1st person pl. pronoun in the nominative case
WAVILY	adv in a wavy manner	**WEAK**	adj WEAKER, WEAKEST lacking strength
WAVINESS	n pl. -ES the state of being wavy	**WEAKEN**	v -ED, -ING, -S to make weak
WAVING	present participle of wave	**WEAKENER**	n pl. -S one that weakens
WAVY	adj WAVIER, WAVIEST full of waves	**WEAKFISH**	n pl. -ES a marine fish
		WEAKISH	adj somewhat weak
WAVY	n pl. -VIES wavey	**WEAKLING**	n pl. -S a weak person
WAW	n pl. -S vav	**WEAKLY**	adj -LIER, -LIEST weak and sickly
WAWL	v -ED, -ING, -S to waul	**WEAKNESS**	n pl. -ES the state of being weak
WAX	v -ED, -ING, -ES to coat with wax (a natural, heat-sensitive substance)	**WEAL**	n pl. -S a welt
WAXBERRY	n pl. -RIES a berry with a waxy coating	**WEALD**	n pl. -S a woodland
		WEALTH	n pl. -S a great quantity of valuable material
WAXBILL	n pl. -S a tropical bird	**WEALTHY**	adj WEALTHIER, WEALTHIEST having wealth
WAXEN	adj covered with wax	**WEAN**	v -ED, -ING, -S to withhold mother's milk from and substitute other nourishment
WAXER	n pl. -S one that waxes	
WAXIER	comparative of waxy	**WEANER**	n pl. -S one that weans
WAXIEST	superlative of waxy	**WEANLING**	n pl. -S a recently weaned child or animal
WAXILY	adv in a waxy manner	
WAXINESS	n pl. -ES the quality of being waxy	**WEAPON**	v -ED, -ING, -S to supply with a weapon (an instrument used in combat)
WAXING	n pl. -S the act of one that waxes	
		WEAPONRY	n pl. -RIES an aggregate of weapons
WAXLIKE	adj resembling wax	
WAXPLANT	n pl. -S a tropical plant	**WEAR**	v WORE, WORN, WEARING, WEARS to have on one's person
WAXWEED	n pl. -S an annual herb	
WAXWING	n pl. -S a type of bird	**WEARABLE**	n pl. -S a garment
WAXWORK	n pl. -S an effigy made of wax	**WEARER**	n pl. -S one that wears something
WAXWORM	n pl. -S a moth that infests beehives	

WEARIED past tense of weary

WEARIER comparative of weary

WEARIES present 3d person sing. of weary

WEARIEST superlative of weary

WEARIFUL adj tiresome

WEARISH adj tasteless

WEARY adj -RIER, -RIEST tired WEARILY adv

WEARY v -RIED, -RYING, -RIES to make or become weary

WEASAND n pl. -S the throat

WEASEL v -ED, -ING, -S to act evasively

WEASON n pl. -S weasand

WEATHER v -ED, -ING, -S to expose to atmospheric conditions

WEAVE v WOVE or WEAVED, WOVEN, WEAVING, WEAVES to form by interlacing threads

WEAVER n pl. -S one that weaves

WEAZAND n pl. -S weasand

WEB v WEBBED, WEBBING, WEBS to provide with a web (an interlaced fabric or structure)

WEBBING n pl. -S a woven strip of fiber

WEBBY adj -BIER, -BIEST weblike

WEBER n pl. -S a unit of magnetic flux

WEBFED adj pertaining to a type of printing press

WEBFOOT n pl. -FEET a foot having the toes joined by a membrane

WEBLESS adj having no webs

WEBLIKE adj resembling a web

WEBSTER n pl. -S a weaver

WEBWORM n pl. -S a web-spinning caterpillar

WECHT n pl. -S weight

WED v WEDDED, WEDDING, WEDS to marry

WEDDER n pl. -S one that weds

WEDDING n pl. -S a marriage ceremony

WEDEL v -ED, -ING, -S to perform a wedeln

WEDELN n pl. -S a skiing technique

WEDGE v WEDGED, WEDGING, WEDGES to force apart with a wedge (a tapering piece of wood or metal)

WEDGIE n pl. -S a type of woman's shoe

WEDGY adj WEDGIER, WEDGIEST resembling a wedge

WEDLOCK n pl. -S the state of being married

WEE adj WEER, WEEST very small

WEE n pl. -S a short time

WEED v -ED, -ING, -S to remove weeds (undesirable plants)

WEEDER n pl. -S one that weeds

WEEDIER comparative of weedy

WEEDIEST superlative of weedy

WEEDILY adv in a weedy manner

WEEDLESS adj having no weeds

WEEDLIKE adj resembling a weed

WEEDY adj WEEDIER, WEEDIEST resembling a weed

WEEK n pl. -S a period of seven days

WEEKDAY n pl. -DAYS any day of the week except Sunday

WEEKEND v -ED, -ING, -S to spend the weekend (the end of the week)

WEEKLONG adj continuing for a week

WEEKLY n pl. -LIES a publication issued once a week

WEEL adj well

WEEN v -ED, -ING, -S to suppose

WEENIE n pl. -S a wiener

WEENSY adj -SIER, -SIEST tiny

WEENY adj -NIER, -NIEST tiny

WEEP v WEPT, WEEPING, WEEPS to express sorrow by shedding tears

WEEPER n pl. -S one that weeps

WEEPY adj WEEPIER, WEEPIEST tending to weep

WEER comparative of wee

WEEST superlative of wee

WEET v -ED, -ING, -S to know

WEEVER n pl. -S a marine fish

WEEVIL n pl. -S a small beetle WEEVILED, WEEVILLY, WEEVILY adj

WEEWEE v -WEED, -WEEING, -WEES to urinate

WEFT n pl. -S a woven fabric or garment

WEFTWISE adv in a horizontal direction

WEIGELA n pl. -S a flowering shrub

WEIGELIA n pl. -S weigela

WEIGH v -ED, -ING, -S to determine the weight of

WEIGHER n pl. -S one that weighs

WEIGHMAN n pl. -MEN one whose occupation is weighing goods

WEIGHT v -ED, -ING, -S to add weight (heaviness) to

WEIGHTER n pl. -S one that weights

WEIGHTY adj WEIGHTIER, WEIGHTIEST having great weight

WEINER n pl. -S wiener

WEIR n pl. -S a fence placed in a stream to catch fish

WEIRD adj WEIRDER, WEIRDEST mysteriously strange

WEIRD n pl. -S destiny

WEIRDIE n pl. -S a very strange person

WEIRDIES pl. of weirdy

WEIRDLY adv in a weird manner

WEIRDO n pl. WEIRDOES or WEIRDOS weirdie

WEIRDY n pl. WEIRDIES weirdie

WEKA n pl. -S a flightless bird

WELCH v -ED, -ING, -ES to welsh

WELCHER n pl. -S one that welshes

WELCOME v -COMED, -COMING, -COMES to greet cordially

WELCOMER n pl. -S one that welcomes

WELD v -ED, -ING, -S to join by applying heat WELDABLE adj

WELDER n pl. -S one that welds

WELDLESS adj having no welded joints

WELDMENT n pl. -S a unit composed of welded pieces

WELDOR n pl. -S welder

WELFARE n pl. -S general well-being

WELKIN n pl. -S the sky

WELL v -ED, -ING, -S to rise to the surface and flow forth

WELLADAY n pl. -DAYS wellaway

WELLAWAY n pl. -WAYS an expression of sorrow

WELLBORN adj of good birth or ancestry

WELLCURB n pl. -S the stone ring around a well (a hole dug in the ground to obtain water)

WELLDOER n pl. -S a doer of good deeds

WELLHEAD n pl. -S the source of a spring or stream

WELLHOLE n pl. -S the shaft of a well

WELLNESS n pl. -ES the state of being healthy

WELLSITE n pl. -S a mineral

WELSH v -ED, -ING, -ES to fail to pay a debt

WELSHER n pl. -S one that welshes

WELT v -ED, -ING, -S to mark with welts (ridges or lumps raised on the skin)

WELTER v -ED, -ING, -S to roll about

WELTING n pl. -S a cord or strip used to reinforce a seam

WEN n pl. -S a benign tumor of the skin

WENCH v -ED, -ING, -ES to consort with prostitutes

WENCHER n pl. -S one that wenches

WEND v -ED, -ING, -S to proceed along

WENDIGO n pl. -GOS windigo

WENNISH adj wenny

WENNY adj -NIER, -NIEST resembling a wen

WENT past tense of go

WEPT past tense of weep

WERE a pl. and 2d person sing. past indicative, and past subjunctive of be

WEREWOLF n pl. -WOLVES a person capable of assuming the form of a wolf

WERGELD n pl. -S a price paid for the taking of a man's life in Anglo-Saxon law

WERGELT n pl. -S wergeld

WERGILD n pl. -S wergeld

WERT a 2d person sing. past tense of be

WERWOLF n pl. -WOLVES werewolf

WESKIT n pl. -S a vest

WESSAND n pl. -S weasand

WEST n pl. -S a cardinal point of the compass

WESTER v -ED, -ING, -S to move toward the west

WESTERLY n pl. -LIES a wind from the west

WESTERN n pl. -S one who lives in the west

WESTING n pl. -S a shifting west

WESTMOST	*adj* farthest west
WESTWARD	*n pl.* -S a direction toward the west
WET	*adj* WETTER, WETTEST covered or saturated with a liquid
WET	*v* WETTED, WETTING, WETS to make wet
WETBACK	*n pl.* -S a Mexican who enters the United States illegally
WETHER	*n pl.* -S a gelded male sheep
WETLAND	*n pl.* -S land containing much soil moisture
WETLY	*adv* in a wet manner
WETNESS	*n pl.* -ES the state of being wet
WETPROOF	*adj* waterproof
WETTABLE	*adj* capable of being wetted
WETTED	past tense of wet
WETTER	*n pl.* -S one that wets
WETTEST	superlative of wet
WETTING	*n pl.* -S a liquid used in moistening something
WETTISH	*adj* somewhat wet
WHA	*pron* who
WHACK	*v* -ED, -ING, -S to strike sharply
WHACKER	*n pl.* -S one that whacks
WHACKY	*adj* WHACKIER, WHACKIEST wacky
WHALE	*v* WHALED, WHALING, WHALES to engage in the hunting of whales (large marine mammals)
WHALEMAN	*n pl.* -MEN a whaler
WHALER	*n pl.* -S a person engaged in whaling
WHALING	*n pl.* -S the industry of capturing and processing whales
WHAM	*v* WHAMMED, WHAMMING, WHAMS to hit with a loud impact
WHAMMY	*n pl.* -MIES a supernatural spell bringing bad luck
WHANG	*v* -ED, -ING, -S to beat with a whip
WHANGEE	*n pl.* -S an Asian grass
WHAP	*v* WHAPPED, WHAPPING, WHAPS to whop
WHAPPER	*n pl.* -S whopper
WHARF	*v* -ED, -ING, -S to moor to a wharf (a landing place for vessels)
WHARFAGE	*n pl.* -S the use of a wharf
WHARVE	*n pl.* -S a round piece of wood used in spinning thread
WHAT	*n pl.* -S the true nature of something
WHATEVER	*adj* being what or who it may be
WHATNOT	*n pl.* -S an ornamental set of shelves
WHAUP	*n pl.* -S a European bird
WHEAL	*n pl.* -S a welt
WHEAT	*n pl.* -S a cereal grass
WHEATEAR	*n pl.* -S a small bird of northern regions
WHEATEN	*adj* pertaining to wheat
WHEE	*interj* — used to express delight
WHEEDLE	*v* -DLED, -DLING, -DLES to attempt to persuade by flattery
WHEEDLER	*n pl.* -S one that wheedles
WHEEL	*v* -ED, -ING, -S to convey on wheels (circular frames designed to turn on an axis)
WHEELER	*n pl.* -S one that wheels
WHEELIE	*n pl.* -S a maneuver made on a wheeled vehicle
WHEELING	*n pl.* -S the condition of a road for vehicles
WHEELMAN	*n pl.* -MEN a helmsman
WHEEN	*n pl.* -S a fairly large amount
WHEEP	*v* -ED, -ING, -S to wheeple
WHEEPLE	*v* -PLED, -PLING, -PLES to give forth a prolonged whistle
WHEEZE	*v* WHEEZED, WHEEZING, WHEEZES to breathe with a whistling sound
WHEEZER	*n pl.* -S one that wheezes
WHEEZY	*adj* WHEEZIER, WHEEZIEST characterized by wheezing WHEEZILY *adv*
WHELK	*n pl.* -S a pustule
WHELKY	*adj* WHELKIER, WHELKIEST marked with whelks
WHELM	*v* -ED, -ING, -S to cover with water
WHELP	*v* -ED, -ING, -S to give birth to
WHEN	*n pl.* -S the time in which something is done or occurs
WHENAS	*conj* at which time
WHENCE	*adv* from what place
WHENEVER	*adv* at whatever time

WHERE	*n* pl. -S the place at or in which something is located or occurs
WHEREAS	*n* pl. -ES an introductory statement of a formal document
WHEREAT	*adv* at what
WHEREBY	*adv* by what
WHEREIN	*adv* in what
WHEREOF	*adv* of what
WHEREON	*adv* on what
WHERETO	*adv* to what
WHEREVER	*adv* in or to whatever place
WHERRY	*v* -RIED, -RYING, -RIES to transport in a light rowboat
WHERVE	*n* pl. -S wharve
WHET	*v* WHETTED, WHETTING, WHETS to sharpen by friction
WHETHER	*conj* if it be the case that
WHETTER	*n* pl. -S one that whets
WHETTING	present participle of whet
WHEW	*n* pl. -S a whistling sound
WHEY	*n* pl. WHEYS the watery part of milk **WHEYEY**, **WHEYISH** *adj*
WHEYFACE	*n* pl. -S a pale, sallow face
WHICH	*pron* what particular one or ones
WHICKER	*v* -ED, -ING, -S to whinny
WHID	*v* WHIDDED, WHIDDING, WHIDS to move rapidly and quietly
WHIDAH	*n* pl. -S whydah
WHIFF	*v* -ED, -ING, -S to blow or convey with slight gusts of air
WHIFFER	*n* pl. -S one that whiffs
WHIFFET	*n* pl. -S an insignificant person
WHIFFLE	*v* -FLED, -FLING, -FLES to move or think erratically
WHIFFLER	*n* pl. -S one that whiffles
WHILE	*v* WHILED, WHILING, WHILES to cause to pass pleasantly
WHILOM	*adv* formerly
WHILST	*conj* during the time that
WHIM	*n* pl. -S an impulsive idea
WHIMBREL	*n* pl. -S a shore bird
WHIMPER	*v* -ED, -ING, -S to cry with plaintive, broken sounds
WHIMSEY	*n* pl. -SEYS whimsy
WHIMSY	*n* pl. -SIES a whim **WHIMSIED** *adj*
WHIN	*n* pl. -S furze
WHINCHAT	*n* pl. -S a songbird
WHINE	*v* WHINED, WHINING, WHINES to utter a plaintive, high-pitched sound
WHINER	*n* pl. -S one that whines
WHINEY	*adj* WHINIER, WHINIEST whiny
WHINIER	comparative of whiny
WHINIEST	superlative of whiny
WHINING	present participle of whine
WHINNY	*v* -NIED, -NYING, -NIES to neigh in a low or gentle manner
WHINNY	*adj* -NIER, -NIEST abounding in whin
WHINY	*adj* WHINIER, WHINIEST tending to whine
WHIP	*v* WHIPPED or WHIPT, WHIPPING, WHIPS to strike with a whip (an instrument for administering corporal punishment)
WHIPCORD	*n* pl. -S a strong, twisted cord
WHIPLASH	*n* pl. -ES the lash of a whip
WHIPLIKE	*adj* resembling a whip
WHIPPED	a past tense of whip
WHIPPER	*n* pl. -S one that whips
WHIPPET	*n* pl. -S a small, swift dog
WHIPPIER	comparative of whippy
WHIPPIEST	superlative of whippy
WHIPPING	*n* pl. -S material used to whip
WHIPPY	*adj* -PIER, -PIEST pertaining to or resembling a whip
WHIPRAY	*n* pl. -RAYS a stingray
WHIPSAW	*v* -SAWED, -SAWN, -SAWING, -SAWS to cut with a narrow, tapering saw
WHIPT	a past tense of whip
WHIPTAIL	*n* pl. -S a lizard having a long, slender tail
WHIPWORM	*n* pl. -S a parasitic worm
WHIR	*v* WHIRRED, WHIRRING, WHIRS to move with a buzzing sound
WHIRL	*v* -ED, -ING, -S to revolve rapidly
WHIRLER	*n* pl. -S one that whirls
WHIRLY	*adj* WHIRLIER, WHIRLIEST marked by a whirling motion
WHIRLY	*n* pl. WHIRLIES a small tornado
WHIRR	*v* -ED, -ING, -S to whir
WHIRRED	past tense of whir
WHIRRING	present participle of whir

WHIRRY	*v* -RIED, -RYING, -RIES to hurry
WHISH	*v* -ED, -ING, -ES to move with a hissing sound
WHISHT	*v* -ED, -ING, -S to hush
WHISK	*v* -ED, -ING, -S to move quickly and easily
WHISKER	*n pl.* -S a hair on a man's face WHISKERY *adj*
WHISKEY	*n pl.* -KEYS a liquor
WHISKY	*n pl.* -KIES whiskey
WHISPER	*v* -ED, -ING, -S to speak softly
WHISPERY	*adj* resembling a whisper
WHIST	*v* -ED, -ING, -S to hush
WHISTLE	*v* -TLED, -TLING, -TLES to make a shrill, clear musical sound
WHISTLER	*n pl.* -S one that whistles
WHIT	*n pl.* -S a particle
WHITE	*adj* WHITER, WHITEST of the color of pure snow
WHITE	*v* WHITED, WHITING, WHITES to whiten
WHITECAP	*n pl.* -S a wave with a crest of foam
WHITEFLY	*n pl.* -FLIES a small whitish insect
WHITELY	*adv* in a white manner
WHITEN	*v* -ED, -ING, -S to make white
WHITENER	*n pl.* -S one that whitens
WHITEOUT	*n pl.* -S an arctic weather condition
WHITER	comparative of white
WHITEST	superlative of white
WHITEY	*n pl.* -EYS a white man — an offensive term
WHITHER	*adv* to what place
WHITIES	pl. of whity
WHITING	*n pl.* -S a marine food fish
WHITISH	*adj* somewhat white
WHITLOW	*n pl.* -S an inflammation of the finger or toe
WHITRACK	*n pl.* -S a weasel
WHITTER	*n pl.* -S a large draft of liquor
WHITTLE	*v* -TLED, -TLING, -TLES to cut or shave bits from
WHITTLER	*n pl.* -S one that whittles
WHITTRET	*n pl.* -S a weasel
WHITY	*n pl.* WHITIES whitey
WHIZ	*v* WHIZZED, WHIZZING, WHIZZES to move with a buzzing or hissing sound
WHIZBANG	*n pl.* -S a type of explosive shell
WHIZZ	*v* -ED, -ING, -ES to whiz
WHIZZED	past tense of whiz
WHIZZER	*n pl.* -S one that whizzes
WHIZZES	present 3d person sing. of whiz
WHIZZING	present participle of whiz
WHO	*pron* what or which person or persons
WHOA	*interj* — used to command an animal to stop
WHODUNIT	*n pl.* -S a mystery story
WHOEVER	*pron* whatever person
WHOLE	*n pl.* -S all the parts or elements entering into and making up a thing
WHOLISM	*n pl.* -S holism
WHOLLY	*adv* totally
WHOM	*pron* the objective case of who
WHOMEVER	*pron* the objective case of whoever
WHOMP	*v* -ED, -ING, -S to defeat decisively
WHOMSO	*pron* the objective case of whoso
WHOOP	*v* -ED, -ING, -S to utter loud cries
WHOOPEE	*n pl.* -S boisterous fun
WHOOPER	*n pl.* -S one that whoops
WHOOPLA	*n pl.* -S a noisy commotion
WHOOSH	*v* -ED, -ING, -ES to move with a hissing sound
WHOOSIS	*n pl.* -SISES an object or person whose name is not known
WHOP	*v* WHOPPED, WHOPPING, WHOPS to strike forcibly
WHOPPER	*n pl.* -S something unusually large
WHORE	*v* WHORED, WHORING, WHORES to consort with prostitutes
WHOREDOM	*n pl.* -S prostitution
WHORESON	*n pl.* -S a bastard
WHORING	present participle of whore
WHORISH	*adj* lewd
WHORL	*n pl.* -S a circular arrangement of similar parts WHORLED *adj*
WHORT	*n pl.* -S an edible berry

WHORTLE *n pl.* -S whort

WHOSE *pron* the possessive case of who

WHOSEVER *pron* the possessive case of whoever

WHOSIS *n pl.* -SISES whoosis

WHOSO *pron* whoever

WHUMP *v* -ED, -ING, -S to thump

WHY *n pl.* WHYS the reason or cause of something

WHYDAH *n pl.* -S an African bird

WICH *n pl.* -ES wych

WICK *n pl.* -S a bundle of loosely twisted fibers in a candle or oil lamp

WICKAPE *n pl.* -S wicopy

WICKED *adj* -EDER, -EDEST evil **WICKEDLY** *adv*

WICKER *n pl.* -S a slender, pliant twig or branch

WICKET *n pl.* -S a small door or gate

WICKING *n pl.* -S material for wicks

WICKIUP *n pl.* -S an American Indian hut

WICKYUP *n pl.* -S wickiup

WICOPY *n pl.* -PIES a flowering shrub

WIDDER *n pl.* -S a widow

WIDDIE *n pl.* -S widdy

WIDDLE *v* -DLED, -DLING, -DLES to wriggle

WIDDY *n pl.* -DIES a hangman's noose

WIDE *adj* WIDER, WIDEST having great extent from side to side **WIDELY** *adv*

WIDE *n pl.* -S a type of bowled ball in cricket

WIDEN *v* -ED, -ING, -S to make wide or wider

WIDENER *n pl.* -S one that widens

WIDENESS *n pl.* -ES the state of being wide

WIDER comparative of wide

WIDEST superlative of wide

WIDGEON *n pl.* -S a river duck

WIDGET *n pl.* -S a gadget

WIDISH *adj* somewhat wide

WIDOW *v* -ED, -ING, -S to deprive of a husband

WIDOWER *n pl.* -S a man whose wife has died and who has not remarried

WIDTH *n pl.* -S extent from side to side

WIDTHWAY *adv* from side to side

WIELD *v* -ED, -ING, -S to handle or use effectively

WIELDER *n pl.* -S one that wields

WIELDY *adj* WIELDIER, WIELDIEST easily wielded

WIENER *n pl.* -S a frankfurter

WIENIE *n pl.* -S a wiener

WIFE *n pl.* WIVES a woman married to a man

WIFE *v* WIFED, WIFING, WIFES to wive

WIFEDOM *n pl.* -S the status or function of a wife

WIFEHOOD *n pl.* -S the state of being a wife

WIFELESS *adj* having no wife

WIFELIKE *adj* wifely

WIFELY *adj* -LIER, -LIEST of or befitting a wife

WIFING present participle of wife

WIG *v* WIGGED, WIGGING, WIGS to provide with a wig (an artificial covering of hair for the head)

WIGAN *n pl.* -S a stiff fabric

WIGEON *n pl.* -S widgeon

WIGGED past tense of wig

WIGGERY *n pl.* -GERIES a wig

WIGGING *n pl.* -S a scolding

WIGGLE *v* -GLED, -GLING, -GLES to move with short, quick movements from side to side

WIGGLER *n pl.* -S one that wiggles

WIGGLY *adj* -GLIER, -GLIEST tending to wiggle

WIGHT *n pl.* -S a living being

WIGLESS *adj* having no wig

WIGLET *n pl.* -S a small wig

WIGLIKE *adj* resembling a wig

WIGMAKER *n pl.* -S one that makes wigs

WIGWAG *v* -WAGGED, -WAGGING, -WAGS to move back and forth

WIGWAM *n pl.* -S an American Indian dwelling

WIKIUP *n pl.* -S wickiup

WILCO *interj* — used to indicate that a message received will be complied with

WILD *adj* WILDER, WILDEST living in a natural state

WILD   *n* pl. -S an uninhabited or uncultivated area

WILDCAT   *v* -CATTED, -CATTING, -CATS to search for oil in an area of doubtful productivity

WILDER   *v* -ED, -ING, -S to bewilder

WILDFIRE   *n* pl. -S a raging, destructive fire

WILDFOWL   *n* pl. -S a wild game bird

WILDING   *n* pl. -S a wild plant or animal

WILDISH   *adj* somewhat wild

WILDLIFE   *n* pl. WILDLIFE wild animals and vegetation

WILDLING   *n* pl. -S a wilding

WILDLY   *adv* in a wild manner

WILDNESS   *n* pl. -ES the state of being wild

WILDWOOD   *n* pl. -S natural forest land

WILE   *v* WILED, WILING, WILES to entice

WILFUL   *adj* willful **WILFULLY** *adv*

WILIER   comparative of wily

WILIEST   superlative of wily

WILILY   *adv* in a wily manner

WILINESS   *n* pl. -ES the quality of being wily

WILING   present participle of wile

WILL   *v* -ED, -ING, -S to decide upon **WILLABLE** *adj*

WILL   *v* past sing. 2d person WOULD, WOULDEST, or WOULDST — used as an auxiliary followed by a simple infinitive to express futurity, inclination, likelihood, or requirement

WILLER   *n* pl. -S one that wills

WILLET   *n* pl. -S a shore bird

WILLFUL   *adj* bent on having one's own way

WILLIED   past tense of willy

WILLIES   present 3d person sing. of willy

WILLING   *adj* -INGER, -INGEST inclined or favorably disposed in mind

WILLIWAU   *n* pl. -S williwaw

WILLIWAW   *n* pl. -S a violent gust of cold wind

WILLOW   *v* -ED, -ING, -S to clean textile fibers with a certain machine

WILLOWER   *n* pl. -S one that willows

WILLOWY   *adj* -LOWIER, -LOWIEST pliant

WILLY   *v* -LIED, -LYING, -LIES to willow

WILLYARD   *adj* willful

WILLYART   *adj* willyard

WILLYWAW   *n* pl. -S williwaw

WILT   *v* -ED, -ING, -S to become limp

WILY   *adj* WILIER, WILIEST crafty

WIMBLE   *v* -BLED, -BLING, -BLES to bore with a hand tool

WIMPLE   *v* -PLED, -PLING, -PLES to pleat

WIN   *v* WON or WAN, WINNING, WINS to be victorious

WIN   *v* WINNED, WINNING, WINS to winnow

WINCE   *v* WINCED, WINCING, WINCES to flinch

WINCER   *n* pl. -S one that winces

WINCEY   *n* pl. -CEYS a type of fabric

WINCH   *v* -ED, -ING, -ES to raise with a winch (a hoisting machine)

WINCHER   *n* pl. -S one that winches

WINCING   present participle of wince

WIND   *v* WOUND or WINDED, WINDING, WINDS to pass around as object or fixed center **WINDABLE** *adj*

WINDAGE   *n* pl. -S the effect of the wind (air in natural motion) on a projectile

WINDBAG   *n* pl. -S a talkative person

WINDBURN   *v* -BURNED or -BURNT, -BURNING, -BURNS to be affected with skin irritation caused by exposure to the wind

WINDER   *n* pl. -S one that winds

WINDFALL   *n* pl. -S a sudden and unexpected gain

WINDFLAW   *n* pl. -S a gust of wind

WINDGALL   *n* pl. -S a swelling on a horse's leg

WINDIER   comparative of windy

WINDIEST   superlative of windy

WINDIGO   *n* pl. -GOS an evil demon in Algonquian mythology

WINDILY   *adv* in a windy manner

WINDING   *n* pl. -S material wound about an object

WINDLASS   *v* -ED, -ING, -ES to raise with a windlass (a hoisting machine)

WINDLE   *v* -DLED, -DLING, -DLES to wind

WINDLESS   *adj* being without wind

WINDLING   *n* pl. -S a bundle of straw

WINDMILL   v -ED, -ING, -S to rotate solely under the force of a passing airstream

WINDOW   v -ED, -ING, -S to provide with a window (an opening in a wall to admit light and air)

WINDPIPE   n pl. -S the trachea

WINDROW   v -ED, -ING, -S to arrange in long rows, as hay or grain

WINDSOCK   n pl. -S a device used to indicate wind direction

WINDUP   n pl. -S a conclusion

WINDWARD   n pl. -S the direction from which the wind blows

WINDWAY   n pl. -WAYS a passage for air

WINDY   adj WINDIER, WINDIEST marked by strong wind

WINE   v WINED, WINING, WINES to provide with wine (the fermented juice of the grape)

WINELESS   adj having no wine

WINERY   n pl. -ERIES an establishment for making wine

WINESHOP   n pl. -S a shop where wine is sold

WINESKIN   n pl. -S a goatskin bag for holding wine

WINESOP   n pl. -S a food sopped in wine

WINEY   adj WINIER, WINIEST winy

WING   v -ED, -ING, -S to travel by means of wings (organs of flight)

WINGBACK   n pl. -S a certain player in football

WINGBOW   n pl. -S a mark on the wing of a domestic fowl

WINGDING   n pl. -S a lively party

WINGEDLY   adv swiftly

WINGER   n pl. -S a certain player in soccer

WINGIER   comparative of wingy

WINGIEST   superlative of wingy

WINGLESS   adj having no wings

WINGLET   n pl. -S a small wing

WINGLIKE   adj resembling a wing

WINGMAN   n pl. -MEN a pilot behind the leader of a flying formation

WINGOVER   n pl. -S a flight maneuver

WINGSPAN   n pl. -S the distance from the tip of one of a pair of wings to that of the other

WINGY   adj WINGIER, WINGIEST swift

WINIER   comparative of winey and winy

WINIEST   superlative of winey and winy

WINING   present participle of wine

WINISH   adj winy

WINK   v -ED, -ING, -S to close and open one eye quickly

WINKER   n pl. -S one that winks

WINKLE   v -KLED, -KLING, -KLES to displace, extract, or evict from a position

WINNABLE   adj able to be won

WINNED   past tense of win (to winnow)

WINNER   n pl. -S one that wins

WINNING   n pl. -S money won in a game or competition

WINNOCK   n pl. -S a window

WINNOW   v -ED, -ING, -S to free grain from impurities

WINNOWER   n pl. -S one that winnows

WINO   n pl. WINOES or WINOS one who is habitually drunk on wine

WINSOME   adj -SOMER, -SOMEST charming

WINTER   v -ED, -ING, -S to pass the winter (the coldest season of the year)

WINTERER   n pl. -S one that winters

WINTERLY   adj wintry

WINTERY   adj -TERIER, -TERIEST wintry

WINTLE   v -TLED, -TLING, -TLES to stagger

WINTRY   adj -TRIER, -TRIEST characteristic of winter WINTRILY adv

WINY   adj WINIER, WINIEST having the taste or qualities of wine

WINZE   n pl. -S a steeply inclined mine shaft

WIPE   v WIPED, WIPING, WIPES to rub lightly in order to clean or dry

WIPEOUT   n pl. -S a fall from a surfboard

WIPER   n pl. -S one that wipes

WIPING   present participle of wipe

WIRE   v WIRED, WIRING, WIRES to fasten with wire (a slender rod, strand, or thread of ductile metal) WIRABLE adj

WIREDRAW   v -DREW, -DRAWN, -DRAWING, -DRAWS to draw into wire

WIREHAIR *n pl.* -S a dog having a wiry coat

WIRELESS *v* -ED, -ING, -ES to radio

WIRELIKE *adj* resembling wire

WIREMAN *n pl.* -MEN one who makes or works with wire

WIRER *n pl.* -S one that wires

WIRETAP *v* -TAPPED, -TAPPING, -TAPS to intercept messages by means of a concealed monitoring device

WIREWAY *n pl.* -WAYS a tube for protecting electric wires

WIREWORK *n pl.* -S an article made of wire

WIREWORM *n pl.* -S a wirelike worm

WIRIER comparative of wiry

WIRIEST superlative of wiry

WIRILY *adv* in a wiry manner

WIRINESS *n pl.* -ES the quality of being wiry

WIRING *n pl.* -S a system of electric wires

WIRRA *interj* — used to express sorrow

WIRY *adj* WIRIER, WIRIEST resembling wire

WIS *v* past tense WIST to know — WIS and WIST are the only accepted forms of this verb; it cannot be conjugated further

WISDOM *n pl.* -S the power of true and right discernment

WISE *v* WISED, WISING, WISES to become aware or informed

WISE *adj* WISER, WISEST having wisdom

WISEACRE *n pl.* -S a pretentiously wise person

WISED past tense of wise

WISELY *adv* -LIER, -LIEST in a wise manner

WISENESS *n pl.* -ES wisdom

WISENT *n pl.* -S a European bison

WISER comparative of wise

WISEST superlative of wise

WISH *v* -ED, -ING, -ES to feel an impulse toward attainment or possession of something

WISHA *interj* — used to express surprise

WISHBONE *n pl.* -S a forked bone in front of a bird's breastbone

WISHER *n pl.* -S one that wishes

WISHFUL *adj* desirous

WISHLESS *adj* not wishful

WISING present participle of wise

WISP *v* -ED, -ING, -S to twist into a wisp (a small bunch or bundle)

WISPIER comparative of wispy

WISPIEST superlative of wispy

WISPILY *adv* in a wispy manner

WISPISH *adj* wispy

WISPLIKE *adj* wispy

WISPY *adj* WISPIER, WISPIEST resembling a wisp

WISS *v* -ED, -ING, -ES to wish

WIST *v* -ED, -ING, -S to know

WISTARIA *n pl.* -S wisteria

WISTERIA *n pl.* -S a flowering shrub

WISTFUL *adj* yearning

WIT *n pl.* -S intelligence

WIT *v* WIST, WITING or WITTING, present sing. 1st person WOT, 2d WOST or WOSTTETH, 3d WOT or WOTTETH, present pl. WITE or WITEN to know

WITAN *n/pl* the members of a national council in Anglo-Saxon England

WITCH *v* -ED, -ING, -ES to bewitch

WITCHERY *n pl.* -ERIES sorcery

WITCHING *n pl.* -S sorcery

WITCHY *adj* WITCHIER, WITCHIEST malicious

WITE *v* WITED, WITING, WITES to blame

WITEN a present pl. of wit

WITH *prep* in the company of

WITHAL *adv* in addition

WITHDRAW *v* -DREW, -DRAWN, -DRAWING, -DRAWS to move back or away

WITHE *v* WITHED, WITHING, WITHES to bind with flexible twigs

WITHER *v* -ED, -ING, -S to dry up and wilt

WITHERER *n pl.* -S one that withers

WITHHOLD *v* -HELD, -HOLDING, -HOLDS to hold back

WITHIER comparative of withy

WITHIES *pl.* of withy

WITHIEST superlative of withy

WITHIN	*n* pl. -S an interior place or area
WITHING	present participle of withe
WITHOUT	*n* pl. -S an exterior place or area
WITHY	*n* pl. WITHIES a flexible twig
WITHY	*adj* WITHIER, WITHIEST flexible and tough
WITING	present participle of wit and wite
WITLESS	*adj* lacking intelligence
WITLING	*n* pl. -S one who considers himself witty
WITLOOF	*n* pl. -S chicory
WITNESS	*v* -ED, -ING, -ES to see or know by personal experience
WITNEY	*n* pl. -NEYS a heavy woolen fabric
WITTED	*adj* having intelligence
WITTIER	comparative of witty
WITTIEST	superlative of witty
WITTILY	*adv* in a witty manner
WITTING	*n* pl. -S knowledge
WITTOL	*n* pl. -S a man who tolerates his wife's infidelity
WITTY	*adj* -TIER, -TIEST humorously clever
WIVE	*v* WIVED, WIVING, WIVES to marry a woman
WIVER	*n* pl. -S wivern
WIVERN	*n* pl. -S a two-legged dragon
WIVES	pl. of wife
WIVING	present participle of wive
WIZ	*n* pl. -ES a very clever or skillful person
WIZARD	*n* pl. -S a sorcerer WIZARDLY *adj*
WIZARDRY	*n* pl. -RIES sorcery
WIZEN	*v* -ED, -ING, -S to shrivel
WIZZEN	*n* pl. -S weasand
WO	*n* pl. WOS woe
WOAD	*n* pl. -S a blue dye WOADED *adj*
WOADWAX	*n* pl. -ES an ornamental shrub
WOALD	*n* pl. -S a yellow pigment
WOBBLE	*v* -BLED, -BLING, -BLES to move unsteadily
WOBBLER	*n* pl. -S one that wobbles
WOBBLY	*adj* -BLIER, -BLIEST unsteady

WOBBLY	*n* pl. -BLIES a member of the Industrial Workers of the World
WOBEGONE	*adj* affected with woe
WOE	*n* pl. -S tremendous grief
WOEFUL	*adj* -FULLER, -FULLEST full of woe WOEFULLY *adv*
WOENESS	*n* pl. -ES sadness
WOESOME	*adj* woeful
WOFUL	*adj* woeful WOFULLY *adv*
WOK	*n* pl. -S a cooking utensil
WOKE	a past tense of wake
WOKEN	a past participle of wake
WOLD	*n* pl. -S an elevated tract of open land
WOLF	*n* pl. WOLVES a carnivorous mammal
WOLF	*v* -ED, -ING, -S to devour voraciously
WOLFER	*n* pl. -S one who hunts wolves
WOLFFISH	*n* pl. -ES a marine fish
WOLFISH	*adj* wolflike
WOLFLIKE	*adj* resembling a wolf
WOLFRAM	*n* pl. -S tungsten
WOLVER	*n* pl. -S wolfer
WOLVES	pl. of wolf
WOMAN	*n* pl. WOMEN an adult human female
WOMAN	*v* -ED, -ING, -S to play the part of a woman
WOMANISE	*v* -ISED, -ISING, -ISES to womanize
WOMANISH	*adj* characteristic of a woman
WOMANIZE	*v* -IZED, -IZING, -IZES to make effeminate
WOMANLY	*adj* -LIER, -LIEST having the qualities of a woman
WOMB	*n* pl. -S the uterus WOMBED *adj*
WOMBAT	*n* pl. -S a nocturnal mammal
WOMBY	*adj* WOMBIER, WOMBIEST hollow
WOMEN	pl. of woman
WOMERA	*n* pl. -S a device used to propel spears
WOMMERA	*n* pl. -S womera
WON	*v* WONNED, WONNING, WONS to dwell
WONDER	*v* -ED, -ING, -S to have a feeling of curiosity or doubt

WONDERER n pl. -S one that wonders

WONDROUS adj marvelous

WONKY adj -KIER, -KIEST unsteady

WONNED past tense of won

WONNER n pl. -S a prodigy

WONNING present participle of won

WONT v -ED, -ING, -S to make accustomed to

WONTEDLY adv in a usual manner

WONTON n pl. -S a pork-filled dumpling used in Chinese cooking

WOO v -ED, -ING, -S to seek the affection of

WOOD v -ED, -ING, -S to furnish with wood (the hard, fibrous substance beneath the bark of a tree or shrub)

WOODBIN n pl. -S a bin for holding firewood

WOODBIND n pl. -S woodbine

WOODBINE n pl. -S a European shrub

WOODBOX n pl. -ES a woodbin

WOODCHAT n pl. -S a European shrike

WOODCOCK n pl. -S a game bird

WOODCUT n pl. -S an engraved block of wood

WOODEN adj -ENER, -ENEST resembling wood in stiffness **WOODENLY** adv

WOODHEN n pl. -S the weka

WOODIER comparative of woody

WOODIEST superlative of woody

WOODLAND n pl. -S land covered with trees

WOODLARK n pl. -S a songbird

WOODLESS adj having no wood

WOODLORE n pl. -S knowledge of the forest

WOODLOT n pl. -S an area restricted to the growing of forest trees

WOODMAN n pl. -MEN woodsman

WOODNOTE n pl. -S a song or call of a forest bird

WOODPILE n pl. -S a pile of wood

WOODRUFF n pl. -S an aromatic herb

WOODSHED v -SHEDDED, -SHEDDING, -SHEDS to practice on a musical instrument

WOODSIA n pl. -S a small fern

WOODSMAN n pl. -MEN one who works or lives in the forest

WOODSY adj WOODSIER, WOODSIEST suggestive of a forest

WOODWAX n pl. -ES woadwax

WOODWIND n pl. -S a musical wind instrument

WOODWORK n pl. -S work made of wood

WOODWORM n pl. -S a wood-boring worm

WOODY adj WOODIER, WOODIEST containing or resembling wood

WOOER n pl. -S one that woos

WOOF v -ED, -ING, -S to utter a gruff barking sound

WOOFER n pl. -S a loudspeaker designed to reproduce low-pitched sounds

WOOINGLY adv attractively

WOOL n pl. -S the dense, soft hair forming the coat of certain mammals **WOOLED** adj

WOOLEN n pl. -S a fabric made of wool

WOOLER n pl. -S a domestic animal raised for its wool

WOOLFELL n pl. -S woolskin

WOOLIE n pl. -S a woolly

WOOLIER comparative of wooly

WOOLIES pl. of wooly

WOOLIEST superlative of wooly

WOOLLEN n pl. -S woolen

WOOLLIER comparative of woolly

WOOLLIES pl. of woolly

WOOLLIEST superlative of woolly

WOOLLIKE adj resembling wool

WOOLLY adj -LIER, -LIEST consisting of or resembling wool

WOOLLY n pl. -LIES a garment made of wool

WOOLMAN n pl. -MEN a dealer in wool

WOOLPACK n pl. -S a bag for packing a bale of wool

WOOLSACK n pl. -S a sack of wool

WOOLSHED n pl. -S a building in which sheep are sheared

WOOLSKIN n pl. -S a sheepskin with the wool still on it

WOOLY adj WOOLIER, WOOLIEST woolly

WOOLY n pl. WOOLIES a woolly

WOOMERA n pl. -S a womera

WOOPS interj oops

WOORALI n pl. -S curare

WOORARI *n pl.* -S curare

WOOSH *v* -ED, -ING, -ES to whoosh

WOOZY *adj* -ZIER, -ZIEST dazed
WOOZILY *adv*

WOP *n pl.* -S an Italian — an offensive term

WORD *v* -ED, -ING, -S to express in words (speech sounds that communicate meaning)

WORDAGE *n pl.* -S the number of words used

WORDBOOK *n pl.* -S a dictionary

WORDIER comparative of wordy

WORDIEST superlative of wordy

WORDILY *adv* in a wordy manner

WORDING *n pl.* -S the act or style of expressing in words

WORDLESS *adj* being without words

WORDPLAY *n pl.* -PLAYS a witty exchange of words

WORDY *adj* WORDIER, WORDIEST using many or too many words

WORE past tense of wear

WORK *v* WORKED or WROUGHT, WORKING, WORKS to exert one's powers of body or mind for some purpose

WORKABLE *adj* capable of being done

WORKADAY *adj* everyday

WORKBAG *n pl.* -S a bag for holding work instuments and materials

WORKBOAT *n pl.* -S a boat used for commercial purposes

WORKBOOK *n pl.* -S an exercise book for a student

WORKBOX *n pl.* -ES a box for holding work instruments and materials

WORKDAY *n pl.* -DAYS a day on which work is done

WORKER *n pl.* -S one that works

WORKFOLK *n/pl* manual laborers

WORKING *n pl.* -S a mining excavation

WORKLESS *adj* unemployed

WORKLOAD *n pl.* -S the amount of work assigned to an employee

WORKMAN *n pl.* -MEN a male worker

WORKOUT *n pl.* -S a period of physical exercise

WORKROOM *n pl.* -S a room in which work is done

WORKSHOP *n pl.* -S a workroom

WORKUP *n pl.* -S an intensive diagnostic study

WORKWEEK *n pl.* -S the number of hours worked in a week

WORLD *n pl.* -S the earth and all its inhabitants

WORLDLY *adj* -LIER, -LIEST pertaining to the world

WORM *v* -ED, -ING, -S to rid of worms (small, limbless invertebrates)

WORMER *n pl.* -S one that worms

WORMHOLE *n pl.* -S a hole made by a burrowing worm

WORMIER comparative of wormy

WORMIEST superlative of wormy

WORMIL *n pl.* -S a lump in the skin of an animal's back

WORMISH *adj* wormlike

WORMLIKE *adj* resembling a worm

WORMROOT *n pl.* -S pinkroot

WORMSEED *n pl.* -S a tropical plant

WORMWOOD *n pl.* -S a European herb

WORMY *adj* WORMIER, WORMIEST infested with worms

WORN *adj* affected by wear or use

WORNNESS *n pl.* -ES the state of being worn

WORRIED past tense of worry

WORRIER *n pl.* -S one that worries

WORRIT *v* -ED, -ING, -S to worry

WORRY *v* -RIED, -RYING, -RIES to feel anxious and uneasy about something

WORSE *n pl.* -S something that is worse (bad in a greater degree)

WORSEN *v* -ED, -ING, -S to make or become worse

WORSER *adj* worse

WORSET *n pl.* -S worsted

WORSHIP *v* -SHIPED, -SHIPING, -SHIPS or -SHIPPED, -SHIPPING, -SHIPS to honor and love as a divine being

WORST *v* -ED, -ING, -S to defeat

WORSTED *n pl.* -S a woolen yarn

WORT *n pl.* -S a plant, herb, or vegetable

WORTH *v* -ED, -ING, -S to befall

WORTHFUL *adj* worthy

WORTHY	*adj* -THIER, -THIEST having value or merit **WORTHILY** *adv*
WORTHY	*n* pl. -THIES a worthy person
WOST	a present 2d person sing. of wit
WOSTTETH	a present 2d person sing. of wit
WOT	*v* WOTTED, WOTTING, WOTS to know
WOTTETH	a present 3d person sing. of wit
WOULD	past tense of will
WOULDEST	a 2d person sing. past tense of will
WOULDST	a 2d person sing. past tense of will
WOUND	*v* -ED, -ING, -S to inflict an injury upon
WOVE	a past tense of weave
WOVEN	past participle of weave
WOW	*v* -ED, -ING, -S to excite to enthusiastic approval
WOWSER	*n* pl. -S a puritanical person
WRACK	*v* -ED, -ING, -S to wreck
WRACKFUL	*adj* destructive
WRAITH	*n* pl. -S a ghost
WRANG	*n* pl. -S a wrong
WRANGLE	*v* -GLED, -GLING, -GLES to argue noisily
WRANGLER	*n* pl. -S one that wrangles
WRAP	*v* WRAPPED or WRAPT, WRAPPING, WRAPS to enclose in something wound or folded about
WRAPPER	*n* pl. -S one that wraps
WRAPPING	*n* pl. -S the material in which something is wrapped
WRAPT	a past tense of wrap
WRASSE	*n* pl. -S a marine fish
WRASTLE	*v* -TLED, -TLING, -TLES to wrestle
WRATH	*v* -ED, -ING, -S to make wrathful
WRATHFUL	*adj* extremely angry
WRATHY	*adj* WRATHIER, WRATHIEST wrathful **WRATHILY** *adv*
WREAK	*v* -ED, -ING, -S to inflict
WREAKER	*n* pl. -S one that wreaks
WREATH	*n* pl. -S a band of flowers **WREATHY** *adj*

WREATHE	*v* WREATHED, WREATHEN, WREATHING, WREATHES to shape into a wreathe
WRECK	*v* -ED, -ING, -S to cause the ruin of
WRECKAGE	*n* pl. -S the act of wrecking
WRECKER	*n* pl. -S one that wrecks
WRECKFUL	*adj* destructive
WRECKING	*n* pl. -S the occupation of salvaging wrecked objects
WREN	*n* pl. -S a small songbird
WRENCH	*v* -ED, -ING, -ES to twist suddenly and forcibly
WREST	*v* -ED, -ING, -S to take away by force
WRESTER	*n* pl. -S one that wrests
WRESTLE	*v* -TLED, -TLING, -TLES to engage in a type of hand-to-hand contest
WRESTLER	*n* pl. -S one that wrestles
WRETCH	*n* pl. -ES a wretched person
WRETCHED	*adj* -EDER, -EDEST extremely unhappy
WRIED	past tense of wry
WRIER	a comparative of wry
WRIES	present 3d person sing. of wry
WRIEST	a superlative of wry
WRIGGLE	*v* -GLED, -GLING, -GLES to turn or twist in a sinuous manner
WRIGGLER	*n* pl. -S one that wriggles
WRIGGLY	*adj* -GLIER, -GLIEST wriggling
WRIGHT	*n* pl. -S one who constructs or creates
WRING	*v* WRUNG or WRINGED, WRINGING, WRINGS to twist so as to compress
WRINGER	*n* pl. -S one that wrings
WRINKLE	*v* -KLED, -KLING, -KLES to make wrinkles (small ridges or furrows) in
WRINKLY	*adj* -KLIER, -KLIEST having wrinkles
WRIST	*n* pl. -S the junction between the hand and forearm
WRISTLET	*n* pl. -S a band worn around the wrist
WRISTY	*adj* WRISTIER, WRISTIEST using much wrist action
WRIT	*n* pl. -S a written legal order

WRITE	v WROTE, WRITTEN, WRITING, WRITES to form characters or symbols on a surface with an instrument **WRITABLE** adj
WRITER	n pl. -S one that writes
WRITHE	v WRITHED, WRITHING, WRITHES to squirm or twist in pain
WRITHEN	adj twisted
WRITHER	n pl. -S one that writhes
WRITHING	present participle of writhe
WRITING	n pl. -S a written composition
WRITTEN	past participle of write
WRONG	adj WRONGER, WRONGEST not according to what is right, proper, or correct
WRONG	v -ED, -ING, -S to treat injuriously or unjustly
WRONGER	n pl. -S one that wrongs
WRONGFUL	adj wrong
WRONGLY	adv in a wrong manner
WROTE	past tense of write
WROTH	adj very angry

WROTHFUL	adj wroth
WROUGHT	a past tense of work
WRUNG	a past tense of wring
WRY	adj WRIER, WRIEST or WRYER, WRYEST contorted **WRYLY** adv
WRY	v WRIED, WRYING, WRIES to contort
WRYNECK	n pl. -S a European bird
WRYNESS	n pl. -ES the state of being wry
WUD	adj insane
WURST	n pl. -S sausage
WURZEL	n pl. -S a variety of beet
WYCH	n pl. -ES a European elm
WYE	n pl. -S the letter Y
WYLE	v WYLED, WYLING, WYLES to beguile
WYND	n pl. -S a narrow street
WYNN	n pl. -S the rune for W
WYTE	v WYTED, WYTING, WYTES to wite
WYVERN	n pl. -S wivern

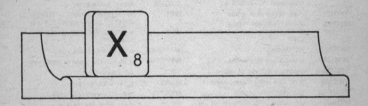

XANTHATE	n pl. -S a chemical salt
XANTHEIN	n pl. -S the water-soluble part of the coloring matter in yellow flowers
XANTHENE	n pl. -S a chemical compound
XANTHIC	adj tending to have a yellow color
XANTHIN	n pl. -S a yellow pigment
XANTHINE	n pl. -S a chemical compound
XANTHOMA	n pl. -MAS or -MATA a skin disease
XANTHONE	n pl. -S a chemical compound
XANTHOUS	adj yellow
XEBEC	n pl. -S a Mediterranean sailing vessel
XENIA	n pl. -S the effect of pollen on certain plant structures XENIAL adj
XENIC	adj pertaining to a type of culture medium
XENOGAMY	n pl. -MIES the transfer of pollen from one plant to another
XENOGENY	n pl. -NIES the supposed production of offspring totally different from the parent
XENOLITH	n pl. -S a rock fragment included in another rock
XENON	n pl. -S a gaseous element
XERARCH	adj developing in a dry area
XERIC	adj requiring only a small amount of moisture
XEROSERE	n pl. -S a dry-land sere

XEROSIS	n pl. -ROSES abnormal dryness of a body part or tissue XEROTIC adj
XERUS	n pl. -ES an African ground squirrel
XI	n pl. -S a Greek letter
XIPHOID	n pl. -S a part of the sternum
XU	n pl. XU a monetary unit of Vietnam
XYLAN	n pl. -S a substance found in cell walls of plants
XYLEM	n pl. -S a complex plant tissue
XYLENE	n pl. -S a flammable hydrocarbon
XYLIDIN	n pl. -S xylidine
XYLIDINE	n pl. -S a chemical compound
XYLOCARP	n pl. -S a hard, woody fruit
XYLOID	adj resembling wood
XYLOL	n pl. -S xylene
XYLOSE	n pl. -S a type of sugar
XYLOTOMY	n pl. -MIES the preparation of sections of wood for microscopic examination
XYLYL	n pl. -S a univalent radical
XYST	n pl. -S xystus
XYSTER	n pl. -S a surgical instrument for scraping bones
XYSTOS	n pl. -TOI xystus
XYSTUS	n pl. -TI a roofed area where athletes trained in ancient Greece

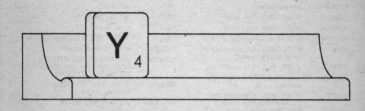

YA	*pron* you	**YANQUI**	*n* pl. -S a United States citizen
YABBER	*v* -ED, -ING, -S to jabber	**YAP**	*v* YAPPED, YAPPING, YAPS to bark shrilly
YACHT	*v* -ED, -ING, -S to sail in a yacht (a vessel used for pleasure cruising or racing)	**YAPOCK**	*n* pl. -S an aquatic mammal
		YAPOK	*n* pl. -S yapock
YACHTER	*n* pl. -S one who sails a yacht	**YAPON**	*n* pl. -S yaupon
YACHTING	*n* pl. -S the sport of sailing in yachts	**YAPPED**	past tense of yap
		YAPPER	*n* pl. -S one that yaps
YACHTMAN	*n* pl. -MEN a yachter	**YAPPING**	present participle of yap
YACK	*v* -ED, -ING, -S to yak	**YAR**	*adj* yare
YAFF	*v* -ED, -ING, -S to bark	**YARD**	*v* -ED, -ING, -S to put in a yard (a tract of ground adjacent to a building)
YAGER	*n* pl. -S jaeger		
YAGI	*n* pl. -S a type of shortwave antenna	**YARDAGE**	*n* pl. -S the use of an enclosure for livestock at a railroad station
YAH	*interj* — used as an exclamation of disgust	**YARDARM**	*n* pl. -S either end of a ship's spar
YAHOO	*n* pl. -HOOS a coarse, uncouth person	**YARDBIRD**	*n* pl. -S an army recruit
		YARDMAN	*n* pl. -MEN a man employed to do outdoor work
YAHOOISM	*n* pl. -S coarse, uncouth behavior	**YARDWAND**	*n* pl. -S a measuring stick
YAIRD	*n* pl. -S a garden	**YARE**	*adj* YARER, YAREST nimble YARELY *adv*
YAK	*v* YAKKED, YAKKING, YAKS to chatter		
YALD	*adj* yauld	**YARMELKE**	*n* pl. -S yarmulke
YAM	*n* pl. -S a plant having an edible root	**YARMULKE**	*n* pl. -S a skullcap worn by Jewish males
YAMEN	*n* pl. -S the residence of a Chinese public official	**YARN**	*v* -ED, -ING, -S to tell a long story
YAMMER	*v* -ED, -ING, -S to whine or complain peevishly	**YARROW**	*n* pl. -S a perennial herb
YAMMERER	*n* pl. -S one that yammers	**YASHMAC**	*n* pl. -S yashmak
YAMUN	*n* pl. -S yamen	**YASHMAK**	*n* pl. -S a veil worn by Muslim women
YANG	*n* pl. -S the masculine active principle in Chinese cosmology	**YASMAK**	*n* pl. -S yashmak
YANK	*v* -ED, -ING, -S to pull suddenly	**YATAGAN**	*n* pl. -S yataghan

YATAGHAN n pl. -S a Turkish sword

YAUD n pl. -S an old mare

YAULD adj vigorous

YAUP v -ED, -ING, -S to yawp

YAUPER n pl. -S one that yaups

YAUPON n pl. -S an evergreen shrub

YAW v -ED, -ING, -S to deviate from an intended course

YAWL v -ED, -ING, -S to yowl

YAWMETER n pl. -S an instrument in an aircraft

YAWN v -ED, -ING, -S to open the mouth wide with a deep inhalation of air

YAWNER n pl. -S one that yawns

YAWP v -ED, -ING, -S to utter a loud, harsh cry

YAWPER n pl. -S one that yawps

YAWPING n pl. -S a loud, harsh cry

YAY adv to this extent

YCLEPED adj yclept

YCLEPT adj called; named

YE pron you

YEA n pl. -S an affirmative vote

YEAH adv yes

YEALING n pl. -S a person of the same age

YEAN v -ED, -ING, -S to bear young

YEANLING n pl. -S the young of a sheep or goat

YEAR n pl. -S a period of time consisting of 365 or 366 days

YEARBOOK n pl. -S a book published each year by a graduating class

YEARLIES pl. of yearly

YEARLING n pl. -S an animal past its first year and not yet two years old

YEARLONG adj lasting through a year

YEARLY n pl. -LIES a publication appearing once a year

YEARN v -ED, -ING, -S to have a stong or deep desire

YEARNER n pl. -S one that yearns

YEARNING n pl. -S a strong or deep desire

YEAST v -ED, -ING, -S to foam

YEASTY adj YEASTIER, YEASTIEST foamy YEASTILY adv

YEELIN n pl. -S yealing

YEGG n pl. -S a burglar

YEGGMAN n pl. -MEN a yegg

YEH adv yeah

YELD adj not giving milk

YELK n pl. -S yolk

YELL v -ED, -ING, -S to cry out loudly

YELLER n pl. -S one that yells

YELLOW adj -LOWER, -LOWEST of a bright color like that of ripe lemons YELLOWLY adv

YELLOW v -ED, -ING, -S to make or become yellow

YELLOWY adj somewhat yellow

YELP v -ED, -ING, -S to utter a sharp, shrill cry

YELPER n pl. -S one that yelps

YEN v YENNED, YENNING, YENS to yearn

YENTA n pl. -S a gossipy woman

YEOMAN n pl. -MEN an independent farmer YEOMANLY adj

YEOMANRY n pl. -RIES the collective body of yeomen

YEP adv yes

YERBA n pl. -S a South American beverage resembling tea

YERK v -ED, -ING, -S to beat vigorously

YES v YESSED, YESSING, YESSES or YESES to give an affirmative reply to

YESHIVA n pl. -VAS or -VOTH an orthodox Jewish school

YESHIVAH n pl. -S yeshiva

YESSED past tense of yes

YESSES a 3d person sing. of yes

YESSING present participle of yes

YESTER adj pertaining to yesterday

YESTERN adj yester

YESTREEN n pl. -S the previous evening

YET adv up to now

YETI n pl. -S the abominable snowman

YETT n pl. -S a gate

YEUK v -ED, -ING, -S to itch

YEUKY adj itchy

YEW n pl. -S an evergreen tree or shrub

YID	n pl. -S a Jew — an offensive term	**YOKE**	v YOKED, YOKING, YOKES to fit with a yoke (a wooden frame for joining together draft animals)
YIELD	v -ED, -ING, -S to give up		
YIELDER	n pl. -S one that yields	**YOKEL**	n pl. -S a naive or gullible rustic
YILL	n pl. -S ale	**YOKELESS**	adj having no yoke
YIN	n pl. -S the feminine passive principle in Chinese cosmology	**YOKELISH**	adj resembling a yokel
		YOKEMATE	n pl. -S a companion in work
YINCE	adv once	**YOKING**	present participle of yoke
YIP	v YIPPED, YIPPING, YIPS to yelp	**YOLK**	n pl. -S the yellow portion of an egg YOLKED adj
YIPE	interj — used to express fear or surprise	**YOLKY**	adj YOLKIER, YOLKIEST resembling a yolk
YIPES	interj yipe	**YOM**	n pl. YOMIM day
YIPPED	past tense of yip	**YON**	adv yonder
YIPPEE	interj — used to express joy	**YOND**	adv yonder
YIPPIE	n pl. -S a politically radical hippie	**YONDER**	adv over there
		YONI	n pl. -S a symbol for the vulva in Hindu religion
YIPPING	present participle of yip	**YONKER**	n pl. -S younker
YIRD	n pl. -S earth	**YORE**	n pl. -S time past
YIRR	v -ED, -ING, -S to snarl	**YOU**	pron the 2d person sing. or pl. pronoun
YIRTH	n pl. -S yird		
YOD	n pl. -S a Hebrew letter	**YOUNG**	adj YOUNGER, YOUNGEST being in the early period of life or growth
YODEL	v -DELED, -DELING, -DELS or -DELLED, -DELLING, -DELS to sing with a fluctuating voice		
		YOUNG	n pl. -S offspring
YODELER	n pl. -S one that yodels	**YOUNGER**	n pl. -S an inferior in age
YODELLER	n pl. -S yodeler	**YOUNGISH**	adj somewhat young
YODH	n pl. -S yod	**YOUNKER**	n pl. -S a young gentleman
YODLE	v -DLED, -DLING, -DLES to yodel	**YOUPON**	n pl. -S yaupon
		YOUR	adj a possessive form of the pronoun you
YODLER	n pl. -S yodeler		
YOGA	n pl. -S a Hindu philosophy involving physical and mental disciplines	**YOURN**	pron yours
		YOURS	pron a possessive form of the pronoun you
YOGEE	n pl. -S yogi	**YOURSELF**	pron pl. -SELVES a form of the 2d person pronoun
YOGH	n pl. -S a Middle English letter		
YOGHOURT	n pl. -S yogurt	**YOUSE**	pron you
YOGHURT	n pl. -S yogurt	**YOUTH**	n pl. -S a young person
YOGI	n pl. -S a person who practices yoga	**YOUTHEN**	v -ED, -ING, -S to make youthful
		YOUTHFUL	adj
YOGIC	adj pertaining to yoga	**YOW**	v -ED, -ING, -S to yowl
YOGIN	n pl. -S yogi	**YOWE**	n pl. -S a ewe
YOGINI	n pl. -S a female yogi	**YOWIE**	n pl. -S a small ewe
YOGURT	n pl. -S a food made from milk	**YOWL**	v -ED, -ING, -S to utter a loud, long, mournful cry
YOICKS	interj — used to encourage hunting hounds		
		YOWLER	n pl. -S one that yowls

YPERITE	*n* pl. -S a poisonous gas
YTTERBIA	*n* pl. -S a chemical compound **YTTERBIC** *adj*
YTTRIA	*n* pl. -S a chemical compound
YTTRIUM	*n* pl. -S a metallic element **YTTRIC** *adj*
YUAN	*n* pl. -S a monetary unit of China
YUCCA	*n* pl. -S a tropical plant
YUGA	*n* pl. -S an age of time in Hinduism
YUK	*v* YUKKED, YUKKING, YUKS to laugh loudly
YULAN	*n* pl. -S a Chinese tree
YULE	*n* pl. -S Christmas time
YULETIDE	*n* pl. -S yule
YUMMY	*adj* -MIER, -MIEST delicious
YUMMY	*n* pl. -MIES something delicious
YUP	*adv* yep
YUPON	*n* pl. -S yaupon
YURT	*n* pl. YURTA or YURTS a portable tent
YWIS	*adv* iwis

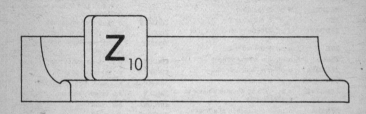

ZABAIONE	n pl. -S a dessert resembling custard
ZABAJONE	n pl. -S zabaione
ZACATON	n pl. -S a Mexican grass
ZADDIK	n pl. -DIKIM a virtuous person by Jewish religious standards
ZAFFAR	n pl. -S zaffer
ZAFFER	n pl. -S a blue ceramic coloring
ZAFFIR	n pl. -S zaffer
ZAFFRE	n pl. -S zaffer
ZAFTIG	adj full-bosomed
ZAG	v ZAGGED, ZAGGING, ZAGS to turn sharply
ZAIBATSU	n pl. ZAIBATSU a powerful family combine in Japan
ZAIRE	n pl. -S a monetary unit of Zaire
ZAMARRA	n pl. -S a sheepskin coat
ZAMARRO	n pl. -ROS zamarra
ZAMIA	n pl. -S a tropical plant
ZAMINDAR	n pl. -S a tax collector in precolonial India
ZANANA	n pl. -S zenana
ZANDER	n pl. -S a freshwater fish
ZANIER	comparative of zany
ZANIES	pl. of zany
ZANINESS	n pl. -ES the quality or state of being zany
ZANY	adj ZANIER, ZANIEST ludicrously comical **ZANILY** adv
ZANY	n pl. -NIES a zany person
ZANYISH	adj somewhat zany
ZANZA	n pl. -S an African musical instrument

ZAP	v ZAPPED, ZAPPING, ZAPS to kill or destroy
ZAPATEO	n pl. -TEOS a Spanish dance
ZAPTIAH	n pl. -S a Turkish policeman
ZAPTIEH	n pl. -S zaptiah
ZARATITE	n pl. -S a chemical compound
ZAREBA	n pl. -S an improvised stockade
ZAREEBA	n pl. -S zareba
ZARF	n pl. -S a metal holder for a coffee cup
ZARIBA	n pl. -S zareba
ZARZUELA	n pl. -S a Spanish operetta
ZASTRUGA	n pl. -GI sastruga
ZAX	n pl. -ES a tool for cutting roof slates
ZAYIN	n pl. -S a Hebrew letter
ZEAL	n pl. -S enthusiastic devotion
ZEALOT	n pl. -S one who is zealous
ZEALOTRY	n pl. -RIES excessive zeal
ZEALOUS	adj filled with zeal
ZEATIN	n pl. -S a chemical compound found in maize
ZEBEC	n pl. -S xebec
ZEBECK	n pl. -S xebec
ZEBRA	n pl. -S an African mammal that is related to the horse **ZEBRAIC** adj
ZEBRASS	n pl. -ES the offspring of a zebra and an ass
ZEBRINE	adj pertaining to a zebra
ZEBROID	adj zebrine
ZEBU	n pl. -S an Asian ox
ZECCHIN	n pl. -S zecchino

ZECCHINO *n pl.* -NI or -NOS a former gold coin of Italy

ZECHIN *n pl.* -S zecchino

ZED *n pl.* -S the letter Z

ZEDOARY *n pl.* -ARIES the medicinal root of a tropical plant

ZEE *n pl.* -S the letter Z

ZEIN *n pl.* -S a simple protein

ZELKOVA *n pl.* -S a Japanese tree

ZEMINDAR *n pl.* -S zamindar

ZEMSTVO *n pl.* -VOS an elective council in czarist Russia

ZENANA *n pl.* -S the section of a house in India reserved for women

ZENITH *n pl.* -S the highest point ZENITHAL *adj*

ZEOLITE *n pl.* -S a mineral ZEOLITIC *adj*

ZEPHYR *n pl.* -S a gentle breeze

ZEPPELIN *n pl.* -S a long, rigid airship

ZERO *v* -ED, -ING, -ES or -S to aim at the exact center of a target

ZEST *v* -ED, -ING, -S to fill with zest (invigorating excitement)

ZESTFUL *adj* full of zest

ZESTY *adj* ZESTIER, ZESTIEST marked by zest

ZETA *n pl.* -S a Greek letter

ZEUGMA *n pl.* -S the use of a word to modify or govern two or more words, while applying to each in a different sense

ZIBELINE *n pl.* -S a soft fabric

ZIBET *n pl.* -S an Asian civet

ZIBETH *n pl.* -S zibet

ZIG *v* ZIGGED, ZIGGING, ZIGS to turn sharply

ZIGGURAT *n pl.* -S an ancient Babylonian temple tower

ZIGZAG *v* -ZAGGED, -ZAGGING, -ZAGS to proceed on a course marked by sharp turns

ZIKKURAT *n pl.* -S ziggurat

ZIKURAT *pl.* -S ziggurat

ZILCH *n pl.* -ES nothing

ZILLAH *n pl.* -S an administrative district in India

ZILLION *n pl.* -S an indeterminately large number

ZINC *v* ZINCED, ZINCING, ZINCS or ZINCKED, ZINCKING, ZINCS to coat with zinc (a metallic element)

ZINCATE *n pl.* -S a chemical salt

ZINCIC *adj* pertaining to zinc

ZINCIFY *v* -FIED, -FYING, -FIES to coat with zinc

ZINCITE *n pl.* -S an ore of zinc

ZINCKED a past tense of zinc

ZINCKING a present participle of zinc

ZINCKY *adj* resembling zinc

ZINCOID *adj* zincic

ZINCOUS *adj* zincic

ZINCY *adj* zincky

ZING *v* -ED, -ING, -S to move with a high-pitched humming sound

ZINGANO *n pl.* -NI zingaro

ZINGARA *n pl.* -RE a female gypsy

ZINGARO *n pl.* -RI a gypsy

ZINGY *adj* ZINGIER, ZINGIEST enjoyably exciting

ZINKIFY *v* -FIED, -FYING, -FIES to zincify

ZINKY *adj* zincky

ZINNIA *n pl.* -S a tropical plant

ZIP *v* ZIPPED, ZIPPING, ZIPS to move with speed and vigor

ZIPPER *v* -ED, -ING, -S to fasten with a zipper (a fastener consisting of two rows of interlocking teeth)

ZIPPY *adj* -PIER, -PIEST full of energy

ZIRAM *n pl.* -S a chemical salt

ZIRCON *n pl.* -S a mineral

ZIRCONIA *n pl.* -S a chemical compound

ZIRCONIC *adj* pertaining to a certain metallic element

ZITHER *n pl.* -S a stringed instrument

ZITHERN *n pl.* -S zither

ZITI *n pl.* -S a tubular pasta

ZIZITH *n/pl* the tassels on the four corners of a Jewish prayer shawl

ZIZZLE *v* -ZLED, -ZLING, -ZLES to sizzle

ZLOTY *n pl.* ZLOTYS a monetary unit of Poland

ZOA a pl. of zoon

ZOARIUM *n pl.* -IA a colony of bryozoans ZOARIAL *adj*